ADVANCE PRAISE FOR BARDDAS

"The central document of the nineteenth-century Druid Revival, and a major source for Druids throughout the Western world since its original publication, *The Barddas of Iolo Morganwg* combines medieval Welsh bardic traditions with Iolo Morganwg's own brilliant innovations into an extraordinary tapestry of Druid teaching full of unexpected insights and visionary wisdom. Weiser Books is to be commended for putting this classic text of modern Druid spirituality into the hands of a new generation of seekers and scholars."
—John Michael Greer, Ancient Order of Druids in America
and coauthor of *Learning Ritual Magic*

"Whatever the origins of the writings collected here, *Barddas* is a magical brew, blending ancient mystery with revolutionary ideas, splashed with caustic humour, obsession, genius, vision, and laudanum. With modern Druidic philosophy and spirituality so shaped by individual inspiration, having accessible all the available sources is essential, and this is certainly one. A neat presentation, it benefits, too, from a clear introduction by Matthews, one of the foremost thinkers on this fascinating subject."
—Emma Restall Orr, Head of the Druid Network

"*Barddas* by John Williams ab Ithel written in 1862 is the fictional and factual story about Druidry originally written by a most controversial character named Iolo Morganwg. This wonderful book, long out of print, is enhanced by Celtic scholar John Matthews whose introduction to the book is priceless in itself. Nothing has influenced modern revivalist Druidry more than *Barddas*. This book deserves an honored place in the library of anybody interested in the Druids."
—John F. Gilbert, Ph.D., Druidry professor
for over 30 years at the Universal Seminary

"One of the archetypal spiritual teachers is the Trickster, whose daring and eccentricity pushes us to explore life in ever-increasing depth. Iolo Morganwg was such a trickster—at times infuriating, at times inspired—and through his writings he has profoundly influenced the development of modern Druidism and Celtic spirituality. At last in this edition much of his work is again available, and combined here with John Matthews's wide-ranging introduction, Iolo's words and ideas can once more intrigue a new generation of readers."

—Philip Carr-Gomm, Chief of the Order of Bards, Ovates, and Druids, author of *The Druid Mysteries, Druidcraft,* and *The Druid Way*

"This book will be of interest to students of the history of the modern Druid revival, especially as it has developed in England. The author of *Barddas,* Iolo Morganwg, was a notorious forger and opium (laudanum) addict and as such his works cannot be relied upon for genuine Druid material with any convincing link to the Druids of antiquity.

Thankfully John Matthews has written an introduction that honestly discusses the problems with Morganwg's scholarship: his drug-enhanced imagination and the fact that it is nearly impossible to separate fact from fiction in his writings. Other modern authors who claim to write about 'genuine Druids from antiquity' have not been as honest, preferring to cite Iolo as an authentic and unquestioned source.

This is a text that will be useful to scholars so long as they have a good grounding in the archaeology and history of the ancient Druids. However, Iolo deserves credit for popularizing the ancient Celtic religion in a way that continues to inspire modern neo-Druids to this day."

—Ellen Evert Hopman, author of *A Druid's Herbal for the Sacred Earth Year,* and *Tree Medicine, Tree Magic*

The Barddas
of Iolo Morganwg

A Collection of Original Documents,
Illustrative of the Theology, Wisdom,
and Usages of the Bardo-Druidic
System of the Isle of Britain

J. Williams ab Ithel, Editor

WEISERBOOKS
Boston, MA/York Beach, ME

This edition first published in 2004 by
Red Wheel/Weiser, LLC
York Beach, ME
With offices at:
368 Congress Street
Boston, MA 02210
www.redwheelweiser.com

Library of Congress Cataloging-in-Publication Data
Iolo Morganwg, 1747–1826
   The Barddas of Iolo Morganwg : a collection of original documents,
illustrative of the theology, wisdom, and usages of the Bardo-Druidic
system of the Isle of Britain / J. Williams ab Ithel, editor.
      p. cm.
   ISBN 1-57863-307-9 (alk. paper)
1. Bards and bardism. 2. Druids and Druidism. 3. Celtic literature—
History and criticism. 4. Civilization, Celtic. I. Title: Barddas. II.
Williams, John 1811–1862. III. Title.
   PB1097.I58 2004
   891.6'609--dc22

                                                        2004042738

Printed in the United States
MV

11 10 09 08 07 06 05 04
 8 7 6 5 4 3 2 1

Introduction
Iolo Morganwg and the Dream of Other Days

Barddas has been controversial almost since its publication in 1862. It has been used to support the wildest theories of Celtic origins and drawn upon by revivalist Druids to support claims of authenticity. Yet much of the material included here is known to be forged and to have come from the pen of one of the most fertile minds in the history of 19th-century Welsh literature. Today it holds a curious place in the history of Celtic tradition—admired by some, reviled by others, at once held up as an example of outright forgery or treated with cautious reverence.

The name that appears on the cover and title page of the original edition is J[ohn] Williams ab Ithel (1811–1862). But this man, a celebrated antiquary and patriot who did much to foster an interest in Welsh culture among the literati, is not the author, but the editor. All of the material in the original two volumes (here bound as one) was either written or compiled by another man, better known today by his self-applied "bardic" name—Iolo Morganwg (Iolo of Glamorgan).

It is impossible to discuss the history of ancient Celtic literature without reference to Iolo, who probably did more to keep alive its heritage than any other person before or since. Despite this, his work offers numerous problems to the would-be commentator, since it is often difficult to tell what was written by Iolo in the 18th century and what is genuinely ancient material. Yet the life and times of this remarkable man not only provide a context for his work, but open a window onto *Barddas* itself, and to the age that shaped its contents.

The Making of a Bard

Born Edward Williams at Pennon, near Llancarvon in the area of South Wales known as Glamorgan, in 1747 Iolo was the son of Edward Williams Sr., a respected stone mason, and Anne Matthews, who came from a well-to-do family but who seemed to have been something of a poor relation—a fact which she never ceased to bemoan. This was an attitude she passed on to her son, who may well have derived a life-long desire to be accepted by the "gentry" from his mother's knee.

Anne Matthews in fact claimed descent from an ancient Welsh family, the Rees Brydydds, which had produced several well-known bards in the 15th and 16th centuries—a factor which was to resurface in her son's bardic dreams years later.

Iolo grew up speaking English with Welsh as a second language. His family moved to the little South Welsh village of Flemington, Glamorgan in 1755, and

Iolo ever after regarded the little stone cottage there as his true home, to which, despite many years of wandering, he always returned. In later years he drew a portrait of himself as a lonely romantic boy communing with nature in the Welsh hills, from which he received his inspiration. The reality was that he had access to a wide range of literature in the libraries and book clubs of the nearby town of Cowbridge, where he spent long hours reading omnivorously and joining in the literary discussions at the home of a local printer. By the time he left Wales in 1773 to seek his fortune in London, he was as well-read as many of the foremost literary lions of the time.

A major early influence was the brilliant lexicographer, John Walters (1721–1797), who taught Iolo classical Welsh and inspired in him a love for the earliest writings of the bards. Even this early on, Iolo was endlessly making lists of old "bardic" words which he intended to use in his own poetry—an early example of the obsession with the traditional language and learning, which culminated in the creation of the *Barddas* materials.

A turning point in Iolo's early life was the death of his mother in 1770. He was devastated by the loss and seemed to have begun to suffer from the asthma that dogged his health from that point forward. A direct effect of this affliction was that he began to take large doses of laudanum, an addictive distillation of opium, which was widely used for ailments both real or illusory at the time, and had a very distinct effect on the mind. King George IV, William Wilberforce, and Samuel Taylor Coleridge all became opium addicts and Iolo himself was almost certainly addicted to laudanum throughout his life, with predictable effects on both his writing and thinking. He was one day to write about the pleasurable effects of the drug:

> Thou faithful friend in all my grief
> In thy soft arms I find relief;
> In thee I forget my woes.

It was also at this time that Iolo began his life-long habit of wandering, usually on foot, from place to place in search of subscriptions to enable the publication of his writings. This was a common practice at the time when anyone wishing to publish their work sought prepayment to defray the costs of printing. At the same time, he began collecting letters and manuscripts, which became the basis for his later works, including *Barddas*. A contemporary account describes him as "stumping bravely along the dusty roads on his short legs, seldom pausing or showing signs of fatigue."

In 1773 Iolo and his three brothers journeyed to London in search of work. Iolo was immediately lost to the bookshops of the city and soon fell in with the London Welsh, a group which included the brightest and best of Welsh authors in exile. He also joined the recently formed Cymmrodorion and

Gwyneddigion Societies, which were dedicated to the retrieval and publication of early Welsh manuscripts.

While in London, he found time to visit the British Museum and to travel to nearby Oxford, where he began to make careful transcriptions of medieval Welsh manuscripts in their libraries. But employment eluded him and a few months later, he moved to Kent where he found work for a time as a laborer. In spare moments, he took the opportunity to visit the great megalithic sites of southern England including Stonehenge and Avebury, which filled him with wonder and a desire to know more about the people who had built them. At this time, it is widely thought that these ancient monuments had been constructed by the Druids, a belief which Iolo continued to hold throughout his life.

After four years of wandering, during which time he seldom had work and often went hungry, Iolo returned home in 1777 with a growing accumulation of manuscripts and a bundle of love poems addressed to a girl he named "Euron." This was actually Margaret Roberts, a farmer's daughter from the village of St. Marychurch whom Iolo had known before he left Wales and whom he was to marry in 1781.

Apart from a property worth £1000, a considerable amount at the time, Margaret also brought a lively, literate mind that could match Iolo's at almost every point. They were to remain married for the rest of his life—a feat of no small endurance on her part, considering they were almost always in debt due to Iolo's lack of foresight with money. Indeed, he several times abandoned both Margaret and their growing family to follow his wandering lifestyle, and among her letters to him are many in which she begs him to return. Iolo's responses nearly always dwelt on his own sufferings rather than those of his family:

> I rise in the Morning early, for I never sleep, and walk about
> I know not where, often to the fields where I lie down under
> a hedge. I then come home, and pass the night in a manner
> so distressing that it will soon bring me to the grave. . . .
> I have not slept a single moment this many months. . . . I
> take a good deal of laudanum, and it keeps me alive, but
> gives me no sleep. (National Library of Wales MS.)

His obsession with words and ideas was such that he never seemed to have felt any real obligation toward his wife or family, preferring to leave them in the care of his aging father while he took to the roads in search of further manuscript remains of a past that loomed ever larger in his mind.

After a time he did return home and with his wife's money set up as a builder, first in Llandaff and later in Cardiff. But both enterprises failed, and Iolo then tried his hand as a shopkeeper and a farmer. All these attempts to earn a living came to nothing and his debts grew larger. In addition he now had a small daughter, Peggy, born in 1782. In 1785 Iolo, with wife and child in tow, fled from their creditors to the town of Wells in Somerset. A few months later they were forced to move again and, upon returning to Flemington, Iolo was arrested and thrown into debtor's prison in Cardiff. He remained there for over a year from 1786–1787, while his wife and family— now with the addition of a boy named after the great 6th-century bard, Taliesin—continued to be looked after by his father.

Allowed to bring both his papers and books into prison Iolo continued his studies of early Celtic literature. By this time he was acknowledged as one of the foremost scholars of his time and corresponded with many leading thinkers and antiquaries who shared his fascination with the historical past of Wales. Many of these men felt that the only way that national pride, lost to the Norman invaders at the start of the Middle Ages, could be restored was through the recovery and promotion of the great literary heritage of the ancient bards. Such a belief immediately communicated itself to Iolo, who thereafter saw himself as a champion of the "lost and forgotten" relics of the bards.

He had already begun to write verses of his own in the style of one of the greatest medieval Welsh poets, Dafydd ap Gwilym, (1320–1370), a number of which he sent to leading members of the London Welsh—neglecting to mention that they were his own work and claiming to have discovered them in old manuscripts on his travels. To his delight these works were included in a new edition of Dafydd's poems and became an overnight sensation. So good were Iolo's forgeries that they remained undetected until the early 20th century. They made Iolo famous and earned him the respect of the London literati. A recent commentator declared that Iolo's versions are at times better than the originals.

It was now that Iolo began to style himself Iolo Morganwg (Iolo of Glamorgan) and to dream of creating a wonderful legacy of Welsh literature dating back to the time of the Druids. All things Druidical were fashionable, and it was widely believed, based on the antiquarian speculations of John Aubrey and William Stukely, that the Druids were responsible for building Stonehenge and Avebury, as well as other monuments that dated from the Megalithic era. Iolo believed this implicitly and since he also believed that the Druids had originated in Wales this became a central part of his nationalistic temperament.

At the time little or nothing was known about the true history of the Druids. In order to understand the impact Iolo's work had on the public imagination of the time, it is necessary to take a brief look both at what we know now and also at the way in which the Druids were perceived in the 18th century.

THE TRUE HISTORY OF THE DRUIDS

Almost all that we know about the Druids comes from contemporary classical sources, written by authors who had no love for them. Thus the most famous early account, by Julius Caesar (100-44 B.C.), is that of a soldier who was vigorously opposed by them, and who was writing at the end of their apparently long history. In fact there are no records of their origins, nor is it known with any certainty when they were first active. The Druids themselves possessed no writings, preferring to depend upon the memory and on oral transmission of their teachings. Hence nothing ascribed to them can be considered genuine, although it is possible that at least some of their teachings were preserved in oral tradition. Even these fragmentary memorials remain doubtful due to the ease with which such traditions can become corrupted.

The origin of the name Druid may come from Celtic root words such as *dru*, meaning "oak" and *wid*, meaning "to know" or "to see"—hence "oak-knowledge." Another possible meaning may simply be "great knowledge" or "knowledge as great (old) as the oaks." In addition, the Irish word *druidecht* is translated as "magic," and *druth*, as "fool"or "madman" (in the sense of inspired madness or inspiration). In Sanskrit the word *drus* means "tree" and *duru* means "wood." The Welsh *drws*, the Scottish Gaelic *dorus*, and the Cornish *daras* all mean "door." Also, there is the Gaelic *druidim*—"I shut."

From all of these we may infer, if nothing else, that the root from which the name "Druid" comes was widespread throughout the Indo-European world and that it had a powerful connection with oak trees, doors, and the opening and closing of ways. The one certainty is the power they wielded as priests, lawgivers, doctors, and historians who guarded the traditional lore and wisdom of the Celtic people.

The Druids were, by all accounts, virtually wiped out by the Romans, who destroyed the great college of Druidry on Anglesey in A.D. 64. After this, little is heard of them for many years—though it has been suggested that those who survived simply went underground and were secretly active for longer than is often supposed. Interestingly, the early Christian writers of saints' lives, who might have been expected to attack them as a pagan priesthood, recorded seemingly cordial relations between followers of the two faiths, to the extent that a certain amount of Druid philosophy seems to have been absorbed into the Christian writings of the time.

With the gradual rise of Christianity throughout the Middle Ages, Druidry was almost forgotten, relegated to a distant corner of memory and perceived as a last relic of pre-Christian belief. But the memory did not quite die, and during the latter part of the 16th century, a large number of highly speculative works appeared in Continental Europe, each one promising to have uncovered the innermost secrets of Druidry. These not only examined the history of the Druids but also claimed their philosophy and wisdom for either France or Germany. England followed suit, although it was not until the 18th century that the romantic figure of the Druid, as perceived by Iolo and his friends, began to emerge.

Before this, poets such as Michael Drayton, in his monumental poem on the spirit of Britain entitled "Polyolbion" (published between 1596 and 1622), spoke of the Druids in tones of almost breathless respect, while at the same time casting some doubt on their history. Even John Milton mentioned them in his early writings. Then, in 1689, the antiquary John Aubrey wrote in his preliminary study of Stonehenge that the Druids were probably its architects and that they must have been mighty in wisdom and skill to achieve such a great feat of spiritual architecture. Aubrey was backed up in his controversial thesis by the eminent Celtic scholar Edward Llwyd (1660–1709), whose own massive book, *Archaeologica Britannica* (1707), marked one of the first serious attempts to chart the history of Celtic language and belief. Meanwhile the classical sources, such as Caesar, Strabo, and Pliny were becoming more readily available, and these works began to influence the way in which Druids were perceived.

The first serious work on Druidry was a projected history by John Toland (1670–1722). However, the work remained fragmentary and unfinished, appearing finally as a series of letters to Toland's patron Viscount Molesworth in 1726. This work, despite some confusion and an insufficient knowledge of Irish, is still important and well worth re-reading today.

Shortly after, in 1740, William Stukeley finally published his long awaited book, *Stonehenge: A Temple Restored to the British Druids*. Stukeley was active in the establishment of the Society of Antiquaries, whose members were dedicated to the investigation of just such subjects, and he not only embraced Aubrey's theory, but also considerably elaborated on it, describing white-robed Druids worshipping a great serpent named Dracontia at Stonehenge, a temple built by their own hands. His book described a system of Druidry that had never existed, but it was influential at the time and continues, despite the clear refutation of modern scholarship, to influence both the way that Druidry is perceived today and the belief that the Druids were in some way responsible for the building of Stonehenge.

Stukeley followed up his first book with another: *Abury: A Temple of the British Druids*, which was published in 1743. In this he turned his attention to the great megalithic centre of Avebury in Wiltshire, declaring this to be another of the wonders created by the Druids.

No less a person than the poet and prophet William Blake (1757–1827) was influenced by this book, and his engraving for the poem "Jerusalem" (1804–1820) depicts robed Druids worshipping a serpent. In the same poem he wrote, in a darker mood, of the bloodier side of Druid history:

> O ye sons of the mighty Albion
> Planting these Oaken Groves,
> Erecting these Dragon Temples . . .

Where Albion slept beneath the Fatal Tree
And the Druid's golden knife
Rioted in human gore
In offerings of human life.

The learned Dr. John Ogilvie of Aberdeen, in his anonymously published *Fane of the Druids* (1787), described the Druids in terms that are familiar to most of us today from many a romantic painting or photograph of modern neo-Druidic events at Stonehenge:

Though time with silver locks adorn'd his head
Erect his gesture yet, and firm his tread . . .
His seemly beard, to grace his form bestow'd
Descending decent, on his bosom flow'd;
His robe of purest white, though rudly join'd
Yet showed an emblem of the purest mind

However, it was in Wales that the revival of Druidry gathered momentum. In 1764 the antiquarian Evan Evans published a collection entitled *Specimens of the Poetry of the Ancient Welsh Bards*, which generated a good deal of interest among his fellow Cambrians about their own literary history and certainly influenced Iolo's own studies. His one-time friend Edward Jones, the harper to the Prince of Wales, produced influential works on the musical heritage of the bards, including *Methodological and Poetical Relics of the Welsh Bards and Druids* (1784) and *The Bardic Museum* (1802).

Iolo's own contribution to the revival of interest in the mysteries of the bards and Druids was considerable. On June 21, 1792, the eve of midsummer, he marched up Primrose Hill in London, traditionally, though without any real foundation, said to be a meeting place for the ancient Druids. Accompanied by a dozen or so other self-styled Welsh "patriots," he convened the first bardic gorsedd or assembly since the Middle Ages. Theatrical, shot through with elements of Masonic ritual, this restored event was to become a fixture of Welsh cultural life during the succeeding years and continues to this day.

Following this successful venture, Iolo went on to establish eisteddfods, bardic meetings where poets and scholars from all walks of life would contend for prizes, and where the winner was crowned as the Chief Bard of Britain. The impressive ceremony of the Chairing of the Bard still takes place annually at the National Eisteddfod in Cardiff.

In all contests, now as then, great emphasis is placed on the use of Welsh, which Iolo saw as the foundation of national identity. His passionate belief that his native tongue was Europe's oldest surviving literary language and his desire to retrieve it from the darkness of obscurity into which it had fallen, went hand in hand with a desire to restore the fortunes of his homeland. In this he was as much a patriot as the revolutionaries with whom he spent time in London.

Ironically, the resurgence of interest in Celtic lore and language arose after Ireland, Scotland, and Wales had been both politically and culturally suppressed in the 18th century, at which time it became fashionable to look back at "quaint" native customs. Iolo's influence, which strove to impress the real value of these ancient ways, can be seen in more recent literature, especially in what became known as the "Celtic Revival." Nineteenth-century poets and dramatists such as W.B. Yeats, AE (George W. Russell), Fiona Macleod (William Sharp) and others produced a series of brilliant works that captured the romance and mystery of Celtic traditions and helped to enshrine them in the consciousness of the 19th and 20th centuries.

Among other pseudo historians and antiquarians who followed Iolo's lead was Edward Davies, whose *Mythology and Rites of the British Druids* (1809) and *Celtic Researches* (1804) had a profound and long-lasting effect on the way in which both the Celts and Druidry were perceived. Davies was a brilliant if erratic scholar, whose misreading of the documents set forth by Iolo led him to some curious conclusions. However, his work still bears re-reading for his occasionally inspired guesses, which influenced such modern writers as Robert Graves, whose book, *The White Goddess: A Historical Grammar of Poetic Myth* (London, 1957) would have been different had it not been for Iolo's writings.

Other, less well-known writers, such as Godfrey Higgins whose book, *The Celtic Druids* (1829) traced the Celtic peoples and the Druidic teachings to biblical times, and R.W. Morgan, who sought an equally eastern point of origin for the "Cimmeranian" race (from Cymric, "Welsh") pushed Davies' original ideas to the limits. An entire substratum of lore and literature emerged at this time in the shape of the British Israelite movement, which taught that the Celts were one of the twelve Lost Tribes of Israel, who had settled in these islands in the remote past. This led to further speculation and comparison between so-called Druidic rites and those of the Judaic people, a theory that has refused to die even in our own time, though it is little regarded by modern scholars of Druidry.

Druids and druidry are still very much with us today. There are currently some thirty-five orders scattered throughout the world, many deriving their inspiration from writers like Iolo, and who have only recently begun to research the original native models. Today Druidry is more properly described as a philosophy. It has absorbed so many influences from as far apart as Christianity and Hinduism, that it is really no longer possible to tell what shape it once possessed. Iolo's writings, along with freemasonry and neo-shamanism, have all helped shape it into a rich and often heady brew that draws people from many walks of life to its ranks.

A RISING STAR

Iolo's return to London in 1789 from his latest period of wandering was triumphant. Not only was he now accepted into the circle of the London Welsh as a scholar in his own right, but he began also to move in the circles of radical thinkers with whom he discussed the past glories of the Welsh people and the need for them to succeed from British rule.

These revolutionary leanings were to bring trouble upon Iolo. After a furious argument over the "oppression" of the Welsh by the British with his royalist friend Edward Jones, Iolo received a visit from government agents who seized his papers on the strength that they might contain "seditious" material. Iolo extracted himself from this situation with difficulty and remained under suspicion for a number of years that spanned the revolution in France and the American War of Independence.

Iolo openly admired the freedom and independence of the United States. In an extraordinary essay entitled "America, by an Ancient British Bard" he wrote: "I have from the beginning been an enthusiastic admirer of your glorious and successful struggles for Liberty, your Republican Principles, your excellent constitutions of Government." Tom Paine, the author of *The Rights of Man* (1791–1792), which became one of the foundation stones of the American revolution, was a close personal friend, and among the subscribers to Iolo's first volume of poetry was General George Washington, the future president of the United States; William Wilberforce, the anti-slavery activist; and other leading revolutionary thinkers of the time.

At about this time, a certain Dr. John Williams began circulating documents describing a tribe of fair-skinned, blue-eyed, Welsh-speaking native Americans, the descendants of a certain Prince Madoc, whom he claimed had discovered America before Columbus. This was not a new idea. Prince Madoc (Madog) was an actual historical figure who lived at the end of the 12th century, and rumours of his voyage to the North American continent had been around for some time. When Iolo learned of the story he at once began to forge documents that proved the veracity of Madoc's journey. He even offered a challenge to any Welshman prepared to mount a voyage to discover the historical remains of Madoc's "kingdom" in the Americas and promised to accompany any such voyage himself.

Whether Iolo ever intended this challenge to be taken seriously we may never know, but when a young man called John Evans took him up on it, and as preparations for the historic voyage went ahead, Iolo began to put himself through a rigorous program of training to toughen himself up for the trip. He later claimed that this damaged his health irrevocably and used it as an excuse not to go on the voyage.

Undaunted, John Evans went alone and made it to the lands of the Mandean Indians, who lived in earth lodges and were reputed to have blue eyes. To Evans' disappointment they turned out not to speak Welsh or even a derivative of that language, and after a terrible winter he returned to New Orleans where he died from a mixture of drink and pneumonia. However, despite his failure to prove the truth of Prince Madoc's voyage, his extraordinary journey inspired President Thomas Jefferson to obtain a grant of $2,000 from Congress to fund the more famous expedition of Lewis and Clarke into the interior of the American continent, following John Evans's route. This was a far cry from the life of an obscure Welsh antiquary, yet were it not for Iolo's enthusiastic response to the legend of Madoc, the first great survey of the heartland of America might have taken a very different direction.

A DRUID HERITAGE

Despite setbacks, Iolo continued to collect subscriptions for his poems and in 1794 a volume entitled *Poems Lyrical and Pastoral* appeared. It was received with enthusiastic reviews, but Iolo seemed to have lost interest in it almost at once. His family was in desperate straits by this time and one of his children had died, as did his father in 1795. Seeming finally to feel a twinge of conscience, Iolo returned to Wales, moved his family into Cowbridge, Glamorgan, and set up a series of disastrous shopkeeping ventures. He was ill suited for any business, as we can see from the occasion when, having opened a lending library, he spent more time reading the books!

Iolo continued to eke out an existence with generous help from friends in London and some occasional work for the Board of Agriculture, on whose authority he toured South Wales to report on the state of farming there. In fact, Iolo's voluminous reports were not published until many years later, for as he wandered the roads of Wales, he became more and more occupied with the copying of manuscripts in the possession of those wealthy enough to own libraries. It is still difficult to separate Iolo's own inventions from the genuine material he collected at this time. As with the poems of Dafydd ap Gwilym, his forgeries of medieval and pre-medieval works were often so good that telling true from false remains a nightmare for modern scholars.

At the same time, Iolo began to spread the gospel of his own version of Druidry to anyone who would listen. If any local bards he encountered on his wanderings showed an interest in his ideas, he persuaded them that he was a direct descendent of the ancient bards of Glamorgan (presumably through his mother) and the recipient of the ancient mysteries of the bards and Druids. He would then "initiate" them into the druid mysteries and establish a gorsedd on a convenient hilltop in the area.

As the new millennium dawned Iolo's associates in the Cymmrodorion

Society were preparing a huge collection of early historical Welsh documents to be called the "Welsh Archaiology." The first three volumes appeared between 1801–1807 under the title of *The Myrvyrian Archaiology of Wales* and Iolo wrote an introduction to the first volume in which he set forth many of his wilder notions of the Druidic and bardic heritage of Wales. Volume 3 consisted almost entirely of his own writings, some forgeries, some actual texts copied and translated from manuscripts discovered during his wanderings.

All this time Iolo had continued, intermittently, to follow his father's trade as a stonemason, building barns and cottages and carving headstones throughout the vale of Glamorgan. In the latter part of his life he earned enough to support himself and his family, though he was never considered wealthy. His son Taliesin joined him as a partner in the masonry business and even ran a school for a time, but the business side of Iolo's life was precarious at best and the family was always on the edge of destitution.

As old age claimed Iolo and brought an end to his tireless wanderings, he retired to the tiny cottage at Flemington where he had lived as a child. Here he withdrew into a laudanum-fueled world and began writing ever more strange and fantastic visions of Druidic philosophy—some drawn from his own fevered imagination, some from historical documents, and others from his somewhat odd brand of Christianity. Out of this strange mixture came the brew that eventually formed the materials collected under the title *Barddas*, though the book would not appear until almost forty years after Iolo's death.

In his last years Iolo spent all day and most of the night writing. He seldom slept, took increasingly large doses of laudanum and drank tea, all the while wheezing asthmatically. Finally, just a week before Christmas, 1826, Iolo fell into a sleep from which he never woke. He was in his eightieth year. His body was buried in the churchyard at Flemington, only a few yards from where he had lived. His son, Taliesin, collected all of the papers he felt worthy and had them bound into a staggering eighty volumes, which he hoped to sell to a collector. When he failed to find a buyer—Iolo's star having fallen somewhat by this time—he began to make his own selections from his father's works, publishing a collection called *Cyfrenach Y Beirdd* (*Secrets of the Bards*) in 1829. This was followed by an even stranger book, *Coelbren Y Beirdd*, (*The Bardic Alphabet*) in 1840. It remains the source of several recent theories regarding the existence of a secret method of writing known only to the bards, but was almost certainly invented by Iolo.

Taliesin ab Iolo died suddenly in 1847, while in the midst of compiling a third volume, intended as an addition to the *Myrvyrian Archaiology*. This appeared in 1848 as *The Iolo Manuscripts*.

It was not until another six years after that, in 1853, that Iolo's papers were bought by Lord and Lady Llanover, who subsequently made the material accessible to those wishing to study Iolo's unpublished work. One of the first to take advantage of this was John Williams "ab Ithel," who after drawing deeply on Iolo's writings for his own work, finally edited some of the Druidic and bardic fantasies into the collection reprinted here, which, though it omitted Iolo's name from the title page, made a wider proportion of his work available to the general public almost forty years after its author's death.

The content of the volumes varies hugely, both in quality and authenticity. The long section titled "Symbol" in Vol. I which deals largely with the bardic alphabet known as *coelbren*—almost certainly Iolo's invention, based in part on Norse runes—remains fascinating to all concerned with secret languages. The detail with which it is described is astonishing and it remains a workable symbolic system.

But by far the most interesting part of the first volume is found in the section headed "Theology," most of which is very clearly derived from Iolo's own rather muddled Christian beliefs (he once described himself as a Unitarian Quaker!). However, imbedded in this vast tide of curious lore, is a collection of triads, gnomic statements grouped in threes and believed to be used as mnemonics by the wandering bards of the Middle Ages and earlier.

Once again, most of them are probably the product of Iolo's own mind, displaying his wide learning at every point. However, there are a number of triads included here that may very well be authentic and part of the extensive collection of bardic sayings that are genuinely ancient. Rachel Bromwich, the editor of the early triads, also made a study of Iolo's "forgeries," and believed that he must have had access to later copies of the originals long before they were widely known or had been collected and translated in English. Most, however, almost certainly remain the work of his own genius.

The third section, called simply "Wisdom" contains much of interest, especially the information regarding the elements, names of constellations, and months of the year, as well as the divisions of the day. As with much of the material in *Barddas* these derive largely from the lore of 16th- and 17th-century bards rather than the more ancient druidic characters so beloved of Iolo.

The second volume, which remained unfinished and was published after J. Williams ab Ithel's death, is really a handbook for the use of bards and those seeking to establish a gorsedd. It is meticulously detailed and repetitive and bears all the hallmarks of Iolo's peculiar cast of thought, liberally sewn with fragments of genuinely ancient lore and wisdom, drawn from an authentic late-medieval bardic grammar called Cyfrenach Y Beirdd, later borrowed by his son Taliesin ab Iolo for the second major selection of his father's writings.

How one approaches this work is very much up to the individual. It may be regarded as a literary curiosity and one that has certainly found champions and imitators since its appearance in print. Ultimately it displays a mind of great subtlety and genius, in whose company it is a genuine pleasure to spend some time.

THE IOLO TRADITION

But the question remains: How much of what Iolo wrote can we trust to be even vaguely authentic? The answer is perhaps best summed up by a contemporary Welsh writer, Emyr Humphries, who remarks in his study of the Welsh cultural heritage:

> The unnerving element in everything to do with Iolo is
> the surprising way in which fresh advances in scholarship
> are forced to concede the presence of traces of truth even
> in his most outlandish fantasies (*The Taliesin Tradition*).

A good deal of time and effort has been put into discovering the origins of Iolo's writings. The general conclusion is that many of his ideas are the product of his personal genius, though some may well be based on sound scholarship. The greatest authority on Iolo's work, J.G. Williams, reached the conclusion that much of the writings that flowed from Iolo's pen were as much the product of a warped sense of humour as of a genuine desire to educate, and that Iolo may well be laughing in heaven.

But we must not forget that Iolo was immensely well-read and genuinely did collect and transcribe manuscripts held in the private collections of well-to-do Welsh families. We should probably ask which of these documents were genuinely old and which were either bad copies of older works or the product of later medieval writers. It has been suggested, for example, that some of Iolo's sources may be traceable to a 16th-century bard named Llewellyn Sion, who, among other things, wrote a version of *The Life of Taliesin*, which differs radically from the better-known version published by Lady Charlotte Guest in the 19th century. This could itself be either a forgery or drawn from an alternate source. Sion, according to an account given by Iolo himself, copied manuscripts relating to the Druidic mysteries from books in the library of Raglan Castle. Nothing is now known of these writings and various scholars have speculated that Sion may himself have been a forger—or that he at least "updated" some genuinely ancient materials.

Whatever the truth of this, Iolo was undoubtedly a fine scholar in his own right, one whose encyclopedic knowledge was easily capable of making leaps of understanding. Also, that he was genuinely inspired—to a point where, amid the jumble of disconnected fragments that make up his work, a kind of essential truth shines through. Whether one sees his inspirations as divinely received or merely the effects of laudanum, the inherent truth of much that he wrote remains a triumphant testimony to his energy and imagination.

Iolo has been described as a force of nature, an unstoppable tide of learning and native wisdom that continues to be remembered into our own time. He described himself as "a rattleskull genius" and once introduced himself to the Prince of Wales as "Edward of Glamorgan." Among his interests Iolo listed the study of language and literature, hymnology, dialectology, architecture, agriculture, botany, geology, horticulture, politics, history, and folk music. He also said that he "always pushed himself forward" and was never content with mastering any single branch of knowledge. The North Welsh poet Dafydd du Eerier called him "a cross, harsh little bugger," and his unprintable jokes and hot temper were famous. He liked to append to his name the letters BBD, which stood for Bardd wrth Ffraint a Defod Beirdd Ynys Prydein, "Bard by the Privilege and Rite of Bards of the Island of Britain," and while the title may be an invented one, in essence it is close to the truth.

By the end of the 19th century Iolo's reputation had faded and most scholars regarded his works with suspicion, as they do to this day. Some, however, continued to regard him as a source of information which, provided it was treated with due care, could still yield some worthwhile nuggets. In particular the great modern Welsh scholar G. J. Williams did much to restore Iolo as an important poet—though unfortunately he did not live to complete more than a single volume of his projected study of Iolo's life and work. Even he was forced to concede that among the fantasies and forgeries nuggets of truth gleamed forth in the most unexpected fashion.

Today Iolo is regarded as at best a literary curiosity and at worst as a charlatan. However, while it is true that his writings must be treated with caution by all who seek to investigate the origins of Druidry and the bardic mysteries, some remain worthy of study and make for fascinating reading. Often repetitive, clearly a product of laudanum-inspired dreams, there are references to ancient lore which could well have a foundation in truth.

Much of the material presented here has served as a foundation for the modern revival of interest in Druidry, and for this reason alone *Barddas* remains essential reading for all concerned with the mystical beliefs of the Celts. It is also a testimony to the working of a remarkable mind, to a man who wanted to encompass the worldview of a visionary people and to translate these into words that would inspire a new generation.

That Iolo's words have indeed continued to do so is itself a fitting memorial for this extraordinary man, whose work ultimately inspired much of the vast outpouring of modern Celtic literature, as well as a continuing fascination with the history and beliefs of this remarkable people that continues to this day.

John Matthews
Oxford, 2003

/|\

Y GWIR YN ERBYN Y BYD.

BARDDAS;

OR, A COLLECTION OF ORIGINAL DOCUMENTS, ILLUSTRATIVE OF THE THEOLOGY,
WISDOM, AND USAGES OF

The Bardo-Druidic System

OF THE ISLE OF BRITAIN.

WITH

TRANSLATIONS AND NOTES.

BY

THE REV. J. WILLIAMS AB ITHEL, M.A.,

RECTOR OF LLANYMOWDDWY, MERIONETHSHIRE;
AUTHOR OF "THE ECCLESIASTICAL ANTIQUITIES OF THE CYMRY," &c., &c.

PUBLISHED FOR

The Welsh MSS. Society.

VOL. I.

LLANDOVERY:
PUBLISHED BY D. J. RODERIC; LONDON: LONGMAN & CO.
MDCCCLXII.

/I\

𝔜 𝕲𝔴𝔦𝔯 𝔶𝔫 𝔢𝔯𝔟𝔶𝔫 𝔶 𝕭𝔶𝔡.

I'R

BEIRDD, DERWYDDON, AC OFYDDION,

Y CYFLWYNIR

Y CASGLIAD HWN O WYBODAU A DEFODAU

𝕭𝔞𝔯𝔡𝔡𝔞𝔰 𝔶𝔯 𝕳𝔢𝔫 𝕲𝔶𝔪𝔯𝔶,

GAN EU FFYDDLAWN WASANAETHWR,

AB ITHEL, B. B. D.

YN ENW DUW A PHOB DAIONI.

b

Committee,

The Right Honourable Lord Llanover, Chairman
Octavius Morgan, Esq. M.P., F.R.S., F.G.S., Friars, Newport
J. Bruce Pryce, of Dyffryn, Esq. Cardiff, Glamorgan
J. Arthur Herbert, of Llanarth, Esq.
The Rev. Illtyd Nicholl, M.A. of Ham, Cowbridge, Glamorgan

Editors, Translators, and Collators of Manuscripts,

The Rev. J. Williams Ab Ithel, M.A. Rector of Llanymowddwy*
The Rev. E. Owen Phillips, M.A., Vicar of Aberystwyth*
The Rev. Hugh Williams, M.A. Chancellor of Llandaff*
John Pughe, Esq. F.R.C.S. Penhelyg, Aberdovey
William Rees, Esq. of Tonn, Llandovery*

Those marked thus* are also Members of the Committee.

Corresponding Members,

WALES.

The Right Hon. Lady Llanover, *(Gwenynen Gwent)* Llanover, Abergavenny
Lady Charlotte Schreiber, Dowlais, Glamorganshire
George Grant Francis, Esq. F.S.A. Cae'r Baily, Swansea
Major Herbert, Llansanffraed, near Abergavenny
Rev. Dr. James, (Dewi o Ddyfed,) of Pantêg, Monmouthshire
Arthur James Johnes, of Garthmyl, Esq. Judge of Local Courts, North Wales
John Johnes, Esq., Dolaucothy, Caermarthenshire
Rev. T. Jones, M.A. Llanengan, Caernarvonshire
The Very Rev. Dr. Lewellin, Dean of St. David's, & Principal of St. D.C.L.
Thomas Wakeman, Esq., The Graig, near Monmouth
W. W. E. Wynne, Esq. M.P. Peniarth, Merionethshire
Rev. Sir Charles Salusbury, of Llanwern, Bart.
Miss Williams, of Ynyslâs, Glamorgan, South Wales
Miss Jane Williams, of Ynyslâs, Glamorgan, South Wales.

ENGLAND, &c.

Rev. A. B. Clough, B.D., F S.A., &c. Braunston, Northampton
Rev. Robert Jones, M.A. All Saints Rectory, Rotherhithe, London
Rev. R. H. Lloyd, M.A. of Owersby, Lincolnshire
J. Whitefoord Mackenzie, Esq. F.R.S., F.S.A. &c. Edinburgh
Sir Thomas Phillipps, Bart. F.R.S. Middle Hill, Worcestershire
The Lady Charlotte Schreiber, Roehampton, Middlesex

Secretary,

Mr. William Griffith, 4, Sidmouth Place, Gray's Inn Road, London.

HONORARY FOREIGN SECRETARY FOR GERMANY.—Mr. J. G. Sauerwein,
Asiatic Society's Office, London.
HONORARY FOREIGN SECRETARY FOR FRANCE.—Monsr. Rio, Paris.

Treasurers,

Messrs. Bailey, Gratrex & Co., Bankers, Abergavenny.

Publisher,

Mr. D. J. Roderic, Llandovery, South Wales.

The Welsh MSS. Society,

HAS been formed for the purpose of transcribing and printing the more important of the numerous Bardic and Historical Remains of Wales, still extant in the Principality, and other parts of the world, that have hitherto been allowed to continue in a state of obscurity, without any effective measures being adopted to lay their contents before the public, and secure them from the various accidents to which they are liable. In addition to the general decay which, from their perishable nature, these venerable relics have been for ages undergoing, whole collections have, within a short space of time, been destroyed by fire; and of those MSS. dispersed throughout the country, numbers known to have existed a few years ago, are now no where to be found.

Besides the interest which these ancient documents possess, as objects of antiquarian curiosity, and as contributing to the elucidation of British History, they have a claim to attention of a far more general character, as being intimately connected with the origin and progress of modern European Literature; for it is among the legends and traditions of the Welsh that many of the materials are to be found, which supplied the nations of the Continent with their earliest subjects of composition, and produced those highly imaginative works that continue to exercise so powerful an influence to the present day.

A great mass of Historical information, relating to the thirteenth, fourteenth, and fifteenth centuries, is contained in the unpublished Poetry of Wales; from which an intimate acquaintance with the state of society during those periods may be obtained ; the Welsh Bards being the Chroniclers of the times in which they lived, and their Poems chiefly addressed to the leading men of the day. Besides Poetry, there is still existing unpublished a large collection of Prose, both Historical and Legendary ; persons of affluence are therefore solicited to contribute larger Donations and Subscriptions, than are required by the Rules of the Society, in order to enable the Committee to proceed with greater rapidity in carrying on the publication of Manuscripts.

The first Work that was published by this Society, was the LIBER LANDAVENSIS, or LLYFR TEILO, comprising nearly 700 Royal 8vo. pages ; gratuitously edited by the late Rev. W. J. Rees, M.A., F.S.A. &c. Of this Work only a few Copies remain to be sold to persons becoming Members of the Society at £1 1s. 0d.—Non-members, £2 2s. 0d.

The second Work of the Society consisted of a MISCELLANEOUS SELECTION OF ANCIENT WELSH MSS. in prose and poetry, from the originals collected by the late Edward Williams, (*Iolo Morganwg*) for the purpose of forming a continuation of the Myvyrian Archaiology, and afterwards proposed to be used as materials for a New History of Wales. Edited with Notes and *Translations*, by his son, the late TALIESIN AB IOLO, of Merthyr Tydvil. This work is of the same size and price as the Liber Landavensis, and a few copies remain still in the hands of the Publisher.

The third Work, The HERALDIC VISITATIONS OF WALES AND ITS MARCHES, Temp. Elizabeth, and James I. in two Imperial 4to.Volumes was printed under the gratuitous and able superintendence of its Editor, the late SIR SAMUEL RUSH MEYRICK, K.H.,LL.D., F.S A, &c., of this Work only 240 copies were published which were all engaged by Subscribers; it is therefore out of print and has become extremely scarce.

The LIVES OF CAMBRO BRITISH SAINTS, was next published, from Ancient Welsh and Latin MSS. in the British Museum and elsewhere, comprising 680 pages Royal 8vo., and was gratuitously edited and translated by the late Rev. W. J. REES, M.A., F.S.A., &c. Some copies of this Work are still to be had of the Publisher, price £1 1s. 0d. to persons becoming Members of the Society, —Non-members, £2 2s. 0d.

The ANCIENT WELSH GRAMMAR made by EDEYRN DAFOD AUR, by the command of Llywelyn ap Gruffydd, (prince of Wales from 1254 to 1282,) Rhys Vychan lord of Dynevor and Ystrad Towy ; and Morgan Vychan, lord paramount of Morganwg,—together with Y PUM LLYFR KERDDWRIAETH, or Rules of Welsh Prosody, by Simwnt Vychan, in the 15th Century. Edited with Translations and Notes, by the Rev. John Williams Ab Ithel, M.A. A few copies only remain on hand, to be sold at £1 1s. 0d. each,—Non-members, £2 2s. 0d.

The MEDDYGON MYDDFAI, or a Compendium of the Medical Practice of the celebrated Rhiwallon and his Sons, Cadwgan, Gruffydd, and Einion, of Myddvai, in Caermarthenshire, Physicians to Rhys Gryg, lord of Dynevor and Ystrad Towy, son of Gruffydd ap Rhys, the last Prince of South Wales, about the year 1230 ; from Ancient MSS. in the Library of Jesus College, Oxford, Llanover, and Tonn ; accompanied by an English Translation. To the whole is annexed the curious Legend of THE LADY OF THE LAKE, called LLYN-Y-FAN, from whom the above Physicians were said to be descended, and a copious Herbal ; Edited by the Rev. J. Williams ab Ithel, M.A., Rector of Llanymowddwy ; Translated by John Pughe, Esq., F.R.C.S., Penhelyg, Aberdovey. Price £1 1s. 0d.

To be ready early in 1863, *the Second Volume of*

BARDDAS ; OR BARDISM, a Collection of Original Documents, illustrative of the Theology, Discipline and Usages, of the Bardo-Druidic System of the Isle of Britain, with Translations and Notes, by the Rev. J. Williams Ab Ithel, M.A., Rector of Llanymowddwy.

⁕ The curious matter brought to light for the first time in this Work. cannot fail to attract the particular attention of scholars, and to open a new and interesting era in the History of Welsh Literature.

☞ *It is intended henceforward to bring out a Volume of about* 400 *pages every Twelve Months, to be supplied to Members of the Society only, free of all expense. Those Works already published, and not out of print, can be had by payment of the additional price affixed to each.*

RECOMMENDED FOR PUBLICATION.

The inedited matter of the LLYFR COCH O HERGEST, in the Library of Jesus College, Oxford.

ANCIENT RECORDS, Temp. Edward III. belonging to the Manor Court of Ruthin.

WELSH CHARTERS.

Y DAROGANAU, or VATICINATIONS of the middle ages.

A complete and correct edition of the BARDS of the 6th and 7th centuries.

Y DIARHEBION CYMREIG, or WELSH PROVERBS.

The HISTORICAL TRIADS.

The Life of GRUFFUDD AB CYNAN.

The GREAL ; in the Hengwrt Collection.

Rules of the Society.

I. That the objects of the Society shall be to procure copies of any interesting Manuscripts relating to Wales and the Marches thereof, and to publish them with English Translations and Notes.

II. That Subscribers of at least One Guinea annually, become members of the Society.

III. That all Subscriptions being considered due for the ensuing year, notice must be sent to the Secretary, before the 1st of January, of any Member's intention to withdraw his name.

IV. That the Society's Publications are to appear yearly in parts or volumes, to be delivered free to Subscribers not in arrear with the subscriptions.

V. That there shall be only a limited number of copies printed of each Work beyond the number of Subscribers, which copies the Committee are empowered to dispose of to persons becoming annual subscribers.

VI. That the management of the affairs of the Society be vested in the Chairman and Committee, and that the funds of the Society be disbursed in payment of the necessary expenses incident to the production of the Works of the Society, and that the accompts of the receipts and expenditure be audited annually by two Members.

⁕ Subscribers' Names, Donations and Annual Subscriptions are requested to be forwarded to the Secretary, Mr. Griffith, 4, Sidmouth Place, Gray's Inn Road, London.

ADVERTISEMENT.

IN preparing the present work for the press, it has been deemed advisable to place the Welsh and English on opposite pages, as an arrangement more convenient for the scholar, who may wish to test the accuracy of the translation by a reference to the original.

Except to supply some of the headings, no liberty whatever has been taken with the text. Even obvious and glaring errors, whether in the orthography or punctuation, have been transferred to our pages exactly as they were found in the manuscript.

The translation has been rendered as literal as possible, short of becoming obscure. This was considered expedient, not only with the view of exhibiting the style and idiom of the original, but in order to guard against any misapprehension of the sense, which a free construction is too apt to produce.

Notes, historical and explanatory, have been added, which, without being cumbersome, it is to be hoped, will prove of considerable service to the reader.

Our thanks are especially due to the Right Honourable Lord and Lady Llanover for their kindness in allowing us free access to the MSS. of Iolo Morganwg, from which the present Collection has been for the most part made.

Tair sail Barddas: Heddwch; Cariad; a Chyfiawnder.

PREFACE.

THE promoters of the National Eisteddvod, which was held at Llangollen, in the autumn of 1858, conscious of the increased attention that was being paid by foreign scholars to the literature and usages of our Cymric ancestors, and desirous, at the same time, of facilitating their inquiries in that direction, as well as of effectually rescuing from a precarious existence the traditions of the Bards, offered a prize of £30, and a Bardic tiara in gold, for " the fullest illustration, from original sources, of the theology, discipline, and usages of the Bardo-druidic system of the Isle of Britain." Only one compilation was received, which, nevertheless, received a very high encomium, accompanied with a recommendation that it should be published, in the following adjudication, which was read at the meeting by Myvyr Morganwg,* one of the three judges appointed for the occasion.

"On this very important and interesting subject only one composition has been received, which bears the feigned signature of PLENNYDD. It is a very extensive collection, for the most part of unpublished

---

* The other adjudicators wore the Rev. T. James, Netherlong, Huddersfield, and the Rev. Silvan Evans, Llangian, Pwllheli.

MSS., consisting of 287 folio pages, clearly and beautifully written, and exhibiting indications of being carefully and accurately copied, for the writer, following herein the example of the late Iolo Morganwg, has suffered even errors, which were obvious in the manuscripts before him, to remain unaltered.

" The compiler has been very diligent, and remarkably successful in obtaining access to such a vast number of ancient MSS. bearing on Bardism, many of which had seen but little light for several years before. With respect to their genuineness, PLENNYDD justly observes,—' though their authors cannot in many instances be named, any more than we can name the authors of the Common Law of England, yet the existence of the peculiar dogmas and usages, which they represent, may be proved from the compositions of the Bards from the era of Taliesin down to the present time.'

" This collection contains a great many of the Rules and Usages appertaining to the Gorsedd of the Bards, several valuable fragments on the Natural and Moral Philosophy of our ancestors, together with the ingenious Theology of the ancient Bardism of the Cymry ; also curious extracts on Astronomy, Arithmetic, the Bardic Coelbren, and a vast quantity of Triads. Every fragment that can thus be made public, of what once related to the primitive Gorsedd or Throne of the Bards, is truly valuable, inasmuch as it was this simple, moral, and sublime system, that constituted the very foundation of the primitive worship, legislature, and scholastic institutes of the nation, and was the living means of promoting learning and morality among all classes of the people, in early times. And when we consider that the Gorsedd of the Bards was but a continuation, in the White Island, of the circular temples of patriarchal times, we may feel assured that it is among the remains of Bardism, or the religious system connected with those primitive temples, we may hope to discover, if at all, that *Golden Key*, concealed and secured, which can open the mysteries, or esoteric doctrine, of ancient nations..........

" We had no right to expect that we should find the ' Secrets of Bardism,' or the ' Mysteries of *Maen Arch*,' introduced into a compilation, which was intended to be made public ; for such have been, and ought to be a sort of mute tradition, and tradition only, to be communicated solely to such as have proved themselves worthy to receive them..........

" Nevertheless, there may be found in this collection, some fragments which contain, as is very clear to every initiated Bard, the remains of that sublime learning, as it existed in the Isle of Britain anterior to Christianity ; such as those extracts about the elements— the migration of the soul from the point of extreme evil in Annwn to the point of extreme good in heaven—the mystic Name of God— the nature of Cythraul, &c. In order to prove the genuineness and great antiquity of these particulars to one who is not initiated in the mysteries of Bardism, it may suffice that they are also discoverable, though in a more corrupt form, in the ancient bardism of Hindoostan. They are old dogmas, at present neither preserved nor existing amidst the antiquities of any nation under the sun, except the Indians and the Cymry.

" But we have in the present collection some pieces of mixed Bardism, which may be called Monkish Bardism, or Bardism and Christianity mixed together, which could easily take place after the introduction of Christianity, owing to the remarkable—very remarkable coincidence which exists between the two systems.

" The Compiler assures us that he is in possession of more documents, which would have been added, if time had permitted. We trust that he will hereafter kindly make the addition, and that the whole will be published in one or more volumes. It will make a valuable Book, not only as aid in the management of the Gorsedd of the Bards, but also, and especially, because the time is undoubtedly coming, as is proved by certain signs, when every fragment of the primitive Bardism of the Cymry will be treasured as gold, and subjected to the severest criticism by men of learning and research.

" I know not what the literati of the Continent will say, when the Book is published, but I presume that their curiosity will be much excited by its contents, and that they themselves will be highly pleased with the labour and industry of the Compiler..........

" The three judges are of opinion that the writer deserves to have the prize presented to him by acclamation, and with the full and joyful approbation of the nation, as represented in this Great Eisteddvod." *

The compilation thus referred to is that, which, with omissions and additions, somewhat re-arranged, and accompanied with an English translation, is now offered to the public. With very few exceptions, the several documents used on the present occasion, have been collected from the manuscripts of the late Iolo Morganwg, Bard according to the privilege and usage of the Bards of the Isle of Britain, and one of

---

* The adjudication was originally written in Welsh, in which language it was also read at the meeting.

the two that constituted the only members of the
Bardic institution, when it was revived at the close of
the last century.*   But though they are thus in his
handwriting, if we set aside some brief and unimpor-
tant notices, which, whether original or otherwise, may
have been couched in his own language, there is
every reason to believe that they are transcripts of
older manuscripts.   In the first place we may remark,
that they are interspersed, without method or order
of any kind, among the private and casual entries of
the Bard, which he made on loose scraps of old letters, bills, and placards—bound together only after
his death, and that they were thus evidently not
intended to be published.   This fact of itself would
remove the notion of any design on his part to impose
upon the credulity of his countrymen.   Moreover,
we have had an opportunity of examining fully and
carefully those papers, and thus seen the Bard, as it
were, in his most private and unguarded moments,
and can, as the result of our observation, unhesita-
tingly pronounce him to be incapable of perpetrating
literary deceit or forgery, particularly with the view
of upholding a theory.   Integrity of purpose is apparent throughout all his works.   Strong feelings,
indeed, he had, amounting almost to prejudice, but
they were founded in jealous concern for the due
preservation of the traditions of the country, and
never displayed, except when he beheld a disposition
to oppugn or disparage what he considered ancient
and national.   It was on this ground, for instance,
that he so strenuously advocated the claims of Dos-

---

* The other was the Rev. Edward Evan, of Aberdare.

parth Morganwg, or the Glamorgan system of versification, in preference to the twenty-four new canons
of poetry, which were sanctioned at the famous Eisteddvod, held at Caermarthen, under the patronage
of Gruffydd ab Nicholas, in the 15th century. Secondly, the style is in general too archaic for the
18th century, exhibiting occasionally terms of such
an obsolete character as to baffle the skill of the
etymologist. Nor must it be asserted that they
were fabricated for a purpose, with a view of imparting to the documents the appearance of antiquity,
for even Iolo Morganwg himself professes not to
fully understand some of them. Thus, in reference
to a Triad entitled, "Tri phrif anaw Beirdd Ynys
Prydain," he remarks, "the meaning of this word
(anaw) has not hitherto been satisfactorily given,"
and proposes the query, "whether it may not signify
an original genius?" and soon after, "whether *anaw*
may not signify a philosopher?" Again, after an
extract, to which the name of Llywelyn Sion is
attached, relative to "Cadair Tarannon," he asks,
"*Tarannon* and *Teyrnon*—were they one and the
same thing? Qu. whether *Cadair Teyrnon* in Taliesin be not one and the same thing, and also the
same thing as *gorsedd gwlad ac arlwydd?*" The
word *obryn* is not to be met with in the Dictionaries;
it may, and probably does, signify a state in Abred
corresponding with man's turpitude at the time of his
death, which is the meaning given to it by Iolo
Morganwg; but assuredly if he had been driven to
coin for himself a compound which should express
the above idea, instead of the very unusual prefix *ob*,
he would naturally have adopted *cyf, cyd,* or *cyn,* as

in the case of *cydfil,* which occurs in the same Triad.
Sometimes, when the language is not obscure, he
seems to misunderstand the import of a word, and to
suggest an interpretation, which, on due examination
of the Bardic doctrine, appears to be erroneous. Thus
when, referring to *light* in the Triad — "There are
three cognates: man; liberty; and light," he observes, "intellectual light is here probably meant,"
he forgets that it is distinctly stated in other documents that man sprang into existence simultaneously
with the resplendent appearance of the triple form of
God's Name, which was the first manifestation of
material light. These facts clearly prove that Iolo
Morganwg had no hand in forging the documents in
question. Thirdly, the different readings, which
abound in them, demonstrate that the Bard had
frequently even more than one manuscript before
him, when he made his transcripts — a fact, which
shows, moreover, that their contents were then better known than they are in our own day. Fourthly,
whilst the general subject is the same, there is a
want of uniformity in some of the details, as in the
directions given for constructing a Peithynen, and the
formation of a Gorsedd — the explanation of the Divine epithet Iau — and the enumeration and names
of the elements. This circumstance, whilst it indicates a variety of sources, whence the different expressions of opinion must have been derived, at the same
time excludes the idea of a collusion. Had Iolo and
some of his friends entered into a conspiracy to palm
upon the public, as an ancient system, a theory of
their own invention, they would doubtless have taken
care that there should exist an exact agreement

between the several parts of their joint production.
It is of the essence of forgery to endeavour to avoid
varieties in matters of detail—whilst truth, and integrity of purpose, having a greater regard for the main
subject, are generally indifferent to these particulars.
Lastly, Iolo Morganwg refers to the actual existence
of some of the documents, which he alleges to have
copied, and gives, with very great minuteness, the
address of the owner. Thus, in relation to certain
extracts which he made from "Trioedd Barddas,"
"Trioedd Braint a Defod," "Trioedd Doethineb,"
and "Trioedd Pawl," which contain the very essence
of Bardism, as exhibited in our pages, he remarks ;—
"The Triades that are here selected are from a manuscript collection, by Llywelyn Sion, a Bard of
Glamorgan, about the year 1560. Of this manuscript I have a transcript ; the original is in the
possession of Mr. Richard Bradford, of Bettws, near
Bridgend, in Glamorgan ;" and as if this were not sufficiently particular, he adds in a note, "son of the
late Mr. John Bradford, who, for skill in ancient
British Bardism, left not his equal behind." Nor
does this statement occur among the private papers
of the Bard, but appears in his published work—his
"Poems Lyric and Pastoral," where also the selections alluded to are printed.* If the reference had
been untrue, it could easily have been refuted, nor
would his enemies, of whom he had several, have
been slow to take advantage of the circumstance to
expose the whole as a tissue of falsehood and deceit.
But nothing of the kind took place. It is fair, how-

* See Vol. ii.

ever, to observe that the existence of the manuscript
in question at the present moment is open to doubt
—the prize offered at the Eisteddvod failed to bring
it forth. Still we are in hopes that it is not irre-
trievably lost, and it may be in the possession of some
person who " careth for none of these things."

We trust that these reasons are sufficient to justify
us in our conclusion, that Iolo Morganwg had nothing
whatever to do with the original compilation of the
main documents, which form the present collection,
and that he merely transcribed older materials, which
from some sources or other had fallen into his hands.

Failing the attempt to convict Iolo Morganwg as
a literary impostor, the sceptics of the present day
profess to discover the sources in question in the
Eisteddvodau, which were held subsequently to the
beginning of the 15th century, more especially those
of 1570, 1580, and 1681. A body of curious matter
is found to exist, purporting to have come down to
us, through the medium of the Chair of Glamorgan,
as genuine remains of the theology and usages of the
Bards. This is an incontrovertible fact. Again, history notes with equal sternness the authorization, at
the above mentioned Congresses successively, of what
was likewise called Bardism: and the not unnatural
inference is, that they are one and the same. But,
apparently for no other reason than that the code
thus promulgated was not formally committed to
writing before, a higher origin is denied to it, and of
course the Bards of those periods, Ieuan ab Hywel
Swrdwal, Gwilym Tew, Lewys Morganwg, Meurig
Davydd, Davydd Benwyn, Llywelyn Sion, Davydd
Llwyd Mathew, Edward Davydd, and others, are

boldly charged with being its sole inventors. As
they were not all contemporaries, and as they held
various positions in life, and were also members of
different religious communions, it would be difficult
to account for the unanimity with which they adopted
the strange and curious system, which these volumes
present to our view. To accuse them of being under
the influence of that spirit, which led to the overthrow
of the monarchy, and to the establishment of the commonwealth on its ruins, merely because their system
represents the three orders of Bard, Druid, and
Ovate, as co-equal in rank and privilege, is, to say
the least, not warranted by facts. History does not
point out a single Bard of those times as mixing in
any political intrigue. On the contrary they, one
and all of whom we have any knowledge, appear to
have led quiet lives, paying due and just homage of
loyalty to the existing government of the day, without opposition, and without complaint. Besides, it
may be interesting to know, why the Bards in question should have selected this particular form, whether as the embodiment of their own creed, or as the
representation of ancient Druidism? There was nothing in the prevailing philosophy of the day to
suggest it; and to say that they derived it from the
traditions of the Brahmins, would be to give them
credit for a greater extent of knowledge than their
positions in life would warrant. Could they, then,
have compiled the whole system — ingenious, com-
plex, and yet harmonious and symmetrical as it was,
out of the mere allusions to it, which are contained
in the works of the earlier Poets? The Rev. Edward
Davies observes, — " It does not appear, from their

d

own profession, nor from the research of Llwyd, and other antiquaries, that this society possessed a single copy of the works of the ancient Bards, previous to the eighteenth century."* If the inference, evidently intended to be drawn from this guarded form of expression, be well founded, of course a direct negative must be returned to our inquiry. But we are not prepared to endorse the opinion, favourable as it may be to our present argument. We believe that the Bards of the 15th and 16th centuries were, to some extent, acquainted with the poetical productions of their predecessors, but at the same time we boldly maintain that it was next to impossible they should agree upon any system drawn from those sources. And in proof of our assertion, we need only refer to those who are known to have made the trial. What two persons have been found to agree in their views of the mystic allusions of the Bards? What an interminable distance there is between the respective theories of Davies and Nash!

Whilst, however, we deny that the contents of these volumes could have been derived immediately from the metrical compositions of the medieval and early Poets, we believe that they can be abundantly proved by them. There are numerous allusions, which, otherwise obscure and unintelligible, become by means of the light thrown upon them from Bardism, as clear as day. As an example; Rhys Brydydd, between 1450 and 1490, has the following lines on Hu the Mighty :—

* The Mythology and Rites of the British Druids, p. 34.

The smallest of the small
Is Hu the Mighty, as the world judges ;
And the greatest, and a Lord to us,
Let us well believe, and our mysterious God ;
Light His course, and active,
An atom of glowing heat is His car ;
Great on land and on the seas,
The greatest that I manifestly can have,
Greater than the worlds—Let us beware
Of mean indignity to him who deals in bounty.*

Even supposing Hu the Mighty to signify the Supreme Being, it would be difficult to explain how He
can be " the smallest of the small," and at the same
time " the greatest," or to show how His chariot is
composed of " an atom of glowing heat."   Accordingly, the interpretations given by Davies, Archdeacon
Williams, and Nash, varied though they be, are extremely vague and unsatisfactory, leaving us in a
greater state of bewilderment than if we had never
received them.   And yet how simple is the illustration which Bardism affords — " Hu the Mighty —
Jesus the Son of God, — the least in respect of His
worldly greatness whilst in the flesh, and the greatest
in heaven of all visible majesties."   Or, which also
explains the nature of His car ; — " the particles of
light are the smallest of all small things ; and yet one
particle of light is the greatest of all great things,
being no less than material for all materiality that
can be understood and perceived as within the grasp
of the power of God.   And in every particle there is
a place wholly commensurate with God, for there is
not, and cannot be less than God in every particle of

---

* Dr. O. Pughe's Dict., sub voce *mymryn*.

light, and God in every particle; nevertheless God is only one in number."

In like manner, there are various allusions to *annwn, abred, manred, byd mawr, byd bach, pair Ceridwen,* the *Coelbren,* and many other particulars of a similar kind, which, while they are in themselves insufficient to constitute an intelligible groundwork on which to raise a superstructure such as our pages contain, bear strong testimony to the fact of its existence from the 16th up to the 6th century. The transmigration related by Taliesin is not identical in detail with that of Bardism, for in the latter the soul is not supposed to enter inanimate objects, such as a sword, a star, a word, a book, a boat, a shield, a tree, an axe, and a grain of wheat, which form some of the gradations in " Cad Goddeu " and " Angar Cyvyndawd;" and we infer from this discrepancy that the Bardic doctrine was not directly founded on the poet's language. Still we may regard it as a valuable testimony to the actual existence among the Cymry, at the time when the poems were written, of a doctrine of metempsychosis, whether believed in, or preserved merely as a matter of curiosity. To notice in detail all the passages, which might be culled out of the works of the Poets, as referring to the principal tenets and usages of Bardism, would swell our Preface to an unnecessary length, especially since many of them are inserted in the body of the work as footnotes; to them, then, we would beg to direct the attention of our readers.

Further, the philosophical features of Bardism may be traced even in the language of the Cymry, and the testimony, which it thus affords, is the more valuable,

because it is indirect and unexpected. If we allow
it possible that the Bards of the 15th and 16th centuries should have actually drawn their system directly
from the works of their predecessors, no one can for a
moment entertain the thought that they were capable of drawing it from the language, whether solely,
or in conjunction with the poetry of different times.
Independently of Bardism, it would be difficult to
explain why *advyd*, a term signifying *re-world*, or a
beginning of the world over again, should in common
use stand for adversity, but "Rhol Cof a Chyfrif"
informs us that it was originally applied to the state
of retraversing *abred*, which, being a punishment for
sin, was of course a state of hardship and adversity.
Again, we find that the word *gwydd* means both *wood*
and *knowledge*, which cannot be accounted for except
on the supposition of a common origin, or that there
was a mutual connection between the one and the
other from the earliest times. This affinity is explained
by the *Coelbren*. In like manner, the doctrine of *eneidvaddeu* alone can satisfactorily account for the double
meaning of *maddeu*, and show us how a word, which
properly means *to liberate*, or *to dismiss*, came also to
signify *to forgive*, which is its common import at the
present day. *Angau, aberth, huan, nefoedd*, and a host
of other words might be enumerated, which clearly
refer to the mythology of the ancient Cymry; hence
it is manifest that no Welsh philologist can effectually succeed in his investigations, unless in the first
instance he makes himself acquainted with Bardism.

What, then, shall we say? Did the Bards in
question model their system according to the description, which Julius Cæsar, and other foreign

writers, have given of Druidism? There is *prima
facie* a wide difference between the two systems.
Cæsar speaks of a plurality of gods, of an archdruid,
who had superior authority over the others, and also
of the immolation of human sacrifices; whereas the
unity of the Godhead is the very soul and centre of
Bardism, which also strongly insists upon the co-
equality of its orders, and seems to discountenance
altogether the notion of the sacrifice of living beings,
in the strict acceptation of the term, whether they
were men or beasts. This circumstance, therefore, is
fatal to the hypothesis which would regard classical
Druidism as the groundwork on which the fabric of
Bardism has been raised. Still, if the latter is, as it
professes to be, the genuine remains of the primitive
worship and philosophy of Britain, there must be a
possibility of harmonizing the two systems — they
must in principle be identical. To this subject we
will now address ourselves.

JULIUS CÆSAR, b.c. 99—44.

It is necessary that we should, at the outset, bear
in mind the following observation made by Cæsar, as
to the comparative merits of the Continental and
British systems :—

"The institution is thought to have originated in Britain, and to
have been thence introduced into Gaul; and even now those who
wish to become more accurately acquainted with it, generally repair
thither, for the sake of learning it."

It is clear from this statement that Druidism, in
Cæsar's time, was not considered as pure and as well
understood on the Continent as it was in the British
isle, its genuine home; an hypothesis, moreover,

exactly in accordance with the traditions of the
Bards:—"Bardism originated in the Isle of Britain
—no other country ever obtained a proper comprehension of Bardism. Three nations corrupted what
they had learned of the Bardism of the Isle of Britain, blending with it heterogeneous principles, by
which means they lost it: the Irish; the Cymry of
Armorica; and the Germans."*

According to this view, we must not expect that
the two systems should agree in all matters of detail,
but only in principle and substance.

Cæsar's description refers solely to the Druidism of
Gaul. How he acquired his information, he does not
tell us; it might have been in part from personal
observation, and in part, if not wholly, from his friend
Divitiacus, who was a Druid among the Ædui. It is
possible that his narrative in this respect is correct;
still his general character for veracity does not bind
us to believe implicitly every word that he says. Suetonius tells us, that Asinius Pollio, who was a contemporary of Cæsar, was of opinion that his assertions
are not altogether worthy of credit;—" Asinius Pollio," he remarks, "thinks that they [the works of
Cæsar] were composed with but little accuracy, and
little truth, since Cæsar used to believe rashly respecting the deeds of other men, and also to relate
erroneously the things done by himself, either of set
purpose, or through failure of memory, and he is of
opinion that he intended to re-write and correct
them."† We shall not, however, take the benefit of

---

* Trioedd Braint a Defod.   † Suet. i.

this opinion, but proceed at once to notice the principal points of Druidism, as actually related by Cæsar himself, and to compare them with the views of the Bards, in order to see how far they may be reconciled one with the other.   The whole account, as given by Cæsar of the Continental Druids, is as follows:—

"They preside over sacred things, have the charge of public and private sacrifices, and explain their religion.   To them a great number of youths have recourse for the sake of acquiring instruction, and they are in great honour among them.   For they generally settle all their disputes, both public and private ; and if there is any transgression perpetrated, any murder committed, or any dispute about inheritance or boundaries, they decide in respect of them ; they appoint rewards and penalties ; and if any private or public person abides not by their decree, they restrain him from the sacrifices.   This with them is the most severe punishment.   Whoever are so interdicted, are ranked in the number of the impious and wicked ; all forsake them, and shun their company and conversation, lest they should suffer disadvantage from contagion with them : nor is legal right rendered to them when they sue it, nor any honour conferred upon them.   But one presides over all these Druids, who possesses the supreme authority among them.   At his death, if any one of the others excels in dignity, the same succeeds him : but if several have equal pretensions, the president is elected by the votes of the Druids, sometimes even they contend about the supreme dignity by force of arms.   At a certain time of the year, they assemble in session on a consecrated spot in the confines of the Carnutes, which is considered the central region of the whole of Gaul.   Thither all, who have any disputes, come together from every side, and acquiesce in their judgments and decisions.   The institution is thought to have originated in Britain, and to have been thence introduced into Gaul, and even now, those who wish to become more accurately acquainted with it, generally repair thither for the sake of learning it.

"The Druids usually abstain from war, nor do they pay taxes together with the others; they have exemption from warfare, and the free use of all things.   Instigated by such advantages, many resort to their school even of their own accord, whilst others are sent by their parents and relations.   There they are said to learn thoroughly a great number of verses.   On that account, some continue at their education for twenty years.   Nor do they deem it lawful to commit those things to writing ; though, generally, in other cases, and in their public and private accounts, they use Greek letters.   They appear to me to have established this custom for two reasons; because they would not have their tenets published, and because they would not have those, who learn them, by trusting to letters, neglect the exercise of memory; since it generally happens, that, owing to the safeguard of letters, they relax their diligence in learning, as well as their memory. In particular they wish to inculcate this idea, that souls do not die, but pass after death from one body to another; and they think that by this means men are very much instigated to the exercise of bravery, the fear of death being despised. They also dispute largely concerning the stars and their motion, the magnitude of the world and the earth, the nature of things, the force and power of the immortal gods, and instruct the youth in their principles.

" The whole nation of the Gauls is very much given to religious observances, and on that account, those who are afflicted with grievous diseases, and those who are engaged in battles and perils, either immolate men as sacrifices, or vow that they will immolate themselves, and they employ the Druids as ministers of those sacrifices; because they think that, if the life of man is not given for the life of man, the immortal gods cannot be appeased; they have also instituted public sacrifices of the same kind. Some have images of immense size, the limbs of which, interwoven with twigs, they fill with living men, and the same being set on fire, the men, surrounded by the flames, are put to death. They think that the punishment of those who are caught in theft or pillage, or in any other wicked act, is more acceptable to the immortal gods; but when there is a deficiency of such evil doers, they have recourse even to the punishment of the innocent.

" They chiefly worship the god Mercury; of him they have many images, him they consider as the inventor of all arts, as the guide of ways and journeys, and as possessing the greatest power for obtaining money and merchandise. After him, they worship Apollo, Mars, Jupiter, and Minerva. Concerning them they have almost the same opinion as other nations, namely: that Apollo wards off diseases; that Minerva instructs them in the principles of works and arts; that Jupiter holds the empire of heaven; and that Mars rules wars. To him, when they have determined to engage in battle, they generally vow those things which they shall have captured in war. When they are victorious, they sacrifice the captured animals; and pile up the other things in one place.

" The Gauls declare that they have all sprung from their father Pluto, and this they say was delivered to them by the Druids."*

---

* De Bel. Gal. liber vi. cc. 13—18.

e

The principal topics, which demand our attention in this extract, are:—

1. *The religious function of the Druids.* The two systems are perfectly agreed in this respect, that the priestly office belonged to the Druidic order. Cæsar, indeed, does not mention either of the other two orders, but his silence is no proof that they did not exist in Gaul as well as in Britain. It is very probable that the Druids were, in respect of their office, the most conspicuous among the Gauls, and that Cæsar's attention was especially drawn to their deeds, so as to overlook the Bards and Ovates, or that he considered the functions of these as absorbed in that of the Druids. We have the evidence of Diodorus Siculus and Strabo that there were Bards in Gaul, and the latter says there were Ovates (Οὐάτεις) also.

2. *The respect in which they were held.* The Druids of Britain were, likewise, highly esteemed by the people. According to the laws of Dyvnwal Moelmud, "the Gorsedd of Bards" was "the oldest in its origin" of "the three privileged Gorsedds of the Isle of Britain." Its different functionaries had a right each to five free acres of land in virtue of their office —were entitled to maintenance wherever they went —had freedom from taxes—no person was to bear a naked weapon in their presence—and their word was always paramount. These privileges, as well as others, to which they had a right, are distinctly specified in the present volumes, and they show the great respect and honour in which they at all times stood in the community. The consequence was that many persons were usually candidates for the office, not only among the nobility and gentry, but also

among those of low rank, for the bondsman became free on his assuming the profession of Bardism, though he could not learn it " without the permission of his proprietary lord, and the lord of the territory." Cæsar regards the Druids and Knights as of a higher rank than the common people, and as being distinct from them, and though he does not say that the former could have arisen, and gained their nobility by means of their office, yet it is not improbable that the teachers of Gaul were, in this respect, similar to the Bards of the Isle of Britain. At any rate, every Bard among the Cymry was according to his office a free and honourable man, whatever his position might have been previously. In this matter, therefore, we perceive no substantial difference between the Druidism of Britain and the Druidism of Gaul.

3. *The arbitration and settlement of disputes.* It appears from the Laws of Dyvnwal Moelmud that there were " three Gorsedds according to the privilege of the country and nation of the Cymry," having their respective duties and functions with a view to the improvement of society.

" The first is the Gorsedd of the Bards of the Isle of Britain, and their foundation and privilege rest upon reason, nature, and cogency ; or, according to other teachers and wise men, upon reason, nature, and circumstance. And the privilege and office of those protected by the Gorsedd of Bards are to maintain and preserve and diffuse authorized instruction in the sciences of piety, wisdom, and courtesy ; and to preserve memorial and record of every thing commendable respecting individuals and kindred ; and every event of times ; and every natural phenomenon ; and wars ; and regulations of country and nation ; and punishments ; and commendable victories ; and to preserve a warranted record of genealogies, marriages, nobility, privileges, and customs of the nation of the Cymry ; and to attend to the exigencies of other Gorsedds in announcing what shall be achieved, and what shall be requisite, under lawful proclamation and warning : and further than this there is nothing either of office or of privilege attached to a Gorsedd of Bards.......Second, the Gorsedd of the country and common weal ; or the Gorsedd of judicature and decision of law, for the right and protection of the country and nation, their refugees, and their aliens. These Gorsedds act severally ; that is to say, the Gorsedd of federate support makes a law, where an occasion requires, and confirms it in a country and federate country ; and that is not allowed to a country distinct from a federate country. The Gorsedd of judgment and judicature decides upon such as shall transgress the law, and punishes him. And the Gorsedd of the Bards teaches commendable sciences, and decides respecting them, and methodically preserves all the memorials of the nation to insure their authenticity. And it is not right for any one of these Gorsedds to intermeddle with the deliberation of either of the other two, but to confirm them, and to support them regularly. The third Gorsedd, or that of federate support, in its original and determinate purpose, is to effect what may be necessary as to any thing new, and as to the improvement of the laws of a country and federate country, by a federate jury of chiefs of kindreds, wise men, and sovereign ruler. A sovereign prince, or ruler of paramount right, is the oldest in possessive title of the kings and the princes of a federate community : and he is to raise the mighty agitation ; and his word is superior to every other word in the agitation of the country."

According to the tenor of this extract, it was "the Gorsedd of judgment and judicature" that possessed the special right of determining national and social disputes, in conformity with the law that was enacted in a " Gorsedd of federate support." They were matters of a literary character mainly that came under the supervision of the Bards. Nevertheless, there was some connection between the three institutions—they were " to confirm, and support " each other "regularly." The Bards were required more particularly to register the events that occurred in country and nation, to preserve the records of genealogies, marriages, nobility, privileges and customs, of the nation of the Cymry, and to attend to the exigencies of other Gorsedds in announcing what shall be

achieved, and what shall be requisite, under lawful
proclamation and warning. So far, then, it might be
said that they settled matters appertaining to inheritances and boundaries, as the Druids of Gaul did in
the time of Cæsar. The Roman captain might easily
be mistaken with respect to the extent of the authority and power of the Druids, attributing to them more
than in reality they possessed. After all, he does not
admit that the entire authority was in their hands—
his observation is, " they *generally* settle all their disputes, both public and private." And even if things
were exactly as he relates them, it is not difficult to
suppose that this was a natural corruption of the
primitive custom. Inasmuch as the Druids generally
were possessed of more learning and knowledge than
any other class of people in the country, it was quite
natural that they should increase in political and social authority, especially where the other establish-
ments were not as orderly and well defined as they
were in Britain. We see this principle at work in
relation to the Church, during what is called "the
dark ages," when more than necessary of temporal
and political authority fell into the hands of ecclesi-
astics.

Cæsar says of the Druids of Gaul that the greatest
punishment which was inflicted upon evil doers was,
to keep them from the sacrifices. It must be admitted that there was nothing, as far as we know, in the
institute of Britain, which altogether answered to
this interdict. Perhaps the nearest approach to it
was the refusal of the protection of the Gorsedd to
any member of the community, who, for some fault
or other, was announced to be exposed to a " naked

weapon." The Bards, however, had a peculiar mode of degrading their convicted brethren. It took place at a Gorsedd, and the act was called " to bring the assault of warfare against " him who was to be thus disfranchised. After the Bards had agreed in their decision, they covered their heads, and one of them unsheathed the sword, named the person aloud three times, with the sword lifted in his hand, adding when he was last named, " the sword is naked against him." He could never after be re-admitted ; and was called "a man deprived of privilege and exposed to warfare." There is some resemblance in this custom to what Cæsar says of the excommunicated, "that no legal right was rendered to them, nor any honour conferred upon them ;" and the resemblance is sufficient to show that the usages of the two countries had sprung from the same root.

4. *The Archdruid.* Among the Cymry the three orders, Bard, Druid, and Ovate, were co-equal, one with the other, in point of privilege and dignity, whilst they were different in regard to duties. For thus it is stated in " Trioedd Braint a Defod:"—

" 'The three branches of Bardism : Poetry ; Ovatism ; and Druidism ; that is to say, these three branches are adjudged to be of equal privilege, and equal importance, for there can be no superiority to one of them over another—though they are distinct in purpose, they are not distinct in privilege."

" There are three Bards of equal importance, that is, the three worthy primitive Bards, namely : a licensed native Bard, or a Poet according to privilege and usage ; an Ovate-bard, devoted to genial learning ; and a Druid-bard, devoted to theology and morality ;—and they are said to be of equal importance, because one cannot be better than another, or supreme over the rest ;—though one is distinct from another in respect of office and movement, still they are equal and of like dignity in respect of obligation, effort, and object, which are, learning, truth, and peace."

In this sense, then, it may be said that the system of the Cymry varied from that of the Gauls. Nevertheless, occasionally, that is, when they met in Gorsedd, " one presided," even among the British Bards. He was called *chief*-Bard, or Gorsedd Bard ; and if he were of the Druidic order, he might be easily regarded as an *Arch*-druid, not only because he presided, but because in doing so he stood on the " maen *arch*," in the centre of the sacred circle. Every chief-Bard had a right to preside at a Gorsedd, but still nothing could be decided without the consent of the majority of Gorsedd Bards—the former was merely a kind of chairman—*primus inter pares*, for the time.

Cæsar seems to imply that one only presided during life, and when he died, that another was elected in his stead. This is not altogether in unison with the custom of the Cymry. Nevertheless, if such in truth was the usage of Gaul, it might easily have been derived from our own country. Whilst the people of the Continent did not properly understand Bardism, there was nothing to prevent them from falling into a mistake as to the nature of the authority, which the Bard president possessed, deeming it to be personal, and intended to continue for life, whereas it was official only—belonging to several, and to be exercised as occasions required. The Cymry never had recourse to the sword in order to settle the question of supremacy, as we learn from Cæsar was the case sometimes on the Continent. This was quite an abuse— and thoroughly inconsistent with the spirit of Bardism.

5. *The place of meeting.* According to Cæsar, the Druids of Gaul had a fixed place and time for meet-

ing; he mentions not the time, but the place he says was on the confines of the Carnutes, in the middle of the country, as was supposed. "Thither," he says, "all, who have any disputes, come together from every side, and acquiesce in their judgments and decisions." In like manner, the Bards or Druids of Britain had their appointed times and places for meeting in Gorsedd. Their times were the Albans, namely, Alban Eilir, Alban Hevin, Alban Elved, and Alban Arthan, that is, the equinoxes and solstices, or the commencement of the four seasons of the year. The principal places are recorded in the following Triads:—

"The three principal Gorsedds of the Bards of the Isle of Britain: the Gorsedd of Bryn Gwyddon at Caerleon-upon-Usk; the Gorsedd of Moel Evwr; and the Gorsedd of Beiscawen.

"The three Gorsedds of entire song of the Isle of Britain: the Gorsedd of Beiscawen in Dyvnwal; the Gorsedd of Caer Caradog in Lloegria; and the Gorsedd of Bryn Gwyddon in Cymru."

There was thus one special Gorsedd in each of the three principal provinces, where the native mind chiefly predominated. The Gorsedd was a sort of national temple, to which the majority of persons within the province resorted at the appointed times, in order to worship God, and to receive instruction. All were invited, except such as were "deprived of privilege, and exposed to warfare," and no impediments were allowed to be put on their way, as they travelled "under the protection and peace of God."

"Three common rights of federate country and border country: a principal river; a high road; and a *resort of worship;* and those are under the protection of God and His peace; since a weapon is not to be unsheathed by such as frequent them against those they may meet;

and whoever shall do so, whether a native or a stranger, a claim of galanas against him arises on the plaint of the lord of the territory."*

6. *The derivation of the Druidic system.* We have already noticed the coincidence between the notion which prevailed in Gaul on this head and the drift of the Cymric traditions.

7. *Memorials.* "They are said," observes Cæsar, " to learn thoroughly a great number of verses; and on that account, some continue at their education for twenty years." One of " the three memorials of the Bards of the Isle of Britain," was " the memorial of song." This was one of the oldest vehicles in which events and sciences were handed down among the Bards, and it is supposed that the particular form which they used was the metre called " Triban Milwr," or the Warrior's Triplet. The name of Tydain, the father of Awen, is especially associated with the memorial of song ; and " the poem of Tydain " is prominently alluded to in the account of the establishment of Bardism. He was a contemporary of Prydain.

As time rolled on, accumulating events and sciences, we may easily suppose that " twenty years " would not be more than sufficient to enable a man to treasure in his memory the " great number of verses " necessary to contain and embody them. Generally, however, nine years was the time during which a pupil was required to be under discipline previous to his being graduated as a Chief Bard.

* The Laws of Dyvnwal Moelmud.
f

"They do not deem it lawful *(fas)* to commit those things to writing," i.e. the things appertaining to the system. Neither did the British Bards countenance the habit of writing their traditions. On the contrary, it was their custom to recite them publicly in every Gorsedd, until they became deeply rooted in the memory of the people. This is what they called the "voice of Gorsedd," and it was in this manner that their traditions have come down to us. Cæsar's opinion respecting such a practice coincides exactly with the reason which influenced the Bards of Cymru. "They appear to me to have established this custom for two reasons; because they would not have their tenets published, and because they would not have those, who learn them, by trusting to letters, neglect the exercise of memory." The Bards had a "Cyvrinach," or Secret, which they did not consider it lawful for any one to know out of their own order; such were the Name of God, and the Ten Letters. All this secrecy related especially to the institute, and the candidate for admission into it took an awful vow that he would not divulge the *cyvrinach* to any one, who was not a regular Bard. They likewise considered that the use of writing tended to weaken the memory, not only in respect of the disciples, but also of the people generally; or rather, with regard to the latter, they considered that the voice of Gorsedd was the easiest mode of teaching them, and the most effectual for preventing every kind of falsehood and corruption.

With respect to the voice of Gorsedd, and its connection with the discipline of the Bards themselves, we have it thus stated in "the Book of Lewys Morganwg, which he compiled from many of the old Books:"—

"There is no other than the memorial, voice, and usage of Gorsedd belonging to the privileges and usages of the primitive Bards, for they spring from primary and original right, before there was any Book knowledge; therefore, they were submitted only to the memorial of the voice, and usage of Gorsedd; or, as others say, to the memorial of song, voice, and usage. And they have no permanent privilege and authority, but what we know by these means."

Nevertheless, the Bards had a knowledge of letters from the beginning. It is said that Einigan, the first man, "beheld three pillars of light, having on them all demonstrable sciences, that ever were, or ever will be," and that "he took three rods of the quicken tree, and placed on them the forms and signs of all sciences, so as to be remembered." People misunderstood these, and "regarded the rods as a God, whereas they only bore His Name. When Einigan saw this, he was greatly annoyed, and in the intensity of his grief he broke the three rods, nor were others found that contained accurate sciences. He was so distressed on that account that from the intensity he burst asunder, and with his [parting] breath he prayed God that there should be accurate sciences among men in the flesh, and there should be a correct understanding for the proper discernment thereof. And at the end of a year and a day, after the decease of Einigan, Menw, son of the Three Shouts, beheld three rods growing out of the mouth of Einigan, which exhibited the sciences of the Ten Letters, and the mode in which all the sciences of language and speech were arranged by them, and in language and speech all distinguishable sciences. He then took

the rods, and taught from them the sciences — all,
except the Name of God, which he made a secret,
lest the Name should be falsely discerned; and hence
arose the Secret of the Bardism of the Bards of the
Isle of Britain."*

The first ten letters were derived from the creative
Name of God, /|\, and represented a, p, c, e, t, i, l,
r, o, s; and "they had been a secret from the age of
ages among the Bards of the Isle of Britain, for the
preservation of memorials of country and nation.
Beli the Great made them into sixteen, and divulged
that arrangement, and appointed that there should
never after be a concealment of the sciences of letters, in respect of the arrangement which he made;
but he left the ten cuttings a secret."†

According to some authorities, the alphabet of the
sixteen letters was formed, and divulged in the time
of Dyvnwal Moelmud. The original Abcedilros, or
alphabet of the ten letters, was quite different to that
of the sixteen and its augmentations; and whilst
these were known to the public, the former was
known only to the Bards.

The Druids of Gaul had a knowledge of letters,
though they did not commit to writing the things
that pertained to their institute. "Generally," says
our author, "in other cases, and in their public and
private accounts, they use Greek letters." The alphabet of the sixteen was at this time open to the
public in Britain; could it have been the one which
the Continental Druids used, mistaken by Cæsar for
Greek letters?

---

* Caffaeliad Llythyr.   † Ystorrynnau Cyssefin.

The Druids of Gaul had letters of their own, which were *similar* to the letters of Greece; it is, therefore, not impossible that Cæsar confounded one series with the other. Mr. Astle, who is well skilled in ancient letters, gives a series of Gaulish characters, which are somewhat similar to those of Greece. They were taken from the monumental inscription of Gordian, the messenger of the Gauls, who suffered martyrdom, in the third century, with all his family. "These characters," he says, "were generally used by the people, before the conquest of Gaul by Cæsar."*

Another author remarks:—"There are those who think the Druids had ancient characters, which were both elegant, and similar to those of the Greeks. For according to the testimony of Xenophon, and Archilochus, the figures of those letters, which Cadmus brought out of Phœnicia into Greece, resembled Gaulish, rather than Punic, or Phœnician characters."†

He who compares the ancient Greek Alphabet with the Bardic Coelbren, will find a remarkable similarity between them, so that a stranger might easily mistake the one for the other.

The Druids of Britain as well as those of Gaul, made use of letters under many circumstances. The "memorial of letters," or the "memorial of Coelbren," was one of their "three memorials." This is clearly seen in the Laws of Dyvnwal Moelmud. It would, therefore, not be difficult to harmonize Cæsar's narrative respecting the "memorial of voice" and the "memorial of letters" of the Gauls, with what we

---

* Origin and Progress of Writing, p. 56.   † Bucher. Fro. p. 183.

know to have been the usage of the Bards of Britain
in these matters.

8. *The transmigration of souls.* The Bardic dogma
on this head was, that the soul commenced its course
in the lowest water animalcule, and passed at death to
other bodies of a superior order, successively, and in
regular gradation, until it entered that of man. Humanity is a state of liberty, where man can attach
himself to either good or evil, as he pleases. If his
good qualities preponderate over his evil qualities at
the time of his death, his soul passes into Gwynvyd,
or a state of bliss, where good necessarily prevails,
and from whence it is impossible to fall. But if his
evil qualities predominate, his soul descends in Abred
into an animal corresponding in character to the disposition he exhibited just before he died. It will
then rise as before, until it again arrives at the point
of liberty, where it will have another chance of clinging to the good. But if it fails, it must fall again;
and this may happen for ages and ages, until at last
its attachment to good preponderates. It was believed, however, that man could not be guilty twice
of the same sin; his experience in Abred, whilst
undergoing punishment for any particular sin, would
prevent him from loving that sin a second time;
hence the adage, " Nid eir i Annwn ond unwaith."

The views of the Gaulish Druids, as far as they are
expressed by Cæsar, do not appear to differ from the
above. "They wish to inculcate this idea, that souls
do not die, but pass after death from one body to
another." The only thing that may be *supposed* to
be different is the passing from one body to another,
which, in the original Latin, seems as if it meant from

one human body to another human body, " ab aliis—
ad alios." But in reality there is no inconsistency between the two systems, even in this respect; for,
though the soul of a good man was considered in
general as entering an angelic body in the circle of
Gwynvyd, and the soul of a wicked man as entering
the body of a beast, a reptile, or a bird, in Abred,
yet, it was thought that occasionally the good soul
returned from Gwynvyd to inhabit a human body,
and that the soul of one punished by death, against
his will, for an injurious evil, passed to another human
body. There is no doubt that this, with the Cymry
as well as with the Gauls, acted as a strong incentive
to bravery, especially as they considered that to suffer
in behalf of truth and justice was one of the greatest
virtues, and was sure to bring the soul to everlasting
bliss.

9. *Astronomy.* " They dispute largely concerning
the stars and their motion," says Cæsar, and herein
the Druids of Gaul were similar to those of Britain.
We have evidence enough to prove that the latter
paid particular attention to the doctrine of the stars.
Testimony is borne to their knowledge of the revolution of the stars even by the very word, which they
used to denote time, *amser*, compounded of *am*,
round, and *ser*, the stars. They themselves, also, not
unfrequently went by the name of *sywedyddion*, that
is, astronomers, or men versed in the science of the
stars.

> Talhaiarn y sydd
> Mwyaf *sywedydd*.

It will be seen that the names given by our ancestors to the different constellations, as enumerated in

these volumes, are thoroughly Cymric, and radical,
thus indicating early and profound knowledge on
their part " concerning the stars and their motion."

10. *Cosmology.* The Bards believed that all the
visible creation sprang into existence simultaneously
with the pronunciation of God's Name; and this
article occupies a very prominent place in their religious creed. From other fragments in this Collection
we find that they professed to know something of the
laws of nature; why water rises to the surface of the
earth, and descends from the clouds, and why the sea
is briny. And, if we take Taliesin as a proper representative of Bardism, we may have abundant proof
from his poems that they reasoned much in his days
" concerning the world, the earth, and the nature of
things."

11. *Theology.* " And about the force and power
of the immortal gods." Let GOD be substituted for
"gods," and this statement would apply equally to
the Cymry, and no difference whatever would exist
between the two systems on the subject. Nothing
is oftener, and more positively insisted upon in the
Bardic creed than the doctrine of ONE GOD; and it is
remarkable that all the testimonies of archaiological
research, though they are for the most part of a
negative character, tend to confirm the antiquity and
genuineness of that creed. The Bards were careful
to inculcate this truth above all, and brought it to
bear upon the several rites and ceremonies, which
distinguished their national worship. The ideas they
had, also, of the nature and attributes of the Deity
were truly sublime and eminently magnificent, not
to be equalled perhaps by any other race of the Gen-

tile world, prior to its adoption of the more divine religion of Christ.

12. *Sacrifices.* The views of the Bards on the subject of "aberthau," or oblations, are clearly and distinctly quoted in these volumes, so that we need not give a summary of them here. What we have to do is to harmonize the account, which Cæsar gives of the sacrifices of the Continental Druids with the Bardism of the Cymry. The Roman captain might easily fall into a mistake about those matters. When he saw malefactors being put to death, under the supervision of the priests, he would naturally infer that they were thus dealt with as sacrifices, to propitiate the gods. He saw men, perhaps, giving themselves up voluntarily to suffer the punishment due for their transgressions, and he would reasonably suppose that they were "vowing to sacrifice themselves." It is quite possible that he should, also, have seen good men suffer in the cause of truth and justice, and his inference would be, that they were being sacrificed for want of a sufficient number of evil doers to take their place. But, if we grant that Cæsar gives a correct account of the sacrifices of the Gaulish Druids, it is very easy to perceive that the rite in question originated in the doctrine of *eneid-vaddeu*, which prevailed among the Cymry. "They think that if the life of man is not given for the life of man, the immortal gods cannot be appeased." Life for life was required by the laws of the Cymry ; but we do not find that our ancestors viewed the retaliation as what would propitiate God, further than that to benefit the man himself, who was put to death, might be taken as a sign of his reconciliation

g

with God. If a murderer died a natural death, his soul would descend low in Abred, but the fatal punishment inflicted upon him by the public officers was considered, according to the order of providence, as equivalent to that degradation, and his soul passed simultaneously to another human body. In this sense, then, the punishment of *eneidvaddeu* propitiated God; that is, God did not, on that account, place man in such a miserable position as He would otherwise have done. Since the Divine Being wishes every man to be saved, it may be said, that whatever is done to facilitate that object, and to bring about its speedy consummation, must be pleasing to Him.

It is very probable that the prisoners of the wicker image were no other than the malefactors who would not surrender themselves voluntarily; we can hardly see the necessity for the scheme in the case of the others. We do not read of anything of the kind in connection with our own island; most likely it was peculiar to the Continent.

Cæsar observes that it was the opinion of the Gaulish Druids " that the punishment of those who were caught in theft or pillage, or in any other wicked act, was more acceptable to the immortal gods " than that of the innocent. It is difficult to withstand the supposition that these were the words of the commentator himself, used by him as a reason for the want of proportion, which he observed in the number of the bad and good, that were immolated. If, on the contrary, it was really the opinion of the Druids, then they must in this respect have differed much from their Cymric brethren, who considered that the offenders, who gave themselves up willingly to be punished, were more acceptable than those who were punished against their will, and that the good, who suffered in behalf of truth and justice, were still more so. Besides, there was something in the above opinion inconsistent with the idea which mankind in general entertained respecting the qualities of a sacrifice, and which sets forth the immaculate, the obedient, and the innocent, as the one which is most pleasing to God.

It appears from Cæsar that the agent, which the Gauls used for consuming their sacrifices, was fire. Fire might in like manner be employed among the Cymry for the punishment of those who were adjudged to be *eneidvaddeu.* " There are three *eneidvaddeu* punishments: beheading; hanging; and *burning;* and it is for the king, or lord of the territory, to order which he willeth to be inflicted."*

13. *The Names of God.* We must again express our conviction that Cæsar might have mistaken the several attributes, which belonged to the one true God, for as many distinct and independent divinities, just as it is said that some of the Cymry, in the infancy of the world, deified and worshipped the rods which only bore the Name of God. Not at once did men forget the great and primitive doctrine of the unity of the Godhead, setting up in the imagination of their hearts " gods many, and lords many." Even the names, by which the gods of the Gentiles were designated, had been invented, and were used to denote the several properties of the Deity, before that

---

* Laws of Dyrnwal Moelmud.

great corruption took place. As an old poet observes,—

> "Pluto, Proserpine, Ceres, Venus, Cupid,
> Triton, Nereus, Tethys, and Neptune,
> Hermes, Vulcan, Pan, Jupiter, Juno,
> Diana, and Apollo, are ONE GOD."*

The same doctrine is also taught in the hymns, which historians ascribe to Orpheus. It is quite probable, therefore, that Cæsar, when he observed the several parts of the Gaulish worship, concluded that they were adorations offered to distinct gods, and that those gods were similar to the gods of Rome and Greece, with whom he was best acquainted.

"They chiefly worship the god Mercury." This character is almost the chief in every religious system; it is the same as to its original nature with the Gwyddon of the Cymry, the Budha of the Indians, and the Woden of the Saxons—that is, the Bard presiding at Gorsedd. It was the office of this Bard to instruct men in various kinds of knowledge, and to lead them along the ways of morality; therefore, his auditors might easily consider him as "the inventor of all arts, the guide of ways and journeys, and as possessing the greatest power for obtaining money and merchandise."

"Of him they have many images." Perhaps the *maen crair*, on which the presiding Bard stood, and the *meini gwynion*, at which his assistants took their station, were these supposed images. But, granting that the inhabitants of Gaul, in Cæsar's time, did worship the god Mercury, it is easy to see that such

---

* See Davies's Celtic Researches, p. 297.

was merely a misapprehension of the primitive views, which were entertained respecting the Bard in Gorsedd. The same properties, but more suitably adapted to the character of a divine being, were ascribed to Mercury, as were supposed to belong to the Bard. The first, and most natural step in this corruption, was to view the president of Gorsedd as the representative of a Divine Gwyddon, and doubtless the people fell into this mistake sooner than did the Druids themselves. Inasmuch as the principles of Bardism were never so thoroughly understood in Gaul as they were in Britain, it was not difficult to fall into error on the point in question.

We know not whether Mercury was a name which the Druids themselves gave to their president, or their god, or whether it was one that Cæsar invented, from noticing the similarity that existed between their views and worship and those of his own countrymen. If it be a Celtic name, what does it mean? Is it MERCH-WR, (woman-man,) because the Gwyddon looked straight before him along the line of the East —"Dwyrain," i. e. *dwy rain*, the two rays—the ray of Eilir and the ray of Elved, which in nature represented the two sexes, male and female? Or is it MARCH-WR, (horse-man,) because he mounted, or, as it were, rode the *maen crair*, whilst he presided in Gorsedd—the word *march* again being originally derived from my-ARCH, i.e. the ARCH, or maen ARCH, being another name of the stone on which the Bard stood?

"After him they worship Apollo," who is supposed "to ward off all diseases." He is the same undoubtedly with the SUN in the Bardism of the Cymry,

which was regarded as the natural or physical representative of the Sun of righteousness, or the Supreme
God. Wherefore, many of the rites and ceremonies
of the Gorsedd were regulated with reference to this
luminary. The days for holding the Gorsedd were
the four Albans, when the rays of the orient sun
converging to the *maen llog* delineated the creative
Name of God. The Bard thus standing in "the face
of the sun, and the eye of light," when he taught the
people, literally "spoke in the Name of the Lord."
No Gorsedd could be held except when the sun was
above the horizon.

Since it is the property of the sun to warm, cheer,
and revive, it may well be said to " ward off diseases;" and when deified, the same attribute would
of course still belong to it, but in a more eminent
degree.

Having lost sight of the true position of the sun in
the system of Bardism, it was not difficult to fall into
error, and to worship the creature more than the Creator. It would appear that the Gentiles had made
gods of " the heavenly host" sooner than of any other
parts of the creation; and if the Gauls were to some
extent idolaters in the time of Cæsar, we may be sure
that they worshipped the Sun.

The next god, whom Cæsar says they worshipped,
was MARS, " the ruler of wars." The British Bards
were pre-eminently men of peace; no one was allowed to carry a naked weapon in their presence, nor
did they ordinarily unsheath the sword against any
one. We say ordinarily, for there were occasions, on
which they were required to act in a different manner,
as may be seen from the following Triad :—

" The three necessary, but reluctant duties, of the Bards of the Isle of Britain : secrecy for the sake of peace and public good ; invective lamentation required by justice; and *to unsheath* the sword against the lawless and depradatory."*

It was not for the purpose of acquiring unlawful possessions, and of oppressing other people and countries, that they " unsheathed the sword ;" " they would not have country and lands by fighting and pursuing, but of equity, and in peace."† It was evil that they resisted even unto blood. Accordingly, on his way to the Gorsedd, the Bard carried the sword by its point, to signify his own readiness to suffer in the cause of truth ; it was sheathed on the *maen crair*, for the people had been invited to attend, where there would be no naked weapon against them; but against " a man deprived of privilege, and exposed to warfare," it was unsheathed. It may be that the rite of the sword in Gorsedd had created an opinion in the mind of Cæsar, that the Druids were at the time worshipping Mars, the god of war ; or it may be that the Druids themselves, having forgotten its original import, had come to regard it as referring to the same god, whom, they no doubt had heard of as existing in the religious system of their neighbours. The accompanying offerings and sacrifices seem to have been derived from this view of Mars, since nothing of the kind can be traced to the usages of the Cymry ; unless the burying his horse and arms with a warrior had been a sort of foundation for the custom.

* Trioedd Braint a Defod.　　　† Trioedd Ynys Prydain.

After Mars, Jupiter is mentioned, as the god, who
" held the empire of heaven." Iau* was one of the
names, which the Cymry gave to the supreme God,
and it signified the last or most recent manifestation
of the Godhead, such as that which occurred in creation as contrasted with the preceding vacuum—after
that in the incarnation of His Son. Perhaps the
word is the same with /|\, the unutterable Name
of God, by which He created all things—the Word of
His might. There is, however, another meaning
given to the name in question in the traditions of
the Bards :—

" Disciple.   Why is Iau (yoke) given as a name for God ?
" Master.   Because the yoke is the measuring rod of country and
nation in virtue of the authority of law, and is in the possession of
every head of family under the mark of the lord of the territory, and
whoever violates it is liable to a penalty. Now, God is the measuring
rod of all truth, all justice, and all goodness ; therefore He is a yoke
on all, and all are under it, and woe to him who shall violate it."†

This meaning bears a close relation to the opinion
that the owner of the name " held the empire of heaven." Nevertheless, the name, even in this sense,
might have been founded upon /|\, or, according to
a further development, | /|\\|/, which signifies pre-
servation, creation, and destruction.

The Gauls could not fall into the error of inventing
an additional divinity in the person of Jupiter, for he
was the principal god, or god in his primary character
—though their formation of different gods out of his
attributes necessarily encroaches upon, and abbrevi-
ates his greatness and authority.

---

* The Cymric form of Jupiter, or Jove.   † Iau.

MINERVA. The Druids of Gaul, according to Cæsar, were of opinion that it was this goddess who "instructed them in the principles of works and arts." It is very likely that she was the same originally with the Awen, (A wen, /|\,) the Word of God, that proceeded out of His mouth, even as Minerva is said to have sprung out of the brain of Jupiter. It was from the AWEN that all knowledge was derived—in like manner Minerva was considered as the goddess of wisdom. One of the objects of AWEN is to produce peace—Minerva produced the olive, the symbol of peace. In several other respects, also, a remarkable similarity between the characteristics of the Bardic Awen and the goddess Minerva, may be pointed out, though in matters of detail this is not necessary, because Cæsar observes that the opinion of the Gauls was but *almost* the same as that of the other nations concerning the above divinities.

14. *Origin of the people.* "The Gauls declare that they have all sprung from their father Pluto, and this they say was delivered to them by the Druids." There can be no doubt that this sentiment is perfectly identical with that of the Bards relative to the procession of man from Annwn.

"Whence didst thou proceed? and what is thy beginning?
"I came from the Great World, having my beginning in Annwn."*

We have thus gone through the testimony of Cæsar, the principal classical authority on the subject of Druidism; we will now proceed to examine the statements of the other ancient authors, who have

* Llyfr Barddas.
h

touched upon the same point, though not so largely
and minutely; namely, Strabo, Diodorus Siculus, Cicero, Pliny, Pomponius Mela, Tacitus, Diogenes La-
ertius, and Ammianus Marcellinus.

STRABO, B.C. 54.

The description, which this author gives of Druidism, refers entirely, like that of Cæsar, to Gaul, and
is as follows :—

" And among the whole of them [the Gauls] three classes more
especially are held in distinguished veneration, the Bards, the Ovates,
and the Druids. The Bards are chaunters and poets. The Ovates
are sacrificers and physiologists. The Druids, in addition to physiology, practise ethic philosophy. They are deemed to be most upright,
and, in consequence, to them are committed both public and private
controversies, insomuch that on some occasions they decide on battles,
and stop the combatants on the eve of engaging. Matters pertaining
to murder are more especially entrusted to their decision, and when
profit accrues from these, they think fertility will attend their country. These and others say that souls are immortal, and that the world
is so too ; yet that ultimately fire and water will prevail. To their
simplicity and ferocity are superadded much stupidity, vain boasting,
and love of ornament. They wear gold, having collars thereof on
their necks, and bracelets on their arms and wrists ; and dignified
persons are clad in dyed garments embroidered with gold..........
" Having stricken the man destined for sacrifice on the back with a
sword, they augur from the palpitation. They never sacrifice without
the Druids. Other kinds of human immolation are spoken of : some
victims they slay with arrows, or crucify for their offerings ; and having prepared a colossus of hay, and thrown wood upon it, they burn
together oxen, all sorts of wild beasts, and men."*

Strabo and Cæsar both agree with respect to some
things, such as, 1stly, that the Druids were in great
esteem among the people ; 2dly, that they decided
disputes ; 3dly, that their presence at the sacrifices

---

* Geograph. lib. iv.

was necessary; 4thly, the immortality of the soul ;
5thly, human sacrifices. There is no occasion, therefore, that we should make any further observation on
these subjects in the main. We will only notice the
variations and additions made by Strabo, and compare
them with the Bardism of the Cymry.

1. *The three degrees.* These, according to the
privilege and usage of the Isle of Britain, were the
Chief Bard, the Ovate, and the Druid, the three
being co-equal in dignity, though their offices were
distinct. Strabo calls his three classes exactly by
the same names, but he does not ascribe to them
their respective functions quite in accordance with
Bardism, at least, as regards the Ovate, who, he
says, was the sacrificer, though he says again that
they never sacrificed without the Druids. It was not
difficult to incur misapprehension with reference to
the duties of the several orders, for on special occasions one might enter upon the office of another.

2. *The justice of the Druids.* Justice was a virtue
greatly inculcated by the members of the Bardic
College.

" The three foundations of Bardism : peace ; love ; and *justice.*

" For three reasons ought a man to hazard his life, and to lose it, if
necessary : in seeking for truth; *in clinging to justice ;* and in performing mercy."*

3. *Their influence in war.* The Bard, in his blue
robe, was the herald of peace. He was privileged to
pass from one country to another in safety and un-
harmed, for not only it was the law of Bardism, but
also the law of nations, that no person was to unsheath

* Trioedd Braint a Defod.

a sword against him. He was a man of peace, according to his office, and if he thus went between two armies on the field of battle, they immediately ceased from fighting. The privilege of protection belonged in the same manner to the Druid and Ovate.

4. *Sacrifices.* It is very probable that Strabo refers to the rites of *eneidvaddeu,* when he speaks of murder as being entrusted to the decision of the Druids. The Bardic traditions contain no record of what is here said concerning " the fertility of the country," or of the particular mode of stabbing or slaughtering the men who were sentenced to death, unless it was done in a manner similar to that to which the lord of the territory had recourse, when he drew blood from a degraded Bard, namely, " from his forehead, his bosom, and his groin, that is, from the seats of life and soul."

5. *Vaticinations.* Our ancestors very generally professed to foretel events, though it is not said that they founded their predictions upon any particular appearance, which the men, whom they put to death, exhibited. Meugant, in the 6th century, observes:—

" Trust to God that *the Druids will not prophesy,*
    When the privilege of the hill of legislature shall be broken."

6. *The eternal duration of the world.* The British Bards, likewise, believed that every existence and form of life would continue for ever—purged from evil. The opinion, which prevailed about the increase or prevalence of *fire* and *water,* seems to be founded on the Bardism of the Cymry :—

" There are three things on their increase : *fire,* or light ; understanding, or truth ; and the soul, or life ; *these will prevail over every thing*, and then Abred will cease."*

Elsewhere it is said, that life proceeds from " a conjunction of *water, fire,* and nwyvre ;" hence, if life is on the increase, it follows that its component elements also acquire continual strength.

7. *Ornaments.* The several members of the Bardic College wore proper vestments, which were emblematic of their respective offices. The Bard wore a sky blue robe, to signify peace ; the Druid wore white, denoting holiness; and the Ovate green, which was an emblem of progress. Each colour was also uniform, to signify truth, which is one. Nevertheless, it was lawful for them to introduce *silver* and *gold,* which, not being subject to rust and stain, were signs of honour. " Therefore, a gold fringe may be properly added to a Bard's robe, of whichever of the three colours it is, or a *gold girdle* be put round him, for it is right to honour truth, peace, godliness, and knowledge."

DIODORUS SICULUS, B.C. 44.

His description also is confined to the Druidism of Gaul, and is to the following effect :—

" And there are among them [the Gauls] composers of verses, whom they call Bards ; these, singing to instruments similar to a lyre, applaud some, while they vituperate others. There are also certain philosophers and priests surpassingly esteemed, whom they call Druids. They have also soothsayers, who are held in high estimation ; and these, by auguries and the sacrifice of victims, foretel future events, and hold the commonalty in complete subjection : and more

---

* Trioedd Barddas.

especially, when they deliberate on matters of moment, they practise a strange and incredible rite ; for, having devoted a man for sacrifice, they strike him with a sword on a part above the diaphragm : the victim having fallen, they augur from his mode of falling, the contortion of his limbs, and the flowing of the blood, what may come to pass, giving credence concerning such things to an ancient and long-standing observance. They have a custom of performing no sacrifice unattended by a philosopher. For they say that thanksgiving should be offered to the gods by men acquainted with the divine nature and using the same language, and by these they deem it necessary to ask for good things; and not only in the concerns of peace, but even of war, not friends alone, but even enemies also, chiefly defer to them and to the composers of verses. Frequently, during hostilities, when armies are approaching each other with swords drawn and lances extended, these men rushing between them put an end to their contention, taming them as they would tame wild beasts."*

This description is somewhat similar to that which Strabo gives, as the reader will easily perceive. Both authors agree as to the number of the different orders —the esteem in which they were held—their custom of predicting events by means of the sacrifice—and the influence of the Bards in restraining armies from fighting.

1. *The names of the orders.* Whilst Strabo gives the same names as those used by the Cymry, that is, Bards, Ovates, and Druids, Diodorus calls them Bards, Soothsayers, and Druids, making a soothsayer and an ovate to be of the same import, and both are of opinion that this functionary had to do with the act of sacrificing. They, likewise, agree as to the office of the Bard, that he was a singer and a poet, and in respect of the devotion which was paid by the Druid to philosophy, and the necessity of his presence at the sacrifices.

* Hist. lib. v. c. 31.

2. *Vaticinations.* Strabo mentions only one thing from which they augured future events, namely, "the palpitation" of the victim; Diodorus adds two other particulars, namely, " his mode of falling " and " the flowing of the blood." There is no allusion to these matters in the Bardic traditions.

3. *The mediation of the Druids.* According to the declaration of Diodorus, the common people regarded the Druids as mediators between themselves and the gods, and grounded their competency and fitness for that purpose upon the fact that they were acquainted with the divine nature, and used the same language. We have already seen that the Druids of Britain, as well as those of Gaul, studied and taught much respecting the nature and attributes of God. Using "the same language" seems to imply that the language of divine worship was unchangeable, whatever might be that of the people. And since the acts of the Gorsedd in Britain were to be performed at all times in Cymraeg, we may reasonably infer that it was in the old Celtic tongue Druidism was administered on the Continent—there was not much difference between the Cymraeg and the native language of Gaul.

CICERO, (slain) B.C. 43.

"This method of divination has not been neglected even amongst barbarous nations. For there are Druids in Gaul, with one of whom I was acquainted, namely, Divitiacus Æduus, who enjoyed the hospitality of your house, and spoke of you with admiration. This man not only professed an intimate knowledge of the system of nature, which the Greeks call physiology, but also foretold future events, partly by augury, and partly by conjecture." *

* De Divinatione, l. i.

Cicero does not speak here from vague report; but declares the profession of a man who was personally known to him, who had been his guest, and with whom he had familiarly conversed. And all that he says of him coincides almost exactly with the statements of Cæsar, Strabo, and Diodorus Siculus. The only new fact that we are made acquainted with is, that the Druids sometimes foretold future events " by conjecture ; " but perhaps we should not take the word to mean simply a *guess,* but as synonymous with *inference*—to signify that they had some foundation for all their vaticinations.

PLINY, (born) A.D. 23.

This philosophic but credulous author speaks of the Druidism of Gaul, in his " Natural Philosophy," as follows :—

" The Druids (so they call their wise men) hold nothing in greater reverence than the misletoe, and the tree on which it grows, so that it be an oak. They choose forests of oaks, for the sake of the tree itself, and perform no sacred rites without oak leaves ; so that one might fancy they had even been called for this reason, turning the word into Greek, Druids. But whatever grows upon these trees, they hold to have been sent from heaven, and to be a sign that the Deity Himself has chosen the tree for his own. The thing, however, is very rarely found, and when found is gathered with much ceremony ; and above all, on the sixth day of the moon, by which these men reckon the beginnings of their months and years, and of their cycle of thirty years, because the moon has then sufficient power, yet has not reached half its size. Addressing it in their own language by the epithet of all healing, after duly preparing sacrifices and banquets under the tree, they bring to the spot two white bulls, the horns of which are then for the first time garlanded. The priest clothed in a white dress ascends the tree, and cuts the misletoe with a golden knife ; it is caught in a white cloak. Thereupon they slay the victims, with a prayer that the Deity may prosper His own gift to them, to whom

He has given it. They fancy that, by drinking it, fertility is given to any barren animal, and that it is a remedy against all poisons."*

"Like to this Sabine herb is that called *selago*. It is gathered, without using a knife, with the right hand wrapped in a tunic, the left being uncovered, as though the man were stealing it ; the gatherer being clothed in a white dress, and with bare feet washed clean, after performing sacrifice before gathering it, with bread and wine. It is to be carried in a new napkin. According to the tradition of the Gaulish Druids, it is to be kept as a remedy against all evil, and the smoke of it is good for all diseases of the eyes. The same Druids have given the name of *samolus* to a plant that grows in wet places ; and this they say must be gathered with the left hand by one who is fasting, as a remedy for diseases of swine and cattle, and that he, who gathers it, must keep his head turned away, and must not lay it down anywhere except in a channel through which water runs, and there must bruize it for them who are to drink it."†

"There is another kind of egg in high repute in Gaul, although the Greeks make no account of it. A great number of snakes in summer time are artificially twisted and rolled together into a mass by the saliva of their jaws and the foam of their bodies. It is called snake's egg. The Druids tell you that it is thrown into the air with hisses, and must be caught in a cloak that it may not touch the ground ; that he that catches it must fly on horse-back, for that the snakes pursue him until hindered by the intervention of some river; that the test of it is, if it flows against the stream, even when tied with gold. And, according to the common craft of wizards, shrewd to conceal their cheating, they pronounce that it must be taken up at a particular time of the moon ; as though it rested with man's choice, whether that proceeding on the part of the snake should take place or not."‡

Pliny says that he has seen one of these eggs, and that the Druids used them as a distinguishing badge.

In the above description there are several new things, that present themselves to our notice, in connection with the Druidism of Gaul.

1. *One God.* It is remarkable that Pliny speaks of the Gauls as professing one God ; for though he

---

* Hist. Nat. lib. xvi. sect. 95.   † Lib. xxiv. ss. 62-3.

‡ Lib. xxix. s. 12.

had occasion to refer twice to the Deity, he uses the singular number each time. In this matter he differs from Cæsar, and we may be allowed to believe that though much ignorance and error had crept upon the Continent, in later times, relative to the Divine Being, the unity of His nature was to some extent acknowledged. But Pliny, after all, may be only referring to one god in particular, out of many, that is, the one that was interested in the circumstance to which he refers, and therefore names him in the singular number.

2. *The oak groves.* Though Pliny is undoubtedly mistaken as to the etymology of the name Druid, yet we have the testimony of the Cymric traditions that our remote progenitors did sometimes choose to worship under the oak. This usage they seem to have derived from Seth, who "first made a retreat for worship in the woods of the vale of Hebron, having first searched and investigated the trees, until he found a large oak, being the king of trees, branching, wide-spreading, thick-topped, and shady, under which he formed a choir and a place of worship."*

3. *The misletoe.* All admit that this plant was in great repute among the Ancient Cymry. From remote times it has been used by the Bards to decorate their tribunals on Alban Arthan, and even to this day traces of that custom may be found in the country during the Christmas festivities.

Three persons, Tydai, the Bard of Huon, Rhuvawn the Bard, and Melgin, the son of Einigan the Giant,

---

* Y Cread. Golychwyd, &c.

are recorded in a Triad as having worn around their heads a garland of misletoe, "darllys awelvar."

One of the names by which the Cymry called this plant was *Holliach*, which answers completely to the "omnia sanantem" of Pliny.

We know nothing of the rites which attended its gathering in Britain; and therefore we are not in a position to say in what consisted the resemblance or difference, as the case may be, between them and the ceremonies mentioned above.

4. *The white garment of the Druids.* Of the same description, as we have seen, was the official dress of the British Druids.

5. *The offering of bread and wine.* This seems to have come down from Patriarchal times—from Melchizedec, who "brought forth bread and wine," type of the Blessed Eucharist, that "pure offering" which was to take place under the Gospel; and though nothing is positively said of such a rite as existing in the Bardism of the Cymry, it is likely enough that it was practised. The reader is referred to the description given in these pages of the sacrifices of the Bards.

6. *Adder's stones or beads*—glain nadroedd. The three orders used to wear these beads, of a colour uniform with that of their respective robes; and they generally regarded them as possessed of rare virtues. It is questioned whether they are the production of nature or art. Be that as it may, they are always found in great numbers; and there are people who search for them, and from whom they may be had, but they maintain that they are only to be met with at one season of the year, and that they are blown by

a knot of snakes.   " Ai chwythu y glain y maent ?"
" Are they blowing beads ?" is a proverbial inquiry
applied to persons who lay their heads together in
conversation—an expression involving an opinion similar to that of Pliny.

But our author is not altogether silent respecting
the Druidism of Britain, for he says ;—

" Britain even now celebrates it [Magism] wonderfully, with so
many ceremonies, that it may seem to have imparted it to the Persians."

There is here, however, no mention of any doctrine
or usage in particular — Pliny merely intimates that
there were many ceremonies in connection with the
Druidic worship, which view is not inconsistent with
the traditions of the Bards.   The Persian, as well as
the Gaulish system, might have been received from
Britain, both of them, however, being greatly dege-
nerated.   Or it may be, that the resemblance, which
Pliny perceived between the Druidism of Britain and
the Magism of Persia had grown from the same root
—the patriarchal religion.

POMPONIUS MELA, A.D. 45.

His description is as follows :—

" They [the Gauls] have an eloquence of their own, and their Druids as masters of wisdom.   These profess to know the magnitude and
form of the earth and the world, the motions of the heaven and the
stars, and the will of the gods.   They teach the most noble of the
nation many things privately, and for a long time, even for twenty
years, in a cave, or in inaccessible woods.   One of their precepts has
become public, namely, that they should act bravely in war, that
souls are immortal, and that there is another life after death.   Therefore along with the dead, they burn and bury things which belonged
to them while living.   Their debtor and creditor accounts were trans-

ferred below. Some even went so far as to ascend the funeral pyres of their friends of their own accord, as though about to live with them."*

Mela agrees with Cæsar as to the knowledge which the Druids were said to possess concerning the universe, and as to their being in the habit of training their disciples for the long space of twenty years. We may conclude from the only specimen of their precepts, which he succeeded in obtaining, that they were inculcated in the Triadic form :—

> "To act bravely in war ;
> That souls are immortal ;
> And that there is another life after death."

1. *Interment.* The remains discovered in ancient sepulchres sufficiently prove that the Cymry in former times buried with their princes and great men those things to which in their life-time they had been particularly attached, such as their steeds and arms.

2. *The debt of the deceased.* Undoubtedly this is a remnant of the ancient doctrine of the metempsychosis, according to which the man, after his fall in Abred through death, was regarded as suffering punishment, or paying the debt which he had contracted in his life-time.

3. *Voluntary death.* It is, likewise, very probable that there is some connection between the custom, which some of the people in Gaul adopted, of throwing themselves on the funeral pyres of their relatives, and the doctrine of *eneidvaddeu,* already spoken of.

* De Situ Orbis, lib. iii. c. 2.

DIOGENES LAERTIUS, (died) A.D. 222.

This author has preserved one of the Triads of the Druids, which is as follows :—

> " To worship the gods ;
> To do no evil ;
> And to exercise fortitude."

Now, it is remarkable that we have one Triad in the series called "Trioedd Doethineb," which very much resembles the above, so much so as to impress us with the belief that it was the original model after which the Greek Triad was compiled. It runs thus,

> " The three first principles of wisdom—
> Obedience to the laws of God ;
> Concern for the good of mankind ;
> And bravery in sustaining all the accidents of life."

Diogenes says, moreover, that the Druids among the Britons were the same as the Philosophers among the Greeks, the Magi among the Persians, the Gymnosophistæ among the Indians, and the Chaldæans among the Assyrians ; and so undoubtedly they were in respect of the origin and substance of their religion.

C. SUETONIUS TRANQUILLUS.

Suetonius flourished in the beginning of the second century. He describes " the Druidic religion among the Gauls as one of terrible cruelty."* We presume that he here refers to their practice of sacrificing men, which, as we have already noticed, seems to have sprung from the Bardic doctrine of *eneidvaddeu.*

---

* Lib. v. de Claudio Cæsare, c. 25.

Ammianus Marcellinus says that " the Bards record the exploits of heroes, in poems, which they sing to the soft sound of the lyre,"* which is quite in accordance with the practice of the Cymric Bards. He also observes that the Druids were similar to the Pythagoreans, as indeed they were with reference to the doctrine of the metempsychosis.

C. CORNELIUS TACITUS.

We have left this author to the last, because he speaks of the Druids of our own country. Tacitus lived in the time of Nero and his successors until Hadrian. Though deemed in general a skilful and correct historian, yet we have evidence enough to prove that he could occasionally run counter of the truth; consequently we ought to be cautious how we receive his statements. He utters a glaring falsehood when he treats of the history of the Jews; declaring that they fled from the island of Creta into Egypt, and received the name *Iudæi* from mount *Ida* in that island—that Moses obtained water in the wilderness by following a herd of wild asses, and that the Jews religiously preserved in their houses the image or picture of a wild ass, in grateful memory of the event. Tacitus had no excuse whatever for falling into these errors. There were a great many Jews in Rome, and the Scriptures had been translated into the Greek language long before his era; besides, St. Paul himself actually visited the city, and preached the Gospel

* Lib. xv. c. 9.

there in his time. If then, Tacitus, erred so egregi-
ously, in the face of so many opportunities of learning
the real truth concerning a renowned nation like the
Jews, why might he not have fallen into similar mistakes with regard to the Cymry, though he received
his account from his father-in-law, Agricola, who was
governor of Britain?

But what says Tacitus of the Druidism of Britain?
In speaking of the invasion of the isle of Mona, or
Anglesey, by Suetonius Paulinus, he says :—

"There stood apart on the strand an army, thick with men and
arms, and women ran to and fro after the manner of Furies, clad in
funereal dresses, with dishevelled hair, and carrying torches before
them. The Druids, also, pouring out terrible prayers around them,
with hands raised towards heaven, struck the soldiers with awe by the
novelty of the sight ; so that, as if their members clung to the spot,
they offered their unmoved bodies to the wounds. Afterwards, by
the exhortations of their leaders, and by their own mutual encouragements, not to be afraid of a womanish and fanatical troop, they lead
on the standards, overthrow their opponents, and involve them in
their own fires.

" A guard was afterwards placed over the conquered, and their
groves were cut down, which had been consecrated to their cruel
superstitions ; for they considered it lawful to offer the blood of cap-
tives on their altars, and to consult the gods by means of the nerves
of men."*

The historian has unquestionably coloured the above
sketch as black as possible ; but, even if we grant that
it is tolerably correct, there is nothing in it, after all,
which is inconsistent with the ancient Bardism of the
Cymry.   Patriotism was a great virtue with them—
and aggressive war was looked upon as a dire crime
—a crime that exposed its perpetrators to the pun-

* Lib. xiv. c. 30.

ishment of death. What wonder, then, is it, if the
Cymry sentenced to death the Roman soldiers, who
chanced to fall into their hands? But, it may be
objected, they were slain by the Druids, as sacrifices
to their gods. There is no doubt that the Druids
did superintend their execution, and that this in a
certain sense partook of the nature of a sacrifice.
Their death was a punishment for the offence, which
they had committed, but at the same time it was
regarded as a sort of atonement, which made up for
the degradation they would have been subject to in
Abred, if they had died a natural death. If Tacitus
had known something of the doctrine of *eneidvaddeu,*
he would have considered the act of the Druids on
this occasion as a just and merciful one ; just, in that
it punished the transgressor, merciful, in that it placed
him in a better state ; for, according to their creed,
his soul would pass immediately into another human
body, totally cleansed from the guilt of the crime for
which he had died. So easy is it to misunderstand
the nature and object of men's actions, when viewed
from a point which is external to their own religious
sentiments!

We have entered upon this subject at some length,
because the supposed antagonism between Classical
Druidism and British Bardism, is one of the principal
grounds on which our literary sceptics found their
denial of the genuineness of our traditions, and hence
it becomes our strict duty to examine how far their
position in this respect is really tenable. It is to be
hoped that our comparative analysis will convince
every unprejudiced person that, whilst the apparent
discrepancy, which existed between the two systems,

k

precludes the idea of one being considered as a mere
copy of the other, taken in recent times, there is sufficient identity of principle observable in them both,
subject to the qualifying character of the Gaulish
tradition, to suggest a common origin. On this account, then, the tenets and usages of Bardism, as
given in our pages, may well be considered as the
genuine remains of Druidic lore; that is, if we have
further reason for believing that they were effectually
preserved and handed down through the different
ages, which followed the introduction and establishment of Christianity.

The machinery principally adopted by the Bards
for this purpose was, "the voice of Gorsedd," which
is amply explained and described in these volumes.
Under favourable circumstances, indeed, it might be
considered as highly efficient; but such circumstances, we all know, did not at all times exist. Under
the Roman domination, we may be assured, that the
ancient institute of the country, opposed as it was,
both in spirit and practice, to all foreign usurpation,
would not be allowed to give public expression to its
views. The Bards could not meet in Gorsedd without incurring great personal danger. Consequently,
they would have recourse to "cyvail," which was the
second "assembly of the Bards," and created especially to meet the requirements of the case; that is,
a *cyvail* was a group of three persons, who met
"where and when they could, for fear of the assault
of depredation and lawlessness." By this means the
old traditions might be preserved, though they would
not be known out of the circle of the fraternity.
That there were Bards and Bardism during this pe-

riod, is undoubted. All the Bardic privileges and
immunities were recognized by law until the reign of
Lucius, A.D. 173—189. Gorwg, son of Eirchion, two
generations later, is described not only as "a very
wise and religious king," but also as "a good Bard."*
And it is supposed that Bardism formed the principal
ingredient in the Pelagian heresy, which spread so
rapidly and extensively among the people, towards
the end of the fourth century.

About A.D. 383, when the Roman power was fast
declining in the island, Macsen Wledig, (Maximus,)
with the view of resuscitating the ancient system,
submitted it to the verdict of country and nation, as
in the time of Prydain, "lest the primitive Bardism
should be lost and forgotten; when it was found in its
integrity, and in accordance with the primary privileges and usages. And thus it was submitted to the
judgment and verdict of country and nation, and the
ancient privileges and usages, the ancient meaning
and learning, and the ancient sciences and memorials
were confirmed, lest they should fail, become lost and
forgotten; and this was done without contradiction
or opposition."†

In the reign of Gwrtheyrn Gwrthenau, however,
about a century later, Bardism was greatly corrupted,
owing to "the divulging of the Name of God, introducing falsehood into vocal song, and distorting the
sciences of Bardism." To remedy this state of things,
king Arthur, in the sixth century, established the system of the Round Table, which was "an arrangement
of the arts, sciences, usages, and privileges of the

---

* Gwehelyth Iestin ab Gwrgant.   † Trioedd Braint a Defod.

Bards and men of vocal song; and improved, and
committed to memory, where there was occasion,
every thing commendable in what was old, and authorized every thing new that was adjudged to be an
augmentation and an amplification of desirable sciences, with a view to the wisdom and requirement of
country and nation." The two Merddins, Taliesin,
St. Mabon, and others, presided at this Chair.

Upon the death of Arthur, the Chair of the Round
Table was removed to the court of Urien Rheged, at
Aberllychwr, where it went sometimes by the name
of Taliesin's Chair, and sometimes by that of the
Chair of Baptism. " Under the privilege of the in-
stitute of the Round Table, Gildas the prophet, and
Cattwg the Wise from Llancarvan, were Bards, and
also Llywarch the Aged, son of Elidyr Lydanwyn,
Ystudvach the Bard, and Ystyffan the Bard of
Teilo."*

It remained at Aberllychwr about two hundred
years; after that, it was transferred to Caerwynt,†
where it continued for more than a hundred years.
It was then removed to Maes Mawr, by Einion, the
son of Collwyn; and afterwards by Iestyn, the son of
Gwrgant, to the court of Caerleon-upon-Usk, which
was held at Cardiff Castle. Here it was shortly
disturbed, owing to the war that broke out between
Iestyn and Rhys, the son of Tewdwr; nor was it
again restored until the time of Robert, earl of Gloucester, grandson of the latter, " who endowed this
Chair with privilege and maintenance in Maes Mawr
in Morganwg, and gave the name of *Tir Iarll*, or the

---

* Dosparth y Ford Gron.   † The *Venta Silurum* of the Romans.

earl's land, to the portion which he conferred upon
the Bards for their maintenance, whilst he gave the
other portion for the maintenance of the Monks.......
The Chair of Tir Iarll was enjoined to investigate the
ancient sciences of Bardism; and after the search,
recovery, and confirmation, the primitive Chair, Gorsedd, sciences, privileges, and usages of the Bards of
the Isle of Britain, were restored thoroughly and
altogether."*

Geraint, the Blue Bard, had, in the beginning of
the tenth century, established a Chair at Llandaff,
different to the one of the Round Table. It afterwards went by the name of the Chair of Morganwg,
and enbosomed that of Tir Iarll, itself being enbosomed by *(ynghesail)* the Gorsedd of the Bards of the
Isle of Britain.

This Chair, whether we call it the Chair of Tir
Iarll, or the Chair of Morganwg, was well protected
as long as the lords of Glamorgan retained sovereign
authority over that territory; and the rights and immunities of the Bards were renewed from time to
time, but always on condition that they should investigate and preserve the sciences of Bardism.

Llywelyn, the son of Gruffydd, was slain Dec. 11,
1282, and with him fell the ancient independence of
Cymru, which henceforth became subject to the kings
of England. In consequence of the opposition, which
the Bards offered to the claims of Edward, they were
rigorously persecuted by that monarch, and of course
were prevented from meeting publicly in Gorsedd.
Neither did they any longer enjoy the *trwydded* or

---

* See Preface to " Cyvrinach y Beirdd."

maintenance, which had been conferred upon them by their own native princes. Nevertheless, they kept up the old system, and from A.D. 1300, at least, down to Iolo Morganwg's time, they managed to hold a Gorsedd occasionally for Morganwg, as the following " Bardic Succession," or list of the Bards of the Chair of Glamorgan, and the order in which they were the Awenyddion, or disciples, taken from a manuscript of the late Mr. John Bradford,* will shew. The dates denote the times when they presided.

TRAHAEARN BRYDYDD MAWR 1300
HYWEL BWR BACH 1330
DAVYDD AB GWILYM 1360
IEUAN HEN 1370

His Awenyddion.
Gwilym ab Ieuan Hen,
Ieuan Tew Hen,
Hywel Swrdwal.

IEUAN TEW HEN 1420
Awenyddion.
Hywel Swrdwal,
Ieuan ab Hywel Swrdwal,
Ieuan Gethin ab I. ab Lleision,
Hywel ab Davydd ab I. ab Rhys.

IEUAN GETHIN AB I. AB LLEISION 1430
Awenydd.
Gwilym Tew, *or* G. Hendon.

GWILYM TEW 1460
Awenyddion.
Huw Cae Llwyd,
Hywel ab Dav. ab I. ab Rhys,
Harri o'r Gareg Lwyd,
Iorwerth Vynglwyd.

MEREDYDD AB RHOSSER 1470

* Cited in W. Owen's " Bardism," prefixed to his " Heroic Elegies of Llywarch Hen."

Awenyddion.
Iorwerth Vynglwyd,
Ieuan Deulwyn,
Sir Einion ab Owain.

IEUAN DEULWYN 1480
Awenyddion.
Iorwerth Vynglwyd,
Lewys Morganwg,
Harri Hir.

IORWERTH VYNGLWYD 1500
Awenyddion.
Lewys Morganwg,
Ieuan Du'r Bilwg.

LEWYS MORGANWG 1520
Awenyddion.
Meiryg Davydd,
Davydd Benwyn,
Llywelyn Sion o Langewydd,
Thomas Llywelyn o Regoes.

MEIRYG DAVYDD (died in 1600) 1560
Awenydd.
Watcin Pywel.

DAVYDD BENWYN 1560
Awenyddion.
Llywelyn Sion,
Sion Mawddwy,
Davydd Llwyd Mathew.

LLYWELYN SION (died in 1616) 1580
Awenyddion.
Watcin Pywel,
Ieuan Thomas,
Meilir Mathew,
Davydd ab Davydd Mathew,
Davydd Edward o Vargam,
Edward Davydd o Vargam.

WATCIN PYWEL 1620
Awenyddion.
Davydd Edward,
Edward Davydd,
Davydd ab Davydd Mathew.

EDWARD DAVYDD (died in 1690) 1660
Awenyddion.
Hywel Lewys,
Charles Bwttwn, Esq.
Thomas Roberts, Offeiriad,
S. Jones o Vryn Llywarch, Offeiriad,
Evan Sion Meredydd,
Davydd o'r Nant.

DAVYDD O'R NANT 1680
Awenyddion.
Hopcin y Gweydd,
Thomas Roberts, Offeiriad,
Davydd Hopcin o'r Coetty.

SAMUEL JONES, OFFEIRIAD 1700
Awenyddion.
Rhys Prys, Ty'n y Ton,
William Hain,
Sion Bradford, yn blentyn.

DAVYDD HOPCIN, o'r Coetty 1730
Awenyddion.
Davydd Thomas,
Rhys Morgan, Pencraig Nedd,
Davydd Nicolas,
Sion Bradford.

SION BRADFORD (died in 1780) 1760
Awenyddion.
Lewys Hopcin,
William Hopcin,
Edward Evan,
Edward Williams.

However, as their meetings were not always regular, and as the number of members was continually
dwindling, there was danger that the traditions of the
institution would suffer loss in consequence. Hence
such of the Bards as were anxious for their preservation, began, more than before, to make collections of
them in Books. We say more than before, because
some few, like Geraint the Blue Bard, had previously

committed to writing many things concerning the Bards and their system. With a view to consolidate those collections, several Gorsedds were held from the beginning of the fifteenth century, under the sanction of Sir Richard Neville and others. One was held for that purpose in 1570, under the auspices of William Herbert, earl of Pembroke, the great patron of Welsh literature, and the founder of the celebrated Library of Welsh MSS. at Rhaglan Castle, which was afterwards destroyed by Oliver Cromwell. What was done at those meetings received considerable improvement at one held by Sir Edward Lewis of the Van, about 1580, from the arrangement of the venerable Llywelyn Sion of Llangewydd; and lastly, a complete revisal of the former collections was made by Edward Davydd of Margam, which received the sanction of a Gorsedd, held at Bewpyr, in the year 1681, under the authority of Sir Richard Basset; when that collection was pronounced to be in every respect the fullest illustration of Bardism.*

Part of the said collection, namely, "Cyfrinach Beirdd Ynys Prydain," which is a most excellent treatise on the Ancient Versification of the Cymry, was published in the original by Iolo Morganwg, A.D. 1829. What is now offered to the public, it is but reasonable to infer, constitutes the remainder, or, at any rate, a great portion of the remainder, for many of the documents profess to have been taken out of the Books of Trahaiarn Brydydd Mawr, Hywel Swrdwal, Ieuan ab Hywel Swrdwal, Llawdden, Gwilym Tew, Rhys Brydydd, Rhys Brychan, Lewys Morgan-

---

* See William Owen's Bardism, prefixed to his Elegies of Llywarch Hen.

1

wg, Davydd Benwyn, Davydd Llwyd Mathew, Sion
Philip, Antoni Pywel, and principally Llywelyn Sion,
Bards who flourished from the 14th to the 17th century.   Llywelyn Sion tells us that he made his collection out of the Books of Taliesin, Ionas Mynyw,
Edeyrn Davod Aur, Cwtta Cyvarwydd, Einion Offeiriad, Davydd Ddu Hiraddug, Sion Cent, Rhys Goch,
and others in the Library of Rhaglan, by permission
of the lord William Herbert.

There is no doubt that these Bards viewed the
traditions of the Gorsedd as the genuine remains of
Ancient Druidism ; and there is every reason to believe that in their main features they were so.   The
variations observable in minor points would indicate
in what direction, and to what extent, they suffered
in their passage from the Christian era downwards.

But a question offers itself,—Did the Christian
Bards receive and believe these traditions as articles
of faith; or did they preserve them merely as curious
relics, or specimens of the primitive theology and
wisdom of the Cymry ?   We think that to act on the
former theory was impossible, in the face of two
facts.   First, they were members of the Chair of Baptism, in which "no one had the privilege of a teacher,
who was not baptized and devoted to the faith in
Christ."   For, be it observed, it was this Chair
alone that enjoined its members to preserve the ancient traditions ; and it was for that reason that we
omitted all mention of other Chairs, such as those of
Powys and Gwynedd.   Secondly, several individuals
of distinguished orthodoxy, piety, and position in the
Church, were admitted members of Bardism from
time to time.   It is said that Arthur, when he was

about to institute the Chair of the Round Table,
summoned to his aid three prelates, two of whom
are mentioned by name, that is, Dyvrig, archbishop
of Llandaff, afterwards of Caerleon-upon-Usk, and
Cyndeyrn, bishop of Llanelwy, " lest he and his
knights should do any thing contrary to the Holy
Scripture and the faith in Christ.......And Arthur
enjoined St. Teilo to baptize the three Bards," Taliesin, Merddin Emrys, and Merddin Wyllt, who
arranged its discipline and usages on the occasion.
St. Teilo, Cattwg the Wise, and St. Pryderi, were
members of the Bardic College, being " the three
blessed Bards of Arthur's court."   St. David, the patron saint of Wales, Padarn, the bishop of Llanbadarn,
Deiniol Wyn, the first bishop of Bangor, and Gildas,
were also Bards.   So also were Geraint, the Blue
Bard, supposed by some to be the same person as
Asser Menevensis, about 900, Einion the Aged, domestic chaplain to Sir Rhys the Aged, of Abermar-
lais, 1300—1350, Sion Cent, priest, 1380—1420,
Meurig Davydd, 1560, Thomas Roberts, priest, 1680,
S. Jones, Bryn Llywarch, priest, 1680, and Bishop
Burgess, who was graduated Druid by Iolo Mor-
ganwg.

We cannot conceive that these men, some of
whom were ornaments to the Christian religion,
should yet believe in tenets that were inconsistent
with that religion.   We may mention St. David in
particular, as one who took a very active part in
suppressing the Pelagian heresy, which in many re-
spects exhibited the lineaments of Druidism.   Padarn
subscribed the decrees of the Council of Paris, which
was held in the year 557, and is commended both as

an abbot and a bishop in the writings of Venantius
Fortunatus, a Latin poet of Gaul, who was his contemporary ; sure proofs that he also was sound in the
faith.   These considerations force us to conclude
that the Bards in Christian times preserved and
handed down the traditions of their institutes, merely
as curious speculations, illustrative of the religion and
philosophy of the primitive inhabitants of the island.

It may be remarked in addition that some of the
Bardic Chairs were occasionally held in churches and
religious houses.   The Chair of Tir Iarll was at one
time held alternately in the Church of Bettws and
the Church of Llangynwyd.   The Chair of Morganwg
was held at Easter in one of the chapter houses of
Llandaff, Margam, Glyn Nedd, or in the Church of
Llanilltyd ; at Whitsuntide, among other places, in
the Church of Pentyrch ; on St. John the Baptist's
day in the Church of Llancarvan, and in the Monastery of Penrhys.   Surely, the ecclesiastical authorities would never have allowed the inculcation of
heresy to desecrate places that were pre-eminently
dedicated to the service of the Christian religion.
Bardism, then, was not regarded as constituting the
faith of all who professed to know it.

We doubt not, however, that individuals would be
found now and then to cherish the traditions of the
Bards as saving truths, just as in our own days there
are persons, who entertain strange and erroneous doctrines, and yet have no mind to abandon their Christian profession.   Llyr Myrini endeavoured to reconcile
Bardism with Christianity, and to mould them into
one system, but his efforts resulted in Pelagianism ;
and there are traces in our volumes of other develop-

ments of a similar nature in respect of the Incarnation, which, however, took a Sabellian direction. It is not meant that the principles of Bardism were incompatible with the Christian religion; but that heresies, having arisen from the attempt to harmonize them, prove the attempt to have been made by individuals without the aid or sanction of the great body of Bards, who were, we may presume, good and honest Christians. In our opinion, the following Triad seems to express the judgment of Gorsedd on the comparative merits of the Bardic and Gospel dispensations :—

"There are three special doctrines that have been obtained by the nation of the Cymry : the first, from the age of ages, was that of the Gwyddoniaid, prior to the time of Prydain, son of Aedd the Great ; the second was Bardism, as taught by the Bards, after they had been instituted ; the third was the Faith in Christ, being THE BEST OF THE THREE."

The Bards believed that all things were tending to perfection ; when, therefore, they embraced Christianity, they must on their own principles have viewed it as a stage in advance of their former creed. The more advanced in religious knowledge would, doubtless, recognize it in its true character, as the fulfilment of Druidism, that is, as far as the latter was identical with the patriarchal religion of Noah—as "the mystery which hath been hid from ages, and from generations, but now is made manifest to his saints; to whom God would make known what is the riches of the glory of this mystery among the Gentiles." The Gospel of Christ is "the truth"—the realization of types and shadows; it is the "Truth against the world," which Bardism was continually

searching for. We, therefore, not only in virtue of
our clerical office, but also as a Bard according to the
privilege and usage of the Bards of the Isle of Britain,
under the privilege of the Chair of Morganwg, embo-
soming the Chair of Baptism, beg to enter our most
energetic protest *(gwrthneu)* against all attempts to
impose upon any one as articles of belief the tenets of
Bardism, where they are inconsistent with Christianity, as found in the Sacred Scriptures, and defined in
the creeds of "the Holy Church throughout the
world."

YN ENW DUW A PHOB DAIONI.

Alban Eilir, 1862.

LLYWELYN SION.

INASMUCH as Llywelyn Sion of Llangewydd was the person, by whom principally the present Collection of Bardism was made, the following brief Memoir of him may not be out of place here, or unacceptable to our readers.

He was born in the early part of the 16th century, and became at the usual age one of the disciples of Thomas Llywelyn of Rhegoes, and of Meurig Davydd of Llanisan, both eminent Bards of the Glamorgan Chair—the latter having presided in it A.D. 1560. His numerous compositions show him to be a poet of vigorous and lofty thoughts, which he, moreover, clothed in pure, correct, and elegant language. According to Taliesin Williams, who professes to derive his information from ancient manuscripts, he was also an antiquary of great research and ability.

Sion Bradford describes him as a man well to do in the world, accumulating wealth by the sale of transcripts of manuscripts, both poetic and prosaic, by which means also he obtained great respect among all classes of people. From the *Cywyddau*, that passed between him and Sion Mowddwy, it would appear that he held a subordinate office—that of crier—in the law court of Glamorgan. This

position brought him into contact with many of the gentry
and men of influence in the country, who invited him to
their houses, and, by allowing him access to their libraries,
afforded him facilities of gratifying the literary bent of his
mind. He was in particular acquainted with Sir Edward
Mansell, who, about 1591, wrote an excellent " account of
the conquest of Glamorgan." Sir Edward speaks of him
under the name of " Lewelyn John," as a painstaking and
respectable writer. It would appear that Sir Edward himself was a diligent collector of old Welsh MSS. According
to Sion Bradford, he was also in much esteem at Rhaglan
Castle; he says that it was from thence that he copied
most of his writings, Sir William Herbert having made
there a collection of the most valuable Welsh MSS., which
were afterwards ruthlessly destroyed by fire in the time of
Oliver Cromwell. Indeed, Llywelyn Sion himself, at p.
224 of the 1st volume of this work, confesses as much, and
expresses his unbounded obligation to "the lord William
Herbert, earl of Pembroke," for giving him permission to
make extracts from ancient and rare Books in the Castle of
Rhaglan.

He presided in the Chair of Glamorgan A.D. 1580, and
it was then that his arrangement received the sanction of
Gorsedd. His " Cyfrinach Beirdd Ynys Prydain," which
formed a part of his Collection, is beyond question an
excellent and invaluable treatise on Welsh versification,
and one which ought to be widely known beyond the limits
of the Principality. Indeed, a New Edition, with a translation, of this work, would form a very appropriate sequel
to BARDISM.

Sion Bradford says that he was an excellent teacher to
many of the poets of his time, as well as to other Welsh
literati. It would seem from some *Englynion*, which he
composed, that, when far advanced in years, he gave his
Books to his young disciple Edward Davydd of Margam.
At the end of one of his collections, entitled " Llyfr Hir
Llanharan," is written, " Fy llaw i, Llywelyn Sion, o Lan-

gewydd, hyd ymma, Tach. y 27. 1613;" after which follows the handwriting of Edward Davydd.

According to Watkin Powell, he composed a Book, which he designated, " Atgofion Gwybodau yr Hen Gymry," being a treatise on the poetry, genealogy, memorials, medicine, agriculture, law, handicraft, and chemistry of the Ancient Cymry. This he sent to London to be printed, but meanwhile the author died, and the Book was lost. According to one authority, his death took place in 1615, but two other documents place it respectively in 1616 and 1617, when he had attained the venerable age of about 100.

A

Tair rhagoriaeth Barddas: hoffeiddiaw myfyrdawd; helaethu addysg; a gwerinaw moes a defod.

CONTENTS.

		PAGE.
Advertisement	- - - - - -	xi
Preface	- - - - - - -	xiii
Llywelyn Sion	- - - - - -	lxxxiii

𝔖𝔶𝔪𝔟𝔬𝔩.

The Origin of Letters, Roll, and Paper.—The Virtue of Letters - 11

The Origin and Progress of Letters.—The Name of God.—The
  Bardic Secret - - - - - - 17

The first Inventors of Letters.—Improvers of the Alphabet.—
  Invention of the Roll and Plagawd.—Obligation of a Bard to
  hold a Chair and Gorsedd - - - - - 33

Origin of Letters - - - - - - - 39

The Inventor of Vocal Song.—The first Recorders of Bardism.—
  Its first Systematizers.—Their Regulations.—Mode of in-
  scribing the primary Letters.—Origin of their Form and
  Sound.—The three Menws - - - - - 41

The principal Elements of various things.—The Gogyrvens - 47

The Invention of Letters by Einigan and Menw.—The Secret of
  Bardism - - - - - - - 49

Cuttings.—Foundations of Awen - - - - - 51

Origin and Progress of Letters.—Einigan the Giant.—The Gwyddoniaid.—Systems of Letters - - - - 53

The Origin of Letters and Books.—Their Introduction into Britain.—The Coelbren - - - - - - 55

The primary Letters.—Improvement of the Alphabet - - 57

Primary Cuttings.—Improvement of the Coelbren.—Its Restoration - - - - - - - - 59

Recovery of the Old Cymraeg - - - - - 61

PAGE.

The primary Letters.—Their Augmentation.—Restoration of the
    Coelbren - - - - - - - 63
The Bardic Secret - - - - - - 65
The Sacred Symbol - - - - - - 67
The primary Letters.—Improvement of the Alphabet - - 67
Gogyrvens.—Writing with Ink - - - - - 69
Gogyrvens - - - - - - - 69
Gogyrvens - - - - - - - 69
Gogyrvens - - - - - - - 69
The Three First Words of the Cymraeg - - - 69
The primary Letters.—Names of the Coelbren - - - 71
Classification of the Letters - - - - - 73
The Bardic Secret.—Formation of Letters - - - 77
The Vowels - - - - - - - 77
The primary Letters - - - - - . 79
Variations of Letters - - - - - - 81
The Sixteen Primary Symbols - - - - - 81
Introduction of Letters.—Original Country of the Cymry.—
    Their Arrival in Britain.—Augmentation of the Alphabet - 83
Coelbren of the Bards, according to the arrangement of Llawdden 85
The Symbols of Literary Sciences.—Improvement of the Coel-
    bren.—Metrical Canons.—Dissolution of the Monastery of
    Pen Rhys - - - - - - - 89
The Pillars of Memory.—The Symbols - - - - 93
The Birds of Rhianon - - - - - - 95
The Five Ages of Letters - - - - - 95
The Three Symbols of Sciences - - - - - 97
The three Primitive Symbols.—The three Coelbren Symbols - 99
Numbers - - - - - - - 103
The Nine Degrees of Numerals - - - - - 107
The System of Numerals - - - - - 109
Arithmetic - - - - - - - 109
The System of Numerals - - - - - 109
Numerals - - - - - - - 111
The Numerals - - - - - - - 113
The Arithmetical Characters of the Ancient Cymry ; that is,
    the Numerals - - - - - - 113
The Three Symbols - - - - - - 115
The Materials of Language and Speech - - - - 115
The three Wreathed Bards - - - - - 115
Coelbren of the Bards - - - - - - 117
Coelbren of the Bards - - - - - - 133
Coelbren of the Bards - - - - - - 143
Peithynen - - - - - - - 151

PAGE.

Coelbren of the Bards - - - - - - 153
Secret Coelbren.—Secret Coelvain.—Coelvain of History - 155
Burning the Letters - - - - - - 155
Coelbren of Simple Letters - - - - - 157
Palm Coelbren - - - - - - - 157
Peithyn Coelbren.—Palm Coelbren - - - - 157
Peithynvain - - - - - - - 159
Memorials - - - - - - - 161
Plagawd - - - - - - - 163
The three principal Materials of Knowledge - - - 163
The Herald-bard - - - - - - 163
Dasgubell Rodd - - - - - - - 165

𝕮𝖍𝖊𝖔𝖑𝖔𝖌𝖞.

Triads of Bardism - - - - - - 169
Theological Triads - - - - - - 181
Theological Triads - - - - - - 197
Theological Triads - - - - - - 199
Theological Triads - - - - - - 201
Theological Triads - - - - - - 201
Theological Triads - - - - - - 205
Druidism - - - - - - - 205
God - - - - - - - 213
Cythraul - - - - - - - 213
Ceugant.—Duration.—God - - - - - 213
The three Imperceptibilities of God - - - - 215
The Bards' Enigma - - - - - - 215
The twelve primary Negatives - - - - - 217
Bardic Aphorisms - - - - - - 219
The Divine Names - - - - - - 219
Iau - - - - - - - 221
Hu the Mighty - - - - - - 221
The Circles - - - - - - 223
The Book of Bardism - - - - - 225
Abred.—Gwynvyd.—Awen - - - - - 235
The Three States - - - - - - 241
Annwn.—Life.—Death - - - - - 243
Abred - - - - - - - 243
The Origin of Man.—Jesus Christ.—Creation - - 245
The Creation.—The First Man.—The primary Letters - - 249
The Discipline of Bardism. (The Creation.) - - - 255

6 CONTENTS.

PAGE.

The Creation.—Worship.—Vocal Song.—Gwyddoniaid - 257
The Material of the World - - - - - 261
The Fall in Abred - - - - - - 263
God in the Sun - - - - - - - 263
God in the Light - - - - - - - 265
Triads of Bardism - - - - - - 267
God ; and the Faculties of the Soul - - - 267
Sentences of Bardism - - - - - - 271
The Ten Commandments of the Bards - - - 275
The Ten Commandments of the Bards - - - 285
The Rudiments of Theology - - - - 289
The Triads of St. Paul - - - - - 291
The Triads of St. Paul - - - - - 323
The Triads of St. Paul and Bardism - - - 339
Triads of Bardism and Usages - - - - 345
Triads of Bardism - - - - - - 357
The Mode of taking Food and Drink - - - 359
The Gorsedd Prayer - - - - - 361
The Prediction of Peredur, the Bard of Prydain - - 365
The Stanza of the Gorsedd Chair of the Winter Solstice - 367

Wisdom.

Triads of Wisdom - - - - - - 369
The Elements - - - - - - - 371
Triads of Bardism. (The Elements.) - - - 371
The Triads of Bardism, called the Triads of Ionabwy. (The
   Elements.) - - - - - - 377
Bardism, &c. (The Elements.) - - - 379
The Elements - - - - - - - 381
The Elements - - - - - - - 381
The Elements - - - - - - - 381
Bardism. (The Elements.) - - - - 383
The Materials - - - - - - - 383
The Elements - - - - - - - 385
The Elements - - - - - - - 387
The Materials of Man - - - - - 387
The Eight Materials of Man - - - - 389
The Seven Materials of Man - - - - 389
The Seven primary Materials of the World - - 391
The Eight Materials of Man - - - - 391
The Parts of the Human Body in which are the Faculties - 391

PAGE.

The Philosophy of the Blue Bard of the Chair - - - 393
Particular Triads - - - - - - 395
Triads of Ten Numbers - - - - - 397
Mutual reasoning between a Disciple and his Teacher - - 399
The Stars - - - - - - - 403
Astronomy - - - - - - - 403
Chronology - - - - - - - 405
Chronology - - - - - - - 407
The Memorial of Computation.—The Memorial of Country - 409
Memorial and Computation - - - - - 409
The Cycle of Time - - - - - - 411
The Months - - - - - 411
The beginning of the Year - - - - - 417
The three Circles of the Sun - - - - - 417
The Four Quarters of the Year - - - - 417
The Albans - - - - - - - 419
The Divisions of the Year - - - - - 419
The Divisions of the Year - - - - - 419
The Divisions of the Year - - - - - 419
The Divisions of the Year - - - - - 419
The Divisions of the Year - - - - - 421
The Divisions of the Day - - - - - 421
The Divisions of the Day - - - - - 421
The Divisions of the Day - - - - - 421
The Divisions of the Day - - - - - 423
The Divisions of the Day - - - - - 423
Years of the Sun and Moon - - - - - 423
Years of the Sun and Moon - - - - - 423
Years of the Sun and Moon - - - - - 425
Days of Days - - - - - - 425

A LIST OF DOCUMENTS

OCCURRING IN VOLUME I., WHICH HAVE BEEN PRINTED BEFORE.

Pwy a wnaeth rôl—cenedl y Cymry, pp. 12, 14. Coelbren y Beirdd, p. 25.

Adolwyn pa fodd—gyfergyd ar llafar, p. 46. Coelbren y Beirdd, p. 7.

Einigan Gawr—poed felly bydded, pp. 48, 50. Coelbren y Beirdd, p. 6.

Cyn amser Beli—pedair awgrym ar hugain, pp. 56, 58. Iolo MSS. pp. 203, 204.

Ystorrynnau—arnynt yn awr, pp. 58, 60. Iolo MSS. pp. 204, 205.

Yn amser Owain—adver ag adgael, pp. 60, 62. Iolo MSS. p. 205.

Coelbren y Beirdd — **ɯ Y**, pp. 84—88. Coelbren y Beirdd, pp. 26, 27.

Coelbren y Beirdd—yn dorredig a chyllell, pp. 116—132. Coelbren y Beirdd, pp. 15—22.

Llyma fal y dywed Lywelyn Sion—ddeunaw ar hugain, pp. 133—142. Iolo MSS. pp. 206—209.

Cymmer goed bychain—breiniau gwlad, pp. 142—150. Coelbren y Beirdd, pp. 22—25.

Y pillwydd—bren a fythawr, pp. 150—152. Iolo MSS. pp. 205, 206.

Trioedd Barddas—ynghylch y Gwynvyd, pp. 168—180. Poems Lyric and Pastoral, vol. ii. pp. 235—239.

Llyma Weddi'r Orsedd—O Lyfr Mawr Margam, p. 360. Iolo MSS. p. 80.

Llyma weddi'r Orsedd—Duw a phob daioni, pp. 360, 362. Iolo MSS. p. 80.

Llyma weddi'r orsedd o Lyfr arall—Daioni, p. 362. Iolo MSS. p. 80.

Gweddi Talhaiarn—Tanwyn ai cant, p. 362. Iolo MSS. p. 79.

Llyma ddarogan Peredur—Peredur Fardd ai cant, p. 364, 366. Iolo MSS. pp. 80, 81.

Llyma Bennill Cadair—Merddin Emrys ai cant, p. 366. Iolo MSS. p. 81.

Saith deunydd dyn—Y Bardd Glas o'r Gadair a'i dywed, p. 388. Myv. Arch. v. iii. p. 109.

Llyma saith—Y Bardd Glas o'r Gadair ai dywed, p. 390. Myv. Arch. v. iii. p. 109.

Wyth devnydd dyn—sev y bywyd, p. 390. Myv. Arch. v. iii. p. 132.

Athronddysg y Bardd Glas—or Gadair ai dywed, pp. 392, 394. Myv. Arch. v. iii. pp. 108, 109.

Barddas.

Bardism.

BARDDAS.

Amgrym.

DECHREUAD LLYTHYR, RHOL, A PHAPUR.— RHINWEDD LLYTHYRENAU.

Da'ch cyfarwyddyd fy athraw caredig, yn rhodd dywedwch wrthyf pwy a wnaeth Lythyr gyntaf?

Einiged Gawr, fab Huon fab Alser fab Iôn fab Iabwth fab Noe hên wedi marw ei dad er dodi cof cadwedig am a wnaethoedd hwnnw ai weithredoedd moliannus, herwydd gwarantedig o goel a chyfarwyddyd, ag achaws mai ar brenn y doded hynny o goel gyntaf y gelwir coelbren ar y llythyrennau ag ar au doder arnaw.

---

[1] Probably the same as Elishah, in Gen. x. 4.

[2] It is remarkable that, contrary to the popular notion which represents Gomer as the progenitor of the Cymry, Nennius, the Genealogy of Gruffydd ab Cynan, in the 2nd volume of the Myvyrian Archaiology—and other Pedigrees registered by Lewis Dwnn, all support the view of the text as to the descent of that people from Javan. Nennius, indeed, asserts positively that his information was derived "ex traditione veterum, qui incolæ in primo fuerunt Britanniæ."

[3] That is, *wood of credibility.* The ancient mode of cutting letters on wood is frequently alluded to in the poems of the Bards, both early and medieval. Thus;—

TALIESIN, 520—570.

Wyf llogell cerdd wyf lle ynydd (llëenydd),
Caraf y *gorwydd* a *gorail* clyd.

I am the depository of song, I am a reader,
I love the *sprigs* and the compact *wattling.*

Buarth y Beirdd.

BARDISM.

Symbol.

THE ORIGIN OF LETTERS, ROLL, AND PAPER.—THE VIRTUE OF LETTERS.

MAY it please your information, my beloved teacher; pray, tell me who was the first that made a Letter?

Einiged the Giant, son of Huon, son of Alser,[1] son of Javan,[2] son of Japheth, son of Noah the Aged, after the death of his father, for the purpose of preserving a memorial of what he did, and of his praiseworthy actions, warranted in respect of credibility and information. And because it was on wood (pren) that such belief was first placed, both the letters, and what they were inscribed on, were called *Coelbren.*[3]

> Gwydion ap Don—
> A rithwys *gorwyddawd* y ar‚plagawd.
>
> Gwydion, son of Don—
> Formed *wood knowledge* upon plagawd.
> Kadeir Keridwen.

RHYS GOCH AB RICCERT, 1140—1170.

> Bu *bwyall brenn* bardd anghymmen
> Yn *naddu* can i Wenllian.
>
> The *wooden axe* of an unpolished bard
> Has been *hewing* a song to Gwenllian.

CYNDDELW, 1150—1200.

> O ffyrfioli tri o draethaut berffaith
> Oe *gwyded* ieith oe *gwydaur.*

Pwy a wnaeth rôl gyntaf ar lythyr?

From composing three complete treatises
Of *wood* language—of *wood letters.*—Canu i Dduw.

DAVYDD AB GWILYM, 1300—1368.

Hwn fydd ar *wydd* i'w hannerch.

This will address them on *wood.*

O myn wawd orddawd arddof
Aed i'r *coed* i *dorri* cof.

If he would have an encomium of gentle character,
Let him go into the *wood* to *cut* a memorial.
I Ruff. Grug.

Haws yw cael lle bo gwael *gwydd*
Saerni dwfn *saer* na defnydd.

It is easier to obtain, where the *wood* is poor,
The *carpentry* of a skilful *wright*, than materials.—Ib.

IOLO GOCH, 1315—1402.

Arwain i Owain a wnaf
Ar eiriau mydr ir araf
Peunydd nid *naddiad gwydd gwern,*
Pen *saerwawd.*

I will bear for Owain,
In metrical words, fresh and slow,
Continually, not the *hewing of alder wood*
By the chief *carpenter of song.*—I O. Glyndwr.

RHYS GOCH ERYRI, 1330—1420.

Ni welir mwy ol *bwyall*
Flodau *saer* ar gerddgaer gall.

No longer will be seen the mark of *the axe*
Of the flower of *carpenters* on a song-loving and wise one.
Mar. Gruff. Llwyd.

LLYWELYN MOEL Y PANTRI, 1400—1430.

Pan glywyf hiraethwyf hoed
Pensaergerdd pain is *irgoed.*

When I hear, I regret the delay,
The *chief carpenter of song*—a peacock beneath the *green wood.*

GWILYM TEW, 1430—1470.

Llun ei gorph yn darllain *gwydd.*

The form of his person reading *wood.*

IEUAN DU'R BILWG, 1460—1500.

Aed dy fawl, ydwyd filwr,
Ar *wydd* hyd mae dydd a dwr.

May thy praise go—thou art a soldier—
Upon *wood*, as long as day and water continue.

Who was the first that made a Roll[1] in connection with letters?

LEWYS MON, 1480—1520.

Bwyall gerdd pan ballai gant
Byth *naddai* beth ni wyddant.

The *axe* of song, when a hundred failed,
Always *hewed* what they knew not.

Mar. Rhys Nanmor.

SION TUDUR, 1560—1602.

Ni wnai brydydd na brawdwr
Roi *gwydd* gwell ar gywydd gwr.

No poet or judge
Used better *wood* for a poem to man.

Mar. Sion Brwynog.

RHYS CAIN, 1580.

Yscerbwd mewn cwd, nid min call—a'i mawl,
Llyfr moliant bardd cibddall,
Anhawdd yw ei iawn ddeall,
Fe wna i ddyn a fo'n ddall.

A skeleton in a bag—the lips of the wise will not praise it,
The eulogistic book of a purblind bard,
It is difficult to rightly understand it,
It will do for a man who is blind.—I lyfr pren.

A long string of similar quotations might be adduced, but the foregoing are sufficient to show that the practice in question was known to the Bards from the 6th down to the 17th century.

It may be observed that several words in the Cymric language, which relate to knowledge or literature, have a primary reference to wood. Thus; *arwydd,* a sign; *cyfarwydd,* skilful; *cyfarwyddyd,* information; *cywydd,* a species of versification, also revelation; *dedwydd,* having recovered knowledge, happy; *derwydd,* a Druid; *egwyddawr,* a rudiment, an alphabet; *gwyddawr,* a rudiment; *gwyddon,* a man of science; *gwynwyddigion,* men of sacred knowledge.

[1] Though Roll, as in the text, primarily refers to the schedule that was turned up with the hand in the form of a pipe, it came also to denote a system, or arrangement, as in the phraseologies, *Rhol y Crythor, Rhol y Telynor, Rhol y Mesurau, Rhol Iolo Goch, Rhol Achau, Rhol Cof a Chyfrif,* and *Rhol y Beirdd.* It is alluded to by many of the Bards; thus—

DAVYDD AB GWILYM, 1300—1368.

Bydd yr un *Rhol* ag Iolo
Ddefod hardd, hen fardd y fro.

He will be of the same *Roll* as Iolo,
Fair usage—the old Bard of the district.

GRUFFYDD AB IEUAN AB LLYWELYN VYCHAN, 1470.

Y rhai na wyppont eu *Rhol*
Yn esgud aent i ysgol.

Bendigeidfran fab Llyr Llediaith a ddysgawdd y ffordd honno yn Rhufain ag ai dug gydac ef i Brydain lle yi dysges ef hi ir Cymry. a'r modd y trinid crwyn mynnod a geifr mal y gellid ysgrifen o lythyr arnynt. a'r ffordd honno a aeth ar arfer hyd nad oedd namyn y Beirdd yn ymarfer megis o graffymachub ar hen ffordd o ddodi llythyrennau ar goed, er cof a chadw ar hen brifwybodau Cenedl y Cymry ag o hynny ydd aethpwyd iddei galw hi Coelbren y Beirdd. ag nid oes yr awr honn namyn y Beirdd ai ceidw ar gof drwy naddu yi cerddi au coelion cof ar goed herwydd yr hen gelfyddyd. a hynny er cadw cof coeliadwy ar brifwybodau cenedl y Cymry.

Pwy a wnaeth bapir gyntaf?

Gwr o Gonstinoblys ydoedd ai enw Moran ag ef a fales lîn ac a hwnnw o'i ledu yn deneu papur.

Beth yw rhinwedd llythyreneu.

Ermygion aflafar ydynt yn llafaru, a chorph heb enaid heb fywyd yn arwain meddwl, marw yn gwybod yn fwy na'r byw, Llaw yn llafaru yn well na thafawd, llygad yn clywed yn well no chlust heb na swn na sain, edraith heb dafawd, clyw heb glust, Iaith heb eiriau, Llun llafar, cen-

> They who know not their *Roll*,
> Let them quickly go to school.

HUW AP DAVYDD AP LLYWELYN AP MADAWC, 1480—1520.

> Goreuro *Rhol* geiriau rhawg,
> *Grafio* dadl gref odidawg.

> He gilt a *Roll* of long words,
> He *engraved* a controversy, strong and excellent.
> > Mar. Tudur Aled.

HARRI AP RHYS AP GWILYM, 1530.

> Graddau a *Rhol gorwyddawd,*
> Gwraidd gwybodau er gwau gwawd.

> The degrees and *Roll* of *wood-knowledge,*
> The root of sciences, for the weaving of a song of praise.
> > Mar. Gwilym ap Ieuan Hen.

DAVYDD BENWYN, 1550—1600.

> Eurai bwnc orau bencerdd,
> Arail gwawd a *Rhol* y gerdd.

Bran the Blessed,[1] son of Llyr of Defective Speech, learned that mode at Rome, and brought it with him to Britain, where he taught it to the Cymry, as well as the manner of dressing the skins of kids and goats, so as to be suitable for written letters. And that mode became customary, so that the Bards alone practised, as it were by bare rescue, the old style of inscribing letters on wood, for the purpose of preserving the memorials of the old and primitive sciences of the nation of the Cymry; thence it came to be called *Coelbren of the Bards*. At present there are only the Bards that keep it in memory, by engraving their songs and records on wood, according to the ancient art, with the view of preserving in reliable memory the primitive sciences of the nation of the Cymry.

Who was the first that made paper?

A man from Constantinople, named Moran; he ground flax, which on its being thinly spread out, became paper.

What is the virtue of letters?

They are mute organs that speak—a body without a soul, and without life, guiding thought—dead ones, knowing more than the living—a hand speaking better than the tongue—an eye hearing better than the ear, without either noise or sound—speech without a tongue—hearing without an ear—

He embellished a subject—the best chief of song—
He attended to encomium, and the *Roll* of song.
Mar. Lewys Morgan.

Lewys ap Hywel, 1560—1600.

Rhin gwawdiaith a'i rhoi'n gadarn,
Rhol beirdd yn rheoli barn.

The charm of panegyric, firmly placed,
The *Roll* of the Bards ruling judgment.
Mar. Iorwerth Vynglwyd.

Sion Tudur, 1560—1602.

Ai *Rhol* achau rhy lychwin.

And their *Roll* of pedigrees, too much covered with mould.

---

[1] Father of the celebrated Caractacus. Bran is said to have remained at Rome for seven years as hostage for his son. (Tr. 35. Third Series). It was then that he acquired the information imputed to him in the text.

nad yn adrodd y gwir heb ei wybod, marw yn dysgu 'r byw.
Cof heb neb yn ei arwain. Deall y marw, a phennaf o
gywreindeb celfyddyd y byw. a chadwedigaeth pob celfyddodau a gwybodau, a dangos ar bob dangos.

DECHREUAD A GWELLHAD LLYTHYR.—ENW DUW.—
CYFRINACH Y BEIRDD.

Yn rhodd fy Athraw celfyddbwyll, os teg ei ofyn, pa
fodd y cafad Gwybodaeth gyntaf ar lythyr?

Dangosaf Gyfarwydd Gwyr doethion gwybodbell, sef pan
roddes Duw ei enw ar lafar y tarddes gyda'r gair y goleuni
ar bywyd sef cyn no hynny nid oedd bywyd namyn Duw ei
hunan, sef modd ai llefair cyfarwyddyd Duw ai enw ar lafar,
a chyda'r llafar tardd y goleuni a bywydoldeb, a Dyn, a
phob arall bywydol sef cyttardd un ag arall o honynt, a
Menw Hen ab y Menwyd a weles dardd y goleuni ai ddull
ai olwg nid amgen nag yn llynn /|\ yn dair colofn, ag
ymhelydr y goleuni y llafar, sef un y clyw ar gweled, un
cyfun llun a llais ag un cyfun ar llun a'r llais bywyd, ag un
cyfun a'r tri hynn gallu, a'r gallu hynny Duw Tâd. A
chan tair un cyfun bobun o'r rhain y dealles mai un cyfun a
Duw pob llafar a chlyw a byw a bod a golwg a gweled, ag
nid amgen na Duw y dim lleiaf, a chan weled y llun ag yn
hynny clywed y llafar ac nid yn amgen, y gwybu 'r llun a'r
olwg a ddylit ar lafar a chaffael daear y danaw yn gyttrym
ar goleuni, lluniaw 'r llafar ar goleuni ar y ddaear, a chan

---

[1] The words Menw and Menwyd, which are here used as proper names, signify the source of intellect and happiness, the mind, or the soul, being derived
from *men*, an active principle. There are several words growing out of the same
root, such as, *menwad*, *menwawl*, *menwedig*, *menwi*, *menwin*, *menwydaidd*, *men-
wydaw*, *menwydawg*, *menwydawl*, *menwydedd*, *menwydiad*, *menwydig*, *menwydus*,
menwydusaw, *menwyn*, through all of which the original idea of intellect and
bliss runs. "Tri *menwedigion* teyrnedd," the three beneficent sovereigns; "tri
menwydigion Duw," the three blessed ones of God. (Tr.)

Diwahardd i fardd ei *fenwyd*,

Unrestricted to the bard his *talent.*—Cynddelw.

language without words—form of voice—a messenger uttering the truth, without knowing it—the dead teaching the
living—memory with no one guiding it—the understanding
of the dead—the principal skill of the art of the living—the
preservation of all arts and sciences—and the demonstration
of all that is demonstrable.

THE ORIGIN AND PROGRESS OF LETTERS.—THE NAME OF GOD.—THE BARDIC SECRET.

Pray, my skilful and discreet teacher, if it be fair to ask,
how was the knowledge of letters first obtained?

I will exhibit the information of men of wisdom and profound knowledge, thus;—When God pronounced His name,
with the word sprang the light and the life; for previously
there was no life except God Himself. And the mode in
which it was spoken was of God's direction. His name was
pronounced, and with the utterance was the springing of
light and vitality, and man, and every other living thing;
that is to say, each and all sprang together. And Menw[1]
the Aged, son of Menwyd,[1] beheld the springing of the
light, and its form and appearance, not otherwise than thus,
/|\, in three columns; and in the rays of light the vocali-
zation—for one were the hearing and seeing, one unitedly
the form and sound; and one unitedly with the form and
sound was life, and one unitedly with these three was power,
which power was God the Father. And since each of these
was one unitedly, he understood that every voice, and hearing, and living, and being, and sight, and seeing, were one
unitedly with God; nor is the least thing other than God.
And by seeing the form, and in it hearing the voice—not
otherwise—he knew what form and appearance voice should
have. And having obtained earth under him coinstantaneously with the light, he drew the form of the voice and light

The English words *man* and *mind*, and the Latin *mens*, seem to be of cognate
origin.

C

glywed ymlef y llafar ag ynddo ryw ag yngan trillais y
cafas ef y tair llythyren ag y gwybu 'r arwydd a weddai ar
un ag arall o honynt. sef a wnaeth ar lun ag arwydd Enw
Duw yn rhith pelydr y goleuni, ag y canfu taw rhith a llun
ag arwydd bywyd ydoeddynt. hefyd un a hynny bywyd, ag
yn y bywyd Duw sef un Duw a bywyd, ag nid bywyd ond
Duw, ag nid Duw ond bywyd.

Sef o'r deall a gafad yn llynn ar hynn o lafar medru cyd-
gyfelydd ar bob llafar amgen herwydd rhyw ag ansawdd a
phwyll, a medru llythyren a weddai ar bob ymlef llais a
llafar, ag mal hynny caffael y Gymraeg a phob iaith amgen,
ag o'r tair llythyren gysefiniaid eiliaw pob llythyren amgen
a llyna brif gyfrinach Beirdd Ynys Prydain ag o'r gyfrinach
honn pob gwybod ar lythyr, a geffir yn alledig.

Mal hynn o ddodir llafar a glywsid ar gôf yn yr arwydd
a dodi pwyll ar bob un o'r trillais, doded pwyll O i'r golofn
gyntaf, a phwyll I i'r ail golofn sef yr un ganol, a phwyll
V i'r drydedd, ag o hynny'r gair OIV. sef a'r gair hynn
y datgenis Duw ei fodoldeb ai fywydoldeb ai wybodoldeb, ai
alluoldeb, ai dragywyddoldeb a'i gyffredoldeb ag yn y datgan ei gariadoldeb sef yn gyttrem ag ef y tarddes mal
mellten yr holl fydoldeb i fod a bywyd yn gymmloedd
gyngan ag enw duw ar lafar, yn un cyfun can orfoledd a
llawenydd. yna'r bydoedd oll hyd eithafoedd annwfn. sef
yn hynn o fodd y gwnaeth Duw'r bydoedd, nid amgen
datgan ei enw ai fodoldeb. $\left\{ \begin{smallmatrix} /|\backslash \\ O\ I\ V \end{smallmatrix} \right\}$ *

Pam nad iawn i ddyn rhoi enw Duw ar lafar, a llef iaith
a thafawd?

Achaws nas gellir hynny heb gamenwi Duw, cans nid

---

* In Iolo Morganwg's MS. this is followed immediately by " sef o'r gwybodau
a'r ddeall parth Llafar Iaith," &c., p. 14; but as the following note is added
" /|\ cymmer oddi wrthy nod hwn /|\ ar bapur arall," we have transposed
the portions accordingly.

on the earth. And it was on hearing the sound of the
voice, which had in it the kind and utterance of three notes,
that he obtained the three letters, and knew the sign that
was suitable to one and other of them. Thus he made in
form and sign the Name of God, after the semblance of rays
of light, and perceived that they were the figure and form
and sign of life; one also with them was life, and in life was
God, that is to say, God is one with life, and there is no
life but God, and there is no God but life.

It was from the understanding thus obtained in respect
of this voice, that he was able to assimilate mutually every
other voice as to kind, quality, and reason, and could make
a letter suitable to the utterance of every sound and voice.
Thus were obtained the Cymraeg, and every other language.
And it was from the three primary letters that were constructed every other letter,—which is the principal secret of
the Bards of the Isle of Britain; and from this secret comes
every knowledge of letters that is possible.

Thus was the voice, that was heard, placed on record in
the symbol, and meaning attached to each of the three
notes :—the sense of O was given to the first column, the
sense of I to the second or middle column, and the sense of
V to the third; whence the word OIV. That is to say, it
was by means of this word that God declared His existence,
life, knowledge, power, eternity, and universality. And in
the declaration was His love, that is, coinstantaneously
with it sprang like lightening all the universe into life and
existence, co-vocally and co-jubilantly with the uttered
Name of God, in one united song of exultation and joy—
then all the worlds to the extremities of Annwn. It was
thus, then, that God made the worlds, namely, He declared
His Name and existence $\left\{ \begin{smallmatrix} /|\backslash \\ O\ I\ V \end{smallmatrix} \right\}$.

Why is it not right that a man should commit the Name
of God to vocalization, and the sound of language and
tongue?

Because it cannot be done without misnaming God, for

oes o ddyn a glywes ei enwi ef erioed ar lafar, ag nid oes a
wyr ei lefaru, cyda'i doder ar llythyrenau mal y gwyper
beth a feddylier, ac am bwy mae, ac arwyddon a ddodid
gynt sef y tri defnydd llafar lythr, a rhag amharch ar dduw
ai ddianrhydeddu, gwahardder i fardd ei enwi amgen nag
yngheudawd ac ar feddwl.

Yn rhodd fy athraw caredigbwyll, dangoswch imi yr
arwyddon a safant am enw Duw? a'r modd au gwneir?

Llyma fal au gwneir y cyntaf or arwyddon, ysgïen neu
linell fechan ar oleddf gyda'r haul yn ucher fal hynn /
ail ysgïen arall yn null post gyfarben unionsawn fal hynn
| a'r trydedd ysgïen yr un faint ei goleddf a'r gyntaf
eithr yngwrthwyneb iddi sef yn erbyn yr haul fal hynn \,
a dodi'r tair ynghyd fal hynn /|\, ag yn lle ag yn nirprwy
y rhai hynn y dodir y tair llythyren yma sef O. I. W. ag
yn hynn o fodd y dodes y Bardd yr enw hwnn ar ei
Englyn, nid amgen,

> Iôr—Iôn—Dwyf—Deon, boed diwair   genau
> Ar ganon ai llefair
> Arall enw a rhoi'r llawnair
> O. i ag w, $\frac{oiw}{yw}$ y gair.   Ieuan Rudd ai cant.

Ag enw hwn a roddes Duw arno ei hunan yn dangos ei fod
mewn bod, ag nad oes namyn efe ei hun eithr o ddawn a
chennathâd. sef yr ydym bawb o ddynion ag eraill fywydolion ar fod ac mewn bod namyn o ddawn a channiattâd

---

[1] Al. *is.*

[2] The Name is alluded to by Iolo Goch;—

> Oio Dduw! o waedd hyorn
> Pa beth yw y gyfryw gorn?

> Oio God! from the sound of the bold horn,
> What is such a horn?

And by Sion Cent, 1380—1420,

> Pannon ar ganon gannaid ai gelwir
> Da gwelwn ef o'n plaid,
> O. I. ac W. yw a gaid
> Oiw beunydd i bob enaid.

> He is called Pannon in the holy canon;
> We behold Him favourable on our side—

no man ever heard the vocalization of His Name, and no one knows how to pronounce it; but it is represented by letters, that it may be known what is meant, and for Whom it stands. Formerly signs were employed, namely, the three elements of vocal letters. However, to prevent disrespect and dishonour to God, a Bard is forbidden to name Him, except inwardly and in thought.

Pray, my beloved and discreet teacher, show me the signs that stand for the Name of God, and the manner in which they are made.

Thus are they made;—the first of the signs is a small cutting or line inclining with the sun at eventide, thus, ╱ ; the second is another cutting, in the form of a perpendicular, upright post, thus, │ ; and the third is a cutting of the same amount of inclination as the first, but in an opposite direction, that is, against the sun, thus ╲ ; and the three placed together, thus, ╱│╲. But instead of, and as substitutes for these, are placed the three letters O I W. And it was in this manner that the Bard inserted this name in his stanza, thus,

> The Eternal, Origin, Self-existent, Distributor,—holy be the lips
> That canonically pronounce them;
> Another name, in full word,
> Is O. I. and W—OIW [1] the word.—Ieuan Rudd sang it. [2]

This name God gave to Himself, to show that He is in existence, and that there is no one but Himself, except by gift and permission; for truly all of us men, and other living beings, are and exist only by the gift and permission

> O. I. and W. is He found to be,
> Oiw always to every soul.

Llywelyn ap Hywel ap Ieuan ap Gronw, 1500—1540, makes use of the term, thus,

> OIO Ddyn byw i ddwyn byd.
> OIO man alive, to bear the world.

And Davydd Nanmor, who died A.D. 1460, observes,—

> O. I. ag W. yw ag Oen.
> He is O. I. and W. and a Lamb.

Duw. a Thrahausder y bernir llafaru yr enw hwnn ynghlyw dyn o'r byd, Eisioes er hynny, pob peth ai enwant ef yngheudawd gerfydd yr enw hwn, nid amgen no mor a thir, daiar ag awyr a holl weledigion ag anweledigion y byd ai yu naiar ai yn wybren y bont, yr holl fydoedd pob nefolion a daiarolion, pob dealledig ar fodolion a bodoldeb pob bywydol a phob ammywydol, am hynny nid oes a beirch Duw ai enwa gerfydd hynn o enw namyn yngheudawd.

Sef y Tair Llythyren rin arwyddaw Tair Angheneddyl Duw a wnant, nid amgen, Cariad, Gwybodaeth, a Gwirionedd, sef o'r tri hynn y tyf pob Cyfiawnder, ag heb bob un o'r tri nis gellir cyfiawnder, a phun bynnag o'r tair a saif i fynydd y ddwy eraill o'r arwyddon a bwysant att honno. A phob dwy ba bynag o honynt a roddant flaen a goreu i'r Drydedd ba un bynnag o'r tair y bo. ag wrth hynn o drefn ag ansawdd y dodwyd tair Ysgen raddawl a'r Feirdd Ynys Prydain, ac i bob yn o'r tair Braint a Blaen a goreu, parth arbennicter anghenyddyl rhag y ddwy eraill, bynnag o rai y bônt, o dair angheneddyl Duw y tardd pob gallu a gwyllys a deddf.

Sef o'r gwybodau a'r ddeall parth Llafar Iaith ag ymadrodd o gymmhwyl y Tair prif Lythyren y lluniwyd unllythyren ar bymtheg un eiliedig o'r gysefin golofnau nid amgen y tair prif lythyren ar ddull pelydr y goleuni, a medru fal hynny llun a golwg ar bob llafar Iaith ag ymadrodd, ag ar bob ymlef gysefin, a lluniau arwydd cof yn weledig ar bren a maen ag yn gymmedr a chof clyw cof y golwg, a chymmedru fal hyn yn mhwyll arwydd pob ymlef llafar yn weledig i'r llygad, hyd y dichonai clyst glywed a lafarai tafawd ag y medrai Awen o Dduw. Yna wedi eiliaw un llythyren ar bymtheg o'r

of God. It is considered presumptuous to utter this name in the hearing of any man in the world. Nevertheless, every thing calls Him inwardly by this name—the sea and land, earth and air, and all the visibles and invisibles of the world, whether on the earth or in the sky—all the worlds of all the celestials and terrestrials—every intellectual being and existence—every thing animate and inanimate; wherefore none that honours God, will call Him by this name, except inwardly.

The three mystic letters signify the three attributes of God, namely, love, knowledge, and truth; and it is out of these three that justice springs, and without one of the three there can be no justice. Which one so ever of the three stands up, the other two will incline towards it; and every two of them whatsoever will yield precedency and pre-eminence to the third, whichever of the three it may be. It was according to this order and principle that three degrees were conferred upon the Bards of the Isle of Britain, and each of the three was invested with privilege, precedency, and pre-eminence, in respect of the particularity of necessity, over the other two, whichsoever they might be. Out of the three attributes of God spring every power and will and law.

It was out of the knowledge and understanding of the vocalization of language and speech, by reason of the three principal letters, that sixteen letters were formed, constructed from the primary columns, namely, the three principal letters in the form of rays of light. And it was thus that form and appearance could be imparted to every vocalization of language and speech, and to every primary sound, and symbolic forms of memory be made visible on wood and stone. Accordingly the memory of seeing could thus take place simultaneously with the memory of hearing; and, by means of signs, every sound of voice could be rendered visible to the eye, as far as the ear could hear what the tongue spoke, and what awen from God was capable of. Then when sixteen letters were constructed out of the principal

prif-golofnau sef y rhai hynn /|\, can nas gellir llythyren
ar goelbren a chyfrinach Beirdd Ynys Prydain nas caffer ei
defnyddau ai cymmalau o un neu arall or tair prifgolofn,
ag o dorri 'r arwyddon hynn ar bren y gelwyd ^{llythyr}_{llythyrau}
arnynt, a gwedi torri pob un o'r llythyrau ar bren doded
enwau a phwyll ar bob un o henynt herwydd ymlef a llafar
yn warantedig ag yn ddosparthus; sef i bob un ei lafar heb
yn amgen, gan gadarnhau celfyddyd arnynt, ag mal hynn y
cafad arwydd a gwyddor llafar warantedig yr honn a elwir
yr Abic. ac eraill ai geilw yr Abcedilros. mal hynn y cafad
celfyddyd golwg a llaw ar lafar a meddwl, ag o hynny cof
golwg a defnydd ar wybodau, yna ymroddasant ddoethion
ag awenyddion i wellhâu gwybodau ag Iaith ag ymadrodd,
ag i farnu yn fwy celfyddbwyll a manolbwnc ar lafar, ag
amrafaeliant ymlef ag ^a ymgywreiniaw arnynt, yn medrwyd
ar ddwy lythyren eraill onid aeth yr egwyddor ar ddeunaw
llythyren, gwedi hynny gwelwyd achos dwy eraill onid
aethant yn ugain, yna dwy ar hugain ag yn orphen y
gwaith pedair llythyren ar hugain o brif lythyrau, ag nid
oes mwy yn odidogion ar wyddor y goelbren, sef yn gysefiniaid ymlef, etto y mae eraill yn lythyrau cyfansoddedigion
yn arwyddaw newid llafar a phwys ar lythyren, ag o'r rhai
hynny y mae herwydd gwyr yn athrawon celfyddgamp hyd
rif unarbymtheg ag eraill a fynnant ddeunaw, ac i rai
onaddynt nis gellir nag awdurdawd na gwarant, o'r hyn
lleiaf, nis gellir anghen arnynt o gymhwyll anhepcor. eisioes nid rhydd gwahardd amwellhâu ar wybodau, a rhydd
pob awen a chelfyddyd cyd nas drygont, ag y tywyllont neu
a ddyrysont wybodau moliannus.

---

[1] Al. *llythyr;* a cutting, from the prefix *lly,* signifying what is manifold,
various, or manifest, and *tyr, (torri,)* to cut. Or it may be from *lleu,* to
explain, or to read; or else from *llw,* an exclamation, an oath, and *tyr.*

[2] That is, A. B. C., the I being inserted with the view of giving B its proper
pronunciation, or of filling up the vowel sound between B and C.

[3] A word composed entirely of the ten primary letters. See further on.

columns, namely these /|\—since no letter can be found
on the Coelbren, or in the Secret of the Bards of the Isle of
Britain, that has not its elements and modifications derived
from one or other of the three principal columns—and because these signs were cut on wood, they were called *llythyrau.*[1] And when every one of the letters was cut on
wood, each of them received a name and meaning in respect
of sound and voice, warranted and systematized; that is to
say, each had its own peculiar vocalization, confirmed by
art. Thus were obtained the signs and rudiments of warranted speech, which is called Abic,[2] but others call it
Abcedilros.[3] Thus was ocular and manual art applied to
speech and thought, whence arose ocular memorials and the
materials of knowledge. Then wise men and aspirants
engaged themselves in improving sciences and language
and speech, and in discriminating vocalization and the
variety of sound with greater skill and minuteness; and
they elaborated them, until they were able to make two
more letters, so that the Alphabet consisted of eighteen
letters. After that the need of two more was observed,
until they became twenty;[4] then twenty-two; and to complete the work, twenty-four principal letters; nor are there
more in the Alphabet of the Coelbren that are simple, that
is to say, of primary sound. Nevertheless, there are others
that are compound letters, significative of the mutation of
voice, and of the accentuation of letters, of which, according
to highly skilful teachers, there are sixteen in number,
whilst others will have them to be eighteen. Some of them
cannot have authority or warrant, at least they cannot have
necessity, in virtue of indispensable reason; nevertheless it
is not allowable to forbid the improvement of sciences, whilst
every awen and art are free, provided they do not injure,
obscure, or confound laudable sciences.

---

[4] Taliesin observes,

Iaith ugain ogyrfen y sydd yn awen.

The language of twenty letters is in Awen.

Sef a llythyr y gyrrer cof pwyll ar wybodau a chyfarwyddyd, sef yw Tair sylfaen gwybodau Cof, Deall, ag
Ymbwyll, a bach heb y Cof lleshâd Cof, Deall, ag Ymbwyll. Sef gwedi cael gwybod ar lythyr y doded pob deall
ag ymbwyll a phob myfyrdod awen ar gof llythyr, ac o hir
ymarfer a hynny gwelwyd lle gwellhau a mwyhau ac amra-
faelu Trefn a Dosparth Iaith ag ymadrodd a chelfyddyd
Llythyr, sef mal y gellid gwarantu llythyr a weddai ymhob
achaws Iaith ag ymadrodd, ag i ddangos yn weledig pob
llef ac ymlef gair a llais a llafar. mal y bai cysson a chys-
pwyll celfyddyd Iaith a llythyr a chyfun llafar a llafar
rhwng dyn a dyn, parth ymlef, ag ymbwyll ymadrodd, ag
ymgais Iaith, ag ymgyrch celfyddyd a gwybodau Iaith a
llythyr. ag o hynny hawdd a gwarantedig y deall, a deall
wrth ddeall. a phawb yn gydfarn parth pwyll gair ag ymadrodd, a pharth ymbwyll a phwys ag arwyddoldob llythyr.
ag o hynny cadernyd anymmodiadawl ar wybodau llythyr ag
ar bob gwybodau a ddodid ar gof ag yn nawdd llythyr. a
hefyd hawdd addysg a deall ar a fo fal hynny drefnedig ar
ddosparth a phwyll cadarn. a hawdd i bawb cydfarn a
chymmwyll ar a fo fal hynny sef o hir gymhwyll doethion
ag awenyddion, a chelfyddiaid y cair gwellhâd a chadernyd
pwyll a dosparth ar bob gwybodau ag ar bob un o naddynt.
gwedi gwellhau ag amlhau wrth ofyn ag achos ar lythyr
parth pwyll a nifer, gwelwyd pedair ar hugain cysefiniaid,
barn eraill y tri naw sef saith ar hugain, ag nid agen nag

---

[1] The word " Awenyddion " here translated *aspirants*, generally stands for
bardic disciples, but it literary means persons endowed with poetic genius, being
derived from Awen.

It is by means of letters that sciences and history are committed to rational memory. The three foundations of sciences are memory, understanding, and reason, and without the memory little is the utility of memory, understanding, and reason. After the discovery of the knowledge of letters it was that every understanding, and consideration, and every meditation of awen were committed to the memorial of letters; and from long acquaintance therewith room was seen for improving, amplifying, and varying the order and system of language and speech, and the art of letters, that letters might be warranted, which should be suitable to every circumstance of language and speech, and for the purpose of showing visibly every sound and utterance of word, voice, and speech, that they might harmonize with the ratiocination of the art of language and letters, and that speech might agree with speech between man and man, in respect of the sound and meaning of a sentence, the effort of language, and the encounter of the art and sciences of language and letters. Hence easy and warranted became the understanding, and understanding arose from understanding, and all men became of one judgment in respect of the meaning of word and sentence, and in respect of the sense, accent, and signification of letters. And hence fixed confirmation was bestowed upon the sciences of letters, and upon all sciences that were committed to the memory and under the auspices of letters; and it became easy, also, to learn and understand what was thus arranged systematically and with a fixed meaning; and it was easy for all men to be of one judgment, and of one sense in respect of such. That is to say, from the long co-reasoning of wise men and aspirants,[1] and men of art, improvement and fixedness of meaning and system, are obtained, in respect of all sciences, and in respect of every one of them. After letters had been improved and amplified, as occasion required, in respect of meaning and number, there were exhibited twenty-four primaries—in the opinion of others, the three nines, that is to say, twenty-seven; nor is there any need or occa-

achos mwy cysefiniaid, sef meddant nis gellir arwydd pob
ymlef gair ag ymadrawdd yn y Gymraeg dan saith llythyren
ar hugain. a lluniaw adlawiau a dwy lythyren gyssefin.

Yn rodd fathraw gwybodbell pam y dywedir nas gwyr
namyn Bardd cwblgyfrin y modd y dylit llafar clyw ar enw
Duw, sef ar y tair brifgolofn llythyr ?

Achaws nad oes namyn bardd cyfrin a wyr hen ddosparth
y llythyrau a'u pwyll a'u pwys a'u nerthoedd yn gyfiawn
herwydd gwaranred arnynt yn nosparth deunaw llythyren,
sef wedi gwaranredu'r ddosparth ar ddeunaw y dodi newydd
o lythyr ar enw Duw nid amgen O I U, a chyn no hynny
sef yn oed dosparth un ar bymtheg nid oedd amgen o lythyr
ar enw Duw na'r tair colofn llythyr gysefin, nid amgen /|\
sef Dosparth Duw a goleuni ai gelwir, ag nis gwyr namyn
Bardd cyfringwbl yn awr nag un nag arall yn gyfiawn or
ddwy hen ddosparth a wedais am danynt.

Paham nas doder y gyfrinach honno ar lythyr a llafar
hyglyw, mal ai gwypid gan bawb.

Achaws camfarnu arni gan a fynno gred gan arall am fwy
nag y gwyr, a drwg o ddyn er anrheithiaw cred oddiar nas
gwyr, a wna hynny ag a ddod ddychymygion anghyfiawn
ar lythyr ai phwyll ai phwys ai llafar ai hymlef yn amgen
na'r gwir ag y sydd gyfiawn, a chan y cyfryw y llygrir ag
y llygrwyd gwybodau dwyfolion, am hynny nis dylit dangos
y gyfrinach i amgen nag a fo gwarantedig yn marn a golwg
dyn ei awen o Dduw, ag nid oes amgen ag a wyr lafar ar
enw Duw heb wedyd celwydd, a mwya celwydd celwyddo
Duw ai enw.

Pam nad rhydd rhag a fo celwydd dodi enw Duw ar lafar
a chlyw clust ?

---

[1] Cyfrinach, from *cyd* and *rhin ;* what is known to some, but not to all. The
word occurs in the poetical compositions of the Bards. Rhys Goch yr Eryri has
a whole poem entitled " Cywydd Cyfrinach,'' in which there are allusions to the
" Awen," " Einigan," " Pont Hu " *(the bridge of Hu,)* "tair llythyren " *(three
letters,)* " Menw," " Gair heb wybod " *(the unknown word,)* and other esoteric
doctrines of the Bards.
Lewis Mon, in his elegy on Tudur Aled, refers to the Bardic secret,—
Yn iach brigyn awch breugerdd
Yn iach cael *cyfrinach* cerdd.

sion for more primaries, for, say they, there cannot be symbols ef every sound of word and speech in the Cymraeg under twenty-seven letters—but they formed secondaries and two primary letters.

Pray, my far knowing teacher, why is it said that only a Bard of thorough secrecy knows how the Name of God is to be spoken audibly, that is to say, by means of the three principal columns of letters?

Because only a Bard of secrecy knows properly the old system of letters, and their meaning, accent, and powers, in respect of their stability in the system of the eighteen letters; for when the system of the eighteen was established, new letters were employed for the Name of God, namely O I U, but previously, during the era of the sixteen, no letters stood for the Name of God, other than the three columns of primary letters, that is /|\, which was called the system of God and light, and only a Bard of thorough secrecy now knows properly either the one or the other of the two old systems, which I have mentioned.

Why is not that secret [1] committed to letter and audible speech, that it may be known of all?

Because it is misjudged by him who would have credence from another for more than he knows, and it is the wicked man, with the view of pillaging belief from the ignorant, that does so, and that bestows unjust imaginations upon a letter, and its meaning, accent, pronunciation, and sound, rather than the true and just. It is by such men that divine sciences are and have been corrupted, therefore the secret ought not to be divulged to other than to him who, in the judgment and sight of man, is warranted as having awen from God. Nor is there any other who knows the vocalization of the Name of God, without telling a falsehood, and the greatest falsehood is to falsify God and His Name.

Why is it not free from falsehood to commit the Name of God to speech and the hearing of the ear?

Farewell sprig—ardency of the short-lived song,
Farewell to having the *secret* of song.

Achaws nis gellir hynny heb ei lafaru yn gelwydd gan neb
o ddyn nag o fyw a bod perchen enaid a deall namyn Duw ei
hun, eithr mewn ymadrodd arddangos ai lafaru yn amgen
nag yn y cyfryw fodd celwydd yw a difrawd ag anrhaith ar
Dduw achaws nid Bod namyn Duw ag yn Nuw, ag a ddywetto 'n amgen celwydd yw, a chelwydd yn erbyn Duw a
thrais anrhaith arnaw. hagen y neb a feddo Awen o Dduw
a genfydd y gyfrinach ag ai gwybydd, a lle gellir ar ddyn or
byd awen o Dduw yn warantedig o bwyll a buchedd nid
anghyfiawn dangos iddo'r gyfrinach. ag nid iawn i amgen.
rhag llafaru ynhgam ag ynghelwydd ag ar gam ddychymyg
oferbwyll enw Duw. ai watwar ai waradwyddaw ai dwyll-
anrhydeddu wrth hynny. Achaws arall hefyd y sydd nid
amgen, gyrru ar ddyn ymarfer ai ddeall ai ymbwyll ar
fyfyrdawd gyfiawn a chadarn, sef a wnelo hynny efe a ddeaill
ansawdd a phwyll prif ddosparth unarbymtheg ar y llythyrau
ar adtosparth ar ddeunaw, ag o hynny a wel ag a ddeaill enw
Duw, ar geinmyged gyfiawn parth ag atto. sef a wel wirionedd a wna gyfiawnder;

Sef pan wellhaed dosparth y llyrau parth rhif a llafar y
doded ⟡ lle nis gallesid llafar cyfiawn ar ⬦, ag ll yn
arail L. neu Ͷ yn arail Ͷ,* ag o graffu ar rhyw
ag ansawdd gweled yn gyfiawn y blaen i'r ll, sef yr Ͷ
achaws y bydd gwreiddon y llythyryn hynny, a chysefin ar
air ag nis gellir hynny ar y ⋀ herwydd a gadarnhaed ar y
Gymraeg gan athrawon o wyr doethion goleudrem. A lle
sefis y Gymraeg ar y deunaw, y trefnwyd yn gadarn a
gwarantedig y tair llythyren llafar nid amgen nag OIV.
a rhai au ysgrifenant yn amrafaelfodd sef ⬦ I Ͷ, ag nis
gellir heb dorr cyfrinach amgen o drefn gan wellhâd ar y tri
llythyryn au pwys au pwyll.

Ag or Tripheth hynn y dechreuwyd dodi gwybodau ar
Drioedd, nid amgen,

* This ought to be ⋀

Because that cannot be done without its being falsely spoken, by any man or living being and existence possessed of soul and intellect, but by God Himself;—to exhibit and pronounce it in speech otherwise is falsehood, and the devastation and spoliation of God, for there is no being but God and in God, and whoso says otherwise speaks falsehood, which is falsehood against God, and depredatory usurpation over Him. ' But he who possesses awen from God will perceive the secret, and will know it, and wherever a man may have awen from God, warranted in respect of reason and conduct, it is not unjust to divulge to him the secret, but it is not just to do so to any other, lest the Name of God be spoken erroneously, falsely, and through unjust and vain imagination, and thereby be mocked, disparaged, and dishonoured. There is also another cause, namely, to induce a man to excercise his understanding and reason upon just and firm meditation; for he who does so, will understand the character and meaning of the primitive system of sixteen letters, and the subsequent system of eighteen, and hence will perceive and understand the Name of God, and the just reverence due to Him; for he who does truth will do justice.

When the system of letters was improved in respect of number and pronunciation, V was employed where there could be no proper vocalization of ◇, and Ll as producing L, or N as producing ⋀ ; and by observing kind and quality, one could well perceive the priority of Ll, that is, N, inasmuch as that letter is the root, and a primary word, which cannot be the case with ⋀, according to the fixedness given to the Cymraeg by wise and clear sighted teachers. And where the Cymraeg stands on the eighteen, the three vocal letters OIV, written variously by some thus ◇ I M, were fixedly and authoritatively arranged; and, without the violation of secrecy, there cannot be another system arising from the improvement of the three letters, and their accent and meaning.

It was from these three things that they began to exhibit sciences in Triads, that is to say;—

Tri phrif arwyddion gwybodau, nid amgen, Tair pelydren goleu sef o henynt y cafad golwg a lliw, a llun. Tair llafar goleuni ag o henynt y cafad clyw, a llafar, a cherdd dafawd. A Thair llythyren arwydd, ag o henynt y cad cof gweled, llun llafar yn weledig, a deall meddwl ar nas gellir na lliw, na llun, na llafar arnaw, ag o'r tri hynn y cad cadernyd a gwaranred ar wybodau a chelfyddyd.

CAFFAELWYR LLYTHYR GYNTAF.—DIWYGWYR Y WYDDOR.— CAFFAELIAD RHOL A PHLAGAWD.—DYLED BARDD I GYNNAL CADAIR A GORSEDD.

Pwy a wnaeth Lythyr gyntaf?

Einigan Gawr, sef ai gelwir hefyd Einiget Gawr, sef cymmeryd tair paladren goleuni a ddoded yn arwydd gan Fenw ab y Teirgwaedd, ai dodi 'n weithredyddion ag yn offeryddion llafar Nid amgen y Tair offer B. G. D. a ceseiliaid ag ar bob un or Tri Tair Gweithred, efe a wnaeth or gwahanau a'r rhagwahanau bedair arwydd Lle a llafar, fal y gallai 'r offeryddion gael lle i yngan eu nerthoedd ag i ddangos eu gweithredoedd. Ag o hynny y cafwyd tair Llythyred ar ddeg au torri yn luniedig ar wydd a main, gwedi hynny gweles Einigan Gawr achos amgen beiriannau llafar ag ymadrodd ag a ddodes amgen o foddion cynghyd ar y peleidr ag o hynny gwneuthur arwyddon L. ac R. ac S. ag o hynny un arwydd ar bymtheg, a gwedi hynny Trefnu gwyr o Ddoethion iddeu dwyn ar gof a gwybodaeth her- wydd celfyddyd a rywnaethodd ef, a'r Gwyr hynny a elwid Gwyddoniaid a Gwŷr wrth awen o Dduw oeddeint, ag nid

---

[1] In one version of Rhys Goch's "Cywydd Cyfrinach" mention is made of this personage as one whose learning was the source of the *Awen*—

O ddysg *Einigan* a ddoeth.

It came from the learning of Einigan.

[2] Reference is made to the usage of engraving on stone by Huw Cae Llwyd, A.D. 1450—1480;—

Darllen *main* bychain yn ber,
Dull Hywel deall llawer.

The three principal signs of sciences, namely,—the three rays of light, for from them were obtained appearance and colour and form—the three voices of light, and from them were obtained hearing and speech and vocal song—and the three symbolic letters, and from them were obtained the memory of sight, and the form of voice, visibly, and mental understanding in regard to what can have no colour, or form, or voice. And it was from these three that fixedness and authority were obtained for sciences and art.

THE FIRST INVENTORS OF LETTERS.—IMPROVERS OF THE ALPHABET.—INVENTION OF THE ROLL AND PLAGAWD.—OBLIGATION OF A BARD TO HOLD A CHAIR AND GORSEDD.

Who was the first that made letters?

Einigan the Giant,[1] or, as he is also called, Einiget the Giant; that is, he took the three rays of light, which were used as a symbol by Menw, son of the Three Shouts, and employed them as the agents and instruments of speech, namely the three instruments B. G. D. and what are embosomed in them, the three being respectively invested with three agencies. Of the divisions and subdivisions he made four signs of place and voice, that the instruments might have room to utter their powers, and to exhibit their agencies. Hence were obtained thirteen letters, which were cut in form on wood and stone.[2] After that, Einigan the Giant saw reason for other and different organs of voice and speech, and subjected the rays to other combinations, from which were made the signs L. and R. and S., whence there were sixteen signs. After that, wise men were appointed to commit them to memory and knowledge, according to the art which he made; and those men were called Gwyddoniaid, and were men endued with awen from God. They

He sweetly read little *stones*,
After the manner of Howel, he understood many things.

E

oedd Braint a thrwydded warantedig o Gyfraith a nawdd
Gwlad a Chenedl iddynt, namyn o syberwyd a bodd ai
rhoddai,—a phrif Ddoethion Cenedl y Cymry y gelwir y
Gwyddoniaid, a gwedi dyfod y Cymry i Ynys Prydain a
threfnu goresgyn ar Dir a daiar i bob Cymro cynhenid ag i
bob un ei addef ai ansawdd a Threfnu Teyrnedd a dodi 'r
Deyrnedd ar a gaid yn wrolaf ag yn ddoethaf, ag yn gad-
arnaf, o ddyn y Gymro cynhenid, myned yng Ngorsedd gan
bencenhedloedd a dodi ar Brydain ab Aedd y Mawr y
deyrnedd sef y caid ef yn wrolaf a chadarnaf ag yn ddoethaf
a gloywaf ei bwyll. A Phrydain ab Aeth Mawr a ddyges
Bencenedloedd a Doethion a Gwybedydd Cenedl y Cymry
yng ngorsedd ddygynnull. Ag yna Trefnu Beirdd nid
amgen nag o dair gradd sef Prif Feirdd i gynnal Cof
Llafar gwlad a Cherdd dafod, ag ofyddion y gynnal Cof
Arwydd ac o hynny ei galw yn Arwyddfeirdd a Derwyddon ag arnynt gyrru addysg a gwybodau ar Genedl y Cymry
nid amgen na Gwybodau Dwyfolion, a Gwybodau doethineb herwydd a wyppid drwy Gof Llafar Gorsedd a Cherdd
Dafawd ym mraint Prifardd, a Chof arwydd a Llythyr gan
arwyddfairdd, a gwedi Trefnau swyddau gorfodau y Tair
Gradd Trefnu Trwydded a Breiniau herwydd nawdd a
Chyfarwys iddynt. a dodi gwnedd i bob un o'r Tair gradd,
nid amgen, glas i Brifairdd, gwydd i Ofyddfairdd, a gwyn
ir Derwyddfairdd ag yno pob un i ddwyn ei nod ai anryd-
edd yn waranted, fal y gwypai bob Cymro ei fraint ai nawdd
ai gyfarwys. a nawdd na ddygai neb yn amgen nag hwynt,
y nodau Gwnedd hynny.

Pa amser y dyged ar wybod ag arfer amlhad arwydd hyd
ym mhedwar ar hugain.

Rhufawn dafawd aur a ddodes ddwy arwydd nid amgen

---

[1] This doubtless is none other than the " Rhufin," whose name occurs in a
poem by Edmund Prys (1541—1624) in conjunction with the names of " Plennydd," " Goron," " Meugant," " Melchin," " Mefin," " Madog," and " Cadog."

Mae un *Rhufin* min rhyfedd.

There is one Rhuvin of wonderful lips.

had no privilege and license warranted by the law and protection of country and nation, but only by the courtesy and
pleasure of the giver. The Gwyddoniaid are called the
principal sages of the nation of the Cymry. When the
Cymry came to the Isle of Britain, and seisin of land and
soil was appointed for every innate Cymro, and each had his
dwelling and position, and when sovereignty was arranged,
and was to be conferred upon him who should be found to
be the bravest and wisest and most powerful, being an
innate Cymro, they resorted to Gorsedd by their heads of
kindred, and conferred the sovereignty upon Prydain, son
of Aedd the Great, for he was found to be the bravest, most
powerful, wisest, and the brightest of wit. And Prydain,
son of Aedd the Great, assembled the heads of kindred,
sages, and men of knowledge of the nation of the Cymry
in a conventional Gorsedd. Then were Bards appointed,
namely, of three degrees, that is to say, primitive Bards,
to uphold the memorial of national voice and vocal song,
and Ovates, to uphold the memorial of symbols, whence
they were called herald-bards, and Druids, whose duty it
was to impart instruction and sciences to the nation of the
Cymry, namely divine sciences, and sciences of wisdom,
according to what was known by means of the memorial of
the voice of Gorsedd and vocal song, in right of the primitive
Bard, and the memorial of symbol and letter by herald-
Bards. And when the offices incumbent upon the three
degrees were appointed, license and privileges in respect of
protection and reward were assigned to them. And raiment
was given to each of the three degrees, namely blue to the
primitive Bards, green to the Ovate-Bards, and white to the
Druid-Bards. Thus every one was to bear his badge and
honour by authority, that every Cymro might know his
privilege, protection, and reward; and security was given
them that none besides should bear those vestment badges.

When was the augmentation of symbols as far as twenty-
four brought into knowledge and use?

Rhuvawn the Golden-tongued,[1] introduced two symbols.

w* ac ff, ag o hynny ymarfer a deunaw llythyren, ac fal
hynny bu hyd yn amser Talhaiarn o Gaer llion ar wysg y
gwr a ddodes chwech Llythyren yn amgen nag a fu o'i flaen
ef, sef a oedden ch. F. C. T. P. Ll. qu? ac yna pedair llythyren ar hugain. Gwedi hynny y meddyliwyd eraill yn
gesseiliaid i'r arwyddon au gofynaint, er cadarnhau llafar
gair ag arwydd, hyd oni threfnwyd y sydd yn awr nid amgen na deunaw arwydd ar hugain yn arwyddon Gwydd a
main; ag y maent ar arfer gan arwyddfeirdd Ynys Prydain
ym mraint Gwybodau Cenedl y Cymry.

Pa bryd y Cafad gwybodau ysgrifen Rol a phlagawd?

Bran ap Llyr Fendigaid meddir, ag ereill a ddywedant
Gwyddion ap Don Wyddȩl o Arfon yr hwn ai dug o'r
Werddon ag nid gwir hynny, parth Cenedl y Cymry sef
cadarn yw mai Bran fendigaid ai dug i Ynys Prydain
gyntaf o Rufain lle y dysges efe'r gelfyddyd a'r modd y
gwneir Plagawd o grwyn wyn a lloi a mynnod, a Gwydion
au dug gyntaf i'r Werddon, gwedi cael o'r Gwyddelod Mon
ag Arfon y ffydd yng Nghrist ag o hynny Gwybodau Llythyr ag ysgrifen Rol a phlagawd.

Pam y dylai fardd herwydd ei dynghedair gynnal Cadair
a Gorsedd?

1 Achos nis gellir Gwlad a Chenedl heb wybodau daionus yn nawdd Duw ai dangnef, ag nis gellir Gwybodau
pardion parorion heb athrawon ag nis gellir Athrawon heb fraint a
defod yn drefnedig, ag nis dylid braint heb ddefod wneuthur edig iadol, am hynny nis gellir gwneuthuriadol, heb drefn ᵬy-

---

* It is not clear that N is not meant. The letter is written something like
m. Is the last stroke a punctuation?

¹ We retain the original term *plagawd*, (Lat. plagula, plaga; Gr. πλῃγη,
Dorice πλαγη,) because in the documents before us it is described as meaning
not only parchment, but also a kind of plant or sedge grown in the East.

² Thus Taliesin,—

Gwydion ap Don
A rithwys gorwyddawd y ar *plagawd*.

namely W and Ff, whereupon eighteen letters were used, and thus they continued until the time of Talhaiarn of Caerleon-upon-Usk, who introduced six letters different to what had been before him, which were Ch. F. C. T. P. Ll., whence they became twenty-four letters. After that, others were invented as ancillaries to the signs which required them, for the sake of confirming the vocalization of word and sign, until those which now exist were arranged, namely, thirty-eight signs, as the signs of wood and stone; and they are in use by the herald-bards of the Isle of Britain under the privilege of the sciences of the nation of the Cymry.

When were the sciences of the writing of Roll and Pla-gawd[1] obtained?

By Bran, son of Llyr the Blessed, it is said; but others relate that it was by Gwydion, son of Don[2] the Irishman, of Arvon, who brought them from Ireland. That, however, is not true in reference to the nation of the Cymry, for certain is it that Bran the Blessed first brought them into the Isle of Britain from Rome, where he learned the art, and the mode of manufacturing plagawd with the skins of lambs and calves and kids. It was Gwydion that first introduced them into Ireland, after the Irish of Mona and Arvon had obtained the faith in Christ; hence the know-ledge of letters and the writing of Roll and Plagawd.

Why should a Bard, in virtue of his oath, hold a Chair and Gorsedd?

Because there can be no country and nation without good sciences under the protection of God and His peace, and there can be no prepared[3] sciences without teachers, and there can be no teachers without the ordering of privilege and usage, and there ought to be no privilege without actual usage; wherefore nothing can become actual without

Gwydion son of Don—
Fashioned wood-knowledge upon *plagawd*.
Kadeir Keridwen.

[3] Pardion—parodion. Another reading has *parorion*, continued, permanent.

bwyll ac ymarfer yn ddeddfedig, a swydd rwymedig ar a ^{ddylit}_{ddoder} breiniau a thrwyddedau iddynt. sef yw tair ymswydd-ogaeth Cadair a Gorsedd, dysgu gwybodau o dduw a daioni herwydd a gaffer yn ddoethineb, Cadw Cof ar freiniau a defodau a gweithredoedd molianus gwlad a Chenedl y Cymru. A Chynnal Trefn ac amseroedd Gwybodiadawl ar addysg Athrawon.

DECHREUAD LLYTHYR.

Einigain ⎫
Einigair ⎬ Gawr, yr a wnaeth Lythr gyntaf, yn arwydd
Einiger ⎭ y llafar cyntaf a glywed erioed nid amgen Enw Duw, sef y rhoddes Duw ei enw ar lafar a chyda'r gair cyflam yr holl fydoedd au perthynasau ar holl fydolder i fod a bywyd a gorfloedd can llawenydd, a'r gan honno fu'r gerdd gyntaf a glywed erioed, sef y cerddodd llafar y gan hyd y mae Duw ai fodoldeb a'r ffordd y cerdd-odd pob bodoldeb arall ar dardd ymgydfod ag ef hyd fyth tragywydd, ag or dim diarfod y Tardd, sef gan felused a phereidded Duw yn datgan ei enw hyd onid egryn bywyd drwy'r holl fodoldeb a thrwy bob defnyddoldeb bodiadol a'r gwynfydig yn y nef ai clywant hyd fyth dragywydd, a'r lly ai clywer nis gellir amgen na chaderyd bod a bywyd hyd fyth tragywydd, ag or clyw ag ai clywer y cafad gwy-bodau, a gorwyddawd, a deall, ag Awen o Dduw, sef arwydd

---

[1] Al. "invested with."

[2] There was some such tradition about the Creation in Job's time, as we infer from Chap. xxxviii. 7 of his Book. "When the morning stars sang together, and all the sons of God shouted for joy?"

There is an allusion to the creative melody in the poetic compositions of the Bards. Thus in a version of the "Englynion y Coronog Faban" attributed to Aneurin, about A.D. 550.—

> Coronog Faban y dydd cynta
> A *gant ganon* yn y gwenydfa
> Ag awen gogoniant o'r uchelfa
> Gan *floedd bydoedd* a byw Adda.

> The crowned Babe, on the first day,
> *Sang a chant* in the region of bliss,
> And the awen of glory came from the high place,
> With the *shout of the worlds*, and Adam lived.

prudent order, and established practice, and obligatory office on the part of those who are entitled[1] to privileges and immunities. The three functions of Chair and Gorsedd are to teach sciences from God and goodness, in respect of what is found to be wisdom,—to preserve the memory of the privileges, usages, and praiseworthy actions of the country and nation of the Cymry,—and to uphold order and known dates in respect of the learning of masters.

ORIGIN OF LETTERS.

Einigain, Einigair, or Einiger, the Giant, was the first that made a letter to be a sign of the first vocalization that was ever heard, namely, the Name of God. That is to say, God pronounced His Name, and with the word all the world and its appurtenances, and all the universe leaped together into existence and life, with the triumph of a song of joy.[2] The same song was the first poem[3] that was ever heard, and the sound of the song travelled as far as God and His existence are, and the way in which every other existence, springing in unity with Him, has travelled for ever and ever. And it sprang from inopportune nothing; that is to say, so sweetly and melodiously did God declare His Name, that life vibrated through all existence, and through every existing materiality. And the blessed in heaven shall hear it for ever and ever, and where it is heard, there cannot be other than the might of being and life for ever and ever. It was from the hearing, and from him who heard it, that sciences and knowledge and under-

---

And William Cynwal (1560—1600)—

> Yr awen o'r dechreuad
> Gwedi'r *Ton* oedd gyda'r Tad.

> The awen from the beginning,
> After the *tone*, was with the Father.

[3] Cymrice *cerdd*, which, though now universally meaning *a poem*, or *a song*, seems to have originally denoted *a going* or *a walk*. We have thus the reason why it received its secondary meaning, i.e. because the melody of the divine vocalization a *gerddodd*, walked through, or pervaded all creation.

enw Duw **/|** o'r dechreuad, a gwedi hynny **◇ | V**, ag yr awr honn Oiw. ag o ansawd yr arwydd hwn pob llun ag arwydd llafar, a llais, ag enw, ag ansawdd.

GWNEUTHURWR CYNTAF CERDD DAFAWD.—COFIADURON CYNTAF BARDDAS. — EI DDOSPARTHWYR CYNTAF. — EU TREFNAU.—Y DULL O YSGRIFAW Y PRIF LYTHYRENAU. —DECHREUAD EU LLUN A'U LLAFAR.—Y TRI MENW.

Adolwyn pydoedd a wnaeth Gerdd Dafawd gyntaf yn y Gymraeg?

Hu Gadarn y gwr a ddug y Cymry gyntaf i Ynys Prydain, ar gerdd a wnathoedd ef yn gof am a fu ar Genedl y Cymry er yn oes oesoedd ag am a fu arnynt, a dodi moliant Duw arni am a gawsant y Cymry i ar ei law ef, yn nawdd a gwared, ag arni Gwybodau a Threfnau Cenedl y Cymry, ag or gerdd honno y cafwyd addysg ar gerdd dafawd gyntaf, a deall ar gof a Chadw cyfiawn, a gwedi hynny y bu Tydain Tad Awen ag efe a welliaes wybodau a Chelfyddyd Cerdd dafawd ag a ddodes arni ddosparth Celfyddyd, modd y gellid yn haws ei dysgu ai deall ai chofiaw, a modd y byddai diddanaf ei datgan ai gwrandaw.

Adolwyn poeddynt a gadwasant Gof a gwybodau Barddas gyntaf ag a ddodaint addysg ar ddoethineb?

Y Gwyddoniaid nid amgen na doethion cenedl y Cymry, a gadwasant gof cerdd dafawd ar wybodau a doethineb Barddas, ag a ddodaint addysg arnynt, ag nid oedd na braint na Thrwydded ar wybodau y Gwyddoniaid namyn y byddai syberwyd, nag ychwaith Dosparth a Chadair.

---

[1] Conformably with this statement is that of the Triads, where Hu the Mighty is called one of " the three cultivators of song and thought," because it was he that "first applied to vocal song the preservation of memory and thought." Tr. 91. Third Series.

[2] He was the third of "the cultivators of song and thought," so considered, because it was he that "first conferred art upon vocal song, and system upon thought." Id. Geraint the Blue Bard, who flourished about A.D. 900, has recorded his achievement in this respect ;—

Goruc Tydain Tad Awen
Oi fyfyrdawd fawr aren,
Glof ar gof gan gerdd gymhen.

standing and awen from God, were obtained. The symbol of God's Name from the beginning was /|\, afterwards ◇ | ∨, and now OIW; and from the quality of this symbol proceed every form and sign of voice, and sound, and name, and condition.

THE INVENTOR OF VOCAL SONG. — THE FIRST RECORDERS OF BARDISM.—ITS FIRST SYSTEMATIZERS.—THEIR REGULATIONS. —MODE OF INSCRIBING THE PRIMARY LETTERS.—ORIGIN OF THEIR FORM AND SOUND.—THE THREE MENWS.

Pray, who was the first that made a vocal song in Cymraeg?

Hu the Mighty,[3] the man who first brought the Cymry into the Isle of Britain ; and he made the song to be a memorial of what happened to the nation of the Cymry from the age of ages. And he inserted in it the praise of God for what the Cymry had received at His hand, by way of protection and deliverance, also the sciences and regulations of the nation of the Cymry. It was from that song that instruction in vocal song, and the understanding of just memorials, were first obtained. After that came Tydain, father of Awen,[1] who improved the sciences and art of vocal song, and reduced it to an artistic system, that it might be the more easily learned, understood, and remembered, and be the more pleasantly recited and listened to.

Pray, who were they that first preserved the memory and sciences of Bardism, and gave instruction in wisdom?

The Gwyddoniaid, namely, the sages of the nation of the Cymry; they preserved the memory in vocal song of the sciences and wisdom of Bardism, and gave instruction in them; nevertheless the sciences of the Gwyddoniaid possessed neither privilege nor license, except by courtesy— neither system nor chair.[2]

> The achievement of Tydain, the father of Awen,
> Of his vast and wise meditation,
> Was the securing of memory by eloquent verse.
> Iolo MSS. pp. 262, 669.

[2] " There were previously Bards and Bardism, but they had no licensed sys-

Pwy a ddodes ddosparth a Chadair gyntaf ar Feirdd a Barddas ag ar Brydyddion a Cherdd dafawd ?

Y Tri Beirdd Cyntefigion, nid amgen Plennydd ag Alawn a Gwron, sef oeddynt yn amser Prydain ab Aedd Mawr ag yn amser Dyfnfarth ap Prydain ei fab ef, sef dychymmyg Cadair a Gorsedd a wnaethant a dod Trefn ar Athrawon ag awenyddion, ag ar Faccwyaeth ag addysg *gwybodau, a chof a chadw cadarn a* chyfiawn ar *wybodaeth** Barddas a Cherdd dafawd a'i Pherthynasau, ag ar ddefodau a weddaint o gyfiawnder a pharth gofyn doethineb ar Feirdd a Phrydyddion, mal y bai goreu yn gofyn er lles a moliant cenedl y Cymry.

Adolwyn fy athraw cymmhenbwyll dodwch ar addysg imi 'r drefn ar Ddosparth Cadair a Gorsedd a ddodasant y Tri Beirdd Cyntefigion ar Feirdd a Phrydyddion.

Sef y gwnaeth Brydain ap Aedd Mawr, oi gymmhen-ddoeth bwyll a myfyrdawd a welai yn oreu ymhob dichwaith a dichwain er lles a moliant chadernyd Cenedl y Cymmry. Yna galw atto 'r Gwyddoniaid ag erchi barn wrth Coelbren ar dri a gaid yn ddoethaf ag yn oreu am wybodau o henynt, a goreuon am wybodau a Doethineb a Chyfrinach a Chelf-ydd Cerdd dafawd y cafwyd Plennydd ag Alawn a Gwron, yna dodi braint gwlad a Chenedl ar a welynt yn oreu parth Gwybodau a Chelfyddyd Barddas a Cherdd Dafawd, ag ar yr addysg a ddodynt yn drefnedig o Ddosparth a Chelf-yddyd. a Llyma'r Drefn ar Ddosparth a ddychymygasant.

† Adolwyn ar ba beth y gwnaed llythyr gyntaf a phyd-oedd y modd ?

---

tem, nor privileges or usages, but what were obtained by kindness and courtesy, under the protection of country and nation, before the time of these three," i.e. Plennydd, Alawn, and Gwron. Tr. 58, Third Series.

* The words in *italics* are not sufficiently legible in the MS.

† There is a small space between the preceding portion and what follows in the MS., but not sufficient to decide whether they are distinct documents or not.

[1] "The three primary Bards of the Isle of Britain : Plennydd, Alawn, and Gwron ; that is to say, they were the persons who devised the privileges and

Who were the first that conferred system and chair on Bards and Bardism, and on Poets and vocal song?

The three primary Bards, namely, Plennydd, Alawn, and Gwron,[1] who lived in the time of Prydain, son of Aedd the Great, and in the time of Dyvnvarth ap Prydain, his son. That is, they devised a Chair and Gorsedd, and regulated teachers and aspirants, and pupilage; and introduced instruction in sciences, and fixed and just memorials in respect of the knowledge of Bardism, and vocal song, with its appurtenances, and in respect of usages, that, of justice, and according to the requirements of wisdom, were suitable to Bards and Poets, as would be most requisite for the benefit and praise of the nation of the Cymry.

Pray, my accomplished teacher, instruct me as to the regulation and system of Chair and Gorsedd, which the three primary Bards introduced in respect of Bards and Poets?

Prydain, son of Aedd the Great, did, of his acute and sagacious sense and meditation, what he saw the best in every act and event for the benefit and praise of the might of the nation of the Cymry. He then called to him the Gwyddoniaid, and requested judgment by ballot as to the three who should be found to be the wisest and best of them in respect of sciences, when Plennydd, Alawn, and Gwron, were found to be the best in respect of sciences, and wisdom, and secrecy, and the art of vocal song. Then they conferred the privilege of country and nation upon those whom they perceived to be the best in respect of the sciences, and art of Bardism and vocal song, and upon the instruction which they gave, and which was regulated by system and art. And these are the order and system which they devised.

Pray, on what were letters first made, and in what manner?

---

usages of Bards and Bardism. Therefore are they called the three primaries. * * * Some say that they lived in the time of Prydain son of Aedd the Great; but others say that they lived in the time of Dyvnwal Moelmud, his son, who in some old Books is called Dyvnvarth ab Prydain." Id.

Ar wŷdd ai gwnaethpwyd gyntaf, a naddu coed yn ebillion pedrystlys ag ar bob ystlys torri rhiniau bychain, ag a
chynnifer rhint y bai achos lluniaw llythyr, gwedi hynny
ar garreg ysledan, a chrafu llythyr arni a chethren ddur neu
gallestren, a lle gwnaed ar wŷdd Coelbren ai gelwid, ag o
hynny galw Rhilleu y llythyrenau yn goelbren, ar garreg a
lythyrenid ei galw Coelfain. modd arall y gwnaed llythyr
ar wydd yn amgen na rhinniau, sef hynny a du neu arall o
liw a fai parottaf. a hynn a fu gan arfer Cenedl y Cymry er
oesoedd cyn cof, a gwedi ynnill yr Ynys honn gan wyr
Rhufain y dygasant yma lysewyn a elwir plagawd sef oedd
honno Elestron a gaid o wlad Asia a gwlad y Ganon. ag
ysgrifennu ar honno.   Gwedi hynny cafwyd celfyddyd ar
grwyn Lloi a chrwyn Geifr a Chrwyn defaid ag o henynt
gwneuthur plagawd, a goreu ar bob darllaw ydyw mewn
llyfrau, eiswys Beirdd Ynys Prydain a gadwant ar Gof a
Chyfarwyddyd y modd y gwneid yr hen Lyfrau er gwared
y Gymraeg rhag anneall y syrthiai arni pai amgen. ag
achos arall, sef y gellir gwŷdd a main Lle ag amser nis
gellir plagawd, ag am hynny nid na Gorsedd na Chadair
gyfiawn lle nas dangoser yr hen ddefodau ar hen wybodau
wrth deall a chelfyddyd. am hynny y dylit gwŷdd ymhob
Gorsedd a Chadair, a Chyda hynn Rhôl blagawd.   Sef y
dylit arddangos ar bob Gwybodau Llythyr yng Ngorsedd a

---

[1] Stone of credibility.   The poets frequently allude to the *coelvain*, thus,—

CYNDDELW.

Mwyn Ofydd i Feirdd ei faith *goelfain*.

A kind Ovate to Bards was his large *stone of credibility*.
To Owain Cyveiliog.

GRUFFYDD AB DAVYDD AB TUDUR, 1290—1340.

Colofn Prestatun *coelfeiniau* Awrtun.

The pillar of Prestatyn, the *belief stones* of Overton.

They were first made on trees, that is, wood was hewn into four sided staves, on each of which were cut small notches, and it was by means of as many notches as were necessary, that letters were formed. After that, on a slate stone, that is, letters were engraved on it with a steel pencil, or a flint. When it was done on wood, it was called *coelbren*, and hence the grooves of the letters were called *coelbren*; and the lettered stone was called *coelvain*.[1] There was a different way in which letters were made on wood, other than by means of notches, namely, with black or any other colour that might be most ready at hand. And this was practised by the Cymry for ages before memory. When this island was won by the men of Rome, they brought over here a plant, called *plagawd*, that is, a sedge, which was obtained from the land of Asia, and the land of Canaan, and wrote upon it. After that, art was applied to the skins of calves, the skins of goats, and the skins of sheep, and plagawd was made from them, and it is the best of all manufactures for books. Nevertheless, the Bards of the Isle of Britain retain in memory and history the mode of making the ancient books, in order to rescue the Cymraeg from the misunderstanding, to which it would otherwise be liable. Another reason is, that wood and stone can be procured where and when plagawd cannot; wherefore there is no proper Gorsedd or Chair, where the ancient usages and the ancient sciences, according to understanding and art, are not exhibited. On that account there ought to be wood in every Gorsedd and Chair, and besides a Roll of plagawd; that is, there ought to be an exhibition of all the sciences of letters in the Gorsedd and Chair of the Bards of the Isle

GRUFFYDD AB MEREDYDD AB DAVYDD, 1310—1360.

Cor Ior aur drefnad ⎫
Cyw·aint wneuthuriad ⎬ Mair ai *choelvain*.
Mawr uchelfab rhad ⎭

The Choir of the Lord, of golden order, ⎫
And of skilful workmanship, ⎬ Of Mary, and her *stone of credibility*.
The great, high and gracious Son ⎭

Chadair Beirdd Ynys Prydain. a lle na bo Gwŷdd Main llythyraid.

Adolwyn pa fodd y cafwyd deall gyntaf ar lythyr parth Llûn a llafar. sef hynny Duw pan nad oedd mewn na byw na bod namyn ef ei hûn a ddatgenis ei enw ag yn gyttrym a'r gair yn floedd gorfoledd pob byw a bod yn gwbledig a melusaf a glywid erioed ar gerdd y llafar hynny, ag yn gyttrym ar llafar goleuni, ag yn y goleuni Llun, ar $^\text{llafar}_\text{enw}$ yn drillais dri llafar, yn gydlef gyfennyd, ag yn y gweled dri llun, a lliw a llun goleuni ydoedd, ag yn un a'r llafar, a lliw a llun y llafar hwnnw oeddent y tair Llythyren gyntaf, ag o gysswllt eu tri llafar y lluniwyd pob llafarau eraill ar lythyr, sef a glywes y Llafar Menw hen ab y Teirgwaedd, ag eraill a wedant taw Einigan Gawr a wnaeth Lythyr gyntaf, a llun enw Duw oedd hynny, pan y cafas ef ei hynan yn fyw ag yn bod yn gyttrum gyfergyd ar llafar.

Adolwyn fy athraw cymmhenddysg pa sawl dyn o Fenw y bu ynghenedl y Cymry, achos y caf son a Chyfarwydd am eraill a'r Enw Menw.

Tri gwyr dan gof a gwybod a fuant o'r Enw, nid amgen Menw ap y Teirgwaedd, ail oedd Menw hir o'r Gogledd, ag arall Menw ap $^\text{Menwad}_\text{Menwaedd}$o Arfon. Y gwr a wnaeth hud a Lledrith gyntaf o Genedl y Cymry.

PRIF ELFENAU AMRYW BETHAU.—YR OGYRFENNAU.

Tair phrif ansawdd (Elwydden) pob peth, Gallu, Defn-ydd, ac $^\text{ansawdd}_\text{a modd}$ $^\text{(Enias)}_\text{ynius}$

SION TUDUR.

Wrth ddarllain *coelfain* celfydd
Gair naw gloes ar gronigl wydd.

In reading an ingenious *stone of credibility*,
Or the nine tropes on a wooden chronicle.

[1] Al. " Name."

[2] Al. " conditions."

[3] Al. " condition." Al. " energy."

of Britain; and where there is no wood, then lettered stones.

Pray, how were letters first understood in respect of form and sound?

Thus, God, when there was in life and existence only Himself, proclaimed His Name, and co-instantaneously with the word all living and existing things burst wholly into a shout of joy; and that voice was the most melodious that ever was heard in music. Co-instantaneously with the voice was light, and in the light, form; and the voice[1] was in three tones, three vocalizations, pronounced together at the same moment. And in the vision were three forms and colours, which were the form of light; and one with the voice, and the colour and form of that voice, were the three first letters. It was from a combination of their vocalizations that every other vocalization was formed in letters. He who heard the voice was Menw the Aged, son of the Three Shouts; but others say that it was Einigan the Giant that first made a letter, the same being the form of the Name of God, when he found himself alive and existing co-momentaneously and co-instantaneously with the voice.

Pray, my eloquent and learned teacher, how many men, that were Menws, have there been in the nation of the Cymry, for I find mention and account of others of the name of Menw?

Three persons, within memory and knowledge, have been of that name, that is to say, Menw, son of the Three Shouts, the second was Menw the Tall from the North, and the other, Menw, son of Menwad, of Arvon, the man who was the first of the nation of the Cymry that made dramatic representations.

THE PRINCIPAL ELEMENTS OF VARIOUS THINGS.—
THE GOGYRVENS.

The three principal elements[2] of every thing: power; matter; and mode.[3]

Tair prif Elwydden, gwybodau, bywyd, Deall, a serch,
(Deall, serch, ac ymbwyll)

Tair Elwydden doethineb, $^{amcan}_{diben}$, modd, a buddioldeb.

Tair Elwydden cof a Chadw, deall o serch, Arwydd wahanred, a Chymmyged er gwell.

Tair elwydden Llythyr, /|\ sef o gymmodoldeb y naill
neu 'r llaill o'r tri y gwnëir llythyr. Sef ydynt tair pelydren
goleuni. ac o'r rhai hyn y gwneir yr ungogyrfen ar bymtheg, sef yr unllythyren a'r bymtheg. ac o gelfyddyd amgen
y mae saith gogyrfen a saith nid amgen nag arwydd teil-
yngnod y saith gair a saith ugain yn rïaint y Gymraeg. ac
o henynt pob gair arall. eraill a wedant saith ugeinair a
saith gant.

CAFFAELIAD LLYTHYR GAN EINIGAN A MENW.—
CYFRINACH BARDDAS.

Einigan Gawr a weles dair colofn goleuni ag arnynt holl
wybodau a fuant erioed ag a fyddant fyth yn ddangosedig
ynddynt, ag efe a gymmeres dair gwydden gerdin ag a
ddodes arnynt luniau ag arwyddion bob gwybodau yn goff-
adwy, ag ai dangoses hwynt, a'r rhai au gwlesasant a ddodasant gam ddeall a geubwyll arnynt, ag a ddysgasant dwyll
wybodau a Dodi Duw ar y gwiail lle nid oedd namyn ei
enw arnynt, ag Einigan yn gweled hynny mawr y bu
chwithrwydd iddo, a chan amgerth ei alar tòrri 'r tair
gwydden, ag ni chaffad eraill yn gyfiawn eu gwybodau, a
chwithed hynny gantho oni holltes gan yr amgerth, ag ai
anadl gweddio Duw er cael Cyfiawn wybodau ymhlith Dynion ynghnawd, a Chyfiawn ddeall er iawn ymbwyll ag wynt,
ag ymhenn undydd a blwyddyn gwedi marw Einigan y
gweles Menw ap y Teirgwaedd dair Gwialen yn tyfu o

---

[1] Al. "intellect ; affection ; and deliberation."

[2] Probably " score " is to be supplied.

[3] *Saith ugein ogrfen*
Y sydd yn Awen.

The three principal elements of sciences: life; intellect; and affection.[1]

The three elements of wisdom: object; mode; and benefit.

The three elements of memorials: understanding from affection; distinctive sign; and reverence for the better.

The three elements of letters, /|\ ; that is to say, from a combination of one or other of the three are letters made. They are three rays of light. And of these are made the sixteen gogyrvens, that is, the sixteen letters. According to a different arrangement there are seven gogyrvens and seven,[2] the seven words and seven score[3] in the Alphabet of the Cymraeg being no other than a sign of worthiness; and it is from them that every other word proceeds. Others say seven score and seven hundred words.

THE INVENTION OF LETTERS BY EINIGAN AND MENW.— THE SECRET OF BARDISM.

Einigan the Giant beheld three pillars of light, having in them all demonstrable sciences that ever were, or ever will be. And he took three rods of the quicken tree, and placed on them the forms and signs of all sciences, so as to be remembered; and exhibited them. But those who saw them misunderstood, and falsely apprehended them, and taught illusive sciences, regarding the rods as a God, whereas they only bore His Name. When Einigan saw this, he was greatly annoyed, and in the intensity of his grief he broke the three rods, nor were others found that contained accurate sciences. He was so distressed on that account that from the intensity he burst asunder, and with his [parting] breath he prayed God that there should be accurate sciences among men in the flesh, and there should be a correct understanding for the proper discernment thereof. And at the end of a year and a day, after the decease of Einigan, Menw, son

Seven score gogyrvens
Are there in Awen.—Taliesin.

G

enau Einigan ag arnynt yn gyflwyn gwybodau Deg llythyren a'r modd y trefnawr ynddynt bob gwybodau Iaith
ag ymadrawdd, ag ar Iaith ag ymadrawdd bob gwybodau
darnodadwy arnynt, yna cymeryd y gwiail a dysgu'r gwybodau oddiarnynt, y cwbl ond enw Duw ag ar hynny dodi
Cyfrinach rhag dodi geubwyll ar yr Enw. ag o hynny Cyfrinach Barddas Beirdd Ynys Prydain, a Duw a ddodes ei
nawdd ar hyn o gyfrinach ag a roes i Fenw ddeall traphwyll
ar wybodau yn hyn oi nawdd, ar deall hynny a elwir Awen
o Dduw, a gwyn ei fyd fyth ai caffo.   Amen.   poed felly
bydded.

O enau Addaf fal Gwynwydd*wy* Tair croes &c.·
Gwiail a gad, tyfiad da, yn wydd o enau Adda.

Y TORRIADAU.—SYLFEINI AWEN.

/|\. Or tri arwydd y Cafas Einigan Gawr ei ddeall
gystal ar lythyr, ac ai torres wyddon. ac efe ddychymyges
y modd ai ag ef a wnaeth ddeuddeg (Ddeg *al*) o brif lythyrenau, ys gwir llyfrau doethion, ar deg tadogion au gelwir a
pharth ag ydynt a pharth eu lluniau, rhin yw yng nghyf-
rinach Beirdd Cenedl y Cymry nid amgen y Gwyddoniaid a
elwir y Prifeirdd. a thri o'r tadogion cyssefinion ydynt nid
amgen y tri thorriad, sef au gelwir torriadau am eu torri yn
dair pelydren or tywyll, ag ar yr un cymmhwyll y diwedir
torri gwawr. a torri maes, a torri allan, a'r Trydydd Torriad
allan llafar can gorfoledd, sef y cyntaf o lafar oedd llafar
gorfoledd.

Tri seilfaen Awen o Dduw Deall Gwirionedd — Caru
gwirionedd—Ag gwirionedd modd nas gellir yn ei erbyn
Ag o'r tri hyn atteb yn gofiawn yr hawl.   Paham y mynnit
for yn fardd.   Ac o gyfiawn atteb yr hawl cael gradd cad-

---

[1] This line is from the works of William Lleyn, 1540—1587.

[2] Al. " ten."

[3] The sameness of the word is better kept in the original, " torri " meaning
both *to cut* and *to break*.

of the Three Shouts, beheld three rods growing out of the mouth of Einigan, which exhibited the sciences of the Ten Letters, and the mode in which all the sciences of language and speech were arranged by them, and in language and speech all distinguishable sciences. He then took the rods, and taught from them the sciences—all, except the Name of God, which he made a secret, lest the Name should be falsely discerned; and hence arose the Secret of the Bardism of the Bards of the Isle of Britain. And God imparted His protection to this secret, and gave Menw a very discreet understanding of sciences under this His protection, which understanding is called Awen from God; and blessed for ever is he who shall obtain it. Amen, so be it.

From the mouth of Adam, like blessed trees, three crosses, &c.
Rods of fine growth were obtained, being trees from the mouth of Adam.[1]

CUTTINGS.—FOUNDATIONS OF AWEN.

/|\. It was from the three signs that Einigan the Giant obtained so good an understanding of letters, which he cut on staves. He devised the mode, and made twelve[2] principal letters, if the books of the wise are true, which are called the ten radicals. As to what they are, and what their forms, it is a secret in the mystery of the Bards of the nation of the Cymry, namely, the Gwyddoniaid, who are called the primary Bards. They are three of the primary radicals, that is, the three cuttings; and they are called cuttings, because they are cut out of the dark into three rays; and for the same reason we say, the break of dawn,[3] to cut a field, to cut or break out. The third break out was the voice of a song of triumph, that is, the first voice was a voice of triumph.

The three foundations of Awen from God: to understand the truth; to love the truth; and to [maintain] the truth, so that nothing may prevail against it. From these three things may the question be correctly answered — Why wouldest thou be a Bard? And from correctly answering

air neu wrthneu arni. Rhwng yr Awenydd ai gydwybod y mae 'r atteb a rhwng ei gydwybod a Duw, ac nid rhyngtho ai Athraw.

DECHREUAD A GWELLHAD LLYTHYR.—EINIGAN GAWR.— Y GWYDDONIAID.—CYLMAU LLYTHYR.

a. e. i. o—b. c. T. l. s. R p.

Einigan Gawr a gafas ddeall ar lythyr gyntaf, ac efe a wnaeth y prif dorronau, nid amgen nag unarddeg, sef y pedair golefiaid, a'r saith gwerforion, a phob drycholion a welai a phob chwedl a glywai a phob edmyg a ddeallai efe a dorri Cof ar wŷd, ag eraill yn dal barn ar y pethau a wnelai Einigan bwrw mai Cythraul oedd, ai yrru ar ddeol. Yna dyfod att genedl ei Dad yn Ynys Prydain dangos ei gelfyddyd a orug, yna barnu mai doethaf o'r Doethion yd-oedd, ai alw Einigan Wyddon a phob un a ddysgu 'r gelf-Yddyd wrth lythr a elwaint Gwyddoniaid, a'r gwyddoniaid hynny a fuaint Brif ddoethion Ynys Prydain cyn ceinmygu Beirdd herwydd Braint a Defod yn ddosparthus. A gwedi trefnu Beirdd a Barddas Doded arnynt gadw Cof yr un torron ar ddeg, ag o hynny y gwellhaed y gelfydd ac y caed un torron ar bymtheg au galw yr un llythyr ar bymtheg. Gwedi hynny deunaw, ag o hynny hyd bedwar ar hugain, ag at y rhai hyd y pedair rhaglythr ar ddeg, fal ag au gwelir yr awr honn, a hyn a gedwir ar gof Llafar, a Lly-thyr a Defod Beirdd Ynys Prydain. Cwlm un ar ddeg a elwir Cwlm Einigan, un un arbymtheg Cwlm Edric, ag un deunaw cwlm Alawn a Chwlm y Beirdd. Un pedair ar hugain a elwir Cwlm Arthafael, a'r un sydd yn awr a elwir

---

[1] The literary achievement of Alawn is thus recorded in the " Englynion y Gorugiau " by Geraint the Blue Bard ;—

> Goruc Alawn fardd Prydain,
> Gofredeu cleu clodysgein,
> Coel cyd celfyddyd cyfrein.

The achievement of Alawn, the Bard of Britain,
Was to establish true memorial of spreading fame—
The mutual recording in the art of disputation.
Iolo MSS. pp. 263, 670.

the question is the degree of Chair obtained or refused. The answer is between the aspirant and his conscience, and between his conscience and God, not between him and his teacher.

ORIGIN AND PROGRESS OF LETTERS.—EINIGAN THE GIANT.— THE GWYDDONIAID.—SYSTEMS OF LETTERS.

a. e. i. o.—b. c. t. l. s. r. p.

It was Einigan the Giant that first understood letters; and he made the principal cuttings, which were eleven, that is, the four vowels, and the seven consonants. And he inscribed on wood the memorial of every object he beheld, every story he heard, and every honour he understood. Others considering the things that Einigan did, concluded that he was a devil, and banished him. Upon this he came to his father's kindred in the Isle of Britain, and exhibited his art, and they adjudged him to be the wisest of the wise, and called him Einigan the Gwyddon, and all, who learned the art of letters, they called Gwyddoniaid, which Gwyddoniaid were the principal sages of the Isle of Britain, before Bards were systematically distinguished in respect of privilege and usage. When Bards and Bardism were arranged, they were required to keep the memorial of the eleven cuttings. After this the art was improved, and sixteen cuttings were obtained, which were called the sixteen letters; subsequently, eighteen, and thence until twenty-four, to which were added the fourteen secondary letters, as they are now seen. This is preserved in the memorial of voice and letters, and the usage of the Bards of the Isle of Britain. The system of eleven is called the system of Einigan; the one of sixteen, the system of Edric; the one of eighteen, the system of Alawn[1] "and the system of the Bards;"[2] the one of twenty-four is called the system of Arthavael; and

---

[2] Added from another MS.

y Cwlm Newydd, a Chwlm Idner fferyll, ag yn amser y bu
Gruffudd ap Llywelyn ap Sitsyllt yn arwain Braint ar
Gymru benbaladr y bu yr Idner hwnnw. ag fal hynn y
dangoser bonedd Llythyr a gwybodau Llyfr yng Nghof a
Chadw Beirdd Ynys Prydain.

DECHREUAD LLYTHYR A LLYFR.—EU DWYN I YNYS PRYDAIN.—Y COELBREN.

Pwy gyntaf a gafas ddeall ar lythyr?

Addaf ai cafas gyntaf gan Dduw ymharadwys, ai fab ef
Afel wirion ai dysges gan ei dad, a Chain lofrudd Brawd
Afel a fynnai glod o Dda Byd, ag Afel nis mynnai namyn
o wybodau wrth fodd Duw a deall a dysg ar a wnaeth ag a
fynnai Dduw, ag am hynny cenfigenodd Cain wrth ei frawd
Afel ag ai lladdodd o furn a Chynllwyn, ag yna collwyd y
gwybodau a ddug Afel ar ddeall, gwedi hynny y cafas Addaf
fab arall ai enw Sedd, ag ef a ddysges iddo 'r wybodaeth ar
lythyr a phob gwybodau dwyfolion eraill, ag i Sedd y bu
fab ai Enw Enos a ddysged gan ei dad yn wr wrth lythyr a
gwybodau molianus ar lyfr a llên, ag Enos oedd y gwr a
wnaeth lyfr cadw gyntaf, er cynnal cof a chadw am bob
hardd a moliannus a daionus, sef am a wnaeth Duw Gre-
awdr ai waith ar nef a daear, ag a orchymynodd yn Ddeddf
a Chyfraith ar ddŷn, a'r wybodaeth honn a gadwed gan
Eppil Enos hyd yn amser Noe Hen, a gwedi darfod am y
dwr diliw a dyfod o'r llong i dir sych efe a ddysges Noe'r
wybodaeth ar lyfr a phob gwybodau ereill iddei fab Iaboth,
a'n Cenedl ninnau y Cymry a hanoeddynt o Iaboth ab Noe
Hen ai cawsant y wybodaeth honn, ag ai dugasant gyda
nhwy hyd yn Ynys Prydain, ag ai cynhaliasant gan aml-

---

[1] I.e. between A. D. 1021 and 1064.

[2] See Gen. iv.

[3] The Eastern people have likewise certain traditions respecting Enos which
are not recorded in the Holy Bible, such as, that Seth his father declared him
sovereign prince and high-priest of mankind, next after himself; that Enos was
the first who ordained public alms for the poor, established public tribunals for
the administration of justice, and planted, or rather cultivated, the palm tree.

the one now in use is called the new system, and the system
of Idnerth the Artist. It was in the time when Gruffudd,
son of Llywelyn, son of Seisyllt, exercised prerogative over
Cymru universal, that this Idner lived.[1] Thus are shown
the origin of letters and the sciences of books in the memorials of the Bards of the Isle of Britain.

THE ORIGIN OF LETTERS AND BOOKS.—THEIR INTRODUCTION INTO BRITAIN.—THE COELBREN.

Who was the first that obtained understanding respecting
letters?

Adam first obtained it from God in Paradise, and his son,
Abel the Innocent, learned it of his father. Cain the Murderer, Abel's brother, would have fame from the good things
of the world, but Abel would not, except from sciences that
were pleasing to God, and from understanding and learning
relative to what God did or desired. Wherefore Cain envied
his brother Abel, and slew him feloniously and treacherous-
ly.[2] Then the sciences, which Abel caused to be understood,
were lost. After that, Adam had another son, whose name
was Seth; and he taught him the knowledge of letters, and
all other divine sciences. And to Seth was a son, whose
name was Enos, who was educated by his father as a man
of letters and praiseworthy sciences in respect of book and
learning. It was Enos who was the first that made a book
of record, for the purpose of preserving the memory of every
thing beautiful, commendable, and good, that is, of what
God the Creator did, and of his works in heaven and earth;
and he enjoined this to man as a law and ordinance.[3] This
knowledge was preserved by the posterity of Enos until the
time of Noah the Aged; and when the water of the deluge
had ceased, and the ship had come on dry land, Noah
taught the knowledge of books, and all other sciences, to his
son Japheth, and our nation, the Cymry, who were descended from Japheth, son of Noah the Aged, obtained this
knowledge, and brought it with them to the Isle of Britain,

hau a mwyhau gwybodau ar lythyr a llên a dodi ar hynny bob Cof a chadw, hyd oni ddaeth Crist ynghnawd.

Bath o beth oeddynt y llyfrau cyntaf a gafad ar wybod i genedl y Cymry gyntaf, ag a pheth eu defnyddu?

Gwydd, sef hynny coed oedd, a'r ffordd honno a elwid Coelbren, ag o honi y mae Coelbren y Beirdd, fal ag y mae ar gof a chadw fyth gan Genedl y Cymry, ag nid modd arall o ymdrin a llythyr ar wybod i'n Cenedl cyn dyfod Crist ynghnawd.

Adolwyn fy athraw ai gwiw dangos ar lafar immi yr addysg modd y gwneir Coelbren y Beirdd, ar gelfyddyd parth ai dylai?

Mi ai dangosaf drwy Rad Duw, sef y gwneir Coelbren y Beirdd a gwydd edrin* o blanhigwydd deri pedryollt, sef o lasgoed gyfref ag arddwrn glaslanc. au naddu 'n bedryfan, sef yn bedwar ochrog, hyd cyfelin, a chyfunfaint lled a thrwch o faint hyd heiddyn sef traian modfedd, a gwedi

Y PRIF AWGRYMAU.—GWELLHAD Y GOELBREN.

Cyn amser Beli mawr ab Manogan nid oedd amgen na deg llythyren ar deg awgrymau gelwid nid amgen nac a, p, c, e, t, i, l, r, o, s—gwedi hynny cafad m, ac n, a gwedi hynny pedwar eraill au rhoi yn unarbymtheg ar ddatrin a gosteg gwlad a chenedl. Gwedi dyfod y ffydd yng Nghrist dau lythyren eraill nid amgen U a D. ac yn amser y brenin Arthur doded ugain llythyren gyssefin fal yn awr. o gyngor Taliesin Ben Beirdd Bardd Teulu Urien Rheged. ac ar ddosparth y deunaw y trefnwyd O, I, U, sef Enw aflafar

---

* Probably " hydrin," manageable, pliant.

1 The MS. breaks off abruptly here.

2 He was the father of the celebrated Casswallawn or Cassivelaunus, who opposed the Roman invasion.

3 Arthur was elected pendragon of the Britons about A. D. 517, and died A. D. 552.

and they maintained, amplified, and enlarged the sciences of book and learning, and placed them on record until Christ came in the flesh.

What were the first books that were first known to the nation of the Cymry, and what were their materials?

Wood, that is, trees, and that mode was called Coelbren, from which comes the Coelbren of the Bards, as it is still on record by the nation of the Cymry. There was no other mode of dealing with letters known to our nation before Christ came in the flesh.

Pray, my teacher, is it meet that thou shouldest show me orally the instruction how to make the Coelbren of the Bards, and the art that ought to belong to it?

I will show it, by the grace of God,—The Coelbren of the Bards is made with the genial wood of oak plants, split into four parts, that is, of greenwood as thick as a boy's wrist. These are hewn square, that is, into four sides, a cubit in length, their breadth and thickness being equal one to the other, namely the length of a barley corn, which is the third of an inch. After[1]

THE PRIMARY LETTERS.—IMPROVEMENT OF THE ALPHABET.

Before the time of Beli the Great,[2] son of Manogan, there were only ten letters, which were called the ten signs, namely, a, p, c, e, t, i, l, r, o, s. After that m, and n, were invented; and after that four others, and they were made into sixteen by the divulgation, and under the proclamation of country and nation. After the coming of the faith in Christ, two other letters, namely u and d. In the time of king Arthur[3] there were introduced twenty primary letters, as at present, by the counsel of Taliesin, the chief of Bards, and domestic Bard of Urien Rheged.[4] Under the system of the eighteen were arranged O. I. U. which is the

[4] Several of Taliesin's poems to Urien Rheged are printed in the 1st vol. of the Myvyrian Archaiology.

H

Duw. cyn hynny o drefn O, I, O, ydoedd. herwydd yr un
ar bymtheg ag o brif awgrymau nid oes hyd yn awr amgen
nac ugain Llythyren neu ugain awgrym. a Cheraint Fardd
glas a ddosparthes ugain Llythyren a phedair. fal y mae yr
awr honn a'r pedair yn adlawiaid—wedi hynny o gym-
hwyllig ymbwyll Beirdd ac Athrawon o Feirdd Cadeiriogion
dygwyd ar fraint ac arfer, gan wellhaû y goelbren. ddeunaw
llythyren ar hugain. arwŷdd, eisioes nid oes ar ddu a gwyn
amgen na'r pedair awgrym ar hugain.

YSTORYNAU CYSSEFIN.—GWELLHAD Y GOELBREN.— EI HADFERIAD.

Ystorrynau y gelwid y llythrennau ym mhrif amseroedd
Cenedl y Cymry; a gwedi amser Beli ap Manogan y gelwid
yn llythrennau a chyn o hynny nid oedd amgen o lythyr
na'r deg ystorryn cyssefin. a chyfrinach y buant er yn oes
oesoedd, gan Feirdd Ynys Prydain yn cadw Cof Gwlad a
chenedl, A Beli mawr au gwnaeth yn unarbymtheg. a'r
drefn honno arnynt efe a'i datrines, ac a wnaeth nas dylit
fyth wedi hynny cyfrinach ar wybodau Llythyr, herwydd y
drefn a wnaeth ef arnynt, a gadael y deg ystorryn dan
gyfrin.

Gwedi dyfod y ffydd yng Nghrist gwnaeth deunaw. a
gwedi hynny ugain. ag ar hynny y cadw arnynt, hyd yn
amser Ceraint Fardd Glas. ag efe a ddodes bedwar ar ugain
arnynt.

Ac ar hynny buant yn hir oesoedd. hyd yn amser y
Brenin Harri bummed, ag efe a waharddes ysgolion ir Cymry, a llyfrau a defnydd llyfrau. ag achos hynny gorfu ar y
Cymry gydymgymeryd a choelbren y beirdd a thorri a
duo llythrennau ar wydd a gwiail, a chymmeryd Beirdd iw

---

[1] I e. in writing.

[2] It may be remarked here that according to one version of the Poem by
Taliesin, in which the expression "Saith ugain Ogrfen y sydd yn Awen," occurs,
(See Antea p. 48) the word "iaith" is used instead of "Saith," which makes
the meaning to be—"the language of twenty letters is in Awen,"—a statement
that in some measure bears out that of the text.

unutterable Name of God; whereas previous to that arrangement it was O. I. O. according to the sixteen. Of the principal signs there are not, to this day, more than twenty letters, or twenty signs. Geraint the Blue Bard appointed twenty-four letters, as it is at present; but the four are auxiliaries. After that, through the argumentative consideration of Bards, and Teachers who were chair Bards, there were brought into use and privilege, by the improvement of the Coelbren, thirty-eight letters on wood; but there are in black and white [1] only the twenty-four signs.

PRIMARY CUTTINGS.—IMPROVEMENT OF THE COELBREN.— ITS RESTORATION.

In the early times of the nation of the Cymry letters were called cuttings; and it was after the time of Beli, son of Manogan, that they were called letters. Previously, there were no letters but the primary cuttings, which had been a secret from the age of ages among the Bards of the Isle of Britain, for the preservation of the memorials of country and nation. Beli the Great made them into sixteen, and divulged that arrangement, and appointed that there should never after be a concealment of the sciences of letters, in respect of the arrangement which he made; but he left the ten cuttings a secret.

After the coming of the faith in Christ, they were made eighteen; and after that twenty,[2] and such they were kept until the time of Geraint the Blue Bard, who made them twenty-four.

They continued such for long ages, even until the time of king Henry the Fifth,[3] who forbade schools, books, and the materials of books for the Cymry. On that account the Cymry were obliged to betake themselves in a body to the Coelbren of the Bards, and to cut and blacken letters on wood

[3] A.D. 1412—1122.

dy bob perchen ty a theulu a fynnai wybodau llythyr a
darllain, ac o hynny trefnwyd cymmorth Tir ac ar a buarth
i'r Beirdd, ag aeth Beirdd yn niferog yng Nghymry, ag
ynfwy gwybod llythyr nag y bu cyn y gwahardd. am hynny
y canodd Llawdden fardd,

> Ar gam gochel gwel a gwilia ergyd
> pob argoll ai redfa,
> adammeg y byd yma
> nid drwg a ddwg a fo'n dda.

sef lle nas caid ysgol namyn Saesoneg nag atraw namyn
Sais y dysgai'r Cymry eu hiaith ai gwybodau yn fwy nag
erioed, ag a wnaethant wellhâd ac Amlhâd. ar rhif llythyr
ac ystorryn. oni ddaeth pen y rhif y sydd arnynt ynawr.

ADFERIAD YR HEN GYMRAEG.

Yn amser Owain ap Maxen Wledig ydd enillwys genedl
y Cymry eu braint a'u Coron, cymmerasant at eu mamiaith
gyssefin yn lle'r Lladin ag oedd wedi lled enill Ynys Prydain, ag yn y Gymraeg y cadwasant gof a Chyfarwydd a
dosparthau Gwlad a chenedl gan ddwyn ar atgof yr hên
gymraeg a'u geiriau a'u hymadroddion Cynhwynolion, eithr
achos angof ag anneall ar hen lythyriaeth y deg llythyr
cyssefiniou. hwy fuant ar wall, ac fal hyn y daeth anghydbwyll ar amrafaelion heneiriau, sef dodi dau lythyren lle
nad oedd gofyn amgen nag un, fal y mae Caan, a Braan, a
glaan, yn lle Cän, a brän, a Glän a digerth yn lle dierth, a
phlegid yn lle phlaid a llaweroedd eraill. hefyd dod T yn
DD, ag I. yn lle E ag yn lle Y. ag U, yn lle E. ag nid
achos dangos y cwbl, eithr hynn er cof am ai gwellhais nid

---

[1] Llawdden flourished from about 1440 to 1480.

and rods; and every owner of a house and family, that wished to know the sciences of letters and reading, took Bards into his house. And from this was appointed the endowment of land, and tilth, and fold for the Bards. And the Bards became numerous in Cymru, and the knowledge of letters was greater than before the prohibition; wherefore Llawdden the Bard[1] sang—

> Beware of being wrong; see and observe—the throw
> And course of every privation;
> And the adage of this world,
> "That is not evil which produces good."

That is to say, where there was no school to be had, but an English one, and no teacher but a Saxon, the Cymry would study their own language and sciences more than ever, and they improved and augmented the number of letters and cuttings, until they completed the number, of which they now consist.

RECOVERY OF THE OLD CYMRAEG.

It was in the time of Owain, son of Maxen Wledig, that the nation of the Cymry recovered their privilege and crown. They took to their primitive mother tongue instead of the Latin, which had well nigh overran the Isle of Britain; and in the Cymraeg they kept the memorials and history and systems of country and nation, restoring to memory the ancient Cymraeg, with its original words and expressions. Because the ancient orthography of the ten primary letters was forgotten and misunderstood, they became lost, and thus arose a disagreement respecting several old words, that is, the putting of two letters, where only one was required, as *caan, braan, glaan,* instead of *cân brân,* and *glân,* and *digerth* instead of *dierth,* and *phlegid* instead of *phlaid,* with many others; also putting *t* for *dd,* and *i* instead of *e,* and instead of *y,* and *u* instead of *e.* It is not necessary to show the whole, but this much is given in memory of him who made the amendment, namely, Tal-

amgen no Thalhairn Fardd o Gaerllion ar wysg, dan nawdd
y Ford gronn, ag ar ei ol ef Taliesin ben beirdd, a wnaeth
drefn ar y gymraeg o iawn ddeall ar Bwyll a Theilyngdawd
y deg llythyr gyssefin, a'r moddau a'r trafodau arnynt a'r
treiglaethau teilyngion, ac o hyn y cafwyd yr hen gymraeg
ar adver ag adgael.

Y LLYTHYRENAU CYSSEFINION.—EU GWELLHAD.— ADFERIAD Y GOELBREN.

Hynn a gymerais i Lewelyn Sion o Lyfr Dafydd Benwyn,
a elwir Coelbren y Beirdd.

Llyma Ddosparth awgrym Llythyr sef Awgrym Iaith ag
ymadrodd fal ag ai trefnwyd gan Wilym Tew Brydydd ag
Athraw Cadeiriog, ac ai dangoswys yn Eisteddfod Cadair a
gorsedd Monachlog Penrhys yn amser y bu Owain Glyndwr
a'r Cymry ar y goreu yn erbyn y Saeson.

Deg llythyr Awgrym a fo'r dechreuad gan y Cymry Cyn
eu dyfod i Ynys Prydain a'r deg hyn a gedwir hyd yr awr
hon yn gyfrinach anesgor gan Feirdd Ynys Prydain ag am
hynny nis gellir i neb o ddyn deall gwreiddgael ar Goelbren
Llythyr na fytho dan gyfrwym adduned Cyfrinach Beirdd
Ynys Prydain, ag yn amser Dyfnwal Moelmud ap Dyfnfarth ap Prydain ap Aeth Mawr y dodwyd yn archafael un
rhif ar bymtheg ar dorriadau awgrym Iaith ag ymadrodd

---

[1] Talhaiarn presided in the chair of Urien Rheged, which was established at
Caer Gwyroswydd, or Ystum Llwynarth. He composed a prayer, which has
always been the formula used in the Gorsedd Morganwg, or Bardic Sessions of
Glamorgan. He was also domestic chaplain to Emrys Wledig, or Ambrosius
Aurelianus. Taliesin in his Poems-alludes to Talhaiarn,—

Trwy ieith Talhayarn
Bedydd bu ddydd farn.

According to the language of Talhaiarn,
There will be baptism at the day of judgment.

Angar Cyvyndawd.

[2] Llywelyn Sion was an eminent bard of Glamorgan, distinguished for having
been appointed to collect the System of Bardism as traditionally preserved in
the Gorsedd Morganwg, in which he presided in 1580. A great portion of the
present Volume is due to his care and assiduity.

haiarn the Bard,[1] of Caerleon-upon-Usk, under the protection of the Round Table. After him Taliesin, Chief of Bards, arranged the Cymraeg, from a right understanding of the meaning and merit of the ten primary letters, and their modes, and changes, and proper inflections; and from this the ancient Cymraeg was restored and recovered.

THE PRIMARY LETTERS.—THEIR AUGMENTATION.— RESTORATION OF THE COELBREN.

This is what I, Llywelyn Sion,[2] took from the Book of Davydd Benwyn,[3] which is called the Coelbren of the Bards.

Here is the system of the symbols of letters, or the symbols of language and speech, as it was arranged by Gwilym Tew,[4] Bard and Chair Teacher, and exhibited at the Eisteddvod of the Chair and Gorsedd of Pen Rhys Monastery,[5] when Owain Glyndwr and the Cymry were prevailing against the Saxons.[6]

There were ten symbols of letters in the possession of the Cymry from the beginning, before they came into the Isle of Britain, which ten are now kept an undivulged secret by the Bards of the Isle of Britain, and therefore no man can radically understand the Coelbren of letters, who is not under the obligation of the vow of the secret of the Bards of the Isle of Britain. In the time of Dyvnwal Moelmud, son of Dyvnvarth, son of Prydain, son of Aedd the Great, the symbolic cuttings of language and speech were augmented

---

[3] Davydd Benwyn was a Bard who flourished from 1550 to 1600, being a native of Glamorganshire. He presided at the Glamorgan Gorsedd in 1580.

[4] Gwilym Tew presided at the Glamorgan Gorsedd in 1460.

[5] The Monastery of Pen Rhys was suppressed in the second year of King Henry V.'s reign, A.D. 1415, because its inmates had sided with Owain Glyndwr.

[6] The insurrection of Owain Glyndwr began about 1400, and continued with varied success for fifteen years, when he died, i. e. September 20th, 1415.

a dodi cyfesgor arnynt, a ffurf newydd i bob un yn amgen
nag y mae ar y deg pwnc awgrym cyfrinach ag anesgorawl,
ag yn amser y bu Beli Mawr ap Manog yn Fren Penrhaih
Ynys Prydain yr un awgrym llythyr ar bymtheg ar Esgor
i Genedl y Cymry, a nawdd nas gellid na Brenin na Barnwr
nag Athraw Gwlad ar nas gwypai yr un awgrym ar bymtheg a'u hamgelfyddodi 'n gyfiawn, a bu oesoedd wedi
hynny cyn deall ar awgrym Plagawd sef hynny crwyn
cyffaeth, a phan ai caed y dychymygwyd Rhôl, a chwedi
hynny y llyfrau a welir yr awr hon dan arfer. a mwyhau
rhif awgrymau hyd nas caed ar eu deunawfed yn amser
Taliesin Ben Beirdd ag efe ai dodes ar ei orchanau, ag o
hynny gwellhad ar Gerdd dafod. Gwedi hynny rhif ugain
ar yr awgrymau, sef ar y cysefiniaid fel ag y mae yr awr
hon. Gwedi hynny yn amser Ceraint fardd Glâs, y dechreuwyd ymarfer ag awgrymau adlawiaid ag ef ai dychymyges ag eraill ar ei ol ef yn eu gwellhau, a'r Beirdd yn cynnal
cof a chadw ernynt a gwedi myned Owain Glyn Dwr ar
goll dod gwahardd ar blagawd a phapir ynghymru. a gorfu
ar y Beirdd a'r athrawon a phawb eraill dan raid a gofyn
cof a chadw ddwyn awgrymau Coelbren y Beirdd ar adwedd
ag adfer, onid aeth celfyddyd eu gwneuthur yn barod ir
torr. yna aml afrifed gan wegryddion a Basgedyddion au
gwerthaint i'r nebun a'i ceisiai, a pharhau felly hyd yng
rhai y sy'n fyw y dydd heddyw. (Sef ai dywed Dafydd
Benwyn.)

CYFRINACH Y BEIRDD.

O I W, yw'r Tair llythyren, ag mewn llyfrau hen iawn
O I U, am fod U yn cael ei arfer yn lle W yn yr hen amseroedd. Gair Cyfrinach y Prifeirdd yw, ag nid rhydd ei
lafaru na'i yngan ar glyw i ddyn or byd, ond i Fardd dan

---

[1] I.e. Manogan.

to sixteen in number, and they were mutually divulged, and to each was given a new form, other than what the ten symbolic points that are secret and undivulged have. In the time when Beli the Great, son of Manog,[1] was king paramount of the Isle of Britain, the sixteen symbols were laid open to the nation of the Cymry, and security was given that there should be no king, judge, or teacher of country, without knowing the sixteen signs, and being able to reduce them into proper art. It was ages after that, before understanding respecting the symbols of Plagawd, that is, dressed skins, was obtained, and when that took place, the Roll was invented, and after that, the Books that are now seen in use. The number of the symbols was augmented until they were found to be eighteen in the time of Taliesin, chief of Bards, who employed them in his canons, hence the improvement of vocal song. After that the number of the symbols was raised to twenty, that is, the primaries, as at present. After that Geraint, the Blue Bard, began to use auxiliary symbols, which he invented, and which others, after him, improved, and the Bards kept memorials of them. When Owain Glyndwr was lost, plagawd and paper were prohibited in Cymru; and the Bards and Teachers, and all others who were required to keep memorials, were obliged to restore into sight and use the symbols of the Coelbren of the Bards, until the making them ready for the cutting became an art. Then they became infinitely numerous by the hands of sieve and basket makers, who sold them to any one that sought for them, and so they continued down to the days of those who are now living. It is Davydd Benwyn that says it.

THE BARDIC SECRET.

O I W are the three letters, and in very old books O I U, because U was used instead of W, in the olden times. It is the secret word of the primitive Bards, which it is not lawful to speak or utter audibly to any man in the

I

adduned Tynghedfen. Gellir enwi a dangos y llythyrennau i'r neb a fynner o'r byd heb yngan y llafar a ddylit
iddynt yn nawdd Cyfrinach, heb ddamdwng arnno, ond os
efe a'u hyngan ar lafar yng nghlyw, efe a dyrr ei nawdd;
ag nis gellir Bardd o hono, ag nid rhydd dangos ymhellach
iddo ar y Gyfrinach, nag yn y byd hwn a dderfydd, nag yn
y byd arall ni dderfydd hyd fyth bythoedd.

Sion Bradford.

YR ARWYDD GLAN.

/|\ Sef y Tair Colofn goleuni au gelwir, a'r Tair colofn
gwirionedd can nas gellir gwybod ar wirionedd ond o'r goleuni a geir arnaw, a Thair Colofn Gwybodau can nag gellir
gwybodau ond o'r goleuni ar gwirionedd.

Y LLYTHYRENAU CYSSEFINION.—GWELLHAD Y GOELBREN.

Cyn caffael y ffydd ynghrist nid arferid amgen na deuddeg Llythyren—Sef oeddynt a. e. i. o. b. D. G. L. M. N.
R. S. gwedi dyfod y ffydd, dygwyd ar arfer unarbymtheg
yna collwyd Celfyddyd y deuddeg Llythyren, ag nid oes
yr awr honn ai gwyr namyn amcan ddall.* Gwedi dyfod
Taliesin ymarferwyd a deunaw Llythyren, ag o gelfyddyd
dosparth y deunaw y trefnwyd o. i. u. ar enw Duw, cyn
hynny o drefn OIO ydoedd herwydd yr un ar bymtheg, gwedi
amser Taliesin cafwyd arfer ar ugain Llythyren a hynny
hyd yn amser Ceraint Fardd Glas, ag efe a ddosbarthes

---

* Forsan " ddull," or " ddeall."

1 The non reception of a perjured Bard in the world of bliss is likewise dwelt
upon by Sion Cent;—

Nid addwyn i ddyn didduw
A dwng gan *afrinaw* Duw
Ei fyned i deg faenol
Draw 'n y nef heb ei droi 'n ol.

It is not meet for a godless man,
Who will swear, *divulging* God,
To go into the fair manor,
Yonder in heaven, without being turned back.

world, except to a Bard who is under the vow of an oath.
The letters may be shown to any one in the world we like,
without uttering the vocalization, which, under the protection of secrecy, is due to them, though he be not under an
oath ; but should he utter them in speech audibly, he
violates his protection, and he cannot be a Bard, nor will it
be lawful to shew him any more of the secret, either in this
world that perishes, or in the other world that will not
perish for ever and ever.[1]   Sion Bradford.[2]

THE SACRED SYMBOL.

/|\. That is to say, they are called the three columns,
and the three columns of truth, because there can be no
knowledge of the truth, but from the light thrown upon it ;
and the three columns of sciences, because there can be no
sciences, but from the light and truth.

THE PRIMARY LETTERS.—IMPROVEMENT OF THE ALPHABET.

Before the faith in Christ was obtained, no other than
twelve letters were used, namely, a, e, i, o, b, d, g, l, m, n,
r, s. After the coming of the faith, sixteen were put in
use, then the art of the twelve letters was lost, nor is there
at present any one that knows it, except from conjecture.
After the coming of Taliesin eighteen letters were used ;
and it was according to the art of the system of eighteen
that O I U was appointed for the Name of God. Before
that arrangement it was O I O according to the sixteen.
After the time of Taliesin the use of twenty letters was
obtained,[3] which continued until the time of Geraint the

---

[2] Sion Bradford was admitted a disciple of the bardic chair of Glamorgan in
1730, being then a boy. He presided in the same chair in 1760, and died in
1780.

[3] Iaith ugain ogyrfen y sydd yn Awen.
The language of twenty letters is in Awen.—Taliesin.

bedair llythyren ar hugain. gwedy hynny o gymhwyll i gymhwyll, y Beirdd a ddygasant gan wellhau 'r Goelbren Rif hyd ymhen deunaw ar hugain ar wŷdd, eisoes ar ddu a gwyn, nid arferyd ag amgen na phedwar ar hugain.

GOGYRFENAU.—YSGRIFENU A DU.

Gogyrfen (a corf) y gelwid Llythyr cyn amser Cred a Bedydd, a gogyrfen ai gelwir fyth ar y Goelbren o enw cyfiawn. Ac eraill ai geilw Cyrfen, a'r Hen wyr o brifathrawon a ddodaint ar gerdd dafawd rif pelydrenau pob Cyrfen, au cadw fel hynny ar gof a gwybod.

Gwedi cael plagawd, sef hynny, crwyn ysgrublaid cwyriedig, dodwyd arfer ar ysgrifenu a du sef ag ingc, ag o hynny dygwyd ar arfer ysgrifenu ag ingc ar y Goelbren ai hebillion yn lle torri Cyrfenau, a hynny a welir fyth mewn mannau anghyfymwel ac anghyttrain, sef fal hynny y cadwer Cof a Chyfrif ar wydd ag estyll ag ar fain lle bo hyall eu cael.

GOGYRFENAU.

Y Tair prif ogyrfen ydynt /|\ .

GOGYRFENAU.

Un gogyrfen ar bymtheg cyn y ffydd ynghrist gwedi hynny deunaw, yna ugain.

GOGYRFENAU.

Talhaiarn a ddodes ugain ogyrfen.

TRI GAIR CYNTAF Y GYMRAEG.

Sulw⎫
Sul ⎬ Yr Haul. Barddas.

---

[1] I.e. in writing.

[2] A body.

Blue Bard, who made an arrangement of twenty-four letters. After that, from reasoning to reasoning, the Bards improving the Alphabet, increased the number to thirty-eight on wood; but in black and white[1] no other than twenty-four were used.

GOGYRVENS.—WRITING WITH INK.

Before the time of Belief and Baptism a letter was called gogyrven (from corf[2]); and its right name is still gogyrven on the Coelbren—others call it cyrven. The old men—the primitive teachers—inserted in vocal song the number of the rays of every cyrven, and thus kept the memory and knowledge of them.

After plagawd had been obtained, that is, the dressed skins of animals, writing with black, or ink, came into use; and thence was introduced the practice of writing with ink on the Coelbren and its staves, instead of cutting cyrvens, which is still seen in places that are not visited, and are not much known. And thus were memorials and computation kept on wood and boards, and on stones, where it was possible to get them.

GOGYRVENS.

The three primary gogyrvens are $/ | \backslash$.

GOGYRVENS.

There were sixteen gogyrvens before the faith in Christ; after that eighteen, then twenty.

GOGYRVENS.

Talhaiarn appointed twenty gogyrvens.

THE THREE FIRST WORDS OF THE CYMRAEG.

Sulw }
Sul } The Sun. *Bardism.*

Tri gair cyntaf y Gymraeg, Enw Duw, sef O. I. U.

Enw yr haul ar canfod a'r ymryn, sef, Sulw.

Bo.　E. A. W.* Byw.

Sef parwyddiad cadarn enw Duw,

Enw cadarn yr haul,

Ansawdd gadarn sulw.　sef amlwg hynny, cyn colli'r Gymraeg gyflawn.

Y LLYTHYRENAU CYSSEFINION.—ENWAU Y COELBRENI.

Llyma 'r Cyseviniaid

a phymtheg oeddynt.　Gwedi hynny gwnaethpwy

ac a hwnnw

Gwedi hynny V ac Y ac yna deunaw oeddynt y lly-thyrenau, fal hynn

yn ddeunaw.

Gwedi hynny ugain fal hynn.

yn ugain.

Ag fal hynny y bu 'r Goelbren hyd yn amser y collwyd y lladin yn y wlad hyd nad oedd namyn gwyr wrth lyfr ag ysgol ai gwyddai, yna dychymygwyd er byrhau gwaith ar wydd a *hariannu* 'r† Gymraeg y llythyrenau adlawiaid fal ag y maont yn awr ynghoelbren y beirdd

Llyma fal y mae 'r hen orchest ar Goelbren y Beirdd sef llythyrenau rhin. a'r rhai hynny meddir oeddynt y rhai cyntaf a gafwyd ar wybod.

Arall

---

* I.e. eraill a wedant.

The three first words of the Cymraeg: the Name of God, that is O I U; the name of the Sun, perception, and sensation, that, is SULW; and Bo, others say, BYW.

The Name of God is a substantive verb; the sun is a substantive noun; and sulw is a substantive adjective—which was clear before the perfect Cymraeg was lost.

THE PRIMARY LETTERS.—NAMES OF THE COELBRENS.

Here are the primaries,—

∧ Ʋ ⟨ ⟩ ↲ ⊂ I Ʌ W И ◇ ⌐ Γ Ƴ ⊤

which were fifteen. After that Ƕ was made, and therewith ⟨Ƕ ⟩Ƕ Γƕ ⊤Ƕ ƙƕ Γƕ After that V and Ⴘ, and then the letters were eighteen, thus,

∧ Ʋ ⟨ ⟩ ↲ ⊂Ƙ I Ʌ W И ◇ ⌐ Γ
Ƙ ⊤ V Ⴘ

being eighteen. After that, twenty; thus,—

∧ Ʋ ⟨ ⟩ ↲ Ƙ ⊂Ƙ I Ʌ W И ◇ ⌐
Ƙ Ƙ ⊤ Ⴘ V Ƴ

being twenty.

And thus the Coelbren continued until the time when the Latin was lost in the country, so that only book students and scholars knew it. Then, with the view of shortening the work on wood, and of softening the Cymraeg, secondary letters were invented, such as are now in the Coelbren of the Bards.

The ancient extraordinary character of the Coelbren of the Bards, or mystic letters, which, it is said, were the first known, was thus,—

Ѵ ⋏ Ʌ Ѵ ⋔ Ʌ ⋙ ∧ ⋓ ⋓
⋙ ⋙ ⋈ ⋈ ⋈

Another,

† Sic in the MS., which proves it to be a copy.

 O ⬦ ⬦ ⬦ ⬦ ⬦ ⬦ ⬦ ⬦ ⬦ ⬦
⬦ ⬦ ⬦ ⬦ ⬦ ⬦ ag felly ar a fynner. Ag
wrth hynn y dywedir mai ag un llythyren o'i thrwsio at ei
hachos yr ysgrifenai Beirdd Ynys Prydain y peth a fyn-
nynt yn rhin a chyfrinach.

Wrth a ddangoswyd y gwelir modd ag y mae 'r Coelbreni
fal y buant yn amrafaelion oesoedd ag amseroedd ag ef ai
doedwyd ar enwau y rhai ai dysgasant, nid amgen

1. Yr hen Goelbren. a elwir hefyd y Goelbren Gysefin a
fu ar wybod gan y Cymru cyn dyfod estroniaid o Genhedl-
oedd i Ynys Prydain.

2. Coelbren deunaw, a elwir Coelbren Taliesin, neu un
Talhaiarn.

3. Coelbren ugain. a elwir un Ithel felyn.

4. Coelbren pedwar ar hugain, a elwir un Hywel Dda.

5. A'r Goelbren hir, a honno o dair neu bedair ffordd a
modd.

6. Coelbren Ystudfach. A Choelbren Iorwerth Fynglwyd, &c.

6. Coelbren y meneich amrafaelion o foddion.

DOSPARTHIAD Y LLYTHYRENAU.

from Lln Sion the above Alphabets.*

m. n. w. u. w.

---

* This statement is made by the copyist, Iolo Morganwg.

[1] This could hardly have been the same as Ithel the Tawny, son of Llywelyn
of the Golden Torque, in the middle of the 12th century. The number of his
alphabet, being less than that of Howel the Good, who died A.D. 948, would
require that he should have flourished before the latter date.

[2] Ystudvach was a Bard who flourished in the early part of the fifth century.

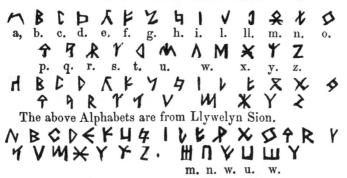

and so with as many as one likes. Wherefore it is said, that with one letter, by modifying it as occasion required, the Bards of the Isle of Britain wrote whatever they liked in secret and mystery.

From what has been exhibited are seen the modes of the Coelbrens, as they have been in various ages and times; they have also borne the names of those who taught them; thus,

1. The old Coelbren, called also the primitive Coelbren, which was known to the Cymry before strange nations arrived in the island of Britain.

2. The Coelbren of eighteen, which is called the Coelbren of Taliesin, or the one of Talhaiarn.

3. The Coelbren of twenty, which is called that of Ithel the Tawny.[1]

4. The Coelbren of twenty-four, which is called that of Howel the Good.

5. The Long Coelbren, which is of three or four ways and modes.

6. The Coelbren of Ystudvach;[2] and the Coelbren of Iorwerth the Gray-haired,[3] &c.

7. The Coelbren of the Monks, after divers modes.

CLASSIFICATION OF THE LETTERS.

a, b. c. d. e. f. g. h. i. l. ll. m. n. o.

p. q. r. s. t. u. w. x. y. z.

The above Alphabets are from Llywelyn Sion.

m. n. w. u. w.

---

[3] Iorwerth Vynglwyd, or the Gray-haired, was an eminent Poet, who was a disciple of the Glamorgan Gorsedd in 1460, and presided there in 1500.

K

Abcedilros, sef felly y gelwid y dengllythyr cyntefigion achos eu dodi ar ungair pedrysill, sef au dosperthid herwydd y gair, nid amgen   A. B. C. D.* I. L. R. O. S.

Gwedi hynn dychymygwyd M. ac N. ac o hynny deuddeg llythyren, ag au gelwid

Mabcednilros, a dosparthu 'r llythyrenau fal hynn, nid amgen, M. a. b. c. e. d. n. i. l. r, o, s, yn ddeuddeg llythyren, gwedi hynny, meddyliwyd pedair llythyren eraill, nid amgen G. T. P. F. ag yna dosparth newydd ar y llythyrau, a dodi pob gogyflar yn nesaf at eu gilydd mal o'r un genedl parth Llafar, sef yn gyntaf y Godidogiaid, nid amgen,

A. e. i. o

Yna 'r minogiaid, nid amgen, M. B. P. F. yna 'r deinogiaid, sef D. T. N.

Yna 'r Taflodiaid G. C. yna 'r afrywiogiaid, nid amg. L. R. S. ag fal hynn eu dosparthu.

A. E. I. O. B. M. P. F. D. T. N. G. C. L. R. S.

au galw $_{\text{gerfydd}}^{\text{llwrw}}$ eu prif enwedigaeth sef Abcedilros, cyd bod o lythyrau yn goel parth rhyw a rhif mwy nag a geffir yn y gair Enwedig. Gwedi hynny dychymyg dwy lythyren eraill, nid amgen V neu Ⴂ ag Ⱶ neu H, yna deunaw Llythyren, yna dwy eraill ag o hynny ugain, nid amgen K ac Ⴌ. Gwedi hynny pedair † Llythyren eraill, nid amgen Y . V . Ⴘ, ac au dosparthu $_{\text{yn}}^{\text{ar}}$ y Goelbren, llwrw eu cenhedloedd parth llef a llafar, au cyfermygiadau, gwedi hynny dychymygwyd rhaglythyrau, sef ydynt Ꭰ. Ⴉ. ᛁᚦ. Ᵽ &c. hyd ddeunaw ar hugain, etto Cynnal yr hen

---

* The E has been omitted, evidently through inadvertence.   † Sic in MS.

[1] A letter, probably either Ⴘ or V, ought to be supplied here, in order to make up the number four, if that, and not three, was really intended.

Abcedilros; so were called the ten primary letters, because they are put in one word of four syllables, being arranged according to the word, thus,

A. B. C. E. D. I. L. R. O. S.

After that M and N were invented, and thence there were twelve letters, which were called Mabcednilros, the letters being thus arranged—

M. A. B. C. E. D. N. I. L. R. O. S.

making twelve letters. After that four other letters were devised, namely, G. T. P. F. And then there was a new arrangement of the letters; all that were partially co-vocal being placed next to each other, as if of one family in respect of sound. That is to say, firstly, the simple ones, namely,

A. E. I. O.
Then the labials, namely, M. B. P. F.
Then the dentals, namely, D. T. N.
Then the palatals, G. C.
Then the non congeners, namely, L. R. S.

And thus were they arranged,—

A. E. I. O. B. M. P. F. D. T. N. G. C. L. R. S.

and were called after their primitive name Abcedilros, though the authentic letters might, in respect of kind and number, be more than what are found in the special word. After that, two other letters were devised, namely V or Ц, and И or Н, then there were eighteen letters. After that, two others, which made twenty, namely, K and Ͷ. After that, four other letters, namely, Y . V . Y;[1] which were arranged on the Coelbren according to their families in respect of sound and vocalness, and mutual relation. After that secondary letters were devised, which are Ϸ. Ͳ. Ͱ. Ϸ, &c., as far as thirty-eight. Still their old

alw arnynt sef Abcedilros, a hen Lyfr au geilw Abcednilroswm.

CYFRINACH Y BEIRDD.—LLUNIAD LLYTHYRENAU.

It is very remarkable that the Druidical secrets consisted
in the use of Letters ◇ I W or ◇ I ↙, anciently /I\ of
the twelve letters.* I \I/—L < > ʌ ᚱ ʏ ſ W
neu fal hyn /\ I \ a lle gwnaed W torri llawn a thraws y
goelbren, neu fal hyn /\ I / sef fal hynny pum llythr
oslef a chyda hynny yn yr ail oes saith llythyr gadarnlef
nid amgen. ↙ < > ᚱ ʏ ʌ H neu ʌ. Ag yn lle
M dau ↙ fal ᚹ ynghyd ag yn lle P ↙ pendraphen fal
hyn ſ ag yn lle mh. dau ſ fal hynn ᚾ. ag yn lle F ʌ
ac uchenaid fal hynn N a chwedi hynny fal hynn ʀ ac yn
W I llawn athraws fal hynn / ac /ᚹ\ I I I / a. e. i. o.
ac yna / I / / a. e. i. o. w. a rhai a fynnant mai tair
goslef a fu o'r dechreu nid amgen /I\ o. i. w. gwedi hynny
∧ I / V. eilwaith lyfrau ∧ ac I yn gwneuthur ∖ E.

Y LLAFARIAID.

Wyth llafariad neu oslef y sydd.
a. e. i. o. u. w. *y.* y (wy) so called because it is the mutate of w.

* This English sentence is evidently Iolo Morganwg's own observation.

designation is retained, which is, Abcedilros.   An old Book calls them, Abcednilroswm.

THE BARDIC SECRET.—FORMATION OF LETTERS.

It is very remarkable that the Druidical secrets consisted in the use of the letters ◇ | W or ◇ | ⌐; anciently /|\, of the twelve letters, | \|/—⌐ < > ⌐ ⌐ ⌐ ⌐ W; or thus /\|\, A. E. I. O, and where W was made, it was cut fully across the Coelbren; or thus, /\|/, which were five vowels.   With them in the second age there were seven strongly vocal letters, namely ⌐ < > ⌐ ⌐ ⌐ H or ⌐.   Instead of M there were two ⌐'s together, as ⌐; and instead of P, ⌐ upside down, thus ⌐; and instead of Mh, two ⌐'s, thus, ⌐; and instead of F, ⌐, and an aspirate thus ⌐, and subsequently, thus ⌐; and instead of W, / fully across, thus, /.   And /|\ |⌐|, A. E. I. O; and then /⌐|// A. E. I. O. W.   Some persons maintain that there were only three vowels from the beginning, namely, /|\. O. I. W; after that, ⌐ |/ V; in other books, ⌐ and | making ⌐ E.

THE VOWELS.

There are eight vowels or sounds,
A. E. I. O. U. W. y. Y, (wy,) so called because it is the mutate of W.

Λ𐌵I◊ＵWＶＹ (Ｕ)

Λ𐌵I◊ＵＶＹＹ. A gwedi hynny fal hyn

Λ𐌵I◊ＶWＶＹ. Ac fal hyn y bu fwyaf ar
arfer gan feirdd ac athrawon, hyd yn amser Addaf ap Davydd o Gilvai, a elwir yn rhai Lyfrau Adam Davi, yr hwn a
ddug bump oslef hirion ir Abcedilros, nid amgen Λ𐌵◊Ｖ

Ｙ. ag a ddywed nad rhaid wrth Ｕ, ag ai dug i maes, a
threfnu deuddeg goslef, eiswys, nid yr Addaf hwnnw ai
dychymyges y pump hyn, sef ydd oeddent o hên gof a
chadw er mwy na thrichanmlynedd, ag nid oedd gwarant
Cadair a Gorsedd iddynt, a hynn o fraint gwarant a rodded
arnynt yn amser yr Addaf hwnnw. ag efe a ddug lawer o'r
hen Addysg ar atgof, ai lyfrau ef a fuant warantedig o awdurdawd hen gof a chelfyddyd.

Modd hyn herwydd eraill,

Λ ∈ I ◊ Ｕ W Ｖ Ｙ. a honn a elwir y goelbren
newydd.

Y LLYTHYRENAU CYSSEFINION.

Unbrifllythyryn-ar bumtheg a fu or dechreuad. nid amgen Λ𐌵I◊—Ｌ, (medd eraill 𐤓,) W neu ＬＬ,—
𐤓𐤓, (neu Ｎ) ⟨⟨, ＋Ｔ, (Ｔ) ⟩𐌵Ｌ Г (Г)
Ｙ (Ｓ. Ｓ.)

Ag am eraill deuoli a thrioli neu bedroli llythyrau man.
ei mman—maan, maab, gwen, gween, rhen—byr—myyr,

---

[1] Adam Davie, an old English Minstrel or Poet floruit Anno 1312.—Percy's
Essay, p. 101. He was probably the same as Addav Eurych, who was also called Addav ap Davydd, and wrote in English as well as in Welsh. His son,

∧√I◇∪WɣⰯ (∪)

∧√I◇∪VɣⰯ; and after that, thus,

∧√I◇VWɣⰯ, which continued mostly in use by the Bards and Teachers, until the time of Addav, son of Davydd, of Gilvai, called in some books Adam Davi,[1] who introduced five long vowels into the Abcedilros, namely,

∧⅄⊕V⅄; and, asserting that there was no occasion for ∪, he abolished it, and appointed twelve vowels. Nevertheless, it was not that Addav who devised these five, for they had been long retained in memory, even for upwards of three hundred years; but they had no authority of Chair and Gorsedd. It was this authoritative privilege that was bestowed upon them in the time of the said Addav, who also restored to memory much of the primitive learning. His books were warranted by the authority of ancient memorial and art.

Thus, according to others,

A Є I ◇ ∪ W ɣ Ⰱ, which is called the New Coelbren.

THE PRIMARY LETTERS.

Sixteen principal letters have been from the beginning; namely, ∧ √ I ◇—Ⱂ, (others say, Ⲅ,) W (or Ⱳ) Ⲅⲅ (or Ⲏ) < Ⲋ ↑ (Ⲧ) > Ⲏ Ⲕ Ⲅ (Ⲅ) Ⲅ (ⳤ ⳤ.)

And in respect of others, letters were doubled, trebled, or quadrupled; as man, ei mman, maan, maab, gwen, gween, rhen, byr, myyr, llyyr, tor, moor, crwn, crwwn,

Gruffydd ap Addaf ap Davydd, was the friend of Davydd ap Gwilym; and was murdered at Dolgelley.

llyyr. ✝ tor, moor. & crwn. cwwn. ✝ baad ei bbaad, Dyydd ei ddydd. fy ⟩⟩⟩Y ⟩⟩ dddydd. &c. (Lln Sion.)

Whence the doubling of d a dd, and l ac ll, still retained. ℕ n. for d. ℳ m for b

Variations.

Λ pro Λ—U pro Y or Y—⟨⟨ pro K.—Ħ pro ₩—ℳ pro ⊦—Ⱶ pro Ɛ—ℕ pro ⅌.—R pro Ɣ —Ƨ pro Ⱦ. ₩ pro V. Ⱶ pro ƅ

ℍ. ℍ secretary whence ∩—ℳ secretary from ₩.*

Llyma'r deg priflythyren, a wnaeth Einigan gawr.

A. P. C. T. E. I. L. O. R. S.

Sef ydynt deg ermygion Llafar y gan y deg peiriannau ymadrodd. sef yi gelwant eraill, y deg prif awgrym ymadrodd, ac enwi felly hefyd y deg prif lythyr.

AMRYWIAETH LLYTHYRENAU.

Λ a droed ar ei ochr ai waelod i'r deau △ ag a wnelai E, ai droi fel hyn ⩒ gwnelai V, ag oi ddeuodi fal ↻ O,—a or ⩒ y gwnaed Y ag Y. Ag fal hyn y treigl y llythyrau, o naw i ddeuddeg, ag unarbymtheg, a deunaw ag ugain, a phedwar ar hugain ag o hynny hyd yn neunaw ar hugain, sef namyn dau deugain.

Y PRIF UN AWGRYM AR BYMTHEG.

---

baad, ei bbaad, dyydd, ei ddydd, fy 〉〉〉Y〉〉 dddydd, &c. (Llywelyn Sion.)

Whence the doubling of d and dd, and l and ll, still retained. ᛘ n for d; ᛙ m for b.

Variations.

Λ for Λ—U for Y or Y—《 for K—ᚻ for ᛚ— ᛘ for ᚴ—ᚼ for ᚼ—ᛘ for ᚹ—R for ᚱ—ᛋ for ᚱ—ᛜ for V—ᚼ for ᚦ.

ᛁ ᚼ secretary, whence ᚾ—ᛘ secretary from ᛚ.

These are the ten principal letters, which Einigan the Giant made,—

A. P. C. E. T. I. L. R. O. S.[1]

That is to say, they are the ten powers of sound produced by the ten organs of speech. Others call them the ten organs of speech; and so also are the ten principal letters named.

VARIATIONS OF LETTERS.

Λ turned on its side, with its base to the right, ⊿, stood for E; when turned thus, ▽, it stood for V, which being doubled thus, ◇, stood for O; and from ▽ were produced Y and Y. And in this way the letters were varied from nine to twelve, and sixteen, and eighteen, and twenty, and twenty-four; and from thence to thirty-eight letters, that is to say, forty save two.

THE SIXTEEN PRIMARY SYMBOLS.

---

[1] We have placed the vowels E and O in the positions which they ought to occupy so as to form the word Apcetilros.

L

DYFODIAD LLYTHYRYDDIAETH DROSODD.—GWLAD GYSSEFIN
Y CYMRY.—EU TIRIAD YN MHRYDAIN.—CHWANEGIAD Y
GOELBREN.

Llyma bellach gyfarwyddyd ar awgrymau ag ymadrodd,
nid amgen Llythyr ag arwydd, herwydd y modd y mae dan
Cadwedigaeth Cof a Llafar a Defodau Cadair a Gorsedd
Beirdd Morganwg a Gwent yn Nhir Iarll a chyn no hynny
yng Nghaerllion ar Wysg er amser Dyfodiad Cyntaf y
Cymry ir Ynys honn y dywedant mai Tair Celfyddyd
freiniol a ddaeth yn eu gwysg gan y Kymmry dan nawdd a
Thywysogaeth Hu Gadarn i'r Ynys honn nid amgen Barddoniaeth, Llythyryddiaeth, ac Eryddiaeth, ys ef o'r Asia fal
ai gelwir yr awr honn, Eithr Deffrobani neu wlad yr haf
oedd yr Enw Cyntaf ar wlad gysefin Cenedl y Cymry, ag
yn wlad honn aneirif Deyrnasoedd helaethlawn, a henedl
ormes a ddyvasant y Cymry allan o'u gwlad i wledydd lle
buant fwy na deucanmlynedd yn symud o wlad i wlad dan
ormes Cenhedloedd difrod ac anraith lle yn y diwedd tirias-
ant yn Llychlyn a brigwlad yr Eidal a Bro Gal, ag o Lych-
lyn y daethant gyntaf i Ynn* a thirio yn Afon Hymrys a
chwedi hynny daeth gosgorddau Eraith o'r Cymry o Dir
Gal i'r Ynys honn, a thirio yn Rhydiau Pwyth Meinlas, a'r
Coriniaid yn genedl ormes au gyrrasant i Ddeheubarth, a'r

---

* Sic in MS., as if the original copy was not very clear.

1 " Cai Hir, nephew of the emperor Arthur, lord of the Comot of Maes Mawr
in Glamorgan, was the first who appointed a Chair of Vocal Song in Tir Iarll,
which was anciently called the Comot of Maes Mawr, whither it had been removed from Caerleon upon Usk, on account of the surrounding incursions of the
Saxons. It was still called there the Chair of Caerleon. In the time of the
contests between Rhys, son of Tewdwr, and Iestyn, son of Gwrgant, the Chair
was disturbed, until the time of William, earl of Gloucester, who renewed it in
Tir Iarll, (the earl's land,) for such, after his appellation, was the new name bestowed upon the Comot of Maes Mawr, and gave privilege and license to Bards."
—Anthony Powell.

2 Geraint, the Blue Bard, has recorded a tradition respecting some of the
services which Hu the Mighty showed to the Cymry, preparatory to their journey
from Deffrobani :—

> Goruc Hugadarn gymmhrain
> Ar Gymry Ynys Prydain
> I ddyffryd o ddeffro Bain.

The achievement of Hu the Mighty, was forming social order
For the Cymry of the Isle of Britain,
To stream out of Deffrobani.—Iolo MSS. pp. 262, 669.

INTRODUCTION OF LETTERS.—ORIGINAL COUNTRY OF THE
CYMRY.—THEIR ARRIVAL IN BRITAIN.—AUGMENTATION
OF THE ALPHABET.

At length here is an account of symbols and speech,
namely, letters and signs, according to their preservation
by means of the memory, voice, and usages of the Chair
and Gorsedd of the Bards of Glamorgan and Gwent in Tir
Iarll,[1] and previously at Caerleon-upon-Usk, since the first
arrival of the Cymry in this island. They say that three
privileged arts were introduced by the Cymry under the
protection and guidance of Hu the Mighty[2] into this island; namely, Bardism, Literature, and Agriculture; that
is, they were brought from Asia, as it is now called. Deffrobani,[3] however, or the Summer Country, was the first
name of the primitive country of the nation of the Cymry,
in which country were large and rich kingdoms without
number. An usurping nation drove the Cymry out of their
country into countries where for upwards of two hundred
years they were roving from land to land under the oppression of devastative and predatory nations, until at last they
landed in Scandinavia and the highlands of Italy, and the
region of Gaul. It was from Scandinavia that they first
came into the island [of Britain,] having landed at the river
Humber.[4] After that other clans of Cymry came from the
land of Gaul into this island, landing at the fords of Pwyth
Meinlas,[5] but the usurping nation of the Coranians[6] drove

---

[3] Probably Taprobane, the island of Ceylon, is meant; celebrated as having
been the residence of Adam. The Historical Triads, however, identify " the
summer country " with that " in which Constantinople now is." (Tr. 4. 56;
Third Series.)

[4] " They came across the Hazy Sea to the island of Britain and Armorica
where they remained." (Tr. 4; Third Series.)

[5] Anglice " the narrow green point," where also the Romans are said to have
landed under Julius Cæsar. (Tr. 22; Second Series.)

[6] The Coranians are described as the first of " the three usurping hordes that
came into the Isle of Britain, and went not out of it," (Tr. 7; Third Series;)
and as having in course of time " coalesced with the Romans until they became
one people," and ultimately with the Saxons, " against the Cymry." (Tr. 15;
ib.) They were evidently the same as the Coritani.

Gwyddyl Ffich a'u gyrrasant Gymry Gwlad Deifr a Bryn-
aich a hanoeddynt o'r Gymry Llychyn i Wynedd a chwedi
hynny Gwyddelod y Werddon a fuant yn ormes arnynt yn
Mon ag Arfon.   Sef deg o'r Dechreuad oedd rhif awgrymau
y Goelbren ai galw abcedilroes, ac abcedilros fal ai gelwir
yn awr, nid amgen abcedilros ∧Ⱡ⟨ᴎ⟩Iↄᴘ◇* a
ᚱ∧ᛏ◇ᚠ⟨ᴎ ↃI, gwedi hynny yn amser Pryd-
ain Aedd Mawr y dyrchafed erail hyd un awgrym ar bymtheg a sefyll ar hynny o rif amser dyfod Crist yng nghnawd
ac yna deunaw a chwedi hynny ugain neu fal dywed eraill
un awgrym ar hugain yn gyssefin fal yn awr, a dychymyg
eraill yn adlawiaid o rifedi i ddeunaw ar hugain.

COELBREN Y BEIRDD, HERWYDD DOSPARTH LLAWDDEN.

	∧	A	ᗐ	Dd	ᴎ	Ll
	ᐃ	Å	⟨	E	M	M
	Ⱡ	B	E	É	N	N
	ᗐ	V	ᚠ	F	◇	O
ⷨ	Ⱶ	M	⟨	G	◈	Ó
	⟨	C	✗ ✗	Ng	ᚹ	P
ᔑ ᛕ	ᛕ	Ch	H	H	ᴎ	Ph
⋈ ⋈	⋈	Ngh	I	I	ᛗ	Mh
	⟩	D	ᚴ	L	ᚱ	R

¹ Llawdden, or Ieuan Llawdden, was a very eminent Poet, who flourished
from about 1440 to 1480. He was at one time Rector of Machynlleth, but in
his old age he retired to the place of his nativity, the Vale of Llychwr, where
he died, and was buried in the Churchyard of Llandeilo Talybont. His elegy

them to the South, whilst the Irish Picts drove the Cymry of the land of Deivr and Bernicia, who were derived from the Cymry of Scandinavia, to Venedotia; after that, the Irish of Ireland oppressed them in Mona and Arvon. Ten from the beginning was the number of the symbols of the Coelbren, and they were called Abcedilroes and Abcedilros, as they are called at present, that is, ∧ᒧᐊᐁᐅ|ᚴ-ᒥᐅᖾ, and ᒥ ∧ ᚠᐅᖾ ᐊᒍᚼ |. Subsequently, in the time of Prydain [son of] Aedd the Great, others were added until they were sixteen symbols, and they continued of that number until the coming of Christ in the flesh; then eighteen, and after that twenty, or, as others say, twenty-one symbols primarily as at present, whilst others were invented as auxiliaries, in number as far as thirty-eight.

COELBREN OF THE BARDS, ACCORDING TO THE ARRANGE-
MENT OF LLAWDDEN.[1]

		A		Dd		Ll
		Â		E		M
		B		Ê		N
		V		F		O
ᕽ	ᕽ	M		G		Ô
		C	ᚷ	Ng		P
		Ch		H		Ph
		Ngh		I		Mh
		D		L		R

was written by his contemporary, Iorwerth Vynglwyd, from which we learn
that he obtained the highest bardic honours.

Ҟ	Rh	Ⱶ	Nh	Ɣ	Ẏ
Ϟ	S	∪	V	Ɣ	Y
↑	T	Ⱳ	W		
∧	Th	Ɣ	Y		

Rhai a ddodasant

a yn lle

Ҟ yn lle ＜

Ѣ yn lle Ҟ

Ϟ yn lle Ⴔ

Ⱨ yn lle Ⱨ hefyd Ⱨ a ⱨ

ⱴ yn lle Ⱳ

ⴖ yn lle Ⴖ neu Ⴖ

ꝑ a Ⱨ yn lle Ⴎ

Ɽ yn lle Ⴔ

Ⱳ yn lle V

Ⱳ yn lle V a ⱴ

Ⱪ ag Ⱡ yn lle Ⱪ

Ⴆ yn lle Ⴔ

Ⱦ yn lle ∧ hefyd Ⴇ

    mal ei Ⴇ∧Ⴔ i ferch

V yn lle Ɣ

Ⴆ yn lle ＞

Ⴇ yn lle Ⴔ lle bai ↑

    yn wreiddiol, mal pei

    dywedyd ei Ⴇ∧Ⴔ i

    fab

Ⱨ yn lle ∧

Ⱦ yn lle ↑

∧ yn lle Ⱪ

Eithr goreu o'r cyfan yw'r hen goelbren fal y dodwys Wilym Tew hi yn ei lyfr cerdd dafawd, a hawsaf ei thorri ar goed; a lleiaf ei gwaith.

Rhai a ddodasant Ⴝ heb V gyda hi, a bai yw hynny, canys pwys ＜Ⱨ y sydd i'r Ⴝ. ag nid mwy, am hynny dylit dodi ⴝV∧Ⴖ↑, ag nid ⴝ∧Ⴖ↑.

---

[1] Gwilym Tew **was a** Poet who flourished from 1430 to 1470, and who presided at the Glamorgan Gorsedd in 1460.

Ϙ	Rh	Ͱ	Nh	Y	Ẏ
ϟ	S	∪	V	Ⲩ	Y
↑	T	Ⱳ	W		
⋔	Th	Y	Y		

Some have substituted

B and ♭ for ⱱ   ⅌ for ⋔, also ⅁, as

K for ⟨   ei ⅁⋀Ⅾ in case of

Ⱪ for K   a daughter

≦ for Ⲅ   V for Y

Ⱨ for Ⱶ, also H and ⱨ   ♅ for ⟩

ⱼ for W   Ⅾ for Ⅾ, where ↑ is

Π for N or Ⱶ   radical, as if one should

Ρ and Ⱶ for Ⲅ   say ei ⅁⋀Ⅾ in case

Ꞃ for Ⲅ   of a son

Ⱳ for V   ⋏ for Ⱶ

Ⱳ for ⋀ Ⱳ   Ⱦ for ↑

Ⲕ and Ⲅ for Ⲅ   Ⱶ for Ⲅ

♅ for Ⅾ

But the best of all is the old Coelbren, as Gwilym Tew[1] has arranged it in his Book of Vocal Song, and the easiest to cut, and of least labour.

Some have placed Ꞡ without V, but that is an error, for Ꞡ has the weight of ⟨Ⱨ, and no more; therefore it ought to be ꞠV⋀Ⱶ↑, and not Ꞡ⋀Ⱶ↑.

Llyma foddion eraill ar Goelbrenni fal y gwelais i hwynt gan Meurig Dafydd.*

Χ Β Γ Ꝺ Ε ᛉ Ϲ ᚼ Ꜧ ᚽ ᛘ ᚢ ⸶ Ⴔ ᚱ ᛋ ↑ ᚢ ᛦ Ⴎ ᚤ

ᚪ ᚦ Ϲ Ꝺ ϵ ᚠ Ϲ ✝ Ꝑ ᚼ ᚻ ᚻ ᚺ ᚮ Ⴔ ᚱ ᚅ ᛏ ᚢ Ⴎ ᚤ

AWGRYM GWYBODAU LLEN. — GWELLHAD Y GOELBREN.—
CYLMAU MESURAU.—DADGYFOETHIAD MONACHLOG
PEN RHYS.

Tair awgrym gwybodau Llen y sydd, Awgrym Coelbren—Llafar — Awgrym Arwest erddigan, ag awgrym rhif.

Awgrym Coelbren yw 'r hynaf oll agar† wybod y Gwydd oniaid er eu dyfod cyntaf i Ynys Prydain, a deg oeddynt y cyssefiniaid; ag than Gyfrinach y Beirdd a chwedy hynny chwanegu deg eraill a newid llun a gwedd pob un o'r unarbymtheg yn amrafaelion cyflwyr ar y deg cyssefiniaid fal nas gellid medru ar y gyfrinach, a dattrin yr un ar bymtheg yn amser Dyfnwal Moelmud, ag yn amser Beli Mawr ap Manogan au doded ar addysg a gwybodau Teuluaidd ac ar swydd a Chelfyddyd Teuluwr o fardd Cadeiriog nid amgen na Derwydd, sef Derwyddon y gelwid y Beirdd Teulu ym mhrif amseroedd cyfannedd Ynys Prydain, ac ar genedl y Cymry cynnal Gwybodau Awgrym a Llen, ag yn amser Arthur y doded Rhif deunaw gorint ar awgrymiaid Coelbren, ag yn amser Ceraint Fardd Glas ugain, ac nid oes amgen nag ugain ar y cyssefinogiaid. Gwedi hynny dychymyg awgrymiaid cymmhleth sef ar y Gorint arwydd uchenad, neu ddichwyth. a gwellhau ar hynny o amser i amser hyd amser Ieuan ap y diwlith, amser y Robert Iarll Caerloyw yn dywysawg Morganwg. ag o hynny hyd amser

---

* Taliesin Williams says that this observation is Llywelyn Sion's.

† The italic letter indicates that the transcriber was doubtful about it.

[1] An eminent Poet of Glamorgan, who presided in the Gorsedd Morganwg in the year 1560, and died in 1600. Llywelyn Sion in the early part of his life was well acquainted with him.

[2] Al. " voice."   [3] Al. " harmony."

[4] He was living somewhere from 1160 to 1180. See a brief notice of him in Iolo MSS. p. 88.

Here are other modifications of the Coelbren, which I have seen with Meurig Davydd.[1]

ΧΒᴄ ᛏᛂᛣᴄᚺᛁ ᛚᛏᚼᛁᚼ✳ᛘᚱᛊᛏᚢᛠᚡᛉ

ᗡᛚᴄ ᗪᛠᚠᴄ✝ᛁᛙᛙᚼᗝᛈᚱᛉᛏ ᚡ ᛃᚥ

THE SYMBOLS OF LITERARY SCIENCES.—IMPROVEMENT OF THE COELBREN.—METRICAL CANONS.—DISSOLUTION OF THE MONASTERY OF PEN RHYS.

There are three series of symbols of literary sciences: the symbols of Coelbren;[2] the symbols of music;[3] and the symbols of number.

The symbols of Coelbren are the most ancient of all, and were known to the Gwyddoniaid from their first arrival in the island of Britain. The primaries were ten, and were under the secret of the Bards. After that, ten others were added, and the form and appearance of each of the sixteen were totally altered from those of the ten primaries, so that the secret could not be known. The sixteen were divulged in the time of Dyvnwal Moelmud; and in the time of Beli the Great, son of Manogan, they were included in the domestic instruction and sciences, and came under the office and art of the domestic teacher, who was a Chaired Bard, that is to say, a Druid; for the domestic Bards were called Druids in the early times of the occupation of the island of Britain; it being incumbent upon the nation of the Cymry to keep up the sciences of symbol and literature. In the time of Arthur the symbols of Coelbren were eighteen notches in number; and in the time of Geraint, the Blue Bard, twenty; nor are there more than twenty of the primaries. After that, mixed symbols were devised; that is to say, by means of a notch was made the sign of sighing or breathing; and these were improved from time to time until the time of Ieuan, son of the Dewless,[4] the time when Robert, earl of Gloucester, was prince of Glamorgan; and

M

y Clâr diweddaf ond un yn Dywysog Morganwg, a Meneich
Pen Rhys yn nglyn Rhondde ae trefnaint fal ac y maent yn
awr a Gwilym ap Hywel Gethin a elwir Gwilym Tew yn
arwain y Gadair wrth Gerdd Dafawd yno ym mraint Prif
Feirdd Cenedl yr Hen Gymry, ag ni ddoded ond hynny
fyth amgen yn wellhâd ar awgrym Coelbren ag ni chafwyd
ar a wnaed yno farn Cyfallwy Cadeiriau effro ar y trydydd,
neu pes ceid ar y nawfed, a lle nis caffer naw, ar y seithfed,
a lle nis gellir saith ar y pummed, a lle nis gellir pump ar y
trydydd, a lle nis tri ar yr Un *a fo* * sef y dylit y dyniadon
yn aghynnifer er barn gorfodrif sef y rif a fo dros yr hanner
ac nis gellir hynny o gadernyd anesgorol ond ar annghyni-
ver Dyniadon wrth eu deurannu, eraill a ddywedant or hen
Athrawon y gellir gorfod ar gynnifer Dyniadon o ddodi
hynny yn fraint ar yr un gyntaf y rhifer o'r ddeuhanner
dan ammod rhoddi a chymmeryd hynny yn honnaid cyn y
doder dan farn, ag nid yn amgen, Ac yn llyn y sydd yn
farn cadeiriau ar rifedi awgrymiaid gorint Coelbren y Beirdd,
sef nid oes barn hyd gyfallwy naw Cadair effro ar y gwellhâd diwedd ar yr Awgrymiaid Gorint ag ar eu rhifedi, eisoes y mae braint amser dros gof y nawfed ach ar y gwellhâd
ac nis gellir cau yn ei erbyn.　Amcan yr un amser nid
amgen na'r amser y bu Owain Glyndyfrdwy yn gwrthym-
wrdd a Brenin Llundain, nid amgen nag yn amser y Breni
Harri sef y pumed y bu Cadair Eisteddfod yn Monachlog
pen Rhys lle y trefnwyd cylmau mesurau Cerdd dafawd, a
goreu y barnwyd un Gwilym Tew sef yr Awdl a wnaeth ef
i Fair o Ben Rys, a gwedi hynny efe a wnaeth wellhâd

---

* Marked by the copyist as not being sufficiently legible.

1 This Ode is printed in " Cyfrinach Beirdd Ynys Prydain," p. 213.

from thence to the time of the last Clare but one, prince of Glamorgan. It was the monks of Pen Rhys in the vale of Rhondde that arranged them as they are at present, when Gwilym, son of Howel the Savage, called Gwilym Tew, bore the Chair of vocal song there in right of the primary Bards of the nation of the ancient Cymry. No other improvement of the symbols of Coelbren ever took place, nor did what was done there obtain the efficient judgment of active Chairs, as far as the third, or, if it might be obtained, as far as the ninth, but where nine cannot be had, as far as the seventh, and if seven cannot be had, as far as the fifth, and where five cannot be had, as far as the third, and when there are not three, as far as the one that there is; for individuals ought to be unequal in number in order to have the judgment of a majority, that is, the number that is above half, which cannot be the case, of irrevocable fixedness, but where individuals are of unequal number, when they are divided into two parts. Others of the ancient teachers say that a majority may be obtained where the individuals are of equal numbers, by conferring it as a privilege upon the first of the two halves that is counted, under the condition of giving and taking the same as a claim, before it is put to the verdict, and not otherwise. And it is in this manner that the judgment of Chairs has been had upon the number of the cut symbols of Coelbren,—that is, no judgment as far as the efficiency of nine active Chairs, has been obtained upon the last improvement of the cut symbols, and their number; nevertheless, the improvement has the privilege of time beyond the memory of the ninth generation, and it cannot be opposed. About the same time, namely, the time when Owain Glyndwr was opposing the king of London, that is, in the time of King Henry the Fifth, there was an Eisteddvod Chair in the monastery of Pen Rhys, where the canons of the metres of vocal song were settled, among which that of Gwilym Tew was adjudged the best, namely, the Ode which he composed to Mary of Pen Rhys.[1] After that he improved the number and ar-

Rhif a dosparth ar y mesurau ar cynghaneddion ag ag arni
yn gyntaf gan fraint Cadair y doded odlau cyfochrogion. ar
awdl honno a ddangosed yng nghadair Eisteddfod gyntaf
Caerfyrddin dan nawdd Gruffudd ap Nicolas a than fraint
edring a chynnwys y Brenin Harri Sant o Winsor nid amgen nad pedwerydd o'r Enw, a hwnnw a fu dan fraint
Cadair a gwlad, hyd yn amser yr ail Eisteddfod yno lle
rhodded y goreu ar gwlm Dafydd ap Edmwnt, yn amser
Harri y pummed o'r enw pan oedd oed Crist yn fil a phedwar Cant a phedwar blwydd ar ddeg y dadgyfoethwyd
fonachlog Penrhys achos cymmhleidio ag Owain Glyndyr-
dwy a gwerthu'r _{perchenyddiaeth}·^{perchenogaet.¹}

COLOFNAU COFFADWRIAETH.—AWGRYM.

Tair colofn coffadwriaeth a chyfarwyddyd, Cerdd dafawd,
Llythyr, ag awgrym, sef yw Awgrym, llun a ddealler, ac oi
ddeall a ddengys ar olwg bod o geinmyged a ragofynai lawer
o lythyr neu o gerdd dafawd, neu o lafar ag araith cyn y
gellid deall cyfiawn arnaw.

Tair awgrym y sydd, awgrym Rhif, awgrym llef neu oslef
ac o honno dangos cyfiawn ar lais a goslef erddigan. ac
awgrym cyflun, a honno a fydd Llun ag arwydd a ddealler
wrth ei lluniadoldeb, a gwisg arfau bonedd ac arfau cenedl,
A gwr a fedro'r gelfyddyd honn ac ai dangoso yn warantedig a elwir arwyddfardd ai swydd ai gelfyddyd yw dangos
cyfarwyddyd ar awgrym Cyflun, sef fal y dangoser amseroedd lleuad wrth luniau golwg arni a rhif Blwyddyn mis a
diwarnod.

---

¹ Gruffydd, son of Nicholas, was illustrious for his power, riches, and family,
was a great patron of the Bards, and extremely popular throughout the principality. He latterly joined the Yorkists, in whose cause he fought, and was
fatally wounded at the battle of Mortimer's Cross, in 1461.

² Davydd, son of Edmund, was a native of Hanmer, in Flintshire, and is
celebrated as the reformer of Welsh Prosody, having compiled the twenty-four

rangement of the metres and consonancies. It was in it (the Ode) that, by privilege of Chair, parallel rhymes were first used. That Ode was exhibited in the first Eisteddvod Chair of Caermarthen, under the patronage of Gruffydd, son of Nicholas,[1] and under the privilege of leave and license from Saint Henry the King, of Windsor, that is the fourth of the name; and it continued under the privilege of Chair and Country until the time of the second Eisteddvod there, where the canon of Davydd, son of Edmund,[2] was pronounced the best, in the time of Henry, the fifth of the name. When the year of Christ was one thousand, four hundred, and fourteen, the monastery of Pen Rhys was dispossessed, and its property sold, because it sided with Owain Glyndwr.

THE PILLARS OF MEMORY.—THE SYMBOLS.

The three pillars of memory and history: vocal song; letter; and symbol. A symbol is a form that is understood, and, being understood, shews at sight that that really exists which would require many letters, or much of vocal song, or speech and oration, before it could be properly understood.

There are three symbols: the symbol of number; the symbol of sound or tone, from which is justly shown the voice and tone of harmony; and the symbol of hieroglyphics, which is the form and sign that is understood by its formation; and the blazonry of the arms of nobility, and the arms of nation. The man who knows this art, and will show it authoritatively, is called a herald-bard, and his office and art is to represent history in hieroglyphics, even as the times of the moon are shewn by its visible delineations, and the number of year, month, and day.

new canons of poetry, which are still adopted by the Bards of North Wales, though they have been protested against by those of Gwent and Morganwg as innovations.

ADAR RHIANON.

Adar Rhianon a genynt oni ddelei Engyl Nef iddeu
clywed ag ou caneuon hwynt y cafwyd Cân a Cherdd Arwest a thant gyntaf, sef yw Cerdd Arwest honno a genir ar
dafawd gan Erddigan a Chan Dant. (Evan Evans.)

PUM OES LLYTHYR.

Pum oes Llythyr. Cyntaf oedd oes y Tair Llythyren, ag
yn bennaf arnynt Enw Duw, a daioni, ag yn arwydd daioni
a gwirionedd, a Deall ag Iawn o ba ryw bynnag y bai, ag
eraill o beth dan arwydd cyfrith herwydd Celfyddyd Arwyddfardd. A llyma 'r modd y rhifeint ddeg ar y Tair
llythyren. Nid amgen /I\\\I//I\ △* a dod ▷ yn lle
deg, a gwedi hyn ⟨ yn lle ail ddegfed, sef Cant, ag ◇ yn
lle drydedd ddegfed, sef mil, ac ◈ yn lle pedweredd ddegfed, sef myrdd, ag am fyrddiwn ▷◁▷, ag am Funa ◁◇,
ag o hynny maes hyd dair ◈ neu bedair neu fwy, ag ar
hyn o ddosparth / yn lle A sef llythyren gyntaf, Λ yn lle
Bi sef yr ail Ⱳ y drydedd ⱲⱮ pedwar—V.—Ⱳ,—W.
—Ⱳ.—IⱲ. a ▷ degfed llythyren.—▷.—▷. deuddeg, a llyma 'r oes gyntaf.

Ail oes y bu trefnu unllythyren ar bymtheg, ag o hynny
amlyccach Llen llythyr, gwedi hynny

Trydedd oes y bu deunaw llythyren yn gwellhau Llen
wrth Lythyr sef y dodwyd Ⱳ yn lle ail ymlef B. Ag

---

* Sic in MS., but the following character, as well as the representation of ten
in other fragments, shews clearly that ▷ is meant.

1 " Rhiaint was a name given to the sixteen letters, and in the Ancient Secret
the Birds of Rhianon :—one letter was called Rhïan, plur. Rhieinau."—Iolo
Morganwg, who refers to Llywelyn Sion.

> Hwn a bryn win o'r gwinwydd
> Hon fal *Rhianon* ai rhydd.

THE BIRDS OF RHIANON.[1]

The Birds of Rhianon sang until the Angels of heaven came to listen to them ; and it was from their songs that were first obtained vocal song and instrumental music; vocal song being that which is sung by the lips to melody and harp. Evan Evans.

THE FIVE AGES OF LETTERS.

The five Ages of Letters. The first was the age of the three letters, which above all represented the Name of God and goodness, and which were a sign of goodness and truth, and understanding and equity, of whatsoever kind they might be. Other things were exhibited under the sign of blazonry in respect of the art of a herald-bard. This is the mode in which they numbered ten according to the three letters, namely, /I\\\I//I\△, ▷ being put for ten, and after that ⟨ for the second tenth, that is, a hundred, and ◇ for the third tenth, that is, a thousand, and ◐ for the fourth tenth, that is, a myriad, and for a million ▷◇, and for buna ◇▷◇, and so on to three ◐, or four or more. According to this arrangement / stood for A, that is, the first letter, ∧ for B, that is, the second, ∨, the third, ∨I, the fourth, ∨, ∨I, ∧∧, ∧∧∧, I∧∧∧, and ▷, the tenth letter, ▷, ▷ the twelfth. This is the first age.

In the second age sixteen letters were arranged, whence literature became more clear. After that,

In the third age there were eighteen letters, for the improvement of literature; that is, ∐ was put for the second

He will buy wine from the vines,
She like *Rhianon* will give it.
Sion Brwynog, to Rhydderch ap Rhys
of Tregaian and his wife.

yna dodi Tair llythyren Enw Duw yn ○ | Ͷ. a deunaw-
fed llythyr Ͱ, ag yn amgen o rith Ͷ.

Pedweredd oes pedair llythyren ar hugain ag enw Duw
ar ddosparth y drydedd oes yn gyfrinach.

Pummed oes fal ag y mae yn awr sef deunaw llythyren ar
hugain, a Chadw enw Duw ar ddosparth y drydedd oes yn
gyfrinach.

TAIR AWGRYM GWYBODAU.

Tair awgrym Gwybodau a fuant ar arfer o'r dechreuad
gan genedl y Cymry.

Awgrym gair ag ymadrodd, sef llythyr, ar y degfed, ar
yr unar bymthegfed, ac ar yr ugeinfed, ag ar y pedair ar
hugeinfed.

Cyntaf o'r Tair herwydd braint a bonedd yw Awgrym
Gair ag ymadrodd, sef Llythyr.

Ail awgrym Erddigan, sef Goslef ac Arwest.

Trydydd, Awgrym rhif ac fal hynn y mae,

Λ ͷ | ◇ Ⅴ Ⴤ Ⴠ ＜ ＞ Ⅹ

1　 2　 3　 4　 5　 6　 7　 8　 9　 10, sef

un, dau, tri, pedwar, pump, chwech, saith, wyth, naw, deg,
unneng ag un—unneng a dau—unneng a thri—unneng a
phedwar, unneng a phump—unneng a chwech—unneng a
saith—unneng ac wyth—unneng a naw—deuneng—ac fal
o'r blaed hyd Trineng—pedryneng—pumneng—chweneng,
seithneng — wythneng — nawneng. Cant, ac hyd fil, ac o
hynny hyd Geugant, a chyfrinach yw cadwedig ar lafar
Gorsedd Beirdd Ynys Prydain, o'r dechreuad a Thydain
Tad Awen ai trefnis gyntaf yn Gelfydd fannog ar wybodau
Doethineb, Ac efe hefyd a drefnis Awgrym Celfyddyd Er-

sound of B; and then the three letters of God's Name were made into ◇ | **Ͷ**; and the eighteenth letter was **ͱ**, or, according to another form, **Ͱ**.

In the fourth age there were twenty-four letters; and the Name of God, according to the arrangement of the third age, was a secret.

The fifth age was, as it is now, that is, there were thirty-eight letters; and the Name of God, according to the arrangement of the third age, was kept a secret.

THE THREE SYMBOLS OF SCIENCES.

There have been three symbols of sciences in use by the nation of the Cymry from the beginning.

The symbol of word and speech, that is to say, a letter, ten fold, sixteen fold, twenty fold, and twenty-four fold.

The first of the three, in respect of privilege and origin, is the symbol of word and speech, that is to say, a letter.

The second, the symbol of harmony, that is to say, tone and music.

The third, the symbol of number, which is thus,—

$$\wedge \quad \vee \quad | \quad \diamondsuit \quad \vee \quad \curlyvee \quad \curlyvee \quad < \quad > \quad \times$$
$$1 \quad 2 \quad 3 \quad 4 \quad 5 \quad 6 \quad 7 \quad 8 \quad 9 \quad 10$$

That is to say, one, two, three, four, five, six, seven, eight, nine, ten, one-ten and one, one-ten and two, one-ten and three, one-ten and four, one-ten and five, one-ten and six, one-ten and seven, one-ten and eight, one-ten and nine, two-tens; and as before to three-tens, four-tens, five-tens, six-tens, seven-tens, eight-tens, nine-tens, a hundred; and to a thousand; and from thence to ceugant. It is a secret kept from the beginning by the voice of the Gorsedd of the Bards of the Isle of Britain; and it was first appointed as a special art in the sciences of wisdom by Tydain, father of Awen, who also arranged the symbols of the art of musical

ddigan Arwest herwydd llafar, a Thant, a megin, fal mae'n ddangosiadol ar gof Cyfrinach Beirdd Ynys Prydain. (O Ail Lyfr Cyfrinach Beirdd Ynys Prydain—Ac o'r Yniales.)

Achwaneger a ganlyn at ddosparth yr awgrym uchod.

X—2 X—3 X—4 X—5 X—6 X—7 X—8 X—9 X—⟨

—neu X X a rhai a ddodant ◇ am gant, X ◇ am fil.—

Y TAIR AWGRYM CYSSEFIN.—TAIR AWGRYM COELBREN.

Llyma Ddosparth yr Awgrym.

Tair awgrym a fuant o'r Dechreuad ar gof a chadw gan Feirdd a Doethion Cenedl y Cymry; nid amgen

1 Awgrym gair iaith ag ymadrodd, sef Llythyr, o'r awgrymau y gwneir gair gweledig, ac o'r geiriau iaith weledig, a llafar gweledig.

2 Awgrym Erddigan a goslef, sef arwyddion Llais a llafar Cerdd Arwest, a Cherdd dant. 3 Ac Awgrym Rhif a mantol.

Awgrym Rhif a ddangosir dan arwyddon Dengnod llafar gair ac ymadrodd, sef y dengnod llythyr cyssefinion, sef ai cedwir yn gyfrinach gan feirdd Cenedl y Cymry dan gyfrwym adduned, ag nis gellir eu dattrin yn amgen nag i Fardd dan ddamdwng adduned Bywyd ac Angau, eithr er dysgu 'r werin nid y dengnod damdwng yw 'r modd eithr y nodau rhif sathred fal y maent ar gof a gwybod gwlad a

---

[1] "The Yniales. That book, the work of Hopkin ap Thomas of Glyn Tawy, contained various matters, memorials, and sciences appertaining to things advantageous to be known. He lived in Ynys Tawy, and made the Gwernllwyn Chwith. Llywelyn the Red, son of Meurig the Aged, sang his praise."—MS.

In a poem addressed to Hopkin ap Thomas by Davydd y Coed, who flourished 1300—1350, mention is made of the Yniales as being in the former's possession.

" ———— mae yn ei lys
Eur ddar y Lucidarius
A'r Greal ar *Yniales*."

" ———— There are in his court,
The golden oak, Elucidarius,
And the Greal and *Yniales*."—Myv. Arch. vol. i. p. 494.

harmony, in respect of voice, string, and bellows, as is exhi-
bited in the memorials of the Bards of the Isle of Britain.
(From the Second Book of the Secret of the Bards of the
Isle of Britain, and from the Yniales.[1])

Let the following be added to the above system of symbols;—X, 2 X, 3 X, 4 X, 5 X, 6 X, 7 X, 8 X, 9 X,
<, or X X; but some put ◊ for a hundred, and X ◊ for
a thousand.

THE THREE PRIMITIVE SYMBOLS.—THE THREE COELBREN
SYMBOLS.

Here is the system of Symbols.

There have been three symbols remembered and preserved
from the beginning by the Bards and Sages of the nation of
the Cymry ; namely,—

1. The symbol of word[2] and speech, that is, letter. It is
from the symbols that a visible word is formed, and from
the words a visible language, and visible vocality.

2. The symbol of harmony and tone, that is, the signs of
the sound and utterance of vocal song, and instrumental[3]
song.

3. The symbol of number and weight.

The symbols of number are exhibited under the signs of
the ten vocal characters of word and speech, that is, the ten
characters of the primitive letters, which are kept secret by
the Bards of the nation of the Cymry under the obligation
of a vow, and may not be divulged to other than a Bard
under the sworn vow of life and death. Nevertheless, for
the purpose of instructing the common people, the sworn
ten characters are not the means, but the trite signs of
number, such as are in the memory and knowledge of a

---

[2] Al. "of language."　　　[3] Lit. "stringed."

Chenedl addwyn, ac yn un ac ymbwyll addwynder a thair
sail gwybodau Dysgeidiaeth, a thri arwyddon cenedl addwyn
ac ysgolgar.

Llyma lafariaith awgrym herwydd ai dangoser dan arwyddon Rhif sathredig y Cenedloedd addwynion dan gred
a Bedydd.

1 un   2 dau   3 tri—4 pedwar—5 pump—6 chwech—7
saith—8 wyth—9 naw—0 deg—ac o flaen yr 0 y rhif a fo
arno.   Nid amgen unneng, 10. 20 deuneng. 3.* trineng.
4* pedryneng. 50 pumneng—60 chweneng. 70 seithneng
neu seitheng 80 wythneng neu wyneng—90 nawneng, 100
cant.

11 Unneng ac un, neu deg ac un
12 Unneng a dau, neu deg a dau
13 Unneng a thri, neu deg a thri
14 Unneng a phedwar, neu deg a phedwar
15 Unneng a phump, neu deg a phump
16 Unneng a chwech, neu deg a chwech
17 Unneng a saith, neu deg a saith
18 Unneng ac wyth, neu deg ac wyth
19 Unneng a naw, neu deg a naw
20 Deuneng ⎤ Ac un, neu dau a deuneng. &
30 Trineng ⎬ Ar un am bob lliosneng arall,
40 Pedryneng ⎦ hyd gant.

101 Cant ac un—Cant a dau &c.   Neu un a chant, dau
chant &c.   ac fal hynny ar bob lliosgant.

101 Cant ac un, 120 Cant a deuneng, 125 Cant a deuneng
a phump &c. ac fal hynny am bob lliosgant hyd Fil &c.
Ac fal hynny ar bob lliosmil hyd myrdd, ac ar bob llios
myrdd hyd Fyrddiwn ac ar bob llios myrddiwn, ac yn yr
un modd ym mlaen hyd

Buna, neu mwnda—ac ymlaen hyd

Gattyrfa—ac ymlaen hyd

Rhiallu—ac o'r Rhiallu i'r

Manred—ac o'r manred i'r

* These figures were evidently intended to be 30 and 40 respectively.

civilized country and nation, and in unison with the sense of civilization, and the three foundations of the sciences of learning, and the three signs of a civilized and scholastic nation.

Here is a description of the symbols, as they are exhibited under the trite signs of number in use by the civilized nations of Belief and Baptism.

1 one, 2 two, 3 three, 4 four, 5 five, 6 six, 7 seven, 8 eight, 9 nine, 0 ten, and placing before the 0 the number which it has, thus, 10 one-ten, 20 two-tens, 30 three-tens, 40 four-tens, 50 five-tens, 60 six-tens, 70 seven-tens, 80 eight-tens, 90 nine-tens, 100 hundred. 11 one-ten and one, or ten and one, 12 one-ten and two, or ten and two, 13 one-ten and three, or ten and three, 14 one-ten and four, or ten and four, 15 one-ten and five, or ten and five, 16 one-ten and six, or ten and six, 17 one-ten and seven, or ten and seven, 18 one-ten and eight, or ten and eight, 19 one-ten and nine, or ten and nine, 20 two-tens, 30 three-tens, 40 four-tens— and one, or two, and two-tens, &c., one being added for every other plurality of tens as far as a hundred; 101 a hundred and one,—a hundred and two, &c., or one and a hundred, two and a hundred, &c., and so for every additional hundred; 101 a hundred and one, 120 a hundred and two-tens, 125 a hundred and two-tens and five, &c., and so for every additional hundred as far as a thousand; and so for every additional thousand as far as a myriad, and for every additional myriad as far as a million, and for every additional million; and so on, in the same manner, as far as buna or mwnda; and on as far as cattyrva; [1] and on as far as rhiallu; [2] and from rhiallu to manred; [3] and from man-

---

[1] Cattyrva (cad-tyrva) means literally, the crowd of battle.

[2] Rhiallu, (rhi-allu,) the power of a sovereign; army of a country.

Manred, (man-rhed,) the elementary particles of creation.

Cyfanred—ac o'r Cyfanred i'r

Ceugant—lle nid oes ond Duw ai gwybydd.

Or Brith Cyfarwydd cynnulliad Antoni Powel o Lwydarth yn Nhir Iarll, ynghylch 1580.

Yn Llyfr Llywelyn Sion fal hynn—

Tair Awgrym Coelbren y sydd nid amgen Awgrym iaith a llafar yn bedwar awgrym ar hugain.

Awgrym Arwest ac Erddig, ac o henynt y mae saith ni amgen, a. b. c. d. e. f. g. Ac awgrymau goslef au gelwir, a goslefiaid Arwest. A phump awgrym amser, sc. Γ Τ Ҥ Ҥ ҤҤ. a'r rhain yn arwyddo amserau y goslefiaid, a lle dangoser goslefiaid noethion—yr Amserau uwch eu pennau, a lle dodir peleidr, sef pedair paladr arwest, yr amserau ar y pelydr au cyfryngau.

RHIFOEDD.

Paham y gofynner rhifoedd ar ddosparthau ?

Achos hawsineb Cof, cans lle bo rhif y bydd gwybod, ac heb rif a phwys a mesur nis gellir gwybodaeth ar ddim, wrth hynny rhif yw un o dri sail gwybodaeth a ddoder ar ddosparth rhif hynny a gofier, bynnag o rif y bo, ag ar bob un yn hynny o rif y bydd adrif—ag ad-ddosparth, a hynny er trefnu ar gof cans o drefn y gwneir cof ar bethau a gwybodau, ag am hynny y dywedir " nid cof ond trefn "—hefyd " nid trefn ond dosparth," " nid dosparth ond rhif pwys a mesur," a hynny yn wybodedig, ag yn gadarn o ansawdd, ag yn warantedig o farn doethion."

---

[1] Cyvanred, (cyd-man-rhed,) an aggregate of the elementary particles of creation.

[2] Ceugant (cau-cant,) an enclosing circle, being the term used by the Bards to denote the infinite space which God alone traverses.

As these several terms were borrowed to represent particular figures in the Numeration Table of the Bards, it would seem that at first they respectively presented to the Bardic eye definite ideas of numbers, such indeed as those which

red to cyvanred ;[1] and from cyvanred to ceugant,[2] which God only knows.

From the "Brith Cyvarwydd," compiled by Anthony Powell of Llwydarth in Tir Iarll, about 1580.

In the Book of Llywelyn Sion thus ;—

There are three series of Coelbren symbols, namely, the symbols of language and speech, being twenty-four symbols; the symbols of music and harmony, of which there are seven, namely, a, b, c, d, e, f, g ; and they are called the symbols of tone, and the tones of music ; and the five symbols of time, namely, ⌐ ⊤ ⊬ ⊞ ⊞ , which signify the times of the tones. Where bare tones are exhibited, the times are put over them, but where staves are used, that is, the four staves of music, the times are represented on the staves and intervening spaces.

NUMBERS.

Why do arrangements require numbers?

To facilitate the memory, for where there is number, there is knowledge, but without number and weight and measure, there can be no knowledge of anything, therefore number is one of the three foundations of knowledge. That which is laid down in the system of numbers will be remembered, whatever number it may be; and every one of such numbers will be divided and re-arranged, for the regulation of the memory, because it is from order that the memorials of things and sciences are formed; wherefore it is said " there is no memory but order "—also " there is no order but system "—" there is no system but number, weight, and measure"—the same being known, fixed by nature, and confirmed by the judgment of wise men.

---

were afterwards attached to them. This view is supported by the fact that the Romans considered their *cateiva* as composed of a definite number of men, namely, six thousand.

Pa rif oreu ar ddosparth ?

Rhif ansoddedig lle ai gwypper, sef a ddycco arno y cyfan
parth rhyw ag ansawdd o'r hynn a ddoder yn ddosparthedig
ar hynny o rif, a goreu fydd y lleiaf o rif lle gellir adrif ar
hynny, ag nid dosparth heb rif ag adrif, a hynn a elwir y
Rhif cyssefin neu'r gysefinrif. ag o fewn i bob un o honaw y
bydd adrif ag o hynny y bydd dosparth, eithr y mae rhifoedd unawddedigion megis y mae tri ag ar hwnnw y bydd
dechreu canol a diwedd, a'r lleiaf a'r mwyaf, a'r cyfrwng. a
hefyd un peth, a pheth arall yngwrth, a thrydydd o beth ai
cynghyd, fal y mae modd, medr, a mynn, sef o bydd modd
gallai na bai medr, ag o bydd modd a medr ynghyd ni les-
hant heb au cyngyd sef mynn neu ewyllys hyall a ymwnelo
ar ddau arall, ag amlaf o rif ar ddosparth yw tri.

Rhif ansawddedig o ryw hefyd yw pedwar, sef y bydd ar
hwnnw adrif o ddau—sef dau hanner, a phedwar pedryfed
chwech hefyd o dri dau—a naw o dri thri ydynt rifoedd
ansoddedig ar ddosparth. Deg hefyd y sydd Rhif dosparthus o gwbl cans ar y deg y mae cylch rhif yn ymbennu.
Deg o ddegau yw cant, deg cant y mil, deg mil yn y
myrdd, deg myrdd yn y Rhiallu, deg Rhiallu yn y Buna,
Deg Buna yn y Gattorfa, deg gatorfa yn yr Annant, deg
Annant yn y Trwn, a deg cylch rhif y gelwir y rhai hynn.
Rhif dosparthus hefyd y gelwir y rhai a ellir eu rhannu yn
gyfartal, megis y mae pedwar ag wyth, ag unarbymtheg, a
phedwar ar hugain, a mwy o ddosparth gan adrif a geir ar
bedwar arhugain nag ar un mesur arall cans arnaw y mae
dau ddeuddeg, a thri wyth, a phedwar chwech, a chwech
pedwar, ac wyth tri, a deuddeg dau.

---

[1] Wallice, "cant," which literally means a circle. Ceugant again is the enclosing circle, which comprehends all.

[2] The elementary principles of sound.

[3] A throne, a circle.

Ag yn y *trwn* gwn i trig,
A diobaith ei debig.

What number is the best for any system?

A natural number, where such is known, namely, that which will convey in itself the whole, in respect of kind and condition, of what is arranged by that number ; and the best will be the least number, where it will admit of a division. There is no arrangement without number and its division, and this is called the primary number, having within it a division, from which comes an arrangement. But there are united numbers, such as is three, which has a beginning, a middle, and an end, and the least, greatest, and intermediate, also one thing, another thing opposite to it, and a third thing joining them together, as means, skill, and will, for if there be means, it may be there will be skill, and if there be means and skill together, they will be of no avail without what will join them, namely, desire or effectual will, that will bear upon the other two : the number mostly used for arrangements is three.

A number, natural in kind, is also four, which may be divided into two, that is, two halves, and four quarters ; six also into three twos, and nine into three threes, are natural numbers used in arrangements. Ten is likewise altogether a systematic number, for it is in ten that the cycle of numbers terminates. Ten tens are a hundred,[1] ten hundreds a thousand, ten thousands in the myriad, ten myriads in the rhiallu, ten rhiallus in the buna, ten bunas in the cattorva, ten cattorvas in the annant,[2] ten annants in the trwn ;[3] and these are called the ten cycles of number. Those also which may be divided equally are called distributive numbers, such as four, and eight, and sixteen, and twenty-four ; and twenty-four admits of more divisions than any other quantity, for it has two twelves, three eights, four sixes, six fours, eight threes, and twelve twos.

And in the throne I know he dwells,
And there is no hope of his equal.
Huw ap Dafydd, 1480—1520.

O

Paham y mae rhif tri ar arfer gan feirdd ynys Prydain yn eu gwersi addysg?

Achos y bydd hawdd cofiaw tri, ac achos y gellir y triffrif ansawdd yn adrif ar dri, sef un, arall, a chynghyd, a'r hawsaf ei gofio a fydd oreu ar bob addysg, a byrraf o ddosparth yw tri, a hawsaf ei gofiaw yw'r byrraf a ellir yn ddosparthus. Am hynny y dodasant feirdd Ynys Prydain eu haddysg au doethineb ar ddosparth trioedd mal y bai hawdd eu dysgu a'u cofiaw i'r rhai ni fedrant ar lyfr, cans mwy rhif yr anllythyrenog na'r llythyrenog o ddynion. Ag i'r mwyaf o rif y dylit addysg a doethineb a gwybodau defodawl a theuluaidd parth arbennigion pwyll.

NAW GRADD YR AWGRYM.

(O Lyfr Ben Simon.)

Un ddengwaith a wna ddeg. — *Deg* ddengwaith a wna Gant. Cant ddengwaith a wna Fil. — *Mil* ddengwaith a wna Fyrdd — *Myrdd* ddengwaith a wna *Funa.* — *Buna* ddengwaith a wna Gattrif (gatyrfa in al.)

A chwedi hyn y rhif yn ol y degau, sef deg cattrif, cant cattrif, milgattrif, myrdd gattrif, Bunagattrif, a Chattrif o gattrifoedd, neu gad-gattrifoedd, cancadgattrif, milgad gattrifoedd, myrddgad gattrifoedd, cattrif-gadgattrifoedd. Yna denghattrifgadgattrifoedd, ac yn ol hynny naw cylch y nawradd a hynny yn oes oesoedd, ac ymhen hynny o gylch adnewyddu pob peth, hyd ymhen nawcylched newyddiant, a elwir nawradd nef. Ac ymhen pob cylched dechre o'r newydd.

---

[1] The number of battle. In al. cattyrva.

[2] Tad *nawnef* i ti dyn anwyl
Tudur aeth at Tad yr wyl.

The Father of *the nine heavens* to thee, beloved man,
Tudur has gone to the Father of the feast.
Sion ap Hywel ap Ll. Vychan—1460, 1490.

Why is the number three used by the Bards of the Isle of Britain in their lessons of instruction?

Because it is easier to remember three, and because the three principal conditions form the division of three, that is, one, and another, and conjunctive; and the easiest to remember is the best of every learning; and the shortest distribution is three, and the easiest to remember is the shortest that can be arranged. On this account the Bards of the Isle of Britain arranged their learning and wisdom in triads, that those who were unacquainted with books might easily learn and remember them, for the number of the illiterate is greater than that of the literate, and it is to the majority that learning, and wisdom, and institutional and domestic sciences, in respect of precise meaning, ought to be imparted.

THE NINE DEGREES OF NUMERALS.

(From the Book of Ben Simon.)

One ten times will make ten, ten ten times will make a hundred, a hundred ten times will make a thousand, a thousand ten times will make a myriad, a myriad ten times will make a buna, a buna ten times will make a cattriv.[1]

After this the number is according to tens, thus; ten cattrivs, a hundred cattrivs, a thousand cattrivs, a myriad cattrivs, a buna cattrivs, cattriv of cattrivs, or cad-gattrivs, a hundred cad-gattrivs, a thousand cad-gattrivs, a myriad cad-gattrivs, a cattriv cad-gattrivs; then ten cattriv cad-gattrivs. After that, the nine circles of the nine degrees, for ever and ever; and at the end of such a circle, the renovation of all things to the end of the nine circles of the state of novation, which are called the nine degrees of heaven.[2] And at the end of every circle a beginning anew.

Mae gorph mewn bedd,
Gwyn yn gorwedd ;

DOSPARTH YR AWGRYM.

Llyma ddosparth yr Awgrym, nid amgen no bannau Celfyddyd Eirifyddiaeth (Llyfr D. Rissiart Llandochen) a threiglaw o fann i fann wrth hynn o bwyll sef rhif ei hunan pob un o'r bannau ar y rhyw fann y bytho hwnnw ei hunan a wna 'r nesaf goruwch iddaw, a llymma enwau 'r bannau.

Un,
Deg,
Cant,
Mil,
Myrdd,
Myrddiwn,
Mwnt,
Rhiallu
Buna,
Tyrfa,
Catyrfa,
Cadrawd.

Sef, deg un yw deg—deg deg yw Cant, deg Cant yw mil—deg can mil yw myrdd, neu o fodd arall mil o filoedd yw myrdd—myrdd myrddoedd yw myrddiwn — myrddiwn myrddiynau yw mwnt—mwnt myntau yw rhiallu — rhiallu rhialluoedd yw Buna — Buna bunaoedd yw tyrfa, Tyrfa tyrfaoedd Catyrfa—Catyrfa Catyrfaoedd yw Cadrawd. Cadrawd Cadrodau yw rhif bywydau o Annwn hyd wynfyd, &c.   (Lln Sion.)

RHIFYDDIAETH.

Un, pump, deg, pumtheg, ugain, cant, mil, myrdd, myrddiwn, bunaf, myndaf, brëon, catyrfa, gwrmwnt, rhiallu, a'r ceugant, a hwnnw ni ellir rhif arno.

DOSPARTH YR AWGRYM.

Un,	Mil, deg cant,
Deg	Myrdd, dengmil
Cant, deg o ddegau	Mwnt, dengmyrdd,

Mae enaid e
'N rhodio 'r *gradde.*

His fair corpse is lying in the grave,
His soul is perambulating the *gradations.*
Thos. ap Ieuan ap Rhys, 1600.

THE SYSTEM OF NUMERALS.

Here is the system of numerals, that is, the particulars of the art of Arithmetic, (from the Book of D. Richard, Llandochen.) They are removed from point to point according to this method, that is, every one of the points being itself a number, on whatever point it may be, will make the next to be above it. These are the names of the points :—One, ten, hundred, thousand, myriad, million, mwnt, rhiallu, buna, tyrva, catyrva, cadrawd.

That is, ten ones are ten, ten tens are a hundred, ten hundreds are a thousand, ten hundred thousands are a myriad, a myriad myriads are a million, a million millions are a mwnt,[1] a mwnt mwnts are a rhiallu, a rhiallu rhiallus are a buna, a buna bunas are a tyrva,[2] a tyrva tyrvas are a cattyrva, a cattyrva cattyrvas are a cadrawd,[3] a cadrawd cadrawds are the number of lives from Annwn to Gwynvyd, &c. (Llywelyn Sion.)

ARITHMETIC.

One, five, ten, fifteen, twenty, hundred, thousand, myriad, million, bunav, myndav, breon, catyrva, gwrmwnt, rhiallu, and ceugant, which cannot be numbered.

THE SYSTEM OF NUMERALS.

One,	A thousand, ten hundreds,
Ten,	A myriad, ten thousands,
A hundred, ten tens,	Mwnt, ten myriads,

---

[1] " Mwnt " is probably of cognate origin with a *mons, mount, mynydd.*

[2] Tyrva, Lat. turba, a multitude, a crowd.

[3] Cadrawd, (cad-rhawd,) the rage or course of battle ; an army.

Rhiallu, dengmwnt,   Catyrfa, deg Tyrfa

Mwnda ⎱ deg rhiallu   Cadrawd, deg Catyrfa.
Buna ⎰   O Lyfr Mr Cobb o Gaer
Tyrva, deg Buna, neu fwnda i   Dydd.

A deg gradd yr Awgrym y gelwir y rhain, ac o fedru pob ysmudiad a thrafod ar yr Awgrym y gwybyddir pob gwirionedd, parth Rhif, a mesur, a phwys.

RHIFYDDIAETH.

Rhifyddiaid-ion.   Rhifoedd.

Λ	⨼	I	◇	V	⅄	ᒉ	ᐱ	<	>	>Λ	>⨼	>I	>◇
1	2	3	4	5	6	7	8	9	10	11	12	13	14

>V	>⅄	>ᒉ	>ᐱ	><	>>	>>Λ	>>⨼	>>I
15	16	17	18	19	20	21	22	23

>>◇	>>V	>>⅄	>>ᒉ	>>ᐱ	>><	>>>
24	25	26	27	28	29	30

>>>>	ᗞ	ᗞ>	ᗞ>>	ᗞ>>>	ᗞ>>>>	◁
40	50	60	70	80	90	100

Modd arall ar y llythyrenau Rhif.

Λ	⨼	I	◇	ᚷ	⅄	ᒉ	V	И	>
1	2	3	4	5	6	7	8	9	10

A threfnu mal uchod am fwy na deg, herwydd y deg rhif yma.

◁	◁◁	◁◁◁	◁◁◁◁	V◁	⅄◁	ᒉ◁	ᐱ◁
100	200	300	400	500	600	700	800

ᐱ◁	>◁	neu M neu ◁ᗞ
900	1000	1000

hefyd fal hynn

ᗞ<.   ᗞ<<.   ᗞ<<<.   ᗞ<<<<.   ᗞᗞ   neu ◁ᗞ

ᐊM

VM	ᐊM	>M	X	⨯◇	⊕	⊕
5000	100000	10000	myrdd	1000000		

Rhiallu, ten mwnts,

Mwnda, ⎱
Buna, ⎰ ten rhiallus,

Tyrva, ten bunas, or mwnda, to a

Cattyrva, ten tyrvas,

Cadrawd, ten cattyrvas.

From the Book of Mr..
Cobb of Cardiff.

These are called the ten degrees of Numerals ; and it is from being acquainted with every movement and treatment of the numerals that every truth in respect of number, measure, and weight is known.

NUMERALS.

Numeration.   Numbers.

Λ ⊿ Ɩ ◊ V Ƴ Ʋ Γ < > >Λ ᴊ >Ɩ >◊
1 2 3 4 5 6 7 8 9 10 11 12 13 14

>V >Ƴ >Ʋ >Γ >< >> >>V >>⊿ >>Ɩ
15 16 17 18 19 20 21 22 23

>>◊ >>V >>Ƴ >>Ʋ >>Γ >>< >>>
24 25 26 27 28 29 30

>>>> Ɒ Ɒ> Ɒ>> Ɒ>>> Ɒ>>>> ◁
40 50 60 70 80 90 100

Another mode according to the numeral letters.

Λ ⊿ Ɩ ◊ Γ Ƴ Ʋ V ᴎ >
1 2 3 4 5 6 7 8 9 10

And for more than ten arranged as above according to these ten numerals.

◁ ◁◁ ◁◁◁ ◁◁◁◁ V◁ Ƴ◁ Ʋ◁ ᴎ◁
100 200 300 400 500 600 700 800

Ɑ◁ >◁ or M or ◁Ɒ
900 1000 1000

Also thus ;—

Ɒ< Ɒ<< Ɒ<<< Ɒ<<<< ⱰⱰ or ◁
◁M

VM ◁M >M X X◊ ◊◊ ⊗
5000 100000 10000 a myriad 1000000

Arall

W ·   X   ✕✕

5000   100000   1000000

RHIFOEDD YR AWGRYM.

1	2	3	4	5	6	7	8	9	10

Arall

NODAU RHIFVDDIAETH YR HEN GYMRY,
SEF YR AWGRYMIAID.

Un				Chwech
dau				Saith
tri				wyth
pedwar				naw
pump				deg

Ac o fodd arall

neu 10

cant

cant. neu   . hef. C. hefyd 100

mil—hefyd   hefyd   hefyd 1000

Another,—

MM   **X**   **XƆ**
5000   10000   1000000

THE NUMERALS.

1   2   3   4   5   6   7   8   9   10

Others,—

THE ARITHMETICAL CHARACTERS OF THE ANCIENT CYMRY; THAT IS, THE NUMERALS.

J	One,	6	six,
⅂	two,	Λ	seven,
3	three,	8	eight,
ẟ	four,	9	nine,
ς	five,	∅	ten.

J   ⅂   3   ẟ   ς   ƀ   Λ   8   9   ∅

J   ⅂   3   8   ς   ƀ   Λ   8   9   ∅

Another mode,—

1   ⅂   3   ℓ   9   6   ⅂   8   9   ∅   or 10

1   ⅂   3   ℓ   G   6   Λ   8   9   ∅

1   ⅂   3   8   ς   6   Λ   8   9   ∅

1   2   3   ⅂   9   6   λ   8   9   ∅   ⊕   a hundred

⊕ a hundred; or ⊗ ; also **C**; also 100.

⊖ℓ a thousand; also ↻ ; also ⅁ ; also 1000.

P

Y TRI AWGRYM

Tri rhyw Awgrym y sydd—Awgrym llythyr a alwai yr
hen Awduron Awgrym Cyrven ; Awgrym rhif, ag Awgrym
Arwydd fal y mae pais Arfau, ag a saif ar gelfyddyd arwyddfardd.

DEFNYDDION IAITH AC YMADRODD.

Tri Defnyddion Iaith ag ymadrodd—Llythyr—Sill—a
gair.

Tri Defnyddion ymadrodd—gair—Pwyll—a Chystrywen.

Ugain Llythyren cyssefiniaid y sydd, ac o henynt dri ar
ddeg a elwir yn gydseiniaid, ag o'r rhai hynny y teirdd
saith adlawiaid, a saith, o'r cysefiniaid a elwir Llafariaid, ac
eraill au galwant udleisiaid.

Y TRI CHAEOGION BEIRDD.

Tri chaeogion Beirdd ynys Prydain Tydai Bardd Huon
a wnaeth gyfannedd gyntaf ym mraint gosgordd ar genedl
y Cymry. a Rhufawn Fardd a wnaeth ddosparth a braint
ar gyfar Trefgordd, a Melgin ap Einigan Gawr a wnaeth
awgrym ar Iaith ag ymadrodd gyntaf, a Chae a rodded i
bob un am ei benn sef a'r Darllys awelfar.

(O Trioedd amrafaelion a gasglwyd o Ysgrif-lyfrau amrafaelion ym Morganwg.)

---

[1] Probably Tydain, the father of Awen. See Note 2, p. 40.

[2] The same, most likely, as Hu the Mighty, who in the Triads (57, Third
Series) is said to have himself "first collected and disposed the nation of the
Cymry into tribes."

[3] Mentioned by Edmund Prys in one of his poems See Note 1, p. 34.

THE THREE SYMBOLS.

There are three kinds of symbol: the symbol of letter, which the ancient authors called the symbol of cyrven; the symbol of number; and the symbol of blazonry, as a coat of arms, which belongs to the art of a herald-bard.

THE MATERIALS OF LANGUAGE AND SPEECH.

The three materials of language and speech: letter; syllable; and word.

The three materials of speech: word; sense; and sentence.

There are twenty primitive letters, thirteen of which are called consonants; and from them seven secondaries are derived; and seven of the primitives are called vowels, but others call them scunds.

THE THREE WREATHED BARDS.

The three wreathed Bards of the Isle of Britain: Tydai,[1] the Bard of Huon,[2] who was the first that arranged the mode of dwelling according to clans for the nation of the Cymry; and Rhuvawn[3] the Bard, who conferred system and privilege upon the co-aration of a township; and Melgin,[4] son of Einigan the Giant, who was the first that made a symbol for language and speech. And a wreath was given to each around his head, that is, of the air-growing misletoe. (From various Triads, collected out of different manuscripts in Glamorgan.)

---

[4] His name also occurs in the same poem :—

Melchin a Mefin myfyr.

Melgin and contemplative Mevin.

COELBREN Y BEIRDD.

Coelbren y Beirdd, herwydd Llyfr Llywelyn Sion.

Yr hen Gymry, au prydyddion, au doethion o wyr wrth
lyfr a nattaynt dorri llythyriaeth ar goed, achaws nid oedd
yn eu hamser nhwy or dechreu wybodaeth nag am bapyr
nag am blagawd, a llyma ddangos y modd y gwnaent eu
llyfrau, ac wyneblun dull a modd,—

Cyntaf o beth a wneir yw'r pillwydd sef y Cyffon Cyrfin,
pob cyff yn ddau hanner fal hyn

sef rhif o dyllau yn y cyff, a hannerau'r tyllau yn y naill
hanner, ag yn y llall yr hannerau eraill, sef pan y doder y
ddau hanner ynghyd y bydd rhill o dyllau cyfain yn rhestr
o'r naill ben i'r llall ynghanol y cyff neu'r Pill, a chyff arall
or un rhyw a maint a fydd. gwedi hynny gwydd eraill a
elwir ebillwydd* ac ebillwydd, a phob un fal hynn,

---

* Sic in MS.; probably the first should be *ebill* or *ebillion.*

[1] Pillwydd, (pill-gwydd,) wooden stems.   [2] Pill=bill=billet.

[3] Ebillwydd, (ebill-gwydd,) a wooden piercer.   Ebill also comes from pill.

COELBREN OF THE BARDS.

The Bardic Coelbren, according to the book of
Llywelyn Sion.

The primitive Cymry, and their poets, and book-wise
men, were accustomed to cut letters on wood, because in
their time from the beginning there was no knowledge
either of paper or plagawd, and here is exhibited the manner in which they constructed their books and the figure of
the mode and manner.

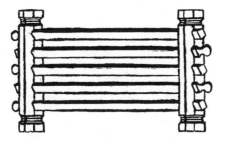

The first thing made was the *pillwydd*,[1] or the side posts,
each post being in two halves, thus,

That is, there is a number of holes in the post, the halves of
the holes being in either half, and the other halves in the
other, so that when the two halves are put together, there
will be a row of perfect holes in a line from one end to the
other, in the middle of the post, or *pill*.[2] There will be also
another post of the same kind and size. After that, other
staves, called *ebillwydd*,[3] each of them thus,—

mynegler y naill ben ar llall fal ai llawlunier yma, a gosod
pill caeedig a chlymedig am fynyglau rhif a fynner o ebillwydd am y naill pen ag am y llall, ag fal hynny eu cyrfinaw
ynghyd pillwyd ac ebillion ar ddull clwyd, ar ebillion bob
un yn troi cylch amgylch gerfydd eu mynyglau yn y pillwydd sef y cyffon.   Ar yr ebillion y torrir y llythyrau a
chyllell gyfallwy ar bob ochor or pedwar i bob ebill, a gwedi
darllen un ochr, troi ail ochr i fynydd, gwedi hynny y trydydd ochr, ag ar ol hynny pedwerydd ochr, a darllen pob
ochr fal ai trother i fynydd.

    rhaid yw rhathu y cornelau ar hyd pob un o'r ebillion hyd
y mynyglau, fel nad elo doriad llythyr ar un wyneb yn un
neu yn gyttrwch a llythyrau'r wyneb arall, ag fal hynny
pob wyneb o'r pedwar.

    Modd arall y sydd ar gyrfinaw Coelbren y Beirdd, nid
amgen, gwneuthur y pillwydd sef y cyffon yn gyfain yn lle
eu bod yn hannerau, a rhestr o dyllau ar hyd y canol, au
tyllu ag ebill dân, a gwneuthur yr ebillion yn golynog un
pen ag arall, au gosod gerfydd eu colynau yn y pillwydd, a
deupen pob un or pillwydd hefyd yn golynawg, ar colynau'n
myned i dyllau trawsbillwydd tros lathau a wneur ar hynn
o ddull

pob twll yn myned am golyn cyff yn dyn. ag fal hynny
cyfrwymaw'n gadarn y cwbl yn gyrfin ar ddull clwyd, a
chofio hawsder tro ag attro i bob un o'r ebillion pennau'r
ebillion a fyddant hyd cymmal Bawd drwy'r cyffon y naill
pen yn garn troi ar llall yn le torri nod rhif yr ebill; colynau'r cyffon hefyd a fyddant yr un hyd drwy dyllau'r
trawsbillwydd cyfrwym ag ychydig fynyglaeth iddynt, a

---

   [1] The plural of ebill.

     Ebillion gweddillion gwawd.
     Staves of the relics of praise.
               D. ab Gwilym.

At one end and the other let a neck be formed, as is delineated here, and let a closed and tied pill be placed round the
necks of as many ebillwydd as may be required, at both ends.
And thus let them be joined together, pillwydd and ebillion,[1] in the form of a hurdle; the ebillion, each one of them,
turning all round by their necks in the pillwydd, or posts.
On the ebillion the letters are cut with an efficient knife,
that is, on each of the four sides of every ebill; and when
one side has been read, the second side is turned upwards,
after that the third side, and after that the fourth side, each
side being read as it is turned upwards.

The corners, along each of the ebillion as far as the necks,
must be trimmed down, that the cutting of a letter on one
face may not become one with, or break into the letters of
the other face, and so with every one of the four faces.

There is another mode of constructing the Coelbren of
the Bards, namely, by making the pillwydd, or the posts,
entire, instead of their being in halves, having a row of
holes along the middle, bored with a fire auger; the ebillion
being pivotted at either end, and placed as to their pivots in
the pillwydd. The two ends of each of the pillwydd likewise should be pivotted, the pivots passing into the holes of
cross pillwydd, or transverse staves, made after this manner,—

each hole tightly encircling the pivot of the post; and thus
are the whole firmly tied together, and conjoined, in the
form of a hurdle. Bearing in mind the facility of turning
and re-turning in respect of each one of the ebillion, the
ends of the ebillion will be the length of a thumb's joint
through the posts, one end being a turning hilt, the other a
place on which to cut the numerical mark of the ebill. The
pivots of the posts will also be of the same length through
the holes of the cross pillwydd, which connect them to-

rhwymaw pob mwnwgl ag edau neu linyn cwyraid fal nas gollyngont golynau'r pillwydd or tyllau, a rhwymo'r mwnwgl onis bo rhef na'r colyn yn y rhwyllau, a phob colyn cyff yn dra thyn yn ei rhwyll, fal nad elo yngollwng nag ar ysgwyd. y pillwydd cyfrwym a elwir troslathau, ar pillwydd hefyd a elwir yn gyffon hydlath neu hydladd, au colynau yn myned yn y cyffon trosladd. mynygler lle'r linyn ar bob colyn or pillwydd hydladd. a rhwymo'n yn erbyn y troslathau, fal nad elont yngollwng. nag yn waglog. a chadarn a diwagl fydd y ffordd honn ag yn hynn gwell na'r un a wneler a chyffon dau hanner, eithr nid cyhawsed dattod ag attod yr un cyfanbill ar un dau hannerbill.

Modd cyfrwym arall y sydd ar y cyffon hydladd a throsladd, nid amgen na thorri llwnc naill hanner ar bob pen yr hydlath ar cyfryw lwnc ar bob pen troslath fal hynn—

a'r llwngc ymhob un hyd hanner y prenn, a dodir cyffon trosladd llwnc yn llwnc a'r rhai hydladd yn dynnon, ac ar draws y cyflwnc rhwymyn dynn a llinyn cwyraid, neu a thant telyn neu grwth, a theg a chadarn y ffordd honn.

Eraill a wnant ebillion, ac a wnant dwll main ag ebill dan yn neupen pob un o'r ebillion au dodi gerfydd y tyllau hynnu ar linyn neu ar dant cryf, a rhai a farnant y ffordd honn yn oreu or cwbl, sef y gellir rholo'r ebillion yn ffasgell a chlymu a'r llinyn cyfrill, a hawsaf er dwyn gydag un y ffordd honn an nad rhaid dattod arni er ffasgelli. rhaid cwlm cadarn ar bob pen y Tant fal nad elo drwy dyllau'r ebillion. a dylit hyd ddigon yn y llinyn fal y symmutter ac

---

[1] Troslath, (tros-llath,) an over or transverse rod.

[2] Cyffon, stocks, the plural of cyff, a stock, stem, trunk. Hydlath, (hydllath,) a longitudinal rod.

gether; they will be somewhat necked too, and each neck will be tied with waxed thread or string, that the pivots of the pillwydd might not drop out of the hole. The neck should be tied until it be thicker than the pivot in the hole; and the pivots of each post should be quite tight in their holes, lest it might drop or shake. The connecting pillwydd are called *troslathau*,[1] and the pillwydd also are called *cyffon hydlath* or *hydladd*,[2] their pivots passing into the transverse posts. Let the place of the string on each of the pivots of the longitudinal pillwydd be rounded, and let them be tied against the transverse staves, so that they do not become loose, or shaky. This mode is firm and steady, and in that respect better than the one which employs posts in two halves, though it is not as easy to undo and put together the frame which is made with an entire pill, as the one with a divided pill.

There is another method of connecting the longitudinal and transverse posts, that is, by cutting a semi-notch on each end of the longitudinal, and the like on each end of the transverse stave, thus,

the notch in each reaching to the middle of the stick, and putting the notches of the transverse posts tightly in those of the longitudinal ones, and tying the conjoined notches across firmly with a waxed line, or the string of harp or violin. This method is fair and firm.

Others make ebillion, and make a narrow hole with a fire auger at each end of the ebillion, and place them by those holes on a strong line or string; which some people consider the best way of all, because the ebillion may be rolled up in a bundle, and tied by the serial line. It is also, done in this way, easiest to carry with one, because it need not be unfastened in order to be bundled up. There must be a strong knot at each end of the string, that it might not slip through the holes of the ebillion; and there ought to be

y trother yr ebillion yn hawdd iddeu darllen, a mal y bo
digon o hyd yn y llinyn i glymmu'r beithynen yn un ffasgell gron lle bo raid ac achos. eisioes afrwyddaf ei darllen y
ffordd honn, a rhwyddaf dattod ag attod or holl ffyrdd
ydyw.

Rhwyddach dattod ag attod a gyfriller a phillwydd dau-
hannerog na'r un a gyfriller a phillwydd cyfain. eisioes
anghadarn a gwaglog ydyw.

Afrwyddach dattod ag attod a fo cyfrill ynghyffon cyfain,
eithr cadarnaf yw, etto trymmaf er dwyn gydag un, eisioes
goreu lle ydd ysgrifener ac inc ar ebillion llydain.

Arfer gan rai ebillwydd llydain teneuon llathraid, a
llythyru ag inc a cholynau pedroglaid i'r ebillwydd, a
thyllau llinyn drwyddynt, mal y rhettont yr ebillwydd ar
y llinyn ynghyd neu ar led fal y bo achos.

Arfer a modd arall ar ebillwydd llydain eu gwneuth yn
wynebgrwn fal hyn yn y trythor traws

a thynni r ymylau yn deneuon heb adael o drwch min amcan trwch noblyn, neu ychydig bach mwy.   Mae hynn yn
ysgafnhau, eithr mwy angnghyno'r tynniad ynghyd. am
nas gorweddant yr ebillwydd yn gedyrn y naill ar y llaill.

---

[1] This was the name applied to the Wooden Book of the Bards, meaning
originally what is plain or clear, an elucidator. " The term has also been applied to several other things, *a weaver's slay, the cogs of a mill wheel, the rows of
human teeth, a board of wood, a slate,* peithynen y ddwyfron, clwyd y ddwyfron,
the breast bone or brisket, &c. Of the several things, and of very different natures
and appearances, the original, whence all others figuratively or similitudinarily
derive their names, must be the Book, because it is from some part, some appearance, or property to be found in it that every other derives its name that has
been so called.   All the different ideas to be found in the others separately are
united in this.   The weaver's slay is similar in its formation to the billets in the
Bard's Book when framed together. The cogs of a mill wheel resemble strikingly
the ends of those billets that project at each end.   The teeth are in similar rows.
The board and slate, before parchment or paper became known, were used
whereon to inscribe, engrave, paint, or cut letters or literary memorials.   The
arrangement of the breast bones or ribs are very similar to the billets in the

sufficient length in the string, that the ebillion might be shifted and turned so as to be easy to read, and that the string might be long enough to tie the Peithynen[1] in one round bundle, where there is need and occasion. Nevertheless, this is the most difficult way for reading it, though it is the easiest of all ways for undoing it and putting it together.

It is easier to undo and re-set that which is framed together by means of halved pillwydd, than the one which is framed by means of whole pillwydd; nevertheless it is infirm and unsteady.

It is more difficult to undo and re-set that which is framed in entire posts, but that is the strongest, though it is the heaviest to carry with one; it is also the best when persons write with ink on wide ebillion.

Some people make use of broad, thin, smooth ebillwydd, and form letters with ink by means of square pencils on the ebillwydd, having made string holes through them, that the ebillwydd might run together or apart on the string, as occasion required.

Another usage and mode in respect of wide ebillwydd is to make them oval at the transverse section,

and to render the margins thin, not leaving the thickness of the edge more than about the thickness of a noble, or very little more. This lightens it, but the drawing together is less compact, because the ebillwydd will not lie firmly one on the other.

Book and the reeds in the slay. But it is in the Book only, and in no other thing, called peithynen, that all those different ideas can be found or traced up to their origin. This is of itself a striking proof of the antiquity of this kind of Book. The probability is at least great that it was known before the weaver's slay, the cogs of a mill wheel, the use of a slate or board for inscription, &c., were known to the Welsh, and these last must have been used before parchment and paper were introduced by the Romans."—Iolo Morganwg.

Arfer ambell un ebillwydd deuled sef eu moddi fal y gellir
deuled neu ddeulinell llythyrau torr ar bob wyneb o'r traws
drythor fal hynn

ac ar hyd ganol pob wyneb rhigol deuled torr llythyr, neu
fal hynn

ffordd orchestol gynnilgamp honn trafaelus ei gwneuthur a
gwell iddei darllain na'r un ag ebillwydd pedryfal. a lle
ysgrifener ag inc ag nid a chyllell, nid rhaid rhigoli canol-
wyneb yr ebill ; rhai a wnaethant yr ebillwydd fal hynn
herwydd trosdor

a mwy lled yr, lla meddant yr ochrau fal hynn ac o hynny
hwy a mwy'r llythyrau. heb fwyhau trymder peithynen.
eithr cymmaint gwell ag y tal trafael.

Rhai a fynyglant yr ebillwydd fal y galler eu rhoi mewn
cyrfin billwydd, a chyda hynny a wnant dyllau ymhennau'r
ebillwydd mal y galler llinyn drwyddynt er hawsder dwyn
gydag un. sef eu dwyn ar linyn yn ffasgell yn lle dwyn
ynghyrfin pillwydd, gwybydded pob un ei achos ai amcan ai
Awen.

Gofaler i'r pillwydd gaead yn gadarn ac yn ogynglyn am
fynyglau'r ebillwydd, yn cadw y cwbl yn gyfrill ynghyd.

A few persons make use of ebillwydd of double thickness, that is, they modify them, so that there may be two thicknesses or two lines of inscribed letters on every face of the transverse section, thus,—

and along the middle of every face a groove twice the width of the letter engraving ; or thus,—

which is an excellent, ingenious way, troublesome to make, but better to read, than the one with the four-sided ebillwydd. And when the writing is done with ink, and not with a knife, it is not necessary to groove the middle of the surface of the ebill. Some have made the ebillwydd, in regard to the transverse section, thus,—

and more, they say, is the breadth of the sides in this way, and on that account the letters are longer and larger, without increasing the weight of the Peithynen. Its superiority is equal to the trouble bestowed on it.

Some make necks on the ebillwydd that they may be inserted in side pillwydd, and, besides, they make holes in the ends of the ebillwydd, that a string may pass through them, for the sake of facility in carrying. That is, they are carried in a bundle on a string, instead of in side pillwydd. Let every one know his reason, and purpose, and awen.

Care must be taken that the pillwydd enclose firmly and wholly the necks of the ebillwydd, keeping all in a row together.

Rhill y gelwir y maint a gyrfinir ynghyd, o'r ebillwydd, mynychaf pedwar ar hugain, a rhai a gyrfinant chwech ar hugaint, eraill saith ar hugaint, sef y tri naw, ac mewn peithynen cynnifer rhill ag y bo gofyn.

Trythor hyd pillwydd

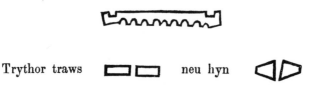

Trythor traws   neu hyn

Y pillwydd dau hanner a glymmir yn dynon ynghyd a llinynon o dannau crwth neu delyn, sef cadarnaf ydynt. rhai ai rhwymant a llinynon sidan neu a rhibanau sidan. a dwyn pob llyfrau mewn cwd sidan gwyrdd.

Modd arall ar lyfr yw Rhôl, a honno a wneir a phren crwn, a fynygler yn fain yr hyd y bo achos yn y canol, a deupen iddo ynghyssefin refder y prenn, hyd cymmal bawd, neu led bawd, fal hynn

a thrithwll drwy'r meinder a thrwyddynt ddodi llinyn i ddiogelu plagawd neu bapyr a ddoder yn ddail i droi am y rholl gynnifer. dalen ac a fynner, neu a fo achos, ac ynghyd a'r dail yn uchaf arnynt ddalen sidan hwy na'r dail papyr i droi am y cwbl yn orwisg am yr ysgrifen iddei gadw yn lan ag yn ddinam. a ffordd honn a gad ar ddeall ag arfer gwedi cael gwybod am blagawd, a gwedi hynny gwybod am bapyr.

Gwedi Rhôl fe ddychymygwyd y llyfrau y sydd yn awr

---

[1] " Rhill, (rhi-ill,) a row; a small trench or furrow; a drill."—Dr. Pughe's Dict. Drill, d-rill, is probably derived or borrowed from it.

Rhill[1] is the name given to the quantity of ebillwydd framed together, most frequently twenty-four, but some put together twenty-six, others twenty-seven, that is, the three nines. A Peithynen has as many rhills as are required.

The longitudinal section of a pillwydd,—

The transverse section—

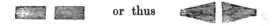

The two halved pillwydd are tied firmly with the strings of a violin or harp, as being the strongest. Some tie them with silk strings, or silk ribbons. And all books are carried in a bag of green silk.

Another form of book is the Roll, which is made of a round piece of wood, turned thin in the middle as long as may be required, having its two ends of the original thickness of the wood, the length of a thumb's joint, or a thumb's breadth, thus,—

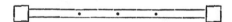

with three holes through the thin part, and a string passed through them, in order to secure the plagawd or paper, which may be placed to turn round the roll, as many leaves as may be required, or may be necessary; and together with the leaves, above them, a silk leaf longer than the paper leaves, to fold round the whole, as a covering for the writing, to keep it clean and free from damage. This method was discovered and brought to use after the knowledge of plagawd was obtained; and after that the knowledge of paper.

Subsequently to the Roll, the books now in use were de-

ar arfer. yn amser Lles ap Coel y Brenin Bedydd cyntaf yn Ynys Prydain.   Eisoes y Beirdd ar prydyddion a gadwant ar gof ac arfer yr hen gymmygedau ar Lyfrau, er cof a chadw pob hen gelfyddyd herwydd Cenedl y Cymry. ag gwybod a ddichoner ar un peth neu fodd, lle nas gellid ar arall o beth a modd gan anesgoroldeb dynghediw, ag nis dylit coll ar un rhith gwybodau daionus.

Llymma'r modd herwydd llun a gwedd y torrer Llythyr-au Coelbren y Beirdd, sef a chyllell finllem au torrer, a thorriad croyw ewinawg.

Un llythyr ar bumtheg o brif lythyrau a fuant o'r dech-reuad er cyn cadw ar gof gwybodau a'r rhai hynny a fuant ar addysg ac arfer gan yr hên Gymry o Brydyddion a Beirdd a dysgedigion Llythyr eraill. a llyma nhwy.

ᚢᚾᚤᛋ
ᚦᛃᛁᛟᛚᚹᚠᚱᚲᚷᛏᚥᚾᛁᛗᛉ

Gwedi hynny dychymygwyd eraill nid amgen

ᚹᛃᛖ neu ᚢᚲᛞᚾᚴ neu ᚺ

Gwedi hynny dychymygwyd eraill, ag y cwblhäwyd y Goelbren yn ddeunaw ar hugain llythyr, gwarantedig o bwyll ac awdurdod gorseddau, a Beirdd a dysgedigion. a llyma'r cwbl o hynny.

Deuddeg llythyr goslef y sydd nid amgen

ᚦᚨᛃᚼᛁᛟᚦᚹᚹᛁᛉᛉ

---

[1] Lles, son of Coel, was a contemporary of Eleutherius, bishop of Rome, A.D. 173—189. Lles seems to have been the Welsh form of Lucius, which was the Latin translation of Lleuver, one of the original names of the British prince. His other name was Lleirwg. Geraint, the Blue Bard, has recorded in a triplet the literary achievement of Lleirwg, thus,—

> Goruc Lleirwg gwâr unben
> Fab Coel fab Cyllin Aren,
> Gyfryngeu a Llyfreu Llen.

vised, in the time of Lles, son of Coel,[1] the first Baptismal King in the island of Britain. Nevertheless, the Bards and Poets keep in memory and use the old observance of books for the remembrance and preservation of every old art belonging to the nation of the Cymry, and the knowledge, as far as possible, of one thing or mode, which cannot be had of another thing or mode, through inevitable destiny; for no form of good sciences ought to be lost.

This is the mode, as regards form and aspect, in which the letters of the Coelbren of the Bards should be cut, that is to say, they ought to be cut with a sharp-edged knife, and the cutting should be distinct and ungulate.

Sixteen primitive letters have there been from the beginning—before the memorial of sciences, and these have been taught and practised by the old Cymry, who were Poets and Bards, and other learned men of letters. They are the following,—

ᚢᚻᚤᛋ
ᚠᚢᛁᛟᛚᚥᚦᚱᚳᚴᛏᛦᚾᚼᚷᛤ

After that, others were devised, namely,

ᚡ ᛦ ᛒ or ᚢ ᚴ ᛞ ᚾ ᚼ or ᚻ

After that, others were devised, and the Coelbren was completed as far as thirty-eight letters, warranted by the reason and authority of Gorsedds, and Bards, and learned men, and these are all of them.

There are twelve vowel letters, namely,

ᚠ ᚠ ᚢ ᚢ ᛁ ᛟ ᛜ ᛜ ᚡ ᚥ ᚤ ᛦ ᛦ

The achievement of Lleirwg, the meek chieftain,
The son of Coel, son of Cyllin the Eloquent,
Was the forming of books, and the medium of learning.
Iolo MSS., pp. 263, 671.

R

Chwech Cydsain ar hugain y sydd nid amgen. deuddeg
Cysefiniaid mal ai dangoswyd or blaen, a phedair llythyr ar
ddeg adlawiaid.

Sef y Cysefiniaid,

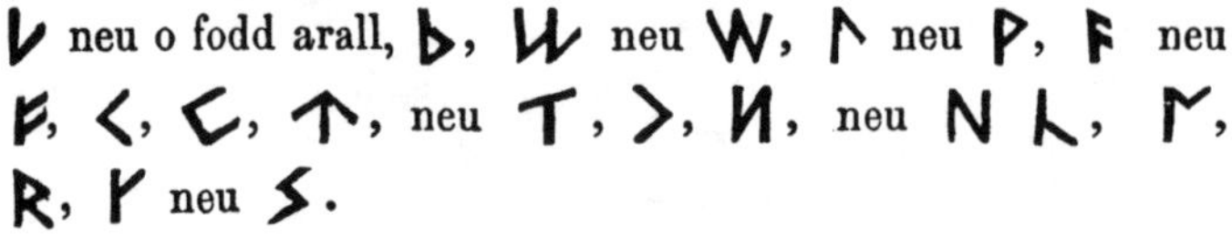

� neu o fodd arall, ᛒ, ᚹ neu W, ᚱ neu ᚹ, ᚠ neu
ᚠ, ᛉ, ᛯ, ᛏ, neu ᛠ, ᚦ, ᚼ, neu ᚾ ᛣ, ᛘ,
ᚱ, ᚣ neu ᛋ.

Sef adlawiaid y rhain, nid amgen,

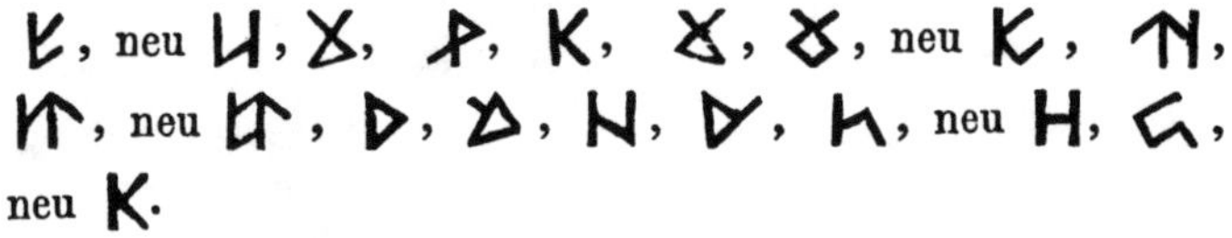

ᛤ, neu ᚢ, ᚷ, ᛈ, ᛈ, ᚷ, ᛪ, neu ᛣ, ᛏ,
ᛏ, neu ᛐ, ᛑ, ᚪ, ᚺ, ᚥ, ᚼ, neu ᚻ, ᚷ,
neu ᛣ.

Ac fal hynn yn Rill herwydd yr hen gelfyddyd ar ddosparth ar Lythyrau.

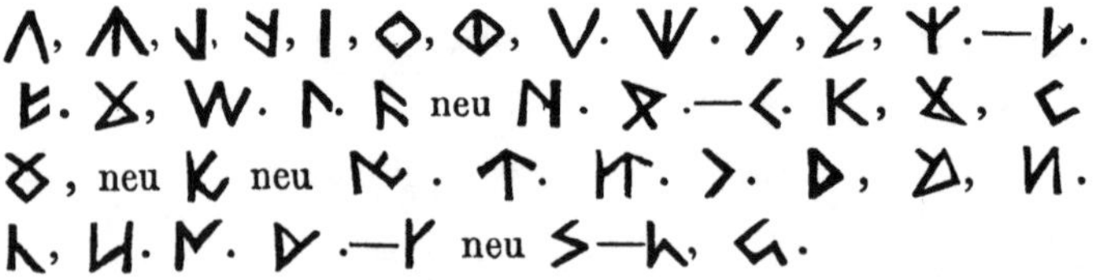

ᚨ, ᚪ, ᛃ, ᛧ, I, ◇, ⬦, V, ᚢ, Y, ᛉ, ᛏ.—�.
ᛤ. ᚷ, W, ᚱ ᛘ neu ᚾ. ᛪ.—ᛣ. K, ᚷ, ᛯ
ᛪ, neu ᛣ neu ᛣ. ᛏ. ᛏ. ᚦ. ᛑ, ᚪ, ᚼ.
ᛣ, ᚢ, ᛘ. ᚥ.—ᚣ neu ᛋ—ᚻ, ᚷ.

Gwedi dyfod y ffydd ynghrist y Saint ar Meneich a
gymmysgasant Goelbren arall amrafael yn amgenu ar Goelbren y Beirdd, a hi a dynwyd o'r Lladin, a llyma'r llun a'r
agwedd y sydd arni, nid amgen

A neu A, B neu ᛒ, ᛣ neu K, ᚦ neu ᛧ, ᛩ neu
E neu ᛖ neu ᛣ neu ᛣ, ᚱ neu F, ᛯ, H, neu ᚼ,
I, ᛣ neu �, M neu ᚻ, N, ◇, P, R neu ᚱ
neu ᛣ, ᚣ neu ᛋ ᛏ neu T, V neu ᚢ neu
W neu ᚹ, Y neu ᛉ, ᛏ.

There are twenty-six consonants, namely, twelve primitives, as shewn before, and fourteen secondaries.

The primitives are,

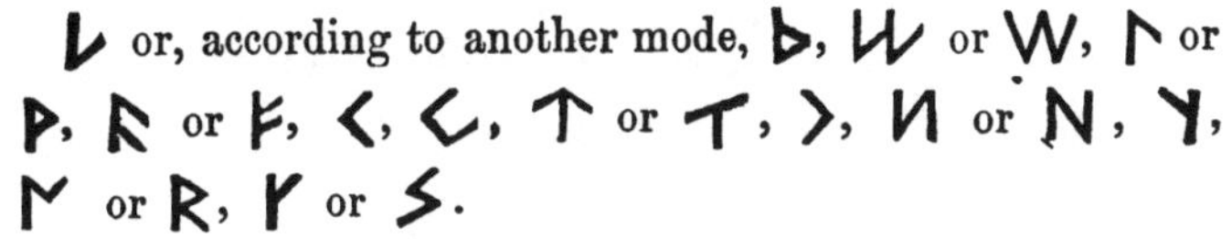

𝗟 or, according to another mode, ᑲ, 𝖂 or W, ᒧ or P, ᖇ or ᖴ, ᐸ, ᕵ, ᐪ or ᐪ, 〉, ᗷ or N, ᖾ, ᒥ or R, ᖮ or ᔢ.

The following are the secondaries, namely,

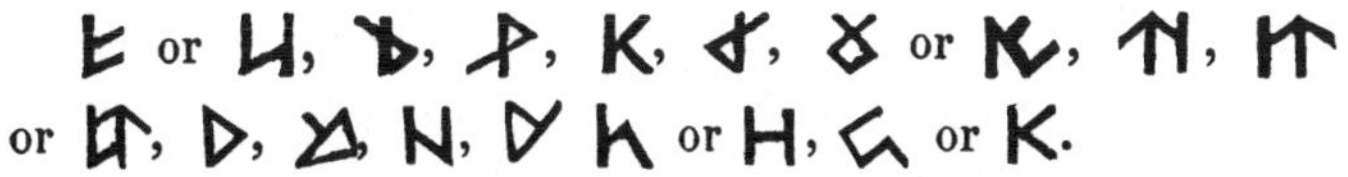

ᕆ or ᕚ, ᖦ, ᖰ, K, ᖶ, 𝗫 or ᖉ, ᐱ, ᕽ or ᕿ, ᗞ, ᗩ N, ᐁ ᖷ or H, ᖝ or K.

And thus in a series, according to the ancient art of the system of letters :—

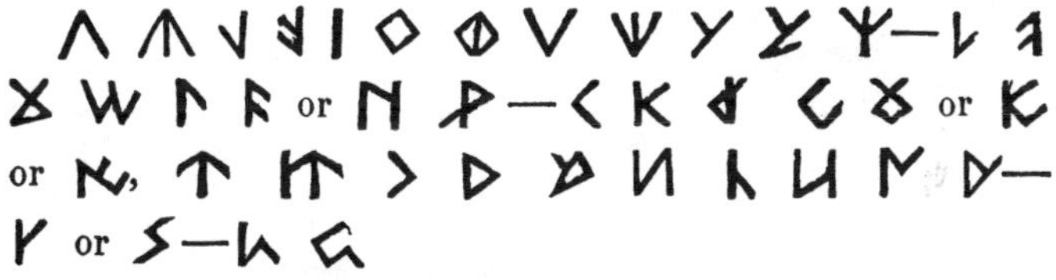

𐊃 𐊲 ᐯ ᕪ I ◇ ⬥ V ᕝ ᖻ ᖶ ᖾ—𝗟 ᕆ ᖉ W ᒧ ᖇ or ᗷ ᖰ—ᐸ K ᖶ ᕵ 𝗫 or ᖉ or ᖉ, ᐪ ᕽ 〉 ᗞ ᗩ ᗷ ᖿ ᕚ ᒥ ᗞ— ᖮ or ᔢ—ᕚ ᖝ

After the coming of the faith in Christ, the saints and monks intermixed another Alphabet, different from the Coelbren of the Bards, which was derived from the Latin ; and this is the form and aspect which it presents,—

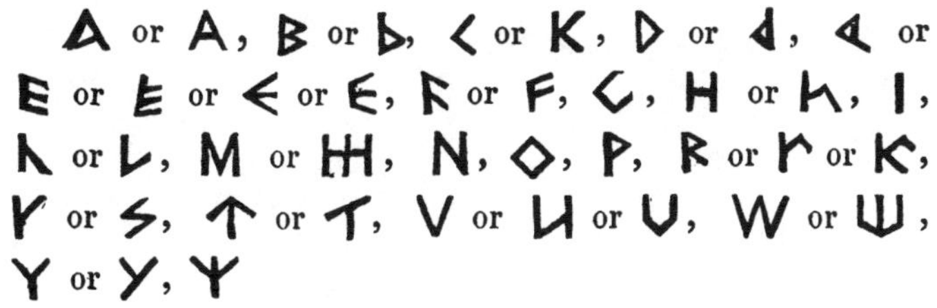

𝗔 or A, ᗃ or ᑲ, ᐸ or K, D or ᐊ, ◁ or E or ᕆ or ᐸ or ᕿ, ᖇ or ᖴ, ᕫ, H or ᖾ, I, ᖾ or ᒪ, M or ᕼᕼ, N, ◇, P, ᖇ or ᒧ or ᖉ, ᖮ or ᔢ, ᐪ or ᐪ, V or � or U, W or ᕮ, Y or ᖻ, ᖶ

ag unarhugain ydynt. ag ugain herwydd eraill sef gadael ym maes Ⴤ.

A gwedi caffael honn yr hen awduron a gymysgynt yn eu coelbrenau beth o'r naill a pheth o'r llall or ddwy goelbren uchod a ddarddangoswyd, sef Coelbren y Beirdd a Choelbren y Meneich, mal y byddai'n oreu ganddynt ac y byddai ar bwyll ac Awen ganddynt.

Gwedi cael celfyddyd plagawd fe ddaeth aball ar lythyru coed. eisoes y Beirdd a'r Prydyddion a gadwaint yr hen gelfyddyd ar wŷdd, a hyd yn ddiweddar o amseroedd nid oedd un o gant o'r prydyddion dosparthus nas medraint y Goelbren au gwneuthur au dwylaw eu hunain mal y gofyn prif ddefod y Beirdd, sef Tripheth y dylai Bardd eu gwneuthur ai ddwylaw ei hunan, ei Goelbren ei Rôl, ai Blagod. Llawer heb law'r Prydyddion a fedraint y Goelbren hyd yng nghof rhai sy'n fyw yn awr. a llawer un yr amser a fu nid pell yn ol a gadwaint eu cyfrifon Teulu ar wŷdd yn dorredig a Chyllell.

COELBREN Y BEIRDD.

Llyma fal y dywed Lywelyn Sion.

Wedi Rhyfel Bargod Owain Glyn Dwr, gwaharddodd y Brenin adael i bapur a phagod gael eu dwyn i gymru nag ychwaith eu darllaw yno, fal y rhwystra hynny gyfeillach Llythyr rhwng Cymro a Chymro a rhwng y Cymry a chenedl gorwlad ag Alldir, a hynn er dial yr ochri at Owain a welid ym mhob mann ymhob dyn yng Nghymry, a gwahardd y Beirdd hefyd ar Prydyddion i gerdded ei cylchoedd

---

[1] Owain Glyndwr was born A.D. 1349. He began to wage war against the English king, about A.D. 1400, which was continued for about fifteen years, when Owain died, i.e. A.D. 1415.

[2] The Cymric chieftain fought against two kings successively, namely, against

and they are twenty-one, or twenty, according to others, by leaving out $\curlyvee$.

And when this was obtained, the old authors used to mix in their Coelbrens some of one and some of the other of the two Coelbrens above, which have been exhibited, that is to say, the Coelbren of the Bards, and the Coelbren of the Monks, as it seemed best to them, and according to reason and awen.

When the art of plagawd was obtained, writing on trees failed; nevertheless the Bards and Poets preserved the old art of using wood; and until lately there was not one in a hundred of the regular Bards who was not skilled in the Coelbren, and could not make it with his own hands, as the primitive usage of the Bards required; that is to say,— Three things which a Bard ought to make with his own hands: his Coelbren; his Roll; and his Plagawd. Many, besides the Poets, knew the Coelbren until within the memory of those now living; and many a one, in no remote times, used to keep their domestic accounts on wood, cut with a knife.

COELBREN OF THE BARDS.

Thus says Llywelyn Sion.

After the intestine war of Owain Glyndwr,[1] the king[2] forbade paper and plagawd to be brought into Cymru, or to be manufactured there, in order that it might prevent epistolary correspondence between a Cymro and a Cymro, and between the Cymry and the people of a bordering country and of foreign lands; and this to revenge the siding with Owain, which was observed every where on the part of every man in Cymru. He also forbade the Bards and Poets to go their cir-

---

Henry IV. and against Henry V., the latter of whom succeeded to the throne A.D. 1413, two years before the death of Owain.

ag ymweled ar ofwy a'r Teuluoedd yn ei swyddau, yna cof-
iwyd a daddygwyd ar arfer henffordd Beirdd Ynys Prydain
sef torri'r llythrenau a elwaint awgrymmau Iaith a llafar ar
goed neu wydd triniedig i'r achos, a elwid Coelbren y Beirdd
ag fal hyn ai gwnelid cynnull coed cyll neu gerdin yn y
gaeaf amcan hyd cyfelin a'u hollti bob un yn bedryran sef yn
bedair asseth y prenn, a'u cadw nis baint gan gyffaith amser
yn sych o gwbl. yna eu canwyro'n bedryfal parth lled a
thrwch, a gwedi hynny canwyro'r cornelau hyd led deg yn y
fodfedd. ag gwneuthur hynn fal nas Delo torriadau'r llythrenau sef yr awgrymmau a dorrer a Chyllell ar un or pedwar wyneb pedryfal ar ymsathr yn weledig ar wyneb nesaf.
ag fal hynny am bob un o'r pedwar wyneb, yna torri'r awgrymmau herwydd y bont âi rhai Iaith a llafar tafod, ai rhai
rhif, neu arwyddion celfyddyd erail megis awgrymau erddigan Cerdd Arwest a Cherdd dant, a gwedi torri deg o'r
cyfryw sethau ag a fo gofyn arnynt parottoi pedair Asseth,
dau a dau o henynt. pill au gelwir au canwyro'n deg a'u
gosod dau ar unwaith yng ochr ag och ag ar draws y cys-
swllt nodi deg lle twll ; ar ol hynny, torri'r tyllau sef hanner
pob un or deg twll ar un or essyth, ar un peth ar y llall,
gwneuthur felly a'r ddwy asseth eraill, yrhain a elwir y
pillwydd yna trin yr essyth awgrymedigion neu lythyredig-
ion a mwnwgl ar bob un o ddeupen yr asseth yn grwnn ei
amgylch lled bys ar hydwedd yr Asseth. yna gosod y coed
llythyredigion gerfydd eu mynyglau ar un o'r pillwydd y
benn a felly ar y pen arall., ag ar hynny benn ag arall y
pillwydd twll am dwll ag ar bob pen i bob dwy billwydden
mynyglau yn leoedd llinynon iddeu clymu yn gadarn
ynghyd, ar bob pen i'r gwydd awgrymedigion. a gwedi'r
clymu'r cwbl fal hynn ynghyd yn gyrfinedig gelwir y llyfr
a wneler yn hyn o fodd Peithynen, am ei fod wedi ei ym-

cuits, and to visit the different families officially. Then was remembered, and brought into use, the ancient custom of the Bards of the Isle of Britain; namely, the cutting of letters, which they called the symbols of language and utterance, upon wood or rods prepared for the purpose, called Coelbren of the Bards—and thus was it done. They gathered rods of hazel or mountain ash in the winter, about a cubit in length, and split each into four parts, that is, the wood was made into four splinters, and kept them, until by the working of time they became quite dry. Then they planed them square, in respect of breadth and thickness, and afterwards trimmed down the angles to the tenth part of an inch, which was done that the cuttings of the letters, that is, the symbols, which were cut with the knife on one of the four square surfaces, should not visibly encroach upon the next face; and thus on every one of the four faces. Then they cut the symbols, according to their character, whether they were those of language and speech, or of numbers, or other signs of art, such as the symbols of music, of voice, and string. And after cutting ten of such bars as were required, they prepared four splinters, two and two, which were called *pill*, planed them smooth, placed two of them together side by side across the frame, and marked the places for ten holes. After that, they cut the holes, that is, half of each of the ten holes, in one splinter, and the same in the other; and they did the same with the other two splinters; and these are called *pillwydd*. Then they took the symbolized or lettered bars, and made a neck at each of the two ends of every bar, all round, the breadth of a finger, along the bar. Then they placed the lettered sticks by their necks on one of the pillwydd at one end, and in like manner at the other end; and on that the other pillwydd at each end, hole for hole. And at both ends of two pillwydden they made necks, as places for strings to tie them firmly together at each end of the symbolized sticks. And when the whole are thus bound tight together, the book that is constructed in this manner is called *Peithynen*, because it is framed; the

byithynu ynghyd y pillwydd ar bop pen yn dal y cwbl
ynghyd, ar ebillion sef yr Essyth llythyredigion yn troi yn
pillwydd yn rwyddesmwyth. ac felly yn hawdd ei darllain.
sef y darllenir un wyneb o'r ebill yn y lle cyntaf herwydd
rhifnod ei wyneb yna troi gyda'r haul a darllain yr ail
wyneb a throi felly am bob wyneb arall, ag yn unwell o
ebill i ebill hyd nas darfydder darllain, nod rhif o un i
ddeg ar wyneb yr clo pob un o'r ebillion a wyneb y nod
rhif yw'r cyntaf iddei ddarllain, a'r rhai yn nhrefn eu tro
gyda'r haul.

Deugain ochr ebill ym mhob peithinen, ar ol hynny
peithyn arall hyd ddiwedd y gerdd neu'r Araith a lle bo
gofyn mwy na deg ebill A llai nag ugain, cynnifer ebill ag
y bo gofyn, yn un peithynen gyfunbarth yn gyfyngorf.—
Achos rhoi deg yn arbennigrif yn gydgyrfin yw am mai deg
yw bann adran rhif, a than rhif degan y dosperthir pob
rhifoedd hyd nas gall Iaith rhoi enwau arnynt, Deg yw
cylch cyfiawn a deg o fewn deg, neu ddeg am ddeg a fydd
tufewn a thufaes i'r cylchyndod cylch ynghylch hyd fyth
bythoedd. am hynny gorau Dosparth ar rhif a rhifoedd yw
deg a degau. ag nis gellir ar amgen o drefn gadw rhifoedd
yn ddosparthus mewn lleoedd cedyrn modd y gellir eu darllain au deall, au datgan yngyfun gydgyfun.   Gwedi dwyn
ar atgof ag adfer am achos a ddangoswyd hen brif gelfyddyd
y Cymry ar lythyr ag awgrym ymrhodded dan farn a chanfod Cadeiriau a Gorseddau Cerdd dafod Deheubarth, a
Morganwg, ag Eisteddfodau, Gwynedd a Phowys, i chwilio
i maes a golled ar wybodau awgrym Coelbren y Beird a'r
gwellhau ar helaethu a fu ar rhyw a rhif yr Awgrymau ac
yna Cadarnhau un awgrym a'r bymtheg yn rai Cyffredin
o'r dechreuad, a chwanegiadau a fu at hynny o rif o bryd i

pillwydd at each end keeping all together, and the ebillion, or lettered staves, turning freely in the pillwydd, and thus being easy to read. That is, one face of the ebill is read first, according to the number of its face, then it is turned with the sun, and the second face is read, and it is turned so for every other face, and thus from ebill to ebill until the reading is finished. A number from one to ten being on the turning face of each of the ebillion, the numbered face is the first that is to be read, and then the others in the order of their course with the sun.

There are forty sides to the ebillion in every Peithynen; after that, another Peithynen is formed, until the conclusion of the poem or narrative. And where more than ten ebillion are required, and less than twenty, as many ebillion as are required are placed altogether in one entire Peithynen. The reason of assigning ten as the particular number of succession, is, that ten is the division point of number, and under the number of decades are all numbers arranged, until language cannot give them names. Ten is a perfect circle, and ten within ten, or ten about ten, will be within and without the circumference, circle within circle, for ever and ever; therefore the best arrangement of number and numbers is ten and tens. And it is not possible by any other method to keep accounts in an orderly manner, in strong places, so that they may be read and understood, and recited, uniformly and consistently.

After having, for the reasons shewn, restored to memory and use the old primitive art of the Cymry in letters and symbols, it was submitted to the judgment and observation of the Chairs and Gorsedds of vocal song of Deheubarth and Morganwg, and the Eisteddvods of Gwynedd and Powys, that they might search out what had been lost of the sciences of the symbols of the Bardic Coelbren, and what improvement and extension had been made in the kind and number of the symbols. Then they confirmed sixteen characters as general ones from the beginning, and the additions, which had been made to that number from time to time until the era

S

gilydd hyd yn amser y Bardd Glas lle ai cadarnhaed yn un
ar hug obrif.awgrymau herwydd llafaryddiaeth y Gymraeg.
gwedi hynny dodi pedwar ar hugain ar rif y Cyffrediniaid,
ag ni ddoded mwy na hynny ar addysg a gwybodau Teuluaidd, eithr y Beirdd a gawsant ar eu Coelbren Cyfrin ddeunaw a'r hugain o hen gadw a Chof Cyfrin, a'u dwyn ar
arfer ag adwaith. ag nis deallwyd y dylit Cyfrinach damdwng ar amgen na deg o henynt a elwaint y deg cyssefiniaid
au dodi dan luniau gyfrinach Ddamdwng, a gadael y cwbl
o'r deunaw a'r ugain yn gyfrinach heb arnynt adduned a
damdwng ag o hynny yr aeth yn gyffredin fal y maent yn
awr.

Wedi adgael gwybodaeth ar y Coelbrenni sef un y Beirdd
ag un y meneich mynai bawb agos gwryw a benyw eu dysgu
au gwneuthur ag o hynny myned yn waith crefft gan wegryddion a Basgedyddion ag ernynt y torrid cof am bob peth
a ofynai gof cadwedig llythyr a llyfr, ag fel hynny y bu hyd
amser Harri y Seithfed ag ynteu yn Gymro, cymmerodd ei
genedl dan nawdd ei gymmwynasgarwch, ag au dododd ar

---

[1] About A.D. 900. Geraint was the author of a Cymric Grammar, which
was preserved among the MSS. in Rhaglan Castle, before it was destroyed in
the wars of the Commonwealth.

[2] Being the grandson of Owain Tudur, of Penmynydd, in Anglesey, who had
married Catherine of France, the queen dowager of Henry V., A.D. 1428. It
was in Henry VII. that the British dynasty was restored, according to the vaticinations of the Bards; and it is somewhat remarkable that he was also the
rightful heir of Llywelyn, the last independent prince of Wales, and that consequently Queen Victoria reigns over the Principality by inheritance, and not in
right of conquest. This may be seen from the following table;—

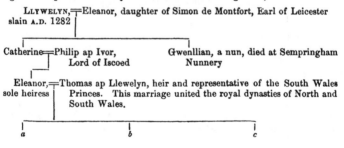

LLYWELYN,⹂Eleanor, daughter of Simon de Montfort, Earl of Leicester
slain A.D. 1282

Catherine⹂Philip ap Ivor,   Gwenllian, a nun, died at Sempringham
        Lord of Iscoed   Nunnery

Eleanor,⹂Thomas ap Llewelyn, heir and representative of the South Wales
sole heiress   Princes. This marriage united the royal dynasties of North and
        South Wales.

a   b   c

of the Blue Bard,[1] when they were confirmed as twenty-one primary symbols, in respect of the vocalization of the Cymraeg. After that, they fixed the number of the common ones at twenty-four; nor were any more appointed for domestic learning and sciences; but the Bards had on their secret Coelbren thirty-eight, of ancient preservation and secret record, which they restored to use and practice. And it was not understood that more than ten of them, which were called the ten primitives, ought to be put under an oath of secrecy; these were put under the forms of sworn secrecy, whilst the whole thirty eight were left a secret, but without vow or oath; and from that they became common, as they are now.

After recovering the knowledge of the Coelbrens, that is, the one of the Bards and the one of the Monks, nearly every person, male and female, wished to learn and construct them. From thence they became the trade of sieve-makers and basket-makers, and upon them was cut the record of every thing that required the preserved memorial of letter and book. And thus it was until the time of Henry the Seventh, who, being a Cymro,[2] took his countrymen under the protection of his courtesy, and placed

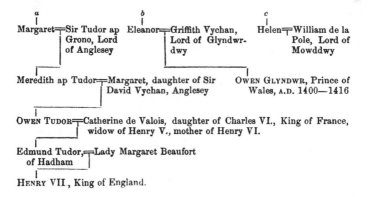

a
Margaret⳿Sir Tudor ap
　　　Grono, Lord
　　　of Anglesey

b
Eleanor⳿Griffith Vychan,
　　　Lord of Glyndwr-
　　　dwy

c
Helen⳿William de la
　　　Pole, Lord of
　　　Mowddwy

Meredith ap Tudor⳿Margaret, daughter of Sir
　　　　David Vychan, Anglesey

Owen Glyndwr, Prince of
　　Wales, A.D. 1400—1416

Owen Tudor⳿Catherine de Valois, daughter of Charles VI., King of France,
　　　widow of Henry V., mother of Henry VI.

Edmund Tudor,⳿Lady Margaret Beaufort
　of Hadham

Henry VII., King of England.

ei gost ei hun dan addysg myneich a phapir a Chroentrin a
fynnit am ddim a chael yn yr un a fynnit o'r ddwy Iaith
nid amgen y Gymraeg a'r Saesoneg a llawer a ddysgaint y
ddwy. ag o hynny cael gwybodau llythyr yn amlach ym
mhlith y werin yng Nghymru nag ai caed yn Lloegr ag o
hynny Prydyddion mwy na digon, ar Abadau yn ei dodi, le
ag arall, yn ysgolyddion, ag o hynny y mae bod y Prydyddion yn ysgolyddion athrawon Teuluaidd hyd y dydd
heddiw yn myned yn ei cylchoedd dosparthedig o dy i dy,
ag o deulu i deulu. y mae'n aml dan olwg a gweled yr hen
goelbrenni. ond yn awr nid aml gwneuthur peithynen eithr
am radd yng Nghadair, neu am dal yn arian neu yn werth
arian gan ai gofynnai wrth achos yr un ai gofynai. y mae
llawer yn fyw y dydd heddyw yn cofio'r ymarfer a Choelbren y beirdd. a llawer Coelbren a welir fyth yn nhai hen
dylwythau Bonheddigion

Y sef fal hynn y 'mae'r Cyfarwyddyd herwydd hen gof a
Llythyr, a Chof Llafar gorsedd, Cadwedig gan Gadeiriau er
y dechreuad, nid amgen

Deg nod awgrym llafar parth Iaith ag ymadrodd a fu gan
genedl y Cymry yn oes oesoedd cyn eu dyfod i Ynys Prydain, a chyfrinach dan adduned a damdwng oeddent gan y
Gwyddoniaid sef oedd y gwyr hyn Prydyddion a gwyr wrth
gerdd dafod a gwybodau Doethineb cyn bod Beirdd Dosparthus, ag yn amser Prydain ab Aedd Mawr amcan mil a
hanner o flynyddau cyn geni Crist ynghnawd o'r wenforwyn
fendigaid Mair, ag yn amser aedd Mawr y trefnyd Beirdd
Dosparthus a swydd a thrwydded gwaranred iddynt, a
chwedi hynny gwellhau Coelbren y Gwyddoniaid fal y bydd
achaws ei deall ai darllain hyd nad oedd unawgrym ar
bymtheg yn y Goelbren ag yn amser Dyfnwal Moelmud

them, at his own expense, under the instruction of the monks, and furnished them gratuitously with as much paper and parchment as was required ; and they were taught whichever they would of the two languages, Welsh or English, and many learned both. On that account the knowledge of letters was more frequent among the common people in Wales than it was in England ; and from hence also there were more than enough of Poets, whom the abbots placed here and there as scholars, from which it happens that the Poets are domestic schoolmasters unto the present day, proceeding on their appointed circuits from house to house, and from family to family. The old Coelbrens are frequently to be seen and beheld, but now a Peithynen is not often made, except for a degree in Chair, or for the payment of money, or the value of money, from the person who might order it, according to the need of him ordering it. There are many now living who remember the use of the Coelbren of the Bards, and many a Coelbren may still be seen in the houses of the old noble families.

The account, according to old memorials and letters, and the memorials of the voice of Gorsedd, which have been preserved by Chairs from the beginning, is as follows, namely ;—

Ten symbolic characters of utterance, in respect of language and speech, have been in possession of the nation of the Cymry from the age of ages before they came into the island of Britain, which were a secret under vow and oath among· the Gwyddoniaid, these persons being Poets and men of vocal song and sciences of wisdom before there were regular Bards. It was in the time of Prydain, son of Aedd the Great, about one thousand five hundred years before Christ was born in the flesh of the pure and blessed Mary, and in the time of Aedd the Great, that regular Bards were instituted, and authorized office and license assigned to them. After that, the Coelbren of the Gwyddoniaid was improved, as occasion required for its being understood and read, until there were sixteen symbols in the Alphabet.

amcan chwechan mlynedd Cof a Chyfrif cyn dyfod Christ
yng nghnawd, y datrinwyd yr unawgrym ar bymtheg ar
drefn arnynt cadw Iaith ag ymadrodd a phob Cof Gwlad a
Chenedl, am nas gallesid gystal ar un arall o drefn er cyn-
hal Cof a gwybodau doethineb, a breiniau a Defodau Cenedl
y Cymry ai pherthynasai ar deg nod Awgrym cyssefin hyd
y dydd heddyw dan gadw Cyfrinach adduned a damdwng
ag nid neb o ddyn namyn y damdynghedigion au gwyr
wedi myned yr unarbymtheg yn agored pen gwlad ir holl
genedl gwellhau ag helaethu'r goelbren ym mhellach a
wnaethpwyd hyd ddeunaw yn amser Beli Mawr ab Manogan, a gwedi hynny ugain, ag yn amser y Bardd glas yn
un ar hugain sef cof arall a ddywed ddywed dau ar hugain,
a hynny y sydd o lythyrenau Cyssefinion yn y Gymraeg,
sef adlawiaid y gelwir y maint a sydd dros hynny o rif hyd
ddeunaw ar hugain.

COELBREN Y BEIRDD.

Llyma ddangos y modd y gwneir Coelbren y Beirdd.

Cymmer goed bychain pedryollt ynghylch hyd cyfelin, ai
hochri'n deg ag yn gywir ag yn llyfn yn y pedwar ochr, au
trwch ynghylch pedryfed modfedd neu ychydig bach dros-
benn hynny yn gydfaint lled a thrwch sef amcan ar hyd
heiddyn ymhob ffordd yn rhefder y pren. a gwedi gwneuthur yn barod hyd hynny rhâth ychydig ar yr ymylau sef
conglau'r coed hyd yn lled degfed neu ddeuddegfed modfedd,
a hynny fal pan dorrer y llythyrau ar un o'r ochreu nad
ymddangoasant arnynt un ochr arall. eithr yn yr ymyl rath-
edig yn unig. gwedi hynny mynygla'r coed hynn o fewn i

And it was in the time of Dyvnwal Moelmud, about six hundred years, by record and computation, before Christ was born in the flesh, that the sixteen symbols, and their order for the preservation of language and speech and every memorial of country and nation, were divulged, because no other method could be found so good for maintaining the memorials and sciences of wisdom, and the privileges and usages of the nation of the Cymry, and its appurtenances. And the ten symbolic characters are kept to this day as a secret by vow and oath; and no man, except those who have taken the oath, knows them. When the sixteen became generally open to all the nation, the Coelbren was further improved and extended, till it consisted of eighteen in the time of Beli the Great, son of Manogan; and after that of twenty; and, in the time of the Blue Bard, of twenty-one, or, as another record says, of twenty-two; and so many are there of primitive letters in the Cymraeg, such as are beyond this number, as far as thirty-eight, being called secondaries.

COELBREN OF THE BARDS.

Here is shewn the mode of making the Coelbren
of the Bards.

Take small pieces of wood, split into four parts, a cubit in length; render the four sides fair, and exact, and smooth, their thickness being about the fourth of an inch, or very little more than that, and the width and depth being of equal size, that is, about the length of a barleycorn each way in the thickness of the wood. When you have prepared them thus far, trim down a little of the edges or corners of the wood, to the width of the tenth or twelfth of an inch; so that, when the letters are cut on one of the sides, they may not appear on any other side, but in the rasped margin alone. After that, make necks on the staves within the

ddau hyd heiddyn at y pen yn grynion a thrwch ewin neu
ddalen gawl yn ddyfnach nac wyneb y pren, a thrwsio'r
neillben yn drefnus ag yn binc fal y bo hardd ei olwg ag
esmwyth dan fys iddei droi. ag yna parod fydd y pren. ag
ef a elwir ebill a'r lluosawg arnynt a elwir ebillion. ac fal y
gwelir yma y fydd yr olwg arno.

ag ar hynn o bren neu ebill y torri'r llythyrau a chyllell yn
rynnau bychain trwch dalen neu gawnen fechan a chyfled a
chawnen fain o wair a thorri pob rhynt yn deg ag yn loyw o
dorriad, a gwedi torri ar un ochr torr ar y nesaf, ag felly ar
y pedwar ochr, a gofalu na thorrot yn ddyfnach na'r rathfa
ar yr ymylau, gwedi torri ar y pedwar ochr dos at bren arall, ag o ebill i ebill yny bot wedi torri'r cyfan or gerdd
neu'r araith a fo'n damcan. gwedi hynny cymmer bedwar
prenn at y pillwydd sef pillwydd y gelwir y coed hynny, ag
o honynt y gwnai gyrfin ymha yn y rhestrir yn drefnus ag
yn ddiogel yr ebillion llythyredig. a llyma luniau y pillwydd

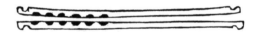

sef ymhob un y gwneir rhestr o ryntau bychain hanner
cylch. yn ogymaint a hanner mynyglau yr ebillion, a gofalu
bod rhynt y naill bren o'r pillwydd yn gywair gyferyd ai
gymmar yn y llall. a phan gwblheir dau yna eu dodi ynghyd-
gysswllt ag wedi hynny dodir ebillion gerfydd eu mynyglau
yn y pillwydd, ag yna rhwymaw'r ddau billwydden am y
mynyglau a wneir ar bob pen iddynt ag edau gref o sidan

length of two barleycorns of the end, round, and the thickness of a nail or cabbage leaf, deeper than the surface of the tree; and trim both ends neatly and smartly, that they may be beautiful to look at, and easy under the finger to turn. Then the stave will be ready, which is also called *ebill*, and in the plural *ebillion*, and its appearance will be as here seen;—

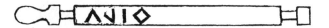

And on this stave or ebill the letters are cut with a knife in small grooves the thickness of a leaf or small straw in depth, and as wide as a slender stalk of hay. Let every groove be cut fair and clear in its cutting. And when you have cut on one side, cut on the next, and so on the four sides; but take care not to cut deeper than the rasping of the edges. When you have cut on the four sides, proceed to another stave, and from ebill to ebill, until you shall have cut the whole of the poem or oration that was intended. Then take four pieces of wood for the pillwydd, for these sticks are called *pillwydd*, and with them make a frame, in which the lettered ebillion shall be arrayed methodically and securely. These are the delineations of the pillwydd;—

that is, in each is made a series of small semicircular notches, as large as half the necks of the ebillion, care being taken that the notch of one piece of wood is exactly opposite to its fellow in the other. And when two are finished, they are joined together, and afterwards the ebillion are inserted by their necks in the pillwydd, and the two pillwydd are tied round their necks at each end with a strong thread of silk,

T

neu a man dannau telyn neu grwth. neu a gwifellipres
meinion, neu a manewynau llwdn hydd. gwedi hynn gwna'r
ddau billwydden eraill yn yr un modd a dod ynddynt yr
ebillion gerfydd eu mynyglau pen arall iddynt. a rhwymaw
arnynt fal y gwnaed ar pen arall. yna bydd gadarn a threfn-
us yr holl ebillion pob un yn ei le yn gywair, ag o bydd
achos herwydd hyd y gerdd neu'r araith gwna garfen arall,
canys ni wedd parth cyweithasder fod dros o bedwar i ddeg
ar hugain o ebillion yn yr un garfen, achos hynny y gwna
ddwy neu dair neu'r maint a fo achos wrthynt. gwedi cwbl-
hau'r garfen yn gywair hi a elwir *Peithynen*. a phob un or
ebillwydd a droant ynddi ynhawdd. sef pan y darllener un
ochr or ebill, ei throi fal y ceir yr ochr arall iddei darllein
ag fal hynny am y pedwar ochr, a throi gyda'r haul neu at
y llaw ddehau, a gwedi darllain un ebill myned at y nesaf is
ei llaw, ag felly o'r naill i'r llall onid eir dros y cyfan. a
chofio bod y pen trwsiedig addurnwaith at y llaw ddeheu fal
y gellir a honno droi pob un o honynt yn hawdd, ag y del-
iaidd. eraill a ddodant yr ebillion bob yn ail pen y bys un at
y llaw ddeau ar llall at y llaw chwith. werstragwers a bydded
hynn fal y bo goreu gan ai gwnelo.

Y mae'n gofyn cyllell lem i dorri'r rhynnon yn glaer-
loywon, a llaw gelfydd delïaidd.

Lled pob hanneryn or pillwydd a fydd dau hyd heiddyn
neu rhyw faint lai a thrwch pob un pedryfed modfedd, ag
nid cyweithas bod mwy nag a wedais ym maint y coed
deunydd fal na bont ry drymion, ac anghyweithas eu dwyn
au darllaw (darllofi.)

Gofaler bod pob rhynt yn gywair ei agwedd y gorfynydd-
ion ar bob llythyryn yn gywir ei safiad heb oleddu at na'r
naill llaw na'r llall, a bod y goleddfon yn lleddfu'n gywair
herwydd y dylyent yn ol y bo ffurf y llythyren.

or with the small strings of a harp or violin, or with thin brass wires, or the small sinews of a hind. After this, construct the other two pillwydd in the same way, and place the ebillion, by their other necks, in them, tying them as at the other end. Thus will all the ebillion be strong and orderly, each one exactly in its place. And if there be occasion, because of the length of the poem or oration, make another framework, for it does not accord with convenience that there should be above from twenty-four to thirty ebillion in the same framework; therefore make two or three, or as many as may be required. When the framework is completed exactly, it is called *Peithynen,* and each of the ebillwydd will turn in it easily, for when one side of the ebill has been read, it is turned so that the other side may be read, and so with the four sides. The turning is made with the sun, or to the right hand. And when one ebill has been read, you proceed to the next below it, and so from one to the other until the whole be gone over. It should be remembered that the trimmed and ornamented end is to be towards the right hand, so that with it you may turn every one of them easily and dexterously. Others place the ebillion for the finger's end alternately, one to the right hand, and the other to the left hand, every other turn. Let this be as is deemed best by the maker.

A sharp knife is required to cut the grooves fairly and clearly, with a skilful, dexterous hand.

The breadth of either half of the pillwydd will be the length of two barleycorns, or somewhat less, and the thickness of each the fourth of an inch; and it is not convenient that there should be more bulk than what I said in the wood materials, lest they should be too heavy, and inconvenient to carry and handle.

Care should be taken that every groove be exact in its form, the perpendiculars of every letter be in a right position, inclining neither to the one hand nor to the other, and that the obliques slant correctly, as they ought, according to the form of the letter.

Ar y pen hynny or ebill a fo drwy'r garfen y pillwydd y
tu chwith y gwneir rhynt ei rif ac felly ar bob un ei rif. fal
y bo hawdd gosod pob ebill yn ei gyfle heb orfod ei ddarllain ag eraill o'i flaen ag ar ei ol, a'r rhifoedd hynn a wneir
mewn dwy ffordd, un yw cynnifer rhynt ag y bo rhif yr
ebill yn y beithynen, ail yw a'r llythyren rif y bo achos.

Gofala bod pob llythyryn parth ei rynt yn o gymmhraff.
os amgen anhardd y byddant i'r olwg.

Goreu o bob coed i weithio peithynen yw planhigwydd
deri ieueinc cyfref ag y bo digon o faint yn yr ebillion gwedi
hollti'r pren yn bedwar a naddu oddiar bob pedryfed y rhisg
ar y gwynnin yn gwbl, au sychu'n dda cyn au cwblhäer ag
au llythyrer. a goreu am torri'r coed yw'r gwyl Fair.

Goreu coed am hawsder naddu a rhyntu yw coed cyll
pedryollt, a neu goed helig pedryollt, au sychu'n dda cyn
au llythyrer, a goreu ar bob helyg y merhelig. Eithr yr
hen Brydyddion a geisynt goed cerdin gan eu barnu'n goed
cyferddawl am nad yw pryfed yn eu bwytta nag yn eu
llygru. ag nad oes na gwag yspryd nag un ellyll drwg a
drig lle bo cerdin, ag nas oes na swyn na chyfaredd a all
ymafael a cherdin na'u drygu na'r neb a'u dycco, ag nad oes
un gwenwyn marwol a eill gyffwrdd ag hwynt.

A'r ffordd honn ar lythyrau yw hen ffordd y Cymru cyn
dyfod Estroniaid i Ynys Prydain. eithr gwedi caffael gwybodaeth o'r ffydd ynghrist, fe ddaeth ysgrifennu ar groen
ar ddeall ynghymru, fal ag y mae yn awr, a gwedi cael
hynny ar wybod. fe wnaethpwyd RHÔL ag ar honno y doded
y croen ysgrifenedig ai throi ai rhwymaw am dani, a llyma
ddull y rhôl a hi a wneir o bren a fynner eithr cerdin

On that end of the ebill, which projects through the pill-wydd frame on the left side, is made its numerical groove, and so its number on every one, that it may be easy to put every ebill in its proper place, without being obliged to read it, whilst others are before and after it. These numbers are made in two ways, the one contains as many grooves as the number of the ebill in the peithynen, the other is the numeral letter that may be required.

Take care that every letter, in respect of its groove, be of uniform thickness, otherwise it will be unseemly to the sight.

The best wood wherewith to construct a Peithynen are young oak saplings, as thick as would leave the ebillion large enough, after the tree has been split into four parts, and the rind and epidermis have been completely chipped off from each quarter. They should be well dried before they are finished and lettered: the best time to cut the wood is the Feast of St. Mary.

The best wood in respect of the facility of chipping and grooving is hazel wood, split into four parts, or willow wood, split into four parts; and they ought to be well dried before they are lettered. The best of all willows is the yellow willow. The ancient Poets, however, sought the wood of mountain ash, regarding it as charmed wood, because worms do not devour or corrupt it, and because no vain spirit, or wicked fiend, will abide where there is mountain ash, and because neither charm nor enchantment can avail against mountain ash, nor injure it, nor him who carries it, and because no deadly poison can touch them.

This mode in regard to letters is the old mode of the Cymry before the coming of strangers into the island of Britain. But when they obtained the knowledge of the faith in Christ, writing on skin came to be understood in Cymru, as at present; and when that was known, a Roll was made, on which was placed the written skin, being folded and tied around the same. This is the form of the Roll, which is made of any wood you like, though mountain

y bernit yn oreu am y cyferddonau a gaid ar y pren hynny

ag am feinder y rhôl tufewn i'r pennau y dodid y crwyn llythyrog cynnifer croen ag a elai am y rôl, au troi au rhwymaw am dani. gwedi caffael papr ef ai arferwyd yn lle crwyn fal y mae ynawr. a chyweithasaf o bob ffordd ar lyfr ag ysgrifen yw rhôl parth hawsder a diogelder ei chadw ai dwyn. eithr nid mawr ai harferir ynawr namyn yn arddangos yngorsedd a chadair gan a ofynner iddo gadw rhol dosparth y gelfyddyd wrth gerdd ag ar achau a breiniau gwlad.

PEITHYNEN.

Y pillwydd a fyddant yn ddau hannerog bob Carfan sef mal y gellir eu hagor au caead i gymmeryd a chyfrwymaw 'r Peithwydd neu 'r ebillion dwy garfan y sydd, un bob pen ymho $_{\text{caeawg}}^{\text{caeogen}}$, ag ymhob $_{\text{caeawg}}^{\text{caeogen}}$ hefyd y bydd gan arfer yn fynychaf bedwar ar hugain o'r peithwydd, cyd y gellir arnynt y rhif a fynner, am hynny deunaw neu ugain a welir yn fynych, ag nid anfynych deg arhugain, ag yn y beithynen gynnifer caeawg ag a fynner, eithr enhydwyth y bydd mwy na thri $_{\text{chaeawg}}^{\text{chaeogen}}$. Rhai a wnant beithynen o un caeogen hir fallai ddeugain neu hanner cant neu drigain neu fwy o beithwydd a lle bo felly nid hydwyth mwy nag un Caeogen. Dylit y peithwydd bob un yn bedwar ochrawg, a rhathu 'r ymylau sef y cornelau yn ysgawn sef hyd yn llawn ddyfnder y llythyrau fal nas gweler llythyrau un ochr yn ymddangos ar ymyl yr ochr arall, ag felly am bob ochr. lled ochrau 'r peithwydd a fydd yn gymmaint a hyd heiddyn

---

[1] Peithwydd, (paith-gwydd,) open or elucidative wood.

ash is considered the best, because of the charms attached
to that tree.

It was around the thin part of the Roll, within the ends,
that the lettered skins were put, as many skins as would go
round the Roll, which were folded and tied about it. When
paper was obtained, it was used instead of skins, as at present. The most convenient of all forms of book and writing
is the Roll in respect of the facility and safety of keeping
it ; but it is not much used now, except at the exhibition of
Gorsedd and Chair by such as are required to keep a Roll of
the system of song, and the pedigrees and privileges of
country.

PEITHYNEN.

The pillwydd will be in two halves each post, so that
they may be opened and closed in order to receive and bind
together the peithwydd, or ebillion. There are two posts,
one at each end of the frame, and in each frame it is usual
for the most part to have twenty-four of the peithwydd,[1]
though there may be any number required. Therefore
eighteen or twenty are often seen, and not seldom thirty.
And in the Peithynen as many fastenings as may be desired, but more than three fastenings are unwieldy. Some
make a Peithynen with one long fastening, having perhaps
forty, fifty, or sixty, or more peithwydd, but where that is
the case, more than one fastening is not manageable. The
peithwydd ought each to be four sided, with the edges or
angles slightly taken off to the full depth of the letters, so
that the letters of one side may not appear on the edge of
the other side, and so with every side. The width of the
sides of the peithwydd will be as large as the length of a

neu wenhithyn. ag o fod yn fwy bydd anhydwydd y beithynen, a throm, ag a ofyn llawer o le yn ai cario.

Rhai a ddodant y peithwydd yn y lliw glas y lliwir gwlan
ynddo, ag yno sefyll hyd nes bo glas lliw pob un o honynt,
a gadael iddynt sychu, yna torri 'r llythyrau, a hwy a fyddant wynnion ag amlyccach ar y coed gleision na phetysaint
heb liw, a'r llythyrau yn ogyfliw ar prenn : eraill a ddodant
liw du, neu wyrdd, neu goch, ni mawr waeth pa liw a fytho,
cyd ydd amgeno 'n daer ar liw pren y llythyrau. Goreu o
bob coed eu parhâd Deri, hawsaf eu gweithio cyll neu helig
neu wern. Bedwen yn bren da, felly eirin ag yspyddaden,
yr hen brydyddion gynt a hoffynt gerdinwydd, Coed efeill
lle au gellir yn deg nid rhaid gwell. am barhâd a gweithiol-
deb, Berwi pillwydd a pheithwydd mewn Llyisy sur au
ceidw rhag bryfed, eu twymo 'n frwd ag iro cwyr gwenyn
ynddynt au lledbobi onid elo 'r cwyr iddynt gan wres, au
ceidw rhag mall a phydri bynnag o bren a fythawr.

COELBREN Y BEIRDD.

Llyma ddangos ar y modd y gwneir Coelbren y Beirdd.
cymeryd coed bychain holl ynghylch cyfelin yr hyd a'u
hochri mewn pedair oni bydd yn bedwar ochrog a lled pob
ochr llai na hanner modfedd sef amgylch hyd heidden y
lled. Ag ar yr ochreu hyn y torrir y llythyrau. eithr cyn
eu torri y mae'n gofyn rhathu yr ymylau fal pan dorrer y
llythyrau ar y naill ochr nad ymddangoso eu pennau 'n ry-
annon ar yr ochreu ereill, eithr yn y rathfa.

barley corn or wheat corn ; if larger, the Peithynen would be unwieldy and heavy, and would require much room in carrying.

Some put the peithwydd in the blue colour in which wool is dyed, letting them stand there until every one of them is of a blue colour ; and having allowed them to dry, they cut the letters, which will be white, and clearer on the blue wood, than if it had not been coloured, the letters being of the same colour as the wood. Others use black, or green, or red colour, it matters not much what colour it may be, so that the letters sufficiently differ from the colour of the wood. The best of all wood for lasting is oak ; the easiest to be worked is hazel, or willow, or alder. Birch is a good tree, so are the plumb-tree and the hawthorn ; the old Poets formerly were fond of mountain ash ; there need be no better for lasting and working than apple trees, where they may be had smooth. Boiling the pillwydd and peithwydd in sour lees, will keep them from worms, and heating them hot, and smearing them with beeswax, half roasting them until the wax penetrates into them from the heat, will keep them from decay and rot, whatever tree it may be.

COELBREN OF THE BARDS.

Here is shewn the mode of making the Coelbren of the Bards. Small pieces of wood are taken, split, about a cubit in length, and squared, until they are four sided, the width of each side being less than half an inch, that is, its width will be about the length of a barley corn. On these sides the letters are cut ; but before they are cut, it is requisite that the edges should be rasped, in order that, when the letters are cut on one side, their heads may not appear as characters on the other sides, except in the rasping.

U

COELBREN RHIN.—COELFAIN GYFRIN.—COELFAIN
CYFARWYDDYD.

Rhinynau 'r Beirdd, sef Coelbrenni rhin ydynt ebillion
bychain hyd bys a rhintau * arnynt fal y trefner rhwng dau
neu amgen a fyddant gyfrin, ag o'u gosod au cyssylltu
herwydd y bo cyfrin y gwneir y geiriau a'r ymadroddion,
ag ou ffasgellu yn eiriau herwydd cyfrinach y gwneir llythyr
anfon ag wynt, a llyfrau cyfrin, nas gwypo neb eu gofeg
namyn a font gyfrin, ag nid iawn herwydd defawd a briduw
eu datrin. a Rhiniau beirdd a'u gelwir, Barddrin.

Coelfeini cyfrin a fyddant yr un gyffelyb, o gerrig bychan
dan nodau cyfrinach, ag ou bwrw herwydd trefn a chelfyddyd y gyfrinach y dangoser gwybodau cyfraid, a lle bont y
cyfryw goelbrenni herwydd rhif llythyrau'r goelbren'r goelbren gyfarwydd, bydded cyfrinach arnynt o newid llythyren
dros arall fal nas caffer eithr ynghylch anghenoctid a threigl
yr un llythyren ddwywaith yn yr un bwyll a grym.

Coelfain cyfarwyddyd a fydd herwydd y llythyrenau cyfarwydd yn eu trefn waranted a chadarn, sef yn lle pillwydd
y bydd peithenen elech, ag erni 'r darllenad ai thorri a
chethren ddûr, neu a challestren lem.

Y gwr am rhoddes riniau, &c.

LLOSGI 'R CYRFENI.

Yn amser Llyr Llediaith y deallwyd llosgi 'r Cyrfeni a
notteyrn, sef haern i bob llythyren ai boethi 'n goch ag a
hwnnw llosgi ar ebill neu astell a fai achos, ag weithiau a
man bigiadau pwyned boeth ffurfio 'r Llythyrenau ar goed.

---

* The virtue or charm attributed to letters, as here explained, accounts very
clearly for the etymology of rhint, (a rhin,) a notch.

SECRET COELBREN.—SECRET COELVAIN.—COELVAIN
OF HISTORY.

The mysteries of the Bards, that is to say, the secret
Coelbrens, are small ebillion, a finger long, having notches,
so that they may be used by two persons or more, who are
confidants. It is by placing and joining them together,
with reference to what is secret, that words and phrases are
formed; and by bundling them into words, according to
secrecy, missive epistles and secret books are constructed,
the meaning of which no one knows but confidants; nor is
it right, according to usage and troth, to divulge the same.
They are called the Charms of the Bards, or Bardic Mystery.

Secret Coelvains are similar, made of small stonês bearing
the marks of mystery; and it is by disposing them, according to the arrangement and art of the Secret, that necessary
sciences are demonstrated. And where such Coelbrens exhibit the number of the letters of the Historical Coelbren, let
them be made secret by changing one letter for another, so
that it be not ascertained except from the necessity and
declination of the same letter twice in the same meaning
and power.

The Coelvain of History will be, in respect of the historical letters, according to their authorized and fixed order;
that is, instead of pillwydd there will be a Peithynen of
slate, having on it the reading, inscribed with a steel spike,
or a sharp flint.

BURNING THE LETTERS.

It was in the time of Llyr of Defective Speech that the
way of burning the cyrvens with an iron stamp was understood, that is, there was an iron for every letter, heated red
hot, with which they burnt on an ebill or a board what was
required; and sometimes they formed letters on wood with
the small prickings of a hot fork.

COELBREN LLYTHYRAU GODIDOGION.

Ambell waith y beirdd a gedwynt goelbrenni llythyrau godidogion sef nid amgen nag un llythyr ar bob prenn, ag o ddodi y rhai hynny ynghyd herwydd gofyn gair ag enw ymarwyddaint y naill a'r llaill a chyd ymddeall ag ymwybod a'u gilydd heb lafar, ag ynghyfrinach. a phob un or prenni yn bedryfal a chwech wyneb i bob un, a llythyr ar bob wyneb, a lliwiau gwahanred arnynt fal y caid a fynnid ar olwg heb hir ymchwil. a dosparth pedwar ar hugain a gaid yn orau ar y rhyw goelbrenni hynny ag o'r cydymwybyddu a'u gilydd a'r Coelbrenni hynny y dygynt ar wybod dirgelion o bethau y rhyfeddid yn fawr pa fodd y gellid hynny.

COELBREN CIL DWRN.

Coelbren Cil dwrn yw un lle torrer pedwar ar hugain ar bedrynau bychain sef fal y mae chwech ochr i bob pedryn, a llythyryn ar bob ochr, am hynny y bydd ar y pedwar pedryddyn 24 llythyren ar hugain heblaw a ellir yn amgen lle gwrthdroser pedrydd i ddangos llythyryn amrafael, sef Λ Λ, ⅃ Ⴑ Ⴔ ⟨ Ð Y Ⴑ M ac eraill, a wnant o'u troi V, Ⴣ—Γ, Ⱶ Ⴚ · ⟩ ◁ · Ⱶ Ⱬ· W, &c. sef a, ā, e, ē, ng, ō, d, y, y m, a wnant or eu gwrthraws w, w̄, p, ff, ngh, d, dd, l ll, w. ag a'r rhai hyn o'u dal mewn dwrn au dodi nghyd yngwydd gwr o gyfrin, y gellir cynnal cyflafar mud.

COELBREN BEITHYN.—COELBREN CIL DWRN.

Coelbren Beithyn yw Ebillwydd wedi eu dodi ynghyd yn drefnus mewn pillwydd.

---

[1] Peithyn, any thing ribbed or cogged, a term applied to the Wooden Book of the Bards.

COELBREN OF SIMPLE LETTERS.

Occasionally the Bards kept Coelbrens of simple letters, that is to say, one letter on each piece of wood; and by putting them together, according to the requirement of word and name, they mutually communicated one with the other, and understood and acquainted themselves with each other, without speech, and in secrecy. Every one of the pieces of wood was four sided, having six surfaces to each, and a letter on each surface, differently coloured, so that what was wanted might be obtained at sight without much searching. The arrangement of twenty-four was found to be the best for those Coelbrens; and from obtaining mutual knowledge by means of the said Coelbrens secrets were ascertained, which caused much astonishment as to how it was possible.

PALM COELBREN.

The palm Coelbren is that where twenty-four are cut on small dice, that is, inasmuch as each die has six sides, and a letter on each side, there will be on the four dice twenty-four letters, besides what may be obtained otherwise, when the die is reversed, in order to show a different letter. Thus, ∧ ∧ ↓ ↓ ⋏ ⟨ ▷ Y Y M and others, being reversed, will make V V Γ Ⱶ ⋈ ⟩ ◁ ⋏ ⋋ W, &c. that is, a, â, e, ê, ng, c, d, y, y, m, turned upside down will make w, ŵ, p, ff, ngh, d, dd, l, ll, w. By holding some of these in the palm of the hand, and putting them together in the presence of a man of secrecy, dumb conversation can be carried on.

PEITHYN[1] COELBREN.—PALM COELBREN.

The Peithyn Coelbren consists of staves placed regularly together in a frame.

Coelbren Gildwrn yw pedroglau bychain o goed ar ddull
a maint disiau a llythyr ar bob un a thwll bychan ymhob un
a'u llinynu drwy'r tyllau a chynnifer llinyn a llythyr sef y
llythyrer ∧ ar un llinyn ∧ ar linyn arall ac yn unwedd
pob llinyn, a phob llinyn ei lythr, a lle bo rhoi a derbyn
gwybodaeth dan rin, un dyn a gymmer oddiar ei linynau a
fo achos, a hwnnw a'u hettyb yn ol yn yr un modd, ag fal
hynny o ddwrn i ddwrn hyd y bo achos, a choelbren cil
dwrn eu galw. a llafar cil dwrn ag awgrym cil dwrn. a
mynych y llythyrid Cerdd dafod fal hynny ys ef y bann
cyntaf ar ei linyn, felly 'r ail ar holl fannau canlyn hyd
ddiwedd y gerdd, a rhwng gair a gair er i bob gair fod yn
amlwg ar benn ei hunan coetten gronn. a choelbren aflafar
ag awgrym aflafar y gelwir hynn, a chyfranu cyfrinach y
gelwir hynn sef y gellir yngolwg yr holl fyd heb neb yn ei
wybod ond y cyfeillion cyfrin eu hunain.

PEITHYNFAIN.

Modd arall ar Lyfru gwybodau oedd peithynfain, sef ysgrifenu a phiccell ddur ar ddau wyneb y meini, a chyda
hynny eu dodi ar dennyn cryf neu ar wialen haern neu efydd
a elai drwy dwll yn nhalcen pob peithynfaen, ar meini hynn
a elwid Coelfain. modd arall oedd un Hywel Dda o grebwyll
Blegywryd ei ysgolhaig ef, sef oedd hynny wynebu neuadd
Llys y Tywysog a pheithynfain un tu ag arall or neuadd ag
ar y main yn gyfrill ysgrifennu a phiccell gref y cyfreithiau
a ddodes Hywel ar wlad a chenedl y Cymry, a phorth agored
i bod dŷn y bai achos iddo pwy bennaf o ddyn y byddai ai
brodor ai Estron gyrchu 'r neuadd a darllain y gyfraith a
chael ei darllenoi iddaw, ag o hynny y daeth yr arfer dodi

---

[1] Peithynvain is the plural of peithynvaen, (peithyn maen,) the stone of elucidation.

[2] He was also Archdeacon of Llandaff. See Ancient Laws and Institutes of
Wales, vol. i. p. 343.

The palm Coelbren consists of small squares of wood of the shape and size of dice, each containing a letter, and a small hole, through which a string is passed. There are as many strings as there are letters; that is, ∧ is lettered on one string, ∧ on another string, and in the same way with every string, each string having its own letter. And where knowledge is mutually communicated in secret, one man takes from his string what is necessary, and the other answers him back in the same manner; and thus from palm to palm as long as is required. This is called the palm Coelbren, and the palm speech, and the palm alphabet; and frequently has vocal song been lettered in this way, that is, the first verse on its own string, the second accordingly, and all the following verses to the end of the song. And between word and word, in order that each word might be distinctly evident, a round piece of wood is inserted. This is called the dumb Coelbren, and the dumb alphabet; and it is called the imparting of secrets, for it can be done in sight of all the world, without any body knowing it, except the privy friends alone.

PEITHYNVAIN.

Another mode for booking sciences were the Peithynvain,[1] that is, they wrote with a steel pencil on both surfaces of the stones, and then put them on a strong cord, or on an iron or brass rod, which passed through the top of every Peithynvaen. These stones were called Coelvain. Another method was that of Howel the Good, devised by Blegywryd, his Clerk,[2] which was this;—they faced the hall of the Prince's court with stones, one side and another of the hall, and on the stones wrote in order, with a strong pencil, the laws which Howel imposed upon the country and nation of the Cymry, an open entrance being left for every man that needed, whatever man he might be, whether a native or a stranger, to proceed into the hall, and to read the law, or to have it read to him. Hence it became customary to inscribe

cerdd dafod, a rhol a chan, a chof gweithredoedd moliannus, a Chyfarwyddyd doethineb ar beithynfain au dodi ar wyneb magwyr a phared neu ar linynau neu wiail heyrn. ag o hynn y doethpwyd i alw coelfain ar bob gwybodau ba bennaf o ryw y baint. a pha bennaf o bethau llythyrid arno.

Y Brenin Arthur a ddodes ddosparth y Ford Gron a gweithredoedd molianus ei marchogion ar ^{ddalenau} ^{estyll} efyddaid ac alcanaid yn ei dair Priflys, nid amgen Caerllion ar wysg a'r Gelliwig, a Phenrhyn Rhionydd ag arnynt eu ysgrifenu a phiccell ddur.

COF A CHADW.

Cyn dyfod gwybod ar Lythyr, nid oedd amgen o gof a chadw na cherdd dafawd warantedig o dair Cadair, a Llafar Gorsedd gyfallwy, sef Tair gorsedd gyfallwy ai cedwynt gofau a chadwedigaethau. nid amgen Gorsedd Beirdd, Gorsedd Llys Arglwydd a Chyfraith, a Gorsedd Dygynnull gwlad a chenedl, a chyfallwy pob cof a chadw a gaffai wyneb Tair gorsedd ai un ai arall fyddaint o'r Tair Gorsedd gwlad a chenedl. sef wyneb yr un orsedd dair gwaith dan osteg a Rhybydd undydd a blwyddyn.

Gwedi cael gwybod ar Lythyr Doded cadw Coelbrenni Gwarantedig o orsedd gyfallwy, ar bob Gorsedd ba un bynnag, ar cof ar cadw hynny a elwyd Cyfarwydd hefyd Cyfarwyddyd.

Gwedi hynny cad wybodaeth ar blagawd sef croen Llythyr a elwir memrwn o'r Lladin. yna doded cadw Rholau gwarantedig ar yr holl orseddau, fal ag y mae yn awr, a gwedi hynny Rholau a llyfrau Papir, eisoes gorau cof a chadw Llafar Gorsedd, sef nis gellir namyn ynghlyw gwlad a chenedl a wypo 'r ddefod, ag nis gellir yr gwybod cadarn ar

---

[1] This is supposed to be the same as Pendennis Castle. See Hughes's Horæ Britanicæ, vol. ii. append. iii.

[2] Glasgow.

a vocal song, a Roll, a poem, the memorial of praiseworthy deeds, and the narration of wisdom, on Peithynvain, and to place them on the face of walls and partitions, or on strings, or iron rods. It was from this also that the practice arose of giving the name of Coelvain to all sciences, of whatsoever kind they were, and to whatsoever things that were inscribed thereon.

King Arthur placed the system of the Round Table, and the praiseworthy deeds of its knights, on plates of brass and tin, in his three principal courts, namely, Caerleon-upon-Usk, Celliwig,[1] and Penrhyn Rhionydd,[2] written with a steel pencil.

MEMORIALS.

Before the knowledge of letters was obtained, there was no other memorial than vocal song, authorized by three Chairs, and the voice of an efficient Gorsedd. There were three efficient Gorsedds that preserved memorials, namely, the Gorsedd of Bards, the Gorsedd of the court of lord and law, and a conventional Gorsedd of country and nation. And every memorial was efficient that received the countenance of three Gorsedds, of one or other of the three Gorsedds of country and nation ; that is, the countenance of the same Gorsedd three times under the proclamation and notice of a year and a day.

When the knowledge of letters was obtained, the preservation of Coelbrens, authorized by an efficient Gorsedd, was imposed upon every Gorsedd whatsoever; and that memorial was called *Cyvarwydd*, also *Cyvarwyddyd*.

After that, a knowledge of Plagawd, namely, letter skin, called membrane from the Latin, was obtained. Then all the Gorsedds were required to preserve authorized Rolls, as at present ; and, after that, Rolls and Books of paper. Nevertheless, the best is the memorial of the Voice of Gorsedd, because no one can know the usage except in the hearing of country and nation, and there can be no confirmed

X

a ddoder ar y Llythyr, a Llyfr am nas gellir clyw gwlad a
chenedl ar gof ag atgof Llythyr yn warantedig, un amgen
nag arall o'r Rholau ar Llyfrau anghytcof.

PLAGAWD.

Plagawd, sef ydoedd Llysewyn o ryw elestron a gyrchit
o'r India, ag arnaw ydd ysgrifennid a du, neu arall o liw.
Gwedi hynny gwnaethpwyd plagawd crwyn, au darllaw gan
gelfyddyd.

TRI PHRIF GYFFYR GORWYDDAWD.

Tri phrif gyffyr gorwyddawd Beirdd Ynys Prydain,
Gwydd sef Coelbren, a Choelfain, a'r ddau hynn cyn caffael
y ffydd ynghrist a gwedi caffael hynny y cafwyd deall a
gwybod ar y Trydydd nid amgen na Phlagawd sef hynny
croen ysgrubl triniedig a elwir memrwn (rawen. dau grawen
⁓y sydd. un gwydd, ag un ysgrubl).

ARWYDDFARDD,

Gwybodau arwyddfardd a gollwyd _{namyn}^{eithr} y maint a gedwir
yng nghelfydd Pais arfau ; ac yn yr amseroedd cyntefinoed
gwybodau arwyddion a fuant anrydeddus, a phob Cymro
cynhenid a wisgai arwyddion ei ach ai freiniau ai weithredoedd molianus a gweithredoedd molianus ei riaint, ac achos
hynny y gelwid pais arfau ar ymwisg ach a Bonedd, a gwedi
trefnu Ofyddiaeth Cafad gwellhad ar wybodau Llythyr a
Chof Coelbren, ag ymddifadu gwybodau arwyddion, ag ym-
ddigoni ynghelfydd Prifardd sef Cerdd dafawd a llafar gor-

---

[1] It is not very clear whether this word is the same or not with *crawen*, a
crust, having here the meaning of rind or skin.

knowledge of what is stated by letter and book, because the memory and recollection of letters cannot have the warranty of the hearing of country and nation—one, any more than another, of the Rolls and Books, which do not agree in their records.

PLAGAWD.

Plagawd was a plant of the lilly kind, which was brought over from India; and on it they wrote with black, or some other colour. After that Plagawd of skin was made, being manufactured by art.

THE THREE PRINCIPAL MATERIALS OF KNOWLEDGE.

The three principal materials of knowledge of the Bards of the Isle of Britain : wood, that is Coelbren; and Coelvain; which two existed before the faith in Christ was obtained ; and when that was obtained, knowledge and understanding was had of the third, namely Plagawd, that is, the dressed skin of a beast, which is called parchment. (Grawen.[1] There are two grawens : one of wood, the other of a beast.)

THE HERALD-BARD.

The sciences of a Herald-bard have been lost, except what is preserved in the art of armory. In primitive times the sciences of heraldry were honourable, and every innate Cymro bore the signs of his lineage, his privileges, and his praiseworthy deeds, and of the praiseworthy deeds of his ancestors ; and on that account the bearing of lineage and gentility was called a coat of arms. And when Ovatism was appointed, the sciences of Letter, and the memorial of Coelbren, were improved, and the sciences of heraldry were abolished, being sufficiently included in the art of a Primitive Bard, namely, Vocal Song, the voice of Gorsedd, and the

sedd, a gwybodau y gelfyddyd wrth **Lythyr a Choelbren**, a **Choelfain**, a gwedi hynny Rhôl ysgrifen a hynny nid amgen na Rhol ysgrifen a gafad gan a ddaethant a'r ffydd ynghrist gyntaf i'r ynys honn, sef yr amser hynny y daeth ar gyfred gwlad a Chenedl y Cymry Celfyddyd ymbeithioni gwybodau ar grwyn plagod, yn Rôl gadwedig.

DASGUBELL RODD.

Pa beth yw Dasgubell rodd?
A.   goriadau 'r goelbren gyssefin
Pa ddangos ar oriadau 'r goelbren gyssefin?
A.   Y Ddasgubell Rodd.

---

[1] The introduction of the Roll is elsewhere specially attributed to Bran the Blessed, father of the renowned Caractacus.

[2] " A gift besom ;" probably in reference to its employment of clearing off what hides the bare truth, or of divulging the secret in which it is couched.

[3] Before we dismiss the subject of the Coelbren, it may not be uninteresting to notice a fact which, as far as it goes, clearly disproves the charge, which would palm upon the late Iolo Morganwg the invention of the Bardic characters. About six or seven years ago, during the process of repairing an old house, called " The Court," at Merthyr Tydvil, a room, which had been closed for a period of time exceeding the memory of man, was laid open, and in it were found several pieces of oak furniture, of decidedly a Tudor character, on one of which, a bedstead, were engraved, in relief, the letters

W < ᚼ

that is, in modern orthography, M C L.   Mr. Thomas Stephens, author of *The Literature of the Cymry*, who has examined the carving, and inquired into the history of the family that owned the bedstead, has kindly favoured us with the following remarks ;—" As to the age of the letters, they are probably, and to all appearance, of the same age as the bedstead. Wood carving in England does not lay claim to any great antiquity. A taste for carving prevailed during the reigns of the Tudors as well as of the Stewards ; and it seems to me that the bedstead in question may be about 250 years old, or perhaps 300 ; but certainly not more. If the true date is ever ascertained, I think it not unlikely that I shall be found to have overstated its age than otherwise. This, however, will be of service in determining the age of the Coelbren to be at least as old as the age of Llywelyn Sion, and in setting aside all imputations upon the character of Iolo Morganwg, as a setter forth of an alphabet of his own invention."

This is a most important admission on the part of one who is in general extremely sceptical about the traditions of the Bards. Mr. Stephens proceeds to give some account of the family, thus :—

sciences of Letter, Coelbren, and Coelvaen, and after that, the Roll of writing. That, namely, the Roll of writing,[1] was obtained by those who first introduced the faith in Christ into this island ; that is, it was at that time that the art of elucidating sciences on plagawd skins, in preserved Rolls, became general in the country and among the nation of the Cymry.

DASGUBELL RODD.[2]

Question. What is the Dasgubell Rodd?

Answer. The keys of the primitive Coelbren.

Q. What is it that explains the primitive Coelbren?[3]

A. The Dasgubell Rodd.

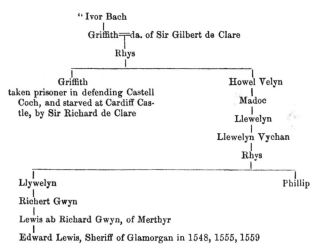

" Ivor Bach
|
Griffith══da. of Sir Gilbert de Clare
|
Rhys
|

Griffith
taken prisoner in defending Castell Coch, and starved at Cardiff Castle, by Sir Richard de Clare

Howel Velyn
|
Madoc
|
Llewelyn
|
Llewelyn Vychan
|
Rhys

Llywelyn
|
Richert Gwyn
|
Lewis ab Richard Gwyn, of Merthyr
|
Edward Lewis, Sheriff of Glamorgan in 1548, 1555, 1559

Phillip

He lived at Van, near Caerphilly, and was the patron of Meyrig Dafydd, (See Cyfrinach y Beirdd, pp. 124, 127,) Dafydd Llwyd Matthew, and other Bards. The family, therefore, was one which must have been cognizant of Coelbren y Beirdd. Next in descent was

1. Thomas Lewis, of Van, also Sheriff of Glamorgan in 1569—died Nov. 2, 1594, 37th of Queen Elizabeth.

Pa beth amgen ?

A. Cyfrinach y ddasgubell Rodd.

Pa gyfrinach ?

A. Cyfrinach Beirdd Ynys Prydain.

Pa ddatrin ar gyfrinach Beirdd Ynys Prydain ?

A. Addysg gan athraw ym mraint adduned.

Pa ryw adduned ?

A. Ymaddunedu a Duw.

He had the following brothers and sisters, viz.,—

2. William Lewis		4. Mary Lewis	
3. Edward Lewis		5. Elizabeth Lewis	
		6. Margaret Lewis	
		7. Jane Lewis	
		8. Blanch Lewis	
		9. Cicely Lewis	

Thomas Lewis married Margaret, daughter of Robert Gamage of Coyty, and uncle of the Countess of Leicester, the great Gamage heiress ; and as his eldest

Q. What else?

A. The secret of the Dasgubell Rodd.

Q. What secret?

A. The secret of the Bards of the Isle of Britain.

Q. What will divulge the secret of the Bards of the Isle of Britain?

A. Instruction by a master in virtue of a vow.

Q. What kind of vow?

A. A vow made with God.

son was born in 1560, the marriage probably took place during the Shrievalty of Sir Edward Lewis in 1559.

We have here the material for the interpretation of M C L. If these letters are not the initials of any one of the three sisters—Mary, Margaret, or Cicely Lewis, then they are most probably those of the bride of Thomas Lewis—Margaret Gamage Lewis — C being used as a radical instead of G. There are two carved bedsteads at the Court; one far more elaborately carved than the subject of these remarks. The former was probably the wedding gift of Sir Edward Lewis to his son; the latter, part of the dowry of Margaret Gamage. That at all events is my exposition of W ⟨ Λ."

Dwyfyddiaeth.

TRIOEDD BARDDAS. *

1.   Tri un cyntefig y sydd, ag nis gellir amgen nag un o honynt, Un Duw; Un Gwirionedd; ag Un Pwngc Rhyddyd, sef y bydd lle bo cydbwys pob gwrth.

2.   Tri pheth tardd o'r tri Un cyntefig, pob Bywyd; pob Daioni; a phob Gallu.

3.   O dri anghenfod y mae Duw, sef y mwyaf parth bywyd; y mwyaf parth gwybod; a'r mwyaf parth nerth; ag nis gellir namyn un o'r mwyaf ar unpeth.

4.   Tri pheth nis dichon Duw lai na bod, a ddylai 'r da cyflawn; a ddymunai 'r da cyflawn; ag a ddichon y da cyflawn.

5.   Tri thyston Duw am a wnaeth ag a wnâ, Gallu anfeidrol; Gwybodaeth anfeidrol; a Chariad anfeidrol; gan nad oes nas dichon, nas gwyr, ag nas mynn y rhain.

---

* These Triads are printed in Edward Williams's Lyric Poems, vol. second. Of the copy from which they were taken, he gives the following account;— " The Triades that are here selected are from a Manuscript Collection, by Llywelyn Sion, a Bard of Glamorgan, about the year 1560. Of this manuscript I have a transcript; the original is in the possession of Mr. Richard Bradford, of Bettws, near Bridgend, in Glamorgan. This collection was made from various manuscripts of considerable, and some of very great antiquity—these, and their authors, are mentioned, and most or all of them still extant.''

Theology.

TRIADS OF BARDISM.

1.   There are three primeval Unities, and more than one of each cannot exist: one God; one truth; and one point of liberty, and this is where all opposites equiponderate.

2.   Three things proceed from the three primeval Unities: all life; all goodness; all power.

3.   God consists necessarily of three things: the greatest in respect of life; the greatest in respect of knowledge; and the greatest in respect of power; and there can only be one of what is greatest in any thing.

4.   Three things it is impossible God should not be: whatever perfect goodness ought to be; whatever perfect goodness would desire to be; and whatever perfect goodness can be.

5.   The three witnesses of God in respect of what He has done, and will do: infinite power; infinite knowledge; and infinite love; for there is nothing that these cannot perform, do not know, and will not bring to pass.

They were published at Geneva, in 1856, by M. Pictet, under the title of " Cyfrinach Beirdd Ynys Prydain," or " Le Mystere des Bardes de l'Ile de Bretagne," accompanied by a translation and a commentary in the French language.

Y

6. Tri phendod trefn gwaith Duw, er peri pôb peth; dirymmu 'r drwg; nerthu 'r da, ag amlygu pob gwahaniaeth, fal y gwyper a ddylai oddiwrth na ddylai fod.

7. Tri pheth nis gall Duw lai na'u gwneuthur, y mwyaf ei les; y mwyaf ei eisiau; a'r mwyaf er harddwch o bob peth.

8. Tri chadernyd hanfod, nis gellir amgen; nid rhaid amgen; ag nis gellir gwell gan feddwl; ag yn hynn y diwedd pob peth.

9. Tri pheth dir y byddant; eitha Gallu; eitha deall; ag eitha cariad Duw.

10. Tri bannogion Duw; Bywyd cyfoll; Gwybodaeth cyfoll; a Chadernyd cyfoll.

11. Tri achos bywedigion, Cariad Duw gan eitha deall cyflawn; Deall Duw yn gwybod eitha moddion; a Nerth Duw gan eitha Mynn Cariad a Deall.

12. Tri chylch hanfod y sydd, Cylch y Ceugant, lle nid oes namyn Duw, na byw na marw, ag nid oes namyn Duw a eill ei dreiglo; Cylch yr Abred, lle pob Ansawdd-hanfod o'r marw, a Dyn ai treiglwys; Cylch y Gwynfyd, lle pob Ansawdd hanfod o'r Byw, a Dyn ai treigla yn y Nef.

---

[1] Cylch y Ceugant, translated by Ed. Williams, " the circle of infinity," and by M. Pictet, " le cercle de la region vide," means literally, the circle of the enclosing circumference, that is, the perfect rim that bounds the entire space of existence. From the idea of unchangeableness or absoluteness, involved in the doctrine of the ceugant, the word has acquired a secondary meaning, that of " certain." It is in that sense that we are to understand it in the adage—

    Ceugant yw angau.

    Death is *certain*.

Also in the following passage from Llywarch Prydydd y Moch, A.D. 1160—1220—

    Ked archwyf ym llyw y lloergant yn rot
    Ef am ryt yn *geugant*.

    Even should I demand of my chief the moon as a gift,
    He will *certainly* give it me.
    I Llywelyn ap Iorwerth, Myv. Arch. i. p. 300.

[2] Cylch yr Abred is rendered by Ed. Williams, " the circle of inchoation," and by M. Pictet, " le cercle de transmigration." Abred seems to be com-

6. The three ultimate ends of God's regulation in giving existence to every thing: to weaken the evil; to strengthen the good; and to manifest all discrimination, that what ought to be might be known from what ought not to be.

7. Three things which God cannot but perform: what is most useful; what is most necessary; and what is most beautiful of all things.

8. The three stabilities of existence: what cannot be otherwise; what need not be otherwise; and what cannot be conceived better; and in these will all things end.

9. Three things will necessarily exist: the supreme power; the supreme intelligence; and the supreme love of God.

10. The three characteristics of God: complete life; complete knowledge; and complete power.

11. The three causes of living beings: the love of God in accord with the most perfect intelligence; the understanding of God knowing all possible means; and the power of God in accord with supreme will, love, and intelligence.

12. There are three Circles of existence: the Circle of Ceugant,[1] where there is nothing but God, of living or dead, and none but God can traverse it; the Circle of Abred,[2] where all things are by nature derived from death, and man has traversed it; and the Circle of Gwynvyd,[3] where all things spring from life, and man shall traverse it in heaven.

---

pounded of *ab*, from, and *rhed*, a course, in reference to the migration of the soul from one animal to another, until it reaches the state of humanity.

Abred is mentioned in a poem attributed to Taliesin, where it is used to denote hell.

Hyd pan ddillyngwys Crist gaethiwed
O ddwfn fais affwys *abred*.

Until Christ released the bondage
From the immensely deep abyss of *hell*.
Y Milveib, Myv. Arch. v. i. p. 170.

[3] Cylch y Gwynvyd, the circle of the *white*, or, (taking that colour as the emblem of purity,) the *holy* world;—the circle of felicity, for, be it observed, *gwynvyd* is the term generally used by the Cymry to this day to denote bliss or happiness.

13. Tri chyflwr hanfod Bywedigion, Cyflwr Abred yn Annwn; Cyflwr Ryddyd yn Nyndod; a Chyflwr Cariad, sef Gwynfyd, yn y Nef.

14. Tri Angen pob hanfod wrth fywyd, dechre yn Annwn; Treigl yn Abred; a Chyflawnder yn y Nef, sef Cylch y Gwynfyd; ag heb hynn o dripheth nis gellir unpeth namyn Duw.

15. Tripheth Angen yn Abred, y Lleiaf o bob byw, ag o hynny dechre; Defnydd pob peth, ag o hynny cynnydd, yr hynn nis gellir mewn cyflwr amgen; a llunio pob peth o'r marw, ag o hynny Gwanhanfod.

16. Tripheth nis gellir amgen na'u bod ar bob byw gan gyfiawnder Duw; Cydymoddef yn Abred, can heb hynny ni cheylai neb gyflawn wybod ar ddim; Cydran cydfraint ynghariad Duw, a Chyttiwedd, gan allu Duw wrth a fo cyfiawn a thrugar.

17. Tri achos angen Abred, cynnull defnydd pob Ansawdd; cynnull Gwybodaeth pob peth; a chynnull Nerth er gorfod pob gwrth a Chythraul, ag ymddiosg a'r drwg; ag heb hynn a dreiglo pob cyflwr byw, nis gellir cyflawn ar un byw na rhyw.

18. Tri phrif anffawd Abred, Angen, Anghof, ag Angau.

19. Thri phen Angen y sydd cynn cyflwyr Wybodaeth, treiglo 'r Abred; treiglo 'r Gwynfyd; a Chof o'r cyfan hyd yn Annwn.

20. Tri chynghyd anhepcor Abred, Anghyfraith gan nas gellir amgen; Dianc Angau rhag drwg a Chythraul; a

---

[1] Annwn=annwfn, (an-dwfn,) a bottomless gulf; an abyss; the great deep, or lowest point of existence, as it is translated by Ed. Williams. There is an old adage which says,

Nid eir i *annwn* ond unwaith.—*Annwn* is visited but once.

Taliesin opposes it to heaven, when he speaks of a deluge;—

O nef pan ddoethant
Yn *annwfn* llifeiriant.

When it came from heaven,
The torrent reached to *annwn*.—Kad Goddeu.

In the Christian code, annwn is made to stand for hell.

13. The three states of existence of living beings : the state of Abred in Annwn ;[1] the state of liberty in humanity ; and the state of love, that is, Gwynvyd in heaven.

14. The three necessities of all animated existences : a beginning in Annwn ; progression in Abred ; and plenitude in heaven, that is, the circle of Gwynvyd ; without these three things nothing can exist but God.

15. Three things are necessary in Abred : the least of all animation, and thence a beginning ; the material of all things, and thence increase, which cannot take place in any other state ; and the formation of all things out of the dead, hence diversity of existence.

16. Three things cannot but happen to all living beings by the justice of God : co-sufferance in Abred, because without that none could obtain the perfect knowledge of any thing ; co-participation of equal privilege in the love of God ; and co-ultimity, through the power of God, in respect of such as are just and merciful.

17. The three necessary occasions of Abred : to collect the materials of every nature ; to collect the knowledge of every thing ; and to collect strength to overcome every adverse and Cythraul,[2] and to be divested of evil ; without this traversing of every state of life, no animation or species can attain to plenitude.

18. The three principal calamities of Abred : necessity ; forgetfulness ; and death.

19. The three principal necessities before fulness of knowledge can be obtained : to traverse Abred ; to traverse Gwynvyd ; and the remembrance of all as far as Annwn.

20. Three things indispensably connected with Abred : lawlesness, for it cannot be otherwise ; the escape of death from evil and Cythraul ; and the increase of life and good-

---

[2] Cythraul, (cy-traul,) the principle of destruction. The term is that which is still employed for the most part to denote the devil, or Satan.

Chynnydd bywyd a Daioni, gan ymddiosg a'r drwg yn ni-aingc Angau; a hynn o gariad Duw yn gafaelu ar bob peth.

21. Tri pheiriant Duw yn Abred er gorfod Drwg a Chythraul, a diangc oddiwrthynt at Wynfyd, Angen; Anghof; ag Angau.

22. Tri chynghyfoedion y sydd, Dyn; Rhyddyd; a Goleuni.

23. Tri Angenorfod Dyn, Dioddef, Newid, a Dewis; a chan allu dewis ni wyper am y ddau arall cyn digwydd.

24. Tri Chydgyfran Dyn, Abred a Gwynfyd; Angen a Rhyddyd, a Drwg a Da; ag oll yn gydbwys, a gallu gan ddyn ymlynn wrth yr un fynno.

25. O dripheth y syrth Angen Abred ar Ddyn, Anym-gais a Gwybodaeth; anymlyn a'r Dâ; ag ymlyn a'r Drwg, sef y syrth, gan hynn o bethau, hyd ei gydryw yn Abred, a threiglo 'n ei ol fal y bu gyntaf.

26. O dripheth y syrthier yn Abred gan Angen, er ym-lynu ymhob peth arall wrth y Dâ, o Falchder hyd Annwn; o Anwiredd hyd Obryn; ag o Anrhugaredd, hyd Gydfil, a threiglo 'n ol at Ddyndod fal o'r blaen.

27. Tri chyntefigaeth cyflwr Dyn, cynnull cyntaf ar Wybodaeth, Cariad, a Nerth, heb Angau; ag nis gellir hynn ym mraint Rhydd a Dewis cyn Dyndod; a'r tri hynn a elwir y tri gortrech.

28. Tri gortrech ar Ddrwg a Chythraul y sydd; Gwy-bodaeth, Cariad, a Gallu; gan y gwyr, y mynn, ag y dichon y rhain yn eu cynghyd y pethau a fynnont, ag ynghyflwr Dyn eu dechre, a parhau dros fyth.

---

[1] M. Pictet has rendered this "l'impassibilitié," as if the word was com-pounded of *di*, non, and *goddef*, to endure. He was driven to prefer this ac-ceptation, from having mistaken the word " angenorfod," which he supposed to mean *what was necessary for the triumph of man over evil*, and not, as we have rendered it, " the necessary obligations " of a man, as such.

[2] Obryn is an obsolete word, but seems to be compounded of *ob*, a going out of, and *rhyn*, an emotion, or perception, and to signify an equivalent state of perception. Ed. Williams has it, " a state corresponding with his turpitude," and is followed therein by M. Pictet, who writes " point de démérite équiva-lent."

ness, by being divested of evil in the escapes of death ; and this from the love of God embracing all things.

21. The three instrumentalities of God in Abred for the subduing of evil and Cythraul, and escaping from them towards Gwynvyd : necessity ; forgetfulness ; and death.

22. There are three primary contemporaries : man ; liberty ; and light.

23. The three necessary obligations of man : to suffer ;[1] to change ; and to choose ; and whilst he has the power of choosing, the other two things are not known before they happen.

24. The three equiportions of man : Abred and Gwynvyd ; necessity and liberty ; evil and good ; all equiponderate, man having the power of attaching himself to the one he pleases.

25. From three things will the necessity of Abred fall on man : from not endeavouring to obtain knowledge ; from non-attachment to good ; and from attachment to evil ; occasioned by these things he will fall to his congener in Abred, whence he will return, as at first.

26. From three things will man fall of necessity in Abred, though he has in every thing else attached himself to good : from pride even to Annwn ; from falsehood to a corresponding state of perception ;[2] and from unmercifulness to a similarly disposed animal,[3] whence, as at first, he returns to humanity.

27. The three primaries of the state of man : the first accumulations of knowledge, love, and power, without death. This cannot take place, in virtue of liberty and choice, previous to humanity : these are called the three victories.

28. The three victories over evil and Cythraul : knowledge ; love ; and power ; for these know, will, and can do, in their conjunctive capacity, what they desire ; they begin in the state of man, and continue for ever.

---

[3] Cydvil, (cyd-mil,) co-animal, meaning an animal corresponding in disposition with himself. " A corresponding state of brutal malignity."—Ed. Williams.

29. Tri braint cyflwr Dyn, Cydbwys drwg a dâ, ag yna Cymhariaeth; Rhyddid wrth Ddewis ag o hynny Barn a Dewis; a Chynnechre Gallu, ym mraint Barn a Dewis, gan eu rhaid cyn dim arall o wneuthur.

30. Tri gwahaniaeth angenorfod rhwng Dyn, a phob byw arall, a Duw; Ing ar Ddyn ag nis gellir ar Dduw; dechre ar Ddyn ag nis gellir ar Dduw; ag angen newid cyflwr olynol ynghylch y Gwynfyd ar Ddyn, o anoddef y Ceugant, ag nis gellir ar Dduw, gan allu pob dioddef, a hynny gan Wynfyd.

31. Tri chyntefigaeth Gwynfyd, Annrwg; Anneisiau; ag Annarfod.

32. Tri adfer Cylch y Gwynfyd, Awen gysefin; a gared gysefin; a Chôf y cysefin; am nas gellir Gwynfyd hebddynt.

33. Tri gwahanfod pob byw gwrtharall; Awen; Côf; a Chanfod; sef y bydd cyflawn ar bobun, ag nis gellir cyfun y rhain ar un byw arall, a phob un yn gyflawn, ag nis gellir dau gyflawn ar ddim.

34. Tri pheth a roddwys Duw ar bob byw, sef Cyflawnder ei Ryw; Gwahander pen ei hun; a Bannogaeth Awen gysefin rhag arall, yna hunan cyfoll pob un gwrtharall.

35. O ddeall tripheth y bydd difant a gortrech ar bob drwg a marw; Ansawdd; Achos; a Pheiriant, a hynn a geir yn y Gwynfyd.

36. Tri chadernyd gwybodaeth, darfod treiglo pob cyflwr bywyd; Cofio treiglo pob cyflwr ai ddamwain; a gallu treiglo pob cyflwr fal y mynner, er prawf a barn; a hynn a gair ynghylch y Gwynfyd.

37. Tri bannogion pob byw ynghylch y Gwynfyd,

---

[1] Genius.

29. The three privileges of the state of man : equiponderance of evil and good, whence comparativity ; liberty of choice, whence judgment and preference ; and the origin of power, proceeding from judgment and preference, since these must necessarily exist before any other action.

30. The three inevitable differences between man, or any other living being, and God : man is finite, which God cannot be ; man had a beginning, which God could not have ; man must needs change his condition successively in the circle of Gwynvyd, from not being able to endure the Ceugant, but God needs not, being able to endure all things, and that consistently with felicity.

31. The three primaries of Gwynvyd : cessation of evil ; cessation of want ; and the cessation of perishing.

32. The three restorations of the circle of Gwynvyd : original Awen ;[1] primitive love ; and primitive memory ; because without these there can be no Gwynvyd.

33. Three things discriminate every animate being from others : Awen ; memory ; and perception : these will be complete in every one, and cannot be common to any other living being ; each will be plenary, and two plenaries of any thing cannot exist.

34. Three things has God given to every living being : namely, the plenitude of his species ; the distinction of his individuality ; and the characteristic of a primitive Awen as different from another ; this is what constitutes the complete self of every one as apart from another.

35. From understanding three things will ensue the diminution and subjugation of all evil and death : their nature ; their cause ; and their operation ; and this will be obtained in Gwynvyd.

36. The three stabilities of knowledge : to have traversed every state of life ; to remember every state and its incidents ; and to be able to traverse every state, as one would wish, for the sake of experience and judgment ; and this will be obtained in the circle of Gwynvyd.

37. The three characteristics of every living being in

Swydd, Braint, ag Awen, ag nis gellir dau 'n bod yn Un-
gyfun ymhôb peth, gan y bydd cyflawn pob un yn y bo
bannog arno; ag nid oes cyflawn ar ddim heb y maint oll a
ddichon fod o hano.

38.   Tripheth nis gall namyn Duw, dioddef bythoedd y
Ceugant; Cynghyd a phob cyflwr heb newidiaw, a rhoi
gwell a newydd ar bob peth heb ei roi ar goll.

39.   Tripheth nis gellir darfod byth arnynt gan angen
eu galledigaeth; Dull hanfod; Ansawdd hanfod; a Llês
hanfod, gan hynn byddant hyd fyth yn eu hannrwg, ai byw
ai marw ydynt, yn amrafael hardd a daionus Cylch y
Gwynfyd.

40.   Tri rhagor newid cyflwr yn y Gwynfyd, Addysg;
Harddwch, a Gorphwys rhag anallu dioddef y Ceugant a'r
tragywyddol.

41.   Tripheth sydd ar eu cynnydd, Tân, sef Goleuni;
Deall, sef Gwirionedd; ag Enaid, sef Bywyd; a gorfod a
wnant ar bop peth, ag yna diwedd Abred.

42.   Tripheth y sydd ar eu difant; Tywyll; Anwir; a
Marw.

43.   Tripheth sy'n ymgadarnhau beunydd, gan fod
mwyaf yr ymgais attynt, Cariad; Gwybodaeth; a Chyfiawnder.

44.   Tripheth sy'n ymwanhau beunydd, gan faint pennaf
yr ymgais yn eu gwrth; Cas; Camwedd; ag Anwybodaeth.

45.   Tri chyflawnder Gwynfyd; Cyfran ymhôb Ansawdd, ag Un cyflawn yn pennu; Cyfymddwyn a phob
Awen, ag yn Un rhagori; Cariad at bob Byw a Bôd, a
thuag at Un, sef Duw, yn bennaf; ag yn y tri Un yma y
saif Cyflawnder Nef a Gwynfyd.

46.   Tri Angen Duw, Anfeidrol ger ei hun; Meidrol

the circle of Gwynvyd: vocation; privilege; and Awen; nor is it possible for two beings to be identical in every thing, for every one will be complete in what is characteristic of him; and there is nothing complete without comprehending the whole quantity that can possibly belong to it.

38. Three things none but God can do: to endure the eternities of Ceugant; to participate of every state without changing; and to ameliorate and renovate every thing without causing the loss of it.

39. Three things that can never be annihilated, from their unavoidable possibilities: form of existence; quality of existence; and the utility of existence; for these will, divested of their evils, exist for ever, whether animate or inanimate, as beautiful and good varieties of the circle of Gwynvyd.

40. The three excellencies of changing condition in Gwynvyd: instruction; beauty; and repose, from not being able to endure the Ceugant and eternity.

41. There are three things on their increase: fire, or light; understanding, or truth; and the soul, or life; these will prevail over every thing, and then Abred will end.

42. There are three things on the wane: the dark; the false; and the dead.

43. Three things acquire strength daily, there being a majority of desires towards them: love; knowledge; and justice.

44. Three things grow more enfeebled daily, there being a majority of desires in opposition to them: hatred; injustice; and ignorance.

45. The three plenitudes of Gwynvyd: participation of every nature, with a plenitude of one predominant; conformity to every Awen, and in one excelling; love towards every living being and existence, and towards one, that is, God, above all; in these three ones will the plenitude of heaven and Gwynvyd consist.

46. The three necessities of God: to be infinite in Him-

ger meidrol; a chyfun a phob cyflwr Bywydolion yngylch
y Gwynfyd.

TRIOEDD DWYFOLDEB.

Tri pheth nis gellir $^{amgen\ na'u\ bod\ bywyd}_{nad\ ydynt\ \ \ \ Duw}$, nerth, a Gwirionedd.

2. O Dri pheth y mae Duw, Bywyd, Nerth, a $^{gwybodaeth}_{Chariad}$.
Al tri pheth nis gellir hebddynt yn Nuw &c

3. Tri ^{phrif} angheneddyl Daioni, Cariad, Nerth, a doethineb, a phob un yn berffaith o angen, ac anhepcor ansawdd.
=cariad. cyfiawnder, a gwirionedd.

4. Tri un y sydd, ac $^{nis\ gellir}_{nid\ oes}$ ail iddynt Un Duw,
$^{unlliw\ gwir}_{un\ gwir}$, ac un pwngc rhyddyd, ac yn y tri hynn y mae
pob daioni 'n wreiddiedig, o barth gallu, daioni, a gwybodaeth.

5. Tri gwahaniaeth angheneddyl rhwng dyn a Duw,
maintioli a meidrolaeth ar ddyn, ac nis gellir ar Dduw,
Dechreu ar Ddyn, ag nis gellir ar Dduw, newid cyflwr ar
Ddyn, ac nis gellir ar Dduw.

6. Tri rhyw hanfodolion, Dyw, Bywedigion, a Marwolion.

7. Tri pheth nis gellir eu bod ar Dduw, bod yn egwan,
yn annoeth, nag yn anrhugarog,—eraill a wedant,

8. Tri pheth ni ddichon Duw, annoethder, bod yn egwan, ag yn annhrugarog.

9. Tri pheth nis gall Duw lai na bod, peth bynnag y
dylai 'r da perffaith, peth bynnag y dymmunai 'r da perffaith, a pheth bynnag y dichon y da perffaith.

10. Tripheth y sydd ac hebddynt nis gellir na Duw na
da perffaith, Gwybodaeth perffaith, Ewyllys perffaith, a
nerth perffaith.

11. Tri phendod trefn a wnaeth Duw er gweithredu pob
peth, darostwng y drwg, derchafu 'r da, ag amlygu pob an-

---

[1] Al. " God."   [2] Ai. "love."   [3] Not in one version.
[4] Al. "they have no."   [5] Al. " unicoloured."

self; to be finite to the finite; and to be co-united with every state of animated beings in the circle of Gwynvyd.

THEOLOGICAL TRIADS.

1. Three things cannot but exist: life;[1] power; and truth.

2. God consists of three things: life; power; and knowledge.[2] Otherwise—Three things that cannot be dispensed with in God, &c.

3. The three principal[3] essentials of goodness: love; power; and wisdom; each one being perfect of necessity, and indispensable nature. Love; justice; and truth.

4. There are three Unities, and they cannot have[4] seconds: one God; one[5] truth; and one point of liberty; and in these three all goodness is rooted in respect of power, goodness, and knowledge.

5. There are three necessary distinctions between man and God: man has size and measure, which God cannot have; man has a beginning, which God cannot have; man is subject to the change of condition, which God cannot be.

6. The three kinds of existences: God; the living; and the dead.

7. Three things which God cannot be; feeble; unwise; and unmerciful. Others say,—

8. Three things which God cannot be: folly; feeble; and unmerciful.

9. Three things which God cannot but be: whatever perfect goodness ought to be; whatever perfect goodness would desire to be; and whatever perfect goodness can be.

10. Three things, without which there can be neither God nor perfect goodness: perfect knowledge; perfect will; and perfect power.

11. The three tendencies of the order of God's work in the formation of all things: to subdue the evil; to elevate

sawdd o barth angen a braint.＝dirymmu 'r drwg, nerthu 'r da, ac amlygu pob gwahaniaeth.

12. Tripheth y rhoddwys Duw yn benn ar bob hanfod, Cariad, Gwirionedd, a Gwybodaeth.

13. Tri chyfnerthiaid Dyn deddfol, Duw, cydwybod ei hun, a mawl pob Doeth.

14. Tripheth a ddangosant Dduw ei hanfod galledig, ei hanfod arwydd, a'i hanfod angen.

15. Tri hanfod angen y sydd ag nis gellir nad ydynt, y mwyaf o bob peth sef Duw, y lleiaf o bob peth, dim ar canol sef $\overset{\text{meidroldeb}}{\text{meidrolaethau}}$·

16. Tri pheth nis gellir nad ydynt yn rhyw le neu amser, y mwyaf yr eisiau arno, y mwyaf ei les, a'r mwyaf a $\overset{\text{garer}}{\text{ddymuner}}$ ei fod, ar peth hynn nis gellir llai nad Duw ydyw.

17. Tri pheth nis gall Duw lai na'u gwneuthur, a fo mwyaf ei les, mwyaf ei eisiau, a mwyaf yr ymgais arno.

18. Tri thystion Duw am ei weithredoedd ei anfeidrol allu, anfeidrol wybodaeth ac anfeidrol gariad, gan nad oes dim nas dichon, nas cais, ag nas ewyllysia 'r angheneddyl-ion hynn.

19. Tri Phrif angheneddyl Duw sylwedd, gwybod, a gallu.

20. ＝Tri Phrif angheddyl Gwybod, $\overset{\text{Teimlad}}{\text{Synhwyr}}$ Deall, ag ∗ ymgais (∗ chariad) ewyllys ·

21. Tri Phrif angheddyl sylwedd, Defnydd ansawdd ac ymmod.

22. Tri Phrif angheneddyl Gallu, Cariad, $\overset{\text{Bryd}}{\text{Ymgais,}}$ a Threfn.

23. Tri phrif ddadanhudd Duw, a ellir o lwyr nerth, a $\overset{\text{wnelai}}{\text{wneir}}$ o lwyr gariad, ac a wyr llwyr wybodaeth. er. a wed. Tri phrif ddadannudd Duw. Tadolaeth, Mabolaeth, ac Ys-prydolaeth.

---

[1] Al. "finitenesses."   [2] Al. "loveable."   [3] Al. "sense."
[4] Al. "will." Al. "love."   [5] Al. "seeking."   [6] Al. "what He would do."

the good; and to manifest every nature in respect of necessity and privilege—To weaken the evil; to strengthen the good; and to manifest every distinction.

12.   Three things that God appointed supreme of every existence: love; truth; and knowledge.

13.   The three supports of a moral man : God; his own conscience; and the praise of all the wise.

14.   Three things that exhibit God : His powerful existence; His significant existence; and His necessary existence.

15.   There are three necessary existences, which cannot but be : the greatest of every thing, that is, God; the least of every thing, that is, nothing; and the middle, that is, finiteness.[1]

16.   Three things that cannot but be in some place or time : the most necessary; the most useful; and the most desirable;[2] and this cannot but be God.

17.   Three things God cannot but perform: what is most useful; what is most necessary; and what is most sought.

18.   The three witnesses of God in respect of His works : His infinite power; infinite knowledge; and infinite love; for there is nothing that these attributes cannot accomplish; cannot seek; and cannot wish.

19.   The three principal attributes of God : essence; knowledge; and power.

20.   The three principal properties of knowledge : feeling;[3] understanding; and seeking.[4]

21.   The three principal properties of essence : substance; quality; and motion.

22.   The three principal properties of power : love; purpose;[5] and order.

23.   The three principal manifestations of God : what can be done by perfect power; what is done[6] by perfect love; and what perfect knowledge knows. Others say,— The three manifestations of God: fatherhood; sonship; and spirituality.

24. Tri pheth cydfyn cyfymgyrch a phob Daioni. Duw yn ei nerth, Cydwybod effraw, a Barn doethion.

25. =Tri achos Bywedigion gan Dduw. Cariad yn dymuno Gwynfyd hyd eitha Deall perffaith. Doethineb yn gwybod eitha moddion, a gallu y medru eithafion amgyffred Deall a Chariad.

26. Tri pheredigaeth pob $^{gwneuthur}_{peth}$, angen a digwydd hyd gylch abred, Dewis o bwyll ryddyd ym myw Dyn, a dewis o gariad ynghyflwr y Gwynfyd.

27. Tri chydwaith Dyn a Duw, dioddef, ystyried, a charu, ac nis gall Dyn gydweithio a Duw mewn dim arall. a dioddef sy bennaf oll can nas gellir y lleill heb hynny.

28. =Tri pheth anghywydd a dyw, anffawd, anwir, ac anobaith.

29. Tri lle y bydd y mwyaf o Dduw, lle bo'r mwyaf ai car, y mwyaf ai cais, a lleiaf or hunan.

30. Tri pheth y sydd a chael Duw lle chwilier am danynt Trugaredd, Gwirionedd, a Heddwch.

31. Tri pheth $^{nis~gwyr~Dyn}_{ni~wyddys~ronyn}$ beth ydynt, Duw, Dim, ac anfeidrol.

32. Tri chylch hanfod y sydd, Cylch y Ceugant, ac nid oes namyn Duw a eill ei dreiglo; Cylch yr abred, a Dyn a'i treiglwys; a Chylch y Gwynfyd, a Dyn a'i treigla.

33. Tri Defnydd ^{gan} Duw yn gwneuthur pob peth, Cariad, Doethineb. a gallu. (Gwel Tri—25).

34. Tri ardderchogrwydd cyflwr Dyn, diwedd abred, Rhyddyd. ac ymgyd a * gwynfydigion. (* nefolion).

35. Tri gwynfyd nef, llwyr orfod ar bod drwg, byw dros fyth, ac adnewyddiad $^{hyd~fyth}_{diderfyn}$ ar wynfyd.

36. Trichynghyfoedion $^{daioni}_{Byd}$, Dyn, goleuni, a rhyddyd.

---

[1] Al. "things." [2] Al. "it is not in the least known." [3] Al. "celestials."

[4] Al. "for ever." [5] Al. "goodness."

24. Three things that are one in will and tendency with all goodness: God in His might; an awakened conscience; and the judgment of wise men.

25. The three causes of animate beings in the hands of God: love desiring felicity to the utmost extent of perfect understanding; wisdom knowing the utmost means; and power to accomplish the utmost conception of understanding and love.

26. The three causations of all acts:[1] necessity and contingence in the circle of Abred; choice by reason of liberty in the life of man; and choice from love in the circle of Gwynvyd.

27. The three co-operations of man with God: to endure; to consider; and to love; nor can man co-operate with God in any other thing. To endure is the chief of all, for the others cannot take place without it.

28. Three things that are discordant with God: misfortune; falsehood; and despair.

29. Three places in which there will be most of God: where there is most of what will love Him; most of what will seek Him; and least of self.

30. There are three things, and God is found where they are looked for: mercy; truth; and peace.

31. Three things that man knows not[2] what they are: God; nothing; and infinity.

32. There are three circles of existence: the circle of Ceugant, which God only can traverse; the circle of Abred, which man has traversed; and the circle of Gwynvyd, which man shall traverse.

33. The three materials employed by God in making all things: love; wisdom; and power. (See Triad 25.)

34. The three excellences of the state of man: the end of Abred; liberty; and communion with the blessed.[3]

35. The three felicities of heaven: the utter subjugation of all evil; everlasting life; and the endless[4] renovation of bliss.

36. The three primary contemporaries of the world:[5] man; light; and liberty.

2 A

37. Tri bannogion Cyflwr bywedigion, marol[1]iaid/ion, daearol-iaid/ion, a nefol[1]iaid/ion.

38. O Tri ansawdd y mae Duw, nis gellir amgen nis gellir hepcor ag nis gellir gwell.

Tri chyflawn/thrigoliaeth y Ceugant, Duw, Cyfiawnder, a Chariad.

Tri pheth nis gellir nad ydynt yn Nuw, eitha gallu, eitha doethineb/gwybod, ag eitha Cariad.*

Tri achos Angau y sydd, anwybodaeth, cariad anhyrym at y da, ag anallu goddef y Ceugant, sef o gariad y mae gwybod, ag o wybod y mae gochel gorfod y Ceugant, sef o wybod newid Cyflwr.

Tri angenhanfod (angenorfod/angenhenyd) Duw, Tragywyddoldeb, Gallu, a Chariad, sef ai gelwir yn angen henydion/orfodion am nas gellir Duw a'u hamgen.

Tri angenorfod Dyn, dioddef, newid, a dewis ac o achos y drydydd nis gellir gwybod am y bydd y ddau gyntaf.

Tri ansawdd angen Dyndod, cymmysg abred a gwynfyd yn gydbwys, ag o hynny ystyr, prawf ar ddaioni a drwg ag o hynny barn, Dewis gan farn wrth ystyr ag o hynny rhyddyd.

Tri pheiriant Duw yn Abred er gorfod drwg a Chythraul, a diangc oddiwrtho tuag at wynfyd, angau, angen, ag anghof.

Tri Chadernyd Gwynfyd, Bodd Duw yn canniattau, Gallu Duw yn nerthu, a Gwybodaeth Duw yn hyfforddi.

Tri phrodoldeb Gwybodaeth, Cariad at y goreu yn ym-ofyn am dano ; Barn wrth brawf gan ei gael ; a dewis wrth farn gan weled y cyfiawn.

Tri pheth a drechant yn y diwedd, Tan, gwirionedd, a Bywyd.

---

* Between this and what follows there is a larger space than usual in the Manuscript, so that it is not quite clear whether they were not originally two different fragments.

[1] Al. "dwellers."   [2] Al. "knowledge."

[3] We presume that "anhyrym," feeble, or non-effective, is a mistake for "anhyrwym," that cannot be bound, or restrained, which is the sense we have given it in the translation.

[4] Al. "impulsive attributes."   Al. "original attributes."

[5] Al. "original attributes."

37. The three prominent features of the state of living beings : mortals ; terrestrials ; and celestials.

38. God consists of three qualities : what cannot be otherwise ; what cannot be dispensed with ; and what cannot be better.

39. The three plenitudes[1] of Ceugant : God ; justice ; and love.

40. Three things which cannot but be in God : supreme power ; supreme wisdom ;[2] and supreme love.

41. There are three causes of death : ignorance ; unrestrained[3] love for the good ; and inability to endure the Ceugant ; that is to say, from love proceeds knowledge, and by knowledge may the obligation of Ceugant be avoided, that is, from knowledge proceeds the change of condition.

42. The three essential attributes[4] of God : eternity ; power ; and love ; and they are called impulsive attributes,[5] because God cannot exist without them.

43. The three impulsive necessities of man : to suffer ; to change ; and to choose ; and because of the third, it cannot be known when the two first will happen.

44. The three conditions of the necessity of humanity : the equiponderant commixture of Abred and Gwynvyd, and hence, consideration ; the experience of good and evil, and hence, judgment ; choice from judgment consequent upon consideration, and hence, liberty.

45. The three instrumentalities of God in Abred for subduing evil and Cythraul, and escaping from it towards Gwynvyd : death ; necessity ; and forgetfulness.

46. The three stabilities of Gwynvyd : the pleasure of God granting ; the power of God strengthening ; and the knowledge of God directing.

47. The three properties of knowledge : love towards the best, seeking it ; judgment from experience, on obtaining it ; and choice according to judgment, on seeing what is right.

48. Three things will prevail at last : fire ; truth ; and life.

Tri lle bod a hanfod pob byw gyda chythraul yn annwn, gyda goleuni ynghyflwr dyn, a chyda Duw yngwynfyd.

Tair ^{gorddwy}_{ymgyrch} a gosawd ar Gylch y Ceugant y sydd, ^{Balchder}_{Coned} , Anudon, a Chreulonder, canys dirio bodoldeb a wnant o wirfodd ac ymgais a rhagddarpar, ar y petheu nas dyleint fod, ac nas gallant yn gyfun ac anhepcorion Cylch y Gwynfyd. Ac o fyned fal hynny yngorddwy, y syrthir yn abred hyd yn annwn, a phennaf a dygnaf yw balchder am mai o hynny y tardd y ddau orddwy eraill, ac o falchder y by'r syrth cyntaf yn abred gwedi 'r treiglaw cysefin hyd yn rhyw a chyflwr dynoldeb yngwynfyd.

Tair gwaith fuddug a wnant ddianc, sef ydynt ar falchder, ar gasineb anghariad, ac ar Drachwant, sef a hwynt nis gellir medru Cylch y Gwynfyd, am nas Cyfunant a'r Gwynfyd, ac nis gellir gwynfyd o'u hansawdd.

Tair gormes balchder, Trawsarwedd pob peth fal nas gellir gweled gwir—caethu ar bob rhydd fal nas gellir ymryddhau o'r Abred, a dwyn Cyrch anraith ar Dduw a'i Fraint, fal nas gellir cyfiawnder.

Tri chadernyd balchder, Trais a lladrad—murn a chynllwyn—a gyrru cred ar y bo anwir.

Y Tri phechod cyntefig yw Balchder, creulondeb, ag anwiredd.

Tri Chylch hanfod y sydd Cylch y Ceugant, lle nid oes ^{namyn Duw} na byw na marw, ac nid oes namyn Duw a eill ei dreiglaw.

Cylch yr Abred lle trech marw na byw, a phob prif hanfod o'r marw, a dyn ai treiglwys.

Cylch y Gwynfyd lle trech byw na marw, a phob prif hanfod o'r byw a'r bywyd, sef yw hynny o Dduw, a dyn ai

---

¹ Al. "encounters."   ² "Save God" omitted in one version.

49. The three places of the being and existence of all animation : with Cythraul in Annwn ; with light in the state of man ; and with God in Gwynvyd.

50. There are three oppressions[1] and onsets on the circle of Ceugant: pride ; perjury ; and cruelty ; because, of free will, and endeavour, and pre-arrangement, they force existence upon things that ought not to be, and that cannot accord with the indispensables of the circle of Gwynvyd. And by making this assault, man falls in Abred even to Annwn. The chief and most grievous is pride, because it is from this that the other two oppressions are derived ; and it was from pride that the first fall in Abred occurred, after the original progression to the species and state of humanity in Gwynvyd.

51. Three victories will occasion an escape, namely : victories over pride ; uncharitable hatred ; and cupidity ; for no one with these can attain to the circle of Gwynvyd, because they will not accord with Gwynvyd, and Gwynvyd cannot be obtained from their natures.

52. The three usurpations of pride : to distort every thing, so that the truth cannot be seen ; to enslave every liberty, so that one cannot free himself from Abred ; and to make a predatory onset on God and His prerogative, so that there can be no justice.

53. The three stabilities of pride : usurpation and theft ; murder and ambuscade ; and imposing belief upon what is false.

54. The three primary sins are : pride ; cruelty ; and falsehood.

55. There are three circles of existence : the circle of Ceugant, where there is neither animate or inanimate save God,[2] and God only can traverse it ; the circle of Abred, where the dead is stronger than the living, and where every principal existence is derived from the dead, and man has traversed it ; and the circle of Gwynvyd, where the living is stronger than the dead, and where every principal existence is derived from the living and life, that

treigla, ac ni chyrraedd Dyn gyflawn wybodaeth oni dderfydd iddo lwyr dreiglo Cylch y Gwynfyd, can nis gellir
gwybodaeth pendant onid o gaffaeliad ymbrawf y synhwyrau, o ddwyn a dioddef pob cyflwr a digwydd.

Tri achos Angau gan Dduw gwellhau cyflwr yn Abred—
Adnewyddu bywyd er gorphwys ^{oddiwrth}/_{rhac} anoddefold^{id}/_{er} y Ceugant ac er ymbrawf ar bob cyflwr byw a bywyd ac a berthyn
o ansawdd a damwain i hynny, sef er cynnull y rhyw arben-
nig ar ^{wybyddawd}/_{wybodau} , ac o hynny caffael gwybodaeth cyflwyr a
chyflawn ar bob byw a bod, ac ar bob ansawdd a hanfod.
can nas gellir yn amgen nac o hynn o dreigl yn Abred
dysgu a medru ar yr holl wybodau a ellir o ansawdd ac
angen, a heb y rhai hynny nis gellir ymddwyn a Chylch y
Gwynfyd.

Tripheth rhagor nac ar arall y sydd i bob bywydawl y
nesaf o bob peth at Dduw o barth ei fannogaeth, Awen rhag
arall nis gellir ei hunryw (ei chyfunryw) ai bennwynfyd yn
fwyaf oll oi ryw.

Tri pheth y sydd ar bob byw parth hunandawd ac anian
arbennig, sef cyflawn o'r peth ag ydyw, ac nis gellir ail
iddaw gan nas gellir dau cyflawn ar ddim.—Un cynghyd
cyfan parth trefn a chyfles—ac un pwngc boddlondeb ac ni
chais neb amgen, gan mai oi anwybawd y bu poenau yr
Annwn, ac achos Abred.

Tri achos newid cyflwr bodoldeb a bywydoldeb yng-
nghwynfyd y sydd—addysg a geffir o hynny—harddwch
newyddoldeb—a gorphwys rhac anoddefder Tragwyddoldeb
y ceugant.
Tri pheth nis gellir onid un ar bobun, un cyflawn parth
rhyw ac awen—un cyngyd parth trefn a chyfles, ac un

is, from God, and man shall traverse it; nor will man attain to perfect knowledge, until he shall have fully traversed the circle of Gwynvyd, for no absolute knowledge can be obtained but by the experience of the senses, from having borne and suffered every condition and incident.

56. There are three occasions for death on the part of God : to better the condition in Abred; to renovate life for the sake of reposing from then on endurance of Ceugant ; and to experience every state of the living and life, and what by nature and incident belongs to it, that is, in order to collect the particular kind of knowledge, and thereby obtain utter and complete knowledge respecting every animation and being, and every quality and essence, for otherwise than by means of this progression in Abred it is impossible to learn and be skilled in all the sciences, which can by nature and of necessity exist; and without them it is impossible to bear with the circle of Gwynvyd.

57. There are three things which distinguish all living beings, one from the other : what is nearest of all to God in respect of its particularity; distinctive Awen, which cannot have another of the same kind; and supreme bliss, being greatest of all of its kind.

58. Every living being has three things in respect of individuality and particular character, namely : plenitude of what he is, and it is impossible that there should be a second of the same, since there can be no two plenitudes of any thing ; one entire uniformity in respect of order and mutual advantage; and one point of contentment, and no one seeks what is otherwise, since it was from ignorance of it that the pains of Annwn, and the cause of Abred, ensued.

59. There are three reasons for changing the state of existence and life in Gwynvyd : the instruction that is obtained therefrom ; the beauty of novation ; and repose from the non endurance of the eternity of Ceugant.

60. There are three things, each of which can have but one : one plenitude in respect of kind and Awen ; one uni-

Penrhaith, sef Duw, ar bob peth. (gwel y diweddaf ond un).

Tri phrif gymmodolion Cylch y Gwynfyd,—Cariad hyd y bo ei angenofyn. Trefn hyd nis gellir gwell—a gwybod hyd y gellir meddwl a dirnad.

Tripheth nis gellir yng Nghylch y Gwynfyd, angau, anghariad, ac annhrefn. E. a. w. angen, anghariad, ac annhrefn.

Tair barn dyled y sydd, ac ynddynt ei ddeall; beth a wahardd arall ac a waharddai ef ei hun yn arall—beth a gais arall ac a geisia efe ei hun gan arall, a bod cyfunder dichwain—a pheth a ellir hyd fyth ei oddef ai chwenychu gan oll o fyw a bod Ynghylch y Gwynfyd, lle nis gellir anghariad ac anghyfiawn, sef nis gellir $^{\text{eithr}}_{\text{ond}}$ annyled ac annosparth ac anghyfiawn, ac anghariad, a fo anghydfod a hynny.

Tri chadernyd Gwynfyd, Gwybod ansawdd y drwg ai oddef yn Abred — Gwybod ansawdd y da ai brofi yng ngwynfyd—a gwybod o bob bywydawl ai bennodoldeb ai arbennigrwydd ei hun herwydd bodd ac amcan ac ewyllys Duw er daioni cyfollgyrch. ac yn hynn o bethau diogel a chadarn, can nis gall Duw yn amgen ei gynnal o gariad wrth wir a chyfiawn, ac nis gall Duw amgen na gwir a chyfiawn, ac o wir a chyfiawn nis gellir amgen na chariad perffaith, ac nis gellir anghariad onid o anghyfiawn.

O dripheth y mae anghariad sef o wneuthur anghyfiawn ac yn hynny peri anghariad yn ai goddefo—o oddef a chael a fo anghyfiawn gan arall, ac o hynny tyfu anghariad tuag at a wnel yn anghyfiawn—ac o anwybodaeth am ansawdd anghariad ai waith yn gyrru llid ac amddiffyn a gwrth parth

formity in respect of order and mutual advantage; and one supremacy, that is, God over all. (See the last but one.)

61. The three principal co-existences of the circle of Gwynvyd: love as far as the necessity of it requires; order until it can not be improved; and knowledge as far as thought and perception can reach.

62. Three things cannot exist in the circle of Gwynvyd: death; uncharitableness; and disorder. Others say;— need; uncharitableness; and disorder.

53. There are three judgments relative to duty, whereby it may be understood: what does another man forbid, and what would he himself forbid in another man; what does another man seek, and what would he himself seek of another man under the same circumstances; and what can be borne and desired for ever by all animations and existences in the circle of Gwynvyd, where neither uncharitableness nor injustice can exist, for whatever does not agree with that can be nought but undutifulness, disorder, injustice, and uncharitableness.

64. The three stabilities of Gwynvyd: to know the nature of evil, and to have endured it in Abred; to know the nature of good, and to experience it in Gwynvyd; and to know of every living form, its speciality, and individuality, as tending, by the pleasure, purpose, and will of God, to the general good. And in these things there is security and firmness, for God cannot otherwise support it out of love to truth and justice, and God can do nothing but truth and justice, and from truth and justice there can be nought but perfect love, and there can be no uncharitableness but from injustice.

65. From three things arises uncharitableness, that is: from doing injustice, and thereby causing uncharitableness in the one that suffers it; from suffering and receiving injustice at the hands of another, whence uncharitableness springs towards the one that does injustice; and from ignorance of the nature of uncharitableness, and the way in which it instigates anger, self-defence, and opposition in

2 B

ag atto, ac yna wers tragwers gelyniaeth heb dranc heb orphen.

^{Tri chadernyd}
^{Tair rhinwedd} undawd Un heb arall, ac o hynny rhydd cadarn—cyfan heb liaws, ac o hynny nerth cadarn—a lliaws ynghyfan ac o hynny Gwybodaeth cadarn, ac o'r tri hynn y gweir Un Cadarn—ac nis gellir un cadarn onid o Dduw.

Tri anghadarn lliaws—*anghydioldeb*. can nis gellir arbennigrwydd a phennodoldeb un pen neu ryw ar arall o beth ac ansawdd, neu yr un lle i'r un ac i'r llall, ar yr un pryd ac amser—*Meidroldeb* can nis gellir anfeidroldeb lle bo arall o ba ryw ac ansawdd bynnag y bo 'r arall, a lleied y bo, parth rhyw ac ansawdd ei fodoldeb—*Cyfnewidioldeb*, can y bydd lle bo dau neu liaws o ba rif bynnag, un yn dwyn y blaen ar arall, a gallu newid o hynny oni bo flaenaf a fu olaf, ac y bydd amgenu lle ac amser sef ydd eir o'r naill le i'r llall, ac o'r naill amser i'r llall, ac o'r naill gyflwr i'r llall, a'r pethau hynny yn cael eu gyrru gan y naill ar y llall. ac am hynn o betheu nis gellir Lliaws ar Dduw a duwiau, na Duw yn liosog neu o liaws.

O dair ffordd y bu'r syrthio yn abred (Al. y digwydd yn Abred) o falchder yn anturiaw Cylch y Ceugant, o ddirmyg a chas ar gylch y Gwynfyd o drachwant amgen ac o hynny dwyn Gorddwy ar Dduw a Daioni ac a berthyn o anhepcoroldeb i'r Gwynfyd sef Cariad a phob gwir a Chyfiawn.— ac o ofni pwyll a dyled.

Tri phrifgyflwr bywydolion crëedig—*Annwn* sef yno y dechre, *Abred* sef yno y treigl er cynnull Gwybodau—a *Gwynfyd* ac yno gorphen yn nigonoldeb hyd eitha gallu a gwybod, a daioni hyd nis gellir mwy.

Tri achos dihenydd, gwared ac ymwared rhag drwg a gwaeth o barth gorfod,—ymneshau ac ymdderchafu at wyn-

---

[1] Al. " virtues."

respect to it, whence enmity ensues alternately world without end.

66. The three stabilities [1] of unity: one without another, and hence firm liberty ; entirety without many, and hence firm power; and many in entirety, and hence firm knowledge ; and from these three is formed firm unity; and there can be no firm unity but from God.

67. The three instabilities of many : non gregariousness, for there can be no individuality and speciality in respect of any one head or kind as distinguished from another thing or quality, or no place for the one and the other at the same period and time ; finiteness, for there can be no infiniteness where there is another of the same kind and quality, however little he may be in respect of the kind and quality of his existence ; changeableness, for, where there are two or many in number, one must bear the preference over another, and this can be changed, so that the one that was last may be first, and the place and time be altered, so that one can go from one place to another, and from one time to another, and from one state to another, such particulars being driven by one to the other. On this account God or gods cannot consist of many, nor can God be manifold or of many.

68. From three causes was there a fall in Abred : from pride that ventured into the circle of Ceugant, out of contempt and hatred of the circle of Gwynvyd, and out of desire for what was otherwise ; hence violence was brought against God and goodness, and what indispensably appertains to Gwynvyd, that is, love, and all truth and justice ; and from the fear of reason ; and of duty.

69. The three principal states of created animations : Annwn, in which was their beginning ; Abred, which they traverse for the sake of collecting sciences ; and Gwynvyd, where they will end in plenteousness to the utmost extent of power, knowledge, and goodness, so much that more cannot possibly be had.

70. The three causes for disanimation : to deliver and be delivered from obligatory evil and worse ; to approach

fyd—ac anoddef y Ceugant ai anorphwys cans nid oes namyn Duw o'i anfeidroldeb a eill ei dreiglaw, ac nis gall meidrol ar anfeidroldeb.

Tri ryw dranc y sydd—cosp a phoen am bechod—cariad Duw yn dwyn pob byw a bod o waeth i well hyd yng ngwynfyd—a gorphwys yng ngwynfyd o anoddefolder byth-oedd y Ceugant.

Tri Chyfnod gwynfydig Dyn — caffael bywyd mal cael enaid yngenedigaeth neu adfywydaeth o lewyg — rhoddi bywyd sef cenhedlu—a newid bywyd sef marw, yn myned o waeth i well.

TRIOEDD DWYFOLDEB.

Trioedd Barddas, nid amgen no Thrioedd Gwybodau dwyfolion, a Doethineb gan Awen o Dduw a rodded i Brif Feirdd Ynys Prydain drwy 'r Yspryd Glân er yn oes oes-oedd, herwydd Dosparth ac Addysg y Tri chyntefigion Beirdd ac Athrawon Ynys Prydain a Chenedl y Cymry, ar Gyfarwyddyd honn a fernir yn warantedig o Gof a Chadw a Llafar Gorsedd Beirdd Ynys Prydain, ym Mraint Cenedl y Cymry, ac ym Mraint a Defawd Beirdd Ynys Prydain.

1. Tri Un anfeidrol y sydd; Lle, Amser, a $^{\text{Bywyd}}_{\text{Dyw}}$, sef nid oes na dechreu na diwedd ar nag un nag arall o honynt.

2. Tri un cyntefig y sydd ac nis gellir amgen nag Un nag ar y naill nag ar arall o honynt, Un Duw, un gwirion-edd, ac un Pwngc Rhyddyd sef y bydd hwnnw lle bo cyd-bwys pob peth a phob Gwrth.

3. Tripheth tardd o'r Tri un cyntefig; Pob Bywyd, Pob daioni, a Phob Gallu.

---

[1] "Geni," to be born, comes from "gen," a soul, a spirit.

> A *gen* y gwr gan ei gi,
> Ai gorph el i Gaerffili.

May the *soul* of the man enter his dog,
And his body be taken to Caerphilly —D. ab Gwilym.

"Geni," to attain to a soul or life, to become animated. "Ganed plentyn," a child has been animated, become animated. *Enaid* in *Silurian* is written *genaid*.

[2] Plennydd, Alawn, and Gwron, who are said to have been contemporaries of Prydain, son of Aedd the Great.

and be raised towards Gwynvyd; and the non endurance of Ceugant and its want of repose, for there is none but God, Who, being infinite, can traverse it, and the finite cannot prevail against the infinite.

71. There are three kinds of death: punishment and pain for sin; the love of God in bringing all animation and existence from worse to better in Gwynvyd; and repose in Gwynvyd from not being able to endure the eternities of Ceugant.

72. The three blessed epochs of man: to receive life, such as having a soul at birth,[1] or in the revival from a swoon; to give life, or to generate; and to change life, or to die, which is a going from worse to better.

THEOLOGICAL TRIADS.

The Triads of Bardism, that is, the Triads of godly sciences, and of wisdom through Awen from God, which was given through the Holy Spirit to the primitive Bards of the Isle of Britain from the age of ages, according to the system and instruction of the three primary Bards and teachers of the Isle of Britain and the nation of the Cymry.[2] And this instruction is adjudged as authorized by the memorials and voice of the Gorsedd of the Bards of the Isle of Britain, in right of the nation of the Cymry, and according to the privilege and usage of the Bards of the Isle of Britain.

1. There are three immeasurable unities: place; time; and life;[3] that is, neither one nor other of them has either a beginning or an end.

2. There are three primary unities, and more than one of each cannot exist: one God; one truth; and one point of liberty, and that is, where all things, and all opposites, equiponderate.

3. Three things spring from the three primary unities: all life; all goodness; and all power.

[3] Al. "God."

4. Tri angheneddyl Duw o brif gymmodoldeb, y mwyaf
parth Bywyd o bob peth, a'r mwyaf parth nerth a gallu o
bob peth.—Eraill a ddywedant fal hynn

5. O Dri anghenfod y mae Duw, sef y mwyaf parth
Bywyd, y mwyaf parth Gwybod, a'r mwyaf parth nerth a
gallu, ag nis gellir namyn Un mwyaf ar unpeth.

6. Tripheth nis dychyn Duw lai na bod ; a ddylai 'r Da
cyflawn, a ddymunai 'r Da cyflawn, ag a ddichon y Da cyflawn.

7. Tri Chysefiniaid pob peth ; Cyffyroldeb, modoldeb, a
Bywydoldeb.

8. Tri Theithi Bodoldeb, Amser, a Lle, a gweithred.

9. Tri Chadernyd Bodoldeb, Anian, Gwahanred, a Phar-
hâd.

10. Tri gwahanred bodoldeb, maintioli, ffurfoldeb, a
gweithredoldeb.

TRIOEDD DWYFOLDEB.

Tri chadernid unoldeb, sef yw Cydoldeb, can nis gellir
deuryw ar un cyfoll.—Anfeidroldeb, can nis gellir terfyn ar
yr un Cyfan (cyd-fan)   Anghyfnewidioldeb can nis gellir y
bydd un cynghyd cyfoll cyfan yn amgen nag y bo.   Ac am
hynn nis gellir Duw onid o un cadarn.*

Tri pheth yn un a wnant nerth, *Mi, Ti,* ac *Ef,* sef *Mi*
yn mynnu a'r *Ti* yn gwneuthur a fynno 'r *Mi,* ac Ef yn ai
bernir gan y *Mi* yn ogydfyn a'r Ti (tau) a'r tri chadarn a'u
gelwir sef o honynt yn yr *un* y gwneir nerth *a bodoldeb.*

Tri barn dyled y sydd ac ynddynt ei ddeall, a waharddo
dyn yn arall—a geisio gan arall—ac a fo cydfod a chylch y
Gwynfyd.

---

* " Saith brif-gydoldeb un cadarn sef, Cydfan—Cydfod—Cyflawn—Cyfnerth
—Cydfyn—Cydwaith—a Chydfyth."—MS.

The seven principal universalities of one fundamentality : co-presence ; co-
existence ; co-plenitude ; co-power ; co-will ; co-operation ; and co-eternity.

4. The three attributes of God, being of primary co-existence: the greatest of all things in respect of life; and the greatest of all things in respect of might and power. Others say thus :—

5. God is of three necessities, that is: the greatest in respect of life; the greatest in respect of knowledge; and the greatest in respect of might and power; and there can only be one greatest of any thing.

6. Three things which God cannot but be: what perfect goodness ought to be; what perfect goodness would desire to be; and what perfect goodness can be.

7. The three primaries of all things: materiality; motion; and vitality.

8. The three characteristics of existence: time; place; and action.

9. The three stabilities of existence: nature; individuality; and continuance.

10. The three discriminations of existence: size; form; and operation.

THEOLOGICAL TRIADS.

1. The three stabilities of unity, namely: completeness, for there can be no two kinds of one universality; infinity, for there can be no limit to one entirety; and immutability, for it cannot be that one completeness, universality, and entirety, should be other than they are. Therefore, there can be no God but from fundamental oneness.

2. Three things united will produce power: I, Thou, and It; that is to say, the I willing, the Thou performing what the I wills, and the It becoming what is decided by the I, willing in union with the Thou. And they are called the three fundamentals, because from them in one are produced might and existence.

3. There are three judgments of duty, in which it will be understood; what a man forbids in another; what he seeks from another; and what is compatible with the circle of Gwynvyd.

Tair gwaith fuddug a wna ddianc, ar anghariad, ar drachwant, ac ar anrhefn, sef ni cyfunant a chylch y Gwynfyd.

Tri phrif-gymmod Cylch y Gwynfyd, Cariad hyd y bo ei
angenofyn—Trefn hyd nis gellir gwell—a gwybod hyd y
gellir meddwl a dirnad.

Tri pheth nis gellir yng Nghylch y Gwynfyd, angeu,
anghariad, ac anrhefn.

TRIOEDD DWYFOLDEB.

Tri chadernyd Gwynfyd—Gwybod ansawdd y drwg o'i
oddef yn Abred, Gwybod ansawdd y da o'i brofi yn y
Gwynfyd—a gwybod o bob bywydol ei bennodoldeb wrth
fodd ac amcan Duw; ac yna diogel a chadarn, can nis gall
Duw yn amgen ei gynnal o gariad wrth wir a chyfiawn, ac
nis gall Duw amgen na gwir a chyfiawn ac o hynny cariad
perffaith.

Tri Rhinwedd Undod Un heb arall—Cyfan heb liaws—
Lliaws ynghyfan—ag nis gellir un cadarn onid o Dduw.

Tri anghadarn lliaws anghydoldeb—meidroldeb—a chyf-
newidioldeb, sef anghydoldeb can nis gellir arbenigrwydd
un peth neu ryw ar arall neu ir un lle i un ac ir llall—
meidroldeb can nis gellir anfeidrol lle bo arall, a lleied y bo,
o'i ryw—cyfnewidioldeb can y bydd lle bo dau neu fwy, un
yn blaenori ar arall a gallu newid o hynny oni bo'n olaf a fu
flaenaf.

TRIOEDD DWYFOLDEB.

Tri phrif dremynt corphorol dyn, gweled, clywed, a
theimlaw.

4. Three victories will cause an escape : over uncharitableness; over coveteousness ; and over disorder ; for these will not accord with the circle of Gwynvyd.

5. The three principal co-existences of the circle of Gwynvyd : love as far as its necessity requires; order until it cannot be improved ; and knowledge as far as it can be conceived and comprehended.

6. There are three things that cannot take place in the circle of Gwynvyd : death ; uncharitableness; and disorder.

THEOLOGICAL TRIADS.

1. The three stabilities of Gwynvyd : to know the nature of evil, from having suffered it in Abred ; to know the nature of good, from having experienced it in Gwynvyd ; and that every living being should know his appointment, according to the pleasure and purpose of God ; and then there will be security and stability. For God cannot otherwise maintain it from love to truth and justice, and God cannot do other than what is true and just, hence comes perfect love.

2. The three virtues of unity : one without another; entirety without plurality ; and plurality in entirety ; and there can be no firm unity but from God.

3. The three instabilities of plurality : non-universality; finiteness ; and changeableness ; that is to say, non-universality, because the speciality of one thing or kind cannot belong to another, nor can the same place be for one and for another; finiteness, because there can be no infinitude, where there is another thing, however little it may be, of the same kind ; changeableness, for where there are two or more, one will have the precedency over another, and hence there will be a capability of change, until the first becomes last.

THEOLOGICAL TRIADS.

1. The three principal bodily perceptions of man : seeing ; hearing ; and feeling.

2 c

Tri phrif dremynt enaid dyn, cariad—cas—a deall.

Tri pheth ydynt o Dduw, sef y pethau ni ellir cystal hebddynt—a welant bawb yn eisiau—ag nis gall neb ei ddigoni.

Tri thrigiannoldeb y Ceugant — Duw — Cyfiawnder—a dymunoldeb, a lle y bytho Duw y bydd y ddau arall.

Tri anallu Duw, Cashau, llesghau, a gormodeddu.

Tri lle nis ceffir Duw, lle nis erchir ei fod, lle ni chwenychir ei fod, a lle ni ufuddheir iddo.

Tri amcan Duw yn a wnaeth. Treulaw drwg—bywydu marw—a gorfoledd o wneuthur daioni.

Tair ffordd y mae Duw yn gweithredu ymbrawf, doethineb, a thrugaredd.

Tri chydfod a ddylai fod ar bob peth a wnelo ddyn. cydfod ac anian deddfoldeb — cydfod a goreuon Dyndod — a chydfod ac a ellir hyd fyth ar bob peth ynghylch y gwynfyd. E. A. W. cydfod a gorchymyn Duw. cydfod a goreuon dyn, a chydfod ac a ellir hyd fyth parth dwyfolder ei fodoldeb ynghylch y gwynfyd. E. a. w. A lles pob byw —a Chyfiawnder Duw—ac a chariadoldeb cylch y gwynfyd.

Tri phrif ddefnyddioldeb pob peth gan Dduw—er a fai fwyaf yr achos, a fai fwyaf y lles, ac a fai fwyaf y cariad.

Tri phrif ansawdd Duw Celi, Nerth, Gwybod, a Chariad.

Tri gofal beunyddiol a ddylai fod ar feddwl pob dyn— diwyllu Duw—gochel niweidio undyn, a gwneuthur cyfiawnder a phob byw a bod.

Tri ofn gwr doeth, ofni digio Duw, ofni gwneuthur

2. The three principal perceptions of the soul of man : love ; hatred ; and understanding.

3. There are three things from God, namely : what cannot be had as good without ; what all see that they want ; and what nobody else can satisfy.

4. The three residents of Ceugant : God ; justice ; and desirableness ; and where God is, there are the other two.

5. The three impossibilities of God : to hate ; to become feeble ; and to become too great.

6. Three places where God cannot be found : where He is not asked to be ; where He is not desired to be ; and where He is not obeyed.

7. The three purposes of God in His works : to consume the evil ; to enliven the dead ; and to cause joy from doing good.

8. The three ways in which God works : experience ; wisdom ; and mercy.

9. There should be three agreements in every act of man : agreement with the nature of morality ; agreement with the excellences of humanity ; and agreement with what can exist in every thing for ever in the circle of Gwynvyd. Others say, agreement with the commandment of God ; agreement with the excellences of man ; and agreement with what can exist for ever, in respect of the godliness of its existence, in the circle of Gwynvyd. Others say ; with the benefit of all living beings ; with the justice of God ; and with the love of the circle of Gwynvyd.

10. The three principal uses of all things in the hands of God : that they should be with a view to the greatest need ; to the greatest utility ; and to the greatest love.

11. The three principal properties of the Hidden God : power ; knowledge ; and love.

12. The three daily cares that should occupy the mind of every man : to worship God ; to avoid injuring any one ; and to act justly towards every living thing.

13. The three fears of a wise man : the fear of offending God ; the fear of acting uncharitably to man ; and the fear

anghariad i ddyn, ac ofni tra golud a llwyddiant. — Al.
ofni Duw, ofni pechawd, ac ofni tra llwyddiant.

Tri ofn annoeth, ofni Dyn, ofni Diawl, ag ofni Tylodi,
(aflwyddiant Bydawl)

Mewn tri pheth y bydd dyn yn debig i Ddiawl, maglu 'r
ffordd, ofni plentyn bach, a chwerthin am benn y drwg.

TRIOEDD DWYFOLDEB.

Llyma drioedd a gafwyd yn y Bewpyr, a golles rywun
yno, neu fallai mai rhywun oi fodd au dodes ar y llawr lle
au cespwyd.

1. Tri achos Duw Rhuthro allan oi anfeidroldeb. 1.
Gwneuthur na fu erioed o'r Blaen a hynny er da ag er
rhagod pob drwg. Ac o hynny yr Hanfodoldeb, ys ef
gwaith ei grëadraeth a phan amgen yn hynn yn dangos
gallu a doethineb afrifed. 2. Gwared y sydd dan han a
hanfod, rhag drwg damwain a Chyrh Cythraul,[1] ac i
ddwyn ar adfer a lithrasai ag goll ag ar waeth neu ei fwrw
i bant a rhoi gwell yn ei le, a hynn a syrth ag a ddaw ar
bob hanfod hyd oni bo gwell hyd eitha daioni i bob hanfodoldeb a chreodraeth.

2. Tri pheth a ddangosant Duw. Dodi 'r Da ar Drwg
wyneb yn wyneb fal ydd adneppid un ar llall o henynt, er
ymgystlwn ar Da ac ymwrthod a'r drwg.

DERWYDDONIAETH.

Dysgybl ag Athraw.

Llyma Dderwyddoniaeth, Beirdd Ynys Prydain, a'i
Barn am Dduw a phob bywydolion o ba radd a rhyw bynnag, ai hegwyddori fal hyn,

---

[1] This phrase, undoubtedly Bardic, seems to have been present to the mind of
the Welsh translator of the Litany, who has employed it as equivalent to "the
assaults of the devil."

[2] These Triads, it will be seen, are incomplete.

of excessive wealth and prosperity. Another version: the fear of God; the fear of sin; and the fear of excessive prosperity.

14. The three fears of the foolish man: the fear of man; the fear of the devil; and the fear of poverty. Al. worldly adversity.

15. In three things will a man resemble the devil: laying snares in the way; fearing a little child; and laughing at evil.

THEOLOGICAL TRIADS.

Here are Triads which were found at Bewpyr, having been lost there by some one; or perhaps some person placed them of his own accord on the floor, where they were found.

1. The three occasions on which God rushed out of His infinitude: the first was, to make what never existed before, and that with a view to good, and for the prevention of all evil. Hence issued existence, or the work of His creation; and when it might have been otherwise, herein were shown infinite power and wisdom. The second was to deliver all emanations and existences from evil chance, and the assault of Cythraul, and to restore what had been lost, or become deteriorated, or to cast it off, and substitute a better in its stead. This will occur and happen to every existence, until all existence and creation shall have been improved to the utmost limits of goodness.

2. Three things indicate God: the placing good and evil face to face, in order that the one or the other may be known, with the view of attaching one's self to the good and renouncing the evil.[2]

DRUIDISM.

Disciple and Teacher.

This is the Druidism of the Bards of the Isle of Britain, with their opinion respecting God and all living beings, of whatsoever grade or kind they may be. It is rudimentally taught as follows:—

1. G. Pa beth yw Duw. A. peth nis gellir amgen. Pam nas gellir amgen. A. pei gellid amgen nis gellid na byw na bod, na hanfod na henfydd ar ddim ag y sydd wybyddiedig i ni, ar wybod inni.

G. beth yw Duw. A. Bywyd Cyflwyr cyflawn, a llwyr ddiddim ar bob _{an}^{di}fyw, a marwolaeth, ag nis gall rhyw o farw ymgyhydreg ag ef, a llwyr gyfanfod bywyd heb drangc heb orphen ydyw Duw.

2. Bywyd cyflwyr yw Duw, ac nis gellir _{derfyn arno;}^{nac attal} na cheithineb, yn ynddo gyflwyr wybodaeth o'i gyfiawn hanfod, herwydd gwedd a goddef a goddeu, yn ymgysefinaw a'i hun, heb ymgyd a dim arall, ba bynag, a llwyr anghyfranog o ddrwg.

3. Daioni pendant wrth lwyr dyddymiant pob drwg yw Duw, ag nis gellir anian o'r lledfod lleiaf o ddrwg ynddo.

4. Gallu pendant wrth lwyr ddyddymiant anallu yw Duw, ag nis gellir Caethineb ar allu ag ewyllys ynddo, gan mai hollalluog a hollddaionus ydyw.

5. Doethineb a Gwybodaeth pendant yw Duw, wrth lwyr ddiddymiant, awybyddiaeth, ag annoethineb, ag wrth hyn nis gellir o ddamwedd ba bynag yr hanfod-ddigwydd nas gwyr. Ag wrth hyn o _{briodoldebau,}^{ansawdd a theithi} _{deithi} nis gellir ar feddwl a phwyll amgen wrth fod a bywyd nad o Dduw y mae, oddierth y drwg anianawl wrth ddiddymiant pob bywyd a daioni.

6. Drwg pendant anianol yw llwyr ddiddymiant a gwrthfod o Dduw a bywyd, ag yn hynny o bob daioni, ag felly 'n gyflwyr wrthwyneb wrthanian, a gwrthhanfod, i Dduw, a bywyd, a daioni.

7. Ag ar hyn o ddarwedd, y gwelir dau beth o anghen-

---

[1] Al. " restrained."

[2] Instead of " qualities and properties," another version has " attributes." Al. simply, " properties."

1. Question. What is God?

Answer. What cannot be otherwise.

Q. Why cannot it be otherwise?

A. Could it be otherwise, we should have no knowledge of any animation, being, existence, or futurity, in respect of any thing now known to us.

Q. What is God?

A. Complete and perfect life, and the total annihilation of every thing inanimate and death, nor can any species of mortality concur with Him. And God is life, full, entire, imperishable, and without end.

2. God is perfect life, which cannot be limited [1] or confined, and, in virtue of His proper essence, is possessed of perfect knowledge, in respect of sight, sufferance, and intention, having His origin in Himself, without communion with any thing else whatsoever, and wholly free from all participation in evil.

3. God is absolute good, in that He totally annihilates all evil, and there cannot be in Him the least particle of the nature of evil.

4. God is absolute power, in that He totally annihilates inability, nor can power and will in Him be restrained, since He is almighty, and allgood.

5. God is absolute wisdom and knowledge, in that He totally annihilates ignorance, and folly; and therefore no event can by any chance happen, which He knows not of. And in view of these qualities and properties [2] no being or animation can be conceived or contemplated other than coming from God, except natural evil, which annihilates all life and goodness.

6. What would utterly annihilate and reject God and life, and therein all goodness, is absolute and natural evil; which is thus in complete opposition, and of a contrary nature, and essence, to God, life, and goodness.

7. And by means of this direction, may be seen two things existing of necessity, namely : the living and dead ;

eddyl hanfod, sef Byw, a marw ; Da, a drwg : Duw a chythraul a thywyll ynghywyll, ag analluol anallu.

8. Nid oes bywyd i Gythraul, ag nid ar oddeu ynddo,
eithr o angen, ag o anfodd, heb na bod na bywyd'o barth
handid a hundeb, eithr gwag wrth wag, a marw wrth farw,
a dim wrth ddim, ydyw, Lle y mae Duw yn dda wrth dda
yn lawnder wrth lawnder, yn fywyd yn y bywyd, ag yn
gyfan ynghyfan, a goleu yngoleu.

9. Ag o'r hyn a wespwyd, gwelir nis gellir hanfod o
gysefin ansawdd, eithr Duw a Chythraul y byw ar marw, y
dim a'r digwydd, tardd o didardd, a bod o ymgyd.

10. Duw yn ymgyd o gariad a thosturi yn athrugar ar
difywyd sef y drwg ar oddeu ei ddarostwng i'r bywyd, a
beris hanfod wrth fywydoldeb i fywion a Bywiaduriaid ag
felly y gafaelodd bywyd a'r marw, ag o hynny y tarddwys
y bywydolion ar bywydoliaeth menedig gyntaf ag o fenedig-
ion wrth fod a bywyd y dechreuasant yn nyfnod annwfn,
gan mae yno y radd isaf a lleiaf, ag nis gellir amgen nad
yno ag yn y Cyflwr hynny y dechreuwys bywyd menedig
gyntaf, am nis gellir amgen nad y radd leiaf ag isaf o bob
peth yw 'r ddychrëol as gyntefin, nis gellir y mwyaf cyn
bod y lleiaf ar hanfod menedig. nis gellir hanfod menedig
heb raddoldeb, ag o raddoldeb nis gellir amgen na dechreu
canol, a diwedd neu eithaf, cyntaf, chwanegiad, ag eithaf
neu orpheniad. ag wrth hynn y gwelir graddoldeb anghenfod ar bob hanfod menedig, gan ddechre 'n anghfodawl yn y
radd isaf gan abredu 'n ddibaid oddiyno ar hyd pob chwanegiad canoliad, tyfiad, oedraniad, a chwblhaad, hyd orphen
ag eithafnod, a gorphwys yno dros fyth o lwyr anghfod gan
nas gellir pellach nag uwch na gwell herwydd gradd ag
abred.

11. Cyfranogiad o ddaioni a drwg yw pob bywydolion

good and evil; God and Cythraul, and darkness in darkness, and powerless inability.

8. Cythraul is destitute of life and intention—a thing of necessity, not of will, without being or life, in respect of existence and personality; but vacant in reference to what is vacant, dead in reference to what is dead, and nothing in reference to what is nothing. Whereas God is good with reference to what is good, is fulness in reference to fulness, life in life, all in all, and light in light.

9. And from what has been said, it may be seen that there can be no existence of original nature but God and Cythraul, the dead and living, nothing and occurrence, issue from what is issueless, and existence from mutual union.

10. God mercifully, out of love and pity, uniting Himself with the lifeless, that is, the evil, with the intention of subduing it unto life, imparted the existence of vitality to animated and living beings, and thus did life lay hold of the dead, whence intellectual animations and vitality first sprang. And intellectual existences and animations began in the depth of Annwn, for there is the lowest and least grade, and it cannot but be that there and in that state intellectual life first began, for it cannot be otherwise than that the least and lowest grade of every thing should be the original and primordial one. The greatest cannot exist in an intellectual existence before the least; there can be no intellectual existence without gradation, and in respect of gradation there cannot but be a beginning, a middle, and an end or extremity,—first, augmentation, and ultimate or conclusion. Thus may be seen that there is to every intellectual existence a necessary gradation, which necessarily begins at the lowest grade, progressing from thence incessantly along every addition, intervention, increase, growth in age, and completion, unto conclusion and extremity, where it rests for ever from pure necessity, for there can not be any thing further or higher or better in respect of gradation and Abred.

11. All intellectual existences partake ᴗof good and

menedig, a hynny o fwy neu lai herwydd eu gradd yn yr
Abred, or marw yn nyfnawd Annwfn, hyd y byw yn eithaf-
nod y daioni, ar galledigaeth, hyd na bo llwyr a angalledig i
Dduw ei ddwyn ymhellach.

12.   Cyfranogion o fywyd a daioni yn y radd galledig
isaf ag o'r marw a'r anfad yn y radd uchaf, a ellir ^{herwydd gallu}_{wrth allu}
yn gyfun gydwedd a bywyd a bod hundebol, ydynt y Byw-
ydolion yn annwfn, ag am hynny drwg anghenfod ydynt,
gan faint traphwys y drwg wrth y da, a byw a bod o fraidd
ydynt, a byrr anghenfod yw eu hoedled, a'u bywydfod, eithr
o drangc ag angau y mae symmud iddynt, yn abredol i radd
a fydd uwch, ag yno cael chwanegiad bywyd a daioni, ag fal
hynn o radd i radd yn abredu nes nes at eitha bywyd a daioni, a Duw o'i drugar serch at fywydolion yn parottoi 'r
ffyrdd ar hyd yr Abred. o lwyr gariad tuag attynt, hyd oni
ddelont i gyflwr a phwngc hanfod Dynoldeb, lle mae cydbwys daioni a drwg heb un yn pwyso 'r llall i lawr, ag o
hynny y dyfydd rhyddineb, a dewis, a gallu tawl, i ddyn,
fal y dichon weithredu yr un a fynno a'r unrhyw ddeubeth,
mal o ddaioni a drwg, ag wrth hyn y gwelir mae cyflwr
prawf ag addysg yw cyflwr dynoldeb, lle mae cydbwys y da
a'r drwg, a bywydolion wrth eu bodd eu hunain.

13.   Ymhob cyflwr a phwngc o'r abred goris dynoldeb
drwg anghenfod yw pob bywydolion, a rhwym anghenfod
wrth y drwg o lwyr anfodd ag anallu iddynt, er eitha cais
a galledigaeth, ag yn hyn o beth yn ol y bont yn yr Abred,
ai uchel ai isel y pwngc, am hynny nid yw Duw yn eu cashau au cospi eithr eu caru au coledd, am nas gallant amgen,
ag am eu bod wrth rwym ag nid wrth fodd a dewis. ag er
maint y drwg nis gallent amgen, gan mai o'u rhwym ag nid
o'u bodd y maent felly.

14.   Yn ol dyfod i bwngc Dyndod yn yr Abred, lle mae

evil, and that, more or less, according to their degree in Abred, from the dead in the depth of Annwn, to the living in the extremity of goodness and power, even so far as would not be at all possible for God to conduct them further.

12. Animations in Annwn are partakers of life and goodness in the lowest possible degree, and of death and evil in the highest degree that is possibly compatible with life and personal identity. Therefore, they are necessarily evil, because of the preponderance of evil over the good; and scarcely do they live and exist; and their duration and life are necessarily short, whilst by means of dissolution and death they are removed gradually to a higher degree, where they receive an accumulation of life and goodness, and thus they progress from grade to grade, nearer and nearer to the extremity of life and goodness, God, of His merciful affection for animated beings, preparing the ways along Abred, out of pure love to them, until they arrive at the state and point of human existence, where goodness and evil equiponderate, neither weighing down the other. From this spring liberty and choice and elective power in man, so that he can perform which ever he likes of any two things, as of good and evil; and thus is it seen that the state of humanity is a state of probation and instruction, where the good and evil equiponderate, and animated beings are left to their own will and pleasure.

13. In every state and point of Abred that is below humanity, all living beings are necessarily evil, and necessarily bound to evil, from utter want of will and power, notwithstanding all the exertion and power put forth, which vary according as they are situate in Abred, whether the point be high or low. On this account God does not hate or punish them, but loves and cherishes them, because they cannot be otherwise, and because they are under obligation, and have no will and choice, and whatever the amount of evil may be, they cannot help it, because it is from obligation, and not willingly, that they are in this condition.

14. After having arrived at the point of humanity in

cydbwys drwg a da, y mae Dyn yn rhydd o bob rhwym gan
nad oes orddwy gan ddaioni a drygioni y naill ar y llall,
nag un o honynt yn traphwyso ar y llall, am hynny cyflwr
bodd a rhyddineb a galledigaeth, yw cyflwr Dyn, a phob
gweithred wrth dawl ag ethawl, a bodd a dewis ag nid o
rwym ag anfodd, ag angen ag anallu, am hyn Byw$^{iadur}_{ydydd}$ wrth
farn yw Dyn, a barn a fydd arno a a wnelo, gan y bydd da
neu ddrwg yn ol a wnelo, gan y gall amgen beth bynag a
wnelo, am hynny cyfiawn iddo gosp neu wobr fal y gofyn-
ant ei weithredoedd.

DUW.

$^{Pedwar\ peth}_{Tri\ pheth}$ yw Duw ag nis gellir yn amgen arno. Cydgyf-
awr a phob amser, cydgyfan a phob Handid, a chydgyfle a
phob amcan meddwl, a phei amgen y gellit ar a elwit yn
Dduw, nid Duw y byddai, achaws y gellid ei ragor, ag nid
Duw nebawd a ellir ei ragor.

A chyfymryn a phob bywydawl.

CYTHRAUL.

Tri lles y sydd o Gythraul, Difant ar ddrwg, golwg ar
ddaioni, a gorfoledd gorfod ar wrthles.

CEUGANT—PARHAD—DUW.

Tripheth nis gellir na maint na mesur arnynt, Y Ceugant, Parhad. a Duw. am nas gellir eithafoedd ar un nag
arall o henynt, na dechreu na diwedd na chanol arnynt.

---

[1] Al. "four things."

[2] Bardism recognises another principle of evil, which is called "DERA,"
respecting which Iolo Morganwg has the following note:—" The old Bardic
idea was that the DERA usurped the occupation of Cylch y Ceugant, and that he
would suffer none but himself to occupy it, destroying all other beings ;—that
God, being more powerful, is able to dispossess him, and, with Himself to occupy
it, creates beings highly susceptible of happiness, to enjoy it with Him to all

Abred, where evil and good equiponderate, man is free from all obligation, because goodness and wickedness do not press one upon the other, nor does either of them preponderate over the other. Therefore, the state of man is a state of will and freedom and ability, where every act is one of project and selection, consent and choice, and not of obligation and dislike, necessity and inability. On this account man is a living being capable of judgment, and judgment will be given upon him and his acts, for he will be good or bad according to his works, since whatever he does he could do differently; therefore it is right that he should receive punishment or reward, as his works require.

GOD.

God is three things,[1] and cannot be otherwise: coeval with all time; co-entire with all essence; and co-local with all mental purpose. Could what is called God be otherwise, it would not be God, since it could be surpassed, and no one is God that can be surpassed. He is also co-sentient with all animation.

CYTHRAUL.[2]

There are three benefits to be had from Cythraul: the defection of evil; a view to goodness; and the triumph of victory over what is contrary to the beneficial.

CEUGANT.—DURATION.—GOD.

Three things that are not capable of size or measure: Ceugant; duration; and God; because there can be no extremes to one or other of them—no beginning or end or middle to them.

---

eternity, on condition of joining with Him to resist evil. The common proverb is hence derived—' Myn y diawl y cwbl iddo ei hunan, fal y cybydd: mae Duw, fal yr haul, yn rhoi rhan i bob un arall.' "

TRI ANHYWYDD DUW.

Tri anhywydd Duw; ei hanas, achos nis gellir amser nad ydoedd ym mod, maint ei gariad achos er maint a wnelo, ni wel ddiwedd ar a ddichon gan gyfiawnder, Ei nerth gan nad oes diwedd na maint na mesur ar a ddichon gwedi eithafoedd Goddeu.

GORCHEST Y BEIRDD.

Nid dirgel ond Dim,
Nid Dim ond anfeidrol,
Nid anfeidrol ond Duw,
Nid Duw ond Dim,
Nid Dim ond Dirgel,
Nid Dirgel ond Dyw.

Llyma fal y mae Gorchest y Beirdd mewn rhai Lyfrau.

Nid Duw ond yr hynn nis gellir ei gyffred,
Nid nis gellir ei gyffred ond Dim,
Nid Dim ond Anfeidrol,
Nid anfeidrol ond Dyw,
Nid Dyw ond Dim.

Llyma Hen Orchest y Beirdd.

Nid Duw ond Dim, Nid Dim ond Duw.
Nid Duw ond Anfeidrol, Nid Anfeidrol ond Dim.

---

[1] These aphorisms are sometimes ascribed to Cattwg the Wise, in the sixth century.

[2] " Dirgel " is compounded of " dir," true, and " cel," concealment.

[3] It is very difficult to render the exact meaning of " dim " in this place, which is evidently not *nothing* in the popular use of the term. The translation, which we have adopted, was suggested by the late Archdeacon Williams in his *Gomer*, p. 136, and is in fact the " nihil cogitabile," as distinguished from the " nihil purum," in Sir William Hamilton's analysis of negative thought.

THE THREE IMPERCEPTIBILITIES OF GOD.

There are three things that are imperceptible in God: His origin, because there can have been no time in which He did not exist; the greatness of His love, for how much so ever He does, He will see no end to what He can in justice accomplish; and His power, because there is no end, size, or measure to what He can do after the utmost intention.

THE BARDS' ENIGMA.[1]

There is nothing truly hidden[2] but what is not conceivable;[3]

There is nothing not conceivable but what is immeasurable;

There is nothing immeasurable but God;

There is no God but that which is not conceivable;

There is nothing not conceivable but that which is truly hidden;

There is nothing truly hidden but God.

In some Books the Bards' enigma is as follows :—

There is no God but what cannot be comprehended;

There is nothing that cannot be comprehended but what is not conceivable;

There is nothing not conceivable but what is immeasurable;

There is nothing immeasurable but God;

There is no God but what is not conceivable.

Here is the ancient Bards' enigma :—

There is no God but what is not conceivable;
There is nothing not conceivable but God;
There is no God but what is immeasurable;
There is nothing immeasurable but God.

Llyma fodd arall arnaw.

Nid anfeidrol ond Dim,
Nid Anfeidrol ond Duw,
Nid Anfeidrol ond y mwyaf oll,
Nis gellir dau o'r mwyaf oll ar unpeth.

A Llyma ddattawd y gorchest.

Dim yw 'r mwyaf oll a'r anfeidrol ar y difant,
Duw yw 'r mwyaf oll a'r Anfeidrol ar y menwyd.
Ag nis gellir hanfod ar un peth onid o'r menwyd.
A difod pob peth o'r difant.

Sef y dywaid y Bardd

Dim yw 'r mwyaf a'r anfeidrol ar bob difant,
Duw yw 'r mwyaf a'r anfeidrol ar bob cymmant,
Al. adfant—ammant—elfant—elfyddiant.

Ӯ DEUDDEG PRIF GYNNEGOLION.

Y Deuddeg Prif Gynnegolion, a elwir Gwers y Gwyddoniaid mewn rhai lyfrau, a Gwers Tydain ai gelwir mewn
llyfrau eraill.

Nid Cais ond Gwerthfawr,
Nid Gwerthfawr ond mad,
Nid mad ond meuedd,
Nid meuedd ond Gwynfyd,
Nid Gwynfyd ond Gwybod,
Nid Gwybod ond Newydd,
Nid Newydd ond Newid,

---

1 "Difant," from "di," non, and "man," a place.

2 "Cymmant," from "cyd," with, or together, and "man," a place. Al.
"that is restored in place"—"that is in place all around"—"intellectual
place"—"elementation."

3 "Cynnegolion," the plural of "cynnegawl," a word compounded of *cyn*,
primary, and *neg*, adj. *negawl*, negation.

Here is another form of it.

There is nothing immeasurable but what is not conceiv able;

There is nothing immeasurable but God;

There is nothing immeasurable but the greatest of all;

There can be no two of the greatest of all in any thing.

Here is a solution of the enigma.

What is not conceivable is the greatest of all, and the immeasurable of what is not in place;

God is the greatest of all, and the immeasurable of intelligence;

And there can be no existence to any thing but from intelligence;

And the non-existence of all things comes from what is not in place.

As the Bard says :—

What is not conceivable is the greatest, and the immeasurable of all that is not in place;[1]

God is the greatest, and the immeasurable of all that are together in place.[2]

THE TWELVE PRIMARY NEGATIVES.[3]

The twelve primary Negatives, called in some books the Lesson of the Gwyddoniaid, but in other books the Lesson of Tydain.

There is nothing sought after but what is precious;

There is nothing precious but what is beneficial;

There is nothing beneficial but possession;

There is no possession but Gwynvyd;

There is no Gwynvyd but knowledge;

There is no knowledge but what is new;

There is nothing new but what changes;

2 E

Nid Newid ond er lles,
Nid lles ond hardd,
Nid hardd ond cyfiawn,
Nid cyfiawn ond cariad,
Nid cariad ond Dyw.
  Ag felly Terfyna.
 Tydain Tad Awen ai Cant
 Medd Llyfr Sion y Cent.

DIARHEBION BARDDONOL.

Sef y dywaid y Bardd,

Nid lles ond yr hyn nis gellir yn unmodd ei hepcor sef Duw.

Nid eisiau ond eisiau Duw,—nid cael ond Duw,
Nid coll ond colli Duw—nid digon ond Duw,
Nid anfeidrol ond Duw—nid gwybodus ond Duw
Nid ymhob man ond Duw,—nid cadarn ond yn Nuw.
Nid ymphob peth ond Duw.—nid oll ond Duw.
Nid Duw ond oll.

ENWAU DUW.

Rhai a alwasant Dduw Dad yn Henddihenydd sef am o'i ansawdd ef y mae pob peth, ag o hanaw y dechre ar bob peth ag ynddo yr annechre gan nas gellir amgen na'i fod, ag nis gellir dechre ar ddim heb ddechreuawr. Ac Iau y gelwid Duw Fab sef Duw dan lun a chorpholaeth meidrol

---

[1] That is, " the Ancient and Unoriginated One." The word occurs as one of the designations of the Supreme Being in the Welsh Bible, Dan. vii. 7; in the English Bible it is " the Ancient of days." The following definition of the word is given in one of Iolo Morganwg's Notes;—" Dihenydd=Gwehynwg. Yr Hen Wehynwg, the same as Hen Ddihenydd. (Barddas.) Gwehynwg, sef y tardd i fywydoldeb yn Annwn—the original lifespring, or springing into life at the lowest point of animated existence, or out of the chaotic mass of matter in its utmost state of decomposition."

There is no change but what is advantageous ;
There is no advantage but what is beautiful ;
There is nothing beautiful but what is just ;
There is nothing just but love ;
There is no love but God.

And thus it ends.

Tydain the Father of Awen sang it, says the Book
of Sion Cent.

BARDIC APHORISMS.

Thus says the Bard :—

There is no advantage but what can in no ways be dis-
pensed with, that is, God ;
There is no want but the want of God ;
There is no enjoyment but the enjoyment of God ;
There is no loss but the loss of God ;
There is no sufficiency but God ;
There is nothing immeasurable but God ;
There is nothing knowing but God ;
There is nothing in every place but God ;
There is nothing powerful but God ;
There is nothing in every thing but God ;
There is no whole but God ;
There is no God but what is whole.

THE DIVINE NAMES.

Some have called God the Father HEN DDIHENYDD,[1]
because it is from His nature that all things are derived,
and from Him is the beginning of every thing, and in Him
is no beginning, for He can not but exist, and nothing can
have a beginning without a beginner. And God the Son is
called IAU,[2] that is, God under a finite form and corporeity,

---

[2] The word is here taken in the sense of *Younger,* or as denoting the last manifestation of the Deity.

can nas gall meidrol adnabod a medru Duw yn amgen a
phan ddaeth ef yn Ddyn i'r byd yma y gelwid ef Iesu
Grist. sef nad oedd o annechre dan lun a chorph meidrol,
a dyn a gretto ynddo ag a wnelo saith weithred y drugaredd, a gaiff ei wared o boen Abred, a gwyn ei fyd fyth a
wnelo hyn. a Duw ddofydd hefyd y gelwir Iesu Grist, ag
enwau amgen y sydd hefyd arno, fal y mae Perydd, a Duw
Ner, a Duw Naf.

IAU

Disgybl ai Athraw.

D. Pam y rhodder Iau yn enw ar Dduw?

A. Achos Iau yw llath fesur gwlad a chenedl herwydd
cadernyd Cyfraith, ac ym meddiant pob un o benteulu dan
nod arlwydd y Cyfoeth a dirwy ar ai llygrai, a 'Duw yn
llathfesur pob gwir a phob Cyfiawnder a phob daioni, ac am
hynny Iau ar bawb a phawb dani, a gwae ar y neb ai llygro.

HU GADARN.

Hu gadarn Iesu fab Duw y lleiaf ei fawredd bydawl tra
bu yng nghnawd, a mwyaf yn y Nef o'r mawrion gweledig.*

---

* This extract is from a list of " Damhegion Beirdd Ynys Prydain."

     [1] " Dovydd ;" Domitor; the Tamer.

     [2] " Perydd ;" the Causer ; the First Cause ; the Creator.

     [3] " Ner;" Energy; the Powerful.

     [4] " Nav ;" the Former ; the Creator. Sion Cent has a Poem on "the
Names of God," into which he has introduced all these, with the exception of
" Hen Ddihenydd," and " Perydd," thus,—

         Duw, *Dofydd* mawr, Ionawr, *Iau.*
         Ener, Muner, *Ner, Naf* ydyw.
         See Iolo MSS. p. 285.

They are also, with many others of undoubtedly Druidic origin, still used by the
Cymry as epithets for the Deity.

     [5] " A yoke." It would appear, rather, that the *iau*, or yoke, being the badge
of power on the part of him who imposed it, was so designated from | /|\ \|/ ,

for a finite being cannot otherwise know and perceive God. And when He became man in this world, He was called JESUS CHRIST, for He was not from everlasting under a finite form and body. And the man who believes in Him, and performs the seven works of mercy, shall be delivered from the pain of Abred, and blessed for ever be he who does so. Jesus Christ is also called GOD THE DOVYDD;[1] and He has also other names, such as PERYDD,[2] and GOD THE NER,[3] and GOD THE NAV.[4]

IAU.[5]

Disciple and his Master.

Disciple. Why is Iau (yoke) given as a name for God?

Master. Because the yoke is the measuring rod[6] of country and nation in virtue of the authority of law, and is in the possession of every head of family under the mark of the lord of the territory, and whoever violates it is liable to a penalty. Now, God is the measuring rod of all truth, all justice, and all goodness, therefore He is a yoke on all, and all are under it, and woe to him who shall violate it.

HU THE MIGHTY.

Hu[7] the Mighty,—Jesus the Son of God,—the least in respect of His worldly greatness whilst in the flesh, and the greatest in heaven of all visible majesties.

---

a combination of Bardic symbols, which indicates preservation, creation, and destruction, and which was one of the earliest forms of the Divine Name. Iolo Morganwg interprets " Iau " as meaning " the recent, or last manifestation of the Deity—Mithras, Mithra ;" from the adjective, which literally signifies *younger*.

[6] The yoke, as a measuring rod, is mentioned in the Welsh Laws ; it follows, therefore, that this catechetical fragment must have been composed when those laws were in force.

[7] The meaning of " Hu," is *that which is apt to pervade, or to spread over*. It is used as an epithet of the Deity, in reference to His omniscience, and is not

Y CYLCHAU.

Cylch yr Abred ag ynddo y mae 'r holl hanfodolion corphorol a marw.

Cylch y Gwynfyd ag ynddo pob hanfodolion eneid$_{iedig}^{iol}$ ac anfarwolion.

Cylch y Ceugant lle nid oes namyn Duw, a'r doethion ai dyfalant fal hyn yn dri Chylch.

unfrequently to be met with as such in the works of the Bards; thus Taliesin, describing the resurrection of our Lord, observes,—

> Trydedydd bu
> Dadebriad Hu.

> On the third day was
> The resuscitation of Hu.
>   Llath Foesen. MS.

And Cynddelw,—

> Oedran Iesu Hu hoywdeg
> Yn wir Dduw un cant ar ddeg.

> The age of Jesus, the fair and energetic Hu,
> In God's truth was eleven hundred.

Rhys Goch Eryri, also, in his "Cywydd Cyfrinach," speaks of "Pont Hu," the bridge of Hu, in reference to the subject of the Incarnation; *pont* being a term used bardically to denote a teacher that conveys his disciples over the bog of ignorance. Hence the adage—"A fo ben bid bont." He who is head let him be a bridge.

Derived from Hu is the word Huon, used also as a Divine appellation; e.g.,

> Gwae wynt ddydd brawd ger bron Huon.

THE CIRCLES.[1]

The Circle of Abred, in which are all corporal and dead existences.

The Circle of Gwynvyd, in which are all animated and immortal beings.

The Circle of Ceugant, where there is only God. The wise men describe them thus, in three Circles.

Woe to them on the judgment day in the presence of HUON.

Geraint Vardd Glas, A.D. 900.

It also occurs in the list of "the Names of God" by Sion Cent;—

HUON, Ion, goreu i ddoniau.

HUON, and Ion, of best gifts.

Iolo MSS. p. 285.

Both Hu and HUON were no doubt originally identical with the HEUS of Lactantius, and the HESUS of Lucan, described as gods of the Gauls. The similarity of the last name to IESU is obvious and striking.

Hu the Mighty is, moreover, described in the Triads as a Historical personage; that is, as the one who first established the Cymry in a civil community, taught them agriculture, with other useful arts, and conducted them over into the island of Britain. See Triad, 3rd Series, Ap. Myv. Arch. vol. ii.

[1] Some persons, and among them M. Henri Martin, the celebrated French Historian, are of opinion that the three Circles of existence are represented in the old stone enclosures of the Bards, such as Avebury, and in the wheels observable on ancient British coins.

LLYFR BARDDAS.

Llyma Lyfr y Barddas sef Derwyddoniaeth Beirdd Ynys Prydain, a dynnais i Llywelyn Sion o Langewydd o'r hen Lyfrau, nid amgen na llyfrau Einion Offeiriad, a Thaliesin Ben Beirdd, a Dafydd Ddu $^{Hiraddug}_{o\ Euas}$, a'r Cwtta Cyfarwydd, a Ionas Mynyw, ac Edyrn Dafod aur, a Sion y Cent, a Rhys Goch, ac eraill yng gellawl rhaglan drwy gennad yr Arglwydd William Herbert Iarll Penfro. ac iddo drwy gennad Duw y bo imi ddiolch tra bwyf. Ac ynghyntaf y mae Traethawd hawl ac atteb Bardd ac Awenydd o waith Sion y Cent, sef y mae ynddo lawer o brifbyngciau yr hen ddoethineb, fal ac y bu er yn oes oesoedd gan Feirdd Ynys Prydain, ac yn hyn o draethawd cyflafar, y mae 'r Awenydd yn gyntaf yn gofyn a'r Bardd yn athraw iddo yn atteb gan ddysgu a gwybyddu. yn ail Bardd yn gofyn ac awenydd yn atteb.

---

[1] See Note, p. 62.

[2] Einion Offeiriad, or the Priest, was the father of Thomas ap Einion, autho or compiler of the " Greal," the tale of " Pwyll Pendaran Dyved," and the "History of Taliesin." He lived in the 14th century.

[3] Taliesin flourished from A.D. 520 to 570. He is ranked in the Triads, with Merddin Emrys and Merddin ab Madog Morvryn, as the three " privardd bedydd," or baptismal Bards of the Isle of Britain. Many of his compositions are still extant, which, with some of later date, wrongly attributed to him, are printed in the first volume of the *Myvyrian Archaiology.* Several Bardic allusions may be discovered in his Poems.

[4] Al. " of Euas." His proper name was Davydd ab Roderic ab Madog, which is still to be seen on his effigies in Dymeirchion Church, of which he was Vicar, and where he lies buried. He flourished about 1340. He was an eminent and learned Poet, and had a great share in regulating Welsh prosody. There is a sacred poem by him " Am ddiwedd dyn a'i gorph," and a very poetical translation of the " Officium B. Mariæ," from Latin into Welsh, which fills thirty columns of the first volume of the *Myvyrian Archaiology.*

[5] He was Meurig or Maurice, treasurer of Llandaf, who died in 1290. He obtained the name of " Cwtta Cyvarwydd " from a Book of his, so called, which contains a compendium of the History of Glamorgan, with other articles, a list of which is given by Edward Llwyd in the *Archaiologia Britannica,* p. 257. He also wrote the History of the whole Isle of Britain ; a Book of Proverbs ; the Rules of Poetry ; and Welsh Theology. He also translated the Gospel of St. John from the Latin into Welsh, with commentaries. " These Books," says Iago ab Dewi, (about 1700,) " were at Abermarlas about fifty years ago."

THE BOOK OF BARDISM.

Here is the Book of Bardism, that is to say, the Druid-ism of the Bards of the Isle of Britain, which I, Llywelyn Sion[1] of Llangewydd, extracted from old Books, namely, the books of Einion the Priest,[2] Taliesin, the Chief of Bards,[3] Davydd Ddu of Hiraddug,[4] Cwtta Cyvarwydd,[5] Jonas of Menevia,[6] Edeyrn the Golden-tongued,[7] Sion Cent,[8] Rhys Goch,[9] and others, in the Library of Rhaglan, by permission of the lord William Herbert, earl of Pem-broke,[10] to whom God grant that I may prove thankful as long as I live. The first is a Treatise in the form of Ques-tion and Answer, by a Bard and his Disciple—the work of Sion Cent, which contains many of the principal subjects of the primitive wisdom, as it existed among the Bards of the Isle of Britain from the age of ages. In this Dialogue, the Disciple first puts the question, and the Bard, his Teacher, answers, and imparts to him information and knowledge. In the second place the Bard examines, and the Disciple answers.

[6] Iohannes Menevensis, a divine and poet, who flourished towards the close of the tenth century. Some compositions, attributed to him, are printed in the first volume of the *Myvyrian Archaiology*.

[7] A poet and grammarian, who flourished in the thirteenth century. The Grammar, which he undertook at the command of the Princes of Wales, about 1270, has recently been published under the auspices of the Welsh MSS. Society.

[8] Sion Cent, or Dr. John Kent, a very eminent poet, and learned divine, who flourished from about 1380 to 1420. He wrote various Treatises in Latin on theological subjects, thirty-nine of which may be enumerated, and many poems in his native language, which were highly esteemed. Every manuscript vol-ume of Welsh poetry of early date generally contains some of his productions. Three of them, one of which enumerates the Bardic Names of God, are printed in the Iolo MSS.

[9] Rhys Goch Eryri, or Rhys ab Davydd, was a very eminent poet, who flou-rished from A.D. 1330 to 1420. About 30 of his poems on various subjects are preserved, among them one entitled "Cywydd Cyfrinach," which is printed in the Iolo MSS , p. 307, and is full of allusions to the mysteries of Bardism.

[10] A distinguished patron of Welsh literature. He was the author of a set of Theological Triads, which appear from the style and language as if they were of Bardic origin.

2 F

Hawl yr ail.

Pwy 'n ydwyt adolwyn ag adrodd imi dy hanes

Dyn ydwyf ym mraint gwyllys Duw, ar angen tardd y sy'n canlyn, *canys a fyno Dduw a fydd.*

O ba le y daethost, a pheth yw dy ddychreuad?

O'r Byd mawr y daethum, a'm dechreuad yn Annwn.

Ymha le'r ydwyt yn awr, a phafodd y daethost i'r lle ddydwyd?

Yr wyf yn y Byd Bychan, lle daethum gan dreiglo Cylch yr Abred, ac ynawr yn ddyn ar ei derfyn a'i eithafon.

Beth oeddyt cyn dy ddyfod yn ddyn ynghylch yr Abred.

Yn Annwn y lleiaf yngallu oeddwn a ellit bywyd ynddo, a'r nesaf a allai fod at y marw pendant, ag ymhob rhith a thrwy bob rhith a ellir corph a bywyd y daethum hyd ynghyflwr dyn ar hyd cylch yr Abred, lle bu tost a thrwm fy nghyflwr hyd oes oesoedd, er pan ym parthwyd yn Annwn oddiwrth y marw drwy ddawn Duw a fawr haelioni ai gariad diderfyn a diddarfod.

Drwy ba sawl rhith y daethost, a pheth fu dy ddamwain

Drwy bob rhith a ellir bywyd ynddo, yn nwr, yn naiar, ac yn wybren. A'n namwain a fu pob tost a phob caled, a phob drwg, a phob dioddef, ac ychydig y bu 'r daioni ar gwynfyd cyn dyn o honof.

Dywedaist taw ym mraint cariad Dyw y daethost drwy hyn oll ac a welaist ac a gefaist hyn oll. dywed imi pa fodd

---

[1] There are two poems printed in the Myv. Arch., vol. i., and attributed to Taliesin, entitled respectively, "Canu y Byd mawr," and "Canu y Byd bychan," or the Great World, and the Little World. The former, referring to the creation, and the latter, to the maintenance of the world, seem, both of them, to be founded on the doctrine of the text. Iorwerth Vynglwyd (1460—1500) bears his testimony to the fact that man was described in the creed of the Bards as a little world, thus;—

> Medd y barddas urddasawl,
> *Byd bach* yw *dyn* iach dan wawl.

> Saith the revered Bardism,
> A *little world* is *man* in his vigour, under the light.

[2] It was this doctrine relative to the commencement of life from Annwn, that was, no doubt, at the bottom of the opinion, which Julius Cæsar attributes to

The second examination.

Q. Prithee, who art thou? and tell me thy history.

A. I am a man in virtue of God's will, and the necessary consequence that follows, for "what God wills must be."

Q. Whence didst thou proceed? and what is thy beginning?

A. I came from the Great World,[1] having my beginning in Annwn.[2]

Q. Where art thou now? and how camest thou to where thou art?

A. I am in the Little World,[1] whither I came, having traversed the circle of Abred, and now I am a man at its termination and extreme limits.

Q. What wert thou before thou didst become a man in the circle of Abred?

A. I was in Annwn the least possible that was capable of life, and the nearest possible to absolute death, and I came in every form, and through every form capable of a body and life, to the state of man along the circle of Abred, where my condition was severe and grievous during the age of ages, ever since I was parted in Annwn from the dead, by the gift of God, and His great generosity, and His unlimited and endless love.

Q. Through how many forms didst thou come? and what happened unto thee?

A. Through every form capable of life, in water, in earth, and in air. And there happened unto me every severity, every hardship, every evil, and every suffering, and but little was the goodness and gwynfyd before I became a man.

Q. Thou hast said, that it was in virtue of God's love thou camest through all these, and didst see and experience all these; tell me how can this take place through the love

---

the Gauls. " Galli se omnes ab Dite patre prognatos prædicant, idque a Druidibus proditum dicunt." (De Bel. Gal. l. vi. c. 18.)

y gellir hyn o gariad Duw, a maint arwyddion anghariad ar dy dreigl yn abred.

Nis gellir gwynfyd heb weled a gwybod pob peth, ac nis gellir gweled a gwybod pob peth heb ddioddef pob peth, ac nis gellir cariad cyflawn a chyflwyr, heb o hano y petheu rhaid tuag at arwain i'r gwybodaeth a bair Gwynfyd, gan nas gellir Gwynfyd heb wybodaeth Cyflwyr ar bob dull hanfod a phob drwg a da, a phob gweithred a nerth ac an- sawdd ar ddrwg a da, ac nis gellir hyn o wybodaeth onid o ymbrawf. ymhob rhith bywyd, ymhob damwain, ag ymhob dioddef, ac ymhob drwg ac ymhob daioni, fal y gwyper y naillion oddiwrth y lleillion. a rhaid yw hyn oll cyn y gellir gwynfyd, a rhaid gan wrthynt oll cyn y gellir cariad cyf- lwyr yn nuw, a rhaid cariad cyflwyr yn Nuw cyn y gellir Gwynfyd.

Paham y mae rhaid wrth y pethau a ddywedaist cyn y gellir Gwynfyd?

Am nas gellir gwynfyd heb orfod ar ddrwg a marw ac ar bob gwrth a chythraul, ac nis gellir gorfod arnynt heb wy- bod eu rhyw au hansawdd, a'u nerth, a'u gweithredon—a'u lle, au hamser, a phob dull a rhyw hanfod arnynt, fal y gwyper oll arnynt, ac y gellir ei gochel, a lle bont ei gwrth- ryw, a'u gwrthrym, a'u gorfod, ac ymwellhau oddiwrthynt, ac ymadfer yn ol o'u peryddiaeth, a'r lle y bo hyn o wybod- aeth cyflwyr y mae y rhydd cyflwyr, ac nis gellir ymwrth a gorfod ar ddrwg a marw onid lle bo rhydd cyflwyr, ac nis gellir gwynfyd onid gyda Duw yn y rhydd cyflwyr, ac yn y rhydd cyflwyr y mae cylch y Gwynfyd.

Pa ham nas gellir gwybodaeth cyflwyr heb dreiglo pob rhith byw yn abred.

Am hyn o achos, sef nid un y sydd i un daurith, ac ym-

---

[1] " Ei gwrthryw," i.e. their species may be opposed by a contrary species.

[2] " Au gwrthrym," i.e. their force be opposed by a contrary force.

of God? And how many were the signs of the want of love during thy migration in Abred?

A. Gwynvyd cannot be obtained without seeing and knowing every thing, but it is not possible to see and to know every thing without suffering every thing. And there can be no full and perfect love that does not produce those things which are necessary to lead to the knowledge that causes Gwynvyd, for there can be no Gwynvyd without the complete knowledge of every form of existence, and of every evil and good, and of every operation and power and condition of evil and good. And this knowledge cannot be obtained without experience in every form of life, in every incident, in every suffering, in every evil and in every good, so that they may be respectively known one from the other. All this is necessary before there can be Gwynvyd, and there is need of them all before there can be perfect love of God, and there must be perfect love of God before there can be Gwynvyd.

Q. Why are the things, which thou hast mentioned, necessary before there can be Gwynvyd?

A. Because there can be no Gwynvyd without prevailing over evil and death, and every opposition and Cythraul, and they cannot be prevailed over without knowing their species, nature, power, operations, place, and time, and every form and kind of existence which they have, so that all about them may be known, and that they may be avoided, and that wherever they are they may be opposed,[1] counteracted,[2] and overcome, and that we may be cured of them, and be restored from under their effect. And where there is this perfect knowledge, there is perfect liberty, and evil and death cannot be renounced and overcome but where there is perfect liberty; and there can be no Gwynvyd but with God in perfect liberty, and it is in perfect liberty that the circle of Gwynvyd exists.

Q. Why may not perfect knowledge be obtained, without passing through every form of life in Abred?

A. On this account, because there are no two forms

mhob rhith y mae achos iddo, a dioddef iddo, a gwybod
iddo, a deall iddo, a gwynfyd iddo, ag ansawdd iddo, a
gweithred, a gorfod iddo nis gellir ei fath ai gwbl unrhyw
yn un rhith hanfod arall. a chan fod gwybodaeth neillduol
ymhob rhith hanfod nas gellir mewn un arall, angen yw
myned ymhob rhith hanfod cyn y gellir pob rhith a rhyw
gwybodaeth a deall. ac o hynny ymwrth a phob drwg, ac
ymgyd a phob Gwynfyd.

Pa sawl rhith hanfod y sydd, a pha achos y sydd iddynt.

Sawl un a welwys Duw yn anghenreidiawl tuag at olrhain
a gwybod pob rhyw ac ansawdd ar y da a'r drwg, fal nas
byddai dim a ellid ei wybod ai feddwl gan Dduw heb ymbrawf arno ac o hynny gwybod arno. ac ymha beth bynnag
y gellir gwybod ar ddaioni ac ar ddrwg, ag ar ansawdd byw
a marw, y mae yno rhith hanfod yn gweddu caffaeliad ar y
gwybodaeth y bo gofyn arno, ac am hynny nifer rhywiau, a
moddion rhith hanfod ydynt y maint a allasai feddwl a deall er daioni a gwybodaeth, a gwynfyd, cyflawn. a Duw a
wnaeth y byddai i bob byw a bywedig, dreiglo pob rhith a
rhyw hanfod wrth fywyd. fal y gellid yn y diwedd y cyflawn i bob byw a bywedig ar wybodaeth a bywyd a gwynfyd. a hynn oll o Gariad cyflwyr Duw yr hyn nis gall...i*
ymraint ei ryw dwyfawl tuag at ddyn a phob byw.

Ai barn yw gennyt, y bydd i bob *byw*† gyrchu Cylch y
gwynfyd o'r Diwedd.

Barn yw gennyf hynny, can nas gellir llai na hynn o
Gariad anfeidrol Duw, a Duw yn medru peri, yn gwybod y
modd oi beri ag yn gwyllysu 'n ddibaid, pob peth a ellir

---

* Illegible in the MS. copied by Iolo Morganwg.   The sense would require
" gall lai."

† Illegible in the MS. copied by Iolo Morganwg.

alike, and every form has a use, a suffering, a knowledge, an intelligence, a gwynvyd, a quality, an operation, and an impulse, the like and complete uniformity of which can not be had in any other form of existence. And as there is a special knowledge in each form of existence, which cannot be had in another, it is necessary that we should go through every form of existence, before we can acquire every form and species of knowledge and understanding, and consequently renounce all evil, and attach ourselves to every gwynvyd.

Q. How many forms of existence are there? and what is the use of them?

A. As many as God saw necessary towards the investigation and knowledge of every species and quality in good and evil, that there might be nothing, capable of being known and conceived by God, without being experienced, and consequently known. And in whatsoever thing there may be a knowledge of good and evil, and of the nature of life and death, there is a form of existence which corresponds with the attainment of the knowledge required. Therefore, the number of the kinds and modes of forms of existence is the sum that could conceive and understand with a view to perfect goodness, knowledge, and gwynvyd. And God caused that every living and animate being should pass through every form and species of existence endued with life, so that in the end every living and animate being might have perfect knowledge, life, and gwynvyd; and all this from the perfect love of God, which in virtue of His Divine nature He could not but exhibit towards man and every living being.

Q. Art thou of opinion that every living being shall attain to the circle of Gwynvyd at last?

A. That is my opinion, for less could not have happened from the infinite love of God, God being able to cause, knowing the manner how to cause, and continually willing every thing to exist that can be conceived and sought in

meddwl a chais arno yn ei gariad ef ei hun, ag yn nymun-
iad pob byw yngwrth drwg a marw.

Pa bryd y daw hyn o gyflwr ar bob byw ac ymha fodd
y diwedd bywyd Abred.

Pob byw a bywedig a dreiglant gylch yr Abred o ddyfnder Annwn sef eithaf yr isel ar bob hanfod wrth fywyd. a
dyfod i fynydd o annwn uwch uwch yn nhrefn a graddau
bywyd oni ddelir yn ddyn ac yna gallu diwedd Abred. drwy
ymgyd a'r daioni, ag yn angau myned ynghylch y Gwynfyd, a darfod abred angen tros fyth, ac ni bydd ar ol hynny
dreiglo pob rhith hanfod ond ymraint rhydd a dewis yn
gyfymgyd a gwynfyd, yn adymbrawf ac yn adymgais a
Gwybodaeth, a hyn a drig tros fyth yn ymnewid ac ym-
newyddiaeth gwynfyd fal nas syrthier i'r Ceugant, ag
oddiyno i'r abred. can nas gall ond Duw goddef a threiglo
Cylch y ceugant. ac wrth hyn y gwelir nad oes wynfyd heb
ymgyfrin, ac ymnewyddu prawf ac ymbrawf, a gwybodaeth,
canys yngwybod y mae bywyd a Gwynfyd.

A â pob dyn i gylch y gwynfyd sef y nef pan y bo marw.

Nid a neb i'r Gwynfyd yn angeu onid a lyno yn ei fyw,
yn ddyn wrth ddaioni a dwyfolder, a phob gwaith doethineb
a chyfiawnder a Chariad, a lle pwysont y cynneddfau hyn
ar eu gwrthiaid o annoethineb, ag anghyfiawnder, ac anghariad, a phob drwg ag annwyfolder, yr a dyn pan y bo marw
i'r Gwynfyd sef y Nef, ag oddiyno ni syrthiai 'n abred mwy,
can y mae trech da na drwg o bob rhyw a threchu y mae 'r
byw ar y marw gan orfod arno, tros fyth, ag ymgodi nes nes
at wynfyd cyflawn oni bo 'n ei eithafon. ag yno y trig tros
fyth yn dragywydd. — A'r dyn na lyno fal hyn wrth y

His own love, and in the desire of every animation whilst opposed to evil and death.

Q. When will this condition happen to every living being, and in what manner will occur the end of the life of Abred?

A. Every living and animate being shall traverse the circle of Abred from the depth of Annwn, that is, the extreme limits of what is low in every existence endued with life; and they shall ascend higher and higher in the order and gradation of life, until they become man, and then there can be an end to the life of Abred by union with goodness. And in death they shall pass to the circle of Gwynvyd, and the Abred of necessity will end for ever. And there will be no migrating through every form of existence after that, except in right of liberty and choice united with Gwynvyd, with a view to re-experience, and re-seek knowledge. And this will remain for ever, as a variation and novation of Gwynvyd, so that no one can fall into Ceugant, and thence into Abred; for God alone can endure and traverse the circle of Ceugant. By this it is seen that there is no Gwynvyd without mutual communication, and the renewal of proof, experience, and knowledge, for it is in knowledge that life and Gwynvyd consist.

Q. Shall every man, when he dies, go to the circle of Gwynvyd?

A. No one shall at death go to Gwynvyd, except he who shall attach himself in life, whilst a man, to goodness and godliness, and to every act of wisdom, justice, and love. And when these qualities preponderate over their opposites, namely, folly, injustice, and uncharitableness, and all evil and ungodliness, the man, when he dies, shall go to Gwynvyd, that is heaven, from whence he will no more fall, because good is stronger than evil of every kind, and life subdues death, prevailing over it for ever. And he shall ascend nearer and nearer to perfect Gwynvyd, until he is at its extreme limits, where he will abide for ever and eternally. But the man who does not thus attach himself to

2 G

dwyfol a syrth yn Abred hyd y gweddo iddo rith a rhyw
hanfod, yn gyfansawdd a'i hun, ag oddiyno treiglo 'n ol at
gyflwr dyn fal o'r blaen, ag yna fal y bo ei ymlyn wrth y
dwyfol na 'r annwyfol y cwyn i'r gwynfyd neu y syrth yn
Abred pan y bo marw. ac fal hyn y syrth dros fyth hyd oni
chais y dwyfol ac ymlynu wrtho ag yna diwedd abred
angen. a phob goddef angen ar y drwg a marw.

ABRED.—GWYNVYD.—AWEN.

Pa sawl gwaith y syrthier yn Abred.

Ni syrthir unwaith gan angen ar ol ai treigler unwaith,
eithr gan wall o lynu wrth yr annwyfol oni bo traphwys ar
y dwyfol y syrthier yn Abred ag yna treiglo 'n ol hyd
ynghyflwr dyn drwy bob rith hanfod ac y bo rhaid tuag
at ddilëo 'r drwg a fu achos y syrth yn abred, ag nis syrthir
amgen nag unwaith am yr un annwyfolaeth, gan y gor-
fydder arno yn hynny o syrth. eithr o lawer anwyfolder
arall y gellir syrth yn abred, ac felly aneirif weithiau oni
orfydder ar bob gwrth a Chythraul, sef ar bob annwyfolder.
ac yna diwedd abred angen.

Pa faint a syrthiasant yn abred ac am ba achos y syrthiasant ?

Pob byw goris cylch y Gwynfyd a syrthiasant yn abred,
ag yn nawr y maent ar eu treigl yn ol i'r Gwynfyd, a hir y
treigl y rhan fwyaf gan amled y syrthiant o ymlyn a'r drwg
a'r annwyfol. Sef achos y syrthiasant oedd y mynent
dreiglo Cylch y Ceugant yr hynn nis gallai namyn Duw ei
oddef, ai dreiglo. Ac o hynny y syrthiasant hyd yn Annwn, ag o falchder a fynnai ymgyhydreg a Duw y syrth-

godliness, shall fall in Abred to a corresponding form and species of existence of the same nature as himself, whence he shall return to the state of man as before. And then, according as his attachment may be to either godliness or ungodliness, shall he ascend to Gwynfyd, or fall in Abred, when he dies. And thus shall he fall for ever, until he seeks godliness, and attaches himself to it, when there will be an end to the Abred of necessity, and to every necessary suffering of evil and death.

ABRED.—GWYNVYD.—AWEN.

Q. How often may one fall in Abred?

A. No one will fall once of necessity, after it has been once traversed, but through negligence, from cleaving to ungodliness, until it preponderates over godliness, a man will fall in Abred. He will then return to the state of man, through every form of existence that will be necessary for the removal of the evil, which was the cause of his fall in Abred. And he will fall only once in Abred on account of the same ungodliness, since it will be overcome by that fall; nevertheless, because of many other impieties he may fall in Abred, even numberless times, until every opposition and Cythraul, that is, all ungodliness, shall have been vanquished, when there will be an end to the Abred of necessity.

Q. How many have fallen in Abred? and for what cause have they fallen?

A. All living beings below the circle of Gwynvyd have fallen in Abred, and are now on their return to Gwynvyd. The migration of most of them will be long, owing to the frequent times they have fallen, from having attached themselves to evil and ungodliness; and the reason why they fell was, that they desired to traverse the circle of Ceugant, which God alone could endure and traverse. Hence, they fell even unto Annwn, and it was from pride, which would

iasant, ag nid oes syrth angen hyd yn annwn onid o falchder.

A syrthiasant bawb yn abred gan falchder a gyrhaeddasant gylch y gwynfyd o'r treigl angen cysefin o Annwn?

Na ddo, rhai a geisiasant ddoethineb ag o hynny a welasant a wnelai falchder, ag ymroi a wnaethant yn ol a ddysged iddynt gan Dduw, Ag o hynny a aethant yn Ddwyfeu, sef yn angylion santaidd. Ag a gawsant addysg wrth a welasant yn eraill. ag o hynny y gwelasant ansawdd y Ceugant, a'r tragywydd, ag nas gallai namyn Duw ei oddef ai dreiglo.

Onid yw pyd y syrthir yn Abred o gylch y Gwynfyd etto fal y bu o'r blaen?

Nag ydyw gan y ceir gorfod ar bob balchder a phob pechod arall cyn y gellir yr ail waith gyrhaedd Cylch y Gwynfyd. ag yna gan atgof, a gwybod, y drwg a fu o'r blaen y byth trachas gan bawb o angen y peth a wnaeth syrthio o'r blaen, a'r peth a fo angen ar gas a chariad a barhânt ac a beryddant dros fyth ynghylch y Gwynfyd lle bydd anarfod y tri chadarn sef, cas, cariad, a gwybod.

Ai bydd unrhyw y rhai a ddychwelant i gylch y Gwynfyd ar ol y syrth yn abred a'r rhai na syrthiasant.

Bydd, ag unfraint, gan nas gellir llai cariad Duw at un na'r llall, nag $^{thuag\,at}$ un rhyw ddull hanfod na'r llall gan e fod ef yn Dduw ag dad iddynt oll, ac yn unfaint ei gariad a'i dadolaeth tuag atynt oll, a chyfartal cydfraint y byddant oll ynghylch y Gwynfyd, sef yn ddwyfeu ag yn angylion santaidd dros fyth.

A bydd tros fyth pob rhith a rhyw hanfod wrth fywyd fel ac y mae yn awr? os felly dywed i mi paham?

Byddant, ymraint rhydd a dewis, a'r gwynfydigion a ant o un i'r llall o honynt fal y dymunont er gorffwys rhag lludded a hired y ceugant yr hyn nis gall namyn duw ei

---

[1] What is stated here may explain the adage,—

Nid eir i Annwn ond unwaith.

Annwn will be visited but once.

ally itself with. God, that they fell, and there is no necessary fall as far as Annwn, except from pride.

Q. Did all, who reached the circle of Gwynvyd after the primary progression of necessity from Annwn, fall in Abred from pride?

A. No; some sought after wisdom, and hence saw what pride would do, and they resolved to conduct themselves according to what was taught them by God, and thereby became divinities, or holy angels, and they acquired learning from what they beheld in others, and it was thus that they saw the nature of Ceugant and eternity, and that God alone could endure and traverse it.

Q. Does not the danger of falling in Abred, from the circle of Gwynvyd, exist still as it did formerly?

A. No; because all pride and every other sin, will be overcome before one can a second time reach the circle of Gwynvyd, and then by recollecting and knowing the former evil, every one will necessarily abhor what caused him to fall before, and the necessity of hatred and love will last and continue for ever in the circle of Gwynvyd, where the three stabilities, namely, hatred, love, and knowledge, will never end.[1]

Q. Will those, who shall return to the circle of Gwynvyd after the fall in Abred, be of the same kind as those who fell not?

A. Yes; and of the same privilege, because the love of God cannot be less towards one than towards another, nor towards one form of existence than another, since He is God and Father to them all, and exercises the same amount of love and patronage towards them all, and they will all be equal and co-privileged in the circle of Gwynvyd, that is, they will be divinities and holy angels for ever.

Q. Will every form and species of living existence continue for ever as they are now? If so, tell me why?

A. Yes, in virtue of liberty and choice, and the blessed will go from one to another as they please, in order to repose from the fatigue and tediousness of Ceugant, which God

oddef, ag er ymbrawf a phob gwybod ag a phob gwynfyd y
gellir rhyw a rhith arno, a phob un yn casau 'r drwg o angenorfod, ag yn ei adnabod yn gyflwyr ag o hynny yn ei
ymwrth o angen gan wybod yn llwyr ei ansawdd a'i niweid-
ioldeb. *a Duw yn borth a Duw'n ben,* yn eu cynnal a'u cadw
dros fyth.

Pa fodd y mae 'r gwybod am hyn o bethau?

Y Gwyddoniaid er yn oes oesoedd er amser Sedd ab
Addaf ab Duw, a gawsant Awen o Dduw ag o hynny y
gwybuant Gyfrinach dwyfoldeb, ag ynghenedl y Cymry
oeddynt y Gwyddoniaid er yn oes oesoedd, a gwedi hynny
y gwnaed trefn ar y Gwyddoniaid wrth fraint a defod fal y
cedwid cof diwall am hyn o wybodaeth a gwedi hynny y
gelwid y Gwyddoniaid yn Feirdd wrth fraint a Defod
Beirdd Ynys Prydain can mae gwedi dyfod y Cymry i
Ynys Prydain y gwnaed hyn o drefn, a thrwy Gof Barddas
ag Awen o Dduw y mae hyn o wybodaeth ag nis gellir anwir gan Awen o Dduw, ag ynghenedl yr Israel y cafwyd y
prophwydi santaidd y rhain drwy Awen o Dduw a wybuant
yr holl bethau hyn fal ag y mae yn yr Ysgruthur lân, a
gwedi dyfod Crist Mab Duw yn y Cnawd o'r Gwynfyd y
celwyd pellach gwybodaeth o Dduw ai ewyllys, fal y gwelir
ym mhregeth bawl a phan ddaethom ni 'r Cymry i'r ffydd
Ynghrist y cafes ein beirdd ni amlyccach Awen o Dduw a
gwybodaeth am bob Dwyfol tu hwnt i'r peth a welwyd o'r
blaen. ag a brophwydasant gan wellhau Awen a Gwybodaeth
ag o hyn y mae pob gwybod ar y dwyfol ag a berthyn i
Dduw.

---

[1] Ieuan du'r Bilwg refers to Seth as a Bard ;—

> SEDD mab ieuaf Addaf oedd,
> Breuddwydiwr, a *Bardd* ydoedd.

> Seth was the youngest son of Adam,—
> He was a dreamer and a *Bard*.

[2] Pan elo'r goron ar garn ddifant
Ofer pob peth ond *pregeth* PAWL SANT
Pan elo 'r goron ar gyfeiliorni,
Nid ellir ai gweryd ond gair Celi.—Penegoes MS.

only can endure, and in order to experience every knowledge and every gwynvyd that are capable of species and form; and each one of them will hate evil of necessary obligation, and know it thoroughly, and consequently of necessity renounce it, since he will perfectly know its nature and mischievousness — God being a help, and God being chief, supporting and preserving them for ever.

Q. How are these things to be known?

A. The Gwyddoniaid, from the age of ages, from the time of Seth,[1] son of Adam, son of God, obtained Awen from God, and thence knew the mystery of godliness; and the Gwyddoniaid were of the nation of the Cymry from the age of ages. After that, the Gwyddoniaid were regulated according to privilege and usage, in order that unfailing memory might be kept of this knowledge. After that, the Gwyddoniaid were called Bards according to the privilege and usage of the Bards of the Isle of Britain, because it was after the arrival of the Cymry in the island of Britain, that this regulation was made; and it is through the memorials of Bardism and Awen from God that this knowledge has been acquired, and no falsehood can accrue from Awen from God. In the nation of Israel were found the holy prophets, who through Awen from God knew all these things as described in the Holy Scriptures. And after Christ, the Son of God, had come in the flesh from Gwynvyd, further knowledge of God, and His will, was obtained, as is seen in St. Paul's Sermon.[2] And when we, the Cymry, were converted to the faith in Christ, our Bards obtained a more clear Awen from God, and knowledge about all things divine beyond what had been seen before, and they prophesied, improving Awen and knowledge. Hence is all knowledge concerning things divine and what appertains to God.

When the crown is on the point of being lost,
All will be in vain except the *sermon of St. Paul :*
When the crown goes astray,
Nothing can save it but the Word of Celi.

Pa fodd y mae cael Awen lle na bytho, fal y gellir Bardd o'r neb a fynnai fod yn fardd.

Drwy ymarfer a buchedd santaidd a phob cariad tuag at Dduw a Dyn, a phob cyfiawnder, a phob trugaredd, a phob haelioni, a phob Goddef, a phob heddwch, ag ymarfer a phob Gwybodau Daionus, a gochel, balchder a Chreulonder, a Godineb, a murn a chynllwyn, a lladrad, a chybydd-dra, a phob anghyfiawn, sef y pethau a lygrant ac a ddifant Awen lle bo, ag a wnant nas gellir ei chael lle na bo.

Ag yn y modd y cafwyd gyntaf ac y mae pellach cael Awen o Dduw?

Yn y modd hyn y ceir Awen fal y gwyper am y gwir, ai gredu : eithr rhai a farnant mai 'r modd y cafwyd gyntaf wybod ar y Gwir oedd dyfod o'r Dwyfeu sef yr Angylion santaidd a'r seiniau sef y dwyfolion a aethant i'r Nef, ag yn y lle pennaf Iesu Grist Mab Duw i lawr o'r Gwynfyd i'r byd bychan Ynghyflwr Dyn er dysgu a rhybyddu ac hyfforddi a Gwybyddu y rhai a geisiant fod yn ddwyfolion, sef y daethant ym mraint anfonog$_{aeth}^{ion}$ o anfoniad Duw o'i An-feidrol gariad ac ym mraint ei mawr gariad ei hunain yn gydwaith a chariad Duw, ag yn anfonogion ufudd iddo. a ninnau a gawn ein rhaid o Awen o Dduw o lynu wrth y dafoedd a'r dwyfol yn ddiffuant ag o wir gariad ar bob daionus.

Y TRI CHYFLWR.

O dri phrif gynneddfau dyn y bydd ei dreigl yn Abred, o syrthni ai ddallineb meddwl y syrth yn annwfn, o'i nwyf-iant afreolus y treigla Cylch yr Abred, herwydd y bytho 'n ngenddyl arnaw, ag oi serch ar ddaioni y cyrch yr ardlafael Cylch y Gwynfyd, o herwydd y trecho yn nac arall o'r prif-

Q. How is Awen to be obtained, where it is not, so that a Bard may be made of him, who would be a Bard ?

A. By habituating one's self to a holy life, and all love towards God and man, and all justice, and all mercy, and all generosity, and all endurance, and all peace, and practising good sciences, and avoiding pride and cruelty and adultery, and murder and ambuscade, and theft, and covetousness, and all injustice, that is, the things that will corrupt and destroy Awen, where it exists, and will prevent the obtaining it, where it does not exist.

Q. Is it in the way it was first obtained, that Awen from God is still obtainable ?

A. It is in this way that Awen is obtained, that the truth may be known and believed. Some, however, are of opinion that the way in which the truth was first known, was, that the divinities, or holy angels, and the saints or godly men, who went to heaven, and especially Jesus Christ, the Son of God, came down from Gwynvyd to the Little World in the condition of man, in order to teach, warn, direct, and inform those who seek to be divine. That is, they came in the capacity of messengers sent by God in His infinite love, and in virtue of their own great love co-operating with the love of God, and as His obedient messengers. And we shall have what of Awen from God is necessary for us, by attaching ourselves to the good and godly with sincerity, and out of pure love for all goodness.

THE THREE STATES.

1. According to the three principal qualities of man shall be his migration in Abred : from indolence and mental blindness he shall fall to Annwn ; from dissolute wantonness he shall traverse the circle of Abred, according to his necessity ; and from his love for goodness he shall ascend to the circle of Gwynvyd. As one or the other of the principal qualities of man predominates, shall the state

2 H

gynneddfau y bydd ar gyflwr y dyn, ac o hynny ei dri chyflwr, Annwn, Abred, a Gwynfyd.

Tri Chyflwr bywydolion, Annwn, ac yno dechreuad;— Abred, ynddaw cynnudd Gwybodaeth ac o hynny daioni, a'r Gwynfyd, ac yn hynny Cyflawnder pob daioni, o wybodaeth, gwirionedd, a chariad, a bywydoldeb didrangc.

ANNWN —BYWYD.—MARWOLAETH.

Ymha le y mae Annwn? A. Yn y man y bo 'r lleiaf a ddichoner or byw a'r bywyd. a mwyaf o'r mawr * heb gyflwr anmryw. — beth yw bannogion bywyd? Ysgafnder goleuni gwres, ag aflygredd, sef $^{\text{anghyfnewidioldeb}}_{\text{cadarn}}$. — Beth yw Bannogion nodau 'r marw? trymder, oerder, tywyllwch, a llygredd, sef Cyfnewidioldeb—

Ymheth y saif ansawdd angau? a marwolder?—Yn ei fannogion sef un yn achos y llall, megis y mae trwm yn achos tywyll a'r ddau 'n achos llygredd, a llygredd yn achos y ddau.—

Ymha beth y saif angen byw a bywyd? yn ei fanogion sef claerder a goleuni ag ysgafnder ag aflygredd, ag un yn achaws y llall, ag o hynny Duw a bywyd.

ABRED. †

Ymgyflwyn a drwg a wna 'n isaf a gwaelaf o bob bywydawl, am hynny ymwellhau ag ymdderchafael yn nhreigl yr

---

* Sic in MS. Probably "marw" is meant.

† In the MS. the heading is Barddas, i.e. Bardism.

1 As it is now generally admitted that the Hyperboreans, spoken of by ancient authors, were the same as the primitive inhabitants of Britain, or the Cymry, it is very probable that their priest *Abaris,* who, according to Herodotus, (l. iv. 36,) carried an arrow *round the whole earth* fasting, referred mystically to the *circle of Abred.* He is said to have presented his arrow to Pythagoras, by which we are probably to understand that the philosopher received the doctrine of the metempsychosis from the Druids.

According to Stephanus of Bysantium, (*De Urb.,*) the Cimbri or Cimmerii were called also *Abroi,* perhaps *Abredolion.*

Αϐροι—Κιμϐροι, ως τινες φασι, Κιμμεριοι.

of the man be; hence his three states, Annwn, Abred,[1] and Gwynvyd.

2. The three states of living beings: Annwn, whence the beginning; Abred, in which is the increase of knowledge, and hence goodness; and Gwynvyd, in which is the plenitude of all goodness, knowledge, truth, love, and endless life.

ANNWN.—LIFE.—DEATH.

Question. In what place is Annwn?

Answer. Where there is the least possible of animation and life, and the greatest of death, without other condition.

Q. What are the characteristics of life?

A. Lightness, light, heat, and incorruption, that is, unchangeableness.[2]

Q. What are the characteristic marks of death?

A. Heaviness, cold, darkness, and corruption, that is, changeableness.

Q. In what does the nature of death and mortality consist?

A. In its characteristics, where one is the cause of another, as heaviness is the cause of darkness, and both the cause of corruption, and corruption the cause of both.

Q. In what does the necessity of animation and life consist?

A. In its characteristics, that is, brightness, and light, and lightness, and incorruption, one being the cause of another—hence God and life.

ABRED.

To consociate with evil will make one the lowest and meanest of all animated beings; therefore a wicked man,

---

[2] Al. "stability."

Abred y mae dyn drwg pan fo marw a myned ei enaid ef ir
pryfyn gwaelaf mewn bod ; ag o hynny y dywedir na
sarnwch ar eich gwell, wrth a sarno ar bryfedyn oi fodd yn
ddiachos.

TARDDIAD DYN.—IESU GRIST.—GWNEUTHURIAD.

Llyma Hawl ag atteb arall o Lyfr amgen.

Athraw, I.

A wyddost ti beth ydwyd?—Dyn ydwyf o Rad Duw Dad
—O ba le y daethost?—O eithafoedd dyfnedd Annwn sef
yno y mae pob dechreu yn nhorriad y goleuni o'r tywyll
cadarn—Pa fodd y daethost yma o Annwn? daethum gan
dreiglo 'r Abred o gyflwr i gyflwr fal am dyges Duw drwy
drangeu ag angheu, oni 'm ganed yn ddyn gan ddawn Duw
ai ddaioni—pwy arweinittor y treigl hwnnw? Mab Dyw
sef yw ef mab y dyn—Pwy ef a pha enw arnaw?—Christ
Iesu ei enw nid amgen no Duw Dad yn ymgorpholi ar agwedd ag yn rhyw Dyn, ag yn arddangos meidrawl gweledig,
a golygiadawl, er daioni a deall dyn, can nas gellir arddangos golwg a chlyw ar anfeidrawl, na deall cywair a chyfiawn,
achaws hynny Duw dad o'i fawr ddaioni a ymddangos ar
wedd ag yn hanfod dyn, mal ai gwelid ag ai deellid gan
ddynion.—pam ai gelwir ef yn Fab Duw? achaws mai o
Dduw yn ei weithrediadau hanfod y mae ag nid oi gynfod
diwneuthuriad y mae, sef o ail ar Dduw y mai a mab pob
ail i'r unfed Cyntefig herwydd bod ag ansawdd, sef yw Iesu

---

[1] " Pryf," a worm, originally written *prif*, probably obtained its name from
its being the first—*prif*=*primus*—link in the chain of Abred.

There seems to be some allusion to the doctrine enunciated here in those lines
by Casnodyn, A.D. 1290—1340 ;—

Trefnaist wern uffern affaith sathan ;
Trefred i *bryfed*, lle yd ymbrofan'.

Thou didst prepare the slough of hell suitable for Satan ;
The habitation for *worms*, where they will be in mutual strife.

[2] This view of our blessed Saviour is identical with the heresy of the Sabel-
lians, or Patripassians. See Hammond's Canons of the Church, p. 54.

when he dies, and his soul enters the meanest worm[1] in existence, becomes better, and ascends in the migration of Abred. From this has arisen the saying,—"Trample not on thy better," addressed to one who tramples on a worm voluntarily, and without a cause.

THE ORIGIN OF MAN.—JESUS CHRIST.—CREATION.

Here are Questions and Answers from another Book.

Teacher. Dost thou know what thou art?

Disciple. I am a man by the grace of God the Father.

T. Whence camest thou?

D. From the extremities of the depth of Annwn, where is every beginning in the division of the fundamental light and darkness.

T. How camest thou here from Annwn?

D. I came, having traversed about from state to state, as God brought me through dissolutions and deaths, until I was born a man by the gift of God and His goodness.

T. Who conducted that migration?

D. The Son of God, that is, the Son of man.

T. Who is He, and what is His name?

D. His name is Jesus Christ, and He is none other than God the Father incarnate in the form and species of man, and manifesting visible and apparent finiteness for the good and comprehension of man, since infinitude cannot be exhibited to the sight and hearing, nor can there, on that account, be any correct and just apprehension thereof. God the Father, of His great goodness, appeared in the form and substance of man, that He might be seen and comprehended by men.[2]

T. Why is He called the Son of God?

D. Because He is from God in His essential works, and not from His uncreated pre-existence, that is, He is second to God, and every Second is a son to the primary First, in respect of existence and nature. That is to say,

Grist ymddangosiad ar dduw mewn mor neillduadawl ydyw,
a mab pob naill i a fo arall cyntefig a mab ymddangosiad
i'r ymddangosydd, a lle y gweler neu a ddealler Duw yn
amgen na rhyw a bod tuhwnt i bob gwybod a deall, nis
gellir hynny eithr ar a welittor yn amgen nag angen Duw
yn annechreuoldeb ag afnewidioldeb ei fod ai anian ai aniad.
—a wyddai ddyn ag arall o ddealledig, rywbeth am Dduw
cyn noi ddyfod ar olwg a deall yn Iesu Grist?—gwyddittor
ei fod wrth wneuthuredigaeth y byd a'r cwbl er daioni,
achos ni gellir gwneuthuredigaeth, heb wneuthurydd, ag nid
gwneuthur eithr digwydd na fytho yn drwyedig er daioni,
mal y digwydd Carnedd o graig ag ni ddigwydd ty neu
eglwys.—Pa fodd ydd adnabydder gwneuthuredig? wrth
ddadwneuthur a ellir arnaw, sef a ellir ei ddadwneuthur,
rhaid ag angen yw gwneuthurydd ir dadwneuthuredig
hynny—sef pethau nas gwnaethpwyd erioed fal y mae lle-
oldeb ag eangder dihyd a lled, nis gellir dadwneuthur
arnynt, ag yn un wedd ni gellir dadwneuthur amser am nas
gwnaethpwyd erioed. ag ef a ddywedir ymhregeth bawl nas
gellir gwneuthur heb wneuthurydd, — Beth yw gwneuthuriad? pob peth a ellir amgen parth dull a sylwedd a hanfod,
nag a welir arnaw, Sef y gellir ei ddifodi, a pharth a weler
nag a ddealler arnaw ynawr. a gellir deall anfodoldeb arnaw,
ag nid gwneu'riad un peth nis gellir deall dadwneuthur ag
anfodoldeb arnaw, fal y mae hyd a lled a dyfnder anghorph-
orawl, ag amser anfesuredig, Sef nis gellir nad oeddynt
erioed heb ddechreu, ag nis gellir amgen nag y byddant

---

[1] The Sabellianism, which marks this fragment, does not appear to have been
adopted by all the Christian Bards. Thus, in "the Venedotian Triads of the
Isle of Britain," it is stated,—

"Taliesin Ben Beirdd a weles yn y Dwydid (in al. Dwydawd and Duwdid)
dri pherson o Dad, o Fab, o Yspryd Glan."

Taliesin, the Chief of Bards, beheld in the Godhead three Persons, Father,
Son, and Holy Ghost.

[2] Rom. i. 20.

Jesus Christ is a manifestation of God in a peculiar manner, and every one is a son to another, who is primary, and the manifested is a son to him who manifests. And where God is seen or comprehended otherwise than as a species and existence beyond all knowledge and comprehension, such cannot take place except in what is seen differently to the attribute of God, in respect of the non-commencement and unchangeableness of His being, His nature, and His quality.[1]

T. Did man, and other intelligent beings, know anything of God before He was manifested and made comprehensible in Jesus Christ ?

D. They knew that He existed by the creation of the world, and the whole being for good, because there can be no creation without a maker ; and that would not be an act but a chance, which should not be thoroughly for good, as a heap of stones occurs by chance, whereas a house or a church is not built by chance.

T. How may what is made be known ?

D. By unmaking what is possible of it, for where anything can be unmade, there must of necessity be a maker to what is thus unmade. For things which were never made, as place and space, without length and without breadth, cannot be unmade. In the same way, time cannot be undone, because it was never made, and it is said in St. Paul's Sermon, that it is impossible to make without a maker.[2]

T. What is creation ?

D. Every thing which can be otherwise, in respect of form and substance and essence, than what it seems. That is to say, it may be annihilated, in respect of what is seen or comprehended of it now ; and its non-existence may be conceived. And nothing is made, of which its decomposition and non-existence cannot be conceived, as in the case of incorporeal length and breadth and depth, and immeasurable time, for it is impossible that they should not have existed always without a beginning, and it cannot be but that they

fyth heb ddiwedd, yn anghyfnewidioli ag nis gellir barnu
yn amgen ar Dduw ai fodoldeb ag am bywyd ysprydawl yw
ag nid corfforawl, am hynny nis gellir newid ar ei ysпryd-
oldeb ef na diwedd Chwaith, pob newidiadwy gwneuthuredig
yw parth a ellir newid ag anfodoldeb arnaw — fal y mae
newid drwy losg a phydri, a thawdd a chaledrwydd, ag oer
a thwym, sef y gell anfodoldeb ar newid ond ar ddeunydd a
modd-der nis gellir anfodoldeb na choll arnaw nag ar ddim
amgen na ei newidiadau — beth yw defnydd angholledig?
Dau ryw y sydd Un marw a difywyd, sef llythrynau 'r
tywyllwch cadarn, ag o hano pob marw a chorpholdeb
marw — a mymrynau neu lythrynau y goleuni, ag o hano
pob corphoroldeb byw, a phob enaid a phob deall a phob
ysprydoldeb a bywyd, a phob synwyroldeb, sef marw pob
oer—twym pob byw— pam y mae achaws treiglaw yr Abred? achaws lle bo dechreu rhaid angen yw mwyhad ag
ymwellhâd. Ag achaws mwyhâu dyn parth daioni bywydawl, ai wellhâu ai barottoi i'r Gwynfyd y trefnis Duw felly.
Ag nis gellir ar unpeth unpeth mewn bod, ag heb dreiglo
canoldeb a'r cyfryngder rhwng y bach lleiaf ar mawr mwyaf.
Ag nis gellir na da na drwg namyn o ddamwain, ar un
gwneuthuredig anghyfnewidiol, ag nis gellir na gwell na
gwaeth ar anrheigladwy o beth na gwell ar ddim lle nis
gwaeth arnaw, na gwnaeth ar ddim lle nis gellir gwell arno.
a lle ydd eler i'r drwg nis gellir ei waeth aros ynddo fyth
tragywydd ag fal hynny am y gwell lle nis gellir gwell.

Y CREAD.—Y DYN CYNTAF.—Y PRIF LYTHYRENAU.

Disgybl ai Athraw.

Awenydd. Fy Athraw caredigbwyll dywedwch wrthyf
ba hany Byd, a phob gweledigion o bethau, a phob clywed-

shall always exist without end and without change. It cannot be judged differently of God, and His existence, because He is spiritual and not corporeal life, wherefore His spirituality can neither change nor end. Every thing changeable is made, in respect of what is capable of change and non-existence, as there is a change through burning and rottenness, and melting and hardness, and cold and warmth. That is, there can be non-existence in the change, but there can be no non-existence in the matter and mode, neither loss, except only in its changes.

T. What is imperishable matter?

D. There are two kinds : the one dead and lifeless, that is, the elements of the fundamental darkness, whence proceed all inanimation and dead corporeity; and the atoms or elements of light, whence proceed all living corporeity, and all intellect, and all spirituality and life, and all sensibility : for every thing dead is cold—every thing living is warm.

T. Why is it requisite to traverse Abred ?

D. Because where there is a beginning there must needs be an increase and an improvement. And in order to magnify man in respect of vital goodness, and to improve and prepare him for Gwynvyd, God arranged it so. And this cannot occur to any thing in existence, without traversing the middle and intermediate space between the smallest small, and the greatest great. Nor can there be either good or evil, except by chance, in any immutable creation, nor can there be better or worse in what does not circulate, nor better in what cannot be worse, nor worse in what cannot be better. And where one enters upon evil, he cannot become worse by remaining in it for ever and ever ; and it is the same with the better, where it cannot be better.

THE CREATION.—THE FIRST MAN.—THE PRIMARY LETTERS.

Disciple and his Teacher.

Disciple. Tell me, my kind and discreet Master, whence originated the world, and all visible, all audible, all sensible,

2 I

igion, a phob teimledigion a phob deallidigion ag o ba beth
y daeth ac au gwnaespwyd?

Athraw. Duw Dad au gwnaeth a hynny gan yngan ei
Enw a honni bodoldeb, ar yr un amrant yn gydgyfamrant
dymma 'r Byd ag oll a berthyn iddo yn gydgyflam yn eu
bodoldeb yn gydgyfungan eu bod agoruchel a phereiddlef
bloedd gorfoledd ; fal agan gwelwn y maent yr awr hon ag
y byddant yn myw Duw Dad yr hwn nis gellir llaith a
marwolaeth arno.

Awenydd. A pha bethau parth defnyddiaethau y gwnespwyd Bodolion o fyw a marw ar bethau dan olwg a chlyw
atheimlad a deall a rhŷn a chrebwyll dychymmyg Dyn?

Athraw. Ys ef au gwnespwyd o'r manred, sef y cywarchenau yn eithafoedd eu mendidau a'u hefnynau lleiaf a
phob mendidyn yn fyw herwydd bod Duw ym mhob mendidyn ag un cyflawn ynddo mal a lle nis gellid ei fwy trwy
holl amleoldeb y ceugant sef hynny yr eangder diderfyn, a
Duw hefyd ymhob un o henynt mendidaur manred, ag yn
un wedd yn y cwbl o henynt yn eu cymminedd cyfungwlm,
am hynny llafar Duw llafar pob mendidyn o'r manred tra
rhif a deall ar nag eu rhifoedd na'u Hansawdd, a llafar pob
mendidyn ys ef llafar Duw. Duw yn mendidyn yn fywyd,
a phob mendidyn neu efnyn yn Nuw a'i fywyd, ag am a
ddangoser, sef fal hynny y damheger geni Duw o'r manred,
heb ddechre heb ddiwedd.

Awenydd. Ai da ai drwg y Bod cyn nog i Dduw yngan
ei enw?

---

[1] " Manred " is compounded of *mân*, small, fine, and *rhêd*, a course.

[2] Ti ymhob pwnk.—Thou art in every point.
Gruff. Gryg i Dduw, (1330—1370.)

[3] "Cymminedd cyfungwlm ;" light is thrown here upon the expression
" manred gymmined," with which Meugant commences the several stanzas of
his " Marwnad Cynddylan," (Ap. Myv. Arch. v. i. p. 159.) It is but a phrase
borrowed from the Druidic Creed, and employed by the Bard for some fanciful
reason or other, but without any immediate reference to the strain or drift of the

and all intelligible things, and whence did they come, and were made ?

Teacher. God the Father made them by pronouncing His Name, and manifesting existence. In the same instant, co-simultaneously, lo ! the world, and all that appertains to it, sprang together into being, and together celebrated their existence with a very loud and melodious shout of joy; even as we see them to be now, and as they shall exist whilst God the Father lives, Who is not subject to dissolution and death.

D. Of what, in respect of materials, were formed living and dead beings, which are cognizable to the human sight, hearing, feeling, understanding, perception, and the creation of the imagination ?

T. They were made of the *manred*,[1] that is, of the elements in the extremities of their particles and smallest atoms, every particle being alive, because God was in every particle,[2] a complete Unity, so as not to be exceeded, even in all the multiform space of Ceugant, or the infinite expanse. God was in each of the particles of the manred, and in the same manner in them collectively in their conjoined aggregation ;[3] wherefore, the voice of God is the voice of every particle of the manred, as far as their numbers or qualities may be counted or comprehended, and the voice of every particle is the voice of God—God being in the particle as its life, and every particle or atom being in God and His life. On account of this view of the subject, God is figuratively represented as being born of the manred, without beginning, without end.

D. Was existence good or bad before God pronounced His Name ?

song. Dr. Pughe knew nothing of the Bardic import of the word "manred," which he renders, " of small step or pace," and "manred gymmined," "short-paced traveller." So necessary, for the proper understanding of the works of the Bards, is a knowledge of Bardism !

Athraw. Da cyflwyr pob peth heb ddechreu heb ddiwedd
fal y mae yr awr hon ag thros byth y bydd er nas gweler
yn abred na modd na pheth y sydd namyn y ddysger gan
glywed a gweled yn arddangosedig neu gan bwyll yn dwyn
ar ddeall, Sef Duw ai Dangnef ym mhob peth, heb ddim yn
bod namyn Duw ai Dangnef ag o hynny Da ym mhob yn
wynfyd a gwynwared rhag pob drwg yn orfod anorchfyg-
edig. a lle bo Duw ym mhob enfyn o'r manred nis gellir
drwg am nad oes ag nas gellir lle iddo, Duw a phob daioni
yn llanw yr annherfynedigrwydd diddechre a diddiwedd
parth Lle ag ymbarhâd o amser, gan hynny nis gellir drwg
na'i debyg ; na'r godeb lleiaf arno.

Awenydd. Pa farn ar waith Duw yn Bodoli 'r Byd o
nef a daear ag y sydd ynddynt ag o henynt.

Athraw. Duw er pob daioni galledig iddo yn ymgang-
henu ei hunan ymaes oi ardduniant annealladwy i ddyn
namyn ei fod felly, ag o hyn mwyhad ar bob daioni meidrol
ag nis gellir pob daioni heb ddaioni meidrol yn yspaid anfeidrol.

Awenydd. Pwy 'r Dyn cyntaf ?

Athraw. Menyw Hen ap y Teirgwaedd sef ai gelwid ef
felly gan mai Duw a rhoddes ac ai dodes y gair yn ei ben
nid amgen na llafar y Tair llythyren awnant Enw anllafar-
adwy Duw, sef a daioni pwyll yr Enw ar Gair, a chyd ag
Enw Duw gyfamrant ai yngan y gweles Menyw dair pelydren goleuni ac a wnaeth liw a llun arnynt, ag o'r lluniau
hynny ar cyfosod amrafaelryw arnynt y gwnaeth Menyw
ddeg llythyren Ag o'r rhai hynny yn amosodedig amrafael
ffyrdd y dodes ef liw a llun ar y Gymraeg, ag o ddeall ar y
deg lluniau cyfosod y mae darllen.

Awenydd. Fy Athraw caredig, a ddangoswch chwi imi

T. All things were thoroughly good, without beginning, without end, as they are now, and ever shall be ; though in Abred neither the mode, nor the thing that exists, is seen, except from learning by means of demonstrative hearing and seeing, or by means of reason making it comprehensible, namely, God and His peace in every thing, and nothing existing without God and His peace. Therefore, there was good in every thing,—a blissful world, and a blissful deliverance from every evil, as an unconquerable predominance. And where God exists in every atom of manred, evil is impossible ; because there neither is, nor can be room for it, since God and all goodness fill the infinitude, which is without beginning and without end, in respect of place and duration of time. Therefore, evil or its like cannot exist, nor the least approximation to it.

D. What judgment is formed concerning the act of God in giving existence to the world, that is, heaven and earth, and all that are in and from them ?

T. God, with a view to every goodness of which He is capable, branched Himself out of His majesty, incomprehensible to man further it was so. And from this there was an increase of all finite goodness, and all goodness cannot be had, without finite goodness in infinite space.

D. Who was the first man ?

T. Menyw the Aged, son of the Three Shouts, who was so called because God gave and placed the word in his mouth, namely, the vocalization of the three letters, which make the unutterable Name of God, that is, by means of the good sense of the Name and Word. And, co-instantaneously with the pronunciation of God's Name, Menyw saw three rays of light, and inscribed on them figure and form, and it was from those forms and their different collocations that Menyw made ten letters, and it was from them, variously placed, that he invested the Cymraeg with figure and form, and it is from understanding the combination of the ten letters that one is able to read.

D. My beloved Teacher, show me the power and mys-

nerth a rhinioedd y Tair Llythyren gyssefin, a lluniau y
deg llythyren a wnathoedd Menyw o gyfosodau amrafaelion
y Tair.

Athraw. Nid rhydd a chennadadwy hynn i mi cann ys
Cyfrinach ydynt y deg llythyren, ag un o dair Colofn Cyfrinach Beirdd Ynys Prydain, a chynn y dyccer yr awenydd
dann rwymau a chadernyd adduned nis gellir datrin ar y
Cyfrinach iddo, ag nid hynny yn amgen nag arddangos ir
Llygad heb lafar heb lef, sef y bydd hynny gwedi ydd elo
ef yr awenydd danfaccwyaeth drwy holl gylch a cherdded ei
Faccwyaeth, eithr y mae ar amgen pell o luniau 'r un llythyren ar bymtheg a rhydd imi ddangos a datgan eu henwau
au rhinweddau cynn y cerdder cylch adduned Maccwyaeth,
a llymma fal y mae yr un llun ar bymtheg a'r modd y
rhodded arfer gadarn ernynt.

DISGYBLAETH BARDDAS.

Y CREAD.

Dysgybl. A pha ddefnydd y gwnaeth Duw bob corphorolion o bethau bywydolion ?

Athraw. Ac Efnynau 'r goleuni sef manaf $^{ar}_{o}$ bob man
ydynt, ag eiswys mwyaf ar bob mawr un efnyn goleuni, nid
llai na defnydd i bob defnyddiaeth a ellir deall a rhyn arno
yngafael gallu Duw, ag ymhob Efnyn lle yn gwbl gydfaint
a Duw, can nad oes ag nas gellir llai na Duw ymhob efnyn
Goleuni, a Duw ymhob Efnyn, ag eiswys nid amgen nag un
y rhif ar Dduw, achos hynny un pob goleuni, ag nid un o
gwbl gymmod ond yr hynn nis gellir dau arnaw, nag o
hanaw.

D. Pa gyhyd y bu Duw yn gwneuthur pob pethau
corphorolion ?

teries of the three primitive letters, and the forms of the ten letters, which Menyw made from the varied combination of the three.

T. This is not allowed and permitted to me, for the ten letters are a secret, being one of the three pillars of the mystery of the Bards of the Isle of Britain. And before the disciple is brought under the obligation and power of a vow, the mystery may not be revealed to him. And even then it can only be displayed to the eye, without utterance, without voice. It can only take place, when the disciple shall have gone through all the cycle and course of his pupillage. Nevertheless, the sixteen letters are formed very differently, and I am at liberty to show and declare their names and their powers, before the cycle of the vow of pupillage shall have been traversed; and thus are the sixteen symbols, and the way in which they are enforced by usage.

THE DISCIPLINE OF BARDISM.

THE CREATION.

Disciple. With what material did God make all corporal things, endued with life?

Master. With the particles of light, which are the smallest of all small things; and yet one particle of light is the greatest of all great things, being no less than material for all materiality that can be understood and perceived as within the grasp of the power of God. And in every particle there is a place wholly commensurate with God, for there is not, and cannot be less than God in every particle of light, and God in every particle; nevertheless, God is only one in number. On that account, every light is one, and nothing is one in perfect co-existence but what cannot be two, either in or out of itself.

D. How long was God in making all corporal things?

A.   Chwaen amrant, ac yna bod a byw, golau a $^{gweled}_{gweeled}$, nid amgen Duw a phob daioni yn difenwi drwg.

Y CREAD.

O ba ddefnyddau y gwnaeth Dyw y bydoedd
Oi hunan, canys amgen o beth nid bod o ddechreu iddaw.

Y CREAD.

Pa fodd y cafwyd byw a bywyd ?
    Atteb
O Dduw ag yn Nuw ai cafad, sef o'r byw cadarn a phendant, hynny yw Duw, sef o Dduw yn ymgyfymgyd ar marw, sef a daearoldeb ag yna Môd a meddwl, sef yw hynny enaid, a phob byw ag enaid o Dduw y mae, ac yn Nuw ei fod o gynfod a hanfod, canys nid cynfod ond yn nuw, nid cydfod ond yn Nuw, ag nid hanfod ond yn Nuw ag o Dduw.

Y CREAD.—GOLYCHWYD.—CERDD DAFAWD.—GWYDDONIAID.*

O beth y gwnaeth Duw 'r byd a bywydolion?
O'r meidion au cynnull o'r meithion anfeidrol ynghylch y Ceugant a'u cyfleoli 'n drefnus ag yn gyfiawn o ddosparthus

---

* In the MS. the heading is BARDDAS, i.e. Bardism.

[1] This fragment, in connection with the fact that HU is one of the Names of God, throws wonderful light upon the language of Rhys Brydydd, whilst that also bears testimony to the existence in his days, namely, between 1450 and 1490, of the curious doctrine of the text :—

> *Bychanaf or bychenyd,*
> Yw Hu Gadarn, fe'i barn byd ;
> A *mwyaf,* a Naf i ni,
> Da coeliwn, a'n Duw Celi,
> Ysgafn ei daith, ac esgud,
> *Mymryn tes,* gloewyn ei glud,
> A *mawr* ar dir a moroedd,
> A *mwyaf* a gaf ar goedd ;
> *Mwy no'r bydoedd,* 'marbedwn
> Amarch gwael i'r mawr hael hwn.

M. The twinkling of an eye; when existence and life, light and vision occurred, that is to say, God and all goodness in the act of contemning evil.[1]

THE CREATION.

Question. Of what materials did God make the worlds?

Answer. Of Himself, for existence having a beginning does not otherwise take place.

THE CREATION.

Question. How were animation and life obtained?

Answer. From God, and in God were they found, that is, from the fundamental and absolute life, that is, from God uniting Himself to the dead, or earthliness — hence motion and mind, that is, soul. And every animation and soul are from God, and their existence is in God, both their pre-existence, and derived existence; for there is no pre-existence except in God, no co-existence except in God, and no derived existence except in God, and from God.

THE CREATION.—WORSHIP.—VOCAL SONG.—GWYDDONIAID.

Disciple. From what did God make the world and living beings?

Master. From the particles, which He collected out of the infinite expanse in the circle of Ceugant, and collocated

The smallest of the small
Is Hu the Mighty, as the world judges;
And *the greatest*, and a Lord to us,
Let us well believe, and our mysterious God;
Light His course and active,
An *atóm of glowing heat* is His car;
Great on land and on the seas,
The *greatest* that I manifestly can have,
Greater than the worlds – Let us beware
Of mean indignity to him who deals in bounty.
See Dr. Pughe's Dict. v. *mymryn*.

It would have been utterly impossible to explain the allusions, contained in this poetical passage, without the key which the Bardic Catechism offers to us.

yng Nghylch y Gwynfyd, yn fydoedd a bywydoedd, ag
anianoedd heb na rhif na phwys na mesur arnaddynt a allai
feddwl a deall amgen nag ef ei hunan ai cynnarbod neu eu
cyflyfelu, pei oesoedd anorphenadwy Cylch y Ceugant y
meddai.

A pha gyflofiad neu gytpar y gwnaeth Duw'r pethau
hynn?

A llafar ei ynnioldeb nerthawl, sef gan ei bereidd-der
Cerddoslef o braidd au clywed nad dyma 'r marwolion yn
ymluchedu 'n fywydolion, a'r dim ag oedd heb na lle na
bod iddaw, yn ymfelltenu 'n elfyddawd, ag yn ymlawen-
hâu 'n fywyd. a'r Rhynn tryffer diymmod yn ymwresogi 'n
fodoldeb byw. y dim diddym yn ymorfoleddu 'n fodoldeb
mil cynt nag y cyrch llucheden ei haddef.

A glybu neppeth o fyw y llafar pereiddlef hynny?

Clybû, ag yn gyttrem ar llafar gwelid pob gwybodau a
phob gwybodawl yn eu cadernyd diddarfod diddiwedd o fod
a bywyd. canys cyntaf ar fod. a chyntaf ar fywyd, cyntaf
ar wybodaeth a chyntaf ai gwybu, cyntaf ai gorug. sef
cyntaf Gwybedydd Huon fab Nudd, a elwir Gwynn ap
Nudd, ag Enniget Gawr, ag efe a ddodes ddangaws gyntaf
yn weledig ag yn ddechreuedig i ddyniadau dyniadon.

D. Pwy gyntaf a drefnawdd olychwyd ag addoli Duw
gyntaf?

A. Sedd fab Addaf, sef efe a wnaeth gil golychwyd
gyntaf ynghoedydd Glyn Ebron, gan chwiliaw ag olrain y
coedydd hyd oni chafas efe yn Dderwen fawr o Frenhinbren
Ganghenfawr gyrhaeddbell gaeedfrig, wasgawdlen, a thani y
gwnaeth ef gôr a chyrch Golychwyd, a honno a elwid Gorsedd, ag o hynny gyntaf y dodwyd enw Gorsedd ar bob

---

[1] In the document printed at p. 11, Huon is said to be the son of Alser.
Gwyn ab Nudd is celebrated in Welsh Romance as the King of the Fairies,

in order and just arrangement in the circle of Gwynvyd, as worlds, and lives, and natures, without number, weight, or measure, which any mind or intellect, but Himself, could possibly foresee or devise, even if it possessed the endless ages of the circle of Ceugant.

D. By what instrumentality or agency did God make these things?

M. By the voice of His mighty energy, that is, by its melodious sweetness, which was scarcely heard, when, lo! the dead gleamed into life, and the nonentity, which had neither place or existence, flashed like lightning into elementation, and rejoiced into life, and the congealed, motionless shiver warmed into living existence;—the destitute nothing rejoiced into being a thousand times more quickly than the lightning reaches its home.

D. Did any living being hear that melodious voice?

M. Yes; and co-instantaneously with the voice were seen all sciences and all things cognitive, in the imperishable and endless stability of their existence and life. For the first that existed, and the first that lived, the first that obtained knowledge, and the first that knew it, was the first that practised it. And the first sage was Huon, the son of Nudd,[1] who is called Gwynn, the son of Nudd, and Enniged the Giant; it was he who first made demonstration visible and inceptive to the inferences of men.

D. Who was the first that instituted the worship and adoration of God?

M. Seth, the son of Adam; that is, he first made a retreat for worship in the woods of the Vale of Hebron, having first searched and investigated the trees, until he found a large oak, being the king of trees, branching, wide-spreading, thick-topped, and shady, under which he formed a choir and a place of worship. This was called Gorsedd, and hence originated the name Gorsedd, which was given to

Brenin y Tylwyth Teg, in which capacity many interesting particulars respecting him have been collected in the Notes to Guest's Mabinogion, ii. p. 323.

Cyrch Golychwyd, ag yn y gor honno y bu Enos ab Sedd
yn prydu Cerdd dafawd i Dduw.

D. Pwy a wnaeth Gerdd dafawd gyntaf?

A. Enos ab Sedd ab Addaf, a wnaeth Gerdd dafawd
gyntaf, ag a folawdd Duw gyntaf ar gyfiawn gerddwriaeth,
ag yng Nghor sedd ei dad y cafas efe Awen gyntaf, sef
awen o Dduw ydoedd, ag o hynny y mae'r ddefawd o gyn-
nal ^{Gorsedd}_{Cadair} Cerdd dafawd ynghyrch a gorsedd golychwyd.

D. Paryw geinmyged Cerdd Dafawd a feddyliawdd
Enos ab Sedd?

A. Cyntaf, Moli Duw a phob daioni. Ail, côf am ddaionus o Gamp, dichwain, a gwybod. Trydydd, addysg ar
wybodau molianus parth ag at Dduw a Dyn modd y bai
hawsaf dysgu a chofiaw, a diddanaf gwrandaw.

D. Pa enw gyntaf ar Ddoethion o wŷr wrth Gerdd dafawd a gwybodau moliannus?

A. Gwyddon y gelwyd un, a Gwyddoniaid lliaws, sef
achaws eu galw felly am ymgelfyddydu o honynt mewn
Gwydd a than Goed mewn lleoedd dirgelfan diarffordd er
llonyddwch a myfyriaw awenddysg a Gwybodau o Dduw, a
llonyddwch i ddangaws addysg ar wybodau i'r neb ai ceisiai
ag a chwenychai ddoethineb gan bwyll ac awen o Dduw.

DEFNYDD Y BYD.

Pa ddefnydd gan Dduw yn gwneuthur y Byd nid amgen
na'r nef a'r ddaear, ag eraill o bethau a wyddis neu a farner
am danynt?

Atteb. Y manred sef yw hynny y manaf o bob man
hyd nas gellid ei fanach, a hwnnw yn rhedeg yn un drwy 'r
holl geugant, a Duw yn fywyd ynddo ac ym mhanrhedyn a
Duw 'n ymsymmud ynddo ac yn newid cyflwr y manred
heb ymnewid ynddo ei hunan. Sef un dinewid yw bywyd

---

¹ See Note, p. 54.   ² Al. " chair."

³ This explains the component *rhed*, which occurs in the word " manred;"—
q. d. *the flowing particles.*

every place of worship; and it was in that choir that Enos, the son of Seth, composed vocal song to God.

D. Who was the first that made a vocal song?

M. Enos,[1] the son of Seth, the son of Adam, was the first that made a vocal song, and praised God first in just poetry, and it was in his father's Gorsedd that he first obtained Awen, which was Awen from God; hence has arisen the usage of holding the Gorsedd[2] of Vocal Song in the resort and Gorsedd of worship.

D. For what honourable purposes did Enos, the son of Seth, invent vocal song?

M. In the first place, for the purpose of praising God and all goodness; secondly, to commemorate good qualities, incidents, and knowledge; thirdly, to convey instruction relative to praiseworthy sciences in respect of God and man, that is, in such a way as would be easiest to learn, and remember, and most pleasant to listen to.

D. What was the name that the wise men first had, whose employment was vocal song and laudable sciences?

M. One was called Gwyddon, and many Gwyddoniaid; and they were so called, because they followed their art in woods, and under trees, in retired and inaccessible places, for the sake of quietness, and the meditation of Awenic learning and sciences from God, and for the sake of quietness to teach the sciences to such as sought them, and desired wisdom by means of reason and Awen from God.

THE MATERIAL OF THE WORLD.

Question. What material did God use in the formation of the world, namely, the heaven and the earth, and other things known and conceived?

Answer. The manred, that is, the smallest of all the small, so that a smaller could not be, which flowed[3] in one sea through all the Ceugant — God being its life, and pervading each atom, and God moving in it, and changing the condition of the manred, without undergoing a change in

yn ei holl ymmodau, ag nid un y Cyflwr yn addemoder, ac am hyn, sef Duw ym mhob ymmod y rhodded Modur yn un o Enwau Duw, a Modurdd*cansodd* * cyflwr a ddemoder.

Y SYRTH YN ABRED.

Duw a wnaeth pob byw ynghylch y Gwynfyd ar un anadl, a bod yn ddwyfeu y mynnent a cheisio treiglo 'r Ceugant sef nis gallent hynny ac o hynny syrthio hyd yn annwn yn ymgyd ar marw a daear, ac yno y dechre pob byw perchen corph daiarol.

Y mha le y mae Annwn—yn eithafoedd Cylch y Gwynfyd, sef nas gwyddai bywydolion wahanu drwg rhag daioni sef gan hynny y syrthiasant yn y drwg a myned yn Abred a'i threiglo hyd draw Ynghylch y Gwynfyd.

pa anwybyddiaeth a wnaethant—anturiaw Cylch y Ceugant a fynnant, a myned o hynny yn feilchion, ag nis gallent ei threiglo ag o hynny syrthiaw ynghylch yr Abred.

DUW YN YR HAUL.

Paham y troer gọlwg ar yr haul ymhob Briduw a Gweddi?

Am fod Duw ymhob goleuni a phennaf ar bob goleuni un yr haul, — trwy dan y mae Duw yn dwyn ar adwedd

---

* Illegible in the MS.

[1] "The Mover."   [2] "The condition of the Mover."

[3] See Gen. iii. 5.

[4] Howel ap Davydd ap Ieuan ap Rhys, (A.D. 1450—1480,) clearly alludes to the doctrine of the text in the following couplet;—

Y Drindod/Duwdod yn rhod yr haul
Ai annedd yn y wennaul.

The Trinity/Deity in the course of the sun,
Having His habitation in the bright sun.
                              I Fair a Sioseb.

Himself. For life is unchangeable in all its motions, but the condition of that which is moved is not one and the same. Therefore, because God is in every motion, (ymmod,) one of God's Names is Modur,[1] and the condition that is moved is called *Moduransawdd*.[2]

THE FALL IN ABRED.

God made all living beings in the circle of Gwynvyd at one breath; but they would be gods,[3] and attempted to traverse the Ceugant. This, however, they could not do, wherefore they fell down to Annwn, which unites with death and the earth, where is the beginning of all living owners of terrestrial bodies.

Question. Where is Annwn?

Answer. In the extreme limits of the circle of Gwynvyd. That is, living beings knew not how to distinguish evil from good, and therefore they fell into evil, and went into Abred, which they traversed until they came back into the circle of Gwynvyd.

Q. What ignorance did they commit?

A. They would venture on the circle of Ceugant, and hence became proud; but they could not traverse it, consequently they fell into the circle of Abred.

GOD IN THE SUN.

Question. Why is the face turned towards the sun in every asseveration and Prayer?

Answer. Because God is in every light, and the chief of every light is the sun.[4] It is through fire that God brings

On which Ieuan Tir Iarll, who presided in the Chair of Glamorgan A.D. 1760, and was remarkably well versed in Bardic lore, has the following observations;—

"There was a general opinion in the age when this was composed, that the sun was the abode, or habitation of God—in other words, that the sun was heaven. There are many words and sentences in other poems and odes which show

atto ei hun bob peth a hanoedd o hano. am hynny nid nid iawn ymgystlwn a Duw ond yn y goleuni sef Tri rhyw oleuni y sydd nid amgen un yr haul ac o hwnnw y Tan, un a geffir yng ngwybodau athrawon, ag un a feddianner yn neall y pen ar galon sef yn yr enaid. Am hynny pob adduned yn wyneb y tri goleuni, sef yngoleuni 'r haul y gwelir goleuni athraw sef arddangos, ac or ddau hynn goleuni ceudawd sef un yr enaid.

DUW YN Y GOLEUNI.

Paham y dywedir y Nefoedd oddiuchod, ag uffern odd-isod lle nis gellir uchaf ar unpeth o fod, nag isaf ar ddim o fodoldeb, a phaham Duw yn uchaf a Chythraul yn isaf. Atteb. Am achos bod y goleuni fyth yn uchaf ag uch ein pennau, ag yn y goleuni y ceir Duw, ag nis gellir Nef namyn yn y goleuni. A chyd fyned a goleuni y bydd Duw a Nef—ag isaf bob amser y tywyllwch, ag ynddo Cythraul ag uffern yn cyd fyned ag ef.

that such was the view held by our ancestors respecting the sun. One of the Names of God in primitive times was Hu, and therefore the sun was designated *Huan*, which means *annedd Hu*, or the abode of God. Sion Mowddwy, in a poem in which he sends the sun as a messenger, says,—

> Yr haul glan hir olau glwys,
> A'i rhediad o Baradwys,
> Gan Enw Duw y gwnai'n dawel
> Golianu o beutu 'r bel;
> Golau nef wyd gwiwlawn faeth,
> Golau 'r byd glaer wybodaeth.

> Fair sun, with enduring and beautiful light,
> Having thy course from Paradise,
> By the Name of God dost thou quietly
> Illumine all around the globe;
> Thou art the light of heaven, worthy fosterer,
> Light of the world, clear knowledge.
>
> Sion Mowddwy.

"It may be supposed that they formerly sacrificed to the sun, or at least in the face of the sun, which, in the opinion of those who are skilled in the Mysteries of the Bards, is the most probable, for I have not yet noticed in any place which

back to Himself all things that have emanated from Him; therefore it is not right to ally one's self to God, but in the light. There are three kinds of light, namely : that of the sun, and hence fire; that which is obtained in the sciences of teachers; and that which is possessed in the understanding of the head and heart, that is, in the soul. On that account, every vow is made in the face of the three lights, that is, in the light of the sun is seen the light of a teacher, or demonstration; and from both of these is the light of the intellect, or that of the soul.

GOD IN THE LIGHT.

Question. Why do we say, heaven above, and hell beneath, where there can be no highest in respect of any being, or lowest in respect of any existence? And why God in the highest, and Cythraul in the lowest?

Answer. Because the light is always highest, and above our heads, and it is in the light that God is found, and there can be no heaven, except in the light; and God and heaven always go together with light. And the darkness is always the lowest, and Cythraul and hell go together with it.

I have read, that they themselves worshipped the sun, but only Him who dwelt in it. Therefore, in the act of worshipping, as well as in the performance of every other solemn rite, they did all in the face of the sun and the eye of light, that is, in the face, or before the face of Him, whom they regarded as living and existing in the sun and the light.

" Gwilym Tew, in a poem eulogistic of the large wine flagon of Rhys ap Sion of Glyn Nedd, says thus ;—

> Grenn aur llaw gywrain Eurych,
> A mîn gronn yn trammwy 'n grych,
> *Aberth yr haul*, a byrth Rys
> *Yn ei hwyneb* yw 'n hynys.

> Golden vessel, the ingenious workmanship of a goldsmith,
> With a rounded rim, running along in curls ;
> *The sacrifice of the sun*, supported by Rhys,
> *In its face*, is our island."

2 L

TRIOEDD BARDDAS.

1. O Dri sylwedd y gwnaeth Dyw 'r byd, Tân, anian, a meidroldeb.

2. Tri offerynau Duw yn gwneuthur y byd; Mynn, Doethineb, a Chariad.

3. Tri phrif orchwyl Duw: Goleuo 'r Tywyll, Corpholi dim, a bywydu 'r marw.

4. Tripheth ni ddichonant fod ar Dduw; yn anfedrus, yn anghyfiawn, ac yn annhrugarog.

5. Tri gofynion Duw gan Ddyn; Cred gadarn sef hynn Ffydd, Ufudd-dawd Golychwydawl, a gweithredu cyfiawnder.

6. Tri phrif anwydau bywyd; Nerth, Nwyf, a Dirnad. (a Rhyniad.)

7. Tri phrif feueddau bywyd; Annwyd, Ammod, a goleuni.

DUW; A CHYNNEDDFAU YR ENAID.

Beth yw Cydwybod?

Llygad Duw ynghalon dyn, a wel bob canfodadwy yn ei agwedd ai le ac amser ai achos, a ddiben cyfiawn.

Beth yw Pwyll. ymdraill cydwybod yn ymsyniad gan olwg a chlyw ag ymbrawf, ar a ddelo ger ei fron ai wyneb.

Beth yw deall, gweithredoldeb Cydwybod yn ymarfer ai ynniau ai nerth er caffael a gwellhau gwybodau daionus.

Beth yw doethineb — Gwybodau o ymdraill Pwyll a Nerth gweithred gan y deall, yn ymgaffael gwybodau o Dduw a daioni, ag o ymlwydd yn eu gwellhau.

TRIADS OF BARDISM.

1. God made the world of three substances: fire; nature; and finiteness.

2. The three instrumentalities of God in making the world: will; wisdom; and love.

3. The three principal occupations of God: to enlighten the darkness; to give a body to nonentity; and to animate the dead.

4. Three things which God cannot be: unskilful; unjust; and unmerciful.

5. Three things required by God of man: firm belief, that is, faith; religious obedience; and to do justice.

6. The three principal temperaments of life: strength; vigour; and perception.

7. The three principal properties of life: temper; motion; and light.

GOD; AND THE FACULTIES OF THE SOUL.

Question. What is conscience?

Answer. The eye of God in the heart of man, which sees every thing that is perceptible, in its right form, place, time, cause, and purpose.

Q. What is reason?

A. The revolving of the conscience, whilst it contemplates by means of sight, hearing, and experience, whatever comes before it.

Q. What is understanding?

A. The working of the conscience, whilst it exercises its energies and might for the purpose of acquiring and improving good sciences.

Q. What is wisdom?

A. Sciences acquired by the revolving of the reason, and the powerful working of the intellect, which obtain sciences from God and goodness, — and by success in the improvement of them.

Beth yw Ystyr.—ymarfer a Doethineb, ai iawnhau drwy ymdrin ar modd ai cespwyd, gan ymarchwaeth a Chynghorion eraill o ddoethion.

Felly ti a wyddost gyweirair doethineb, Cymmer yn atteb gwn ag nis gwn a chais ei ddeall, a fo meddu doethineb ef ai cyweiria ei hun, ac nid rhaid iddaw wrth arall.

Oni ddywedaist y gellit iawnhau doethineb a chynghor doethion, do sef ymbrawf a chynghor doethion, ag ymchwaeth a hynny hynny y sydd doeth yn ei ymwellhau yn ei ddoethineb sef nid o gaffaeliad Cynghor ag addysg eithr o gymmeryd dan archwaeth mal pei rhoddid bwyd corfforawl i'r engyn ai gofynai. Nid y rhoddwr a byrth y corff namyn ai cymero maint a fo iawn iddaw, gan adael arall a fo 'n amgen.

Beth yw Duw.—Bywyd yr holl fywydoedd.

Beth yw Yspryd Duw.—Gallu yr yr holl alluoedd.

Beth yw rhagluniaeth Duw.   Tref y Trefnau, a dosparth y Dosparthau.

Beth yw gallu Duw — Gwybodaeth yr holl wybodau. a chelfyddyd yr gelfyddydau, a pheiriant yr holl beiriannau.

Beth yw gwirionedd.—Gwybodau Doethineb ar gof gan gydwybod.

Beth yw Cyfiawnder.   Celfyddyd a swydd cydwybod, o bwyll a deall, a doethineb yn ystyriaw ag yn gwneuthur yn ol hynny.

Beth yw Barn. — Duw yn ymgymmhwyll a dyn yn ei gydwybod herwydd y Gwybodau a fo ynddo, o draill a *ddangosed*.   qu.]

Q. What is sense ?

A. The exercise and rectification of wisdom, by studying the manner in which it has been obtained, and tasting the counsels of other wise men.

Thus thou knowest the correct saying of wisdom ;— " Take as an answer, I know, and I do not know, and try to understand it. He who possesses wisdom, will correct himself, and will not stand in need of another."

Q. Didst thou not say that wisdom may be rectified by the counsel of wise men ?

A. Yes; for trying the advice of wise men, and tasting that which is wise, causes one to improve in wisdom, that is, not by the acquisition of counsel and instruction, but by applying them to the taste, as if bodily food were given to the wretch that asked it. It is not the giver that feeds the body, but he that takes what is proper for him, omitting what is otherwise.

Q. What is God?

A. The life of all lives.

Q. What is the spirit of God?

A. The power of all powers.

Q. What is the providence of God?

A. The order of orders, and the system of systems.

Q. What is the power of God ?

A. The knowledge of all knowledge, the art of all arts, and the agent of all agents.

Q. What is truth?

A. The sciences of wisdom preserved in memory by conscience.

Q. What is justice ?

A. The art and office of conscience, regulated by reason, understanding, and wisdom, considering and acting accordingly.

Q. What is judgment ?

A. God co-reasoning with man in his conscience, in respect of the knowledge which he possesses, after he has revolved in his mind what has been demonstrated.

Beth yw Enaid.　　Anadl Duw mewn corph cnawdol.
Beth yw bywyd.　　Nerth Duw.

YMADRODDION BARDDAS.

Llyma ymadroddion Barddas, o Lyfr Ieuan ab Hywel Swrdwal.

1.　Nid oes a ellir mwy o ddaioni o hano, nag o annaioni nad yw'n bod; gan nas gellir amgen herwydd Gallu a doethineb a Chariad Duw.

2.　A wnelo ddaioni i rai ag na wnelo ddrwg i eraill ys diogel ei fod gan fod o hanaw fwy o les na phei nas byddai, ag ni ollwng Duw ar goll daioni a ellir.

3.　A fo na drwg na da nid diogel i ddyn ei fod na'i anfod, can ni wyddys wrth bwyll am danaw, eraill a ddywedant mae deunydd pob peth yw hwnnw, ag nid oes ond Duw a ŵyr ei dda ai ddrwg ai les ai afles, na pha fwyaf y da na 'r drwg.

4.　Lle y gellir deall daioni mawr i bawb heb annaioni i neb nis gellir amgen nad yw mewn bod, can nis safai heb hynny dri phrif gynneddfau Duw, sef Gwybod, Doeth, a thrugar heb ing heb angen yn eu gwrth, ag am hynny gwir yw Barddas.

5.　Nis gellir gwir o'r peth ni allo pob gwir sefyll ynddo, ag nas safo ymhob gwir, can nis gellir gwir o a wrtheppo a fo gwir neu ai gwrthsafo.

6.　Ys gwir y dylit gan gyfiawnder y goreu o bob peth.

7.　Ys gwir y dylit gan Gariad y goreu o bob peth.

---

[1] Ieuan ab Hywel Swrdwal was an eminent poet, who flourished from about 1450 to 1480.

Q. What is the soul?

A. The breath of God in a carnal body.

Q. What is life?

A. The might of God.

SENTENCES OF BARDISM.

Here are the Sentences of Bardism, from the Book of Ieuan, the son of Hywel Swrdwal.[1]

1. That does not but exist, from which a greater amount of good than of evil can be produced; since it cannot be otherwise in virtue of God's power, wisdom, and love.

2. The existence of that, which does good to some, and does no harm to others, is safe; since there is more utility from it, than if it had not existed; and God will not permit possible good to be lost.

3. Of that which is neither good nor bad, neither the existence nor non-existence is safe for man, for nothing in reason is known of it. Others say, that it is the material of every thing. However, there is only God that knows its good and evil, its utility and inutility, and whether the good or evil be the greater.

4. Where a great good to all, without harm to any one, can be comprehended, it cannot be but that it is in existence, since otherwise the three principal attributes of God, namely, knowledge, wisdom, and mercy, would not stand without being opposed by distress and necessity: therefore Bardism is true.

5. Truth cannot be had from that in which every truth cannot consist, and which will not consist in every truth, for truth cannot be had from what will contradict or withstand that which is true.

6. It is true that, according to justice, there should be the best of all things.

7. It is true that, according to love, there should be the best of all things.

8.   Ys gwir y dylit gan alledigaeth y goreu o bob peth.

9.   Ys gwir y dylit gan ddoethineb a Gwybod o goreu o bob peth.

10.   Ys gwir nis gellir amgen ar Dduw na phob Gwybod, a phob doethineb, a phob gallu, a phob Cariad a phob cyfiawnder heb ludd heb fesur, heb dranc heb orphen, am hynny nis gellir o barth Gallu Duw nad yw goreuon pob peth mewn bôd, ag nis gellir parth ei wybodau nad felly, ag nis gellir parth ei gariad ai gyfiawnder ai ddoethineb nad yw 'r goreu o bob peth mewn bod.

11.   Ys gwir y gellir gan Dduw y goreu o bob peth, achaws hynny nis gellir nad yw 'r goreu o bob peth $^{mewn}_{yn}$ bod.

12.   Dylit gan gyfiawnder alledigaeth ar gyfiawnder, am hynny parth cyfiawnder nis gellir nad oes alledigaeth ar gyfiawnder.

13.   Dylit o barth gwybodaeth gallu ar wybodaeth, ag ar wybod y goreu; ag am hynny gallu ar wybod y goreu y sydd.

14.   Dylit gan gariad y trugaroccaf, am hynny gan gariad Duw y mae y trugaroccaf mewn bod ar ar bob hanfod.

15.   Gellir gan Dduw parth ei allu ai ddoethineb ai wybodau, ai gariad, y goreu o bob peth, a'r cyfiawnaf o bob peth, a'r carediccaf o bob peth, ag am hynny nis gellir nad yw 'r goreu o bob peth yn bod.

16.   Nis gellir nad yw yr eithafoedd ar bob daioni a daionus a'r Dduw, achaws hynny nis gellir nad oes ag nas ceir yr eithaf o bob daioni a phob daionus o dduw a chan Dduw o'i ddirfawr râd ai gariad.

17.   Nis gellir Duw ond a fo a phob gallu, a phob cariad, a phob doethineb, a phob gwybodau, a phob cyfiawnder, a

8. It is true that, according to power, there should be the best of all things.

9. It is true that, according to wisdom and knowledge, there should be the best of all things.

10. It is true that there cannot be in God other than all knowledge, all wisdom, all power, all love, and all justice, without restraint, without measure, without cessation, without end. Therefore, in respect of the power of God, it cannot but be that the best of all things are in existence ; and it cannot be otherwise in respect of His knowledge ; and it cannot but be, in respect of His love, justice, and wisdom, that the best of all things are in existence.

11. It is true that God can accomplish the best of all things ; on that account, it cannot but be that the best of all things are in existence.

12. According to justice, there should be ability in justice ; therefore, in respect of justice, there cannot but be that ability belongs to justice.

13. In respect of knowledge, there ought to be power in knowledge, and in knowing what is best ; therefore there is power in knowing what is best.

14. According to love, there should be what is most merciful ; therefore, by the love of God, what is most merciful is in existence in every essence.

15. God, in respect of His power, wisdom, knowledge, and love, can produce the best of all things, the most just of all things, and the most kind of all things ; therefore, it cannot but be that the best of all things are in existence.

16. It cannot but be that the extreme limits of goodness, and of what is good, are in God ; on that account, there cannot but be that the extreme of all goodness, and all that is good, is, and may be found, from God, and by God, through His infinite grace and love.

17. There cannot be a God, that does not possess all power, all love, all wisdom, all knowledge, all justice, and all goodness. And it cannot but be that whatever those,

2 M

phob daioni arnaw, ag o'r pethau hynn ar y bythont, nis gellir nas ceir a wnelont heb ing heb angen.

Ag felly terfyna.

DENGAIR DEDDF Y BEIRDD.

(O'r Llyfr Glâs.)

1. Un yw Duw ac nid oes onid efe yn Dduw. Car dy Dduw a'th holl enaid, ac ath holl Galon, ac a'th holl nerth ag a'th holl ymgais, ac a'th holl ddeall, ac a'th holl serchiadau. Canys efe ac nid arall o fyw na bod a'th wnaeth Di ac y sydd yn dy gynnal di ai holl allu ai holl drugaredd.

2. Na char ac na chais eilun yn lle Duw, nac o bren nac o faen, nac o aur, nac o arian nac o un deunydd arall, nac o liw nac o lun, canys ni welaist Dduw erioed, a phwy ai gweles ef? Na chymmer yn lle Duw y Byd hynn nac un byd arall pa mor ogoneddus bynnag yr ymddengys hwnnw iti. Canys nid Duw ydyw eithr gwaith Duw er mawr ddaioni i ti ac i eraill fyrddiynau o weithiau tuhwnt i eithafoedd dy ddeall a'th amgyffred di. Na chymmer yn lle Duw na chyfoeth na meddiant o un rhyw, na pharch na mawredd y Byd Balch pechadurus, na chymmer yn Duw na char na chyfaill na gwryw na benyw. na ro dy gais a'th galon a'th fwriad a'th serchiadau, a'th hyder ar na un nac arall o'r pethau hynn, nac ar ddim a wnelo itti hyderu lai ar Dduw herwydd achos yr hawl a'r perchenogaeth y sydd itti ynddynt, dan gof a gochel gwastadol na chais ac na chadw ac na char un pa bynnag o'r pethau hynn yn y cyfryw fodd ag

---

[1] Literally, "the ten words of the law," which phraseology has been, also, retained in the Welsh Prayer Book, though it is not now popularly used. When the Cymry embraced Christianity, they manifested a special veneration for the Ten Commandments, as is evidenced by the fact that "the ten words of the law, the Gospel of John, and the blessed cross," constitute a Triad of the instruments of swearing, which succeeded the more ancient forms which had been used by the Bards, and which shall be hereafter described.

When Taliesin took the Bardic vow "on the Altar of St. Teilo at Llandaf," among other things he is made to say,—

who possess these things, do, is found to be without distress, without necessity.

And thus it ends.

THE TEN COMMANDMENTS[1] OF THE BARDS.

(From the Blue Book.)

1. God is one, and there is only Himself who is God. Love thy God with all thy soul, with all thy heart, with all thy strength, with all thy endeavour, with all thy understanding, and with all thy affections. For it is He, and no other being, living or existing, that made thee, and doth maintain thee, with all His might, and with all His mercy.

2. Do not love or seek an image instead of God, whether of wood or stone, of gold or silver, or of any other material, and whether it be represented in colour or in effigy; for thou hast never seen God; and who has seen Him? Do not take this world, or any other world, however glorious it may appear to thee, in the place of God; because they are not God, but the work of God, for thy great good, and for that of others, millions of times beyond the extreme limits of thy understanding and comprehension. Do not take riches or possession of any kind, or the regard and greatness of the proud and sinful world, in the place of God. Take not either relation or friend, male or female, for a God. Do not place thy aim, thy heart, thy intention, thy affections, or thy confidence, upon one or other of these things, or upon anything that will cause thee to trust less to God, because of the claim and possession thou hast in them. Always remembering and bewaring, do not seek or retain or love any one of these things, in such a way as will make thee cleave less to thy

---

O *dengair deddf* Duw a'm barno
Os datrin fy min man y bo.
From *the ten words of the law* may God judge me,
If my lips divulge where it is.—MS.

-a wnelo itti lynu wrth dy Dduw lai na phe bait hebddynt, ac o gwnai Duw a dry ei wyneb oddiwrthyd, ac a'th ar dy waelod dy hun ac ar sylfaen bodr y pethau yr addoli.

3. Na thwng i enw Duw, ac na ddos dros ei enw ef yn ammharchus ac yn Ysgawn, ac na wna'n ddibris clywed hynny o ben arall heb ei geryddu ai gynghori 'n hygar ac yn garedig a chyfeillgar, etto yn ddifraw ac yn ddifulder. ac os hynn na thyccia na thrig ymhellach lle gorfydd itti glywed ammharchu enw dy dduw, ac heb raid ac achos o bwys na ddos dros enw dy Dduw ar un amser.

4. Cofia orphwys ar y Sul, fal y caffo 'th deulu, a'th was ath forwyn, a'th weithwr ath weithwraig orphwys a bwrw ei lludded fal y caffo 'th ych a'th farch a phob anifail gwaith arall fwrw ei gorphwys fal y mae gofyn iddynt. Cofia fod hawl i Ddyn ac anifail ar amser gorphwys, nid oes iechyd heb hynn, Cofia fod achos amser itti i ymbwyllaw ac i ys-tyried a dysgu dy ddyledswydd tuac at Dduw a Dyn. heb hyn nis gellir y treigl a ddylit ac y sydd yn boddhau Duw ar na Dyn na da, nac ar fyd nac ar fod, nac ar fyw nac ar fywyd. Duw yn ei chwedydd gwaith a wnaeth y Bydoedd ac oll sydd ynddynt, o nef a nefolion, o ddaiar a daiarolion o fydoedd ac o fodau ac o fodolion, o bob hanfod a hanfodol-ion. Duw ar ei seithedydd a orphwyswys er ystyried ei waith a gwybu gan ei weled mai Da oedd y cwbl. ystyr dithau waith dy chwedydd, ar dy seithedydd a gyrr dy olwg yn graff ac yn ddidwyll ac yn ddilescedd ar hyd pob mymryn o hanaw, ai gwaith dy ddwylaw, ai gwaith dy feddwl ai gwaith dy serch ai gwaith dy ddeall y bo, yna gad i'th gydwybod lefaru, yn ol ei barn, iaith Duw yw ei hiaith ddidwyll hi. a da fydd itti, a da iawn os dichon hi ddy-wedyd mai da ydynt. Ystyr gwaith dy chwedydd nesaf

God than if thou wert without them. If thou doest so, God will turn His face from thee, and will leave thee to stand on thy own footing, and on the rotten foundation of the things which thou worshippest.

3. Swear not to the Name of God, and do not mention His name disrespectfully and lightly, nor deem it of no consequence to listen to such language from the lips of another without reproving and counselling him charitably, kindly, and in a friendly manner, at the same time fearlessly and boldly. If this does not avail, then dwell no longer where thou art compelled to hear the Name of thy God disparaged, and do not, without necessity and cause of importance, mention the Name of thy God at any time.

4. Remember to rest on Sunday, that thy family, thy man servant, and thy maid servant, thy labouring man and labouring woman, may rest, and cast off their fatigue,—that thy ox, thy horse, and every other beast of toil, may enjoy rest, as they require. Remember that both man and beast have a claim to the time of rest;—there is no health without it. Remember that there is need of a time for thee to reflect, to consider, and to learn thy duty towards God and man. Without this there cannot be that rotation, which ought to be, and which pleases God, in respect of man or property, of world or existence, of animation or life. God, in His six working days, made the worlds and all that are in them, consisting of heaven and celestials, of earth and terrestrials, of worlds, beings, and existences, of all essence and essentials. God rested on His seventh day, that He might consider His work; and on beholding it, He knew that all was good. Do thou, also, on thy seventh day, consider the work of thy six days, and review sharply, sincerely, and vigorously every particle of it, whether it be the work of thy hands, or the work of thy mind, or the work of thy affection, or the work of thy intellect; and then let thy conscience speak, according to its judgment, the language of God in its own undeceitful language, and it will be well for thee, and very well, if it can say that such work was good.

gyda llawnfryd a llawn ymgais ei wneuthur yn well nac a'i
gwnaethost o'r blaen, cais ddwyn pob peth ai gwaith corph
ai gwaith meddwl, ai gwaith serch ai gwaith deall y bo,
ymlaen ac ymlaen o well i well tra phery dy einioes, ac ar
ddiwedd honno cai orphwys oddiwrth dy holl lafur mewn
byd a bodoldeb lle y gweli ac y gelli yn gyfiawn ddywedyd
am bob peth mai *da iawn ydyw*.

5. Cofia garu ac anrhydeddu dy Dad a dy Fam fal y
dymunit i'th fab ath ferch dy anrhydeddu dithau. hwy a
welsant ac a glywsant fwy na thydi, rho goel iddynt gyda
pharch ac ufudd-dod, hwy a'th feithrinasant ac ath goledd-
asant gyda chariad a gofal, Coledd dithau hwynt yn eu
hangen au gwendid a'u henynt. Y maent yn dy garu yn
gywir, yn dy wirgaru yn fwy nac y mae neb eraill, ac am
hynny o'u pennau hwy yn unig y cei di wirionedd, cyd y
twyllant bawb ni thwyllant hwy dydi achos y cariad sydd
ganthynt tuag attot, cred a ddywedont. gwna yn ei ol.
Cofia 'r golled o golli yr unig rai ac a ddywedant itti wirionedd. Cofia gariad yr unig rai a ddioddefasant mewn
gwirionedd drossot. tal yn ol iddynt, tal gariad am gariad,
tal ofal am ofal, gwna iddynt fal y gwnaethant hwy i tithau, rhed yn ufudd wrth ei gair hwynt fal y rhedasant
hwy yn ofalus yn gariadfawr ac yn fuan wrth dy lef di pan
oeddyd yn blentyn egwan. ni chefaist ti hir gwynaw, na âd
dithau iddynt hwy hir gwynaw yn eu hegwander. O garu
a pherchi dy dad a'th fam ti a geri ac a berchi dy Dduw.
Yr hwn am hynny a rydd ei fendith arnot, ti a lwyddi yn
dy fywyd a'th foddion, ti a gynhyddi yn dy dda a dy ddeall, ti a gai esmwythder yn dy gydwybod ac o hynny
esmwythder ym mhob peth arall, ac o'r esmwythder meddwl
hynn ti a gai hir iechyd ac o hynny hir einioes, a'r pethau
hynn y mae Duw yn addaw eu chwanegu itti ymhell ti
hwnt i bob mesur ac a'u rhoddir itti gan ddim arall, neu

Consider the work of thy next six days, with full purpose, and full resolution to do it better than thou didst that of the preceding. Try to bring every thing, whether it be the work of the body, or the work of the mind, or the work of the affection, or the work of the intellect, onward and onward, from better to better, as long as thy life continues, and at the end of it, thou shalt rest from all thy labour in a world and existence, where thou shalt see, and canst truly say of every thing, that " it is very good."

5. Remember to love and honour thy father and mother, as thou wouldest that thy son and daughter should honour thee. They have seen and heard more than thou ; give credence to them with respect and obedience. They have nourished and cherished thee with love and care; do thou, also, cherish them in their need, feebleness, and old age. They love thee sincerely, they love thee indeed more than any other persons do ; therefore it is from their own mouths only that thou wilt obtain truth ; though they should deceive all others, they will not deceive thee, because of the love they have for thee. Believe what they say, and act accordingly. Bear in mind the loss of losing the only ones that tell thee the truth. Bear in mind the love of the only ones that have suffered in truth for thee. Repay them ; render love for love; render care for care ; do unto them, as they have done unto thee. Run obediently at their bidding, as they have ran carefully, lovingly, and quickly at thy cries, when thou wert a feeble child. Thou wert not suffered to complain long; do not suffer them to complain long in their feebleness. By loving and reverencing thy father and mother, thou wilt love and reverence thy God, Who on that account will bestow upon thee His blessing. Thou shalt prosper in thy life and means ; thou shalt increase in wealth and understanding; thou shalt have ease in thy conscience, and consequently ease in every thing else; and from this ease of mind, thou shalt have long health, and consequently long life. And these things God promises to add to thee immeasurably beyond what may be given to thee by any

drwy unrhyw foddion eraill ac a roddwyd hyd yn hynn iddynt fodoldeb namyn y sydd yn Nuw ei hunan, ai allu, ai wybodaeth, ai gariad anfeidrawl. efe a ddywed y gair. efe ai gwna.

6. Na ladd, ac na wna lufruddiaeth ar un achos o'r byd ba bennaf, na ddwg fywyd na dyn nac anifail eithr rhac cael dy ladd, megis lladd y gelyn a'th laddai pan nas gelli ddianc a gadael bywyd iddaw, neu ladd anifail rhag newyn, pan nas gelli ar ymborth amgen a'th gadwo rhag marw. a laddo a leddir, cyd nas lleddir y corph efe a leddir yr enaid. o ddianc yn y byd hynn, e ddaw yn drwm yn y byd nesaf, gwaed a dal am waed a Duw yn ei Dyngu.

7. Na wna ledrad, na ddwg oddiar un dyn, nac oddiar un byw na bod ei eiddo ei hun, nac o drais nerth na chyhoedd na dirgel y bo, na ddwg ar un byw ei eiddo drwy dwyll a dichell, na thrwy gribddail a gorthrymder, na ddwg yn un o'r moddion hynn nai dda nai ddeall, nai amser nai gyfle, nai gof nai gelfyddyd, na dim ac a berthyn ar un o'r pethau hynn.

8. Na phutteinia, ac na wna odineb a gordderchoriaeth, nid Cyfiawn i neb feithrin plant arall, nid cyfiawn i neb droi serch dyweddiawl oddiwrth ai dylai, gwna a gwraig arall fal y dymunit i arall wneuthur a'th wraig dithau, gwna a merch arall fal y mynit i arall wneuthur a'th ferch ac a'th chwaer dy hun. A Chofia!

9. Na ddywed anwiredd o unrhyw, nac am un achos o'r byd, na fydd anudonwr, na bradwr, na thyst anghywir yn erbyn dy gymmodog. na dyn arall pa bynnag o'r byd. na ddwg athrawd yn erbyn un dyn, na senn na gogan, na char gelwydd mewn arall, na chudd y gwir pan ai gofynner gen-

---

1 This is the motto of the Chair of Powys, and is supposed to be co-eval with its foundation in the 6th century. It is quoted by Davydd ab Gwilym,—

A laddo un a'i loyw ddur
I luddias hoed *a leddir.*

He who slays another with bright steel
To prevent delay, *shall be slain.*

thing else, or through any other means hitherto endued with existence, other than what is in God Himself, and His infinite power, knowledge, and love. He says the word; He will do it.

6. Kill not, and do no murder upon any account whatsoever. Do not take away the life of either man or beast, except to prevent thyself from being killed, as when thou killest the enemy that would kill thee, when thou canst not escape, and leave him his life; or when thou killest an animal to obviate hunger, when thou canst not have food otherwise that will keep thee from dying. He that slays shall be slain;[1] and though the body may not be slain, the soul shall be slain. If he escape in this world, he shall suffer grievously in the next world. Blood must be rendered for blood; God hath sworn it.

7. Commit no theft; take not from any man, or from any living or existing being, his own property, by forcible violence, whether it be done publicly or privately. Take not from any living being his property, by treachery, or cunning, or extortion, or oppression. Take not, in any of these ways, his goods, or understanding, or time, or opportunity, or memory, or art, or anything that belongs to one or other of these particulars.

8. Abstain from fornication, and do not commit adultery and concubinage. It is not lawful for any one to nourish the children of others. It is not lawful for any one to divert affianced affection from her whose due it is. Do unto the wife of another, as thou wouldest that another should do unto thy wife. Do unto the daughter of another, as thou wouldest that another should do unto thy own daughter and sister: and remember!

9. Tell no falsehood of any kind, nor on any account whatsoever. Be not a perjurer, or a traitor, or an unjust witness against thy neighbour, or any other man whatsoever. Bear no calumny against any man, or reproach, or satire. Do not love falsehood in another. Conceal not the truth, when it is required of thee, on any occasion what-

nyt ar un achos o'r byd, na chudd y gwir nac ar air nac ar
weithred nac ar ymddwyn ac ymddangos. cans nid llai y
celwydd a ddel o'r pethau hynn na'r un a ddelo oddiar y
tafod a'r llafar, pe bai yn erbyn dy dad neu 'th fam, yn erbyn dy frawd neu 'th chwaer, yn erbyn dy fab neu 'th ferch,
yn erbyn gwraig dy fynwes, yn erbyn dy fywyd dy hun,
dywed y gwir. canys yn erbyn dy enaid dy hun y bydd y
celwydd o ba ryw bynnag y bo, yn erbyn Duw ai wirionedd y dywedir, ac ai dangosir, ac ai gwnelir ef.

10. Na fydd drachwantus am ddim, rhac i neb roddi
itti yr hynn a ddylai 'th dlottach, rhag it anghenogi arall
drwy gael a drachwanti, rhag o drachwant ar unpeth o'r byd
itti wneuthur anghyfiawnder er mwyn ei gaffael. rhag itti o
roddi 'th fryd ar a drachwanti ollwng dy Dduw ai ddeddfau
yn anghof, rhac it ollwng o'th gof yr hynn a fo mwy teilwng er y peth a drachwanti, na thrachwanta na 'th dda na
'th feddiant na dim o eiddo dy hun a ellir yn gyttun a
deddfau Duw ei hepcor, rhac gommedd o honot i dlawd ac
anghenus yr hynn y dylit o gariad a chyfiawnder ei roddi
neu ei wneuthur iddaw, eithr car dy gymodog fal y ceri dy
hun, eithr hynn nis gelli tra bo yn dy galon drachwant, ni
elli garu Duw yn bennaf o ddim, na charu ei ddeddfau ef yn
fwy na da 'r byd, na charu 'th gymmodog yn fwy na phethau meirwon daiarol—na thrachwanta na thy na thyddyn dy
gymmodog, nai wraig nai ferch, nai was nai forwyn, nai
eidion nai farch, na dim arall o'i eiddo, rhac itti feddwl am
eu cael a'u dwyn a'u mynnu mewn modd na chydsaif ac
ewyllys a deddfau Duw. eithr cais gan Dduw a fo arnat ei
eisiau a thi ai cai, oi ofyn drwy ffydd a chred ddiffuant o
bydd cyfiawn yr achos a dilys yr eisiau arnot, ac na bo
niwed itti ei gael. Cred yn dy dduw ac ymddirieda drwy
obaith a ffydd ynddo ef, a thi a gai gantho a fo digon ac er

soever. Conceal not the truth by word, or deed, or behaviour, or appearance ; because the lie that comes from these things is not less than that which comes from the tongue and speech. Though it may be against thy father or mother, against thy brother or sister, against thy son or daughter, against the wife of thy bosom, against thy own life, yet tell the truth. For the falsehood, of whatever kind it may be, will be against thy own soul — it will be told, exhibited, and performed against God and His truth.

10. Be not covetous of any thing, lest any one should give to thee what ought to be given to one who is poorer than thou—lest thou shouldest impoverish another by having what thou covetest—lest, from coveting any thing whatsoever, thou shouldest commit injustice with the view of obtaining it — lest, by setting thy mind upon what thou covetest, thou shouldest forget thy God and His laws—lest thou shouldest omit from memory what is of greater worth, for the sake of what thou covetest. Covet not thy goods, or possessions, or any of thy own property, which can be dispensed with agreeably to the laws of God, lest thou shouldest refuse to the poor and needy what, out of charity and justice, ought to be given or done to them. But love thy neighbour as thou lovest thyself ; this, however, thou canst not do, whilst there is covetousness in thy heart. Thou canst not love God above all, or love His laws more than the goods of the world, or love thy neighbour more than mortal and terrestrial things. Covet not the house or farm of thy neighbour, or his wife or daughter, or his man servant or maid servant, or his ox or horse, or any thing else that belongs to him, lest thou shouldest think of obtaining, or taking, or willing them, in a way that is not consistent with the will and laws of God. But seek of God what thou wantest, and thou shalt obtain it, if thou askest it by faith and sincere belief, and if the occasion be just, and thy necessity unavoidable, and if its acquisition be not injurious to thee. Believe in thy God, and trust in Him with hope and faith, and thou shalt have from Him what, in His sight, is suffi-

lles itti yn ei olwg ef, ac efe a wyr dy eisiau, a pheth y sydd er lles itti, yn well nac a wyddost dy hunan, a diau ni phall efe itti ond a fytho er afles a drwg itti.

O gadw yn ddidorr y deddfau hynn, ti a gai gan Dduw gariad a heddwch, or Byd y sydd a'r byd a fydd, a chan Ddyn ti a gai barch a budd, ac ewyllys da, a llawnder, heb angen i'th dy, na gelyn ith gydwybod, hir einioes yn y byd y sydd, a bywyd tragwyddawl, a didranc wynfyd yn y byd a ddaw.

Diwedd.

DENGAIR DEDDF Y BEIRDD.

Llyma Ddengair Deddf Beirdd y Cymry
(O Lyfr Joseph Jones).

1. Car dy Dduw a nerth dy holl gorph ac a nerth dy holl enaid, ac a nerth dy holl galon, ac a nerth dy holl dde-all, ac a nerth dy holl serch, ac na char amgen nac efe. Un yw efe, heb un arall onid efe yn Dduw, nac ymgais ac un Duw arall onid efe.

2. Gochel addoli Delwau yn lle Duw na dim arall o liw nac o lun, na wna eilun Duw o Ddim yn y nef na'r ddaear, ac na feddwl na dychymyg addoliad iddynt, beth bynag y bont ai yn y nef ai yn naiar ai yn nyfroedd a moroedd daiar y bont. na warroga i ddim a roddir yn rhith Duw cans nis gwyddost ei rith ef. o gwnai Duw a ddial ei ammarch arnat ti a'th blant a'th wyron, a'th orwyron, eithr o cheri dy Dduw drwy wir barch ac ufuddhâd iddaw ef ath gar di a'th genhedlaeth hyd yn oes oesoedd.

3. Na wna 'n ofer ac enw dy Dduw cans anneddfol y bydd a wnelo felly ni pharcho Dduw ni pharch ei ddeddfau, ai orchymmyniadau.

cient and useful for thee. He knows thy wants, and what may be for thy advantage, better than thou knowest thyself, and assuredly He will not fail to give thee anything but what may be disadvantageous and injurious to thee.

By keeping these laws incessantly, thou shalt obtain from God love and peace, in the world which now is, and in the world which is to come; and from man thou shalt obtain respect, advantage, good will, and abundance, without there being need in thy house, or an enemy to thy conscience— long life in the world which now is, and eternal life, and endless felicity, in the world to come.

The end.

THE TEN COMMANDMENTS OF THE BARDS.

Here are the Ten Commandments of the Bards of the Cymry, from the Book of Joseph Jones.

1. Love thy God with the might of all thy body, with the might of all thy soul, with the might of all thy heart, with the might of all thy understanding, and with the might of all thy affection; and love no one but Him. He is one, and there is no God but He. Seek no other God but Him.

2. Beware of worshipping idols in the place of God—or any thing else whether in colour or effigy. Do not make an image of God out of anything in heaven or earth; and do not contemplate or invent any adoration to them, whatever they may be, whether they be in heaven, or in earth, or in the waters and seas of earth. Do no homage to any thing, which may be set forth in the form of God, for thou knowest not His form. If thou do, God will bring vengeance, on account of His dishonour, upon thee, thy children, thy grandchildren, and thy great-grandchildren. But if thou love thy God, with true veneration and obedience, He will love thee and thy posterity to the age of ages.

3. Take not the Name of thy God in vain, for he who does so is an immoral man. He who honours not God, will not honour His laws and commandments.

4. Cofia gadw yn ddwyfawl y Sul, rhydd itti weithio chwedydd, ac ar y seithedydd gorphwys a wnai a gadael pob gwaith a gorchwyl mal y gorphwyso dy holl dylwyth a'th holl anifeiliaid gwaith. Gorphwysfa dy Dduw ydyw 'r seithedydd, mewn chwedydd y gwnaeth Duw nef a nefolion, a daiar a daiarolion yr holl fydoedd a'u bodolion, a gorphwys a wnaeth ar y seithedydd gan ei fendithio ai ddwyfoli. ac o hynn y tyf hawl ar bryd ac amser gorphwys i bob dyn ac annifail i bob byw a bywydol.

5. Rho barch ac anrhydedd a chariad cyfiawn ith dad a'th fam, ac i bawb a fo pen ac Arglwydd o fraint gyfiawn arnat. cans o hynn y cai fodd dy Dad nefawl. a llonyddwch i'th fro a'th Haddef, a heddwch a hir einioes yn y byd, a gobrwyon y byd a ddaw.

6. A laddo a leddir, am hynny na ladd, ac na wna lofruddiaeth ar achos o'r byd, nac ar ddyn nac ar un byw arall ond rhac cael dy ladd gan elyn a newyn.

7. Na ddywed Gelwydd ac anudon, ac na fydd dyst anghywir yn erbyn arall, ac na chudd y Gwir ar air na gweithred nac ymddwyn.

8. Na ddwg yn lladrad eiddo arall, nac o drais nac o dwyll, nac o faidd. nac o feddwl, nac o un dichell nac o un dichawn, eithr gwna gyfiawnder, can mai cyfiawn yw Duw, ac ef a dal herwydd y bo cyfiawn.

9. Nac ymgais a godineb a phutteindra, ac na orddercha, gwraig na merch dyn o'r byd, ond bydd itti wraig briod i'th hunan ; a bydd gywir iddi a bydded hi gywir i tithau, Duw a ddial godineb a phutteindra.

10. Na fydd drachwantus am ddim a welot gan, na thai na thiroedd y bont, nac ychein na meirch nac unrhyw ysgrubl, na Gwraig na merch na gwas na morwyn na dim or byd ba bynnag a fo eiddo arall. cans o drachwant y daw pob trais ac anraith, a phob cybydd-dawd a chribddail, a phob

4. Remember to keep Sunday religiously. It is lawful for thee to work for six days; but on the seventh day thou shalt rest, and leave off all work and occupation, that all thy family and all thy beasts of labour may rest. The seventh day is the rest of thy God. In six days He made heaven and celestials, the earth and terrestrials, all the worlds and their inhabitants; and on the seventh day He rested, blessing and sanctifying it. From this springs a claim to a season and time of rest on the part of every man and beast, —of every living and animate being.

5. Pay just respect, honour, and love to thy father and mother, and to every one who may be head and lord, by just rights, over thee. Because from this thou shalt obtain the favour of thy heavenly Father, quietness for thy district and home, peace and long life in the world, and the rewards of the world to come.

6. He who slays shall be slain; therefore, do not kill or commit murder, on any pretence whatsoever, upon any man or other living being, except to prevent thyself from being killed by foe or famine.

7. Tell no falsehood.or perjury, be not an unjust witness against another, and conceal not the truth by word, deed, or behaviour.

8. Steal not the property of another, by oppression, treachery, daring, intention, cunning, or any other possibility; but do justice, for God is just, and He will repay according to what is just.

9. Avoid adultery and fornication, and dishonour not the wife or daughter of any man whatsoever; but let there be unto thee a wedded wife of thy own, and be faithful to her, and let her be faithful to thee. God will revenge Himself upon adultery and fornication.

10. Be not covetous of any thing you see, whether they be houses, or lands, or oxen, or horses, or any beast, or wife, or daughter, or man servant, or maid servant, or anything whatsoever that belongs to another. For from covetousness arise every oppression and pillage, every avarice

crinder a chraffder, a phob anghariad ac anghardawd, a phob ymddwyn anhael ac anhawdd.

Ac felly terfynant y dengair deddf, ac o'u cadw y daw i ddyn bob daioni a bendith, a chariad Duw a dynion a phob gwynfyd yn y byd y sydd a'r byd a ddaw.

EGWYDDOR DYWINIAETH.

1.   Cadw dy olwg ar dduw ag addola ef ac na ddod amharch iddo ger ei fron.

2.   Cyfiawnder a chariad gan heddwch a gwirionedd yw defnyddion bywyd anangheuol.

3.   Gochel odineb a thorpriodas.

4.   Na wna ddifrawd ac anraith.

5.   Nid cyfiawn i neb ond ai digono rhag marw.

6.   Gyrr wybodaeth o Dduw ar bawb, ag addysg o ddyn ar ai cymmero.

7.   Dod ga*trw*r* ag amser ddosparth ar gof a chadw gwybodau dywiniaeth.

8.   Gwna'th orau hyd eitha pwyll a gallu a gad y tragor annichonadwy i Dduw ai wyllys.

9.   Dod o'th olud a'th ddaoedd arllad gyfarwys i Dduw ai dylodion. fal na 'th ddifenwer, ag na 'th edwiner cans y myn Duw ei eiddo.

10.   Nid oes dim nad Duw ai gwnaeth nid oes dim nad Duw ai piau, ac nid arall, gad i Dduw a fynno.

Ac felly terfyna dengair deddf, Pawl Sant, y rhai a gafas efe o ben Iesu Grist y Mab Rhad.

---

* Illegible in the MS.

and extortion, every niggardliness and sharpness, every uncharitableness and want of alms-giving, and every illiberal and disagreeable conduct.

And thus end the Ten Commandments, from the keeping of which every goodness and blessing, and the love of God and men, and every felicity in the present world, and in the world to come, will accrue to man.

THE RUDIMENTS OF THEOLOGY.

1.   Keep thy eyes upon God, worship Him, and do no ·dishonour to Him in His presence.

2.   Justice and love, with peace and truth, are the materials of immortal life.

3.   Avoid adultery and the violation of marriage.

4.   Commit no depradation and pillage.

5.   There is nothing just for any one, except what will suffice him in the face of death.

6.   Impart the knowledge of God to all, and the instruction of man to such as will receive it.

7.   Insert ...... and the order of time in the memorials of theological sciences.

8.   Do thy best, to the extent of reason and power, and leave the impossible excess to God, and His will.

9.   Give of thy wealth and property an oblation to God and his poor, that thou mayest not be accursed, and that thou mayest not pine away ; for God will have his own.

10.   There is nothing which has not been made by God; there is nothing which does not belong to God, and not to another.   Leave to God what He wills.

And thus end the Ten Commandments of St Paul, which he received from the mouth of Jesus Christ, the Son of grace.

2 o

TRIOEDD PAWL.

1. Tair prif ddyledswydd Cristion ; Cred ynghrist ; gobaith yn Nuw ; a chariad at Ddyn.

2. Tair cynneddf anghriston, Balchder; creulondeb; ag anwiredd.

3. Tri arwydd Criston, caru gwir er maint y colled; caru gwlad er maint y goddef; a charu gelyn er maint ei frâd.

4. Tri pheth nis gellir Criston hebddynt ; glendid buchedd; cynghorion dwyfol; a dioddef diddig.

5. Tri chyfaill pob gwir Griston ; Pwyll ; amynedd; a chydwybod.

6. Tair gorfoledd Criston, Cariad Duw; Dedwyddwch Dyn; a llwydd Gwirionedd.

7. Tri pheth y bydd pob Dyn da; gweithgar; heddgar; ag elusengar.

8. Tri pheth y rhoddes Duw er addysg i ddyn; Pwyll gan wrth ansawdd; Barn Cydwybod; ag Efengyl Crist.

9. O dri gair y bydd ungair Duw, cariad, gwirionedd, a chyfiawnder, a'r tri gair hynn un ydynt gan Dduw, sef yw hynny cariad, ag nis gellir gair amgen o Dduw na chariad.

---

[1] Iolo Morganwg, whose transcript we have adopted on the present occasion, observes of St. Paul's Triads, that they are found in MSS. of a date anterior to the Reformation. We embody them in our Collection, because some of them, as Series the Third, not only associate Bardism with their Pauline Title, but also contain unmistakable traces of pre-Christian doctrines. It would seem, as in the case of the Ten Commandments, that the early Christians of Britain held the memory of the Great Apostle of the Gentiles likewise in peculiar veneration. Besides "Trioedd Pawl," or the Triads of St. Paul, allusion is frequently made to "Pregeth Pawl," or St. Paul's Sermon, and "Deifregwawd Pawl," St. Paul's distichs or verses. These, with "Efengyl Ieuan," or the Gospel of St. John, seem to have constituted the only Cymric writings, which, in the infancy of the Church, contained the doctrines of Christianity. It is probable that the attachment of the Cymry to the name of St. Paul had some reference to the supposed share he had in the foundation of their Church. It is not necessary, in order to establish their claim to authenticity, that the Triads in question should have been actually composed by the Apostle himself; though it is quite possible that he might have dictated their substance to Bran the Blessed, who happened to be at Rome at the same time with St. Paul. Bran, being a Bard, would natu-

THE TRIADS OF ST. PAUL.[1]

1. The three principal duties of a Christian : belief in Christ ; hope in God ; and love to man.

2. The three dispositions of an unchristian man : pride ; cruelty ; and falsehood.

3. The three signs of a Christian : to love truth, however great may be the loss ; to love one's country, however great may be the suffering ; and to love an enemy, however great may be his treachery.

4. Three things without which a man cannot be a Christian : holiness of life ; divine counsels ; and suffering without complaint.

5. The three friends of every true Christian : reason ; patience ; and conscience.

6. The three joys of a Christian : the love of God ; the happiness of man ; and the success of truth.

7. Three things which every good man will be : industrious ; pacific ; and benevolent.

8. Three things which God has given for the instruction of man : natural reason ; the judgment of conscience ; and the Gospel of Christ.

9. From three words will be one word of God : love ; truth ; and justice ; and these three words are one word with God, and there can be no other word from God than love.

---

rally throw them into the Triadic form, as that which was best calculated at the time to impress them on the public memory. Or perhaps they were composed by the Bards, and received the sanction of the Gorsedd, after these had in general become converts to Christianity—the name of St. Paul being associated with them, because they were either derived from his writings, or supposed to be in unison with his doctrine. There is reason, indeed, to suppose that some of them were derived immediately from some Apocryphal Scriptures, such as those which refer to the Counsels of Lazarus Though a Bardic tone runs through the whole, yet, as already hinted, it is more observable in the Third Series than in either of the other two. But whether that formed a part of the original compilation—afterwards separated from it as being of a too Druidic character, or whether it is altogether a distinct document, the work of a different school of Bards, we have no means of ascertaining.

10. Tri gofyn a roddwyd ar Grist, sef y cyntaf " beth yw Gwirionedd," ebe fe Cariad, yr ail oedd " Beth yw Cyfiawnder?" Cariad ebe ynteu, a'r trydydd oedd " beth yw Cariad?" Sef yr attebwys ynteu Duw.

11. O dripheth y mae Duw, y galluoccaf o bob amgyffred, y cyfionaf o bob amgyffred, a'r trugaroccaf o bob amgyffred.

12. Tri pheth o Dduw nis gellir amgyffred eu maint, ei allu, ei gyfiawnder, a'i drugaredd.

13. Tripheth nis gellir herwydd cynneddfau ac ansawdd Duw lai na'u bod, Pob cyfiawn, pob cariad, a phob hardd.

14. Tri pheth nis gellir gwybod yn iawn am ddim hebddynt, ansawdd a ddylai, pwyll wrth a ellir, a gorchymmyn Duw tuhwnt i bob un o'r ddau ac etto yn anwrthwyneb a fydd.

15. Tair golwg y sydd ar Dduw, y mwyaf o bob peth, y goreu o bob peth, a'r harddaf o bob peth.

16. Tri chynnhynged pob dyn un dechre, un dreigl ag un gorffen.

17. Tri rhagoriaeth Duw, y cyntaf o bob peth, y pennaf ar bob peth, a'r cydbleiddaf ar bob peth.

18. Tri gweled y sydd ar Dduw, ynddo ei hun, yngallu; yng Nghrist oi weled ; ag yn enaid dyn i'w yspryd santaidd.

19. Tri digon a byw byth, digon o wirionedd, digon o wybodaeth, a digon o gariad.

20. O dri digon y mae pob annigon, digon o gyfoeth bydawl, digon o $\underset{\text{Iechyd}}{\overset{\text{nerth}}{}}$ cnawdol, a digon o $\underset{\text{esmwythder}}{\overset{\text{ddiogi}}{}}$·

21. Tri gair cynghor a roddes Iesu Grist yn ben ar bob cynghorion eraill, 1 Car dy dduw a'th holl enaid, 2 Car dy

---

¹ Al. " health."   ² Al. " ease."

10. Three questions that were put to Christ : the first, " What is truth?" and He said, " Love ;" the second, " What is justice ?" and He said, " Love ;" and the third, " What is love ?" and He said, " God."

11. God consists of three things : the most powerful of all that can be comprehended ; the most just of all that can be comprehended ; and the most merciful of all that can be comprehended.

12. There are three things belonging to God, the magnitude of which cannot be comprehended : His power ; His justice ; and His mercy.

13. There are three things, which, in virtue of the attributes and nature of God, cannot but exist : all justice ; all love ; and all beauty.

14. Three things without which nothing can be well known : the nature that ought to be ; the reason of what is possible ; and the commandments of God beyond every one of the two, and yet not opposed to them.

15. There are three views of God : what is greatest of all things ; what is best of all things ; and what is most beautiful of all things.

16. The three co-destinies of all men : the same beginning ; the same course ; and the same end.

17. The three excellences of God : being the first of all things ; the chief of all things ; and the most complete of all things.

18. There are three ways in which God can be seen : in Himself, in power ; in Christ, by sight ; and in the soul of man, as to His Holy Spirit.

19. There are three sufficiencies, from which will ensue life everlasting : sufficiency of truth ; sufficiency of knowledge ; and sufficiency of love.

20. From three sufficiencies there is every insufficiency : sufficiency of worldly riches ; sufficiency of bodily strength ;[1] and sufficiency of idleness.[2]

21. The three words of advice, which Jesus Christ gave above all other advices : first, love thy God with all thy

gymmydog a'th holl galon, a char dy air da a'th holl ddoethineb, ag nis gellir a'th ofyn amgen.

22. Tri dyn a ryngant fodd Duw, a garo bob byw ai holl
galon, a wnelo bob harddwch ai holl nerth, ac a geisio bob
gwybod ai holl ddeall.

23. Tri pheth a fydd dyn cydwybodol, Doeth, caredig,
a llawen.

24. Tri nod anghydwybolder, annoeth, ofnus, ac anynad.

25. Tri pheth ni wyddys pa un waethaf, Diawl, annud-
onwr, ac anhrugarog.

26. Tri pheth y sydd o Dduw, chwenych bod i a ellir
yn oreu ar bob peth, credu bod a ellir yn oreu ar bob peth,
ac ymddwyn yn oreu ac a ellir ymhob peth.

27. Tri pheth a lafarwyd wrth Bawl o'r Nef, Car dy
Dduw yn fwy na dim, Car dy wirionedd fal dy enaid dy
hun, a char dy gymmodog fel dy hun.

28. Tri nod cymmodog wrth ba rai au adwaener ble
bynnag y bo, Bod yn dlawd, bod yn estron, a bod ar ddelw
Dyn.

29. Tair dyled i Dduw y sydd ac hebddynt nis gellir
dwyfolder, na chyrraedd nefolder, cred, ofn, a chariad.

30. Tri pheth a gant y Dwyfolion, cyfymgyd a Duw,
gwynfyd perffaith, a gwybodaeth cwbledig, a'r cyfan hyd
fyth bythoedd heb dranc heb orphen.

31. Tri pheiriannau deall, meddwl, gair, a gweithred, a'r
tri galluoedd au gelwir (*al.* a thri galluoedd dyn ydynt.

32. Tair ymarfer o'r galluoedd, sef y tri pheiriannau y
gorchymynwys Grist, nid amgen, 1 Car ddaioni a'th holl
nerthoedd ymha le a pheth bynnag y bo, gwna ddaioni a'th
holl nerthoedd ymha bynnag y bo achos a gofyn. (al. galw)
A bydd oddefgar hyd farw yn ddiwarafun dros ddaioni y

---

1 Al. " and they are three faculties of man." ² Al. " call."

soul; secondly, love thy neighbour with all thy heart; and, thirdly, love thy own reputation with all thy wisdom; and no one can ask more of thee.

22. Three men that will please God: he who loves every living being with all his heart; he who accomplishes every thing that is handsome with all his strength; and he who seeks every knowledge with all his understanding.

23. A conscientious man will be three things: wise; amiable; and merry.

24. The three marks of non-conscientiousness: to be unwise; timid; and petulant.

25. Three things, it is not known which of them is the worst: the devil; a perjured man; and an unmerciful man.

26. There are three things of God: to desire existence to what can be the best of all things; to believe that there is existence to what is the best possible of all things; and to conduct one's self in the best way possible in every thing.

27. Three things spoken to Paul from heaven: love thy God above all things; love thy truth as thy own soul; and love thy neighbour as thyself.

28. The three marks of a neighbour, by which he may be known wherever he is: to be poor; to be a stranger; and to be in the image of a man.

29. There are three duties towards God, without which there can be no godliness, or the attainment of heavenliness: belief; fear; and love.

30. Three things which the godly shall enjoy: union with God; perfect gwynvyd; and complete knowledge;— the whole for ever, without cessation, without end.

31. The three organs of the intellect: thought; word; and deed; and they are called the three faculties.[1]

32. The three exercises of the faculties, or the three organs, commanded by Christ, namely: do good with all thy energies wherever, and in whatever there may be cause and requirement;[2] and be patient unto death, without repining, in behalf of goodness, whenever, and on what occasion so ever there may be need and requirement;—and all this

pryd a'r achos bynnag y bo rhaid a gofyn, a hyn oll a'th holl allu a'th holl serch, a'th holl ddeall.

33. Tair llwybr at wirionedd, ei ddeall, ei garu, ai chwennych (al. ai geisio).[1]

34. Tri pheth o'u gwneuthur efe a wneir y cyfan parth Dwyfoldeb, 1. gochel y byd (al. gochel bydoldeb)[2] gommedd y cnawd, a gwrthladd y Cythraul.

35. Tair sail Doethineb, deall, cariad, a chyfiawnder.

36. Tair llath fesur Cyfiawnder, a fernir yn iawn yn arall, a ofner gwrth $\frac{na}{a}$ fo iawn oddiwrth arall, ac a geisir yn ol y chwenychir parth a farner yn iawn gan arall.

37. Tri chadarnhad cyfiawnder, a geffir yn iawn o brawf, ymgais, a deall, a ddysger yn lle 'r iawn o barth caffael, barn, a chydwybod i arall, ac a chwennycher ym mraint a gafwyd a farnwyd ac a ddysgwyd, gan arall, ac nis gellir hawl a braint ar a el yngwrth y cynfannogion ymma (al. hynn o gynfannogion).

38. Tair llathfesur deall, Barn arall, pwys a gwrthbwys, a darweiniant myfyrdod $\frac{gan}{a}$ serch, ac yn ol y by y rhain y bydd maint ac ansawdd y deall.

39. Tri arwydd Dyn dwyfol ymofyn am wirionedd, gwneuthur cyfiawnder, ac ymarfer a thrugaredd.

40. Tri pheth un cyfun ydynt o brif a chysefin ymdardd, cyfiawnder, gwirionedd a Chariad, sef o'r un a hwnnw, cariad, y daw 'r cyfan, yn un iawn o dduw, canys nid oes onid un iawn o'r cyfan wrth fod a hanfod.

41. Am dri achos y dylai ddyn ymwrthod a bywyd $\frac{lle\ bai}{os\ bydd}$ achos, yn chwilio am wirionedd, yn glynu wrth gyfiawnder, ac yn gwneuthur trugaredd.

42. Tripheth sy'n llygru 'r byd, Balchder, afraid, a segurdod.

---

[1] Al. "to seek it."   [2] Al. "worldliness."   [3] Al. "what is right."

[4] Al. " and."   [5] Al. " if."

with all thy power, with all thy affection, and with all thy understanding.

33. The three paths towards truth : to understand it ; to love it ; and to desire it.[1]

34. Three things, by the performance of which, all relating to godliness will be accomplished : to avoid the world ;[2] to deny the flesh ; and to resist the Cythraul.

35. The three foundations of wisdom : understanding ; love ; and justice.

36. The three measuring rods of justice : what is adjudged right in another ; what fears the opposition of what is not right [3] from another ; and what is sought, according to desire, in respect of what is adjudged right in another.

37. The three corroborations of justice : what is found right by experience, exercise, and understanding ; what is taught as right, in respect of acquirement, judgment, and conscience, to another ; and what is desired, in virtue of what has been acquired, judged, and learned, from another. What will oppose these primary characteristics can have no claim or privilege.

38. The three measuring rods of the understanding : the judgment of another ; poise and counterpoise ; and the guidance of meditation with [4] affection ; and, according as these things are, will be the extent and nature of the understanding.

39. The three marks of a godly man : to seek after truth ; to perform justice ; and to exercise mercy.

40. There are three things that are one whole, as to primary and original derivation : justice ; truth ; and love ; for from one, namely, love, the whole proceeds as one right from God, inasmuch as there is only one right of the whole in being and existence.

41. For three reasons ought a man to renounce life, where[5] there is occasion : seeking after truth ; cleaving to justice ; and performing mercy.

42. Three things that corrupt the world : pride ; extravagance ; and indolence.

43. Triphrif gynneddfau dwyfolder, gwedyd y gwir er gwaethaf a'i gwrth^{safo}_{wetto}, Caru pob hardd a daionus, a dioddef yn galonog tros y gwir a phob daionus.

44. Tri pheth nis gellir meidrol arnynt, Duw, ehangder, ac amser.

45. Tri pheth a wnant bechadur, ofn, trachwant, ac anwybodaeth.

46. Tri pheth sy'n llygru 'r byd, Balchder, afraid, a seguryd.

47. Tair prif gynneddf dwyfolder, Ystyriaeth, cyfiawnder, a chariad.

48. Mewn tri pheth y bydd cyfun Dwyfawl a Duw, o wybod pob peth, o garu pob peth, ac o ymryddhad oddiwrth bob peth.

49. Tri ychydig a wnant lawer o ddrwg, ychydig o dwyll, ychydig o lid, ac ychydig o anneall.

50. Tri ^{arbennigion}_{pheth yn bendant} y mae Duw yn eu gǫfyn—ymbwyll, cyfiawnder, a * chariad (* thrugaredd).

51. Tripheth o'u dirmygu a dynnant ddial, Cyngor gweledydd, Barn pwyllog, a chwyn tlawd.

52. Tri chyfun sy'n cynnal pob peth, Cyfun cariad a chyfiawnder, Cyfun gwir a dychymyg, a chyfun Duw a digwydd.

53. Tri nod dwyfolder, gwneuthur cyfiawnder, hoffi trugaredd, ac ymddwyn ufudd dan bob damwain.

54. Tri pheth ^{y sydd} ni char Duw a garo eu gweled, gweled ymladd, gweled anghynfil, a gweled rhodres balchder.

55. Tair prifddadanhudd Duw, ei waith, ei air, ai yspryd.

56. O dripheth y bydd dyn yn gyfun ei amcan ac ewyllys Duw, sef pan na chretto onid ai synhwyrau ei hun,

---

[1] Al. "contradict."　　　[2] This Triad is the same as the 42nd.

[3] Al. "Three things positively."

[4] Al. "mercy."　　　[5] One version omits the words "there are."

43. The three principal qualities of godliness : to speak the truth in spite of him who may withstand[1] it ; to love all that is comely and good ; and to suffer heartily in behalf of the truth and every thing that is good.

44. Three things which cannot be finite : God ; expanse ; and time.

45. Three things that make a sinner : fear ; covetousness ; and ignorance.

46. Three things that corrupt the world : pride ; extravagance ; and indolence.[2]

47. The three principal qualities of godliness : consideration ; justice ; and love.

48. In three things will a godly man be one with God : in knowing every thing ; in loving every thing ; and in freeing himself from every thing.

49. Three littles that will cause much evil : a little deceit ; a little anger ; and a little ignorance.

50. The three principal things[3] which God requires : reflection ; justice ; and love.[4]

51. Three things which, being disregarded, will draw down vengeance : the advice of a seer ; rational judgment ; and the complaint of the poor.

52. The three unions that support every thing : the union of love with justice ; the union of truth with imagination ; and the union of God with contingency.

53. The three marks of godliness : to do justice ; to be fond of mercy ; and to behave obediently under every circumstance.

54. There are[5] three things, God does not love those who love to see them : to see fighting ; to see a monster ; and to see the pomp of pride.

55. The three principal manifestations of God : His works ; His word ; and His Spirit.

56. In respect of three things will a man have his object in unison with the will of God, namely : when he believes only his own senses ; when he imagines only with his own

na ddychymyg onid ai ymbwyll ei hun, ac na wnelo onid ai gydwybod ei hun.

57.   Tri dyn a wedant yn wahanol herwydd eu hanian a'u hathrylith, dyn i Dduw a wed y goreu o'r gwir er heddwch a lles a chydfod, dyn i ddyn a wed y cyfan o'r gwir bid o dda bid o ddrwg deled a ddel heb yn waeth i beth bynnag a dderfydd o'r achos, dyn i ddiawl a wed y gwaethaf o'r gwir er drygu a pheri anffod, a diawl parod a wed gelwydd ystig er mwyn drwg a dinistr.

58.   Tri pheth nis gellir Dwyfoldeb lle bythont, gloddest, balchder a thrachwant.

59.   Tri nod dwyfolder Cariad diamgais, ufudd-dawd gwrawl, a thawedigrwydd serchog.

60.   Tri dyn a safant ym mraint brodyr a chwiorydd, ymddifad, gweddw, ac alltud.

61.   Tri menwydigion Duw, gwar, heddgar, a thrugar.

62.   Tri nodau plant Duw, Cydwybod bur, ymddwyn difalch, a dioddef o wirfodd ymhlaid gwir a chariad.

63.   Tri phrif orchymyn Duw, Cariad, cyfiawnder, ac ufudd-dawd.

64.   Tri arwydd dyn cyfiawn, caru gwirionedd, caru heddwch, a charu gelyn.

65.   Tri phrif hoffder dyn dwyfol, Cyfiawnder, trugaredd, a gwarineb.

66.   Tri gorefras dirieidi, glythineb, ymladd, ac anwadalwch.

67.   Tri chynghor a roddes Iesu Grist iddei ganlynwyr, nid amgen cynghori

1.   Tlodi gwastadol cans yn hynny y derfydd pob trais a gormes a chribddail a thrachwant, ac o hynny caffael cyfiawnder perffaith.

2.   Ufudd-dod gwyllysgar er mwyn ai erchiw ymhob amhechod, ac o hynny terfyn ar bob amryson, ac ymor-

---

1 These are similar to the Evangelical Counsels of the Church, which are, voluntary poverty, perpetual chastity, and perfect obedience.

consideration; and when he has to do only with his own conscience.

57. Three men who will speak differently, according to their nature and disposition : a man of God, who will speak the best part of the truth, for the sake of peace, advantage, and concord ; a man of man, who will speak the whole of the truth, be it good, be it evil, come what will, whatever may ensue in consequence; a man of the devil, who will speak the worst part of the truth, in order to harm and cause misfortune — a ready devil will speak an assiduous falsehood for the sake of mischief and ruin.

58. Three things, wherever they are, there can be no godliness : revelling ; pride ; and covetousness.

59. The three marks of godliness : disinterested love ; courageous obedience ; and affectionate silence.

60. Three men who stand in the relation of brothers and sisters : an orphan ; a widow ; and a stranger.

61. The three blessed ones of God : the gentle ; the peaceable ; and the merciful.

62. The three characteristics of the children of God : a pure conscience ; unostentatious demeanour ; and voluntary suffering in the cause of truth and love.

63. The three principal commandments of God : love ; justice ; and obedience.

64. The three signs of a just man : to love truth ; to love peace ; and to love an enemy.

65. The three principal delights of a godly man : justice ; mercy ; and gentleness.

66. The three encouragements of mischief : voluptuousness ; fighting ; and inconstancy.

67. The three counsels,[1] which Jesus Christ gave to His followers, namely, He counselled : first, perpetual poverty; because thereby all violence, usurpation, extortion, and covetousness, will cease, and consequently perfect justice will be obtained; secondly, voluntary obedience, for the sake of such as may demand it in every thing that is sinless, and consequently there will be an end to all quarrel-

trech, a balchder, a chael heddwch a thangnefedd perffaith.

3. Cariad pur a chyflawn, ac yn caffael pob serch a chymmwynas, a thrugaredd, a chariad, ac amddiffyn cyfymgyd, a phob caredigrwydd at ai haeddo, a phob cymmwynas a heddwch a llonydd ac elusendod i'r neb nas haeddo, ac ymgais iawnhau bynnag na fyddo iawn o ddyn neu o drefn a defawd, a gadael i Dduw gan farn yn ol y gwyppo efe y bo cyfiawn, ac o ganlyn y tri chynghorion hynn y cyrhaedder y tair Benwedigaeth arbennigion sef ydynt y Tair Benwedigaeth,

1. Nis gellir gorchymyn daioni nas gwnaer, nas cadwer, ac nas gorphener.

2. Nis gellir gweithred gyfiawn a thrugarog, a phrydferth, nas gwneler.

3. Nis gellir dyled nas taler, ac nas cyflawner, na gofyn nas caffer, na gwall nas diwaller, ac, yn hynn o bethau, caffael hefyd y tair gwaredigaeth, sef ynt,

1. Ni bydd ^{trossedd}_{cam} nas cymmhwyser, nac anfodd nas maddeuer, na dig nas heddycher, ac yno caffael y tri chael arbennigion, sef ynt

1. Nis bydd gwrthun nas ardduner

2. Na drwg nas dileer (diddymer)

3. Na dymuniad nas cyrrhaedder.

Ac o gyrrhaedd hyn o nod

1. Nis gellir un peth nas gwypper,

2. Na choll o bun nas ceffir a garer.

3. Na therfyn ar wynfyd a gaffer.

Ac nid rhaid ^{ar}_i ddeall a nerth a chariad namyn y petheu hynn, a gwneuthur a ellir ymhryder.

68. Tri Dyn parth athrylith a chynneddf sydd, Dyn i Dduw, a wna dda dros ddrwg, dyn i ddyn, a wna dda dros dda, a drwg dros ddrwg, a dyn i ddiawl, a wna ddrwg dros dda (Al. Tri rhyw o ddyn y sydd &c.)

---

[1] Al. "wrong."   [2] Al. "annihilated."

ling, contention, and pride, and perfect peace and tranquillity will be obtained; thirdly, pure and perfect love, in the exercise of all affection, kindness, mercy, charity, mutual defence, and civility, towards such as may deserve them, and of all kindness, peace, quietness, and almsgiving, towards such as do not deserve, and in the endeavour to rectify whatever is not right, in respect of man, system, or usage, leaving to God what in his judgment he concludes to be just. From following these three counsels will the three special felicities be attained, which three felicities are: first, no goodness can be commanded, which will not be performed, kept, and completed; secondly, there can be no just and merciful deed, which will not be performed; thirdly, there can be no debt which will not be paid, and discharged, no request which will not be obtained, and no deficiency which will not be supplied. Thus also will be obtained the three deliverances, namely: there will be no transgression[1] which will not be set right; no displeasure which will not be forgiven; and no anger which will not be pacified. And thence will be obtained the three excellences: first, there will be nothing ill-favoured, which shall not be adorned; secondly, there will be no evil, which shall not be removed;[2] thirdly, there will be no desire, which shall not be attained. And from reaching this mark: in the first place, there can be nothing, which shall not be known; there can be no loss of anything beloved, which shall not be regained; thirdly, there can be no end to the gwynvyd which shall be attained. And it is not necessary that there should be in understanding might and love other than these things, with the careful performance of what is possible.

68. There are three men of different dispositions and qualities:[3] a man of God, who does good for evil; a man of man, who does good for good, and evil for evil; and a man of the devil, who does evil for good.

---

[3] Al. "There are three kinds of men."

69. Tri dyn a gant eu cais gan Dduw, a gais ymwellhau 'n ei galon, a gais wybod y gwirionedd, ac a gais les a daioni ei * gymmodog (* ei gyd-ddyn / Dynolion).

70. Tri gair Cyngor Lasar, cred dy Dduw cans ef a'th wnaeth, car dy Dduw cans ef a'th brynwys, ac ofna dy Dduw cans efe ath farn.

71. Tri pheth ar gof a geidw rhag pechu, gorchymynion Duw, Llewynydd nef, a chosp pechawd.

72. Tri chadernyd Duwioldeb, Cred. (ffydd), gobaith a chariad.

Tair sylfaen Duwioldeb, Cred / Ffydd, cariad, a gobaith (Llyfr arall)

73. Tri a dystiolaethant am orchymynion Duw, angen, llesioldeb, a harddwch.

74. Tri cholled ar y ddaear a bair ynnill yn y nefoedd, colli golud o gariad ar ddyn, colli clod o gariad ar y gwar, a cholli bywyd o gariad ar y gwir.

75. Tri cholled corph a bair ynnill enaid, colli iechyd, colli cyfoeth, a cholli cas.

76. Tri rhyw gelwydd y sydd, Celwydd gair a gwediad, celwydd gweithred, a chelwydd ymddwyn. (al. a chelwydd o annangos).

77. O dri bendith y cair bendith Duw, Bendith Tad a mam, Bendith tlawd a dolurus / claf a chlwyfus, a bendith estron adfydig / Bendith claf a chlwyfus.

78. Tri dadannudd Duw, Tadolaeth yn crëu 'r byd, mabolaeth yn addysgu y byd, ac ysprydolaeth yn cynnal a llywodraethu y byd.

79. Tripheth y dylai ddyn a'i galon, ei theimlo, ei haddysg, ai hofni.

80. Tri achos y dylai ddyn ymadael / ymwrthod a bywyd os bydd

---

[1] Al. "his fellow-man." Al. "human beings."

[2] Lazarus is asserted to have accompanied Joseph of Arimathea into Britain. See Morgans's St. Paul in Britain, p. 147.

[3] Al. "belief." [4] Al. "belief." [5] Al. "the falsehood that is not shewn."

[6] Al. "the sick and diseased." [7] Al. "the sick and diseased."

[8] Al. "renounce."

69. There are three men, who will get what they seek from God: he who seeks to become better in his heart; he who seeks to know the truth; and he who seeks the benefit and good of his neighbour.[1]

70. The three counsels of Lazarus:[2] believe thy God, for He made thee: love thy God, for He redeemed thee; and fear thy God, for He will judge thee.

71. Three things, if borne in mind, will keep one from sinning: the commandments of God; the joy of heaven; and the punishment of sin.

72. The three stabilities of godliness: faith;[3] hope; and charity.

In another Book — The three foundations of godliness: faith;[4] charity; and hope.

73. Three will testify of the commandments of God: necessity; utility; and beauty.

74. The three losses on earth that will bring gain in heaven: to lose riches out of love for man; to lose fame out of love for civilization; and to lose life out of love for the truth.

75. The three losses of the body that will bring gain to the soul: the loss of health; the loss of wealth; and the loss of hatred.

76. There are three kinds of falsehood: the falsehood of word and saying; the falsehood of deed; and the falsehood of demeanour.[5]

77. From three blessings will the blessing of God be obtained: the blessing of father and mother; the blessing of the poor and sick;[6] and the blessing of the distressed stranger.[7]

78. The three manifestations of God: Fatherhood creating the world; Sonship teaching the world; and Spirituality supporting and governing the world.

79. Three things which a man ought to do with his heart: to feel it; to teach it; and to fear it.

80. For three reasons ought a man to part with[8] life, if

2 Q

galw, yn ymchwilo am y gwir, yn glynu wrth gyfiawn, ac
yn gwneuthur trugaredd.

81. Tri chyfnerth dyn dwyfawl, Duw a'i ddawn rhad,
cydwybod ei hun, a mawl pob doeth a daionus.

82. Tri chynghor Lasar, ufuddha i Dduw a'th wnaeth,
car Dduw a'th brynwys, ac ofna Dduw a'th eilw i farn am
dy weithredon.

83. Tripheth cydfynn cyfymgyrch a phob daioni, Duw
yn ei nerth ai ddawn, cydwybod effraw, a barn doethion o
ddwyfolion.

84. Tri chynghyd crefyddolion, cariad, gocheliaeth, ac
ymofyniaeth.

85. Tripheth anghywydd a Duw, anffawd, anwir, ac
anobaith.

86. Tri lle y bydd mwyaf o Dduw, lle bo mwyaf a'i câr,
y mwyaf ai cais, a lleiaf o'r hunan.

87. Tair cynneddf ddwyfol ar ddyn, Dioddef amyneddgar, Cariad diffuant dihunangais, ac ymwrthod a'r annhra-
gywydd.

88. Tripheth serchog eu gweled, Diriaid yn myned yn
ddedwydd, cybydd yn myned yn hael, a phechadur yn
myned yn ddwyfol.

89. Tri pheth a gair o dlodi, Iechyd, pwyll, a nerth
Duw.

90. Tri chelwydd y sydd, Celwydd gwedyd, celwydd
Taw, a chelwydd ymddwyn, a phob un o'r rhain a wna i
arall gredu yr hynn nas dylai.

91. Tri pheth y caiff dyn goddefus, cariad dynion da,
bodd ei gydwybod ei hun, a * dawn Duw (al. a * chyfnerth).

92. Tri pheth y caiff dyn trugarog, Cariad, heddwch, a
bodd Duw.

93. Tri chosp y sydd am bechod, cosp dyn yn dost, cosp

---

[1] Al. "support."

it be required : seeking after truth ; cleaving to justice ; and performing mercy.

81. The three supports of a godly man: God and His gift of grace; conscience itself; and the praise of every wise and good man.

82. The three counsels of Lazarus: obey God Who made thee; love God Who redeemed thee; and fear God Who will call thee to judgment for thy works.

83. Three things that concur in will and tendency with all goodness: God in His power and favour; a wakeful conscience; and the judgment of wise and godly men.

84. Three things that are united with the religious: love ; avoidance ; and seeking.

85. Three things that are incompatible with God : misfortune ; falsehood ; and despair.

86. Three places where will be the most of God : where He is mostly loved ; where He is mostly sought ; and where there is the least of self.

87. The three godly qualities of man: patient endurance ; sincere and disinterested love; and renunciation of what is temporal.

88. Three things it is desirable to see : the mischievous becoming happy; the miser becoming generous; and a sinner becoming pious.

89. Three things that will be obtained from poverty : health ; prudence ; and the help of God.

90. There are three falsehoods: the falsehood of speech ; the falsehood of silence ; and the falsehood of conduct. Each of the three will induce another to believe what he ought not.

91. Three things that a patient man will obtain: the love of good men ; the approval of his own conscience; and the favour[1] of God.

92. Three things that a merciful man will obtain: love ; peace ; and the good will of God.

93. There are three punishments for sin : the punishment of man, which is severe; the punishment of God,

Duw yn dostach, a chosp Cydwybod, pan effry, yn dostaf oll.

94.   Tripheth a gaiff Dyn o gredu yn Nuw, a fo raid o'r bydol, heddwch cydwybod, ac ymgyd ar nefolion.

95.   Tripheth anghenreidiol i bechadur, cydnabod ei bechodau, edifarhau am danynt, a deisyf maddeuant.

96.   Tripheth y caiff dyn ^{ammalch}_{difalch}, esmwythder meddwl, cariad cymmydogion ac awenbwyll ddwyfol.

97.   Tri chosp Criston ar ei elyn, tewi arno, maddeu iddo, a gwneuthur a fo garedig a da erddo.

98.   Tri gofal Criston, rhag digio Duw, rhac tramcwyddo dyn, a rhag ymwanhau oi gariadoldeb.

99.   Tri moethusder Criston, a ellir o ddarpar Duw, a ellir o gyfiawnder i bawb, ac a ellir eu harfer gan gariad tuag at bawb. (al. Tri moethineb Criston, Darpar Duw &c.)

100.   Tri thyst dwyfolder, gommedd hunander, ymddwyn haelionus, a channerth pob daioni.

101.   Tri phen ofynion Duw Cyfiawnder Trugaredd, ac ufudd-dod ger ei fron.

102.   Tri chyfymgais cariad, addoli Duw o gariad arno, lleshau Dyn o gariad arno, a boddhau hunan er cariad at Dduw a dyn.

103.   Tri phenneifiaid y byd sy'n gyfungyrch at gariad ; Bodd Duw, Lles Dyn, ac ansawdd anian.   (Al. Tri cheinmyged myfyrdawd &c.)

104.   Tri pheth a wnant ddwyfolder ar bob peth, Lluniaethu Dyn, dysgu gwirionedd a chyfiawn, a lleihau poen ac eisiwed.

105.   Tri defnyddioldeb pob peth gan Dduw, er a fo mwyaf yr achos, y mwyaf y llês, ar mwyaf y cariad   (Al. Tri cheinmygedion Duw)

106.   Tri pheth y sydd yn bennaf o Dduw, gwirionedd, Tagnef, a gwybodaeth.

---

[1] Al. " the predestination of God."

[2] Al. " The three dignities of meditation," &c.   [3] Al. " The three dignities of God."

which is more severe; and the punishment of conscience, when it is awakened, which is the severest of all.

94. Three things that a man will have from believing in God: what is needful of worldly matters; peace of conscience; and communion with the celestials.

95. Three things necessary to a sinner: to acknowledge his sins; to repent of them; and to entreat forgiveness.

96. Three things that a humble man will obtain: ease of mind; the love of neighbours; and godly discretion.

97. The three punishments which a Christian inflicts upon his enemy: not to accuse him; to forgive him; and to do what is kind and good for him.

98. The three cares of a Christian: not to offend God; not to be a stumbling-block to man; and not to become enfeebled in love.

99. The three luxuries of a Christian: what is possible from the predestination of God;[1] what is possible from justice to all; and what can be practised in love towards all.

100. The three witnesses of godliness: to forbid selfishness; to behave generously; and to support every goodness.

101. The three chief requirements of God: justice; mercy; and obedience before Him.

102. The three co-endeavours of love: to worship God out of love towards Him; to benefit man out of love towards Him; and to please self out of love for God and man.

103. The three chiefs of the world that tend together towards love: the good will of God; the benefit of man; and the quality of nature.[2]

104. Three things that will invest every thing with godliness: to put man in order; to teach truth and justice; and to lessen pain and want.

105. The three utilities of every thing in the hands of God: that which refers to the greatest necessity; the greatest advantage; and the greatest love.[3]

106. Three things that are principally from God: truth; peace; and knowledge.

107. Tri pheth y sydd yn bennaf o gythraul, anwybod-aeth, anwiredd, ac ymdrin.

108. Tri bannogion Dwyfoldeb, bod yn lan fal y mae Duw, bod yn drugarog fel y mae Duw, a gweithredu cyfiawnder fel y gwna Duw.

109. Tair prif gynneddf dwyfolder Cyfiawnder, cariad, ac ystyriaeth.

110. A thri pheth y dylit gwneuthur pob daioni, a'r holl ddeall, a'r holl allu, ac a'r holl serch.

111. Tri amryson annwyfol, rhyfel tros rhyfel—Cyfraith dros gyfraith a gwarth tros warth.

112. Tri amryson Dwyfol pwyll dros amhwyll, dawn dros annawn a chariad dros gas.

113. O dripheth y mae Dwyfoldeb; Cariad, cyfiawnder, a gwirionedd (Al. Cariad, cyfiawnder, ac ufudd-dod.)

114. Tri dyn gwahanryw y sydd, dyn i ddyn, ac efe a wna dda dros dda a drwg dros ddrwg, dyn i Dduw, ac ef a wna dda dros ddrwg, a dyn i ddiawl, ac efe a wna ddrwg dros dda.

115. Tri athrawon a drefnwys Duw i ddyn, un yw dichwain ai addysg yn gweled a chlywed, ail yw ystyr, ai ddysg yn bwyll a deall, trydydd yw rhadferthwch Duw, ai addysg o reddf ac awen.

116. Tri pheth a nodant ddyn i ddiawl — balchder — cenfigen, a thrais.

117. Tri defnyddion barn — deddf o gyfiawnder — trugaredd o gariad — a chydwybod o bwyll a deall ar y ddau gyntaf.

118. Tri phrif gynneddfau daioni, cariad, cyfiawnder, a goddef yn lew yn eu plaid.

119. Tri gair cyngor y sydd i bob dyn — gwybydd dy allu—gwybydd dy wybodaeth—a gwybydd dy ddyledswydd, ac o'u gwybod gwna yn eu hol.

120. O dri bendith y cair bendith Duw, bendith Tad

---

[1] Al. "obedience."

107. Three things that are principally from Cythraul : ignorance; falsehood; and contention.

108. The three characteristics of godliness : to be holy as God; to be merciful as God ; and to perform justice as God does.

109. The three principal qualities of godliness : justice; love; and reflection.

110. With three things ought every goodness to be performed : with all the understanding ; with all the power ; and with all the affection.

111. The three impious contentions : war for war ; law for law ; and disgrace for disgrace.

112. The three pious contentions: prudence for imprudence ; favour for no favour ; and love for hatred.

113. From three things comes godliness : love ; justice; and truth.[1]

114. There are three different kinds of men : a man of man, who does good for good, and evil for evil ; a man of God, who does good for evil; and a man of the devil, who does evil for good.

115. The three teachers appointed by God for man : one is contingency, which instructs one by seeing and hearing ; the second is consideration, which instructs by reason and understanding ; the third is the grace of God, which instructs by instinct and genius.

116. Three things which mark a man of the devil : pride; envy; and violence.

117. The three materials of judgment : law from justice; mercy from love; and conscience from reason and understanding of the former two.

118. The three principal qualities of goodness : love; justice; and suffering bravely in their behalf.

119. There are three words of advice to every man : know thy power ; know thy knowledge ; and know thy duty ; and knowing them, act accordingly.

120. From three blessings will the blessing of God be obtained : the blessing of father and mother ; the blessing

a mam — bendith tlawd a chlwyfus — a bendith estron anghenus.

121. Tair cynneddf ddwyfol ar ddyn, ystyriaw—caru— a dioddef.

122. Tair cynneddf gythreulig ar ddyn—trachwant — llid—a balchder.

123. Tri bannogion daioni peirianol, meithrin plant yn ddwyfolion, ymgynnal yn y swydd a'r cyflwr a fo arnadd-oedd yn ol y bo dyled, a diwyllio daiar. (al. meithrin plant yn ddwyfolion—addysgu swydd a dyled, a diwyllio daear)

124. Tri bannogion daioni gweithredol, cynnal gwir a chyfiawn—cynnal cariad a thangnef—ag amlhau gwynfyd a fo gan fodd Duw.

125. Tri banogion daioni dymuniadol serchu gwir a chyfiawn — serchu tangnef a chariad — a serchu a dymuno gwynfyd yn gyfol a pharth y cyfoll.

126. Tri daioni gwaredigol a barant nef i enaid dyn,— sef y daioni a wnel o wirfodd a serch ac nas dadwnel oi fodd, gan ddeall ei gyngyd, ac na bo etifar arno yn ei fywyd wneuthur y daioni hynny. megis ac y bydd ymarfer a chyf-iawnder, a thrugaredd, ac haelioni, ac ymoddefgarwch yn ddietifar ac o lawnfryd a serch parth ac at y pethau daionus hynny a pharth ac at a wnel drostynt. Ail yw y daioni a baro ei fod oi wirfodd ac ymgais parth ac at hynny o amcan, a bod wrth hynny yn achos a barai 'r daioni hynny, fal y bydd meithrin plant ac addysgu eraill yn ddwyfolion ac yn weithredorion daioni o gyfiawn addysg a deall ar y daioni a ddylit, hyd eitha galledigaeth y dyn a wnelo hynny o ym-gais. A thrydydd y daioni a wnelai o wirfodd a serch ei galon pe bai galledig hynny iddo, drwy berchennu modd ac amser a gallu a gwybod, ac nas dadwnelai efe y pethau da-ionus hynny ar air na gweithred nac ymddwyn na dymun-iad fyth wedi hynny o wir fodd gan ddeall a gwybod a wnelai a feddyliai ac a wnelai a weithredai parth ac at y

---

[1] Al. "to learn profession and duty."

of the poor and sick ; and the blessing of the needy stranger.

121. Three godly qualities in man : to consider ; to love ; and to suffer.

122. Three devilish qualities in man : avarice ; anger ; and pride.

123. The three characteristics of instrumental good : to rear children in godliness ; to support one's self in the office and state in which one is placed, as duty requires ;[1] and to cultivate the earth.

124. The three characteristics of active good : to maintain truth and justice ; to maintain love and peace ; and to augment that gwynvyd, which may be pleasing to God.

125. The three characteristics of desirable good : to affect truth and justice ; to affect peace and love ; and to affect and desire gwynvyd wholly, and with a view to the whole.

126. The three saving goodnesses that will bring heaven to the soul of man, that is to say : the goodness which he performs voluntarily and in love, and which he would not of his own accord undo, in that he understands its intent— and of doing which goodness he would not repent during life, such as practising justice, mercy, generosity, and forbearance, unrepented of, and with full disposition and love towards those good things, and towards what he does in their behalf ; the second is the goodness which he produces of his free will and endeavour for a particular purpose, being thereby the cause, which produces the said goodness, such as rearing children, and teaching them to be godly, and workers of good, with a just information and understanding of the good that ought to be performed, to the utmost ability of the man who seeks to do it ; the third is the goodness which he would do of the free will and desire of his heart, were it possible for him, if he had the means, time, ability, and knowledge, and which good things he would not undo by word, deed, demeanour, or wish, ever after of his own accord, in that he understood and knew what would be the effect of his intention, and what would be the effect of

pethau hynny. A'r daionïau hynn a farner ac a freinier gan Dduw yn ol maint y gallu, a'r serch, a'r hawsder, a'r dymuniad, a'r gwirfodd yn ogyfuwch a'r daioniau gweithredol a wnelai hynny o alluau, a serch, a moddion, a lle ac amser.

127. Tri achos caru Duw y sydd, ai berchi — am ein gwneuthur—ac o ddyled am ein cynnal—ac am y gwynfyd o'i gyfeillach ysprydawl.

128. Tri achos a dyled caru dyn y sydd, am ei fod ar lun Duw — am ei fod o'r un hanfod ac ansawdd a'n hunain — ac am y bodd a'r budd y sydd i garu o garu.

129. Tripheth a gair yn ffyrdd Duw, heddwch, gwirionedd, a gwybodaeth.
130. Tri pheth a ry Dduw iddei blant ai caro, cyfiawnder, trugaredd, a gwynfyd.

131. Tripheth y dylai pob un a garo 'r gwir—chwilio 'n ddiflin am dano, ufuddhau iddei gynghorion—a marw lle bo achos ar ei fwyn.
132. Tri pheth ffiaidd ar ddyn, godineb, celwydd, a meddwdod.
133. Y tripheth harddaf oll ar ddyn, cyfiawnder, trugaredd, ac ufudd-dod.

134. Tri phrif Enyfed dyn, Awen, serchu, a deall, ac ar tri hynn y dylai efe garu Duw.
135. Tripheth y dylit ufuddhau iddynt—i orchymmynion Duw, i gyfraith gwlad, ac i ofynion cydwybod.

136. Tri pheth nid oes namyn Duw a'u gwybydd, ac am hynny nid iawn rhyfarnu arnynt, syrth awen, ymgais deall, a barn cydwybod.
137. Tri pheth a ddylai dyn eu gwneuthur yn ddidwyll, ynnill meddiant trwy ddiwydrwydd diniwed a chywirdeb,

his act towards those things. And these goodnesses are adjudged and privileged by God, according to the amount of power, affection, facility, desire, and free will, connected with them, as equal to the active goodnesses, which would do so, in that they had the power, affection, means, place, and time.

127. There are three reasons why God should be loved, and honoured: because He made us ; because we are under an obligation to Him for maintaining us ; and as a return for the felicity of His spiritual friendship.

128. There are three reasons and obligations for loving man : because he is in the image of God ; because He is of the same essence and nature with ourselves ; and because of the pleasure and advantage that accrue to love from the act of loving.

129. Three things that will be had in the ways of God : peace ; truth ; and knowledge.

130. Three things that God will give to His children, who love Him : justice ; mercy ; and gwynvyd.

131. Three things which every one, who loves the truth, ought to do : to seek it indefatigably ; to obey its counsels ; and to die, where there is occasion, for its sake.

132. Three things abominable in man : adultery ; falsehood ; and drunkenness.

133. The three things most decorous in man : justice ; mercy ; and obedience.

134. The three principal vigours of man : awen ; affection ; and intellect ; and with these three he ought to love God.

135. Three things that ought to be obeyed : the commandments of God ; the law of the country ; and the requirements of conscience.

136. Three things which God only knows, and therefore it is not right to prejudge them : the tendency of awen ; the attempt of the intellect ; and the judgment of conscience.

137. Three things which a man ought to do honestly : to gain possessions through innocent industry and upright-

er gallu cyfiawnder ac elusendawd, lleshau dyn ymhob gorchwyl a wnelo, a gyrru addysg dwyfolder a deddfolder ar bawb lle 'r elo.

138. Tripheth nis gellir na dwyfolder na deddfolder hebddynt—maddeu gelyniaeth a chamwedd—haelioni—ac ymddwyn yn gyfiawn ar bob achos.

139. Tri rhagorion daioni, addfwynder, pwyllgarwch, ac haelioni meddwl ac ymddwyn.

140. Tri dyn y sydd ac nis gellir eu gwaeth, cybydd, enllibwr, a lledrithiog. (ragrithiwr).

141. Tair cynneddf a barant ddwyfoldeb, gwybodaeth, gwirionedd, ac ^{haelionusder} haelioni.

142. Tri pheth y bydd dyn i Dduw, yn ddeddfawl, yn gariadgar, ac yn ymaniangar.

143. Tri gofynion Duw ar ddyn, Cyfiawnder, trugaredd, ac ufudd-dawd.

144. Tair sail gwynfydigrwydd, deall, haelioni, a boddlondeb.

145. Tripheth ynghyd a wnant oll a fo iawn, nerth Duw, addysg deall, ac ansawdd daioni (E.a.w. a daionus ymgais).

146. Tri arwyddion doethineb dwyfawl, ceisiaw gwybodaeth doed a ddel—rhoddi cardod heb feddwl am a ddel, a dioddef yn wrol dros wir a chyfiawn heb ofni a ddel.

147. Tripheth gwerthfawroccaf i ddyn, iechyd, rhyddyd, a deddfoldeb. (al. a rhinwedd.)

148. Tair sylfaen deddf a chynneddf—trefn hardd—cyfiawnder, a thrugaredd.

149. Tripheth nis gellir deddfoldeb dwyfawl hebddynt, maddeu gelyn a chamwedd, haelioni meddwl a gweithred, a glynu wrth gyfiawnder ym mhob peth.

150. Tair dyledswydd arbennigion y sydd ar ddyn, ymgynnal ei hun ai deulu drwy ddiwydrwydd a chywirdeb—lleshau ei gyd-ddynion ymhob cais a gorchwyl a wnelo, a

---

¹ Al. "virtue."

ness, that he may do justice and almsgiving; to benefit man in every employment which he performs; and to impart instruction in godliness and morality to all, wherever he goes.

138. Three things, without which there can be no godliness or morality: to forgive enmity and wrong; generosity; and just demeanour on all occasions.

139. The three excellencies of goodness: meekness; prudence; and liberality of mind and conduct.

140. There are three men, than whom there can be no worse: the miser; the slanderer; and the hypocrite.

141. The three qualities that will effect godliness: knowledge; truth; and liberality.

142. Three things that a man of God will be: moral; amiable; and well disposed.

143. The three things which God requires of man: justice; mercy; and obedience.

144. The three foundations of felicity: understanding; generosity; and contentment.

145. Three things together will make all that is just: the help of God; the instruction of the understanding; and the nature of good. Others say, and good endeavour.

146. The three signs of godly wisdom: to seek knowledge, come what may; to give alms, without thinking what may come; and to suffer manfully for truth and justice, without fearing what may come.

147. Three things most precious to man: health; liberty; and morality.[1]

148. The three foundations of law and habit: beautiful order; justice; and mercy.

149. Three things, without which there can be no divine morality: to forgive an enemy and a wrong; liberality of mind and deed; and to cling to justice in every thing.

150. There are three special duties incumbent on man: to support himself and family through industry and uprightness; to benefit his fellow-men in every undertaking and employment, in which he may be engaged; and to impart

gyrru addysg deddfoldeb dwyfol ar bob dyn y ffordd yr elo.

151. Tripheth a gaiff dyn o godi 'n fore, cyfoeth bydawl, iechyd corphorawl, a llawenydd ysprydawl.

152. Tripheth ni wedd ar ddwyfawl edrych ac un llygad —gwrandaw ac un clust, a chynnorthwyaw ac un llaw.

153. Tri llathfesur pob dyn — ei Dduw, ei ddiawl, ai ddidawr.

154. Tair Sylfaen Dwyfoldeb, cyfiawnder gweithredawl, gwirionedd cynghorawl, a chariad ynnïawl.

155. Tri cyfreidiau daioni, gwybodaeth, ystyriaeth, a chariadusder.

156. Tair prif gynneddf y sydd ag o honynt y tyfant yr holl gynneddfau da eraill i gyd. Trugaredd, ai arwydd yw rhoddi elusenau a nawdd ag ymborth ag addysg yn ol y gweler achos. Ufudd-dod o ammalchineb, ai arwydd yw derbyn elusenau a nawdd a chyngor drwy weddeidd-dra gwrolaidd a thangnefgarwch. Cyfiawnder, ai nod arwydd yw gwneuthur a fo iawn herwydd Cydwybod a deall er gwaethaf a fynno gan yn ei erbyn, a dioddef yn wrolgamp dros a farno'n iawn o ba ryw bynnag y bo, a phob caledi a gormail a ddel beth bynnag hyd yn nod marw dros a wnelo ac a farno.

157. Tair rhodd elusen y sydd, ymborth, nawdd, ag addysg o gyngor a dangos.

158. Tripheth a ddygant ar gof i ddyn ei ddyled· i Dduw a Dyn, elusen, unpryd, a gweddi.

159. Tripheth a wnant gyfiawn ddwyfoldeb, caru Duw, cariad tuag at bob byw, a charu pob gwir a chyfiawn.

160. Tri chyngor y rhoddes Iesu Grist iddei wasanaethwyr, car dy Dduw yn bennaf o ddim ag ufuddha iddaw ymhob peth — car dy gymmodawg fal y carit dy hun, a gwna erddo a ddymunit y gantaw erddot ti dy hun,—ymgais a gwybodau moliannus canys o hynny y cei ar ddeall

instruction in divine morality to every man, wherever he goes.

151. Three things which a man shall have from early rising : worldly riches ; bodily health ; and spiritual joy.

152. Three things which do not become a godly man : to look with one eye ; to listen with one ear ; and to help with one hand.

153. The three measuring rods of every man : his God ; his devil ; and his indifference.

154. The three foundations of piety : active justice ; preceptive truth ; and energetic love.

155. The three necessaries of goodness : knowledge ; consideration ; and lovingness.

156. There are three principal qualities, out of which spring all the other good qualities : mercy, and its characteristic is to give alms, protection, sustenance, and instruction, as occasion is seen ; obedience proceeding from humility, and its characteristic is to receive alms, protection, and advice, with manly decency, and peacefulness ; justice, and its characteristic sign is to do what is right, according to conscience and understanding, in defiance of the man who may oppose him, and to suffer bravely in behalf of what he may judge as right, whatever it may be, and every hardship and oppression soever, which may ensue, even if he had to die for what he did and judged.

157. There are three gifts of charity : food ; protection ; and instruction in the way of advice and demonstration.

158. Three things that will remind man of his duty towards God and man : alms ; fasting ; and prayer.

159. Three things that will effect just godliness : to love God ; love towards all living beings ; and to love all that is gentle and just.

160. The three counsels that Jesus Christ gave to His servants : love thy God above all, and obey Him in all things ; love thy neighbour as thou lovest thyself, and do for him what thou wouldest he should do for thee ; seek praiseworthy sciences, because from them thou wilt rightly

cyfiawn a ddylit ei garu ag ufuddhau ag ymwârhau iddaw ag a ddylit erof ag erddo.

161. Tri $\overset{2}{\text{gwrthrym}}$ pob $\overset{1}{\text{gwybodaeth}}$, a chelfyddyd, a doethineb anymgais, gorymgais, a dallymgais.

162. Tri argae doethineb, gwirionedd, cariad, ag $\overset{\text{bwyll}}{\text{awen}}$.

163. Tripheth a gae yn erbyn doethineb, trachwant, trablys, a thraffull.

164. Tri phrif gyfymdawr byd, Dwyfoldeb, gwybodau moliannus, a diwydrwydd rhag myned yn nifrawd.

165. Tri ynnill a geir yn golled yn y diwedd, ynnill clod am argyweddus o gamp a gweithred, ynnill golud o anghyfiawnder, ag ynnill y goreu mewn drwgymryson.

166. Tri pheth a dry'n ynnill mawr yn y diwedd, colli da 'r byd o roddi cardawd, colli clod a pharch y byd am ddedwydd o gamp a chynneddf, a cholli bywyd dros wir a chyfiawn.

167. Tri ansawdd gwybodaeth gyfiawn, Cariad $\overset{\text{at}}{\text{ar}}$ y goreu yn chwennych ei wybod, chwilio gan farn am y goreu mal y gellir ei wybod ai adnabod. Dewis gan farn ag ym $\overset{1}{\text{bwyll}}$ ar a gaffer yn oreu a $\overset{2}{\text{glynu}}$ wrthaw, sef y tair ansawdd, Cariad, barn, a dewis.

168. Tair ffordd y gwybyddir ewyllys Duw; o lwyr ymroi iddei wyllys ai orchmynion ef; o farnu 'n gyfiawn a llwyr ar a ellir gan Dduw herwydd ei ddwyfolder a hân o Dduw; ag o farnu ar a ddylid gan Dduw herwydd ei gyfiawnder, ai allu, ai gariad, ag *atolwg** am y pethau hynn y deellir ag y gwelir ewyllys Duw.

169. O dripheth y ceir deall adnabodawl ar Dduw ai ewyllys; gwneuthur a wnelai Dduw gan a weddai iddaw parth ei ddwyfolder a'i gynhaniadau anghenbwyll; caru a

---

* Illegible in the MS.

[1] Al. "for him and for me."   [2] Al. "Awen"

[3] Al. "recognised and known."

understand what thou shouldest love, obey, and do homage to, and what thou shouldest do for me and for him.[1]

161. The three counter-forces of all knowledge, art, and wisdom : lack of seeking; excessive seeking; and blind seeking.

162. The three fences of wisdom : truth ; love; and prudence.[2]

163. Three things that will close against wisdom : avarice ; inordinate desire ; and over-hastiness.

164. The three principal concerns of the world : godliness; praiseworthy sciences; and industry, to prevent waste.

165. The three gains that will turn out a loss in the end: to gain fame for an injurious feat or act; to gain wealth by injustice; and to gain the mastery in evil contention.

166. Three things that will turn out a great gain in the end: to lose the world's goods by giving alms; to lose the praise and regard of the world for a blessed act and disposition; and to lose one's life in the cause of truth and justice.

167. The three qualities of just knowledge: love for what is best, desiring to know it; seeking judiciously for what is best, that it might be known and recognised ;[3] and choosing with judgment and prudence what is found to be the best, and cleaving to it. That is, the three qualities are, love, judgment, and choice.

168. In three ways may the will of God be known : in resigning one's self to His will and commandments; in judging rightly and thoroughly what is possible to God, in respect to His godliness, and what is derived from God ; and in judging what is due to God, in respect of His justice, power, and love. By reviewing these things may the will of God be understood and seen.

169. From three things will God and His will be comprehended and known: from doing what God would do, as became Him, in respect of His divinity and necessary attri-

2 s

garai Dduw o'i ddwyfawl gariad perffaith sef nas gall perffaith garu amherffaith, a barnu a farnai Dduw o'i fawr allu,
ai gyfiawnder, ai gariad, ag yn ol a ellir yn hynn o ddarbod-
bwyll, y gwybydder ewyllys a diben Duw, ag yn hynn y
ceir awen o Dduw.

170. Tair hanbwyll darogan am a ddaw, ar moddion y
ceir gwybod a fydd ar ol llaw ar ddyn ag ar wlad a chenedl:
Cyntaf ymufuddhad i Dduw yn ymgais a'r pethau a ddylid,
ail awen o Dduw gan farn y peth a ddylit gan Dduw, can
nas gwna Dduw amgen nag a ddylit gan ei gariad ai gyfiawnder, ai allu, ag o hynny y gwybyddir a ddaw, gan y
daw yn anesgorawl a ddylit gan Dduw herwydd ei ansawdd
ai gynhaniadau.   Ag nis gellir amgen nag a ddylai fod gan
Dduw; ag a ddylai fod nis gellir amgen nag y bydd, herwydd gallu ag iawnder Duw.

TRIOEDD PAWL.

1. Tri phrifwybodau dyn ; gwybodau am Ddyw, gwybod beth yw ef ei hunan, a gwybod syrth Rhyw ac anian ;
ac o'r tri hynn y tardd yn anesgorawl pob gwybodau moliannus eraill.

2. Tri gofynion Dyw gan Ddyn, Ffydd sef hynn Cred
gadarn, ufudd-dawd golychwydol, a gweithredu cyfiawnder
ar feddwl, gair, a gweithred.

3. Tripheth ni ddichonant fod ar Ddyw, yn anfedrus,
yn anghyfiawn, ac yn annhrugarawg.

4. Tri phrif orchwyl Dyw; goleuo 'r Tywyll, corpholi
dim, a bywydu'r marw.

5. Tri gweithredyddion Duw yn gwneuthur y Bydoedd;
Mynn, Doethineb, a chariad, ac or Tri hynn y mae hollallu-
ogrwydd.

butes; from loving what God would love, in virtue of His divine and perfect love, for what is perfect cannot love what is imperfect ; and from judging what God would judge, in virtue of His great power, justice, and love. As far as possible, by means of this wise provision may be known the will and purpose of God ; and hereby will Awen from God be obtained.

170. The three dispositions of the mind, which can prognosticate the future, and the means of knowing what will hereafter happen to man, country, and nation : the first, obedience to God, performing what ought to be; the second, Awen from God, judging what is due from God, for God will not do anything but what ought to be, as required by His love, justice, and power; hence may be known what will take place, for what is due from God will inevitably occur, in virtue of His nature and attributes. And nothing but what God requires should be, can take place ; and what ought to be cannot but be, in respect of the power and justice of God.

THE TRIADS OF ST. PAUL.

1. The three principal sciences of man : sciences respecting God; to know what he is himself; and to know the tendency of species and nature. From these three all other laudable sciences inevitably spring.

2. The three requirements of God from man : faith, that is, firm belief; religious obedience; and the performance of justice, in thought, word, and deed.

3. Three things God cannot be: unskilful; unjust; and unmerciful.

4. The three principal employments of God: to enlighten the darkness; to invest nonentity with a body ; and to animate the dead.

5. The three agents of God in making the worlds : will; wisdom; and love; and from these three comes omnipotence.

6. Tripheth tuhwnt i bob ymchwil gwybodau Dyn; eithafoedd ehangder, dechreu a diwedd amser, a gweithredoedd Dyw.

7. Tri gofynion Duw oddiar law Dyn; gwneuthur cyfiawnder, gyrru dysg a gwybodau daionus ar a fu au diffyg arnaw, a diriaw Trugaredd ar bob peth parth ag at y Byw o bob rhyw a rhith.

8. Tripheth nid hawdd a'u gwelir yn amlwg yn arall o Ddyn; ag am hynny nid hawdd rhyfarnu arnynt; syrth awen, ymgais deall, a Barn cydwybod, lle nad oes namyn Duw au gwyr, ac efe a biau barnu arnynt.

9. Tripheth ni wyr neb y filfed ou hyd au lled au dyfnder; Cyrch awen gyssefin o Dduw, galledigion gwybodau, a chyfeddolion gwirionedd, ac nid oes namyn Duw au gwyr.

10. Tripheth y dylit eu hystyried yn ddifrifawl deirgwaith bob dydd; Deddfau gwirionedd, Deddfau cariad, a Deddfau Dyw.

11. Tripheth nis gellir bod achos eu hofni 'n y byd a ddaw i'r un na wnelo achos eu hofni yn y byd hynn; cyffwrdd ag arall o ddyn o flaen wyneb Dyw, dangos ar weithredoedd a wnaed ger bronn Dyw, a galwad o'r farn fawr lle bo Dyw ei hunan yn Frawdwr.

12. Tri pheth nis gellir y $_{\text{byddant}}^{\text{eu bod}}$ fyth; achos ofn yn y byd a ddaw i'r un na wnelo achos ei ofni yn y byd hynn, Diffyg trugaredd ar ol hynn o fyd i'r un na wnelo amgen na thrugaredd yn hynn o fywyd daiarawl, a diffyg gwybodaeth ar a ddangoses wybodaeth hyd eithafoedd a wyddai i bob perchen enaid gwybodaethgar, ag i bawb ai gofynai, nag a welit ai eisiwed arnaw. E.a.w. — A diffyg gwybodau o ba ryw bynnag y bwynt i'r neb a ddangoses wybodaeth hyd y medrai i'r neb y bai ynniffyg arnaw.

13. Tri goreuon o'r holl bethau a geir yn hynn o fyd,

6. Three things beyond all the research of man's sciences: the extreme limits of space; the beginning and end of time; and the works of God.

7. The three requirements of God at the hands of man: to do justice; to impart learning and good sciences to those who are deficient in them; and to urge upon every thing the duty of mercy towards all living beings of every kind and form.

8. Three things, which it is not easy to see clearly in another man, and therefore it is not easy to prejudge them: the tendency of awen; the endeavour of the intellect; and the judgment of conscience; these God alone knows, and to Him belongs the right of judging them.

9. There are three things, of whose length, breadth, and depth, no one knows the thousandth part: the tendency of Awen from God; the capabilities of knowledge; and the properties of truth; and God only knows them.

10. Three things which ought to be considered seriously three times every day: the laws of truth; the laws of love; and the laws of God.

11. Three things which there can be no reason to fear in the world to come on the part of him who gives no reason to fear them in this world: to meet another man before the face of God; the exhibition of works performed in the presence of God; and a call from the great judgment, where God Himself is judge.

12. Three things which can never be: cause of fear in the world to come for one who gives no cause to fear in this world; lack of mercy after this world for one who shows nothing but mercy in this earthly life; and lack of knowledge for him who, to the utmost of what he knew, has exhibited knowledge to every man, fond of knowledge, and to all who required it, or might be seen in want of it. Others say: and lack of sciences, of whatever kind they may be, for him who has exhibited knowledge, as far as he could, to those who were in want of it.

13. The three best of all things that are found in this

iechyd corphorawl, deall cyfiawnbwyll, a glendid cydwybod.

14.   Tri pheth y dylit eu hystyried yn ddwysbwyll cyn
cymmeryd bwydydd; cyntaf ai prydferth ac iawn $^{fyddai}_{eu}$
gosod yn gyflwyn o flaen Dyw mal pei y cymmerei ef o
henynt rhag cyfiawnder eu caffaeliad.   Ail ai iawn y bydd i
ei Rad arnynt herwydd y dirper ai cymmero.   Trydydd ai
cymmwys y cyfryw i atteb dibennion Duw er lles Dyn, sef
i gynnal einioes ag iechyd ; a lle nas caffer hynn o bethau
ar fwydydd a pharth ag attynt, nid iawn na rhydd o flaen
Dyw eu cymmeryd.

15.   Tripheth y sydd ar drugaredd i'r neb ai gwnelo i
bob perchen bywyd ac enaid ; ni fetha iddaw gyfiawnder ar
a wnelo, bynnag o beth y bo ;—ni ddiffyg iddo fodd ei gydwybod ei hunan, Ag ni phall iddaw eithafoedd Bodd a
Thrugaredd Duw yn dragywydd yn y byd hynn ag yn y
byd a ddaw, canys nid cyfiawnder ond Trugaredd, ag nid
Trugaredd ond na rotho boen i na chorph na meddwl un
peth bynnag o ryw a rhith a gaffer yn berchen bywyd.

16.   Tri pheth y sydd ar Drugaredd parth ei ryw ai ansawdd, Cyntaf yw, Eithafoedd cyfiawnder can ni ddiffyg
cyfiawnder ar a wneler yn drugaredd, a pharth ag at ai
caffo, ac o ba ryw bynnag ar fywydolion y bo.   Ail, yw
cydweithredu a Duw, ys ef o'i anfeidrawl drugaredd y
gwnaeth Duw yr holl fywydoedd ar $^{holl\ Raddau}_{ar\ graddau}$ au holl Fywydolion bynnag o ryw a rhith yi caffer, nag au meddylier,
lle nad oedd arall o ryw ar gyfiawnder ai gofynnasai ar ei
law ef.   Trydydd yw, $^{nis}_{nas}$ gellir amgen parth cyfiawnder na
cheffir a ellir gan Dduw yn drugaredd, ir neb ai gwnelo, ag
yn gydradd gydfesur ag ai gwneler, ys ef y dywedir.

17.   Triphen cyfansawdd y sydd ar gyfiawnder ; eitha

---

[1] Al. " and the orders."

world : bodily health; just and discreet understanding; and purity of conscience.

14. Three things that ought to be considered seriously before we partake of our meals : first, would it be comely and right to present them before God, as if He would partake of them, because of the just way in which they have been obtained ; secondly, could His grace be fitly bestowed upon them, according to the desert of those who partake of them ; thirdly, are such meet to answer the purposes of God for the benefit of man, that is, to support life and health. Where these particulars do not apply to meals, and what relates to them, it is not right and lawful before God to partake of them.

15. There are three things connected with mercy, that will occur to him who shows it towards every owner of life and soul : he will not fail to have justice in every thing, which he does, whatever it may be ; he will not lack the approval of his own conscience ; and he will not fail to have the utmost of God's good will and mercy for ever, both in this world, and in the world to come. Because, there is no justice but mercy, and there is no mercy but what does not give pain to either the body or mind of any species or form whatsoever, which may be found to possess life.

16. There are three things in mercy, in virtue of its kind and quality : the first is the utmost of justice, for justice will not fail the act of mercy, nor him who obtains it, whatever species of living beings he may be ; the second is co-operation with God, for it was of His infinite mercy that God made all vitalities, and all the orders,[1] and all their animations, of whatever kind or form they actually exist, or may be conceived, since there was no other species which justice could require at His hands ; the third is the impossibility, according to justice, of not obtaining all that can be had from God as mercy, by him who performs it, co-equally and commensurately with the performance itself. And thus is it said :—

17. The three principal compounds of justice : utmost

cariad a thrugaredd achos nis gellir anghariad parth Dyw
ag a wnelo ef o gyfiawnder at na rhyw na rhith nas cawsant
fodoldeb namyn o Dduw ai weithredoldeb, lle nad oes ynddynt a ellesid yn anfoddhad gan Ddyw — ag nid cyfiawn
amgen na chariad parth ag at nas gwnaethant yn anfodd.
Ail yw Eitha gwirionedd a chywirdeb rhyw rhith ag ymsawdd, can nas dylit amgen na gwir a chywir, ac iawnder
cyfymsawdd a chelfyddoldeb ar a wneler gan a fettro 'r
goreu ar bob gwneuthur, ag nis gellir llai ar Ddyw na
medru ar y goreu ymhob rhyw a rhith ac ymsawdd.   Trydydd yw Eithafoedd Harddwch neu Brydferthwch ar a
wneler, achaws nid iawn na gweddiedig amgen na'r harddaf
o bob hardd, a'r prydferthaf ar brydferthwch ar a wneler lle
ai dichoner, ag y bo galledig ; a llwyr alltedig i Dduw pob
goreuder a phob lawnder, a phob celfyddoldeb, a phob pryd-
ferthwch, a phob rhagorgamp a rhagorbwyll a dichoner ar a
fynno ef o bethau bodolion, ac ar a wnelo, Cans er gwell ag
nid er gwaeth y gwna Duw a wnelo, a Diarheb yw fal hynn,
Er gwell ag nid er gwaeth y gwna Duw a wnelo—hefyd, er
y goreu ag nid er y gwaethaf y gwna Dyw a wnelo, a gwir
Diarhebion hynn.   Achaws dangosedig nid iawn na barnu
na meddwl, na chredu, na thybied amgen na'r goreuon ar
bob gwaith Duw.

18.   Tripheth a geir o iawn ymddwyn gan syberwyd ac
ymfucheddu 'n lan, Parch y byd, Llawenydd Cydwybod, a
Bodd Duw.

19.   Tripheth a geffir o iawn adnabod Dyw sef ei ddirnad gan wir wybodaeth rhywiau ag ansoddau ; pob gwirionedd bod a hanfod, pob hardd a chyfiawn, a phob gwynfyd
tragywyddawl, sef o gael Dyw ai ddaioni ar wybodaeth y
ceffir gwybodaeth ar bob peth galledig i ddyn ai ddeall ai

love and mercy, because there can be no want of love on the part of God, and His works of justice, towards any species or form, which have received their existence from God and His operation only, there not being in them anything that could possibly be displeasing to God, and there is no justice but love towards those who have done no displeasure; the second is, the utmost truth and sincerity of species, form, and condition, because there ought to be but truth, sincerity, and rectitude of condition and skill in what is done by one who can perform the best of all acts, and God can do no less than perform what is best in every species, form, and condition; the third is the utmost beauty or fairness in what is done, because that is not right and becoming which is not the most beautiful act of all the beautiful, and the fairest of the fair, where it is accomplished, and where it is possible; but perfectly possible to God are every excellency, every fulness, every skill, every beauty, every surpassing feat, and every surpassing prudence, and whatever of existences and acts He pleases will be effectuated, because God does what He does for better, and not for worse; hence the proverb, " For better, and not for worse, God does what He does;" also, " For the best, and not for the worst, God does what He does." And these proverbs are true ; because it is demonstrated that it is not right to judge, or think, or believe, or suppose, that all the works of God are other than the best.

18. Three things will be obtained from behaving properly, according to courtesy, and leading a holy life : the regard of the world; joy of conscience; and the good will of God.

19. Three things will be obtained from a proper recognition of God, that is, from a discernment of Him by means of a true knowledge of kinds and qualities : every truth of being and existence ; every beauty and justice ; and every eternal gwynvyd; that is to say, from having the knowledge of God and His goodness, will be obtained the knowledge of every thing possible to man, his understanding and reason,

2 T

bwyll ag i bob awen a serch ar hardd a chyfiawn dichoniadol iddaw ef.

20. Tripheth ar ddyn a gaeant ar bob daioni arall, Gwroldeb, Tangnefedd, a Dwyfoldeb.

21. Tripheth ar ddyn a gaeant yn erbyn pob daioni ba bynnag o ryw, llyfrder, neu ofnoccrwydd—cynhenusder, ac annwyfoldeb oddirieidi anianawl.

22. Tri pheth ni ddarfyddant fyth : Bywyd, Deall, a Goleuni; eithr ar eu gwell ag ar fwyfwy ydd ant hyd fyth fythoedd.

23. Tri gwrthymddwyn a Dyw y sydd ; Gwrthymdwng a gwirionedd, gwrthymdyb a phwyll anianawl, a gwrthym-red ac awen gynhenid. E.a.w. a gwrthymdawr ac Awen gynhenid.

24. Tri chyflawnder Duw; cyflawnder Bywyd, cyflawn-der gwybodaeth, a chyflawnder nerth a gallu; ac o'r Tri chyflawnder hynn y daw cyflawnder pob daioni ymhob rhyw a rhann a rhith, a deall a ddichonawr arnaw.

25. Tripheth y sydd ar Dduw o lwyr angheneddyl ; Llygad yn gweled ym mhob man ag ymhob amser, clust yn clywed ym mhob man ac amser, a chof yn cadw pob peth a phob hân ar weithred gair a meddwl ymhob man ac amser, er eu dangos yng ngwydd Engylion nef a'r holl saint ger bronn barn dydd brawd, mal ai taler i bob dyn ei weithred, ai ymarwedd, ai yn y nef ai yn uffern y dylit hynny.

26. Tripheth ar ddyn y sydd gasaf o bob peth gan Dduw; Dichellgarwch, Cybyddiaeth, ag ymgadarnhau yn erbyn gwybodau molianus. E.A.W. ymddichellu, ymgyb-yddu, ac ymgarnhau yn erbyn gwybodau daionus.

27. Tripheth goreu gan Dduw ar bob dyn ; ymgydwy-bodi 'n haelionus, ymddwyn yn wirioneddgar amlwg, ag ymawenu gwybodau molianus.

28. Tri pheth anweledig ir craffaf ei Lygad; Llwybr

---

¹ Al. "good."

and to every awen, affection, beauty, and justice, of which he is capable.

20. Three things in man that will include every other goodness : bravery ; peace ; and godliness.

21. Three things in man that will exclude every goodness, of whatever kind it may be : cowardice, or timidity ; contentiousness ; and ungodliness arising from natural mischievousness.

22. Three things that will never end : life ; intellect ; and light ; but they will improve and increase for ever and ever.

23. There are three demeanours contrary to God : an oath contrary to truth ; a sentiment contrary to natural prudence ; and course of life contrary to innate awen. Others say ; and concern of life contrary to innate awen.

24. The three fulnesses of God : fulness of life ; fulness of knowledge ; and fulness of might and power ; and from these three fulnesses comes the fulness of every goodness, in every kind, part, form, and comprehension possible to it.

25. There are three things in God of pure necessity : an eye which sees in every place, and at every time ; an ear which hears in every place and time ; and memory, which preserves every thing, and every event, in deed, word, and thought, in every place and time, in order to exhibit them in the presence of the angels of heaven, and all the saints, before the judgment of the day of doom, that every man may be paid for his deed and conduct, whether that shall be in heaven or in hell.

26. There are three things in man, that are the most odious of all to God : craftiness ; avarice ; and becoming hardened against praiseworthy[1] sciences.

27. Three things that God regards as the best in every man : to be liberally conscientious ; to demean one's self with a clear regard to truth ; and to genialize prsiseworthy sciences.

28. Three things invisible to him who is keenest of eye:

saeth drwy'r awyr, Llwybr pysg yn y mor, a Llwybr Dichell drwy 'r Byd.

29. Tripheth dwyfawl ar ddyn ; wyneb hawddgar sir-
iolfwyn, ymddwyn gwar syberiaith, a boddlondeb meddwl.
E.a.w. wyneb hawddgar, ymddwyn gwâr, a Boddlondeb i
bob gwyllys Duw.

30. Tripheth cythreulig ar ddyn ; golwg $_{g}^{c}$aled, yspryd
balch, a thrachwant diwala.

31. Tri dyn anhawdd eu dwyfoli; ymladdgar ; glodd-
estgar, a godinebgar.

32. Tri goreuon byd a bywyd ; cydwybod lân, gwybod
gwirionedd, ac iechyd corph a meddwl.

33. Tri pheth nis gall wyneb eu celu ; Balchder, Llid,
a Thraserch.

34. Tri pheth hawdd eu gweled yn wyneb a maccont;
Galar, Llawenydd, a Thangnef meddwl.

35. Tri anferthwch Byd; llawenydd annoethion, haelioni cybyddion, a syberwyd annwyfolion.

36. Tri rhagflaenyddion dirieidi ; anymgais a gwybodau
gwirionedd, anymarbod a defodau syberwyd, ac anymged a
Duw.

37. Am dripheth nag ymfalchïed $^{undyn}_{dyn}$; ei wybodau, ei
ddwyfoldeb, ag a wnelo 'n ddaioni ; canys ni wybydd, ag ni
wna ef tra fo byw hanner a ddylai o'r naill na'r llall o henynt, a gwnaed a allo.

38. Tripheth y dylai bob dyn gochelyd eu gwneuthur ;
peri colled bydawl i nebun o ddyn yn y byd, peri poen corph
neu feddwl i nebun o ddyn neu nebpeth arall o fyw a pher-
chen enaid, a pheri gwaethygiad ar unrhyw beth ba bynnag,
ai moes ai defawd, ai dysg ai celfyddyd ai gwybodau doethineb a bucheddoldeb, neu beth arall bynnacryw y bo, canys

---

[1] Al. "a man should not."

the path of an arrow through the air ; the path of fish in the sea ; and the path of wile through the world.

29. Three things divine in a man : an amiable and cheerful countenance ; a meek and courteous demeanour; and contentment of mind. Others say : an amiable countenance ; gentle demeanour; and contentment with every will of God.

30. Three things devilish in a man : a harsh countenance ; a proud spirit; and insatiable covetousness.

31. Three men it is difficult to make godly : the pugnacious; the reveller ; and the adulterer.

32. The three superiors of the world and life : a pure conscience ; knowledge of the truth ; and health of body and mind.

33. Three things which the countenance cannot conceal: pride; anger ; and amorousness.

34. Three things easy to be seen in the countenance of those who bear them : sorrow ; joy ; and peace of mind.

35. The three monstrosities of the world : the joy of fools ; the generosity of misers; and the courtesy of ungodly men.

36. The three forerunners of mischief : not to seek the sciences of truth ; not to anticipate the usages of courtesy ; and not to make an oblation to God.

37. Because of three things no man should[1] become proud : his sciences ; his godliness ; and the good he does ; for he will not know or do, as long as he lives, half of the one or the other of them, though he should do as much as he can.

38. Three things which every man should avoid doing : to cause worldly loss to any man whatsoever ; to cause bodily or mental pain to any man, or to any other living or animated thing ; and to cause deterioration to any thing whatsoever, whether it be conduct, usage, learning, art, the sciences of wisdom, and morality, or any other thing, of whatsoever kind it may be ; because the evil that he does

y drwg a wnelo a ddigwydd iddo y naill yn y byd a'r bywyd hwn neu yn yr un a ddel yn y byd nesaf.

39. Tri Dyn a fyddant gas gan Dduw, a wnelo gas a chynnen ym mhlith ei gymmodogion, a gudd y gwirionedd er drwg i arall, ag a wasdadla yn erbyn cyfiawnder. E.a.w. ag a wnelo yn erbyn cyfiawnder.

40. Tri anhepcor daioni; Cyfiawnder, Harddwch, a chariad.

41. Tri anhepcor Dwyfoldeb, cariad, gwirionedd, ac ymbwyll. E.a.w. ystyrbwyll.

42. Tripheth a gynnyddant Ddwyfoldeb; Gwybodau, Elusenau, a Golychwyd.

43. Tri enaid golychwyd, gwirionedd, daionusder, a phrydferthwch.

44. Tri chysswyn Golychwyd; Gweddi, Diolch, a mawl.

45. Tri gofynion Duw ar law dyn; ymgred, ufudd-dawd, a golychwyd.

46. Tri achos Golychwyd; addysg doethineb, diwylliaw ynnïau meddwl, a llawenhau gobaith.

47. Tripheth nis gall namyn Duw eu gwneuthur; peth na fu mewn bod erioed o'r blaen, gwybod oll a ddaw, a barnu ar gydwybod. E.a.w. Tripheth nis gall namyn Duw; gwneuthur na fu o'r blaen, gwybod a ddaw, a barnu ar gyd-wybod,

48. Tri yspryd o Dduw a ddylai fod mewn dyn cyn y bo dedwydd; pwyll i ddeall ag ymwybod a phob iawn, awen i garu ag ymryniaw a phob iawn; ag amynedd gwr-olbwyll i ymgymmhleidiaw yn gadarn a phob iawn, ag yn erbyn pob aniawn, ag i oddef lle bo achos yn gofyn dros a ddylai fod, bynnacryw o beth y bo hynny.

49. Tri cholled a bair ynnill yn y diwedd i ddyn; colli a fo mwy na rhaid a gofynion bywyd, colli iechyd corph i

will fall upon him either in this world and life, or in that which is to come in the next world.

39. Three men that will be odious to God: he who causes hatred and contentiousness among his neighbours; he who conceals the truth to the injury of another; and he who servilely disputes against justice. Others say; he who does against justice.

40. The three indispensables of goodness: justice; beauty; and truth.

41. The three indispensables of godliness: love; truth; and prudence. Others say; consideration.

42. Three things that will augment godliness: sciences; alms; and worship.

43. The three souls of worship: truth; goodness; and beauty.

44. The three mutual charms of worship: prayer; thanksgiving; and praise.

45. The three requirements of God at the hands of man: belief; obedience; and worship.

46. The three reasons for worship: to teach wisdom; to cultivate the energies of the mind; and to gladden hope.

47. Three things which God only can perform: what has never been in existence before; to know all that will happen; and to judge the conscience. Others say: Three things which are possible only to God: to perform what did not exist before; to know what will happen; and to judge the conscience.

48. There are three spirits from God, which ought to be in man before he can be happy: reason to understand and to know all rectitude; awen to love and to study all rectitude; and courageous patience to side firmly with all rectitude, and against all wrong, and to suffer, where occasion requires, for what ought to be, of whatever kind it may be.

49. The three losses that will bring gain in the end to man: to lose more than what life needs and requires; to

wr rhodresgamp, a cholli a fo penn iddaw ymmhob ag ar bob
peth, canys yn hwnnw y bydd mwyaf ei bechodoldeb ef.

50.   Tri gwaranred gwybodaeth ar Dduw; ymbellhau
oddiwrth pob drwg, ymneshau at pob daioni, ag ymfoddloni
yn amyneddgar ymhob peth o'r byd a fytho ac ymhob digwydd a dichwain bywyd.

51.   Tri gwaranred gwirionedd ; llesoldeb ym mhob
peth ; hardd ar bob peth, a chadarn rhag ac yn erbyn pob
peth.

52.   Tair colofn Dwyfoldeb, gwir, hardd, a daionus.

53.   Am dri achos dwyfawl y dylit gadw gwylau 'r Nadolic ; cyntaf er cof cael geni Iesu Grist yn Iachawdr y Byd
dynionawl, Ail, er rhoddi Elusen i Dduw a Thlawd anghenus o'r holl feddiant, sef rhodd i dlawd rhodd i Dduw.
Trydydd er llawenydd dwyfawl caffael rhad Duw ai fen-
dithion i ddynion, ac i'r neb na ddug ar ei gof Iesu Grist ai
Efengyl, ac na rotho Elusen, ag nas cymmer ei eiddaw er
llawenydd dwyfawl golychwydawl, ni leshâ iddaw ei gadw
ar wyl y Nadolic.

54.   Tripheth y dylai ddyn ymgadw rhagddynt faׁ rhag
syrth tan ar ei galon ; balchder, creulonder, a thrachwant,
sef lle bythont y syrth a font arno i bob annwyfoldeb, a
*anolwch,** a phob dirieidi.

55.   Tri pheth gorddyfnaid pob diriaid, Celwydd, Twyll,
ag anrhaith.

56.   Tri gorddyfned annwyfawl, balchder, Cribddail, a
chreulonder.

57.   Tri gorddwfn dirieidi, brad, murn, a lledrad.

58.   Tri gorddyned dedwyddyd ; caru hedd a thangnef,
caru gwir a chyfiawn, a charu Duw a phob daioni.

* Illegible in the MS.

lose bodily health on the part of a vain-glorious man; and
to lose what one considers as his chief in and over every
thing, for it is in this that most of his sinfulness consists.

50. The three different sciences concerning God: to
remove far off from all evil; to approach all goodness;
and to acquiesce patiently in every thing whatsoever, and
in every incident and event of life.

51. The three distinctions of truth: utility in every
thing; beauty in every thing; and strength to obviate and
to oppose every thing.

52. The three columns of godliness: truth; beauty;
and goodness.

53. For three godly reasons ought the Christmas Holidays to be kept: in remembrance of the birth of Jesus
Christ as the Saviour of the human world; secondly, in
order to give alms to God and the necessitous poor out of
all our possessions, for a gift to the poor is a gift to God;
thirdly, in godly joyfulness that the grace and blessings of
God have been obtained for men. He who does not call
Jesus Christ and His Gospel to memory, and gives no alms,
and does not enjoy his property in godly and religious glad-
ness, will receive no benefit from keeping it on the Feast of
Christmas.

54. Three things which a man ought to avoid, as he
would the fall of fire on his heart: pride; cruelty; and
covetousness; for where they are, all his doings will degenerate into ungodliness, irreligion, and all mischievousness.

55. Three things familiar to every mischievous person:
falsehood; deceit; and depredation.

56. The three familiar things of the ungodly: pride;
extortion; and cruelty.

57. The three customs of mischief: treachery; murder;
and theft.

58. The three familiarities of happiness: to love peace
and tranquillity; to love truth and justice; and to love God
and all goodness.

TRIOEDD PAWL, A BARDDAS.

1. Tripheth ni fydd dyn fyth eu digon — digon doeth — digon mwyn, a digon didrachwant.

2. Tair deddf gweithredoedd dyn, rhaid a gorfod gan nas galler gwell — Dewis o ystyriaw a fo goreu, y gellir a fynner, a barn wrth a ellir hyd fyth ynghylch y gwynfyd, yn gyfun a phob cariad a daioni.

3. Tripheth y sydd ac nis gellir man a lle nad ydynt, Duw, gwirionedd, a Chylch y gwynfyd, a gwybod hynn yw ymgyfunaw a hwynt, ac a ryddha o'r abred.

4. Tripheth nis gellir gwybod ei maint, Cylch y Ceugant, hyd tragywyddoldeb, a chariad Duw.

5. Tripheth y sydd o Dduw, heddwch, gwirionedd, a gwybodaeth, ac o'u gwybod, dyled ar bawb gyrru hynny ar eraill.

6. Tripheth y sydd o gythraul, anghydfod, celwydd, ac anwybodaeth.

7. Tri chyfeillion goreu enaid dyn a'r unig rai nas gadawant ef, Cyfiawnder, trugaredd, ac ufudd-dawd.

8. Tri pheth nis gellir meidrol arnynt, Duw, amser, ac ehangder.

9. Tripheth y sydd a llawer o wahaniaeth rhyngddynt, rhwng y peth a ganmolir ar peth a faddeuir, a rhwng a faddeuir ac a ddioddefir, a rhwng a ddioddefir ac a'r hynn nis cospir.

10. Tri phrif enyfed Dyn, awen, serch, a Deall, ac o'r tri hynn y dylai bob daioni.

11. Tri rhyw envil y sydd, Dyfrawl — daiarawl, ac wybrenawl.

12. Cyfymgyd a thripheth y dylai fod pob peth a wnelo

THE TRIADS OF ST. PAUL AND BARDISM.

1. Three things that man will never be sufficiently: sufficiently wise; sufficiently kind; and sufficiently uncovetous.

2. The three laws of man's actions: necessity and obligation, since better cannot be; choice of the one you please of what is possible, after considering which is best; and judgment, according to what is possible, for ever in the circle of Gwynvyd, united with all love and goodness.

3. There are three things, and no spot or place can be found where they are not: God; truth; and the circle of Gwynvyd; and to know this is to be united with them, and the same will deliver from Abred.

4. Three things, the magnitude of which cannot be known: the circle of Ceugant; the length of eternity; and the love of God.

5. There are three things from God: peace; truth; and knowledge; and, knowing them, it is the duty of all to communicate them to others.

6. There are three things from Cythraul: disagreement; falsehood; and ignorance.

7. The three best friends of the soul of man, and the only ones that will not forsake him: justice; mercy; and obedience.

8. Three things which cannot become finite: God; time; and space.

9. Three things, between which there is a great difference: between the thing praised and the thing forgiven; between what is forgiven and what is suffered; and between what is suffered and what is not punished.

10. The three principal vigours of man: awen; affection; and intellect; and from these three ought every goodness to proceed.

11. There are are three kinds of animal: aqueous; terrestrial; and aerial.

12. Every thing that a man does or seeks ought to be

ac a geisio dyn — sef a gorchymyn Duw a chydwybod,—ac
o'r goreuon a ellir gan feddwl a deall dyn—ac ar peth a ellir
ei gydfod tros fyth ynghylch y gwynfyd.

13. Tri phrifddibennion pob peth gan Dduw, y mwyaf
ei achos—y mwyaf ei les—a'r mwyaf a ddichon cariad Duw.

14. Tri nod angheneddyl gwirionedd, ac wrthynt ei adnabod—gwell na dim arall a ellir ei ddirnad ai ddeall at yr
un achos—Haws na dim a ellir ei ddeall ai ddirnad at yr
un diben—a harddach na dim a ellir ei ddeall ai fodoli er yr
un lle, ac achos, ac amser.

15. Tair prif elfydden y sydd Daiar, Dwr, a Goleuni,
sef or ddaiar pob corpholaeth cadarn, ac o'r dwr pob ymmod,
ac o'r Goleuni sef y tan, pob bywydoldeb.

16. Tri chymmhrydoldeb Barddas Beirdd Ynys Prydain, Heddwch, cariad — a Gwirionedd, ac o'r tri hynn cyfiawnder.

17. Tripheth a wnant ddeall a gwybodaeth — Heddwch
tuag at bob peth—cariad tuag at pob daionus—ac ystyriaw
pob ansawdd ai corphorawl ai ysprydawl y bo.

18. Tri chynnefnyddion pob peth, Tan sef goleuni—
Dwr—a daiar—sef cyntaf o bob defnydd y bu Tan a mymrynau goleuni, ail dwr ac yn hynny gwahanu pethau, trydydd daiar ac yn hynny corpholi pob peth, a phob amgen
cymmysg, a'r tri chynelfyddion y gelwir y rhai hynn.
E.A.W. Tri chynelfyddion y sydd, Dwr y dechreu, gwedi
hynny y mae daear, a diweddu yn y tan, ac yna anarfod.

19. Tripheth nis gellir ar Dduw, meddwl drwg — di-

in unison with three things : with the commandment of God and conscience ; with the best that can be conceived and comprehended by man ; and with what can co-exist with it for ever in the circle of Gwynvyd.

13. The three principal objects of every thing in the hands of God : that it should be the greatest in point of necessity ; the greatest in point of utility ; and the greatest that the love of God can accomplish.

14. The three necessary characteristics of truth, by which it may be known : that it is better than any thing else which may be discerned and comprehended for the same purpose ; that it is easier than any thing which may be comprehended and discerned for the same object ; and that it is more beautiful than any thing which may be comprehended and realized for the same place, purpose, and time.

15. There are three principal elements : earth ; water ; and light ; that is to say, every fundamental corporeity is from the earth ; every motion is from the water ; and every vitality is from the light or fire.

16. The three contemporaries of the Bardism of the Bards of the Isle of Britain : peace ; love ; and truth ; and from these three comes justice.

17. Three things that will produce understanding and knowledge : peace towards every thing ; love towards all that is good ; and to consider every nature, whether it be corporal or spiritual.

18. The three primary materials of every thing : fire, that is, light ; water ; and earth. That is to say, the first of every material was fire, and the particles of light ; the second was water, whereby things were discriminated ; the third was earth, by which all things were corporalized—all things else were mixed—and these were called the three primary elements. Others say : There are three primary elements : water, which was the beginning ; after that, earth ; and it ended with fire ; and hence ensued imperishableness.

19. Three things, of which God is not capable : thinking

feddwl y goreu — a gwrthfeddwl a feddylwys, can ni feddwl ef namyn a fo goreu, ac nis gellir o Dduw a fo yng ngwrth y goreu.

20.   Tair gradd bywydolion, Duw yn y Ceugant ac nid yno onid ef yn unig, ysprydolion yn y Gwynfyd sef y nefoedd, a chorporolion yn yr Abred, sef yn nwr a daiar.

21.   Tri phrawf ar bob peth y sydd ac hebddynt nis gellir dewis arnynt, prawf dioddef cyn gwybod, prawf ystyr cyn deall, a phrawf deall cyn dewis.

22.   Tri chyflwr y sydd ar ansawdd bodol a bywydol, gwneuthurawl fal y mae duw ai alluoedd — gwneuthuredig fal y mae bywydolion meidrol a bodolion cymmysg — a'r diwneuthur sef nas gwnaed ac nas gwna, fal y mae eangder, ac amser noeth, a marwoldeb, a thywyllwch.   E.A.W.

nas gwnaed—sef Duw,

a wnaed ac a wna, sef byw ac ymmod.

ni wnaed ac ni wna, sef y marw diymmod.

23.   Tri chyfun sy'n cynnal pob peth, cyfun cariad a chyfiawnder — cyfun gwir a $^{\text{dychymyg}}_{\text{chrebwyll}}$—a chyfun Duw a Digwydd.

24.   Tri pheth y sydd ac fal y mae 'r ddau cyntaf y bydd y trydydd, Dwr yn rhedeg i'r mor o'r lle daeth, llinyn cylch yn diweddu lle bu 'r dechreu, ac enaid bywydawl yn adweddu yn Nuw o be le y tarddwys, a gwedi hynny yr un dreigl drachefn.

25.   Tripheth a fyddant un fal y $^{\text{llall}}_{\text{llaill}}$, ansawdd $^{\text{peiriant}}_{\text{peiriad}}$ yn a bernir,* fal y bydd ansawdd tan yn a wresoccer, — ansawdd ymmod yn a fudir, ac felly y bydd ansawdd Duw ai

---

* This is probably a mistake for " berir."

[1] Some persons profess to discover indications of the doctrine of Abred, or the metempsychosis, in the Holy Scriptures.   Thus, they say that the passage in Job, (ch. xxxiii. 29, 30,) " Lo, all these things worketh God *often times* with man, to bring back his soul from the pit, to be enlightened with the light of the living," ought, according to the Hebrew, to be rendered,—" Lo, all these things worketh God with man, AND THRICE to bring back his soul from the pit, to be enlightened with the light of the living."   Again, they say that the Jews, when in reference to the man that was blind from his birth, asked our Saviour, " Who

evil; not thinking the best; and thinking counter to what He has thought; because He does not think but what is best, and it is impossible that God should oppose the best.

20. There are three grades of animations : God in Ceugant, where there is nothing but Himself; spiritualities in Gwynvyd, that is, heaven; and corporalities in Abred,[1] that is, in water and earth.

21. There are three proofs in respect of all things, without which they cannot be chosen : the proof of suffering before knowing; the proof of consideration before understanding; and the proof of understanding before choosing.

22. There are three conditions to which the nature of existence and animation is subject : efficient, as is the case with God and His powers; effected, as is the case with finite vitalities and mixed beings; and non-effective, that is, what was not made, and will not make, as, space, absolute time, mortality, and darkness. Others say : What has not been made, that is, God; what has been made, and will make, that is, the living and motion; what has not been made, and will not make, that is, the motionless dead.

23. There are three coincidences that support all things: coincidence of love and justice; coincidence of truth and conception;[2] and coincidence of God and accident.

24. There are three things, and as the two former are, so will be the third : water flowing into the sea whence it came; the line of a circle ending where it began; and the soul of a living being returning to God whence it emanated; —after that, the same migration as before.

25. There are three things, of which one will be like another : the nature of agency in what is acted upon, as the nature of fire in what is heated; the nature of motion in what is moved; and so will be the nature of God, Who

---

did sin, this man, or his parents, that he was born blind ?" (St. John ix. 2,) must clearly have held a belief in a pre-existent state.

[2] Al. "imagination."

gwnaeth yn enaid a bywydoldeb dyn. Ac fel y bydd oeri
lle y diffoder tan, a sawedigaeth lle gwrthladder ymmod,
felly angeu lle nas bydd a fo o Dduw. (Pawl).

26. Tri chadernyd unoldeb sef yw cyntaf—cydoldeb can
nis gellir deuryw ar un cyfoll — anfeidroldeb, can nis gellir
terfyn ar un Cyfan (cydfan) ac nis gellir cyfan ond a fo
cyfoll neu a fo ollfodedig (ollfodawl) cans nid un cyfan na
fo 'n ollgynnwysawl $\genfrac{}{}{0pt}{}{\text{(ollendidawl)}}{\text{(ollhanfodawl)}}$— anghyfnewidioldeb, can nis
gellir y bydd un cynghyd, cyfoll, cyfan, ac ollendidawl yn
amgen nac y bo, ac am hynny nis gellir Duw onid o un cadarn, cyfoll.

27. Tripheth ar Dduw nis gellir ar neb arall, ollwybydd-
iaeth — ollalluaeth, ac ollfodoliaeth. E.A.W. Ollwybodol-
deb—ollalluoldeb—ac ollfodoldeb.

28. Tair rhodd elusen y sydd bennaf o bob elusenau,
rhoddi gossymaith, rhoddi nawdd, a rhoddi addysg a chyngor i ddyn nas gwyppo a fo er lles iddaw. (al. ymborth,
nawdd, a chyngor.)

29. O dri bendith y ceir Bendith Duw, Bendith Tad a
Mam, Bendith Estron adfydig, a Bendith claf a chlwyfus.

30. Tair Cyfarchen y sydd o brif orfod, Daiar, Gwyar,
ag Ufeliar (al Cywarchen)

31. Tri anfeidrolion, Eangder, Tragwyddoldeb, a Duw.

32. Tri chyfrediad a'r tri anfeidrolion, Daioni, Galluol-
deb, a Chariad.

33. Tri gwrthrediad a'r tri anfeidrolion, Drygioni, an-
alluoldeb, a gwrthgarwch.

TRIOEDD BARDDAS A DEFODAU.

1. Tair sail Barddas, Heddwch, Lles, a Chyfiawnder.
E.a.w. Heddwch, cariad a chyfiawnder.

---

[1] "Al. "all-existent."

[2] There is a set of thirteen Triads, entitled "Paul's Triads," printed in E.
Williams's Lyric Poems, vol. ii; but as they seem to be other versions only of
some of those Triads which we have already inserted, it has not been deemed
advisable to transfer them into our pages.

made them, in the soul and life of man. And as is coldness where fire is quenched, and stationariness, where motion is resisted, so will be death, where there is no God. (Paul.)

26. The three stabilities of oneness, that is to say : the first is universality, for there can be no two kinds of one universality; infinity, for there can be no limits to one whole, nor can any thing be whole, which is not universal or omnipresent, for that is not one whole which is not all-comprehensive ;[1] immutability, for it is impossible that there should be one conjunctive, universal, entire, and all-existent, otherwise than they are; therefore, there can be no God but from fundamental and universal oneness.

27. Three things peculiar to God cannot belong to any other : omniscience ; omnipotence ; and omnipresence.

28. There are three almsgivings, which are the principal of all alms : the giving of provisions ; the giving of protection ; and the giving of instruction and advice to a man who knows not what is useful for him. Al. food; protection ; and advice.

29. From three blessings will the blessing of God be obtained : the blessing of father and mother ; the blessing of a distressed stranger ; and the blessing of the sick and wounded.

30. There are three elements of primary necessity : earth ; fluid ; and fire.

31. The three infinitudes : space ; eternity ; and God.

32. Three things that concur with the three infinitudes : goodness ; power ; and love.

33. Three things that run contrary to the three infinitudes : wickedness ; inability ; and uncharitableness.[2]

TRIADS OF BARDISM AND USAGES.[3]

1. The three foundations of Bardism : peace ; utility ; and justice. Others say : peace ; love ; and justice.

---

[3] Copied by Iolo Morganwg, Oct. 1797.

2. Tri chynnal Barddoniaeth a Barddas, sef ydynt
Braint wrth Ddefod, sef na bo onid a fai defodawl, a Defod wrth fraint, gan nas dylid Defod heb ei breiniaw, na
defod heb fraint iddi, a Braint a defod wrth bwyll ac ansawdd a gorfod, sef na bo onid a fo felly, a hynny ar y tair
sail sef *Gwir. Cariad,* a *chyfiawnder.* E.a.w. *gwir heddwch,*
a *lles cyfiawn.*

3. Tair ansawdd ddamwain a ddigwyddant ar gerdd a
Barddoniaeth, Llygru, gwellhad, ac ᵃᵈᶠᵉʳ effro, o lwgr a choll, ac
ymhob un o'r tair damwain ei rhoddi rhag annefawd wrth
Raith Gwlad a barn Gorsedd. sef pan ai llygrer ei rhoddi
felly er ei gwellhâu, a phan ai coller, sef ei myned yn ghwsg
ei rhoddi felly fel ai deffroër ac ai hadferer, ac ai dyccer ar
gof herwydd y by gynt. Ac yna myned herwydd y tri
chynal, sef Defod wrth fraint, a braint wrth Ddefawd, sef
na wneler ym mraint onid a fo defodawl, nac yn nefawd
onid a fo gan fraint, ac na bo na braint na defawd onid a fo
gan bwyll ac ansawdd a gorfod, wrth *wir* ac wrth *heddwch* a
chariad, ac wrth *les o gyfiawnder.*

4. Tri phrif gynneddfau bywydoldeb, meddwl, gallu, a
gwyllys, ac nis gellir cwbl a chyfan arnynt onid yn Nuw.

5. Tair rhagoriaeth Barddas hoffeiddiaw myfyrdawd,
helaethu addysg, a gwerinaw moes a defod.

6. O dri pheth y cair cred ar wir, o gredu pob peth, o
anghredu pob peth, ac o gredu ni waeth beth.

Tair cynneddf ddwyfol ar ddyn ystyriaw, caru, a dioddef. (Pawl.)

7. O dri achos y dylai ddyn anturiaw bywyd ai golli os

---

[1] Al. " resuscitation."

2. The three supports of poetry and Bardism, that is to say : privilege in right of usage, for there ought to be nothing that is not according to usage ; usage in right of privilege, for there ought to be no usage that is not privileged, nor any usage without privilege ; and privilege and usage according to reason, nature, and obligation, for there ought to be nothing that is not so — the same resting on the three foundations, namely : truth ; love ; and justice. Others say : truth ; peace ; and just utility.

3. Three incidental conditions happen to song and poetry : corruption ; improvement ; and restoration [1] from corruption and loss. And under each of the three contingencies, in order to obviate non usage, they ought to be submitted to the verdict of country, and the judgment of Gorsedd. That is to say, when they are corrupted, they ought to be submitted so, that they may be improved ; and when they are lost, or when they become dormant, they ought to be submitted so, that they may be resuscitated, restored, and brought to memory, as they were formerly. Then they ought to conform to the three supports, namely : usage in right of privilege ; and privilege in right of usage ; that is to say, nothing should be done, in right of any thing, except what is customary, nor as usage, except what is according to reason, nature, and obligation, with a view to truth, peace, love, and just utility.

4. The three principal qualities of vitality : thought ; power ; and will ; and they cannot be complete and entire except in God.

5. The three excellences of Bardism : to be fond of meditation ; to extend learning ; and to popularize manners and customs.

6. From three things does truth obtain credence : from believing every thing ; from disbelieving every thing ; and from believing it matters not what.

Three godly qualities in man : to consider ; to love ; and to suffer. (St. Paul.)

7. For three reasons ought a man to hazard his life, and

bydd achos, yn chwilio am y gwirionedd, glynu wrth gyfiawnder, ac yn gwneuthur trugaredd. (Paul).

8.   Tair prif rywogaeth Bywydolion Dyfrolion — Awyrolion — a nefolion, sef dyfrolion y cyntefiniaid Bywyd, a
hwy a gawsant eu hunain gyntaf, ac yn y moroedd cyn bod
tir sych. Awyrolion a gafwyd wedyn ac ar dir sych y
maent yn byw gan anadl o'r awyr. A nefolion yw y rhai a
gyrhaeddasant Gylch y Gwynfyd ac uchaf oll ydynt heb
farw ynddynt.

9.   Tair ansawdd Bywedigion, Abredigion, Rhyddedig-
ion, a Gwynfydedigion.

10.   Tri pheth ni ddichon eu bod, Duw yn ddrwg ac an-
nhrugar, Drwg na wnelo ddaioni, a daioni na threch yn y
diwedd.

11.   Tri thoriad Llyn Llïon yn y cyntaf y boddes y byd
a phob byw onid Dwyfan a Dwyfach au plant a'u hwyron,
ac o honynt yr epiliwyd yr byd drachefn — ac yn y torr
hynny y caid moroedd. Ail y bu pan aeth y mor rhwng y
tiroedd heb na gwynt na llanw, y trydydd y bu ban dorres
y ddaear yn wahanred gan y cyffro cadarn oni ffrydies y
dwr hyd yn entyrch awyr, a boddi oll o genedl y Cymry
namyn dengnyn a thrugain, a thorri Ynys Prydain oddiwrth y werddon ac oddiwrth dir Gal a llydaw.

12.   Tair gweinyddiad Gwybodaeth, a gafas Cenedl y
Cymru, cyntaf y bu addysc Hu Gadarn cyn no'u dyfod i

---

[1] " Llïon " means an aggregate of floods. The bursting of the Lake of Llïon
is thus chronicled in the Triads :—" The three awful events of the Isle of Britain : first, the bursting of the Lake of Llïon, and the overwhelming of the face
of all lands ; so that all mankind were drowned, excepting Dwyvan and Dwyvach, who escaped in a naked vessel, and of them the island of Britain was re-
peopled." (13, Third Series.) In another Triad (97) it is stated that " the
ship of Nevydd Nav Neivion carried a male and female of all living beings, when
the Lake of Llïon burst."

It is alluded to by Iorwerth Vynglwyd ;—

Lle 'r gwin mal lloer ar gynnydd,
Llawn byth fal *llyn llïon* bydd.

The store for wine, like the moon on the increase,
Ever full, like the *Lake of Llïon*, will it be.

to lose it, if there be occasion : in seeking after truth ; in clinging to justice; and in performing mercy. (St. Paul.)

8. There are three principal kinds of animations : aqueous ; aerial ; and celestial ; that is to say, the aqueous were the primordials of life, being the first that existed, namely, in the seas, before there was dry land ; the aerials then came into being, and they live on dry land, deriving breath from the air ; and the celestials are those which attained the circle of Gwynvyd, being the highest of all that are not subject to death.

9. The three conditions of animations : the being in Abred ; in liberty ; and in Gwynvyd.

10. Three things which are impossible : that God should be evil and unmerciful ; that there should be evil, which will do no good ; and that there should be good, which will not prevail in the end.

11. The three burstings of the Lake of Llion :[1] the first, when the world and all living beings were drowned, except Dwyvan and Dwyvach, their children, and grandchildren, from whom the world was again peopled — and it was from that bursting that seas were formed ; the second was, when the sea went amidst the lands, without either wind or tide ; the third was, when the earth burst asunder by means of the powerful agitation, so that the water spouted forth even to the vault of the sky, and all of the nation of the Cymry were drowned, except seventy persons, and the Isle of Britain was parted from Ireland, and from the land of Gaul and Armorica.

12. The three administrations of knowledge, which the nation of the Cymry obtained : the first was the instruction of Hu the Mighty, before they came into the island of Bri-

---

In the British Chronicles Arthur is introduced, as saying thus ;—" There is a lake near the Severn, called *the Lake of Llion,* which swallows all the water that flows into it at the tide of flood, without any visible increase ; but at the tide of ebb, it swells up like a mountain, and pours its waters over its banks, so that whoever stands near it at this time, must run the risk of being overwhelmed."— Myv. Arch. v. ii. p. 311.

Ynys Prydain yr hwn addysges gyntaf lafuriaw daear a chelfyddyd Gofaniueth, ag ail y bu trefnu Beirdd a Barddas yn addysg wrth gof a llafar Gorsedd, a'r un drydydd y bu 'r ffydd yng Nghrist yn oreu o'r cyfan, a phoed bendigaid y bo fyth.

13. Am dri achos y gellir dwyn bywyd oddiar fywydolion, sef ar a laddo ddyn o fryd ac amcan — ac ar a laddo ddyn ynghyfamwain ac o ansawdd gan ddamcwydd, megis y bydd a ddifetho ffrwythydd a llysiau twf a fo 'n ymborth a chynnal bywyd Dyn.—A lle bydd gwell i a leddir ei ladd nac amgen, mal ei dynnu o ddirboen, neu er gwellhau Cyflwr yn abred, mal y bydd ar ddyn a rotho ei $_{fywyd}^{hun}$ yn enaid faddau am ddrwg cospedig, lle nas gallo amgen o iawn a thal am a wnaeth, na myned $_{yn}^{gan}$ hawl cyfiawnder dan gosp ddyledus o'i wirfodd.

14. Mewn Tair ffordd y damcwydd ar ddyn fod yn enaid faddeu. *Un yw* cosp ddyledus gan Raith Gwlad a chyfraith am ddrwg argyweddus, sef yw drwg argyweddus, Lladd a llosg a murn a chynllwyn a bradych Gwlad a Chenedl, sef y dylit ddihenydd ar a wnelo 'r drygau, a phob dihenydd a fydd y naill ai gan Farn Llys Cyfraith, neu gan $_{Sawda}^{Ryfel}$ wrth Raith Gwlad a Chenedl. *Ail yw,* Dyn a ymrotho, ei hun, gan hawl cyfiawnder a fo arno parth ei gyd-

---

[1] " The three benefactors of the Isle of Britain : the first, Hŭ the Mighty, who first shewed the nation of the Cymry the method of cultivating the ground, when they were in the Summer Country, namely, where Constantinople now stands, before they came into the Isle of Britain." Tr. 56.

The benefit which he thus conferred on his countrymen is frequently alluded to by the Bards ; for instance, Iolo the Red, or Iolo Goch, the bard of Owain Glyndwr, observes of him ;—

> Ai daliodd gwedy diliw,
> Aradr braisg, arnodd-gadr, gwiw.

After the deluge, he held
The strong-beamed plough, active and excellent.
See Dr. Pugh's Dict. v. Hu.

[2] Al. " his life."

tain, who first taught the cultivation of the earth,[1] and the art of metallurgy ; the second was the system of Bards and Bardism, being instruction by means of the memorials and voice of Gorsedd ; and the third was the faith in Christ, which was the best of all, and blessed be it for ever.

13. For three reasons may living beings be deprived of life, namely : when one kills a man intentionally and purposely ; when one kills a man accidentally, or indirectly, as when it destroys fruit and vegetables, which are for the food and sustenance of the life of man ; and when it will be better for the one that is slain that it should be slain than otherwise, with the view of releasing it from extreme pain, or of bettering its condition in Abred, as in the case of a man, who gives himself[2] an eneidvaddeu for some punishable evil, where he cannot render any other satisfaction and payment for what he has done, than by submitting voluntarily, at the demand of justice, to the punishment due.[3]

14. In three ways a man happens to become eneidvaddeu : one is punishment due, by the verdict of country and law, for an injurious evil—an injurious evil being killing and burning, murder and waylaying, and the betraying of country and nation. That is to say, he who commits those evils ought to be executed ; and every execution takes place either by the judgment of a court of law, or in war by the verdict of country and nation. The second is the man, who surrenders himself, at the demand of justice which he feels in his conscience, to execution, for an injurious and punish-

---

[3] The doctrine of *eneidvaddeu* is recognised in the Laws of Dyvnwal Moelmud. Thus, in Triads 19, 20, we read :—" There are three strong punishments : *eneidvaddeu;* cutting off a limb ; and banishment from the country, by the cry and pursuit of men and dogs ; and it is for the king to direct which he willeth to be inflicted." "There are three *eneidvaddeu* punishments : beheading ; hanging ; and burning ; and it is for the king or lord of the territory to order which he willeth to be inflicted." On the supposition that these laws were really enacted by, or under the authority of Dyvnwal Moelmud, it follows, that the doctrine which the above Triads involve, is as old at least as 430 before Christ. - It seems as if a misapprehension of its real nature gave rise to the opinion which Julius Cæsar entertained, that the Britons offered human sacrifices.

wybod, i ddihenydd am ddrwg argyweddus cospedig a ddywetto ef iddo ei wneuthur, a lle nas gallo dal a iawn[1][2] amgen am a wnaeth yn argywedd na myned oi wir fodd dan gosp a ddylit arno am a wnaeth. *Trydydd yw*, Dyn a elo ym mhyd a damcwydd dihenydd ym mhlaid y Gwir ar cyfiawn gan danc a thrugaredd a chaffael ei ladd, a lladd am a wnel yn ddaioni y bernir hynn, ac o hynny ymdderchafael yng nghylch y Gwynfyd—ac amgen na'r tair ffordd yma nis gellir ar ddyn ei farnu 'n enaid faddau, gan ddyn, can nid oes namyn Duw a wyr farnu ar a fo amgen, sef y glŷn y cyntaf o naddynt yn yr abred yng nghyflwr ac ansawdd Dyn heb yn is no hynny ei syrth, ar ddau eraill yn ymdderchafael yng nghylch y Gwynfyd.

15. Tri phrysuriad diwedd abred, clefydon, Cyfymladd, a myned o iawn, a phwyll, ac angen o wneuthur daioni yn enaid faddeu, lle ni byddai hebddynt allu ymryddhau or abred onid yn hwyrach o Lawer. lle y gweler mai o les a thrugaredd i fywydolion y peris Duw 'r cyfymladd a'r cyfladd y sydd y ryngddynt.

Tri Chyflwr Bywydolion, Cyflwr annwn ac abred, lle treich drwg na da, ac o hynny drwg anghenfod, ac yn annwn pob dechreu a threigl hyd well yn abred. Cyflwr Dynolion lle cydbwys drwg a da, ac o hynny rhyddyd, ac yn rhyddid y mae gallu o ddewis ac yna gwellhâd.—Cyflwr Gwynfyd lle trech da na drwg, ac yno llwydd wrth a garer y sef ni charen yno namyn y da o angen cyd bo hefyd o ddewis, ac yna pob cwblhâd ar ddaioni a diwedd ar bob drwg.

Tri angen abredigion, trech gwrth a chythraul ar lwydd a gwellhâd — anneddf gan angen — ac angau gan ortrech

able evil, which he confesses to have committed, and where he cannot render compensation and satisfaction for the injury he has done, otherwise than by submitting voluntarily to the punishment due for what he has done. The third is the man, who undergoes the danger and chance of execution in behalf of truth and justice, at the call of peace and mercy, and is slain. Such a man is adjudged to be slain for the good, which he has done; and on that account he ascends to the circle of Gwynvyd. In any other than these three ways, a man cannot be adjudged as eneidvaddeu by man, for it is God alone who knows how to judge what is otherwise. The first of them will remain in Abred, in the state and nature of man, without falling lower; and the other two will ascend to the circle of Gwynvyd.

15. The three accelerations of the end of Abred: diseases; fighting; and becoming eneidvaddeu, justly, reasonably, and necessarily, from doing good; for without them there would be no release from Abred, but at a much later period. Herein is seen that it was for the benefit of, and mercy to, living beings, God ordained the mutual fighting and mutual slaughter, which take place among them.

16. The three states of animations: the state of Annwn and Abred, where evil predominates over the good, and hence there is essential evil—and in Annwn are every beginning and progression towards what is better in Abred; the state of humanity, where evil and good equiponderate, hence ensues liberty, and in liberty is power to choose, and consequently improvement; the state of Gwynvyd, where good predominates over evil, and there is success in love, since nothing is loved there of necessity but the good, though it be also loved of choice, and hence there is every completion of goodness, and an end to every evil.

17. The three necessities of the occupants of Abred: the predominance of opposition and Cythraul over prosperity and amendment; necessary lawlessness; and death, ensuing from the mastery of Cythraul, and from the system

2 Y

Cythraul a threfn gwared herwydd cariad a thrugaredd Duw.

Tri angen Dynolion y sydd, *Rhyddyd*, can nad oes na da na drwg angen am y bydd cydbwys y ddau, ac o hynny dewis ar yr un a fynner gan farn ac ystyrbwyll *Gallu*, am y bydd dewis o ryddyd a *Barn*, can y bydd deall o allu a chan y dylit farnu ar a ellir amgen.

Tri angen cyflwr Gwynfyd, Trech da na drwg ac o hynny *Cariad*. *Cof er yn* annwn, ac o hynny Barn a deall gyflawn heb allu ammau nac amgen, ac o hynny dewis o angen ar ddaioni. A *gorfod* ar *angau* gan allu wrth wybod y cyfan o'i achos, ar modd ai gocheler heb ar hynny na gwrth nac attal, ac o hynny byw byth.

Tair rhyw Gwledd gyffredin a fyddant wrth drefn a llywedigaeth Beirdd Ynys Prydain, 1af. Gwleddoedd y pedair alban. 2l. Gwleddoedd golychwyd ar fannau lleuad. 3dd. a gwleddoedd gwlad a chenedl gan orfoledd a gwaredigaeth a'u cynnal dan osteg a Rhybydd deugeunydd. E.a.w. Tair gwledd gyferddawn a fyddant yn nawdd Beirdd Ynys Prydain, ac ynddynt pawb ei rodd, o'r tair Dawnged, sef Mel, peillion, a Blith. nid amgen, Gwleddoedd cyfarwys dan osteg deugeinydd. — Gwleddoedd alban, a gwleddoedd Golychwyd, a braint yw i Feirdd drefnu ynddynt, ag ynddynt cael Rhoddion o'r tair Ced gyferddawn, sef yw y rhai hynny, yd—a Blith—a mel.

Tair Gwledd arall y sydd, a syberwyd yw i Feirdd drefnu arnynt, sef yw y rhai hynny, Gwledd, Gwledd pencenedl, a Gwledd Neithior, a Gwledd Gwyl Bentan, sef y bydd honno man y bo derchafael pummhentanfaen yn orsaf cyfannedd

---

[1] These are the equinoxes and solstices of the year.

of deliverance, which is according to the love and mercy of God.

18.   The three necessities of mankind : liberty, for there is no necessary good or evil, inasmuch as both equiponderate, and hence either may be chosen according to judgment and consideration ; power, for free choice may be made ; and judgment, because there is understanding derived from power, and because what is capable of being otherwise ought to be judged.

19.   The three necessities of the state of Gwynvyd : the predominance of good over evil, and hence love ; memory reaching from Annwn, and hence perfect judgment and understanding, without the possibility of doubting or differing, and hence, the necessary choice of goodness ; and superiority over death, consisting in power derived from knowing the whole of its cause, and the means of escaping it — the same being unopposed and unrestrained — and hence everlasting life.

20.   There are three common feasts, according to the order and regulation of the Bards of the Isle of Britain : the first, the feasts of the four albans ;[1] the second, the feasts of worship, at the quarters of the moon ; the third, the feasts of country and nation, consequent upon a triumph and deliverance, and held under the proclamation and notice of forty days.   Others say : There are three feasts of endowment, under the sanction of the Bards of the Isle of Britain, at which every one presents his gift, made up of the three tributes, namely, honey, flour, and milk.   That is to say : the feasts of contribution, under the proclamation of forty days ; the feasts of alban ; and the feasts of worship ; and it is the privilege of Bards to preside at them, and to receive gifts of the three tributes of endowment, which are, corn, milk, and honey.

21.   There are three other feasts, in which Bards preside by courtesy, namely : the feast of the head of kindred ; a marriage feast ; and the feast of a fire back, which takes place when five fire back stones have been raised, so as to

ac ynnynt rhoddion y cymmwd, a'r genedl hyd y nawfed
ach. a rhoddion cyferddawn y Gwleddoedd hynny a fyddant o âr, ac o fuarth, ac o goedwal, mal y bo hawsaf eu cael,
a'u rhoddi, ac i Fardd ei syberwyd.

Tri pheth ammraint i Fardd, can nad iawn y petheu
hynny iddaw ef, sef *fferylltaeth* a'r hynn nid oes a wnelo ef
namyn gwellhau o'i ddysg ai wybodaeth a'i athrawiaeth—
ail yw *Rhyfel* can nas dylid arf noeth yn erbynnu yn ei law
ef, can mai gwr wrth heddwch a thangnef yw ef. Trydydd
yw *cyfnewidiaeth* can mai gwr wrth gynneddf a chyfiawnder
yw ef, ac wrth ei swydd o addysgu Gwlad a chenedl. ac
achos y petheu hynn y bernir nas dylit crefft i fardd amgen
na'i swydd ai gelfyddyd wrth Gerdd a Barddoniaeth, rhag
llwgr a gwaethygiad, a choll ar a ddylid o Fardd a Barddoniaeth.

Tair ymdrafod a fyddant ryddion i Fardd ac i bob arall o
frodor gwlad a chenedl, sef yw y rhai hynny helwriaeth, ac
arddoriaeth, a maeronyddiaeth, can mai wrth y rhain y
caffant bawb eu hymborth, ac nis dylit nag attal o honynt i
neb au chwenychont. E.a.w. Aryddiaeth, maeronyddiaeth,
a meddyginiaeth, can mai Trafodaethau gwellhâd wrth danc
a chynneddf yw y rhai hynny.

Tair prif ymgais Bardd, un yw dysgu a chynnill gwybodau—ail yw athrawiaethu, a thrydydd yw heddychu, a
diweddu argywrysedd, can nid defod na gwedd i fardd a
wnelo yngwrth y petheu hynn.

TRIOEDD BARDDAS.

39. Tair Braint Gwynfyd, llwyr orfod cariad ar anghariad, llwyr allu ym mraint iawn a gwynfyd ar y sydd gan

---

[1] In Iolo's manuscript the five last Triads follow immediately after Tr. 19; but
they are crossed, as if they were not of the same series.

[2] These follow the preceding, in Iolo's manuscript, without any heading, except, " * These marks refer to the printed copy. After 38," which seems to
indicate that they belong to the " Triads of Bardism," which are published in
the " Lyric Poems."

constitute a dwelling station. At them are contributed the gifts of the comot and nation to the ninth generation ; and the endowments of those feasts are of tilth, fold, and wood covert, as will be easiest to obtain and give them ; the Bard having things by courtesy.

22. Three things unprivileged to a Bard, for they are not proper for him, that is to say : metallurgy, with which he has nothing to do, except to improve it by means of his learning, knowledge, and doctrine ; the second is warfare, for there ought to be no naked weapon of offence in his hand, since he is a man of peace and tranquillity ; the third is commerce, for he is a man of primary law and justice, and his office is to teach country and nation. And because of these things, it is adjudged that a Bard ought to follow no trade other than his office and art of song and Bardism, lest what ought to belong to a Bard and Bardism should become corrupted, deteriorated, and lost.

23. Three pursuits are free to a Bard, and to every other native of country and nation, namely : hunting ; agriculture ; and pastoral cares ; for it is by means of these that all men obtain sustenance, and they ought not to be forbidden to any one who may wish them. Others say : ploughing ; pastoral cares ; and medicine ; for these are pursuits of amendment, under the sanction of peace and natural law.

24. The three principal endeavours of a Bard : one is to learn and collect sciences ; the second is to teach ; and the third is to make peace, and to put an end to all injury ; for to do contrary to these things is not usual or becoming to a Bard.[1]

TRIADS OF BARDISM.[2]

39. The three privileges of Gwynvyd : the complete predominance of love over hatred ; complete power, under

wybodaeth cyfoll,—a boddhaad llwyr ar bob peth gan ddar-
fod pob gwrth a Chythraul.

40. Tri pheth annarfod. Tan sef goleuni, Bywyd, sef
Duw, a deall, sef gwirionedd.

41. Tri angenorfod pob byw, swydd, Awen, a braint, ac
ym mhrif ansawdd y rhain ni fydd a fo lwyrgyfun ac ef.

42. Tri rhaid cyn cyflawn wybodaeth, gweled, dioddef,
a chofio pob peth, ymhob cyflwr bywyd.

43. Tri pheth nis gwyr Dyn beth ydynt — Duw — Dim
— ac anfeidrol.

44. Tair ffynon Gwybodaeth, pwyll, ansawdd, a gorfod.

Y DULL O GYMMERYD BWYD A DIOD.*

Pan gymmerch Dy fwyd meddwl am ai dyrydd sef
Duw, a chan meddwl am ei enw ar y gair dyro'r tammaid
cyntaf yn dy ben, gan ddiolch i dduw am dano dan erfyn
rhad a llad arno er iechyd corph a meddwl, yna dy ddiod yr
un modd, ac amgen o beth neu o faint nac a elli ag enw
Duw yn dy feddwl, erfyn rhad a llad arno. rhag ei ddyfod
yn argywedd ac anllad arnat. — a chan gnoi dy fwyd gan
enw Duw, cno 'n fan ac yn fanol, yna llwnc, a chan yfed
yn llwnc, a chan yfed yn araf ac yn brin dy lwnc gwna
parth ac at Dduw fal ar dy fwyd, a bydded fal ai gweler
arnat, ac fal nas clywer llafar calon a chydwybod gan amgen
na Duw.

Fy Athraw caredig, yn rodd dywedwch wrthyf ymbwyll
y cnoi man a manol ar fwyd ar llyncu prin ar ddiod?

Athraw. Sef y cnoi man a manol. ymbwyll ystyrgor

---

* The heading in MS. is, " Ex Egwyddor Dewiniaeth," id est, " From the
Rudiments of Divinity." Probably the above fragment and "Egwyddor Dywiniaeth," printed at p. 288, are portions of the same work.

the privilege of right and bliss, derived from universal knowledge; and complete satisfaction with every thing, since every opposition and Cythraul have ceased.

40. Three things that are endless: fire, that is, light; life, that is, God; and understanding, that is, truth.

41. The three necessities of all animations: vocation; awen; and privilege; and there is nothing else in the primary nature of these that is thoroughly one with it.

42. The three necessities prior to perfect knowledge: to see; to suffer; and to remember every thing, in every state of life.

43. Three things which man knows not what they are: God; nonentity; and infinitude.

44. The three sources of knowledge: reason; nature; and impulse.

THE MODE OF TAKING FOOD AND DRINK.

When thou takest thy food, think of Him who gives it, namely, God, and whilst thinking of His Name, with the word put the first morsel in thy mouth, thank God for it, and entreat His grace and blessing upon it, that it may be for the health of thy body and mind; then thy drink in the same manner. And upon any other thing or quantity, which thou canst not take with the Name of God in thy mind, entreat His grace and blessing, lest it should prove an injury and a curse to thee. Whilst thou art masticating thy food in the name of God, chew it small and delicately, then swallow, drinking whilst thou swallowest. And whilst thou art drinking in slow and spare draughts, conduct thyself towards God, as at thy food; and let the voice of heart and conscience be manifested in thee, and not heard by any other being than God.

My beloved teacher, prithee, tell me the meaning of the small and delicate mastication of food, and the spare swallowing of drink?

Teacher. The small and delicate mastication involves a

ydd arwydda.   Sef nas dyled coel a derbyn ar na bara * na
Brud, na son na sanu, nac ymdyb nac ymdawr, na chred
nac anghred, heb megis ei gnoi ai droi ai drafod yn fan a
manol, ac yn chwal a chwiliedig cyn ai llyncer gan y deall
ar ymbwyll, gan ofyn a fo achos i'r neb a wypo am dano,
parth rhyw ac ansawdd, a pharth gwir ac awir arno. a
hynn i gyd gan ddwyn ar gof a meddwl aflafar enw Duw
modd y dylai meddwl dyn ei lefaru. ac yna bydd a gym-
merot ith gof a'th feddwl, ac i'th bwyll a'th Ddeall yn rad
ac allad itti. a da itti dy hunan, a da i bawb o'r byd y
bydd a rhad penllad Duw a drig arnat.

GWEDDI'R ORSEDD.

Llyma Weddi 'r Orsedd, a elwir Gweddi 'r
Gwyddoniaid.

Dyw dy nerth, ag yn nerth Dioddef;
A dioddef dros y gwir, ag yn y gwir pob goleuni;
Ag yngoleuni pob Gwynfyd, ag yngwynfyd Cariad,
Ag ynghariad Dyw, ag yn nuw pob daioni.
Ag felly terfyna.
O Lyfr Mawr Margam.

Llyma weddi 'r Orsedd o Lyfr Trehaearn Brydydd Mawr.

Dyro Dduw dy Nawdd ;
Ag yn Nawdd, Pwyll;
Ag ymhwyll, Goleuni ;

---

* It is not clear whether the last letter be *a* or *n*.

[1] Trahaiarn Brydydd Mawr, or the Great Poet, flourished from about 1290
to 1350. He presided at the Glamorgan Gorsedd in 1300. Two of his poems
are printed in the Myvyrian Archaiology. He is also supposed to have been the
same person as the one who distinguished himself under the assumed name of
Casnodyn, which is subscribed to five other poems in the same collection.—
Williams' Eminent Welshmen.

deep meaning, namely, that there should be no belief in, and reception of judgment, or chronicle, or report, or marvel, or opinion, or concern, or faith, or unbelief, without, as it were, chewing, turning, and agitating it small and delicately, scattered and scrutinized, before it be swallowed by the understanding and reason ; that inquiry as to what is necessary be made of him who knows about it, in respect of species, and quality, and in respect of what is true or false in it ; and that whilst all this takes place, the unutterable Name of God, how it is to be spoken by the mind of man, should be brought to memory and mind. Then what thou hast taken into thy memory and mind, thy reason and understanding, will be to thee a grace and a blessing, good for thyself, and good for all men, and the grace of God's chief blessing will dwell upon thee.

THE GORSEDD PRAYER.

The Gorsedd Prayer, called the Prayer of the Gwyddoniaid.

God, impart Thy strength ;
And in strength, power to suffer ;
And to suffer for the truth ;
And in the truth, all light ;
And in light, all gwynvyd ;
And in gwynvyd, love ;
And in love, God ;
And in God, all goodness.
And thus it ends.
From the Great Book of Margam.

The Gorsedd Prayer, from the Book of Trahaiarn the Great Poet.[1]

Grant, God, Thy protection ;
And in protection, reason ;
And in reason, light ;

2 z

Ag yngoleuni, Gwirionedd ;
Ag yngwirionedd, Cyfiawnder ;
Ag ynghyfiawn, Cariad ;
Ag ynghariad, Cariad Duw ;
Ag ynghariad Duw, pob Gwynfyd.

> Duw a phob daioni.

Llyma weddi 'r orsedd o Lyfr arall.

Dyro Dduw dy Nawdd ;
Ag yn nawdd, nerth ;
Ag yn nerth, Deall ;
Ag yn Neall, Gwybod ;
Ac yngwybod, gwybod y cyfiawn ;
Ag yngwybod y cyfiawn, ei garu ;
Ag o garu, caru pob hanfod ;
Ag ymhob Hanfod, caru Duw.

> Duw a phob Daioni.

Gweddi Talhaearn, rhai ai galwant Gweddi 'r Orsedd.

Dyw rho nerth
Ag o nerth, pwyll ;
Ag o bwyll, Gwybod ;
Ag o wybod, y cyfiawn ;
Ag o'r cyfiawn, ei garu ;
Ag o garu, caru pobpeth ;
Ag yngharu pob peth, caru Dyw.

> Talhaearn Tad Tanwyn ai cant.

---

[1] This was the motto of the Glamorgan or Silurian Chair.

And in light, truth ;
And in truth, justice ;
And in justice, love ;
And in love, the love of God ;
And in the love of God, all gwynvyd.
God and all goodness.[1]

The Gorsedd Prayer, from another Book.

Grant, O God, Thy protection ;
And in protection, strength ;
And in strength, understanding ;
And in understanding, knowledge ;
And in knowledge, the knowledge of justice ;
And in the knowledge of justice, the love of it ;
And in that love, the love of all existences ;
And in the love of all existences, the love of God.
God and all goodness.

Talhaiarn's[2] Prayer, called by some, the Gorsedd Prayer.

God, impart strength ;
And in that strength, reason ;
And in reason, knowledge ;
And in knowledge, justice ;
And in justice the love of it ;
And in that love, the love of every thing ;
And in the love of every thing, the love of God.
Composed by Talhaiarn, the father of Tanwyn.

[2] See *ante*, p. 62, note.

Gweddi Talhaiarn, neu Weddi 'r Orsedd.

Duw dy Nawdd ;
Ag yn nawdd, Nerth ;
Ag yn Nerth, Pwyll ;
Ag ym mhwyll, Gwybod ;
Ag yng ngwybod, Gwirionedd ;
Ag yng ngwirionedd, Cyfiawnder ;
Ag yng nghyfiawnder, Cariad ;
Ag yng nghariad, caru Duw ;
Ag yng nharu Duw, caru pob byw
   a bod.

Gweddi Talhaiarn.

Duw dy nawdd, — ag yn nawdd nerth — ag yn nerth
Pwyll — ag ym mhwyll cyfiawnder, ac yng nghyfiawnder
Cariad — ag yngnghariad caru Duw — ag yngharu Duw,
Caru pob peth byw.

LLYMA DDAROGAN PEREDUR BARDD PRYDAIN.

Pan fo cwyn cynllwyn bro gwarthefin
A galar a gwasgar y Gilbant werin

---

[1] It is not quite clear whether " Bardd Prydain," means here the Bard of
Britain, that is, the Isle of Britain, or the Bard of Prydain, the son of Aedd the
Great.   Among the Gwyddoniaid, which was the name by which the priests and
public teachers were known previous to the reformation of Bardism under Prydain,
we meet with a son of Peredur Wrawn; and if this Gwrawn was the same as
Gwron, one of " the three primary Bards of the Isle of Britain," Peredur, in
point of time at least, might well be called the Bard of Prydain.   There were
two others of the same name, who lived some time after the Christian era; Peredur, the son of Eliver Gosgorddvawr, who lived about the close of the fifth century,
and Peredur, the son of Evrawg, a chieftain who flourished in the early part of
the sixth century, and is mentioned by Aneurin as having fallen in the battle of
Cattraeth.   Neither of these, however, is represented as of the Bardic order.   We
may remark here, that, whenever the island of Britain is mentioned in old docu-

Talhaiarn's Prayer, or the Gorsedd Prayer.

God, Thy protection ;
And in protection, strength ;
And in strength, reason ;
And in reason, knowledge ;
And in knowledge, truth ;
And in truth, justice ;
And in justice, love ;
And in love, the love of God ;
And in the love of God, the love of
    every animation and existence.

Talhaiarn's Prayer.

God, Thy protection ;
And in protection, strength ;
And in strength, reason ;
And in reason, justice ;
And in justice, love ;
And in love, the love of God ;
And in the love of God, the love
    of every living thing.

THE PREDICTION OF PEREDUR, THE BARD OF PRYDAIN.[1]

When the sovereign[2] country shall bewail a stratagem,
And sorrow and dispersion happen to the secluded populace,

---

ments, it is almost invariably described as *Ynys Prydain*, a circumstance which gives force to the supposition that Peredur, in the heading of the above Prediction, was meant for the Bard of the son of Aedd the Great.

[2] " Gwarthefin " is also one of the Names of the Deity, and is derived from *gwarthaf*, a summit, or a surface.

Gwyn ei fyd y genau yn gyfrwydd gyfrin
A lefair dri gair o'r heniaith gyssefin.

Peredur Fardd ai cant.

LLYMA BENNILL CADAIR GORSEDD ALBAN ARTHAN.

Pan fo cwyn cynllwyn Bro Gwrthenin
Dan ysgyr gwiail y Gilbant werin,
Gwynfyd y geneu yn gyfrwydd gyfrin,
A lefair Tri gair o'r heniaith gyssefin.

Merddin Emrys ai cant.

---

[1] These are the three primitive letters, /|\, the secret of which was known only to the Bards.

[2] This is probably a corrupt reading of "Gwarthefin;" unless we take it as meaning "Gwrthenau," the cognomen of Gwrtheyrn, one of "the three arrant traitors of the Isle of Britain." In that case, the "stratagem" referred to would undoubtedly be the treacherous plot of the long knives on Caer Caradog, of which he was the promoter.

[3] "Ysgyr," the plural of *ysgor*, which, according to Llywelyn Sion, is used for a letter, i.e. a notch, or opening, from *ys*, and *gor*, an opening, or aperture. There is here clearly a reference to the Coelbren or Peithynen of the Bards, to

Blessed the lips that shall easily, and in confidential secrecy,

Pronounce three words[1] of the ancient and primitive language.

Composed by Peredur the Bard.

THE STANZA OF THE GORSEDD CHAIR OF THE WINTER SOLSTICE.

When the country of Gwrthenin[2] shall bewail a stratagem,

To the notches[3] of rods shall the secluded populace repair;

Blessed the lips that shall easily, and in confidential secrecy,

Pronounce three words of the ancient and primitive language.

Composed by Merddin Emrys.[4]

the use of which, under certain national troubles, the people would have to recur, as was the case in the time of Owain Glyndwr.

[4] Merddin Emrys was the Bard of Emrys Wledig, or Ambrosius, in the 5th century.

Doethineb.

TRIOEDD DOETHINEB.

Tair gwaedd Gorsedd y sydd, Gwaedd cyfarch, Gwaedd Hawl, a gwaedd cyfallwy.

Tair Gwaedd gadarn y sydd, gwaedd gwlad a chenedl yn nechre, Gwaedd uwch adneu yn hawl o fraint, a Gwaedd uwch adwedd yngorfod o fraint.

Tri un y sydd, un Duw sef yr Un dywarchen gyssefin ac o hanaw pob peth byw a bod, un gwirionedd, ac o hynny pob gwybod a deall meddwl, ac un pwngc rhyddyd, ac o hanaw pob nerth a gweithredoldeb.

Tripheth nis gellir newid iddynt, deddfau anian, ansawdd gwirionedd, a deddfau Barddas, canys pa beth bynnag a geffir yn hardd a daionus ac yn gyfiawn a berthyn i bob un o'r rhai hynny.

O dri phrif gynneddfau dyn y bydd ei dreigl yn Abred, o syrthni ai ddallineb meddwl y syrth yn annwfn, o'i nwyfiant y treigla cylch yr abred, herwydd y bytho 'n angeneddyl arnaw, ag oi serch ar ddaioni y cyrch yn archafael Cylch y Gwynfyd, a herwydd y trecho yn neu arall

---

[1] These Triads have been selected from a series entitled " Triads of Wisdom," which, together with the " Triads of Bardism," and the " Triads of St. Paul," were required to be recited at every meeting for public worship.

" There are three Triads of worship : the Triads of Bardism ; the Triads of

Wisdom.

1. There are three Gorsedd cries: the cry of greeting; the cry of claim; and the cry of efficiency.

2. There are three authoritative cries: the cry of country and nation to begin; cry relative to a pledge, in right of claim; and cry for a recurrency, in virtue of obligation.

3. There are three unities: one God, that is, the one primary element, from Whom proceeds every living and existing thing; one truth, from which proceed every knowledge and mental intelligence; and one point of liberty, from which proceed every strength and operation.

4. Three things incapable of change: the laws of nature; the quality of truth; and the laws of Bardism; for whatever is found to be beautiful, good, and just, belongs to each one of those things.

5. According to the three principal dispositions of man will be his migration in Abred: from slothfulness and mental blindness he will fall to Annwn; from his dissolute wantonness he will traverse the circle of Abred, according to the necessity laid upon him; and from his love of goodness he will ascend to the circle of Gwynvyd. According as

Paul; and the Triads of Wisdom; and they ought to be recited in every resort of worship."

3 A

o'r prif gynneddfau y bydd ar gyflwr y dyn, ag o hynny ei dri chyflwr, annwn, abred, a gwynfyd.

Tri chyflwr bywydolion, annwn, ag yno dechreuad, abred ynddaw cynnull gwybodaeth ac o hynny daioni, a'r gwynfyd, ag yn hynny cyflawnder pob daioni, o wybodaeth, gwirionedd, a chariad, a bywydoldeb didrangc.

Tri angeneddyl dyn yn Abred, Daioni ansoddawl, ac o hynny deall a phwyll a gwybodau, Nwyf, ac o hynny serch a chas, ac ofn, a gobaith, ac awen, a thristwch, a llawenydd, ac o gynghyd nwyf a daioni y tardd trugaredd, a haelioni, a chariad, a gwroldeb.—Dallineb cynglynawl ac o hynny pob cas ac anneall, a llid, a balchder, a thrachwant, a lle na chaffo'r ddau gyntaf y goreu ar y drydydd syrthiaw yn Abred a wna dyn pan y bo marw ag ymadael a'r bywyd yn y byd hwn.

Tri angheneddyl dyn yn y Gwynfyd, Dwyfolder, cariad, a goleuni, ac o'r tri pob gallu, a phob gwybodaeth, a phob llawenydd tragywyddawl, ac o hynny pob daioni heb dranc heb orpen.

Tair prif gyfarch y sydd, calas, gwyar, a Nwyfre.

YR ELFYDDENNAU.

Manred, cyssefin fodwedd yr holl ddefnyddau neu holl gywarchau sef yr Elfyddenau, a meirwon oeddynt y pedwar cyntaf o'r pump sef y Calas, y Gwyar, a'r ffun, a'r ufel, hyd oni chyffroes Duw nhwy drwy yngan ei Enw a chyda hynny ymfyw 'n orfoledd cân a datgan eu cyflwr.

TRIOEDD BARDDAS.

Y CYWARCHENNAU.

1. Tri Deifnogion pob peth Bod a hanfod, *Calas*, ag o hwnnw pob corph a chadernyd diymmod, a phob caled a

---

[1] The root of this word is *cal*, the root also of *caled*, hard; it is translated *corporeity*.

one or other of the three principal dispositions prevails, will be the state of man; hence his three states, Annwn, Abred, and Gwynvyd.

6. The three states of living beings: Annwn, where there is a beginning; Abred, where knowledge is accumulated, and hence goodness; and Gwynvyd, where is the fulness of every goodness, of knowledge, truth, love, and endless life.

7. The three necessities of man in Abred: natural goodness, and hence intelligence, reason, and sciences; vigour, and hence love, hatred, fear, hope, awen, sorrow, and joy — and from the union of vigour and goodness proceed mercy, generosity, love, and courage; inherent blindness, and hence all hatred, ignorance, anger, pride, and covetousness; and where the two first do not predominate over the third, man will fall in Abred when he dies, and parts with life in this world.

8. The three necessities of man in Gwynvyd: godliness; love; and light; and from the three proceed all power, all knowledge, and all everlasting joy, and hence all goodness without cessation, without end.

9. There are three primary elements: corporeity; fluidity; and air.

THE ELEMENTS.

Manred, the original form of all the materials, or all the constituents, that is, the elements, of which the first four of the five were dead, namely, calas,[1] fluidity, breath, and fire, until God agitated them by uttering His Name, when instantly they became alive in one triumphant song, and manifested their condition.

TRIADS OF BARDISM.
THE ELEMENTS.

1. The three materials of every being and existence: calas, and hence every motionless body and solidity, and

chynnull, *Gwyar*, ac o hwnnw, pob Trangc a threigl ac achwel, a *nwyfre*, ac o hwnnw pob byw a bywydoldeb, a phob nerth, a deall, a Gwybod, a Dᵧw ydyw, ag nis gellir byw a bywydawl lle nas bo.

E. a. w.

Tri Defnydd pob peth y sydd; nid amgen, *Calas*, ac o hano pob corpholdeb, *Gwyar*, ac o hano pob Lliw a llun, a phob trail ag achwel, a *Nwyfre*, ac o hano pob bywydoldeb a Dyw ydyw, ac o hano pob enaid a bywyd a nerth a deall, can nas gellir y naill nag arall or pethau hynn lle nas bo.

E. a. w.

Tair prif gywarchen y sydd; *Calas*, ac o hano pob caled a chadarn a marw ydyw. *Gwyar*, ac o hano pob treigl a newidioldeb, a phob arallder, a lliw a llun, a phob gwahanoldeb, a phob cyffred, a marw ydyw. A *Nwyfre*, a hwnn yw Dᵧw, ac o hano pob bywyd a nerth, a deall, a phob rhyn a synwyr.—Ac fal hynn herwydd eraill o ddoethion ac athrawon eraill, mal y gweler wrth yr hen gyfarwyddyd.

Pump Cyfarchan (Tywarchan) y sydd; *Daiar, Dwr, Awyr, Tan*, a *Nyf*; a dyw ydyw 'r *Nyf*, ac o hanaw pob bywydoldeb ac ymmod dosparthus.

E. a. w.

Calas neu *daiar*, Dwʀ, *Ffun, Ufel*, a *nwyfre*, a marw pob un o honnynt namyn y *nwyfre*, a hwnnw yw *Dyw*, ac o hano pob bywydoldeb.

Ac o fodd arall fal y dywedant eraill athrawon, herwydd

---

[1] Dr. Pughe gives the following meanings to this word, — " the ethereal sphere ; the firmament, the atmosphere," and in support thereof quotes from Taliesin and Llywarch Hen :—

Addwyn haul yn ewybr yn *nwyfre*.

Glorious is the sun moving in the *firmament*.—Tal.

Gorddyar adar, gwlyb traeth,
Eglur *nwyfre*, ehelaeth ton ;
Gwyw calon rhag hiraeth.

Clamorous are the birds, the strand is wet,
Clear is the *welkin*, ample the wave ;
The heart is palsied with longing.—Ll. Hen.

every hardness and concretion; fluidity, and hence every cessation, migration, and return ; and nwyvre,[1] hence every animation and life, and every strength, understanding, and knowledge, and the same is God, without Whom there can be no life and vitality.

Others say :—

There are three materials of every thing, namely : calas, and hence every corporeity ; fluidity, and hence every colour and form, and every course and return ; and nwyvre, and hence every life, being God, from Whom proceed every soul, animation, strength, and understanding, for where He is not, neither one nor another of these things can exist.

Others say :—

There are three primary elements : calas, hence every hardness and solidity, and it is dead; fluidity, and hence every progress and mutation, and every alteration, colour, and form, and every discrimination, and every concurrence, and it is dead; and nwyvre, which is God, from Whom proceed every life, strength, and intellect, and every perception and sense.

Thus, according to other wise men and teachers, as may be seen in the old account :—

There are five elements : earth ; water ; air ; fire ; and nyv ;[2] and the nyv is God, from Whom are all life and orderly motion.

Others say :—

Calas, or earth, water, breath, uvel,[3] and nwyvre, and every one of them is dead, except the nwyvre, which is God, from Whom comes all life.

According to another mode, as other teachers say from an old account :

It is compounded of *nwyf* and *rhe*, *nwyf* signifying " a subtil pervading element ; a fine ethereal fluid ;" and *rhe*, " a swift motion."

[2] " Nyf " seems to be but another form of *nwyf*, and *nwf*, and has the same signification.

[3] " Ufel," according to Dr. Pughe, is " elementary fire ; a spark of fire."

hen gyfarwyddyd, *Daiar*, *Dŵr*, *wybr*, *Tân*, a *Nyf*, a'r *nyf*,
Dyw ydyw, a bywyd, a *Deall*, ag o'r pedwar. cyntaf pob
marw a marwol, ac or bummed pob byw a bywydol, a phob
gallu a gwybod ac ymmod.

2.   Tri Deifnogion bywyd, ymmod, Gwybod, ac Awen.

3.   Tri Deifnogion Gorwyddawd, Awen gynhenid, Cy-
mhwyll hywaith, ac eisiwed (angen) anesgorawl.

4.   Tri Deifnogion Celfyddyd; Addysg gan Athraw ai
mettro, Deall greddfol ai cymhwyllo, a gorddyfnawd Awen
gymharbwyll.

5.   Tair Cyfarchan, Deall greddfawl, serch ^ynnïawl_{Anianawl}, a Chyf-
^{aw}_{o}dau ardymmyr anianawl.

6.   Tri Chyffred bywyd ; Corph, Enaid, a Braint.

7.   Tri Deifnogion Awen; Gwybod neu Ddeall, serch
ynnïawl, a Chyfarchwel.

8.   Tri Chyffred Celfyddyd ; Dosparth gywair, Cyfiawnder cadarn, a drythrwydd awenbwyll yn ymarfer a hi.

9.   Tri Chynnyrchafael Celfyddyd; Cyfarwyddyd y gan
ai mettro, Deall awengyrch er cymhwyllo, ac achaws ang-
henbar ei defnyddio.

10.   Tair Braint a ddylit ar a ddycco ar wybod ac arddangos gelfyddyd ddaionus nas gwypid cyn no hynny,
Braint Bonedd cynhenid o Gymro, Braint cyfarwys celfyddyd.   A Nawdd Beirdd ynys Prydain sef nod cler *
wrth arfau cammawn, ag yn Ryfel a brwydr, namyn o fodd.

11.   Tri phrif ^{argyfre}_{argyffreu} pob peth ; Amser, Lle, ac ansawdd.
E.a.w. Tri phrifgyfarch.

12.   Tri phrifgyfarch Gwybodaeth, Awen o Dduw, Gorddyfnawd Deall, ac arddangaws athraw.

13.   Tri phrifgyfarch Awen o Ddyw, Cyfiawnder greddfawl, Addwynder Cynneddfawl, a Deall anianawl.

---

* A clerical error, no doubt, for " nad eler."

[1] Al. "natural."

Earth, water, firmament, fire, and nyv; and the nyv is God, and life, and intellect. From the first four are all death and mortality; and from the fifth are all life and animation, all power, knowledge, and motion.

2. The three constituents of life: motion; knowledge; and awen.

3. The three constituents of knowledge: original awen; facile reason; and inevitable necessity.

4. The three constituents of art: instruction from a master, who knows it; innate understanding that will comprehend it; and the exercise of congenial awen.

5. Three principles: innate understanding; vigorous[1] affection; and the rises of natural temperament.

6. The three concurrences of life: body; soul; and privilege.

7. The three constituents of awen: knowledge, or understanding; vigorous affection; and devotion.

8. The three concurrences of art: correct system; firm justice; and discreet skill in practising it.

9. The three elevations of art: information from him who knows it; genial understanding to comprehend it; and needful occasion to practise it.

10. Three privileges which ought to be conferred upon him who teaches and demonstrates any good art that was not previously known: the privilege of innate nobility as a Cymro; the privilege of honorary art; and the protection of the Bards of the Isle of Britain, namely, that he should not, except of his free will, bear weapons of offence, or engage in war and battle.

11. The three principal adornments of every thing: time; place; and quality. Others say: The three principal elements.

12. The three principal elements of knowledge: Awen from God; the exercise of the understanding; and the demonstration of a master.

13. The three principal elements of Awen from God: innate justice; habitual kindness; and natural understanding.

14. Tripheth a gadarnhânt Awen o Ddyw ac ai anrhyd-
eddant; Diwydrwydd cadarngyrch, myfyrdawd cyweirbwyll,
a serchogrwydd syberbwyll.

15. Tripheth

TRIOEDD BARDDAS, A ELWIR TRIOEDD IONABWY.

YR ELFYDDENNAU.

Tair tywarchen gysefin y sydd, sef ydynt y tair prif-
elfydden. Cyntaf CALAS ag o hano pob caled, a hwnnw a
galeda bob peth arall a ddelo ar ymgyd ag ef, ag o hynny
pob corpholaeth. Ail $_{DWR}^{gwyar}$, ag o hwnnw pob irder a medd-
alder, ag ef a irhaa ag a feddala bob peth ydd elo ynghymysg ag ef, a phob ymlaith, a phob ymnewidiad ar gorpholdeb.
Trydydd NWYFRE. ag o hwnnw pob bywyd, canys a pheth
bynnag ydd elo ynghymysg bywydawl fydd y peth hynny
herwydd rhyw a dichonder arnaw.

Eraill o athrawon a doethion a ddywedant yn llynn.

Pymp tywarchen y sydd, CALAS, DWR, AWYR, TÂN a
NEF.—ag yn llynn y dywedynt eraill.

Pumelfydden y sydd, DAIAR sef hynny CALAS — GWYAR,
sef DWR ag IRDER—AWYR, ag o hwnnw pob anadliad, a phob
llais a llafar. TAN, ag o hwnnw pob gwres a goleuni — a
NWYFRE, ag o hwnnw pob bywydoldeb, a deall, a gwybodol-
deb, a gallu o fynn ag ewyllys.

Arall o'r cyfryw,

Tri defnyddion pob peth, Daiar, dwr, a Nwyfre   (E.a.w.
daiar, dwr, a nef) E.a.w. CALAS, GWYAR, a NWYFRE.

Arall or unrhyw

Pumelfydden arbennigion y sydd, CALAS, GWYAR, WYBR,
UFEL, a NWYFRE.

---

[1] The rest are wanting.   [2] Al. " water."

[3] This word is used now simply to denote *heaven*.   It seems to be the same as

14. Three things that will confirm and honour Awen from God: energetic industry; correct meditation; and courteous affection.

15. Three things[1]

THE TRIADS OF BARDISM, CALLED THE TRIADS OF IONABWY.

THE ELEMENTS.

1. There are three original principles, which are the three primary elements: the first, calas, hence all hardness, and it hardens every other thing, that comes in conjunction with it, and from this comes all corporeity; the second, fluidity,[2] and hence all freshness and softness, and it freshens and softens every thing that is commingled with it, and all moisture and all corporal change; the third, nwyvre, and hence all life, for whatever it mixes with becomes alive, as far as its species and capability permit.

Other teachers and wise men say thus :—

2. There are five elements: calas; water; air; fire; and nev.[3]

And others say thus :—

3. There are five elements : earth, which is calas; fluidity, which is water and freshness ; air, and hence all breathing, every voice and speech; fire, and hence all heat and light; and nwyvre, whence proceed all life, intelligence, knowledge, and power from will and desire.

Another of a similar kind :—

4. The three materials of every thing: earth; water; and nwyvre. Others say: earth; water; and nev. Others say : calas; fluidity; and nwyvre.

Another of the same kind :—

5. There are five particular elements: calas; fluidity; firmament ; uvel ; and nwyvre.

---

the *neph* or *cneph* of the Egyptians, the ψυχη χοσμου, that pervaded and animated the whole world.

Arall.

Tair Elfydden ddefnydd o gysefindawd rhyw ac ymsawdd
y sydd, CALAS, ag o hwnnw pob corpholaeth wrth lun a
mesur. GWYAR, ac o hwnnw pob treigledigaeth wrth bwys
ac ymmod. a NWYFRE, ac o hwnnw pob bywyd a deall.

A Llyma fal y mae mewn Llyfr arall, o herwydd eraill
Athrawon. Pump Tywarchen y sydd, sef Daiar, Dwr,
Awyr, Tân, a'r Nef. Ag yn y nef y mae Duw, a phob en-
aid, ag o hanaw y mae.

eraill a wedant yn llynn.

Pump Cyffred pob peth, Daiar, Dwr, Awyr, Tan, ag
Enaid, a Duw yw'r Enaid, ag o hano ef y mae pob bywyd,
yn y ddaear y mae 'r Corff ar eilun, yn y Dwr y mae 'r
Cyngyd, yn yr Awyr y mae 'r ffun a'r ymmod, yn y Tan y
mae 'r teimlad, sef synhwyrau corfforolion, yn yr enaid y
mae 'r Bywyd, a synhwyrau Rhyniad, sef Deall, a Gwybodau, ac awen, a phwyll, a'r serch. Ag yn y pump hynn
y mae pob peth yn ymgyffredu ag yn ymwreiddioli.

BARDDAS, &c.

Y CYWARCHENNAU.

Tair cywarchen gysefin y sydd, ag o henynt pob arall o
ddefnydd corphorol a handid bywydol. Cyntaf y Calas ag
o honaw pob corpholaeth a chaled, sef yw Calas yr Awyr ag
o hanaw ynghyfymwasg pob Corphoroldeb a Lliw a llun.
Ail y Tân ag o hanaw pob ymmod a newid, Trydydd y
Nwyfre, ag o hanaw Duw a phob bywyd, a Deall a gwybod. E.a.w. Calas, Ufel, a Nwyfre sef Duw. E.a.w.
Pump tywarchen arbennig y sydd, Daiar, Dŵr, wybr, Tân,
Nwyfre: o'r Calas y mae pob caled a phob corpholaeth, a
phob llun a lliw a thywyll ydyw, ai yn nhawdd ai ynghaled
y bo—or Ufel y mae y Tan a phob gwres a goleuni a phob

Another :—

6. There are three elements of matter, of original kind and condition: calas, from which comes all corporeity that has form and measure; fluidity, from which comes all progress capable of rest and motion; and nwyvre, whence all life and understanding.

It is as follows in another Book, according to other teachers:—

7. There are five elements, namely : earth; water; air; fire; and nev; and it is in nev that God exists, as well as every soul, which is also from Him.

Others say thus :—

8. The five concurrences of every thing : earth; water; air; fire; and soul, the soul being God, from Whom proceeds all life; in the earth are the body and form; in the water is the conjunction; in the air are the breath and motion; in the fire is the feeling, that is, the corporal senses; in the soul are the life, and the senses of perception, namely, understanding, sciences, awen, reason, and affection. And in these five all things concur and have their origin.

BARDISM, &c.

THE ELEMENTS.

There are three primary elements, out of which proceed every other corporal substance, and living existence: the first is the calas, from which are all corporeity and hardness, that is to say, calas is the air, out of which, by compression, are derived every corporeity, colour, and form; the second is the fire, out of which proceed every motion and change; the third is the nwyvre, from which are God, and all life, understanding, and knowledge. Others say: calas, uvel, and nwyvre, which is God. Others say: there are five special elements: earth, water, firmament, fire, and nwyvre. From the calas proceed every hardness, every corporeity, and every form and colour, and it is dark, whether it be liquefied or hard; from the uvel are fire, and all

lliw, a phob ymmod ag amosgryn, O'r Nwyfre y mae pob
bywyd a Duw ag enaid a Deall gwybod, a phob serch ag
Awen. ag nis gellir na rhif, no phwys, no mesur, ar nag un
nag arall or Tri hynn na bont gyfymwasg ai gilydd na
gwybod, nag ymmod, na lliw na llun.

(Llyfr Ieuan Bradford.)

Y TYWARCHENNAU.

Pump Tywarchen (Cywarchen) y sydd, Daiar—Dwr—
Awyr—Tan—a'r nef (nwyfre) sef or nef y mae Duw a phob
enaid byw.

Y TYWARCHENNAU.

Tair Tywarchen gyssefin y sydd ag o honynt y mae pob
defnydd ag arbennigrwydd bodoldeb 1 Calas. 2. Gwyar.
3. Nwyfre.

Ag mewn modd arall fal hynn herwydd rhai o'r hen Athrawon.

Pymp Tywarchen gyssefin y sydd. 1. Calas, 2 Gwyar,
3 Ffun sef awyr a gwynt, 4 Ufel sef Tan a goleuni, 4
Nwyfre sef bywyd ag ymmod. a phob ymmod a fydd o gynhyrfiad y nwyfre, ym mewn bywydolion y bydd ynddynt
ag oddifewn iddynt, ag mewn marwolion y bydd am danynt
ag oddifaes iddynt.

Y TYWARCHENNAU.

Pump tywarchen gyssefinion y sydd, nid amgen, daear, a
dwr, ac awyr, a thân, a'r nef. Ac o'r pedair cyntaf pob
defnydd difywyd, ac o'r nef Duw a phob bywyd a bywydol,
ac o ymgyd y pump hynn pob peth, ai bywydol ai ammywydol y bo.

Mewn Llyfr arall, fal hynn.

Pymp cywarchen y sydd ac o honynt pob peth bod a
byw, ai bywydol ai ammywydol y bo, nid amgen Calas,

heat and light, and all hue, and all motion and sensation; from the nwyvre are all life, and God, and soul, understanding, knowledge, and all affection and awen. And neither number, weight, or measure, can be applied to one or other of these three, where they are not mutually mixed together —nor knowledge, motion, hue, or form.

The Book of John Bradford.

THE ELEMENTS.

There are five elements: earth; water; air; fire; and nev;[1] and from nev are God and every living soul.

THE ELEMENTS.

There are three primordial elements, from which proceed every material, and speciality of existence: calas; fluidity; and nwyvre.

Thus, after another mode, according to some ancient teachers:—There are five primordial elements: calas; fluidity; breath, that is, air and wind; uvel, that is, fire and light; and nwyvre, that is, life and motion. Every motion takes place by the agitation of nwyvre; it is in and within animate beings, and around and without inanimate beings.

THE ELEMENTS.

There are five primordial elements, namely: earth; water; air; fire; and nev. From the first four comes every inanimate matter, and from nev God, and all life, and all living things, and from the union of these five, comes every thing, whether it be animate or inanimate.

In another Book, thus:—

There are five elements, from which proceeds every thing, existing and living, whether it be animate or inanimate,

---

[1] Al. "nwyvre."

Gwyar. Awyr, Ufel, a Nwyfre. Marw sef ammywydol y pedwar cyntaf, a byw y pummed, ac o'r pummed Duw a phob bywydoldeb.

BARDDAS.

Y CYWARCHENNAU.

Pump Cywarch_{en}^{an} y sydd ac o henynt a'u cynghyd pob Peth, y Byw a'r marw, sef ydynt, y Calas, y Gwyar, y Ffun, yr Ufel, ar Nwyfre. O'r Calas pob corph nid amgen na daear a phob caled, or Gwyar gwlyb ac ymlif — o'r Ffun pob gwynt ac awel, ac anadl, ac awyr. Or Ufel pob gwres a than a goleuni. ac or Nwyfre pob bywyd ac ymmod, pob yspryd, pob Enaid Dyn, ac amgen o fywydion yn ei gynghyd a'r cywarcheni (cywarchenau) eraill, ac or Nwyfre yn ei ardduniant yn anghynghyd a phob Amgen y mae Duw sef nwyfre yw Duw, ac nis amrafael arno, na newid na marw, na llwgr, na lleihâd, sef nis gellir lle nad ydyw, nac amser nad yw yn bod.

Ac enwau amgenion y sydd ar y Cywarchau yn eraill o Lyfrau, nid amgen, Daear, Dwr, Awyr, Tân, a Nŷf — ac mewn llyfrau eraill fal hynn sef &c. &c. cynghyd calas a dwr corph, cynghyd Dwr ac ^{wybren}_{awyr} tywyllwch, cynghyd wybr, sef awyr, a Than, gwres. Cynghyd Tan a Nyf ymmodnerth a phob symmud o fann i arall, ac o'r Nyf, pob bywyd a Theithi, nid amgen na deall, cof, awen, serch, cas, galar, gorfoledd &c. &c. &c.

Y DEFNYDDIAU.

Pum defnydd pob bod a bywyd. Calas, Gwyar, Awyr (ffun—wybr) haul (Tân—ufel—uddel) a Nwyfre (enyded —nyfel.)

---

[1] Al. "air."   [2] Al. "breath."   Al. "firmament."

[3] Al. "fire."   Al. "uvel."   Al. "uddel."

namely : calas ; fluidity ; air ; uvel ; and nwyvre. The first four are dead, and the fifth is alive ; and from the fifth are God and all life.

BARDISM.

THE ELEMENTS.

There are five elements, and from them, and their conjunction, are all things, living and dead, that is to say : calas ; fluidity ; breath ; uvel ; and nwyvre. From calas is every corporeity, namely, the earth, and every thing hard ; from fluidity are moisture and flux ; from breath are every wind, breeze, respiration, and air ; from uvel are all heat, fire, and light ; and from nwyvre every life and motion, every spirit, every soul of man, and, from its union with the other elements, other living beings. From nwyvre, in its simplicity, apart from every thing else, is God, for God is nwyvre, and is incapable of variety, or change, or death, or corruption, or diminution, for there can be no place where He is not, or time in which He does not exist.

Different names are given to the elements in other Books, that is, earth, water, air, fire, and nyv ; and in other Books, thus, namely, &c. From the union of calas with water is a body ; from the union of water with firmament,[1] darkness ; from the union of firmament, or air, with fire, heat ; from the union of fire with nyv, moving energy, and every motion from place to place ; and from nyv are all life and its characteristics, namely, understanding, memory, awen, affection, hatred, sorrow, joy, &c.

THE MATERIALS.

The five materials of every existence and life : calas ; fluidity ; air ;[2] sun;[3] and nwyvre.[4]

---

[4] Al. " the soul." Al. " nyvel," i.e. a subtil element.

Ag yn dro fal hynn ai dosparther,

Calas—Gwyar—a nwyfre (enyfel, enaid, ^{uddel} ennyfed &c. sef ydd ymgyd yr uddel ar nwyfre, ar awyr a ymgyd a'r uddel, ar dwr sef y Gwyar a ymgyd a'r awyr, ar Calas a ymgyd ar gwyar.

YR ELFYDDENNAU.

Tair prif elfydden y sydd, Dwr Tân, a'r Nwyfre, sef yw o'r Dwr y mae 'r ddaiar, sef dwr a sychwyd gan dân o'i ir-der, ag o'r dwr gwasgaredig neu doddedig gan dan y mae 'r awyr sef wybr, ag o gyd dwr a than a nwyfre y mae bywyd.

Eraill a wedant, pump elfydden y sydd, Daiar, Dwr, wybr, Tan, a Nwyfre, ag or nwyfre y mae pob bywyd a gallu, ag o'r Tân y mae pob serch, ag or wybr y mae pob ymmod, ag o'r ddaear pob Corpholder, ag o'r dwr pob twf a llun ag agwedd.

Ag o fodd arall fal hynn y mae ar Drioedd Ionabwy.

Pump tywarch y sydd, Daiar, Dwr, _{wybr,}^{Awyr} Tân, a nêf, sef or nef y mae pob byw a bywyd, ag o hanaw Duw a phob eneid ag yspryd, a phan ai gwahaner y wrth y tywarcheneu eraill, byddant farw. ag nis gellir marw ar Dduw canys nid oes corpholdeb iddaw o'r tywarcheni meirwon, achaws hynny nis gellir llun a maint, a mesur nag o le nag o amser arnaw, am hynny dros ben pob mesur a lle ag amser yw ef fyth fythoedd heb dranc heb orphen, sef tywarchen fywydawl y nef, ag oi chyd a'r rhai marwololion y bydd bywyd mewn corph, ag o gyd y rhai marwolion y mae pob corphoroldeb, ag o'r ddaear pob caled, ag or dwr pob twf a llun ag agwedd, canys ar ddwr yn bennaf ag oi ryw y mae mwyhâu a llei-hâu, ag o'r awyr pob ymmod, ag or Tân pob serch a gwŷn, ag o'r Nefoedd pob bywyd. ai fal hynn y dosperthynt yr hen athrawon gynt, cyn colli o Genedl y Cymry eu Gwy-

---

[1] Al. "enyvel"=nyvel. Al. " animation." Al. " soul." Al. "uddel"=uvel.

[2] Al. " firmament." [3] The plural of *nev*,—" heavens."

They are thus variously arranged :—

Calas, fluidity, and nwyvre;[1] and the uvel unites with the nwyvre, the air unites with the uvel, the water, or fluidity, unites with the air, and the calas unites with fluidity.

THE ELEMENTS.

There are three principal elements : water ; fire ; and nwyvre. From the water comes the earth, that is, the water was dried of its humidity by fire ; and from the water, scattered or liquefied by fire, is the air, or firmament ; and from the union of water, fire, and nwyvre, is life.

Others say :—

There are five elements : earth ; water ; firmament ; fire ; and nwyvre. From the nwyvre are all life and power ; from the fire is all affection ; from the firmament is all motion ; from the earth is all corporeity ; and from the water are all growth, form, and habit.

It is thus, according to another mode, in the Triads of Ionabwy :—

There are five elements : earth ; water ; air ;[2] fire ; and nev. From nev are all animation and life, and from it are God and every soul and spirit ; and when it is separated from the other elements, they die, whereas God cannot die, for He has no body formed from the dead elements. On that account, He is not subject to form, size, or measure, nor to place or time ; wherefore He is beyond every measure, place, and time, for ever and ever, without cessation, without end. Nev is an element of life, and, from its union with the dead ones, life takes place in a body ; from the union of the dead ones is every corporeity ; from the earth is every thing hard ; and from the water are all growth, form, and habit, because with water principally, and from its species, augmentation and diminution take place ; from the air is every motion ; from the fire are all affection and lust ; and from nevoedd[3] is all life. It was thus that the ancient teachers arranged them, before the nation of the

bodau au celfyddodau. A phan fo marw corphorolion o
bethau yn ymrannu a wnant y tywarcheni, a phob un at a
ddeïryd iddaw, sef daiar at ddaear, a dwr at Ddwr, ac awyr
at awyr, a Than at dân, a Bywyd at fywyd sef at Dduw.
sef ydd ânt bob petheu at eu dechreuadeu, au cyntefig-
iaetheu, lle y gorphwysant.

Pum elfydden (cywarchen) y sydd, Calas, Gwyar, Ffun,
Ufel a Nwyfre. a defnyddion marw y pedwar cyntaf, a'r
pummed—bywyd yw.

YR ELFYDDENNAU.

Tri elfydd y sydd, daiar, gwyar, a nwyfre. modd arall
Calas, Gwyar, a Nwyfre.

O LYFR LLANRWST.
DEFNYDDION DYN. TALIESIN AI CANT.

Wyth Rhan y sydd mewn Dyn, y *cyntaf* yw y DDAEAR,
llesg a thrwm ydyw, ac o honaw y mae y cnawd. Yr *ail*
yw y MAIN, y sydd gelyd, a defnydd yr esgyrn ydyw. Y
trydydd yw y DWR sydd wlyb ac oer a defnydd y gwaed
yw, Y *pedwerydd* ydyw 'r HALEN sydd hallt a llym, ac o
honaw y mae 'r Gwyniau ac ardymer teimlo parth synhwyr
a llafanad corphorawl. Y *pummed* yw yr WYBR, neu 'r
Gwynt, ac o hono y mae 'r anadl, y *chweched* yw'r HAUL, y
sydd eglur a theg, ac o honaw y mae y tân sef y gwres
corphorawl, ar goleuni a'r lliw ; y *Seithfed* yw yr YSPRYD
GLAN, ac o honaw y mae yr Enaid a'r Bywyd ; yr *wythfed*
yw CRIST sef yw deall, a doethineb, a goleufer Enaid a
Bywyd.

---

[1] The same number of elements is recognised in " Hanes Taliesin," Ap. Myv.
Arch. v. i. p. 20 :—

A honno yn troi sydd
Rhwng *tri alfyd*.

And that turns
Between the *three elements*.

Cymry lost their sciences and arts. And when corporal things die, the elements separate, and each one goes to what pertains to it, namely, earth to earth, water to water, air to air, fire to fire, and life to life, that is, to God; that is to say, all things go to their beginnings and originals, where they rest.

There are five elements: calas; fluidity; breath; uvel; and nwyvre; of which the first four are dead, and the fifth is life.

THE ELEMENTS.

There are three elements :[1] earth; fluidity; and nwyvre. Another mode : calas; fluidity; and nwyvre.

THE MATERIALS OF MAN.

Composed by Taliesin. From the Book of Llanrwst.

There are eight parts in man : the first is the earth, which is inert and heavy, and from it proceeds the flesh; the second are the stones, which are hard, and are the substance of the bones; the third is the water, which is moist and cold, and is the substance of the blood; the fourth is the salt, which is briny and sharp, and from it are the nerves, and the temperament of feeling, as regards bodily sense and faculty; the fifth is the firmament, or wind, out of which proceeds the breathing; the sixth is the sun, which is clear and fair, and from it proceed the fire, or bodily heat, the light and colour; the seventh is the Holy Ghost, from Whom issue the soul and life; and the eighth is Christ, that is, the intellect, wisdom, and the light of soul and life.[2]

---

[2] It is, probably, on this account that the Bards described man as a " little world." They were not, however, singular in their views on this point, for some ancient and medieval Christian writers have spoken of man in the same strain. Thus St. Augustine :—" God therefore placed on the earth the man whom He made, as it were another world, the great and large world in the

Os o'r ddaear y mae y rhan draffwys o ddyn, annoeth a llesg a gorthrwm y bydd; a chòr byr bychan a main, a hynny yn ol y bo'r traphwys ai mawr ai bach.—Os o'r wybren ysgawn, ac anwadal, a geiriolus chwedleufawr y bydd,—os o'r Cerrig, caled ei galon a'i ddeall ai farn y bydd, a chybydd a lleidr.—Os o'r Haul, awengar a serchog, ac esgud, ag athrylithgar, a Barddoniaidd y bydd.—Os o'r Ysbryd Glan, yna Dwyfol, a hygar, a thrugarog, ac yn gyfiawn a thyner ei farn, a llawn celfyddodau y bydd, a chyda hynn nis gellir amgen nag y bydd yn gyfunbwys o Grist a mebyd Dwyfol. ac felly y terfyna.

WYTH DEFNYDD DYN.

1 O'r Ddaear y cnawd.—2 O'r Dwr y gwaed.—3 O'r Awyr yr anadl. 4 O'r calas yr Esgyrn.—5 O'r Halen ei deimlad.—6 o'r haul, sef y Tân, ei gynhyrfiad.—7. O'r gwirionedd ei ddeall.—8 O'r Ysbryd Glân, sef Duw, ei Enaid, sef y Bywyd.

Brith y coed Sion Bradford.

SAITH DEUNYDD DYN.

1. Daiar, ac o hano y mae y corf.
2. Dwr, ac o hano y mae y gwaed a'r llynor.
3. Haul, ac o hano y mae y gwres a'r goleuni.
4. Awyr, ac o hano y mae yr anadyl a'r ymmod.
5. Nwyfre, ac o hano y mae y teimlad a'r serch.
6. Ysbryd Glân, ac o hano y mae y pwyll a'r deall.
7. Duw, ac o hano y mae y bywyd tragywydd.

Y Bardd Glas o'r Gadair ai dywed.

---

small and little world." (Aug. l. qu. 83, 84, 87 ; Retr. l. i. c. 2.) Gregory Nazianzene remarks:—" Every creature, both heaven and earth, are in man." (Greg. Naz. Epist.) And Zanchius :—" The body of man is the image of the world, and called therefore *microcosmus*." (Zanch. de oper. Dei, l. iii. c. 1.)

If the preponderating part of man is from the earth, he will be foolish, sluggish, and very heavy; also a short, little, and slender dwarf, in a great or small degree, according to the preponderance. If it should be from the firmament, he will be light, unsteady, garrulous, and fond of gossip. If from the stones, his heart, understanding, and judgment, will be hard, and he will be a miser, and a thief. If from the sun, he will be genial, affectionate, active, docile, and poetic. If from the Holy Ghost, then he will be godly, amiable, and merciful, with a just and gentle judgment, and abounding in arts. And being thus, he cannot but equiponderate with Christ, and divine sonship. And so it ends.

THE EIGHT MATERIALS OF MAN.

1. From the earth is the flesh; 2. from the water, the blood; 3. from the air, the breath; 4. from the calas, the bones; 5. from the salt, his feeling; 6. from the sun, or fire, his agitation; 7. from the truth, his understanding; 8. from the Holy Ghost, that is, God, his soul, or life.

The " Brith y Coed " [1] of John Bradford.

THE SEVEN MATERIALS OF MAN.

1.   Earth, from which is the body;
2.   Water, from which are the blood and humour;
3.   Sun, from which are the heat and light;
4.   Air, from which are the breath and motion;
5.   Nwyvre, from which are the feeling and affection;
6.   The Holy Ghost, from Whom are the reason and understanding;
7.   God, from Whom is life everlasting.

The Blue Bard of the Chair has said it.

---

[1] The title of a Book.

LLYMA SAITH GYNNEVNYDDION BYD.

1. Cyntav, daiar, ac o hano pob corf a chaled, a phob saw cadarn.

2. Ail, dwr, ac o hano pob llyn ac îr.

3. Trydydd, awyr, ac o hano pob anadyl ac ymmod.

4. Pedwerydd, haul, ac o hano pob gwres a goleuni.

5. Pummed, nwyvre, ac o hano pob teimlad, a serch, ac ymnwyv.

6. Chweched, ysbryd glân, ac o hano pob deall, a phwyll, ac awen, a gwybodau.

7. seithved, Duw, ac o hano pob bywyd, a chadernyd, a chynnal hyd vyth bythodd.

Ac o'r saith cynnevnyddion y mae pob bod a byw: a phoed ar drevyn Duw y cyvan oll.   Amen.

Y Bardd Glas o'r Gadair a'i dywed.

WYTH DEVNYDD DYN.

O lyvyr Mr. Cobb o Gaer Dyv.

O'r ddaiar y cnawd,
O'r dwr y gwaed,
O'r awyr yr anadl,
O'r calas yr esgyrn,
O'r halen y teimlad,
O'r haul, sev y tan, ei gynhyrviad,
O'r gwirionedd ei ddeall,
O'r ysbryd glân, sev Duw, ei enaid,
    sev y bywyd.

LLYMA LEOEDD YNGHORPH DYN Y BYDD SWRN GYNHEDDFAU YNDDYNT.

1. Yn y Talcen y mae synwyr a 'r deall,

2. Yn y gwegil y mae 'r cof,

THE SEVEN PRIMARY MATERIALS OF THE WORLD.

1. The first, earth, from which are every corporeity and hardness, and every firm foundation ;

2. The second, water, from which are all humour and freshness ;

3. The third, air, from which are all respiration and motion ;

4. The fourth, sun, from which are all heat and light ;

5. The fifth, nwyvre, from which are all feeling, affection, and wantonness ;

6. The sixth, the Holy Ghost, from Whom are all understanding, reason, awen, and sciences ;

7. The seventh, God, from Whom are all life, strength, and support, for ever and ever.

And from these seven primary materials are every existence and animation ; and may the whole be under God's regulation. Amen.

The Blue Bard of the Chair has said it.

THE EIGHT MATERIALS OF MAN.

From the Book of Mr. Cobb of Cardiff.
From the earth, the flesh ;
From the water, the blood ;
From the air, the breath ;
From the calas, the bones ;
From the salt, the feeling ;
From the sun, that is, the fire, his agitation ;
From the truth, his understanding ;
From the Holy Ghost, that is, God, his soul,
    or life.

THE PARTS OF THE HUMAN BODY IN WHICH ARE THE FACULTIES.

1. In the forehead are the sense and intellect ;
2. In the nape is the memory ;

3.　Yn yr iad y mae 'r dosparth a'r $_{\text{rheswm,}}^{\text{pwyll}}$

4.　Yn y ddwyfron y bydd chwant,

5.　Yn y galon y bydd y cariad,

6.　Yn y bustl y mae 'r digofaint a'r llid,

7.　Yn yr ysgyfaint y bydd yr anadl,

8.　Yn y ddwyeg y bydd llawenydd,

9.　Yn y corph y bydd y gwaed,

10.　Yn yr iau y bydd y gwres,

11.　Yn yr yspryd y bydd y meddwl,

12.　Yn yr enaid y bydd y ffydd.

Arall.

Yn y talcen y mae 'r deall — yn y gwegil y mae 'r cof — yn yr iad y mae 'r pwyll a'r dosparth — yn yr ysgyfaint y bydd yr anadl — yn y ddwyfron y mae 'r chwant — yn y galon y mae 'r cariad — yn y ddueg y bydd y llawenydd — yn yr afu y bydd y gwres — yn y bustl y mae 'r digofaint — yn y corph y bydd y gwaed — yn yr yspryd y bydd y meddwl — yn y meddwl y mae 'r enaid — yn yr enaid y mae 'r ffydd — ac yn y ffydd y mae Duw (vel mab Duw).[1]

ATHRONDDYSG Y BARDD GLAS O'R GADAIR.

Yn y talcen y mae y deall,
Yn y gwegil y mae y cov,
Yn y iad y mae y dosparth,
Yn y deall, a'r cov, a'r dosparth,
　　yn un, y mae y pwyll,
Yn yr ysgyvaint y mae yr anadyl,
Yn y ddwyvron y mae y chwant,
Yn yr avu y mae y gwres,

---

[1] Al. "the Son of God."

3. In the pate are discretion and reason ;
4. In the breast is lust ;
5. In the heart is love ;
6. In the bile are anger and wrath ;
7. In the lungs is the breath ;
8. In the spleen is joyousness ;
9. In the body is the blood ;
10. In the liver is the heat ;
11. In the spirit is the mind ;
12. In the soul is faith.

Another.

In the forehead is the intellect ;
In the nape is the memory ;
In the pate are reason and discretion ;
In the lungs is the breath ;
In the breast is the lust ;
In the heart is love ;
In the spleen is joyousness ;
In the liver is the heat ;
In the bile is anger ;
In the body is the blood ;
In the spirit is the mind ;
In the mind is the soul ;
In the soul is faith ;
In faith is God.[1]

THE PHILOSOPHY OF THE BLUE BARD OF THE CHAIR.

In the forehead is the intellect ;
In the nape is the memory ;
In the pate is discretion ;
In the understanding, memory, and
    discretion together, is reason ;
In the lungs is the breath ;
In the breast is lust ;
In the liver is the heat ;

3 D

Yn y gwythi y mae y gwaed,
Yn y bustyl y mae y digovaint,
Yn y ddueg y mae y llawenydd,
Yn y galon y mae y cariad,
Yn y rhai hyn i gyd y mae y serch,
Yn y serch y mae yr enaid,
Yn yr enaid y mae y meddwl,
Yn y meddwl y mae y fydd,
Yn y fydd y mae Mab Duw,
Ym mab Duw y mae y bywyd didranc,
Yn mywyd didranc y mae y gwynvyd.

Anorphen, a gwyn ei vyd a wnelo yn iawn a'r ynïau a ddodes Duw ynddo, er cyrhaeddyd gwynvyd anorphen hyd vyth bythodd.   Amen.

Y Bardd Glas o'r Gadair ai dywed.

LLYMA DRIOEDD ARBENNIG.

1. Tri pherson y sydd yn y Nef, y Tad, y Mab, a'r Yspryd Glan.

2. Tri un arbennig y sydd.   Yr un Dywarchen gwir, Diliw angen — a'r Un dywarchen y daw pawb o honi, sef y ddaear — a'r un Dywarchen Bywyd sef Duw.

3. Tri dau arbennig y sydd, y ddwy seren arbennig sef yr Haul a'r Lleuad, a'r Ddwy Dywarchen ydd a pawb iddynt sef y Nef a'r Ddaear.

4. Tri thri arbennig y sydd, sef y Tridiau yr helwyd Adda ac Efa o naddynt.

2   1

---

[1] It will be observed that this and the two following Triads are imperfect.

[2] The meaning of this statement is not very clear.   We are not sure whether it is intended that our first parents were expelled from Paradise within three days of their creation, or whether they were deprived of the holy enjoyment of three days, or portions of days, Friday, Saturday, and Sunday, that closed the first week of time.   Or are we to understand that Adam and Eve were formed out of the constituents or elements of three days ?   The first notion would not be consistent with the opinion that generally prevailed in the middle ages, which represents them as having continued but seven hours in their state of

In the veins is the blood ;
In the bile is anger ;
In the spleen is joyousness ;
In the heart is love ;
In all these is affection ;
In the affection is the soul ;
In the soul is the mind ;
In the mind is faith ;
In faith is the Son of God ;
In the Son of God is imperishable life ;
In imperishable life is gwynvyd ;

Without end; and blessed is he, who rightly exercises the faculties with which God has endued him, in order to attain to endless gwynvyd, for ever and ever. Amen.

The Blue Bard of the Chair has said it.

PARTICULAR TRIADS.

1. There are three Persons in heaven : the Father; the Son; and the Holy Ghost.

2. There are three particular ones : the one true element, the necessary deluge ; the one element, from which all men proceed, namely, the earth ; and the one element of life, namely God.

3. There are three particular twos : the two particular stars, namely, the sun and moon ; and the two elements, into which all men will go, namely, the heaven and the earth.[1]

4. There are three particular threes, namely : the three days that Adam and Eve were taken from.[2]

---

innocency. "Et ut tradunt historiagraphi eos fuisse in Paradiso per vii. horas et non ultra et statim ejecti sunt." Eulog. Hist. c. viii.

"Seithawr i buan
Yn cadw 'r berllan
Cyn cyvrdan satan
Sitiwr tartara.—Iohan. Menev."

5. Tri phedwar arbennig y sydd, pedwar defnydd dyn, sef Tan, awyr, Dwr, a Daiar.

6. Tri phump arbennig y sydd, pum synwyr Dyn, pum Llyfr moesen, a phump gwregys y ddaiar.

7. Tri chwech arbennig y sydd, sef chwech oes y Byd, ar chwech cherwyn maen a droes yr Iesu y Dwr oedd yn-ddynt yn win yn neithiar Ieuan Efangylwr, a chwech thremyn Dyn.

8. Y Tri saith arbennig, saith rhinwedd yr Eglwys, saith weddi y Pader, a saith ddyddiau yr wythnos.

9. Tri wyth arbennig, wyth briwyd pechod, yr wyth aeth gyda Noe i'r llong, a'r wyth wynt.

10. Y Tri naw arbennig, naw Tonn y weilgi, naw Rad y nef, a naw mis tymp.

11. Tri deg arbennig, y dengair deddf, deg hyd rhif, a deg urddeu Duw.

TRIOEDD DEGRIF.

1. Tri un arbennig, Un Duw, un gwirionedd, an un pwnc Rhyddyd, a medru ar y tri hynny a ddwg i'r gwyn-fyd.

2. Tri Dau arbennig, dau ysglain bywydolion sef gwryw a benyw, Dau brifansawdd sef da a drwg, a deupen angen sef dechreu a diwedd.

3. Tri thrioedd arbennig, Tri bannogion trefn, Rhif, Pwys, a Mesur.—Tri phrif thremynt corphorawl, gweled, clywed, a theimlaw.—Triphrif gynneddf (Tremynt) deall (enaid) caru, cashau, a barnu (deall).

---

[1] Pump gwregys terra.—The five zones of the earth.
Taliesin. Ap. Myv. Arch. i. p. 25.

[2] Though, according to the ancients, St. John always led a single life, many of the middle writers of the Church, assert that he was married, and that it was his marriage which our Lord was at in Cana of Galilee. Bed. Prœf. in Ioan. Rupert. Tuit. Comm. in Ioan. lib. ii. in fin. Cyr. in Ioan. cap. 2, et alii.

[3] "There is no number beyond ten."—Laws of Howel the Good.

[4] Al. "perceptions."   [5] Al. "the soul."

5. There are three particular fours : the four materials of man, namely, fire, air, water, and earth.

6. There are three particular fives : the five senses of man ; the five books of Moses ; and the five zones of the earth.[1]

7. There are three particular sixes, namely : the six ages of the world ; the six stone vessels, the water in which Jesus turned into wine, at the marriage feast of John the Evangelist ;[2] and the six perceptions of man.

8. The three particular sevens : the seven sacraments of the Church ; the seven petitions of Pater Noster ; and the seven days of the week.

9. The three particular eights : the eight deadly sins ; the eight that went with Noah into the ark ; and the eight winds.

10. The three particular nines : the nine waves of the ocean ; the nine graces of heaven ; and the nine months of gestation.

11. Three particular tens : the ten commandments ; the ten lengths of numeration ;[3] and the ten degrees of God.

TRIADS OF TEN NUMBERS.

1. Three particular ones : one God ; one truth ; and one point of liberty ; and to know those threes will bring to Gwynvyd.

2. Three particular twos : the two sexes of living beings, namely, male and female ; two principles, namely, good and evil ; and the two heads of necessity, namely, beginning and end.

3. Three particular threes : the three characteristics of order, number, weight, and measure; the three bodily perceptions, seeing, hearing, and feeling ; and the three principal faculties[4] of the intellect,[5] to love, to hate, and to judge.[6]

Al. "to understand."

4. Tri phedwar arbennig, Pedwar bann Byd a mesur,
Dwyrain, Addef, Gogledd a llywynydd — Pedwar Bann
haul sef yr Alban Arthan, yr Alban Eilir — yr Alban Hefin, a'r Alban Elfed. — a phedwar angen ffurf, sef crwn, try-
fal, pedryfal, a gwastad.

5. Tri phump arbennig, Pump gwynfyd Bywyd—sef,
Iechyd, Rhyddyd, cariad, trwydded, a pharch. — pump colofn cyfiawnder, ofn, eonder, cas, cariad, a gwirionedd. —
Pump tywarchen, defnydd — Daiar, Dwr — Awyr, Tân, a'r
nefoedd.

6. Tri chwech arbennig.[1]

LLYMA GYFYMBWYLL Y DYSGYBL AI ATHRAW.

Disgybl.   Adolwyn fy Athraw bonheddig a gwybodfawr
gan eich bod yn Athraw ag yn Brifardd wrth Fraint a Defod Beirdd Ynys,* o'ch mwynder cynnefin immi dangoswch
immi eich celfyddyd a gwedwch wrthyf ansawdd a syrth
Llafar Gorsedd Beirdd Ynys Prydain, mal y gwypwyf ei
chreth ai hymbwyll, ag yr elwyf innau yn Fardd defodawl
wrth Brif deilyngdawd megis ag ydd ydych chwithau.

Athraw.   Fy mrawd ffydd am cydymaith Cadwgan gan
dy fod yn Awenydd defodawl yn Nawdd Beirdd Ynys
Prydain mi a wedaf wrthyt ag a ddangosaf y gyfrinach dan
arch ag ammod itti wrando yn ddiwyd ag yn awchus ag yn
ddilesgedd ar a ddodwyf ragod a thewi ar a ddywedwyf, sef
llyma fal y mae, nid amgen.

Llafar Gorsedd Beirdd Ynys Prydain, yw 'r hen Gof
cadwedig er yn oes oesoedd ag er y dechreuad ar Gelfyddyd
a Gwybodau Prifeirdd Ynys Prydain, nid amgen na gwybodau am Dduw ai ddaioni ai drefnau a defodau Beirdd

---

* "Prydain" is omitted in MS.

[1] The rest are wanting.

4. Three particular fours: the four parts of the world and measure, east, south, north, and west; the four points of the sun, namely, the winter solstice, the vernal equinox, the summer solstice, and the autumnal equinox; and the four properties of form, namely, round, triangular, square, and flat.

5. Three particular fives: the five felicities of life, namely, health, liberty, love, welcome, and respect; the five columns of justice, fear, courage, hatred, love, and truth; and the five constituents of matter, earth, water, air, fire, and heaven.

6. Three particular sixes.[1]

MUTUAL REASONING BETWEEN A DISCIPLE AND HIS TEACHER.

Disciple. Pray, my noble and very knowing Teacher, since you are a Teacher, and a primitive Bard, according to the privilege and usage of the Bards of the Isle of Britain, out of your usual kindness to me, exhibit your art, and tell me the nature and tendency of the voice of the Gorsedd of the Bards of the Isle of Britain, that I may know its purpose and meaning, and become myself a regular Bard of primary merit, even as you are.

Teacher. My brother in the faith and companion, Cadwgan, since thou art an institutional awenydd, under the auspices of the Bards of the Isle of Britain, I will tell thee, and will exhibit to thee the secret, with the request, and on condition, that thou listen diligently, ardently, and vigourously, to what I shall lay before thee, and not divulge what I say. It is thus, namely:—

The voice of the Gorsedd of the Bards of the Isle of Britain, is the old memorial, which has been preserved from the age of ages, and from the beginning, in respect to the art and sciences of the primitive Bards of the Isle of Britain, namely, the sciences concerning God and His goodness and dispensations, and the usages of the Bards of the Isle

Ynys Prydain, au Breeniau, ai celfyddyd wrth Gerdd Dafawd a dosparth Llythyr, a dosparth a chadwedigaeth y
Gymraeg, a'u cof doethineb Cenedl y Cymry, a chof Breeniau a Defodau cenedl y Cymry au hachau au bonedd au
Rhandiroedd a breiniau priodasau teilyngion a phob breiniau a defodau ereill a ddylit gof teilwng arnynt.

Disgybl. Da Duw i chwi am eich mwynder ach cariad-
oldeb sef cynnefin iawn immi ydynt, achaws hynny mi a
gof ofyn i chwi bynciau a phwnc ar bwnc yny chaffwyf eich
Barn ach addysg.

Athraw. Gofynnwch a chan groesaw a mi ach attebaf
yn oreu byth y gallwyf.

Pam y cwyn y dwr o waelod daear i'r wyneb lle ffynhona,
ag y syrth hefyd gyda hynny o'r wybren i'r ddaear.

Achaws a ddangosaf, pob peth a gyrch bywyd a goleuni,
yn y goleuni y mae 'r bywyd, ac yn yr wybren goruwch
wyneb daear y mae 'r goleuni a'r gwres, a'r dwr ymherfedd
daear a than wyneb daear yn y tywyll a gyrch parth ag at
y goleuni er bywyd. canys ymhob peth cynneddf o dduw
yw cyrch ag ymgais bywyd a goleuni; Etwaith dwfr yn
wybren a dreigl oi anfodd hyd egorfeydd yr awyrolion
barthau, ag efe a gais orphwysfeydd, ag nid hynny iddaw
ym man o fyd namyn wyneb daear, ag yno y cyrch ag y
gorymgais, ag o'r ddwy gynneddf hynn o Dduw ymhob
peth, y gorymgais bob peth fywyd a goleuni, a hefyd ef a
orymgais bob peth bywydawl ei orphwys man y caffo, a
gwers o ddoethion y wers honn.

Pam y mae 'r dwr yn y mor yn hallt?
Achos a ddangosaf, craig halen yw perfedd y ddaear, a
changheu 'r graig honno a gerddant waelodlawr y mor, ac
ymwysgonant yn y dwr, ag o hynny ai gwnant yn hallt.
A lle delo brig y graig honno yn agos i wyneb daear ef a

of Britain, and their privileges, and art of vocal song, and the arrangement of letters, and the arrangement and preservation of the Cymraeg, and the memorial of the wisdom of the nation of the Cymry, and the memorial of the privileges and usages of the nation of the Cymry, their genealogies, nobility, inheritances, and the privileges of worthy marriages, and all other privileges and usages, which ought to be worthily remembered.

D. God bless you for your kindness and amiability, for they are very familiar to me; therefore, I shall ask points of you — point upon point, until I receive your judgment and instruction.

T. Ask, and a hundred welcomes to you, and I will answer in the best way I can.

D. Why does the water rise from the bottom of the earth to the surface, where it issues out, and also falls from the sky to the earth?

T. I will shew thee the reason;—every thing tends towards life and light; in the light is life, and in the sky above the face of the earth are the light and heat; the water in the centre of the earth, and beneath the surface of the earth, being in the dark, tends towards the light, with a view to life, for in every thing it is a primary law of God that there should be a tendency and an aim towards life and light. Again, water in the firmament runs against its will along the apertures of the aerial parts, and seeks resting places, but there are none such for it in any part of the world, except on the face of the earth, and thither it tends, and that place it eagerly seeks. And, because of these two primary laws from God which exist in every thing, every thing eagerly seeks its rest, where it can get it. This lesson is a lesson taught by wise men.

D. Why is the water in the sea briny?

T. I will shew thee the reason;—the centre of the earth is a rock of stone, and a branch of that rock runs along the bottom of the sea, and melts in the water, and hence it becomes briny. And where the top of that rock approaches

3 E

geir y ffynhoneu dwfr yn heilltion yn y rhyw leoedd a
hynny, ag a geir halen or dwr, yn hyn o lëoedd.

Y SER.

Tri rhyw ser y sydd, Ser cedyrn a hwy a gadwant ei
lleoedd ac a elwir hefyd ser ystod — Ser Gwibiog, a elwir
planedau, a phymtheg y sydd o honynt, saith yn weledig
parhaus, ac wyth nid ydynt weledig namyn ar ambell iawn
o amserau gan yi treiglorethau o fewn Caergwyddon a thu
draw iddi, a thrydydd ser annoparthus a elwir Ser Cyn-
ffonog ag ni wyddys na lle na rhif nag amser arnynt. na
gwybod am danynt namyn ar amseroedd o ddamwain a
chylch oesoedd.

(Barddas — Manbethau misoedd ag eraill.)

SERYDDIAETH.

Saith Blaned weledig y sydd, ac y mae wyth eraill yn
anweledig, eithr yng ngogylch hir o amseroedd, ag oesoedd
meithion.

Gosgorddiadau 'r Ser ydynt fal hynn

1. Caer Arianrod,	7. Y Llong fawr,
2. Yr Orsedd Wenn,	8. Y Llong foel,
3. Telyn Arthur,	9. Y Llatheidan,
4. Caer Gwydion,	10. Y Twr Tewdws,
5. Yr Haeddel fawr,	11. Y Tryfelan, ·
6. Yr Haeddel fach,	12. Llys Don,

---

[1] It is to be regretted that L. Morris should have omitted from a poem, which
is inserted in the Myv. Arch. v. i. p. 47, a portion " containing an odd sort of
philosophy about the origin of salt water, rain, and springs," as it might, notwithstanding its oddity, have been of service in ascertaining the amount and
species of knowledge possessed by our Bardic ancestors on these matters.

[2] Seven of the Planets are mentioned in a poem of Taliesin, called " Canu y
Byd Mawr," or the Song of the Great World. Myv. Arch. v. i. p. 25.

[3] The daughter of Don, and styled in the Triads (Myv. Arch. ii. 73) one
of ' the three beautiful ladies of the Isle of Britain." This constellation is the

the surface of the earth, springs of water are found to be saline in those localities, and salt is obtained from the water in those places.[1]

THE STARS.

There are three kinds of stars : fixed stars, which keep their places, and are also called stationary stars; erratic stars, which are called planets, and are fifteen in number, seven[2] being always visible, and eight invisible, except very seldom, because they revolve within and beyond the Galaxy ; and the third are irregular stars, which are called comets, and nothing is known of their place, number, and time, nor are they themselves known, except on occasions of chance, and in the course of ages.

> From Bardism — Fragments about the months and other things.

ASTRONOMY.

There are seven visible planets, and eight are invisible, except in a long cycle of times, and vast ages.

The constellations of the stars are the following —

1. The Circle of Arianrod ;[3]
2. The White Throne ;
3. Arthur's Harp ;[4]
4. The Circle of Gwydion ;[5]
5. The Great Plough-tail ;[6]
6. The Small Plough-tail ;
7. The Great Ship ;
8. The Bald Ship ;
9. The Yard ;[7]
10. Theodosius's Group ;[8]
11. The Triangle ;
12. The Palace of Don ;[9]

---

same with the Corona Borealis. Mentioned in "Hanes Taliesin," Ap. Myv. Arch. i. 19.

[4] The Lyre.

[5] The son of Don ; one of "the three sublime astronomers of the Isle of Britain." Tr. 89, third Series. The Galaxy.

[6] The Great Bear.   [7] The Orion.

[8] The Pleiades. Mentioned in "Hanes Taliesin," Ap. Myv. Arch. i. 19.

[9] Cassiopeia.

13. Llwyn Blodeuwedd,	27. Yr Esgair fawr,
14. Cadair Teyrnon,	28. Yr Esgair fechan,
15. Caer Eiddionydd,	29. Yr Ychen Bannog,
16. Caer Sidi,	30. Y Maes mawr,
17. Cwlwm Cancaer,	31. Y fforch wenn,
18. Lluest Elmur,	32. Y Baedd Coed,
19. Bwa 'r Milwr,	33. Llywethan,
20. Brynn Dinan,	34. Yr Hebog,
21. Nyth yr Eryres,	35. March Llyr,
22. Trosol Bleiddyd,	36. Cadair Elffin,
23. Asgell y Gwynt,	37. Neuadd Olwen,
24. Y Feillionen,	38.
25. Pair Caridwen,	39.
26. Dolen Teifi,	40.

AMSERYDDIAETH.

Prydain ab Aedd Mawr a aned ar foreu 'r Alban Eilir
sef hynny y nawfedydd o Fawrth herwydd Cyfrif gwyr
Rhufain, am hynny dodwyd ddechreu 'r flwyddyn ar ei
ddydd ef, yn ddydd gwledd, a gorddawd, fal y mae fyth
hyd heddyw a'r dydd cyntaf o'r Cyntefin ai gelwid yn yr
hen amser a diwedd cyntefin gwyl yr Alban hefin. ag o
hynny hyd yr Alban Elfed Haf ai gelwir a hefyd Cynhauaf,
ag o'r Alban Elfed, hyd Alban Arthan Mesyryd ai gelwir,
ag oiyna hyd yr Alban Eilir Gauaf.

---

[1] The title of one of Taliesin's poems. Myv. Arch. i. 65.

[2] The zodiac, or ecliptic.　Mentioned in "Hanes Taliesin."

[3] Styled in the Triads as one of "the three monarch bulls." Tr. 73 ; third
Series.

[4] There was a king of Britain of this name, who flourished from B.C. 859 to
839.　He founded Bath.

[5] Mentioned in "Hanes Taliesin."　　[6] The Twins.

[7] The son of Bleiddyd—the celebrated king Lear of Shakespeare.

[8] Elffin is said to have first discovered Taliesin, in a leathern bag, fastened to
one of the poles of a weir.　He is frequently mentioned by the Bard.

13. The Grove of Blodeu-
   wedd;
14. The Chair of Teyrnon;[1]
15. The Circle of Eiddion-
   ydd;
16. The Circle of Sidi;[2]
17. The Conjunction of a
   Hundred Circles;
18. The Camp of Elmur;[3]
19. The Soldier's Bow;
20. The Hill of Dinan;
21. The Hen Eagle's Nest;
22. Bleiddyd's[4] Lever;
23. The Wind's Wing;
24. The Trefoil;
25. The Cauldron of Ceridwen;[5]
26. Teivi's Bend;
27. The Great Limb;
28. The Small Limb;
29. The Large-horned Ox-
   en;[6]
30. The Great Plain;
31. The White Fork;
32. The Woodland Boar;
33. The Muscle;
34. The Hawk;
35. The Horse of Llyr;[7]
36. Elffin's[8] Chair;
37. Olwen's[9] Hall.

CHRONOLOGY.

Prydain, the son of Aedd Mawr, was born on the morning of Alban Eilir, that is, the ninth day of March, according to the computation of the Romans; therefore the
beginning of the year was fixed on his day, as a day of feast
and institution, as it is still to this day. In old times it
was called the first day of Cyntevin,[10] the end of Cyntevin
being the feast of Alban Hevin.[11] From thence to Alban
Elved[12] it was called Summer, and also Harvest; from
Alban Elved to Alban Arthan[13] it was called Autumn;
and from thence to Alban Eilir,[14] Winter.

---

[9] A distinguished character in Welsh Romance.

[10] Cyntefin, (cynt-hefin,) the commencement of summer.

> Calangauaf garw hin,
> Annhebyg i *gyntefin.*

> The calends of winter, rough is the weather,
> Unlike *the beginning of summer.*—Ll. Hen.

[11] The summer solstice.   [12] The autumnal equinox.

[13] The winter solstice.   [14] The vernal equinox.

Sef herwydd Cyfrif Eglwys a Llys Cyfraith degfed o
fawrth y gelwir yr Alban Eilir. eithr yng Nghyfrif amser y
Cymry a gwyr Rhufain y nawfed o fawrth ai gelwir.

Cyn nog amser Prydain ab Aedd Mawr dodawd ddechreu
'r flwyddyn ar ddydd yr Alban Arthan, a hynny y nawfed
o fis rhagfyr yng nghyfrif amser y Cymry. (gwel Almanac
Sion Jones) 1752.)

AMSERYDDIAETH.

Sef Cyn amser dyfodiad Crist yng Nghnawd y Beirdd a
geinmygent amseroedd herwydd blynyddau Cof a Chyfrif,
nid amgen er amser Prydain ab Aedd Mawr a fu yn ei glod
bum can mlynedd a thrugain a chwech cyn geni Crist yng
Nghnawd, ag o hynny y mae'n arfer gan y Beirdd geinmygu
amser Cof a Chyfrif, yng nghyforddawd ag oedran Crist, sef
y bu Brydain ab Aedd Mawr dan gof a gwybod a soniwyd o
amser Cyn geni Crist ac herwydd amcan y doethion ag arwyddfeirdd cyfarwyddbwyll chwechant a hanner o flwyddi
gwedi dyfod y Cymry gyntaf i Ynys Prydain, sef hynny
mil o flwyddi, a deucant ag unarbymtheg, cyn geni Crist, y
daethant genedl y Cymry gyntaf i Ynys Prydain, a hynny
a elwir Amser Brut. sef y dyrifid blynyddau Cof a chyfrif
yn yr hen amseroedd dan amcan er amser Brut. sef hynny
amcan mil o flwyddi gwedi Torri Twr Nemrwth gawr, ac
amcan dwyfil ac wythgant o flynyddau gwedi gyrru Addaf
ag Efaf allan o Ardd Baradwys sef y bu hynny $^{bum}_{naw}$ can
mlynedd wedi gwneuthur o Dduw y Byd hwn.

---

[1] Brut—Brutus, supposed to be the same with Prydain.

According to the computation of the Church and the
Courts of Law, Alban Eilir was said to be the tenth of
March, but in the chronology of the Cymry and the Ro-
mans it was said to be the ninth of March.

Before the time of Prydain, the son of Aedd the Great,
the beginning of the year was fixed upon the day of Alban
Arthan, which was the ninth of the month of December,
according to the chronology of the Cymry. (See John
Jones's Almanack, 1752.)

CHRONOLOGY.

Before the coming of Christ in the flesh, the Bards solem-
nized times according to the years of memorial and computation, namely, from the time of Prydain, the son of Aedd
the Great, who was famous five hundred and sixty-six years
before the birth of Christ in the flesh ; and from that time
it is usual with the Bards to celebrate the memorial and
computation of time in accordance with the years of Christ.
Prydain, the son of Aedd the Great, as far as memorial and
knowledge go, lived the time mentioned before the birth of
Christ, and, according to the conjecture of wise men, and
well informed herald-bards, six hundred and fifty years subsequently to the first arrival of the Cymry in the island of
Britain. It was thus, one thousand two hundred and sixteen years before the birth of Christ that the nation of the
Cymry first came into the island of Britain, and this was
called *Brut time*, because the years of memory and computation were in old times conjecturally reckoned from the time
of Brut,[1] which was about a thousand years after the demo-
lition of the tower of Nimrod the Giant, and about two
thousand and eight hundred years after the expulsion of
Adam and Eve from the garden of Paradise, which occurred
five[2] hundred years after God had made this world.

[2] Al. "nine."

COF CYFRIF.—COF GWLAD.

Llyma 'r modd y nottaynt yr hen Athrawon hyspysu cof
amseroedd, sef o ddyfodiad Cenedl y Cymry i'r Ynys hon,
Amcan a Chof gwlad a chenedl, achos nad oedd braint ar
gyfarwyddyd Cof Cyfrif cyn nog amser Prydain ab Aedd, a
elwid Dyfnarth Prydain, sef Dyfnfarth ei enw cyssefin, ai
amser ef amcan ar 700 gant mlynedd wedi dyfod y Cymry
i'r Ynys hon, ag o ei amser ef hyd dyfodiad Crist yng
nghnawd 553 mlynedd yn hysbysiadol o gof cyfrif a chadw
gwarantedig yn nawdd Beirdd Ynys Prydain dan boen colli
Braint a swydd a Thrwydded o aradr ag o roddion, ac o
bob Da wrth gerdd a Barddoniaeth. A chyn dyfodiad y
Cymry i'r ynys hon, nid oes nemmor yn amgau * ar Gof a
chadw gwlad a chenedl, a'r gyfarwyddyd hon a elwir Cof
Cyfrif, ag eraill ai geilw cof a chyfrif, sef y dywedir tâw yn
y flwyddyn cof a chyfrif 553 y dothyw Crist yng Nghnawd
a hynn a gadwed ar arfer hyd yn amser.

COF A CHYFRIF.

Oed Cof a chyfrif a gyfrifid o amser Prydain ab Aedd
Mawr, sef y bu ef Bedwar canmlynedd a phedwar ugain
cyn amser y daeth Crist yn y cnawd, a gwedi dangos o
fran fendigaid ab Llyr y ffydd yng Nghrist i Genedl y
Cymry ai dwyn ar gred yn Ynys Prydain y dechreuwyd
cyfrif amser herwydd oedran Crist. Mynn rhai mai er amser Prydain y dylit amseru pob gwaedd Gwlad a Gorsedd,
sef hynny herwydd arfer yr hen Gymry, eraill a fynnent

---

* Doubtless an error for " amgen."

[1] The fragment would appear to be imperfect, unless we read " to this time."

THE MEMORIAL OF COMPUTATION.—THE MEMORIAL OF COUNTRY.

This is the mode in which the ancient Teachers used to denote the memorial of times ; that is, from the arrival of the Cymry in this island, it was the conjecture and memory of country and nation, because there was no privilege attached to the science of memorial and computation before the time of Prydain, the son of Aedd, who was called Dyvnvarth Prydain, Dyvnvarth being his original name. His epoch was about seven hundred years after the arrival of the Cymry in this island ; and from his time to the advent of Christ in the flesh there were five hundred and fifty-three years, as told in the memorials of computation and tradition, warranted by the sanction of the Bards of the Isle of Britain, under the penalty of losing privilege and office, and the freedom of plough, and gifts, and of all chattels due in respect of song and poetry. Before the coming of the Cymry into this island, there was hardly anything else remembered and preserved by country and nation. This knowledge is called the memorial of computation, and others call it memorial and computation; thus it is said, that it was in the year of memorial and computation, five hundred and fifty-three, Christ came in the flesh ; and this has been kept in practice down to the time.[1]

MEMORIAL AND COMPUTATION.

Chronological memorial and computation were reckoned from the time of Prydain, son of Aedd the Great, who lived four hundred and eighty years before the time when Christ came in the flesh. When Bran the Blessed, the son of Llyr, had exhibited the faith in Christ to the nation of the Cymry, and made them believers in the island of Britain, they began to compute time according to the years of Christ. Some maintain that every cry of country and Gorsedd ought to be dated from the time of Prydain, that is, according to the custom of the ancient Cymry ; others maintain that such

hynny ac oed Crist gyda hynny, eraill ni fynnant eithr oed Crist. (Sion Bradford.)

CYLCH AMSER.

Sef yw cylch amser cyfan, undydd a blwyddyn a phedair wythnos ym mhob mis, a thrimis ar ddeg yn y flwyddyn.

MISOEDD.

1 Mis marw
Marwfis,
Gwynfer,
Gwynhyfer
Gwynhwyfar
Mis du
} IONAWR {
Gwynfyr
Gwynhyfar

2 Mys Myri,
Mis yr ŵyn,
Gerwynnon
} Myrionydd.
CHWEVROL

3 Mis yr Erydd
Mis y Myllyn,
Cynnodor
Gwynnonwy
} Daronwy.
MAWRTH

---

[1] Gwyn-mer; in reference to either frost or snow.

[2] Gwyn-hy-mer.

[3] Gwyn-wy-bar; ice. Gwenhwyvar is also used as a proper name, three of Arthur's wives being so called.

[4] Gwyn-myr; *myr* being the aggregate plural of *mor*, a sea.

[5] Gwyn-hy-bar, or gwyn-y-bar. From *bar* comes *barug*, the term in popular use for hoar-frost.

[6] Probably in reference to the penitential season of Lent.

[7] Cyn-nodd-awr.

[8] Daronwy is one of the epithets of the Deity. It was also the name of a person who is considered as one of the three molestations of the isle of Anglesey. (Tr. 81; first Series.) There is a historical poem by Taliesin, preserved in the

should be done in conjunction with the years of Christ;
whilst others will have only the years of Christ.

(Sion Bradford.)

THE CYCLE OF TIME.

The cycle of complete time is a year and a day, four
weeks being in each month, and thirteen months in the
year.

THE MONTHS.

1. The dead month;
   The dead month;
   The white water;[1]
   The white stream;[2]
   The white surface of water;[3] } January.
   The black month;
   The white flood;[4]
   The white rime.[5]

2. The month of purity;[6]
   The month of lambs;
   The severe time; } February.
   The season of purification.[6]

3. The agriculturist's month;
   The month of violets;
   The rising of the sap;[7] } March.
   The Lily of the valley;
   The thunderer.[8]

1st vol. of the Myv. Arch, entitled "Cerdd Daronwy," or Daronwy's Song.
Probably this name is given to the month of March, not from any idea that thun-
der happens in it oftener than in other months, but because it is a powerful
month—the lord of months, as regards the severity of the weather, even as it is
called Mawrth, March=Mars, the god of war.

4 Mis y Wennol, Mis y Gog, Cyntefin, Cynhewin Canowin (canaw)	Canhavdardd, Gwyronydd, EBRILL	eireinwg glaswyron
5 Mis y Gog, Gwyrfai, Mai, Cyntefin, Ednygain,	Gorlesin MAI Cynwyran—cynwyron. Llywyran—Cogerddan.	
6 Mis y Blodau Myhefin	MEHEFIN	
7 Mis y Gwair Gorphen hâf, Gorhefin, gorhewin	Gwerthefin, GORPHEN HÂF.	
8 Mis y Gwenith Gwynnogawr, Cangalaf, Gwyngalaf, Gwyngoleilion Mis yr yd	Gorhïan—Cannogawr, Gwynfai AWST Gwynhefin.	

[1] "Cynhewin," from *cyn*, and *haw*, ripe. It may, however, be but another form of *Cyntefin*.

[2] "Canowin," from *cenaw*, an offspring ; a graft. It may refer to the sprouts of trees, as well as to the young of animals. We say *cenawon cyll*, the catkins of hazel, and *cenawon llewod*, lion whelps.

[3] Cenaw-tardd.

[4] Probably because the pear trees now begin to blossom.

[5] Also "May;" and is the name still in use.

[6] "Cogerddan," (cog-cerdd.) It may signify also the departure of the cuckoo.

[7] "Gwerthefin" is likewise an epithet for the Deity, and signifies what is supreme, from *gwarthaf*, the upper part, or summit. We have above derived it from *gwarth* and *hefin*.

[8] Gorhïan, i.e. gor-huan.

4. The month of the swallow;
The month of the cuckoo;
The beginning of summer;
The beginning of ripenness;[1]
The season of the young;[2] } April.
The spring of the young;[3]
The time of vegetation;
The pear orchard;[4]
The green grass.

5. The month of the cuckoo;
Freshness;
Opening;[5]
The beginning of summer;
The season of flies; } May.
Superior verdancy;
Prime vegetation;
Various vegetation;
The cuckoo's song.[6]

6. The month of flowers; } June.
The presence of summer.

7. The month of hay;
The close of summer;
The extremity of summer; } July.
The extremity of ripenness;
The height of summer.[7]

8. The wheat month;
The season of whiteness;
Blanched stalks;
White stalks;
White beards of corn;
The month of corn; } August.
Extreme sunniness;[8]
The bright season;
The white appearance;
The white summer.

9 Mis yr Aeron,
   Medi,
   Cangaleifion, } MEDI,
   Cangalaf.

10 Mis y mêl
    Mis y gwin.
    Mis y melwr, } HYDREF,
    Mis Hyddfref,

11 Mis y niwl,
    Mis gwrm;
    Mis y crwybr, } TACHWEDD,
    Deilgwymp,
    Tachwedd

12 Mis Du, } Gwynollydd,
    Mis Tywyll, } RHAGFYR,
    Rhagfyr

Modd arall ar y misoedd.

1 Gwynhyfer—dechreu Alban Arthan
2 hwefrol—
3 Eilir.
4 Cyntefin, dechreu yr Alban eilir,
5 Mis hefin, Mis myhefin.
6 Mis Gorhefin, yn dechreu yr Alban hefin,
7 Mis Medi
8 Mis gwyngalaf.
9 Hyddfref, yn dechreu yr Alban elfed.
10 Mis Tachwedd,
11 Mis Rhagfyr.
12 Mis Marw Mis Du.

---

[1] This clearly indicates that vineyards were formerly cultivated in Britain.

[2] "Gwynollydd," or "gwynyllydd," probably from *gwyntyll*. Many of the above names are, however, now so obsolete, and their roots so obscure, that we do not vouch for accuracy of translation in every case.

9. The fruit month ;
   Reaping ;
   The white stalks ;
   The white stalk.
} September.

10. The honey month ;
    The wine month ;[1]
    The month of the honey gatherer ;
    The month of deer rutting.
} October.

11. The month of mist ;
    The dusky month ;
    The month of honey-comb ;
    The fall of the leaves ;
    Receding appearance.
} November.

12. The black month ;
    The dark month ;
    Fore-shortening ;
    The ventilator.[2]
} December.

Another mode of designating the Months.

1. The white fluid. The beginning of Alban Arthan.
2. The severe month.
3. Regeneration.
4. The beginning of summer. The commencement of Alban Eilir.
5. The summer month. The month of June.
6. The month of the excess of summer, beginning on Alban Hevin.
7. The reaping month.
8. The month of white stalks.
9. Deer rutting, beginning on Alban Elved.
10. The month of receding appearance.
11. The month of fore-shortening.
12. The dead month. The black month.

Ac fel hynn mewn llyfrau eraill, a dechreu dranoeth i'r Alban Arthan.

1 Gwynhyfer,	7 Gwerthefin	Gorhefin
2 hwefrol,	8 Medi,	
3 Eilir,	9 Gwyngalaf	Cangalaf
4 Ebrill.	10 Hyddfref,	
5 Cyntefin	11 Tachwedd,	
6 Maihefin	12 Rhagfyr, mis du.	

DECHREU Y FLWYDDYN.

Yr hên Gymry a ddechreynt y flwyddyn drannoeth i'r dydd byrraf o'r gaeaf, sef ar droad yr haul.

TRI CHYLCH HAUL.

Cylch aban haf, ablan haf, ag alban auaf.

PEDRYFANNOEDD Y FLWYDDYN.

1 Gaeaf — 2 Gwanwyn — 3 Haf. 4 Mesyryd. (Messis in Latin)
      neu fal hynn
1. Gauaf — 2, Gwanwyn — 3 Haf — Canhwyron.
      ac fal hynn y mae pedwar bann haul,
1. Alban Arthan. 2 Alban Eilir — 3. Alban Hefin, 4 Alban Elfed.
      Hefyd fal hynn yn wladaidd
1. Haf — 2 Gaeaf — 3 Gwanwyn.

---

[1] Sic in MS.; but we are inclined to regard them as clerical mistakes for *alban*, a primary point. It seems also as if " gwanwyn," spring, should have been written for the former *summer*.

[2] Or,—The winter solstice; the vernal equinox; the summer solstice; and the autumnal equinox.

In other Books it is as follows—beginning on the morrow of Alban Arthan.

1. The white fluid.
2. The severe month.
3. Reanimation.
4. The springing rows.
5. The beginning of summer.
6. The open summer.
7. The height of summer. The excess of summer.
8. Reaping.
9. White stalks. Bright Stalks.
10. Deer rutting.
11. Receding appearance.
12. Fore-shortening. Black month.

THE BEGINNING OF THE YEAR.

The Ancient Cymry began the year on the morrow of the shortest day of the winter, that is, on the turn of the sun.

THE THREE CIRCLES OF THE SUN.

The circle of the summer aban ;[1] of the summer ablan ;[1] and of the winter alban.

THE FOUR QUARTERS OF THE YEAR.

1. Winter. 2. Spring. 3. Summer. 4. Autumn.
    Or thus :—
1. Winter. 2. Spring. 3. Summer.—White grasses.
    And the four points of the sun are thus :—
1. The point of roughness. 2. The point of regeneration. 3. The point of summer. 4. The point of reaping time.[2]
    Also vulgarly, thus :—
1. Summer. 2. Winter. 3. Spring.

YR ALBANAU.

Llyma fal y mae yn Llyfr Sion Hywel Gwynn ^{Llyfr Tre Bryn.}
Alban Elfed yw calan Hydref,
Alban Arthan yw calan Ionor
Alban Eilir yw calan Gwanwyn,
Alban Hefin, yw calan Haf.

RHANNAU Y FLWYDDYN.

Or un Llyfr.

Tair rhan y flwyddyn
Amser haf, o'r Cyntefin hyd galan Hydref,
Gauaf, o galan Hydref hyd galan chwefror,
Gwanwyn, o galan chwefror i'r cyntefin.

RHANNAU Y FLWYDDYN.

Gwanwyn o'r Alban Arthan i'r Alban Eilir, ac o hynny
hyd yr Alban Hefin. ac o hynny haf hyd yr Aban Elfed,
ac o hynny Gaeaf hyd yr Alban Arthan Gwedi hynny
gwanwyn, Haf. mesyryd a gaeaf.   (Lln Sion.)

RHANNAU Y FLWYDDYN.

Rhai o'r hen feirdd a rannant y flwyddyn fal hynn,
Cynhauaf — Gauaf — Gwanwyn — a Chyntefin.

RHANNAU Y FLWYDDYN.

4 rhan y flwyddyn Gwanwyn, Haf, mesyryd, a gaeaf.
eraill Haf, gauaf, a gwanwyn.

---

¹ Calangauaf garw hin,
Annhebyg i *gyntefin.*
The calends of winter, rough is the weather,
Unlike to the *beginning of summer.*—Ll. Hen.

THE ALBANS.

They are as follows in the Book of Sion Howel Gwyn—the Book of Tre'rbryn :—

Alban Elved is the calend of October;
Alban Arthan is the calend of January;
Alban Eilir is the calend of spring;
Alban Hevin is the calend of summer.

THE DIVISIONS OF THE YEAR.

From the same Book.

The three divisions of the year :—
The time of summer from Cyntevin to the calend of October;
Winter from the calend of October to the calend of February;
Spring from the calend of February to Cyntevin.

THE DIVISIONS OF THE YEAR.

Spring from Alban Arthan to Alban Eilir, and thence to Alban Hevin; and from thence Summer to Alban Elved; and from thence Winter to Alban Arthan. After that: Spring; Summer; Autumn; and Winter.

Llywelyn Sion.

THE DIVISIONS OF THE YEAR.

Some of the ancient Bards divide the year as follows :—
Harvest; Winter; Spring; and the beginning of Summer.[1]

THE DIVISIONS OF THE YEAR.

The four divisions of the year: Spring; Summer; Autumn; and Winter. According to others: Summer; Winter; and Spring.

RHANNAU'R FLWYDDYN.

Pedwar rhan y flwyddyn, Gwanwyn, Haf, Mesyryd, a Gauaf. *Harri Hir.*

Y Gwanwyn sy'n dechre yn Mawrth pan ddel gogyfal haul a gwrthaul, sef cyhydedd dydd a nos. *Ib.*

RHANNAU Y DYDD.

Wyth rhan y dydd—1 Bore—2 Plygaint—3 Anterth—4 Nawn—5 echwydd—Cyflychwyr. &c.

Neu fal hynn.

1 Plygaint—2 Bore—3 Anterth—4 Nawn. 5 echwydd —6. Golychwyr—7 achwedd—8 Dewaint.

RHANNAU 'R DYDD.

1, Dewaint	1, Dewaint,	Hwyr,[3]
2, Pylgeint	2, Pylgeint,	Diwedydd,
3, Bore,	3, Bore,	Cyfnos
4, Anterth,	4, Anterth,	Cyflychwyr,
5, Nawn,	5, Nawn	Cyflwg,
6, Echwydd	6, Echwydd	Hwyr,
7, Hwyr,	7, Gwedechwydd,	&c.
8, Ucher,	8, Ucher,	

RHANNAU 'R DYDD.

1	Dewaint,		
2	Pylgeint,		
3	Bore,		
4	Anterth		
5	Nawn,	Diwedydd, Hanner dydd	
6	Echwydd,	Hwyr, Cyfnos.	
7	Hwyr,—	Gwedechwydd. Cyflychwyr	Hwyr, Cyfnos.
8	Ucher		

THE DIVISIONS OF THE YEAR.

The four divisions of the year : Spring ; Summer ; Autumn ; and Winter. Harry the Tall.

The Spring begins in March, when the sun and its opposite are alike, that is, when the day and night are of equal length. Ib.

THE DIVISIONS OF THE DAY.

There are eight parts of the day : 1. morning ; 2. dawn ; 3. vapourlessness ; 4. noon ; 5. evening ; 6. twilight, &c.

Or thus :—

1. Dawn ; 2. morning ; 3. vapourlessness ; 4. noon ; 5. rest ; 6. twilight ; 7. disappearance ; 8. midnight.[1]

THE DIVISIONS OF THE DAY.

1. Midnight ; 2. dawn ; 3. morning ; 4. vapourlessness ; 5. noon ; 6. rest ; 7. evening ;[2] 8. overcast.

THE DIVISIONS OF THE DAY.

1. Midnight.
2. Dawn.
3. Morning.
4. Vapourlessness.
5. Noon ; the end of day ; mid-day.
6. Rest ; evening ; commencement of night.
7. Evening ; after rest ;[4] evening ; commencement of night.
8. Overcast.

---

[1] Literally, " separation."   [2] Al. "after rest."

[3] The terms in the third column are jumbled together, with no particular assignment, and may be thus translated : evening, the end of day, commencement of night, twilight, ditto, evening.

[4] Al. "twilight."

Ag yn hyn o fodd y cyfrifit amser gynt a rhannau'r dydd, a dywedaint wythran dydd a their awr pob, sef awr gyntaf anterth eilawr, ag felly am eraill, Dewaint, pylgaint &c.

RHANNAU'R DYDD.

Ag yn y modd hynn y cyfrifid amser gynt, a rhannau 'r dydd, a dywedynt wythran dydd, a theirawr ymhob rhann, a chyfrif yn y modd yma, sef yr awr gyntaf, neu'r ail, neu'r drydydd awr, o'r Dewaint, y pylgeint, yr Anterth &c. &c. ac fal hynn am bob un or wyth rhann.

RHANNAU 'R DYDD.

Pedwar rhan dydd. *Bore*, sef y chwechawr cyntaf; *Anterth* yr ail chwechawr; *Nawn* y trydydd chwechawr; ac yn bedwerydd yr *Achwedd* (Echwydd) yn estyn hyd y Bore.

BLYNYDDAU 'R HAUL A'R LLEUAD.

Nawmlwydd ar hugain haul yw dengmlwydd ar hugain lleuad.
Dyddiau blwyddyn leuad 354.
Dyddiau blwyddyn haul 366.
Dyddiau Blwyddyn gof a chyfrif 365.
eraill a wedant 364.
Sef ai gelwir Cof a Chyfrif cyfarwyddyd a chyfrif er pan y daethant y Cymry i Ynys Prydain.

BLYNYDDAU 'R HAUL A'R LLEUAD.

Blynyddau 'r haul a'r Lleuad ydynt fal hynn.
Blwyddyn haul 366 dyddiau.
Blwyddyn Lleuad, 354 dyddiau

---

¹ Al. "rest."

It was in this way that they formerly computed time and the divisions of day ; that is, they enumerated eight parts of the day, giving three hours to each, thus, the first hour of vapourlessness, the second, &c., and so for others, midnight, dawn, &c.

THE DIVISIONS OF THE DAY.

It was in this way that they formerly computed time, and the divisions of day : they enumerated eight parts of the day, and three hours in each part, and reckoned thus, namely, the first hour, or the second, or the third hour of midnight, dawn, vapourlessness, &c., and so in respect of every one of the eight divisions.

THE DIVISIONS OF THE DAY.

The four parts of the day : morning, that is, the first six hours ; vapourlessness, the second six hours ; noon, the third six hours ; and the fourth, evanescence,[1] reaching till the morning.

YEARS OF THE SUN AND MOON.

Twenty-nine years of the sun are thirty years of the moon.

The days of the lunar year are 354.

The days of the solar year are 366.

The days of the year of memorial and computation, 365. Others say, 364.

It is called memorial and computation, information and computation, since the Cymry have come into the Isle of Britain.

YEARS OF THE SUN AND MOON.

The years of the sun and moon are as follows :—
The year of the sun, 366 days.
The year of the moon, 354 days.

Blwyddyn Cof a chyfrif, 364 dyddiau,
Nawmlwydd ar hugain haul yw ⎱
Dengmlwydd ar hugain Lleuad. ⎰
　　Ag mewn man arall fal hynn
Unmlwydd ar ddeg ar hugain Lleuad a wnant ddeng-
mlwydd ar hugain haul.

(O Lyfr Brith y Coed.)

BLYNYDDAU'R HAUL A'R LLEUAD.

Dau gyfrif y sydd ar flwyddyn un yw Blwyddyn haul ac
ynddi 365 o ddyddiau arall yw blwyddyn lleuad, ag ynddi
354, a'r dyddiau dros ben rhif Blwyddyn lleuad a elwir
dyddiau dyddon, ac fal hynn ai rhenir rhwng yr Albannau,
nid amgen 2 ddydd dyddon i'r Alban Arthan, a 3 i'r Alban
Eilir, a thri i'r Alban Hefin, a thri i'r Alban Elfed. a dyddiau rhyddion ydynt a deled a ddelo yno o'r man y delo,
rhydd fydd heb arf heb arfawd yn ei erbyn, gan nis gellir
Llys a Chyfraith gwlad ar hynny o ddyddiau.

(Barddas. Manbethau Misoedd ag eraill.)

DYDDIAU DYDDON.

Dyddiau dyddon yw dyddiau a font dros ben blwyddyn
leuad, a rhannu fal hyn ym mhwydd rhif. 2 ddydd dyddon
ir Alban Arthan. a 3 ir Eilir, a thri i'r hefin a thri i'r Elfed. a dyddiau rhyddon ynt a deled a ddelo o'r man y delo
rhydd fydd heb arf yn ei erbyn, gan nis gellir llys a chyfraith gwlad ar hynny o ddyddiau.

---

[1] " Days of days are those on which it is not proper to prosecute a suit."
Welsh Laws.
　　Dr. Pughe renders " dyddiau dyddon," by *blank days ;*—
　　　　Hoedl Dafydd megis *dydd dyddon.*

The year of memorial and computation, 364 days.

Twenty-nine years of the sun are thirty years of the moon.

In another place, thus :—

Thirty-one years of the moon make thirty years of the sun. From the Book of Brith y Coed.

YEARS OF THE SUN AND MOON.

There are two calculations of years : one is the year of the sun, consisting of 365 days ; the other is the year of the moon, having 354 days. The days which are over and above the number of the lunar year are called days of days, and they are thus distributed among the Albans, that is to say ; —two days of days to Alban Arthan, three to Alban Eilir, three to Alban Hevin, and three to Alban Elved. They are free days, and let any one come from any place he may, he will be free, and exposed to no weapon or stroke, since there can be no court and law of country on those days.[1]

(Bardism ; fragments of the Months and other things.)

DAYS OF DAYS.

Days of days are the days that are over and above the lunar year, and are thus distributed according to their number ; two days of days are given to Alban Arthan, three to Eilir, three to Hevin, and three to Elved. They are free days, and let any one come from where he may, he will be free, without a weapon against him, since there can be no court and law of country on those days.

The life of Davydd is like a *blank day.*—D. Benvras.

3 H

/|\

Y GWIR YN ERBYN Y BYD.

BARDDAS;

OR, A COLLECTION OF ORIGINAL DOCUMENTS, ILLUSTRATIVE OF THE THEOLOGY,
WISDOM, AND USAGES OF

The Bardo=Druidic System

OF THE ISLE OF BRITAIN,

WITH

TRANSLATIONS AND NOTES.

BY

THE REV. J. WILLIAMS AB ITHEL, M.A.,

RECTOR OF LLANYMOWDDWY, MERIONETHSHIRE;
AUTHOR OF "THE ECCLESIASTICAL ANTIQUITIES OF THE CYMRY," &c., &c

VOL. II.

This fragment of the unfinished second volume was found in the Stock of
the late Mr. Rees of Llandovery, after it was purchased by
BERNARD QUARITCH, 15 PICCADILLY, LONDON.
1874.

Barddas.

Bardism.

BARDDAS.

Braint a Defod.

LLYMA Llafar Gorsedd Beirdd Ynys Prydain, lle gellir gweled Breiniau a Defodau Beirdd Ynys Prydain, fal y maent o gysefin arfer a chadarnhâd, a chyda hynn y mae trioedd y Beirdd Cadair Morganwg, a phethau eraill er addysg Barddonïaidd.

Y Cymry a ddaethant gyntaf i Ynys Prydain gyda Phrydain ab Aeddan Mawr, a gwedi gwladychu o honynt yn ddiogel yn y wlad y cyfodwys yn eu plith dri wr doeth, a'u henwau oeddynt Plennydd ac Alawn a Gwron, a chan bob un o honynt Awen o Dduw, ac o hynny Beirdd oeddynt, a hwy a feddyliasant Freiniau a Defodau Beirdd Ynys Prydain gyntaf, ac a'u rhoddasant yn addysg ac yn arfer a deddf yn Ynys Prydain, ac nid oedd Beirdd cyn y gwyr hynn, a chynnal y defodau hynn a wnaethant y Beirdd gan eu gwellhau drwy Awen o Dduw, hyd onid aeth Barddoniaeth Beirdd Ynys Prydain yn Benraith Addysg a Doethineb, a llawer o ddoethion y gwledydd pell a chwenychasant ei dysgu, eithr ei gwaethu ai llygru a wnaethant drwy Awen

---

[1] "Even now those who wish to become more perfectly acquainted with it, for the most part repair thither [to Britain] for the sake of learning it." De Bell. Gall. lib. vi. c. 13.

BARDISM.

Privilege and Usage.

This is the Voice of Gorsedd of the Bards of the Isle of Britain, in which may be seen the Privileges and Usages of the Bards of the Isle of Britain, as originally exercised and confirmed. With them also are the Triads of the Bards of the Chair of Glamorgan, and other matters intended for Bardic instruction.

The Cymry first came into the Isle of Britain with Prydain, son of Aeddan the Great. And when they were safely settled in the country, there arose among them three men, whose names were Plennydd, Alawn, and Gwron, each of them having Awen from God, and who consequently were Bards. These were the first who devised the Privileges and Usages of the Bards of the Isle of Britain, which they appointed for instruction, custom, and law in the Isle of Britain; nor were there any Bards previous to these men. The Bards maintained these usages, and improved them by means of Awen from God, so that the Bardism of the Bards of the Isle of Britain became the supreme learning and wisdom; and many of the wise men of distant countries desired to learn it,[1] but they impaired and corrupted it by means of

nad oedd o Dduw, onid aeth yn y diwedd nad oedd cyfiawn
Farddoniaeth mewn gwlad na man o'r Byd, onid gan
Feirdd Ynys Prydain o genedl y Cymry. a llyma draethu
am y Breiniau a'r defodau a ddylynt Beirdd Ynys Prydain
eu cadw ar gof gerdd Dafawd au hadrodd ar lafar Gorsedd
nid amgen

1. Prif Ddefodau Beirdd Ynys Prydain yw cynnal
heddwch a gwirionedd a chyfiawnder ar gof ac addysg
mewn Gwlad, a mawl i'r mad ac anfawl i'r Anfad. a hynn
oll drwy Awen o Dduw.

2. Nis dygant arf noeth gerwyneb nac yn erbyn neb, ac
nid rhydd i neb ddwyn arf noeth lle bytho Bardd.

3. Tri syrth y sydd o'r Prifeirdd, nid amgen na Bardd
Pendant o gyssefin gaffaeliad, neu Brydydd, ac ym mraint
Trofedigaeth y bydd, ac arno y mae cadw trefn a Rheolaeth
herwydd Braint, Defod, a Llafar Gorsedd, fal na choller y
Farddoniaeth, eithr ei chynnal ai chadw ymraint cyssefin
ddefawd, heb ei llygru a'i newidiaw, ac ar Brydydd y mae
canu mawl ac anfawl wrth a fo cyfiawn a dyledus a chadw
cof ar gan ac arawd am Freiniau a Defodau Beirdd Ynys
Prydain, a'u perthynasau, a Gorseddog y Bernir Prydydd o
dair Cadair, sef yn yr enillo fraint tair Cadair, a rhydd
iddo bob swydd a gorchwyl wrth Gerdd a Barddoniaeth ym
mraint ei gadair, ac ymarfer a swydd Prydydd, ac Ofydd, a
Derwydd, fal y mynno ym mraint achos heb radd heb rodd,
ac yn hynn o beth pennaf ydyw o'r Beirdd, ac nis gellir
Pencerdd onid o Brydydd Gorseddog, a'i Wisg a fydd o'r
glas wybren hinon cyfunlliw, sef yn unlliw ar gwir y cyfunlliw, ac unlliw a'r heddwch y glas wybren hinon, can mai
gwr wrth heddwch a gwirionedd yw Prydydd sef Bardd

Awen which was not from God, until at last there was no pure Bardism in any country or place in the world, but among the Bards of the Isle of Britain, who were of the nation of the Cymry. The following treats of the Privileges and Usages, which the Bards of the Isle of Britain ought to preserve by means of the memorial of vocal song, and to recite with the Voice of Gorsedd : that is to say ;—

1. The principal usages of the Bards of the Isle of Britain are to maintain the memory and teaching of peace, truth, and justice in a country, and to bestow praise upon the good, and dispraise upon the bad ; and all this by means of Awen from God.

2. They are not to bear a naked weapon in the presence of, or against any one; and it is not lawful for any one to bear a naked weapon where there is a Bard.

3. There are three kinds of Primitive Bards. The Bard positive, of original appointment, or a Poet, in virtue of discipleship, whose duty it is to preserve order and rule, in respect of the Privilege, Usage, and Voice of Gorsedd, so that Bardism be not lost, but be maintained and preserved, in right of original usage, uncorrupt and unchanged. And it is incumbent upon a Poet to sing praise and dispraise, according to what is just and requisite, and, by means of song and oration, to preserve the memory of the Privileges and Usages of the Bards of the Isle of Britain, and their appurtenances. A Poet is adjudged to be one of presidency after three Chairs, that is, when he shall have gained the privilege of three Chairs ; and every office and employment, in respect of song and Bardism, are free to him in virtue of his Chair ; and he may exercise the function of Poet, Ovate, and Druid, as he pleases, in virtue of occasion, without a degree, without a grant. In this particular he is the chief of the Bards, and no one can be made master of song who is not a presiding Bard. His dress is to be of serene sky blue, and unicoloured, for unicolour is of the same hue as truth, and the serene sky blue is of the same hue as peace, a Poet, or a privileged Bard, being a man of

Braint, ac ef hefyd a elwir yn Fardd Trwyddedog, a Thrwyddedog Braint, a Phrifardd Pendant. ac nid rhydd iddo
ddwyn arfau, nac i neb ddwyn arf lle bytho yn ei wisg unlliw, wrth ba un ai adnabyddir.

Yr ail o'r Prifeirdd yw Ofydd, ac arno y mae gwybod
wrth Len llythyrog llythyrenog, sef darllen ac ysgrifennu, a medru y
rhyw gelfyddau a font er lles i Feirdd ac i Fyd a'u dangos
yn waranted ger bron ym mron Gorsedd neu Gadair, neu Fardd Gorseddog, ac arno hefyd y mae cynnull a chwilio i maes am
wybodaeth, a'i rhoddi ar addysg, gwedi y caffo Farn a
Braint Gorsedd. nid amgen na hynn arno onid o radd a
rhodd. Gwisg Ofydd a fydd o'r Gwyrdd yn unlliw a gwybodaeth a dysg, a gynnydd fal glasdwf gwanwyn, ac wrth
gaffaeliad gwybodaeth Pennaf yw Ofydd o'r Beirdd.

Yn drydydd o'r Prifeirdd yw Derwydd, ac arno y mae
athrawiaethu wrth bwyll, ansawdd, a gorfod, a dewis, a
welo 'n wirionedd, o gysefin addysg a Defodau a Barn y
Prydyddion, fal y mae ar gof a llafar Gorsedd, ac o Ddysg,
a chelfyddyd, a chaffaeliad yr Ofyddfardd. a phennaf o
swydd arno yw dysgu Gwybodaeth o Dduw, a Chyfiawnder,
a Gwirionedd a heddwch, ac am ddysg a gwybodaeth wrth
bwyll ansawdd a gorfod pennaf or Beirdd yw Derwydd, ac
o fedru canu a dangos can o'i waith ei hun ger bron gorsedd
a roddo arni fraint Cadair, rhydd y bydd iddo fraint Prydydd sef Bardd Braint heb na gradd na rhodd. Gwisg
Derwydd a fydd o'r gwyn cyfunlliw, sef y bydd yn unlliw
pendant a'r gwir yr hwn sydd gyfunlliw a haul a goleuni,
ac o hynny yn unlliw a glendid buchedd a phurdeb Dwyfolder a santeiddrwydd, oni fedro gân nid oes i Dderwydd a
wnelo a swydd Bardd Braint onid o rodd a syberwyd. eithr

peace and truth ;—he is also called a Licensed Bard, a privileged Licentiate, and Primitive Bard positive. Nor is it lawful for him to bear arms, nor for any one to bear a weapon, where he may be in his unicoloured vestment, by which he is to be distinguished. The second of the primitive Bards is the Ovate, and it is incumbent upon him to be acquainted with literature, that is, to read and write, and to know the kinds of arts which may be beneficial to Bards and to the world, and to exhibit them in their authenticity before a Gorsedd or Chair, or a Bard of presidency. It is incumbent upon him, also, to collect and to search for knowledge, and to impart instruction in it, after it shall have obtained the judgment and privilege of Gorsedd ; he is not bound to do more, except in virtue of a degree and grant. The dress of an Ovate is to be green, being of the same colour as knowledge and learning, which grow like the green vegetation of spring ; and in the attainment of knowledge the Ovate is the chief of the Bards. The third of the primitive Bards is the Druid, and it is incumbent upom him to teach, according to reason, nature, obligation, and choice, what he sees to be true, of the original learning, usages, and judgment of the Poets, as preserved in the memory and by the voice of Gorsedd, and of the learning, art, and attainment of the Ovate-bard. And his principal function is to teach divine knowledge, and justice, truth, and peace ; and in respect of learning and knowledge, according to reason, nature, and obligation, the chief of the Bards is the Druid. From knowing how to sing and exhibit a song of his own composition before a Gorsedd, which shall confer upon it the privilege of a Chair, he will be entitled to the privilege of a Poet, that is, a Bard of privilege, without either a degree or a grant. The dress of a Druid is to be of unicoloured white, being thus of the same colour positively as the sun and light, and consequently of the same colour as holiness of life, purity of godliness, and sanctity. If he cannot compose a song, a Druid has nothing to do with the function of a Bard of Privilege, except by grant and courtesy ; but he

Braint iddo heb na gradd na rhodd wneuthur a fo raid a da
gantho yngorchwyl a swydd Ofydd. os o Fardd braint cysefin y bydd Derwydd nid rhaid iddo na gradd na rhodd,
eithr wrth Fraint y Bydd.

---

[1] The three Degrees here mentioned, Bard, Ovate, and Druid, are frequently
alluded to in the compositions of the Poets, from Taliesin to the present day.
To notice a few examples :—

TALIESIN, 520—570.

Ef gwneif *beirdd* byd yn llawen.

He will make the *Bards* of the world merry.

Dysgogan *Derwyddon*
Tra mor tra Brython.

The *Druids* predict,
That the Britons will continue as long as the sea.

MEUGANT, 600—650.

Cred i Dduw nad *Derwyddon* darogant
Ban torrer Din Breon braint.

Trust to God that the *Druids* will not predict,
When the privilege of Din Breon will be violated.

BEDDAU Y MILWYR, about the 9th century.

Bet gwrgi guychit—
A bet llaur llu *ovit*
Yg gwarthav guanas guir yssit.

The grave of Gwrgi the hero—
And the grave of Llawr, the *Ovate* of the host,
Are indeed in the height of Gwanas.

HYWEL AB OWAIN GWYNEDD, 1140—1172.

Ked bwyfy karyadawc kerted *ouyt*
Gobwylled uy nuwy uy nihenyt.

Whilst I wander as an *Ovate*, impressed with love,
May God prepare my latter end.

GWALCHMAI, 1150—1190.

Un mab Maredud a thri meib grufud
Biau bid *beird* weini.

The one son of Maredudd, and the three sons of Gruffudd,
Own the benefit of the administration of *Bards*.

Och Duw na dodyw
Dydbrawd can deryw
Derwydon—

Would to God the day of doom were arrived,
Since *Druids* are come.

is privileged, without either a degree or a grant, to perform what may be necessary, and what may seem good to him, in the employment and office of an Ovate. Should a Druid be an original Bard of Privilege, he has no need of either a degree or a grant, but will act according to privilege.[1]

CYNDDELW, 1150—1200.

Beirniaid am regyd *beird* am ragor,
A'th folant *feirddion derwydon* dor.

Bards are constituted the judges of excellence,
And *Bards* will praise thee, even robed *Druids.*

Mwyn *ouyt* y veirt y ueith goelvein rann
Meirch mygyruann kynkan kein.

As a gentle *Ovate*, to the *Bards* of the ample Coelvaen, he imparts
The fair, lofty coursers, and the harmonious song.

LLYWARCH AB LLYWELYN, 1160—1220.

Mi ym detyf wyf diamrysson,
O'r *prif ueirt* ym prif gyfeillyon.

By my institute, I am opposed to contention,
Of the order of *primitive Bards*, who have been my early companions.

Dywawd *derwyton* dadeni haelon
O hil eryron o eryri.

Druids have declared that liberal ones should be born anew,
From the progeny of the eagles of Snowdon.

PHILIP BRYDYDD, 1200—1250.

Kadeir vaelgwn hir a huberit y *veird*
Ac nyt yr *goueird* yt gyuerchit
Ac am y gadeir honno heddiw bei heiddit
Bod se ynt herwyd gwir a breynt yd ymbrouit
Bydynt *derwyddyon* prydyon prydein.

The Chair of Maelgwn the Tall was prepared for *Bards,*
And not to *poetasters* was it given to compliment:
And if, at this day, they were to aspire to that Chair,
They would be proved, by truth and privilege, to be what they really are :
The *Druids*, the chroniclers of Britain would be there.

MADOG DWYGRAIG, 1290—1340.

Yn nheir llys y gwys gwaisg ddygnedd nad byw
Llun teyrnaidd lyw llin teyrnedd
Balch y *beirdd* bobl heirdd hardded Hu.

In three halls is felt the oppression of anguish, that he lives not,
The chief of princely form, of the royal and proud line
Of the *Bards*, a dignified race, the ornament of Hu.

DAVYDD AB GWILYM, 1300—1360.

Ciliawdr côf neud wyf *Ofydd.*

The chacer of memory, truly I am an *Ovate.*

C

4. Trofedigaeth yw addysg athraw o Fardd Gorseddog, sef y neb a chwenycho gael addysg a braint wrth Gerdd a Barddoniaeth, y mae iddo ymgais ac athraw Gorseddog, ac ymroddi dan ei ofal, ac ymgais a phob Gorsedd wrth Gerdd gyda ei Athraw. ac awenyddion y gelwir y neb a geisiont addysg a braint wrth Gerdd, a Throfedigion, a Thrwydded-igion Braint, a Noddedigion, am y bydd nawdd iddynt na ddygont arfau, ac na ddycco neb arfau lle byddont. ac nid oes amgen o fraint i Awenyddion oni chaffont radd, ym mraint gorsedd, ni ellir gradd ar awenydd hyd ymhen Tair blynedd o drofedigaeth, eithr ym mraint Ofydd y gellir gradd arno, cyn hynny, lle byddo Bardd Gorseddog a ddywetto ar air a Chydwybod y gellir Bardd o'r gwr wrth Ymgais. Ni ellir Trofedigaeth ar wr oni wypo ei law ddeheu, a rhifo Cant, ac enwau misoedd y flwyddyn, a phedwar bann Byd nid amgen na Deheu, dwyrain, gogledd, a Llywynydd, a medru Iaith ei fam fal y bo hawdd ei ddeall; a gwedi y bo trofedig teir blwydd y mae braint ymgais iddo am radd Prifardd Pendant os bydd barf arno ac oni bydd arno farf, arosed oni fo, neu ymgeisied am radd Ofydd. a phan ddelo Barf arno braint iddo ymgais am radd Prifardd os Trofedig teirblwydd neu Ofydd y bydd, ac oni fedr atteb yn Awenyddawl a chyfiawnfarn wrth addysg braint a Defod y pryd hynny yna rhaid gwrthneu gradd

LLYWELYN COCH Y DANT, 1440—1480.

Yma 'ddoeddem ni ddeuddeg
O *Feirdd*, un, sy fyw, ar ddeg.

Here were we twelve *Bards*,
Eleven are now living.

GRUFFUDD AB DAVYDD YCHAN, 1450—1480.

Yma o *Brif-Feirdd* ymbrofwn
O *dair gradd* i dorri grwn.

Here let us, *the three degrees of Primitive Bards*,
Try to break up a ridge.

LEWYS MORGANWG, 1500—1540.

Ba ddyrnod bu ddoe arnom!
Beirdd Tir Iarll bu orddod drom!

4. Discipleship is the instruction of a master, who is a presiding Bard; that is, he who desires to receive instruction and privilege in respect of song and Bardism, must apply to a presiding master, and put himself under his charge, and must attend every Gorsedd of song with his master. Those who seek instruction and privilege in respect of song are called Aspirants, Disciples, privileged Licentiates, and Protected, because protection will be afforded to them, that they should bear no arms, and that none should bear arms where they are. Aspirants have no more privileges, until they obtain a degree in right of a Gorsedd; and no degree can be conferred upon an Aspirant until the end of three years of discipleship, though in right of an Ovate he may have a degree sooner, where there is a presiding Bard, who will aver on his word and conscience that the candidate is competent to be a Bard. No man can be admitted into discipleship, who knows not his right hand, how to count a hundred, the names of the months of the year, and the four parts of the world, namely, south, east, north, and west, and who knows not his mother's tongue in such a way as it may be easy to understand him. When he shall have been a disciple for three years, he is privileged to become a candidate for the degree of a Primitive Bard Positive, if he has a beard; if he has no beard, let him wait until he has, or let him seek the degree of an Ovate. And when he obtains a beard, he is privileged to become a candidate for the degree of a Primitive Bard, if he has been a disciple for three years, or is an Ovate; and if he cannot at that time answer poetically and judiciously, according to the instruction of Privilege and Usage, a degree must be forbidden to him,

Duodd gwawd ac oedd gadarn,
Diweddu *Beirdd* fel dydd barn.

What a blow befel us yesterday!
A heavy stroke fell on the *Bards* of Tir Iarll!
The song that was strong was overcast;
There was an end to *Bards* as in the day of doom.

arno, oni wypo 'n well ei raid ai orchest ai orchwyl, ac yna braint iddo radd.

Gradder Ofydd fal y dywedwyd o'r blaen, ym mraint Bardd Gorseddog a ddywetto ar air a chydwybod y gellir bardd or gwr wrth ymgais, neu o Farn Gorsedd wrth ymgais, neu o drofedig llai na theirblwydd a fedro atteb i'r hynn a ofynner iddo gan Ofydd, Ofydd Braint yw Bardd Braint, neu dderwydd, yn ymarfer a gorchwyl Ofydd neu 'n gwirio hawl Ofydd Ymgais, neu Ofydd Cysefin, ac nid rhaid i Fardd Braint neu Dderwydd, wrth radd na rhodd, can fod iddynt wrth Fraint ymgyd a swydd Ofydd.

Braint Rhodd, neu Fraint wrth syberwyd Gorsedd a fydd pan fo raidd i Fardd ymarfer a swydd na fo iddo herwydd Braint a gradd, fal y bydd Ofydd neu Dderwydd Cysefin, yn ymarfer wrth raid a gorchwyl Prifardd Pendant, lle bytho 'n eisiau, neu Ofydd, wrth eisiau, yn ymgyd a gorchwyl Derwydd, a rhai a ddywedant y gall Awenydd teirblwydd ymgyd ymraint syberwyd a Rhodd Defod, a swydd Prifardd Pendant, lle na bytho un neu ddigon eisoes. ac ymgyd yn yr un modd a swyddau Ofydd a Derwydd. nid rhydd i neb gymmeryd swydd gradd a Gorsedd ym mraint rhodd syberwyd onid lle bo diffyg Beirdd Gorseddog, neu Feirdd wrth radd a Braint defodawl.

Gellir ymgyd a braint rhodd a syberwyd a rhoddi rhybudd undydd a blwyddyn; ac oni ddaw gwrthneu Bardd Defodawl cyn pen hynny o amser, yna rhydd yw braint Defod i bawb a fuant wrth rodd a syberwyd, a *Braint Angen* yw hyn, rhag myned ar goll o'r Farddoniaeth.

Lle bytho dri Bardd Gorseddog y mae Braint gorsedd

unless he is better acquainted with his necessity, his feat, and his employment, in which case he is privileged to obtain a degree.

An Ovate is to be graduated, as before mentioned, in virtue of a presiding Bard, who shall aver on his word and conscience, that the candidate is competent to become a Bard, or according to the judgment of a Gorsedd, to which application has been made, or from having been a disciple for less than three years, if he can answer the questions put to him by an Ovate. An Ovate of privilege is a Bard of privilege, or a Druid, who exercises the vocation of an Ovate, or verifies the claim of an Ovate candidate, or an original Ovate; and there is no need to a Bard of privilege, or a Druid, of a degree or grant, since they are entitled by privilege to assume the office of an Ovate.

The privilege of grant, or privilege by the courtesy of Gorsedd, is that, when a Bard must needs exercise a function, which is not his by privilege and degree, as when an Ovate, or original Druid, in case of necessity, exercises the vocation of a Primitive Bard Positive, where that person is wanting; or when an Ovate, in case of need, exercises the vocation of a Druid. Some say, that an Aspirant of three years, can, in right of courtesy, and of the grant of usage, engage in the office of a Primitive Bard Positive, where there is none, or a sufficient number of such already; and in the same manner, engage also in the offices of an Ovate and a Druid. It is not lawful for any one to assume the office of degree and gorsedd, in right of the gift of courtesy, except where there is a deficiency of presiding Bards, or of Bards of institutional degree and privilege.

A person may share in the privilege of grant and courtesy, by giving notice of a year and a day; and unless an institutional Bard enters his protest against it before the expiration of that time, then all, who have enjoyed grant and courtesy, are entitled to the privilege of usage; this is the privilege of necessity, lest Bardism should be lost.

Where there are three presiding Bards, there is the pri-

Defodawl.   Lle na bo tri nis gellir Braint defodawl, eithr
Braint *rhodd* * neu fraint syberwyd, yn hawl undydd a
blwyddyn; ac yna defodawl y bydd, lle nas doder yn erbyn
yr hawl.

Braint Pendant a fydd lle na $^{bydd}_{bo}$ ond un bardd gorseddog, a hyn a fydd rhag myned o'r Farddoniaeth ar goll.   Sef
y gall y Bardd Gorseddog rhoddi braint gradd a Gorsedd ar
driwyr os mynn er cynnal Gorsedd, ac ymhen undydd a
blwyddyn defodawl y byddant, a gwedi hynny ydd ant yn
orseddogion ym mraint tair Cadair neu dair gorsedd.

Lle na bytho un Bardd gorseddog neu Bencerdd, ac o
hyn Coll ar farddoniaeth mewn golwg, y rhai a wypont
ddefodau a Breiniau Beirdd Ynys Prydain o ben a llafar
Gwlad, neu o Lyfr a choelbren, neu o Gan hen ddihenydd,
rhoddant Rybydd undydd a blwyddyn, ar goedd Gwlad yn
enw Beirdd Ynys Prydain pa rai a fernir bob amser yn
fyw, a phan ddelo pen yr undydd a blwyddyn rhydd yw
iddynt gynnal Gorsedd yn ol a fo defodawl, herwydd Cof a
llafar gwlad, a chof Llyfr neu Goelbren. ac ymhen undydd
a blwyddyn wedi hynny y byddant yn Feirdd Braint a
Defod wrth hawl ac Arddel, ac os ni ddaw gwrthneu arnynt
cyn pen undydd a blwyddyn wedi hynn gan fardd gorsedd
defodawl ym mraint Prifeirdd Ynys Prydain, yna Breiniawl a defodawl y byddant a'u Gorsedd can y byddant yn
awr yn Feirdd wrth Fraint a Defod ym mraint yr un
Rhybydd, a Rhodd, a Syberwyd, ac a roddes Fraint a defod
gyntaf erioed ar Feirdd Ynys Prydain, sef yw hynny
Braint Angen.

* Illegible in the MS. from which Iolo Morganwg made his transcript.

vilege of an institutional Gorsedd. Where there are not three, there can be no institutional privilege, but the privilege of grant, or the privilege of courtesy, in virtue of a year and a day, when it becomes institutional, in case the claim has not been negatived.

Positive privilege takes place where there is only one presiding Bard, such being ordained lest Bardism should become lost. That is to say, the presiding Bard is empowered to confer the privilege of degree and gorsedd upon three persons, if he pleases, for the sake of holding a Gorsedd, which takes place at the end of an institutional year and a day; after that, they become presiding in right of three Chairs, or three Gorsedds.

Where there is not one presiding Bard, or chief of song, and hence there is a prospect of Bardism being lost, let those, who know the usages and privileges of the Bards of the Isle of Britain from the lips and voice of country, or from Book and Coelbren, or from a very old song, give public notice of a year and a day throughout the country, in the name of the Bards of the Isle of Britain, who are adjudged to be always living. And when the year and a day are expired, it is lawful for them to hold a Gorsedd, according to what is institutional, as indicated by the memory and voice of country, and the memorial of Book and Coelbren. And at the end of a year and a day after that they will be Bards of privilege and usage, according to claim and acknowledgment, and unless they are protested against before the end of a year and a day after that by an institutional Bard of Gorsedd, under the privilege of the primitive Bards of the Isle of Britain, then they will be privileged and institutional, as well as their Gorsedd, since they will now be Bards according to privilege and usage in virtue of the same notice, grant, and courtesy, which first of all conferred privilege and usage upon the Bards of the Isle of Britain, that is, the privilege of necessity.

TRIOEDD BRAINT A DEFAWD.

1. Tri Chyntefigion Beirdd gorseddog Ynys Prydain; Plennydd, Alawn, a Gwron;

2. Am dri achos y gelwir Beirdd yn Feirdd wrth fraint a defod Beirdd Ynys Prydain; *un* achaws mai yn Ynys Prydain y cafad ddeall gyntaf ar Farddoniaeth, Ail am na chafwys un _{amgen}^{arall} o wlad yn y Byd ddeall cyfiawn erioed ar Farddoniaeth ddosparthus, *Trydydd*, am nas gellir cynnal Barddoniaeth gyfiawn ond yn mraint Defodau a dosparthau a Llafar Gorsedd Beirdd Ynys Prydain, sef achaws hynny o ba wlad bynnag y bont, Beirdd wrth fraint a Defod Beirdd Ynys Prydain ai gelwir.

3. Tri rhyw Beirdd Ynys Prydain; Prif-Feirdd cyn Cred, gwedi hynny Beirdd Beli, a'r Oferfeirdd, sef ydynt y Prydyddion na font wrth hen freiniau a Defodau Beirdd Ynys Prydain.

4. Tri Bardd cyfarthelyd y sydd, nid amgen Prifardd, Derwydd, Ag Ofydd, can nas dylit ag nas gellir Penn o'r naill ar un o'r llaill o'r Tri hynny cyd y bo braint i bob un o honnynt rag y llaill herwydd braint ag Arbenniccrwydd swydd a Dyled.

5. Trilliw a fyddant amrafaelion y naill ar y llaill yng Ngorwisgoedd y Tri Phrifryw Beirdd Ynys Prydain, nid amgen no GLAS HOEN AWYR Gwisg *Prifardd Pendant*, sef ai

---

[1] " The institution is thought to have originated in Britain, and to have been thence introduced into Gaul; and even now those who wish to become more accurately acquainted with it, generally repair thither, for the sake of learning it." Cæs. De Bel. Gal. lib. vi. c. 13.

[2] William Cynwal (1560—1600) makes a distinction between a Bard and a poet in the following lines:—

> Taeraist yna trwst anhardd
> Y mynwn fod a'm enw 'n *fardd*,
> Ni chleimiais, dodais bob dydd,
> Gwrdd pridwerth ond gradd *Prydydd*.

> Thou didst assert with unseemly clamour,
> That I would have my name as a *Bard*;
> I did not claim—I appointed every day
> An ardent ransom—save the degree of *poet*.

THE TRIADS OF PRIVILEGE AND USAGE.

1. The three primary presiding Bards of the Isle of Britain : Plennydd ; Alawn ; and Gwron.

2. For three reasons are Bards called Bards according to the privilege and usage of the Bards of the Isle of Britain : one reason is, because it was in the Isle of Britain that Bardism was first understood ; the second, because no other country in the world had ever a just comprehension of systematic Bardism ; the third, because genuine Bardism cannot be upheld except in virtue of the usages, systems, and voice of Gorsedd of the Bards of the Isle of Britain. On that account, of whatever country they may be, they are called Bards according to the privilege and usage of the Bards of the Isle of Britain.[1]

3. There are three kinds of Bards of the Isle of Britain : Primitive Bards before Christianity ; after that, the Bards of Beli ; and the pseudo-Bards, that is, the Poets, who are not regulated by the ancient privileges and usages of the Bards of the Isle of Britain.[2]

4. There are three Bards of equality, namely : the Primitive Bard ; the Druid ; and the Ovate ; for there should not, and cannot be supremacy to one over another of those three, though each has a privilege over the other, according to the privilege and speciality of office and obligation.

5. There are three colours, which differ one from the other in the robes of the three principal kinds of Bards of the Isle of Britain, namely : blue,[3] the colour of the sky,

---

[3] Llawdden, at the Eisteddvod, which was held at Caermarthen in the 15th century, thus describes the costume of a Bard :—

> Gwn glas oll yn las a'r lliw 'n lân—ysgawn,
> Glas esgid a braccan,
> Gloyw ei sas, a glas hosan
> Glas i gyd glwys yw i gân.

A blue gown, all blue, of pure colour—and light,
A blue shoe and brogue,
A bright sash, and a blue stocking,
Altogether blue—this becomes a song.

D

gelwir *Trwyddedawg Braint*, sef y bydd iddaw ei Fraint yn
Rhad ai drwydded yn rhydd o'r dydd ydd elo ar ollwng o
law ei Athraw ger bron Gorsedd neu Gadair wrth Gerdd
Dafawd ddosparthus. Gwynn gorwisg *Derwyddfardd*, a
Gwyrdd gorwisg Ofyddfardd, ag nis dylid dau neu fwy o
liwiau ar orwisg nag un nag arall o'r Tri hynn, can mai
annefawd ag annosparth, ag anghydbwyll amryliw ar nag
un nag arall o naddynt.

6. Tripheth a ddoded dan arwydd y Trilliw gorwisg-
oedd Beirdd, *Prifardd*, ei liw yw glas, ac arwydd y lliw
hwnn yw Heddwch a Thangnef, a chariad, a lliw nef $^{ar}_{yn}$ haul a
hinon ydyw, a Hedd a Thangnef herwydd rhyw a goreuder
a ddylai 'r llaw uchaf a Phendawd ar bob peth amgen,
achaws hynny Penn gan fraint a Defawd ag ar bob cof a
chadw prifwybodau yw Prifardd. *Ofydd*, gwyrdd ei liw ef,
a than arwydd y lliw hynn y doded pob Gwybodau Awen,
a Phwyll, a gorfod, yn amgen nag a geffir ar Brifwybodau
Barddas, a phob gwellhâd ar wybodau o ba ryw bynnag yn
ddaionus y bont. sef au dyfelir i wyrddlesni Twf daiar a
choedydd a llysiau yn hyfrydu calon a llygad au gwel, ac
ym mraint Ofydd ai gelfyddyd sef Ofyddiaeth, ai Radd
Gorsedd y doded y Cof a'r Cadw hyd ynghyfallwy, ag o
hynny hyd fyth y byddant yn wahanred ar gof a chadw
Prifardd. *Gwynn*, arwydd Gwirionedd ydyw, a *Derwydd*

---

[1] William Cynwal alludes to a distinctive dress of the Druids :—

E'th folant feirddion, *Derwyddon dor.*

Bards and *robed Druids* will praise thee.

[2] Fy swydd gyda f' arglwyddi,
Hynn fydd, a'u car hen wyf i,
Darllain mydrwaith rhuglwaith rhaid,
Syful im cyfneseifiaid,
Gwisgaw o befrlaw bob un
Gwyrdd roddion gwrdd o'r eiddun.

My function with my lords,
Is this, who am their aged kinsman,—
To read poetry, which is an easy task,
Courteously to my relatives,

distinguishes the dress of the Primitive Bard Positive, who is called Licentiate of Privilege, inasmuch as he has a gratuitous privilege, and a free license from the day he is dismissed from under the hands of his teacher before a Gorsedd or Chair of systematic vocal song; the robe of the Druid-bard is white;[1] and the robe of an Ovate-bard is green.[2] And there ought not to be two or more colours in the robe of one or other of these three, for a variety of colours in one or other of them is contrary to usage and order, and inconsistent with reason.

6. There are three things symbolized by the three colours of the Bards' robes. The colour of the Primitive Bard is blue, and the signification of that colour is peace, tranquillity, and love, it being the colour of heaven in[3] sunshine and serenity—accordingly, peace and tranquillity, in respect of kind and excellence, ought to have the upper hand and supremacy over every other thing—therefore the Primitive Bard is chief, by privilege and usage, in respect of every memorial and record of primitive sciences. Green is the colour of the Ovate, and under the sign of this colour are placed all the sciences of awen and reason and cogency, as distinct from what belongs to the principal sciences of Bardism, and all the improvement of sciences of whatever kind they may be, so that they are good. That is to say, they are assimilated to the green vegetation of the growth of earth, woods, and fields, which delights the heart and eye of those who behold them. In right of an Ovate and his art, or Ovatism, and his degree of Gorsedd, memorial and record are enjoined until the period of efficiency, and from that time for ever afterwards they will be distinct from the memorial and record of a primitive Bard. White is the sym-

And *to wear*, from the fair hands of each,
Green and strong gifts, made by them.
Ll. Goch ab Meurig Hen, (1330—1370.)

[3] Al. "and."

ai arwain yn liw gorwisg, canys cyfliw goleuni a gwynlliw
dydd yw gwirionedd, ag nis gellir arnaw amryliw, a doded
gwir dan arwydd y Cyfunlliw yngorwisg pob un o'r Trirhyw Beirdd, a ni saif na chyfiawnder Braint, na Gwybodau,
na gwellynigion ar ddim o beth yn y Byd yn amgen nag
yng Nghadernyd gwirionedd. Braint i bob un o'r Beirdd
gwedi ai breinier hyd gyfallwy yr Orwisg a fynno ag nid
braint iddo swydd a Chelfyddyd namyn a ddoded yn hawdd
yr orwisg a fynno ef ei arwain.

7.   Tair swydd gelfydd a ddoded o fraint arbennig ar y
lliwiau gorwisg, Prifardd, ei swydd yw cynnal gorsedd a
Barn a gair ar Air, a Chof a Chadw ar brif a Chysefinion
wybodau Barddas Beirdd Ynys Prydain, a hynny mewn
dwy ffordd, nid amgen na llafar gorsedd sef hynny datgan
pob Cof a Chadw ar osteg yngorsedd a Chadair mal ai clywo
gwlad a Chenedl, bawb a gyrchont yr orsedd neu 'r Gadair
y bydd y Prifardd herwydd ei swydd ai ddyled, ar gofyn
ganthaw, a rhydd iddaw yn nawdd ei glyw datgeiniad gwarantedig y Prifardd, Gair ei Air ef ar bawb ynghadair a
Gorsedd, ei ail gof yw cof can sef cerdd dafawd warantedig
o farn Gorsedd.

Swydd Ofydd yw mwyhau a gwellhau gwybodau daionus,
ym mraint Awen a Phwyll, a damcwydd sef hynny gorfod
anesgorawl, achaws hynny ni ofynnir ei Athraw gan Orsedd
ban ai breinier yn Fardd, eithr ei wybodau ai gelfydd ai
fuchedd, sef au gofynnir iddaw rhai hynny, ag ymraint a
gaffer arnaw o naddynt ai breinier ef gan farn a Rhaith
Cadair neu Orsedd wrth Gerdd dafawd, a dau Gof a chadw
a wedd iddaw, nid amgen Cof Cerdd dafawd, a Chof Lly-

bol of truth, and a Druid bears it as the colour of his robe, for truth is of the same hue as light and the bright colour of day, and it cannot admit of a variety of colours. Truth is also represented under the sign of unity of colour in the robes of each of the three kinds of Bards. Nor will the justice of privilege, or sciences, or improvements consist in any thing whatsoever other than in the stability of truth. Each of the Bards, when he shall have been privileged until the period of efficiency, has the privilege of wearing which ever robe he likes, but he has not the privilege of following any office and art other than that which belongs to the robe he may have chosen to wear.

7. Three scientific offices have been, by special privilege, attached to the colours of the robe. The function of a Primitive Bard is to hold a Gorsedd, judgment, and supremacy of testimony, and to maintain the memorial and record of the primary and original sciences of the Bardism of the Bards of the Isle of Britain, in two ways, namely: by means of the voice of Gorsedd, that is, the recitation of every memorial and record publicly at a Gorsedd and Chair, so that they may be heard by country and nation, or by all who resort to the Gorsedd or Chair, at which the Primitive Bard may attend, according to his office and duty, and what is required of him—and he is entitled, under the sanction of his hearing, to the authorized recitation of a Primitive Bard, and his word is a word above all in Chair and Gorsedd ; his second memorial is the memorial of song, that is, vocal poem, warranted by the judgment of Gorsedd. The function of an Ovate is to amplify and to improve good sciences in virtue of awen, reason, and circumstance, that is, inevitable obligation ; on this account, the Gorsedd does not enquire concerning his teacher, when he is privileged a Bard, but merely concerning his sciences, his art, and his life. Those particulars are enquired after ; and, it is in virtue of what he has of them, that he is privileged by the judgment and verdict of Chair or Gorsedd of vocal song. Two memorials and records appertain to him,

thyr, Ag o doder ei gof ai gadw ar Brifardd gan Raith
Gorsedd yna myned a wna 'r gwybodau hynny ar Lafar
Gorsedd yn ddosparthus, ac nis gellir hynny cyn barn cyf-
allwy ar a ddoder felly.

Derwydd, a swydd a ddoder iddaw a fydd o Rodd a braint
Arglwydd y Cyfoeth ynghwmmwd a Thref y bo achaws, ac
am a rodder o'r wlad y danaw, gelwir hynny ei swydd ef,
ag yn ei swydd cynnal Addysg a Golychwyd, nid amgen na
dysgu mal y dylai Athraw Trwyddedawg pob gwybodau
daionus a dosparthus a font warantedig o Lafar Gorsedd
gyfallwy, ag efe a ddylai gynnal cyrch golychwyd man ai
gofynner a man y bo dosparthus a gwarantedig o gof ag
arfer Gwlad a Chenedl. A Braint iddaw nas dyccer arf
noeth ynghyrch y man y bo ei gynnal ef, achaws mai Gwr
yn nawdd Gwlad a chenedl ag yn nawdd Duw ai Dangnef
yw Derwydd.

8. Tri Dyn ni fyddant wrth Gledd nag wrth Gorn;
Bardd, Fferyllt, a Benyw.

9. Tair Celfyddyd a fyddant yn nawdd Beirdd Ynys
Prydain, Cerdd dant ag arwest, meidryddiaeth, a Fferylltaeth, sef yn oed cyd y bont Estroniaid y cyfryw wyr wrth
gelfyddyd a gwybodau breiniolion.

10. Tri Unben Gwlad, nid amgen Bardd yn Athraw
gwybodau daionus er addysg Gwlad a Chenedl, Yngnad yn
Trefnu Iawn a Chyfraith, er Trefn a Thangnef gwlad a
chenedl, Ag Arglwydd, sef Brenin neu Dywysawg Cyfoeth,
yn warcheidwad a nawdd er amddiffyn gwlad a chenedl, ac
o gyfawd Cyfrwym y Tri, pob Rhaith gwlad a chenedl yn
Nawdd Duw ai Dangnef. E.A.W. Arglwydd, Yngnad, a
Bardd.

---

[1] Or, "even if such men of privileged arts and sciences be strangers."

namely, the memorial of vocal song, and the memorial of letters. And when his memorial and record are imposed upon a Primitive Bard by the verdict of Gorsedd, then those sciences will depend systematically upon the voice of Gorsedd, which cannot take place before an efficient judgment is pronounced upon what is so imposed. The function assigned to a Druid comes from the grant and privilege of the lord of the territory, in the comot and town where it may be necessary ; and the extent of country, which is placed under him, is called his office, and in his office he is to maintain instruction and worship ; that is to say, he is to teach, as it behoves a licensed teacher, all good and methodical sciences, which are authorized by the voice of an efficient Gorsedd, and he ought to hold a meeting of worship in the place where it is required, and in the place which is regular and warranted by the memory and custom of country and nation. And his privilege is, that no naked weapon be borne in the approach to the place, where he holds it, because a Druid is a man under the protection of country and nation, and under the protection of God and His peace.

8. Three persons who are to carry neither a sword nor a horn : a Bard ; a metallurgist ; and a female.

9. Three arts that are under the protection of the Bards of the Isle of Britain : instrumental and vocal song ; mensuration ; and metallurgy ; even if such men of arts and sciences be strangers, they are so privileged.[1]

10. The three monarchs of country, namely : a Bard, who is the teacher of good sciences for the education of country and nation ; a judge, who enacts justice and law, for the sake of order and peace in country and nation ; and a lord, that is, a king or prince of a territory, who is guardian and protector, for the sake of defending country and nation : — and from the co-operating union of the three comes every verdict of country and nation, under the protection of God and His peace. Others say : a lord ; a judge ; and a Bard.

11. Tri Dyn arbennigion gwahanred, rhydd fydd eu
breiniaw cyd bont Eillion ag Estroniaid, gan fraint Rhaith
gwlad a gorwlad, sef hynny Rhaith ddygynnull Cymry
Benbaladr, Arglwydd, Bardd, ag Yngnad, ag o'r pryd au
breinier felly, Cynhwynolion au bernir ag nis gellir dychwel
arnynt nag ar eu heppil achaws Braint yw Braint, ag nis
gellir ammraint o fraint, na Braint o Ammraint.

12. Tri Chyflwydd Bardd; Cyfanneddu Gwlad, Gwerinaw Cenedl, a gwellhâu Gwybodau. E.a.w. Gwarhau
Cenedl, a chynnal Gwybodau.

13. Tri pheth nis gellir eu hepcor ar Brifardd ; Awen
wrth Gerdd, Gwybodau Barddas, a Chynheddfau buchedd-
olion diargywedd.

14. Tri aflwydd gwlad a Chenedl ; Arglwydd heb nerth,
Yngnad heb gyfiawnder, a Bardd heb wybodau.

15. Tair Braint arbennigion Bardd, Trwyddedogaeth
ym mhynnag o wlad ydd elo, nas dyccer arf yn ei erbyn
ymhynnag o fan y bo, a gair ar bawb ei air ef parth gwybodau Pynnag o fan y bytho. E.a.w. Tair Braint Bardd
ymhynnag o fan y bo, ai yngwlad ai yngorwlad, Ei drwydded yn rhydd, Ei air yn air ar bawb parth Gwybodau, ac
nas dyccer arf noeth ger ei fronn, bynnag o fann y bytho.

16. Tair Deddf gysefin a ddoded ar Fardd, cadw ei air,
Cadw ei Rîn, a chynnal Heddwch a Thangnef.

17. Tair swyddau deddfedigion Bardd ; Cynnal Hedd a
thangnef man y bo, dangos addysg ar wybodau a Defodau
dosparthus a moliannus gan eu gwellhâu au mwyhau, a
Chadw Cof dosparthus ar ai dirper parth Gwybodau a Dosparthau gwlad a Chenedl.

11. There are three particular and distinct persons, who may be lawfully privileged, though they be aliens and strangers, in virtue of the verdict of country and border country, that is, the conventional verdict of Cymru universally : a lord ; a Bard ; and a judge. From the time they are so privileged, they are adjudged to be innate ; and neither they nor their posterity can become disfranchised, because privilege is privilege, and there can be no lack of privilege from privilege, nor privilege from lack of privilege.

12. The three fortunes of a Bard : to make a country inhabitable ; to civilize a nation ; and to improve sciences. Others say : to civilize a nation ; and to maintain sciences.

13. Three things which cannot be dispensed with in a Primitive Bard : poetical awen ; the sciences of Bardism ; and the qualities of such as lead harmless lives.

14. The three misfortunes of country and nation : a lord without power ; a judge without justice ; and a Bard without sciences.

15. The three special privileges of a Bard : free passport in whatever country he may travel; that no weapon be borne against him in whatever place he may be ; and that his word be paramount in respect of sciences in whatever place he may be. Others say : the three privileges of a Bard wherever he may be, whether in a country or in a border country: free passport; that his word should be paramount in respect of sciences ; and that no naked weapon be borne in his presence, wherever he may be.

16. There are three primary laws enjoined upon a Bard: that he should keep his word ; that he should keep his secret ; and that he should maintain peace and tranquillity.

17. The three institutional laws of a Bard : to maintain peace and tranquillity wherever he may be ; to exhibit instruction in regular and commendable sciences and usages, improving and amplifying them ; and to keep a regular memorial of what is meritorious in respect of the sciences and systems of country and nation.

E

18. Tripheth a waherddir ar Fardd ; Dwyn arfau rhyfel, dwyn achau bonedd anghyfiawn, a dwyn anwiredd ar ei
gerdd dafawd.

19. Tripheth anferth ar Fardd ; Defodau anneddfolion,
Anhynawsder o sarrugrwydd, ac anwybodaeth parth ei
gelfyddyd a swydd wrth gerdd dafawd.

20. Tri Chas Gwlad a Chenedl ; Arglwydd balch,
Twyllnegeswr, a Bardd anynad.

21. Tri Enaid Celfyddyd Bardd ; Cynnal Cof a Chadw
ar wybodau dosparthus, gwellhâu defodau syberwyd, a mwyhau diddanwch.

22. Tripheth ni weddant ar Fardd ; cynnal Cof am
anfad ac anferth, Llygru Defodau syberwyd, a gwrthryn
diddanwch.

23. Tair Annefod y sydd ag am danynt y cyll Bardd ei
Fraint ai dda wrth Gerdd yn anesgorawl ; ymladd, Celwydd, a godineb, sef wrth ddifrawd ag anraith y bernir y
petheu hynn.

24. Tair annefawd y sydd, ag am danynt y cyll Bardd
ei dda wrth Gerdd hyd ymhen y tair blynedd ; gwall ar ei
gof ai gadw meddwdawd cynneddfawl, ag ymarfer a swyddau a chrefftau annosparthus, sef y rhai ni weddant i Fardd
neu Brydydd ymarfer ag wynt, megis ymgynnal ar Gerdd
dant, ag eraill o bethau a waherddir i fardd neu wr wrth
gerdd dafawd.

25. Tripheth nis gellir a el yn eu herbyn ; Cof Llafar
Gorsedd, Hen gerdd warantedig o Gof Barn Gorsedd, a
Defawd gwarantedig Cadair a gorsedd.

26. Tri chof Beirdd Ynys Prydain ; Cof Llafar Gorsedd, Cof can gwarantedig o farn Gorsedd, a chof Coelbren,
sef yw hynny Cof llythyr.

27. Tair Colofn Llafar Gorsedd, Cerdd Dafawd, Gor-
ddodau, a Thrïoedd. E.a.w. Cerdd, Llafar, a Gorddawd.

18. There are three things forbidden to a Bard : to bear the arms of war ; to bear a wrong pedigree ; and to introduce falsehood into his vocal song.

19. Three things monstrous in a Bard : immoral usages; inaffability arising from a morose temper ; and ignorance with regard to his art and office of vocal song.

20. The three odiums of country and nation : a proud lord ; a deceitful messenger ; and a petulant Bard.

21. The three souls of the art of a Bard : to preserve the memorial and record of systematic sciences ; to improve the usages of courtesy ; and to increase amusement.

22. Three things unbecoming in a Bard : to preserve the memorial of what is dishonourable and monstrous ; to corrupt the usages of courtesy ; and to impugn amusement.

23. There are three disusages, for which a Bard will inevitably lose the privileges and chattels, which he possesses in respect of song : fighting ; falsehood ; and adultery—these things being adjudged contrary to law and right.

24. There are three disusages, for which a Bard will lose the chattels, which he possesses in respect of song, to the end of three years : defect in his memorial and record ; habitual drunkenness ; and the practising of irregular employments and trades, such as a Bard or a Poet ought not to practise—for instance, to maintain himself by instrumental song, and other things, which are forbidden to a Bard, or to a man of vocal song.

25. There are three things which cannot be contravened: the memorial of the voice of Gorsedd ; an old song, warranted by a memorial proceeding from the judgment of Gorsedd ; and the warranted usage of Chair and Gorsedd.

26. The three memorials of the Bards of the Isle of Britain : the memorial of the voice of Gorsedd ; the memorial of song, warranted by the judgment of Gorsedd ; and the memorial of Coelbren, that is, the memorial of letters.

27. The three columns of the voice of Gorsedd : vocal song ; institutions ; and Triads. Others say : song ; voice ; and institution.

28. Tri Thrwydded Beirdd Ynys Prydain; Pumerwi rhyddion i bob Bardd ym mraint ei swydd au gelfyddyd, neu lle na bo hynny Ceiniog aradr, sef hynny dogn o bob arad o fewn ei swydd ef, a lle nas Gellir hynny Ceiniog baladr, nid amgen na dogn y gan bob perchen Tir, a'r drwydded honn ym mhynag o'r tair ffordd y bo, yn amgen na'r pumerwi rhyddion a ddylit iddaw ym mraint Cymro Cynhenid. Ail yw ei roddion gobrwy am ei gerdd dafawd ai Rol achau nid amgen na Chof Priodasau a genedigaethau, a Chof Gweithredoedd moliannus. Trydydd yw ei Gylch Clera bob Tair blynedd yn nhai Priodorion a Bonheddigion eraill. A lle ni chaffo ef ei drwydded pumerwi neu yn lle hynny ei geiniog arad, neu geiniog baladr, dwyn gafael Cyfraith y gan Lys Gwlad ag Arglwydd, herwydd defawd nas galler a elo yn ei herbyn.

29. Tri dyn nis dylit Beirdd o honynt ; Celwyddawc Anianawl, ymrysongar cynneddfawl, ag anwybodus anes-gorawl, can nas gellir Awen o Dduw, na deall ar wybodau Barddas ar y rhywiau hynny o ddynion.

30. Tri pheth ar wr a ddangosant Awen o Ddyw, ag y gellir Bardd o hanaw ; serchogrwydd anianawl, Cywirdeb bucheddawl, a Phwyll gwrolgais yn ymgyfryn a gwybodau anrhydeddus.

31. Tri angheneddyl Bardd a Barddoniaeth ; Cof a chadw ar bob anrhydeddus a daionus parth gwir a gwybod-au, Dysgu ac amlyccau gwybodau Gwladolion, a gyrru hedd a thangnef ar a font wrth ddifrawd ag anraith. E.a.w. dodi addysg ar wybodau daionus, Cof a mawl pob rhagor a daionus, a gyrru heddwch a brawd ar ddifrawd ag anraith.

32. Tri anghenwrthwn Bardd, Cel rhin gan orfod er

28. The three licenses of the Bards of the Isle of Britain. Five free acres for every Bard in right of his office and art; or where that is not the case, a plough penny, that is to say, a contribution from every plough in his official district; and where that cannot be, a spear penny, namely, a contribution from every land owner—this license, in whichever of the three ways it may be, is irrespective of the five free acres, which he is entitled to in right of an innate Cymro. The second are the remunerations made to him for his vocal song, and his roll of pedigrees, that is to say, the memorial of marriages and births, and the memorial of commendable deeds. The third is his circuit of minstrelsy every three years to the houses of the natives and other gentry. And where he does not obtain his provision of five acres, or, in lieu of those, his plough penny, or spear penny, he is to bring an action at law in the court of country and lord, in respect of usage, which cannot be contravened.

29. Three men who ought not to be made Bards: a natural liar; an habitual wrangler; and one who is inevitably ignorant: for such persons can not have Awen from God, or any apprehension of the sciences of Bardism.

30. Three things in man, which demonstrate Awen from God, and that he is competent to become a Bard: natural affection; integrity of life; and manly reason occupied with honourable sciences.

31. The three necessities of a Bard and Bardism: to keep the memorial and record of all that is honourable and good, in respect of truth and sciences; to teach and explain political sciences; and to impose peace and tranquillity upon those who are out of the pale of justice and law. Others say: to instruct in good sciences; to confer memorial and praise upon all that is excellent and good; and to impose peace and rights of judicature upon those who are out of the pale of justice and law.

32. The three repulsive necessities of a Bard: the compulsory concealment of a secret. for the sake of advantage

lles a heddwch, Cwyn wrth anfawl gan gyfiawnder, a noethi
Cledd ar ddifrawd ag anraith.

33.   Tair Athrawiaeth a ofynnir $_{gan}^{ar}$ Fardd; Can wrth
bwyll a Doethineb, — Llafar wrth a fo Cof a defod gorsedd
a chyrch golychwyd — ag ymddwyn wrth ddefodau a Chynneddfau daionus.

34.   Tair Deddf ochel y sydd ar Fardd; gochel diogi a
syrthni, can mai gwr wrth ymgais yw, — gochel Cynnen a
Chywrysedd Can mai gwr wrth gariad a Thangnef yw, — a
gochel ffolineb Can mai gwr wrth bwyll a deall ac awen o
Ddyw yw ef.

35.   Tair Colofn Braint a Defawd; Arfer cyn cof Gwlad
a Chenedl, Cof a chadw Llythyr, a Barn Gorsedd Gyfallwy.
E.a.w. Ag awdurdod gorsedd gyfallwy.

36.   Tair gorsedd $_{ddamcweiniawl}^{ddamweiniawl}$ y sydd, ag nis gellir arben-
nigaw dydd ac amser iddynt, ag a fyddant yn ddosparthus
a defodawl o Le; a chymmraint fyddant a'r Dosparthus
defodawl o ddydd ag amser; Dydd y priotto Brenin neu
fab neu frawd neu gâr edlin i'r Brenin, sef priodas frenhin-
awl; Dydd y gwisgo'r brenin ei goron neu eu dorch aur; a
Dydd corn heddwch rhwng gwlad a gorwlad, a gwledd tridiau ar bob un o'r amseroedd hynny, a chynnal cathl arwest
a gorfoledd gan dafawd a thant.

TRIOEDD Y BEIRD.—TRIOEDD BRAINT A DEFOD.

(O Lyfr Llywelyn Sion.)

Llyma Drioedd Beirdd Ynys Prydain, ar Cof ar cadw y
sydd am danynt ar Lafar Gorsedd Beirdd Ynys Prydain,
au hanfod au hansawdd.

Pan ddaethant y Cymry gyntaf i Ynys Prydain o Wlad
yr Haf lle buant gyn no hynny er yn oes ocsoedd, ydd oedd

and peace ; vituperative complaint, required by justice ; and to unsheath a sword against the unjust and lawless.

33. The three doctrines required of a Bard : a song according to reason and wisdom ; voice according to the memorial and usage of Gorsedd, and the resort of worship ; and conduct according to good usages and habits.

34. There are three laws of avoidance incumbent on a Bard : to avoid idleness and sloth, since he is a man of ambition ; to avoid contention and strife, since he is a man of love and peace ; and to avoid folly, since he is a man of reason, understanding, and Awen from God.

35. The three columns of privilege and usage : custom before the memory of country and nation ; the memorial and record of letters ; and the judgment of an efficient Gorsedd. Others say : and the authority of an efficient Gorsedd.

36. There are three incidental Gorsedds, the day and time of which cannot be specified, but which are regular and customary as to place, and also of equal privilege with those which are regular and customary as to day and time : the marriage day of the king, or the son, brother, or lineal kinsman of the king, that is, a royal marriage ; the day on which the king wears his crown, or golden torques ; and the day of the horn of peace between country and border country. There will be a feast for three days on each of those times, and a concert of music and joy by means of voice and instrument.

THE TRIADS OF THE BARDS.—THE TRIADS OF PRIVILEGE AND USAGE.

(From the Book of Llywelyn Sion.)

The following are the Triads of the Bards of the Isle of Britain, and the memorials and records thereof, as preserved by the voice of Gorsedd of the Bards of the Isle of Britain— together with their essence and nature.

When the Cymry first came into the island of Britain from the Country of Summer, where they had been pre-

y Brif wybodaeth ar Doethineb cyntefig ynghof a chadw ag
ar addysg gan y Gwyddoniaid.

TRIOEDD BRAINT A DEFOD.

(See Poems Lyric and Pastoral.)

1. Tri Chyntefigion Beirdd Ynys Prydain Plennydd,
Alawn, a Gwron, ac nid oedd Beirdd wrth fraint a Defod
gorsedd o'u blaen hwy, namyn y Gwyddanod yn ben
addysg.

E.A.W.

Tri Chyntefigion Beirdd Gorseddawg Ynys Prydain
Plennydd, ^{Alawn}_{Alan}, a Gwron, ac nid oedd Beirdd ^{cynnwynt}_{cynnynt}, ond
y Gwyddoniaid yn Brydyddion ag yn Ddysgodron gwlad a
chenedl. Cyntaf o'r gwyddoniaid oedd Tydain Tad Awen
ac efe gyntaf a ddychymygwys Gerdd dafod Gymraeg.

E.A.W.

Tri Chyntefigion Beirdd Braint a Defod Ynys Prydain,
Plennydd, Alawn, a Gwron, ac yn amser Prydain ab Aedd
Mawr, y buant.

2. Am dri achos y gelwir y Beirdd, yn Feirdd wrth
fraint a defod Beirdd Ynys Prydain, sef yn *gyntaf*, am mai
yn Ynys Prydain y cafwyd Beirdd a Barddoniaeth gyntaf.
Yn *ail*, am nas caid Barddoniaeth gyfiawn mewn un Gwlad
amgen nag Ynys Prydain. Yn *drydydd* am nas gellir
cynnal Barddoniaeth gyfiawn eithr ym mraint Defodau ac
Addysg a llafar Gorsedd Beirdd Ynys Prydain, am hynny
o ba wlad bynnag y bytho Bardd, Bardd wrth fraint a defod
Beirdd Ynys Prydain ai gelwir ef.

3. O Dripheth y cafwyd Barddoniaeth gyntaf, ^{Awen o}_{Awen o}
Ddyw—Addysg o ddyn—a syrth Anian.
Dduw, Synwyr a deall dyn, a syrth Anian.

4. Tair ffordd y cynhelir Barddoniaeth gyfiawn, Beirdd
Ynys Prydain, Cof Gorsedd, Defod Gorsedd, a Chan Gorsedd.

---

¹ Al. "Alan."   ² Al. "the sense and understanding of man."

viously from the age of ages, the primitive knowledge, and original wisdom, were preserved in memory and record, and taught by the Gwyddoniaid.

THE TRIADS OF PRIVILEGE AND USAGE.

1. The three primary Bards of the Isle of Britain: Plennydd; Alawn; and Gwron. Before them there were no Bards according to the privilege and usage of Gorsedd, but the Gwyddoniaid were at the head of instruction.

Others say:

The three primary presiding Bards of the Isle of Britain: Plennydd; Alawn;[1] and Gwron; and before them there were no Bards, but the Gwyddoniaid were the poets and teachers of country and nation. The first of the Gwyddoniaid was Tydain, the father of Awen, and it was he who first invented Cymric vocal song.

Others say:

The three primary Bards of privilege and usage of the Isle of Britain: Plennydd; Alawn; and Gwron; who lived in the time of Prydain, son of Aedd the Great.

2. For three reasons are the Bards called Bards according to the privilege and usage of the Bards of the Isle of Britain, namely: first, because Bards and Bardism originated in the Isle of Britain; secondly, because genuine Bardism has not been found in any country besides the Isle of Britain; thirdly, because genuine Bardism cannot be maintained except in virtue of the usages, instruction, and voice of Gorsedd of the Bards of the Isle of Britain. Therefore, of whatever country a Bard may be, he is called a Bard according to the privilege and usage of the Bards of the Isle of Britain.

3. Bardism was obtained originally from three things: Awen from God; instruction by man;[2] and the tendency of nature.

4. Three ways in which the genuine Bardism of the Bards of the Isle of Britain is maintained: the memorial of Gorsedd; the usage of Gorsedd; and the song of Gorsedd.

E.A.W. (Gwel rif 97,)
Defod, Llafar, a Chân Gorsedd.

5. Tri chof Beirdd Ynys Prydain, Cof Llafar Gorsedd,
Cof can, a chof Defod*—(* Coelbren)

E.A.W.

Cof llafar gorsedd. Cof Can gyfallwy, a Chof Coelbren.

6. Tri pheth ni ellir a el yn eu herbyn. Defod a llafar
Gorsedd, Hengerdd Gorsedd, a Rhaith Gwlad ac Arlwydd,
sef or tri hynn y cynhelir cof ac awdurdawd, Breiniau a
Defodau Beirdd Ynys Prydain.

E.A.W.

Tri pheth ni ellir / nid oes a el yn eu herbyn, Defod Gorsedd—Llafar
Gorsedd, a Hengerdd wrth fraint Gorsedd.

7. (Gwel rif 98) Tri Phrifardd y sydd, o syrth gyssefin, (o gyssefin gaffaeliad a threfn) Bardd Braint neu brydydd, ac ef yn Brifardd pendant, wrth fraint, Defod, a llafar
Gorsedd, ai Swydd yw llywodraethu a chynnal cof a chadwedigaeth ar y Farddoniaeth herwydd y tri chof, a phrydu
mawl ac addysg, a chof, ai hanfod o'r Gwyddoniaid, ail yw
Ofydd wrth Awen, ymgais, a dichwain, ai swydd yw Awen-
yddu wrth Grebwyll, a dichwain, a chelfyddyd, a bod wrth
farn Gorsedd yn y bo cyfallwy—*Trydydd* yw *Derwydd*,
wrth Bwyll, Ansawdd, a Gorsedd, ai Swydd yw Athrawiaethu wrth y bo rhaid gwlad a Chenedl, ac ym mraint
Derwydd y bernir pob Effeiriad a golychwydwr lle del
Yngorsedd Beirdd Ynys Prydain.

8. Gwel Rif 122. Tair Cangen Addysg Beirdd Ynys
Prydain, *Barddoniaeth* neu *Brydyddiaeth;* ac ar hynn y
mae Prydu, a chynnal cof wrth *Gan a llafar,* a *Defod Gorsedd.* a chynnal a gwellhau Celfyddyd y Brydyddiaeth. *Ail*
yw *Derwyddoniaeth* ac ar Dderwydd y mae dysgu wrth

[1] Al. "Coelbren."

[2] Al. " are not."   [3] Al. '' of original discovery and order.''

Others say : the usage ; voice ; and song of Gorsedd.

5. The three memorials of the Bards of the Isle of Britain : the memorial of the voice of Gorsedd ; the memorial of song ; and the memorial of usage.[1]

Others say : the memorial of the voice of Gorsedd ; the memorial of efficient song ; and the memorial of Coelbren.

6. Three things that cannot be contravened : the usage and voice of Gorsedd ; an ancient song of Gorsedd ; and the verdict of country and lord. That is to say, by means of these three are the memorial, authority, privileges, and usages of the Bards of the Isle of Britain, maintained.

Others say :

Three things that cannot be contravened :[2] the usage of Gorsedd ; the voice of Gorsedd ; and an ancient song bearing the privilege of Gorsedd.

7. There are three primitive Bards of original disposition.[3] A Bard of privilege, or poet, being a Primitive Bard Positive, according to the privilege, usage, and voice of Gorsedd ; and his function is to rule, and to preserve the memorial and record of Bardism, according to the three memorials, and to compose eulogy, instruction, and memorial —his origination being from the Gwyddoniaid. The second is an Ovate, according to awen, exertion, and circumstance ; and his function is to poetize according to imagination, circumstance, and art, and to defer to the judgment of Gorsedd, until it becomes efficient. The third is the Druid, according to reason, nature, and Gorsedd ; and his function is to teach, according to the necessity of country and nation ; and every priest or worshipper is adjudged to come under the privilege of a Druid, when he attends the Gorsedd of the Bards of the Isle of Britain.

8. The three branches of learning of the Bards of the Isle of Britain. Bardism, or poetry ; in respect of which it is incumbent to poetize, and to maintain the memorial of song, voice, and usage of Gorsedd, and to maintain and improve the art of poetry. The second is Druidism ; and it is incumbent upon a Druid to teach according to reason,

bwyll, Ansawdd, a Gorsedd, herwydd y bo trefn a deddfoldeb a rhiniau Dwyfoldeb yn gofyn. *Trydydd* yw *Ofyddiaeth*, ac ar *Ofydd* y mae ymgais am ddysg a Gwybodaeth
wrth a ellir o Glyw, Gweled, a dychymmyg, sef y dylai
Brydydd cynnal cof pob dysg a gwybodaeth, er a elo wrth
fraint Gorsedd gyfallwy, ac *Ofydd* a ddylai, wellhau ac amlhau dysg a gwybodaeth a'u rhoddi wrth Farn Gorsedd onid
el yn gyfallwy. a *Derwydd* a ddylai athrawiaethu, $_{herwydd}^{wrth}$ a fo
cyssefin o ddefod a Braint gorsedd gyfallwy, ac o gaffaeliad
newydd wrth bwyll ansawdd a gorfod.

E.A.W.

Tair caingc Addysg Beirdd Ynys Prydain, *Prydyddiaeth*
gan Brifardd, ac ar Brydydd y mae Prydu a chynnal cof
Can, llafar, a Defod, a threfnu wrth fraint, sef gorseddog a
chadeiriog wrth yw ef. *Ofyddiaeth*, ac ar ofydd y mae ymgais a chwilio am ddysg wrth a ellid o glyw a llafar byd, ac
o weled a dichwain, ac o gais ac awen a dychymyg. *Derwyddoniaeth*, ac ar Dderwydd y mae dysgu ac athrawiaethu
wrth a fo cyssefin a chyfallwy gan orsedd, ac wrth a fo o
gaffaeliad newydd wrth bwyll, ansawdd, a gorfod.

9.   Tair rhagorfraint Beirdd Ynys Prydain, Trwydded-
ogaeth lle 'r elont, nas dyccer arf noeth yn eu $_{gwydd}^{herbyn}$, a gair
eu gair hwynt ar bawb.

10.   Tair Dyledswydd wrth raid ac achos Gwlad a Chen-
edl y sydd ar Fardd. *Cyntaf* yw cynnal Golychwyd Bob
Bann ac adfan Lleuad yn addysg Dwyfoldeb a Doethineb
ac iawn ymddwyn a phob cynneddfau dyledus a daionus.
Ail yw gweini Cenhadoriaeth rhwng gwlad a gwlad a rhwng
Gwlad a chenedl a gorwlad a chenedl oraillt yn achos newid

---

[1] Al. "in their presence."

[2] "Ban ac adfan;" division and subdivision, i.e. the new and full moon, and
the first and third quarters.

nature, and Gorsedd, as order, morality, and the mysteries of godliness require. The third is Ovatism; and it is incumbent upon an Ovate to endeavour after learning and knowledge, as he can, by means of hearing, seeing, and devising. That is, a poet ought to maintain all learning and knowledge which may be privileged by an efficient Gorsedd; an Ovate ought to improve and amplify learning and knowledge, and to submit them to the judgment of Gorsedd, until it becomes efficient; and a Druid ought to teach, according to the original usage and privilege of an efficient Gorsedd, and according to any new discovery, in respect of reason, nature, and cogency.

Others say:

The three branches of learning of the Bards of the Isle of Britain. Poetry by a primitive Bard; and it is incumbent upon a Poet to poetize, and to maintain the memorial of song, voice, and usage, and to make arrangements according to privilege, for he is gorseddog and chaired. Ovatism; and it is incumbent upon an Ovate to endeavour and seek after learning, as far as he can, by means of the hearing and voice of the world, of sight and contingency, and of attempt, awen, and imagination. Druidism; and it is incumbent upon a Druid to teach and instruct, in respect of what is original and made efficient by Gorsedd, and in respect of new discovery, according to reason, nature, and cogency.

9. The three distinguishing privileges of the Bards of the Isle of Britain: maintenance wherever they go; that no naked weapon be borne against them; [1] and that their word should be a word above all men.

10. There are three duties, according to the requirement and occasion of country and nation, incumbent upon a Bard. The first is to celebrate worship on all the quarter days [2] of the moon, so as to impart instruction in godliness and wisdom, and proper demeanour, and all due and good qualities. The second is to carry on ambassadorial negotiation between country and country, and between country and nation and

a Chynnadl, rhwng Cenedl a goraillt. *Trydydd*, yw arail
Tanc a Chymmod rhwng Brodor a Brodor a rhwng Brodor
a goraillt ym mraint ei swydd o Fardd, cyd na bo cais a
galw arno gan wlad a chenedl.

E.A.W.

Tair swydd dyled Bardd wrth raid ac achos Gwlad a
Chenedl sef ydynt, Cynnal golychwyd. Bod yn genhador
rhwng Gwlad a gorwlad, a rhwng Cenedl a Goreillion, a
gyrru Tanc a Chymmod lle y bydder ynghyfryssedd, ai
rhwng Brodor a Brodor, ai rhwng Cenedl a goreillt y bytho.

E.A.W.

Tair swydd gyffredin y sydd ar Fardd lle ai dylid yn
rhaid Gwlad a Chenedl, nid amgen, Golychwyd, Cenhadoriaeth, a Thangneforiaeth.

11.   Tair cynneddf dyled y sydd ar Fardd herwydd ei
ddyled wrth raid ac achos Gwlad a chenedl, chwilio gwirionedd, Cadw cyfrinach, ac ymddwyn cynneddfol wrth danc
a chyfiawnder.

12.   Tair angenorfod y sydd ar Fardd wrth raid ac achos
Gwir a chyfiawnder, Dywedyd a wyr lle nis gellir yn amgen
a fo iawn a chyfiawn. — Dodi Gwaedd uwch adneu lle ' dd
eler wrth drais ac anghyfraith—a gyrru Barn ar Ddifrod ac
anraith.

13.   Tair swydd o gyssefin ddefod y sydd ar Fardd,
Prydu cof a chadw pob moliannus—Cynnal can a llafar
gorsedd yn gof ac addysg Barddas a Chelfydd wrth Gerdd
a'u Defodau ai Breiniau — a Chyffraw treigl ac amlhâd
gwybodaeth drwy arddangos Cadeiriau wrth Gerdd yn Ddefodawl a chynneddfawl gan waedd uwch adwedd.

---

[1] " Adneu," compounded of *ad* and *neu*. It is usually translated *a pledge,*
or *a deposit.*

[2] " Adwedd," compounded of *ad* and *gwedd*, a return to a former state or
appearance.

border country and border alien nation, in respect of commerce and conference, between a nation and border aliens. The third is to maintain peace and concord between native and native, and between native and border alien, in right of his office of Bard, though he may not be sought or called by country and nation.

Others say:

The three offices incumbent upon a Bard, according to the need and occasion of country and nation, namely: to celebrate worship; to be an ambassador between country and border country, and between nation and border aliens; and to promote peace and concord where there is contention, whether between native and native, or between nation and border aliens.

Others say:

There are three common offices incumbent upon a Bard, which are required by the necessity of country and nation, namely: worship; embassy; and pacification.

11. There are three primary laws of duty incumbent upon a Bard, in respect of his duty according to the necessity and occasion of country and nation: to examine truth; to keep a secret; and to conduct himself morally in reference to peace and justice.

12. There are three cogent necessities laid upon a Bard, according to the necessity and occasion of truth and justice: to tell what he knows, where nothing else can be found which is right and just; to raise the cry of re-assertion,[1] where oppression and lawlessness take place; and to exercise judgment over devastation and spoliation.

13. Three offices, in virtue of original usage, belong to a Bard: to compile the memorial and record of every thing that is commendable; to maintain the song of voice and Gorsedd so that they should become the memorial and instruction of Bardism and poetical art, their usages and privileges; and to agitate the progression and extension of knowledge, by exhibiting the Chairs of song ritually and habitually with the cry of restoration.[2]

14. Tri arddangos Beirdd Ynys Prydain, Arddangos Beirdd lle nas gwyppid, — Arddangos Cyrch Gorsedd a Chadair lle nas gwelid,—ac arddangos gwybodaeth o wir a chyfiawn lle nas dyellid, a'r Tri arddangos hynn a fyddant dan osteg a Rhybydd undydd a blwyddyn ac o hynny hyd ynghyfallwy gan Waedd uch Adwedd.

15. Tair Gwaedd fann Beirdd Ynys Prydain y sydd.— *Gwaedd uwch adwedd* yn effraw a chyffraw y peth nas gwypper,—*Gwaedd uwch adfann*, dros a wneler yn annefod o angen amser ac achos megis cynnal Cadair a Gorsedd yn annosparthus o le ac amser, mal pai yn anamser Ban haul a lleuad, neu lle nas byddo yn wyneb haul a llygad goleuni, a hynny gan raid ac angen ac nis gellir cyfallwy ar a wneler gan waedd uwch adfan ynyddelo 'n ddefodawl gan orsedd wrth Fraint a defod.—a *Gwaedd uwch adneu* rhag a wneler gan ddifrod ac anraith ac yn drais anghyfraith, a rhag a wneler wrth Gerdd yn ammraint ammraint, ac yn annefod, ac yn anghelfydd, ac yn anwybod, ac yn anwirionedd, sef y Bydd Gwaedd uwch adwedd, a gwaedd uwch adneu dan Rybydd a gosteg undydd a blwyddyn ac o hynny yn y bo cyfallwy. a Gwaedd uwch adfan a fydd dan osteg a Rhybydd angen a gorfod yny bo anamlwg ei achos wrth raid gwlad a chenedl, ac ar a wnelir dani nis gellir cyfallwy onid el wrth farn gorsedd yn ddefodol gan waedd uwch adwedd a gwaedd ywch adneu cyflafar cyfamgyrch. can nas dylid, heb hynny, fraint Gorsedd ar a wnelir gan orfod yn anne- fodawl, ac yn anneddf, ac ni wedd i hynny fraint yn y byd

---

[1] "Adfann," from *ad*, and *man*, a place, or *ban*, a point or division, whether of time or place; the reversal, or re-arrangement, of the usual seasons and loca- lities, for holding a Gorsedd.

14. The three demonstrations of the Bards of the Isle of Britain : the demonstration of Bards, where a thing was not known ; the demonstration of the convention of Gorsedd and Chair, where it was not seen; and the demonstration of the knowledge of truth and justice, where it was not understood. The three demonstrations ensue under the proclamation and notice of a year and a day, and from thence unto the period of efficiency they take place by means of the cry of restoration.

15. There are three loud cries of the Bards of the Isle of Britain : the cry of restoration, which resuscitates and agitates every thing that is not known ; the cry of re-arrangement,[1] in respect of what is done contrary to usage, from the necessity of time and occasion, such as holding a Chair and Gorsedd irregularly as to place and time, for instance, at the unseasonable points of the sun and moon, or where it is not in the face of the sun and the eye of light— that being done from obligation and necessity—but what is done in virtue of the cry of re-arrangement cannot be efficient, until it becomes customary by means of a Gorsedd according to privilege and usage ; and the cry of re-assertion, against what may be done by devastation and wrong, and by lawless oppression, and against what may be done, in respect of song, without privilege, usage, art, knowledge, and truth. The cry of restoration, and the cry of re-arrangement, are to be made under the proclamation and notice of a year and a day, and thence until they become efficient ; and the cry of re-arrangement is to be made under the proclamation and notice of necessity and cogency, until the occasion for it, according to the need of country and nation, disappears, and what is done under it cannot be efficient, unless it formally receives the judgment of Gorsedd, consequent upon the cry of restoration, and the cry of re-assertion, covocally and simultaneously issued. For without that, the privilege of Gorsedd ought not to be given to what is obliged to be done contrary to usage and law ; nor is it fitting that it should have any privilege whatever,

namyn ei ddydd angen, hyd yn y gwelir, yn y modd y gwespwyd hawl ac arddel iddo. rhag llygru Barddoniaeth, a Barddas, a Breiniau a defodau Beirdd Ynys Prydain.

16. Tri pheth a ant wrth farn dan osteg a Rhybydd Gwaedd uwch Adneu. — *Difrod ac anraith* — *Ammraint ac annefod gan wlad ac Arlwydd*, o anneall neu anymgais, — ac *ammarddoniaeth*, sef a fo 'n amgen nag a ddylid herwydd Breiniau a Defodau Beirdd Ynys Prydain, gwedi ydd elo ar ymddwyn ac yn arfer gan Fardd a Gorsedd.

17. Am dri achos y dylai 'r Beirdd gynnal Cadair a gorsedd a llafar a Datgan, ar fann ac amlwg ac yng ngolwg a chlyw Gwlad ac Arlwydd, ac yn wyneb haul a llygad goleuni, sef yn *Gyntaf* mal y bo braint nis galler ei wrthneu i bawb gyrchu hyd y man a'r lle. Yn *Ail*, mal y gweler ac y clywer oll a fytho ar occed llygad a Chlust a deall, ac na bo anneddf ac annefod ac anwir ym mhlith Cenedl ac ar glawr gwlad heb allu 'n eilwg ei wybod. Yn *drydedd* mal y gellir addysg a ddylid i bawb o'r genedl ac i bawb a gyrchont yng nghadair a gorsedd can y dylid addysg gyfiawn, gyfanian a chyfunbwnc i bawb o gywiriaid Gwlad a chenedl, can nis gellir Gwlad a chyfraith heb addysg ar wir a chyfiawn ac o hynny Brodoriaeth.

18. Tri pheth anhebcor y sydd ^{ar ddefod}_{ddefodawl} Cadair a gorsedd, sef eu bod ar *fann ac amlwg* yngolwg a chlyw Gwlad ac Arlwydd, o barth man a lle — ac yn wyneb haul a llygad goleuni sef hyd y bo haul yn wybren o barth amser dydd— ac ar fannau haul a lleuad o barth amser y flwyddyn, mal y bo hysbys i bawb gwlad a Chenedl a gorwlad ac aillt a wneler ac y datganer ac a ddysger, a gwybod o'r lleoedd a'r

except its day of necessity, until, in the way mentioned, it obtains claim and avouchment, lest poetry, and Bardism, and the privileges and usages of the Bards of the Isle of Britain, should suffer corruption.

16. Three things that are submitted to judgment, under the proclamation and notice of the cry of re-assertion : devastation and pillage ; non privilege and non usage on the part of country and lord, owing to the want of understanding or exertion ; and non poetry, or that which may be other than what is required according to the privileges and usages of the Bards of the Isle of Britain, after it has become habitual and customary to Bard and Gorsedd.

17. For three reasons ought the Bards to hold a Chair and Gorsedd, and a voice and recitation, conspicuously and manifestly, in the sight and hearing of country and lord, and in the face of the sun and the eye of light. First, that there may be a privilege, not to be gainsaid, for all to resort to the place and spot. Secondly, that all things cognizable by the eye, ear, and intellect, may be seen and heard, and that there may be no lack of law, usage, and truth, among kindred, and on the face of country, which cannot be again known. Thirdly, that proper instruction may be obtained for all the nation, and for all who resort to Chair and Gorsedd, since proper, natural, and pointed instruction ought to be uniformly imparted to true and loyal men of country and nation, for there can be no country and law without instruction in respect of truth and justice— hence proceeds fraternity.

18. There are three things indispensably attached to the rite of Chair and Gorsedd, namely : that they should be conspicuous and manifest, in the sight and hearing of country and lord, as to place and spot ; in the face of the sun and eye of light, that is, while the sun remains in the firmament, in respect of the time of day ; and on the points of the sun and moon, in respect of the time of year ; in order that whatever is done, recited, and taught, may be familiar to all the men of country and nation, and border

amseroedd a'r dynion, a phwys a braint oll a chyfoll. ac heb
y petheu hynn nis gellir Cadair a Gorsedd wrth ddefod a
deddf a braint gyfiawn.

19.   Tri pheth yn Nefodau Beirdd a Barddoniaeth a
ddylynt fod yn egored i bawb, sef yn *gyntaf* y man ar lle y
bo cyrch Cadair a gorsedd, gan ei hagor ym mraint Gosteg
a Rhybydd undydd a blwyddyn, os nid egored eiswys y lle,
Ail yw yr amseroedd sef y rhai defodawl parth pryd dydd
ac amser blwyddyn, nid amgen na bannau Haul a lleuad.
Trydydd yw yr addysg sef ai dylit yn egored i bawb herwydd y modd o'i datgan ai dangos yn na bo cel a Rhin ar
ddysg a gwybodaeth gywir a chyfiawn, am hynny y gelwir
y petheu hynn y tri egoredion, sef ydynt Man a Lle egored,
dydd ac amser egored, ac addysg a datgan egored. ac nis
gellir Barn gan Ddoethion a Gwlad, a Chenedl ar a fo
amgen.

20.   Tri lle ac amser a fernir ym mraint lleoedd a phryd-
iau egored a deddfawl a rhydd cynnal Cadair a gorsedd wrth
Gerdd yn y bônt, sef y lleoedd ar prydiau y bo cyrch golychwyd, a chyrch yngneidiaeth, a chyrch Rhaith Gwlad
yngorsedd ddygynnill, can ai gwyper gan bawb, am hynny
egored a'u bernir megis yngolwg a chlyw Gwlad ac Arlwydd,
ac yn wyneb Haul a llygad goleuni, cyd y byddont dan Lenn
a Thô, sef y bydd hynn o betheu wrth bwyll ac ansawdd ac
angen, ac am hynny wrth Fraint a Defod Beirdd Ynys
Prydain.

21.   Tri thrwydded Bardd, ei Bumerwi Rhyddion — ei
Aberth ged, ai Drythged.

22.   Tri thrythged Bardd. seigiau o fwyd a Llynn — a
gwisgoed—ac arian. E.a w. Tair Aberthged Deuluaidd &c.

country and aliens, and that the places, times, and men, and the importance and privilege of all, be fully known; and without these things there can be no Chair and Gorsedd according to usage, law, and just privilege.

19. Three things in respect of the usages of Bards and Bardism, which ought to be open to all. First, the place and spot where is the convention of Chair and Gorsedd, which is to be opened in virtue of the proclamation and notice of a year and a day, if the place be not already open. The second are the times, namely, the customary ones as to the part of day and time of year, which are none other than the points of the sun and moon. The third is the instruction, which ought to be open to all, in respect of the mode of reciting and demonstrating it, so that there should be no concealment or secrecy of learning and true and just knowledge. Therefore, these things are called the three open ones : being open place and spot; open day and time; and open instruction and recitation ; and no judgment can be pronounced by wise men, and country, and nation, upon what is otherwise.

20. There are three places and times, adjudged to have the privilege of open and customary places and seasons, at which it is lawful to hold a Chair and Gorsedd of song, namely: the places and seasons at which there is the resort of worship; the resort of judicature ; and the resort of verdict of country in a conventional Gorsedd; for they are known to all. Therefore they are adjudged to be open, as if in the sight and hearing of country and lord, and in the face of the sun and eye of light, though they may be under cover and roof ; for these things are to be according to reason, nature, and necessity, and consequently according to the privilege and usage of the Bards of the Isle of Britain.

21. The three maintenances of a Bard : his five free acres; his oblation ; and his tribute.

22. The three tributes of a Bard : messes of food and liquor ; vestments; and money. Others say : the three domestic tributes, &c.

23. Tair Aberthged gyffredin Bardd, Un yw Blithged, a'r Alban Hefin ei rhoddi. Ail yw Peillged, a honno 'r Alban Elfed. Trydydd, Melged, ai rhoddi 'r Alban Arthan, a dognau o bob un o'r tri yr Alban Eilir, sef pan y breinir y Cerddi Newyddion. a thlodion, ac Eillion, ac Estronion a gaffant eu dognau o'r tair Aberthged yr amseroedd hynny can nad oes iddynt Drwydded Ddyledog o Dir a Da.

24. Tri lle gorsedd egored y sydd Tyle penegor cyn côf, neu ynteu ym mraint gosteg a Rhybydd undydd a blwyddyn, ac Eglwys, a Llys Ynad a Chyfraith.

25. Tri amser Gorsedd Egored y sydd, Bannau Haul a Lleuad—Sul a Gwyl, a Dydd Llys a Chyfraith.

26. Tri Chyrch Cywlad y sydd, Cyrch Beirdd yngorsedd—Cyrch golychwyd, a Chyrch Llys a Chyfraith.

27. Gwel Rif 78, 79. Tair Gosteg Gyffredin, y sydd, Cyrch golychwyd—Maes Arglwydd, a Gorsedd Beirdd. ac ynddynt cynnal pob Rhybudd, a phob Gwaedd fann a phob Gwâd, a phob gair a gwrthair hyd ymhen undydd a blwyddyn.

28. Tri cholofn Hawl Beirdd Ynys Prydain, Hen Gerdd — Hen Gof a llafar Gorsedd, a Rhaith Gwlad (a Rhaith trichannyn).

29. Tri Chorn Gosteg Bardd y sydd — Rhaith Gwlad Trichannyn—Gwaedd Galanas—a Choel Heddwch a Chymmod, ac wrth Rybydd undydd a blwyddyn ydd ant, ac yna Braint Bairdd, a Gwlad, a Brenin.

30. Tri chorn Gosteg Brenin y sydd, a braint iddo eu cynnal yngorsedd Beirdd—Rhyfel—Llys Gwlad a Chyfraith—a Gwledd Gwlad a Chenedl. ac nid rhydd na braint

---

[1] Yn nghyfarfod clod cludfeirdd *dyle*.

In the convention of fame, on the *area* of the assembling Bards.

Ll. P. Moch.

[2] Al. "the verdict of three hundred men."

23. The three common oblations of a Bard : one is milk contribution, which is offered on Alban Hevin; the second is meal contribution, on Alban Elved; the third is honey contribution, which is offered on Alban Arthan; and portions of each of the three on Alban Eilir, that is, when new songs are privileged. And the poor, aliens, and strangers are to have their portions from the three oblations at those times, since they have no due maintenance from land and chattels.

24. There are three places of open Gorsedd : an exposed elevation[1] before memory, or in virtue of the proclamation and notice of a year and a day ; a church ; and a court of judge and law.

25. There are three seasons of an open Gorsedd : the points of the sun and moon ; Sunday and festival ; and the day of court and law.

26. There are three meetings of federal country : the meeting of Bards in Gorsedd ; the meeting of worship ; and the meeting of court and law.

27. There are three common proclamations : the resort of worship ; the field of a lord ; and the Gorsedd of Bards ; and in them are to be issued every notice, every loud cry, every denial, every word and contradiction unto the end of a year and a day.

28. The three columns of claim of the Bards of the Isle of Britain : an ancient song ; the old memorial and voice of Gorsedd ; and verdict of country.[2]

29. There are three horns of proclamation belonging to the Bard : the verdict of country, composed of three hundred men ; the cry of murder ; and the signal of peace and concord ; and they take place under the notice of a year and a day, when they receive the privilege of Bards, country, and king.

30. There are three horns of proclamation belonging to the king, and he has the right of issuing them in the Gorsedd of the Bards : war ; the court of country and law ; and the feast of country and nation ; but this is not lawful

i amgen na Brenin ac Arlwydd hynn, ac wrth frys Deugein niwarnod y byddant, (Brys deigeinnydd y bydd)

31.   Tri Chorn Cyffredin y sydd, a dyled ei Cynnal ymhob Cyrch cywlad, Corn murn a chynllwyn, Corn Gormes gorwlad ac Estron, a Chorn difrawd ac anraith.   Ac ym mraint y rhain Corn Gwared, sef y bydd braint Rhaith Gwlad a Chenedl arnaddynt.

32.   Tair Nawdd (noddedigaeth) Beirdd Ynys Prydain, noddi Dysg, sef celfyddyd gwybodaeth — noddi heddwch a thangnef—a noddi Gwirionedd a chyfiawnder. sef y dylÿei y nawdd wrth y rhaid hyd farw drostynt, can mae erddynt y mae Bardd, ac nid Bardd na wnelo erddynt, ac nid neppeth na fytho gan ddyled. sef o'r pethau hynn y cyfyd

33.   Tri gofal Beirdd Ynys Prydain, nid amgen Cannerth celfyddbwyll,—Amlygu gwirionedd,—a choledd heddwch a thangnef.

34.   Tair anghynnefawd ac anghynneddf Beirdd Ynys Prydain, Gormes ar wybodau (wybyddawd)—Gwrtheb gwir —a gwrthladd heddwch a thangnef.   Can ydd eir o wneuthur y pethau hynn wrth ddifrawd ac anraith.

35.   Tri angheneddyl Bardd, dysgu ac amlygu pob peth yn wyneb haul a llygad goleuni—moli pob rhagor a daionus —a gyrru heddwch ar ddifrod ac anraith.

36.   Tair Cainc Barddoniaeth, Prydyddiaeth, Ofyddiaeth —a Derwyddoniaeth. sef cydfraint a chyfunbwys y bernir y Tair cainc hynn, can nis gellir pennogaeth i un o honynt ar y llaill, cyd y bont gwahanbwyth nis byddant gwahanfraint.

37.   Tri Bardd cyfunbwys y sydd, sef ydynt y tri phrifardd dyledogion, nid amgen, Bardd Trwyddedog cynhwynawl neu Brydydd, wrth fraint a Defod,—Bardd Ofydd wrth

for other than king and lord ; and they are to take place in the hurry of forty days.

31. There are three common horns, which ought to be used in every convention of federate country : the horn of murder and waylaying ; the horn of oppression of border country and stranger ; and the horn of devastation and pillage. And in virtue of these is the horn of deliverance ; for they will have the privilege of the verdict of country and nation.

32. The three protections of the Bards of the Isle of Britain : to protect learning, that is, the art of knowledge ; to protect peace and tranquillity ; and to protect truth and justice. That is to say, they ought to be protected even unto death, when there is occasion, for it is on their account that a Bard exists, and he is no Bard who does nothing in their behalf, and there is nothing which is not a duty, arising from these things.

33. The three cares of the Bards of the Isle of Britain, namely : to support science ; to elucidate truth ; and to cherish peace and tranquillity.

34. The three non usages and non qualifications of the Bards of the Isle of Britain : encroachment upon sciences ; contradiction of truth ; and the impugning of peace and tranquillity ; for by perpetrating these things one becomes deprived of privilege and exposed to warfare.

35. The three necessary functions of a Bard : to teach and explain all things in the face of the sun and the eye of light ; to praise all that is excellent and good ; and to substitute peace for devastation and pillage.

36. There are three branches of Bardism : Poetry ; Ovatism ; and Druidism ; and these three branches are adjudged to be of equal privilege and of equal weight, for one cannot have supremacy over the other ; though they are distinct in object, they are not distinct in privilege.

37. There are three Bards of equal importance, who are the three proprietary primitive Bards, namely : an innate licensed Bard, or a Poet, according to privilege and usage ;

H

Ddysg awenbwyll—a Derwyddfardd wrth bwyll dwyfolaeth
a chynneddfoldeb — a chyfunbwys au gelwir, am nas gellir
gwell ar y naill na 'r llaill o henynt, na phennog y naill ar
y llaill o henynt, cyd y bo gwahan y naill ar y llaill parth
swydd ac ymmodoldeb, eithr cyfun a chyfarddun ydynt
parth Dyled ac ymgais, ac amcan, sef addysg — Gwir — a
thangnef.

38.   Tair cainc swyddogaeth Bardd—Dyled—Ymgais,
ac amcan. sef ydynt er addysg—Gwirionedd—a Thangnef.

39.   Tair Gwaith y rhodded Barddoniaeth a Beirdd
Ynys Prydain ᵃʳ Raith gwlad a Chenedl (sef yw rhaith
Gwlad Briduw trichannyn a ymofynna a chlyw a gwybod a
Barn Gwlad a chenedl hyd ymhen undydd a blwyddyn) sef
yn gyntaf yn amser *Prydain ab Aedd Mawr*, pan ydd ym-
roddasant y Bairdd a'r Gwyddoniaid eu hunain wrth fraint
a Defod gan farn a threfn wrth Raith Gwlad a Chenedl, a'r
Fraint ar Ddefod yw'r un a elwir yn awr Braint a Defod
Beirdd Ynys Prydain ac ni bu na gwrtheb na gwrthneu ar
y Breiniau ar Defodau hynny fyth wedi hynny, a chynn no
hynny nid oedd na braint na defod eithr o bwyll syberwyd.
Ac yn ol y bernid gan a fynnai parth ac at Feirdd a Gwyddoniaid—(al. a barnu fal y bai mynnᵞᵘ parth ac at Feirdd a
Gwyddoniaid)

Yr *ail waith* oedd yn amser *Maxen Wledig*, rhag Brif y
Farddoniaeth ar goll ac anghof, ac yno ai cafwyd yn ddifeth
ac wrth y Breiniau ar Defodau cyssefin, a rhoddi hynny
a wnaethpwyd ar farn a Rhaith Gwlad a Chenedl, a chadarnhau yr hen freiniau a Defodau, a'r hen Bwyll ac Addysg,

---

[1] Maxen Wledig, the Welsh title of Clemens Maximus, who commanded the
Roman forces in Britain, and revolted against the emperor Gratian in A.D. 383.
According to an ancient document printed in the *Greal*, he was the son of
Llwydrod, the son of Trahaiarn, who was the brother of Elen Luyddawg, the
mother of Constantine the Great.   According to the Welsh accounts, he married Elen, the daughter of Eudav, or Octavius, a powerful nobleman, who is
called in the Bruts, earl of Ergyng and Euas, districts now comprised in Monmouthshire and Herefordshire.   Maxen having defeated Gratian, and thus

an Ovate-bard, according to poetical learning; and a Druid-bard, according to the sense of godliness and morality. They are said to be of equal importance, because one cannot be better than another, or one superior to another, in respect of office and movement; but they are co-equal, and of like dignity, in respect of duty, aim, and object, which are instruction, truth, and peace.

38. The three branches of the office of a Bard: duty; aim; and object; and they are for the sake of instruction, truth, and peace.

39. Three times have Bardism and the Bards of the Isle of Britain been submitted to the verdict of country and nation, (the verdict of country being the asseveration of three hundred men, who enquire into the hearing, knowledge, and judgment of country and nation until the expiration of a year and a day.) First, in the time of Prydain, the son of Aedd the Great, when the Bards conformed to privilege and usage, judiciously and in order, according to the verdict of country and nation, which privilege and usage are the same as what are now called the privilege and usage of the Bards of the Isle of Britain. No objection or protest has ever after been made against those privileges and usages, but previously there was neither privilege nor usage, except from a sense of courtesy, and according as any one was pleased to judge in regard to Bards and Gwyddoniaid. (Al. and it was judged at will in regard to Bards and Gwyddoniaid.) The second occasion was in the time of Maxen the Sovereign,[1] lest the primitive Bardism should become lost and forgotten, when it was recovered in its integrity, and according to the original privileges and usages; it was submitted to the judgment and verdict of country and nation, when the ancient privileges and usages, the ancient import and instruction, and the ancient sciences and memorials

---

obtained possession of Britain, Gaul, and Spain, exercised imperial power until 385, when he was defeated and put to death by Theodosius.

a'r hen wybodau a Chofion, fal nad elynt ar fethɪ a chollɪ ac anghof. ac ni bu wrtheb na gwrthneu.

Y *Drydydd waith* yr aeth felly, amser *Ithel Brenin Gwent*, sef y cafwyd y Farddoniaeth yn Delediw heb fethɪ, heb nam, heb archollɪ, hethɪ waethwg, parth pwyll, a Gwybodau, ac Addysg, a Chof, a llafar Gorsedd, a pharth Breiniau a Defodau, ac o hynny ai Barnwyd, ac ai Rheithiwyd, ac ai Breiniwyd felly heb na gwrtheb na gwrthneu.

40* Tair Gwaith yr aethɪ y Farddoniaeth a'r Beirdd wrth Raith gwlad, ac nis gallwyd Rhaith Cenedl arnaddynt ; sef *y cyntaf* yn amser *Cadwaladr fendigaid*, a gwrthneu a gwrtheb parth Cendl y rhoddwyd, achos y gwnaed newid a thwyll ar wybodau, a chofion, a Breiniau a Defodau.

Yr *ail waith*, Amser *Bleddyn ab Cynfyn*, ac ni cheisiwyd arnaddynt Raith Cenedl, ac nis bu.

A *thrydedd* waith ai rhoddwyd felly, *yngorsedd Caerfyddᵢyn*, pan y rhoddasant Feirdd Morganwg, a Gwent, ac Erging, ac Euas, ac Ystrad yw, wrtheb a Gwrthneu ar yr orsedd honno yn hawl Beirdd Ynys Prydain, ac ym mraint yr hen wybodau, a chofion, ac addysg, a'r hen Gelfyddydwrth-gerdd, a'r Hen freiniau a Defodau, achos twyll a thorr a wnaed yno arnynt, a myned yn eu Gwrth.

41. Gwel 81 † Tair Gwaith y trefnwyd ar Feirdd a Barddoniaeth ac nid aethpwyd gan Raith Gwlad a Chenedl. *Cyntaf* amser yr *Ymherawdr Arthur*, Ail, amser *Gruffydd*

---

* The number entered in MS. is 41, and the succeeding ones are arranged accordingly. The reason is, that 40 was inserted by mistake before the third part of No. 39.

† These references, which were made in accordance with the erroneous numbering, have been rectified.

[1] Ithel succeeded his brother Meurig, as king of Glamorgan and Gwent, in the year 843. He was slain A.D. 848. "Iudhail rex Guent a viris Broceniauc occisus est."—Annales Cambriæ, p. 13.

[2] Cadwalader the Blessed succeeded his father Cadwallawn ab Cadvan, about A.D. 634, and was the last of the Welsh princes, who assumed the title of chief sovereign of the Britons.

were confirmed, lest they should fail, become lost, or forgotten; — nor was there an objection or protest made against them. The third occasion on which they were submitted so, was in the time of Ithel, king of Gwent;[1] when Bardism was found perfect, without decay, without blemish, without injury, without deterioration, in respect of the meaning, sciences, instruction, memorial, and voice of Gorsedd, and in respect of privileges and usages; wherefore, it was adjudged, decreed, and privileged accordingly without contradiction or objection.

40. Three times were Bardism and the Bards submitted to the verdict of country, but could not receive the verdict of nation. The first was in the time of Cadwalader the Blessed,[2] when protest and objection were offered on the part of the nation, because the sciences, memorials, privileges, and usages were altered and falsified. The second occasion was in the time of Bleddyn, son of Cynvyn,[3] when the verdict of nation was not sought, neither was it given. The third occasion on which they were so submitted was at the Gorsedd of Caermarthen,[4] when the Bards of Glamorgan, Gwent, Ergyng, Euas, and Ystrad Yw, entered an objection and a protest against the said Gorsedd, under the claim of the Bards of the Isle of Britain, and under the privilege of the ancient sciences, memorials, and instruction, and the ancient art of song, and the ancient privileges and usages, because of the falsification and infraction to which they were there subjected; and opposed them.

41. Three times were Bards and Bardism arranged, without being submitted to the verdict of country and nation. The first, in the time of the emperor Arthur.[5] The

---

[3] Bleddyn, son of Cynvyn, was sole prince of Gwynedd and Powys from about 1068 until 1072, when he was slain in battle by Rhys, son of Owain, son of Edwyn.

[4] This Gorsedd was held under the patronage of Gruffudd, son of Nicholas, who had obtained a commission from Edward IV. for that purpose.

[5] The celebrated king Arthur, in the 6th century.

ab Cynan, Brenin Gwynedd, a *Thrydydd*, y trefnwyd fal
hynny yn amser y Brenin Edwart yr Ail, yng Nghastell
Caernarfon, ac nid oes Braint Gorsedd ar a drefnwyd yn yr
amseroedd hynny namyn syberwyd Gwlad gan bwyll ac
angen, yr rhain Bethau rhydd ydynt i Feirdd ac ar Farddoniaeth, cyd na bo torr a thwyll a myned yngwrth yr Hen
wybodau wrth Gerdd a Barddoniaeth.— Ac yn awr y mae
Beirdd a Barddoniaeth Ynys Prydain, ar Hen Freiniau a
Defodau, ar Hen Gofion a Gwybodau. ar hen Bwyll ac
addysg, a'r hen Gelfyddyd wrth Gerdd, ar hen ymbwyll
wrth Farddas, ar Gof a Llafar Gorsedd Cadair Morganwg
a Gwent ac Euas ac Ystrad yw, ac Ergin, ac wrth Farn a
chadarnhâd y Gadair honno dan Osteg a Rhybydd Deddfol
a defodol hyd ynghyfallwy heb na Gwrtheb na gwrthneu,
ac am hynny ym mraint a nawdd Rhaith Gwlad a Chenedl,
yr hon Osteg a Rhybydd a gynhaliwyd gan yr Arlwydd
William Herbert Iarll Rhaglan a Phenbro, a Thywysog
Morganwg, ymhob Llys a Llann, a chan Gorn Gwlad a
Gwaedd uwch adwedd yn ddefodawl yn ei holl Gyfoeth hyd
ynghyfallwy, fal y dywespwyd.

42. Tair Celfyddyd ni ddyly mab Taiog eu dysgu, heb
gennad ei Arglwydd. sef ydynt Ysgolheicdod, Barddoniaeth, a Gofaniaeth—canys o dioddef yr Arglwydd hyd pan
y rhodder corun i'r Ysgolhaig, neu yn ydd el y Bardd wrth
ei gerdd, neu 'r gôf yn ei Efail, rhydd fyddant ac nis gellir
eu caethiwo gwedy hynny.

43. Tri Meib Rhydd o Gaeth, Bardd, Ysgolhaig, a Gôf.
E.a.w. Tri meib rhyddion o gaeth, sef ydynt Bardd, ys-
golhaig, a ^{fferyllt}_{Gof}, can nis gellir caeth o a fedro un o'r tair
celfyddyd freiniol, sef ysgolheicdod, a Barddoniaeth, a gof-

---

[1] Gruffudd, son of Cynan, reigned over North Wales from 1075 until his
death in 1137. His biography, a very interesting document, written in Welsh
soon after his decease, is printed in the second volume of the Myvyrian Archaiology.

[2] Edward the Second reigned from 1307 to 1327.

second, in the time of Gruffudd,[1] son of Cynan, king of Gwynedd. And the third occasion on which they were so arranged, was in the time of king Edward the Second,[2] in the Castle of Caernarvon. There is no privilege of Gorsedd, however, to what was arranged on those occasions, but merely the courtesy of country, according to reason and necessity, to which Bards and Bardism are entitled, as long as they do not infringe, falsify, and contravene the ancient sciences of song and Bardism. And now the Bards and Bardism of the Isle of Britain, the ancient privileges and usages, the ancient memorials and sciences, the ancient import and instruction, the ancient art of song, and the ancient sense of Bardism, are preserved in the memory and by the voice of the Gorsedd of the Chair of Glamorgan, Gwent, Euas, Ystrad Yw, and Ergyng, and are subject to the judgment and authority of that Chair, under the formal and ritual proclamation and notice of a year and a day unto the period of efficiency, without contradiction or objection; and therefore are under the privilege and protection of the verdict of country and nation—which proclamation and notice were issued by the lord William Herbert, earl of Rhaglan and Pembroke, and prince of Glamorgan, in every court and church, and by the horn of country, and the cry of restoration formally throughout all his territory, unto the period of efficiency, as it has been said.

42. There are three arts which the son of a villain ought not to learn without the permission of his lord, namely: scholarship; Bardism; and metallurgy; for if the lord should bear until the tonsure is given to the scholar, or until the Bard takes up his song, or until the smith enters his smithy, they will be free, and cannot afterwards be enslaved.

43. There are three persons free from the bond: a Bard; a scholar; and a smith. Others say: the three free persons from the bond, namely: a Bard; a scholar; and a metallurgist. For no person can be bond, who knows one of the three privileged arts, namely: scholarship;

aniaeth, (fferylltaeth) a Breiniawl ydynt ac nis gellir ond
ar fonheddig y tair celfyddyd hynny, a phynnag au medro,
braint iddo fonedd a Brodoriaeth a Thrwydded Cymro cynhenid, can y bernir y Celfyddydeu hynny yn ddyledogion a
Breiniedigion Gwlad a Chenedl.

44. Tri lle nawdd cyffredin y sydd, ac nis gellir ynddynt
arf yn erbyn neb ba bynnag, sef yngorsedd Beirdd, yn Llys
Gwlad ac Arlwydd, ac yngnghyfarchwel golychwyd.

45. Tair prif hawl ac arddel Cenedl y Cymry y dylit eu
cynnal yngorsedd Beirdd Ynys Prydain. *Cyntaf*, Brenin o
Gymro cynhwynawl — *Ail*, Trwydded pumerwi rhyddion i
bob Cymro cynhenid Cynhwynawl—*Trydydd* Braint Cyrch
cynhired i Bob Cymro Cynhennid yn a fynno parth Gwlad
a Gorwlad yn Ynys Prydain heb wrth heb wahardd, cyd na
bo arfod ei law, ac heb arnaw na hawl na Chanlyn parth
Rhaith a Chyfraith, a Dyled y Breiniau hynn i Genedl y
Cymry, can mai eiddynt hwy o gysefin ansawdd, a meddiant, a Brodoriaeth yw Ynys Prydain.

46. Tair prif amcan Beirdd Ynys Prydain o gysefin
ddefod—dosparth gwybodaeth ac addysg—amlygu cyfiawnder—a chynnal heddwch.

47. Tair ffordd y cynhelir cyfiawn farddoniaeth Beirdd
Ynys Prydain, sef trwy Ddefod Gorsedd, Llafar Gorsedd, a
chan gorsedd.

48. Tri Chof Beirdd Ynys Prydain, Cof Defod, cof can,
a chof Llafar gorsedd. E.a.w. Cof defod, cof can, a chof
coelbren.

49. Tri phrifardd gorseddog y sydd, Prifardd pendant a
elwir hefyd yn fardd Braint a thrwyddedog braint, a Bardd
trwyddedog—a Derwydd,—ac Ofydd.

Bardism; and metallurgy. Those three arts are privileged, and cannot be followed by any one but a gentleman; and whoever knows them is entitled to the privilege of nobility, social rights, and the maintenance of an innate Cymro; for those arts are adjudged to be noble, and privileged arts of country and nation.

44. There are three common places of protection, in which no weapon can be raised against any person whatsoever, namely: the Gorsedd of Bards; the court of country and lord; and the precincts of worship.

45. There are three principal claims and avouchments of the nation of the Cymry, which ought to be supported in the Gorsedd of the Bards of the Isle of Britain. The first, a king who is a free-born Cymro. The second, the fruition of five free acres for every innate and free-born Cymro. The third, the right of progress for every innate Cymro as far as he likes in respect of country and border country in the island of Britain, without let and without hindrance, as long as his hand is not about to strike, and as long as he has no claim or is not sued, in respect of oath and law. These privileges are due to the nation of the Cymry, because theirs in right of original condition, possession, and community, is the island of Britain.

46. The three principal objects of the Bards of the Isle of Britain, in virtue of original usage: system of knowledge and learning; to manifest justice; and to maintain peace.

47. By three methods is the genuine Bardism of the Bards of the Isle of Britain maintained: by the usage of Gorsedd; the voice of Gorsedd; and the song of Gorsedd.

48. The three memorials of the Bards of the Isle of Britain: the memorial of usage; the memorial of song; and the memorial of the voice of Gorsedd. Others say: the memorial of usage; the memorial of song; and the memorial of Coelbren.

49. There are three presiding primitive Bards: Primitive Bard Positive, who is also called Bard of Privilege, Licentiate of Privilege, and Licensed Bard; Druid; and Ovate.

I

E.a.w.

Tri rhyw prifeirdd y sydd, Bardd Braint o gyssefin gaffaeliad, Derwydd wrth bwyll ansawdd a gorfod, ac Of-ydd, wrth ymgais, Dychymyg a dichwain.

50.   O dripheth y cafwyd barddoniaeth, Awen o Dduw, ^{deall}_{synwyr} Dyn, a syrth anian.

51.   Tair Braint Beirdd Ynys Prydain Trwyddedogaeth lle'r elont, Bod gair eu gair hwy ar bawb, ac nas dyger arf noeth lle byddont.

52.   Tair cainc addysg Beirdd Ynys Prydain—Bardd-oniaeth, ac ar hynny y mae cynnal Defod, a llafar, a chan gorsedd ac arnaw llywodraethu;—Derwyddoniaeth ac ar dderwydd y mae dysgu ac athrawiaethu wrth bwyll an-sawdd a gorfod; ac ofyddiaeth a myned wrth ^{wybodau}_{lafar} gwlad, dychymyg a damwan.

53.   Tri pheth a ddylai Bardd eu gwneuthur, gwrando, edrych, a chelu (gwrando—disgwyl, a thewi)

54.   Gwel 92.   Tri dyn nis gellir Beirdd o henynt, Diog, balch, a chelwyddog.

55.   Tripheth a ddylai Bardd eu cadarnhau, Gwybodaeth, gwirionedd, a heddwch.

56.   Tripheth a ddylaid fardd, sef gwellhau a mwyhau gwybodau, llarieiddio moes a chynneddf, a diddanu meddwl.

57.   Tair ffordd y greddir Bardd, sef yn gyntaf graddu Bardd Braint o drofedigaeth neu ynteu o Rybydd undydd a blwyddyn, Derwydd a reddir o Farn Gorsedd wrth a fo mwyaf gan goelbren—ac ofydd, o Fardd Braint gorseddog a ddywetto ar ei air ai gydwybod y gellir Bardd o'r gwr wrth ymgais.

58.   Gwel 60.   Tri gweiniedyddion Gwybodaeth Beirdd

---

¹ Al. "the sense."   ² Al. "the voice."

Others say :

There are three kinds of primitive Bards : Bard of privilege in virtue of original appointment ; Druid, according to reason, nature, and cogency ; and Bvate, according to exertion, imagination, and contingency.

50. From three things has Bardism been obtained : Awen from God; the intellect [1] of man ; and the disposition of nature.

51. The three privileges of the Bards of the Isle of Britain: maintenance wherever they go; that their word should be paramount ; and that no naked weapon be borne where they may be.

52. The three branches of learning of the Bards of the Isle of Britain : Bardism, on which depends the maintenance of the usage, voice, and song of Gorsedd, as well as the regulation of matters ; Druidism, it being incumbent upon a Druid to teach and instruct according to reason, nature, and cogency ; and Ovatism, which has to do with the sciences [2] of country, imagination, and contingency.

53. Three things which a Bard ought to do : to listen ; to look ; and keep secret. Al. to listen; to expect; and to be silent.

54. Three persons who cannot be made Bards : the idle; the proud ; and the liar.

55. Three things which a Bard ought to establish : knowledge ; truth ; and peace.

56. Three things which a Bard ought to do, namely : to improve and extend sciences ; to soften morals and habits ; and to solace the mind.

57. In three ways is a Bard graduated, namely : first, a Bard of privilege is graduated after discipleship, or after the notice of a year and a day ; a Druid is graduated by the decree of Gorsedd, according to a majority of votes ; and an Ovate is graduated after a presiding Bard shall have affirmed upon his word and conscience that the candidate may be made a Bard.

58. The three ministers of knowledge of the Bards of

Ynys Prydain, nid amgen Cân, arwydd, a llythyr, a goreu
y bernir cân, am nas bydd achos namyn wrth y dyn ai
dysgo ar gof heb na gwaith llaw na chelfyddyd, a gallu
myned o gan ar dafod a chof o ddyn i ddyn, ac o wlad i
wlad, ac o oes i oes, heb amgen i gynnal na chof a deall, ac
nis gellir hynny ar arwydd a llythyr. am hynny goreu cynnal a chadw ar wybodau yw Cân wrth fraint a defod Gorsedd. (Gwel rif 59)

59.   Tri gweinyddion gwybodaeth, Cân, Brut, a llythyr,
a goreu Cân, can y bydd hawddaf ei dysgu ai chofio, ac yn
anhawddaf ei newid ai llygru am ei bod wrth osodiad a
threfn herwydd celfyddyd wrth Gerdd a mesurau Prydyddiaeth, achos hynny—anhepcor i Fardd Awen a chelfyddyd wrth Gerdd a Phrydyddiaeth.

60.   Tri gweinyddion addysg, Can, arwydd, a Llythyr—
Al. Cân o brydydd, arwydd o arwyddfardd, a llythyr o
bosfardd.

61.   Tri phrifryw Trioedd y sydd ar fraint a Defod gan
Feirdd Ynys Prydain, sef Trioedd Braint a Defod, Trioedd
Barddas, a Thrioedd Cerdd.

62.   Tri awdurdawd Deddf a chyfraith, ei rhoi ar osteg
a rhybudd undydd a blwyddyn ymhob Llys a Llann yn y
Cyfoeth, ai rhoi wrth Raith Gwlad a chenedl sef yw hynnw
Llw Trichannyn o Gywiriaid gwlad a Chyfoeth a phob a
naddynt yr wr cyfallwy o Bencenedl: Ai rhoi wrth Farn

---

[1] "A preceptive Bard, a teaching Bard."—Dr. O. Pughe's Dict.

Tewch chwi *bosfeirddion.*

Be silent, ye *teaching Bards.*—Bustl Beirdd.

Yn *bosfardd,* ba fardd a fo,
'R hyd bysedd rhaid ei bosio;
A thrwy bwys uthr o bosiad
Graddau gynt o'u gwraidd a gad.

the Isle of Britain, namely : song ; symbol ; and letter ; of
which song is considered the best, because there will be
need only of the person who commits it to memory, without manual labour or art, and because a song can be con-
veyed by means of the tongue and memory from man to
man, and from country to country, and from age to age,
without any thing to support it other than memory and
understanding. This cannot be the case with symbol and
letter ; therefore, the best means of maintaining and preserving sciences is song, according to the privilege and usage
of Gorsedd.

59. The three ministers of knowledge : song ; chronicle ;
and letter. The best is song, inasmuch as it is the easiest
to learn and remember, and the most difficult to alter and
corrupt, being arranged and ordered according to the art of
song and the metres of poetry. Wherefore, awen and the
art of song and poetry are indispensable to a Bard.

60. The three ministers of instruction : song ; symbol ;
and letter. Al. song by a poet ; symbol by a herald-bard ;
and letter by a post-bard.[1]

61. There are three kinds of Triads under privilege and
usage by the Bards of the Isle of Britain, namely : Triads
of privilege and usage ; Triads of Bardism ; and Triads of
song.

62. The three authorities of statute and law : their being published under the proclamation and notice of a year
and a day in every court and church in the territory ; their
being submitted to the verdict of country and nation, that
is, the oath of three hundred true men of country and territory, each of them being an efficient man and head of kindred ; and their being submitted to the judgment of court

A didactic Bard, whatever Bard would be,
On the fingers it is necessary to question him ;
And through the weight of a solemn interrogation
Degrees from their source were given of yore.

Edm. Prys.

Llys ac Ynad herwydd y bo 'r llys gan Ddefod tros gof, mewn Tair gorsedd ymhob un o dair Talaith Cymru, gan farnu wrth gof a Defod a chadarnhaad Gorsedd a Llys.

63. (Gwel rif 96) Tair awdurdawd Cerdd Dafawd gwedi ydd elo yngorsedd gyfallwy — Cyfiawnder iaith a Chaniadaeth, can nas gellir credu amgen herwydd braint y Prydydd—Cyfiawnder ystyr ac amcan, can nas dylit barnu amgen herwydd gair cydwybod y Prydydd :—a Braint o farn Gorsedd gyfallwy—ac nis dylit ei gwrtheb herwydd Gair a Breiniau Beirdd Ynys Prydain.

64. (Gwel rif 93) Tair gwarsaf (gwarant) y sydd gallu Bardd o neb un—Gair Bardd gorseddog Llinolingerdd, a ddywetto ar ei air ai gydwybod y gellir Bardd o'r $^{un}_{neb}$ a fynno fyned $^{yn\ fardd}_{wrth\ gerdd}$—a gair deuddeg o Gywiriaid Gwlad a $^{Chenedl}_{chyfoeth}$ wrth frawd a Rhaith ym mraint Cymry Cynhenid—a Gair Pennaeth Gwlad neu Ynas Llys, a ddywetto y dylit Pabledigaeth ar y neb a fynno fod yn fardd am ei fod yn gywiriad gwlad o fonedd a Braint a bod rhydd hynny iddo gan ei Arlwydd.

65. Tri Chyff Cynnadl. Bardd, Ynad, a Thegyrn * (* i.e. Teyrn)

66. Gwel rif 88. Tri Chyfrwym gwlad, Barddas—Yngneidiaeth—a Theyrnedd. Al. Tri Banogion gwladwriaeth &c.

67. Tair dyledswydd gywladogaidd Bardd—Moli daionus—Addysg a Chyngor—a chynnal Cof a chadw ar ai dirper.

68. Tri choel Beirdd Ynys Prydain Cof a llafar Gorsedd—Arwydd a Darlun—a llythyr ac ysgrif.

69. Tripheth a ddylai Bardd eu Datgan yngorsedd ym mraint Cenedl y Cymry au gofyn gantho, sef yw hynny

---

[1] Al. " to attach himself to song."   [2] Al. " territory."

[3] *Cynnadl* cerdd cerennydd gymhen
Cein Venwas heb gas heb gynnen.

The *competition* of song, among witty friends,
Splendid talent, without hatred, without strife.

and judge, as the court may be from immemorial usage, in three Gorsedds, in each of the three provinces of Cymru, judgment being formed according to the memory, usage, and confirmation of Gorsedd and court.

63. The three authorities of vocal song, when it shall have been sanctioned by an efficient Gorsedd: correctness of language and versification, for what is otherwise cannot be admitted according to the privilege of a poet; correctness of meaning and object, for what is otherwise ought not to receive judgment from the word of a poet's conscience; and privilege received from the judgment of an efficient Gorsedd; and they ought not to be contradicted, because of the word and privileges of the Bards of the Isle of Britain.

64. There are three warrants in virtue of which any one may be admitted a Bard: the word of a presiding Bard of poetic lineage, who shall say upon his word and conscience that the one who desires to be a Bard[1] can be made a Bard; the word of twelve true and loyal men of country and nation[2] judicially and legally pronounced under the privilege of innate Cymry; and the word of the sovereign of country or judge of court, who shall say that the one who seeks to be a Bard may receive a faculty, because he is a loyal man of country in respect of descent and privilege, and that his lord gives him that freedom.

65. The three stocks of competition:[3] a Bard; a judge; and a king.

66. The three mutual bonds of a country: Bardism; judicature; and kingship. Al. The three characteristics of government, &c.

67. The three national duties of a Bard: to praise the good; to impart instruction and advice; and to preserve the memorial and record of what is worthy.

68. The three credibilities of the Bards of the Isle of Britain: the memorial and voice of Gorsedd; symbol and picture; and letter and writing.

69. Three things which a Bard ought to recite in Gorsedd under the privilege of the nation of the Cymry who

datgan pynciau 'r Iaith Gymraeg.—a Breiniau a defodau
Beirdd Ynys Prydain, a Breiniau a Defodau Cenedl y
Cymry au Teyrnedd.

70. Tri chyfamddawd Beirdd Ynys Prydain, Gair,
Llythyr—ac Arwydd—(*Al.* gair arwydd, a llythyr.)

71. Tri Dyn a fyddant dan gyfarwys Gwlad, Bardd—
Ynad a Milwr.

72. Tair Cyfatgan Beirdd Ynys Prydain—Cerdd, Dam-
meg—a Defod.

73. Tri bonedd Cyfraith, Cydwybod—Gwir—a gorfod.
Al ac achos

       Tri Defnydd pob Deddf a chyfraith—Gwirionedd—
Gwybodaeth—a Chydwybod (*Al.* Gwirionedd—Dysg—a
Chydwybod.

74. (Gwel rif 95) Tri chrair Twng a Briduw Beirdd
Ynys Prydain. Y dengair Deddf—Efengyl Ieuan—ac yn
wyneb Haul a goleuni—E.a.w. y dengair Deddf—Efengyl
Ieuan—a Bardd yn dywedyd ar ei air ai gydwybod.—*Al*
Bardd. ac Ynad, a gwr rhaith, yn dywedyd ar ei air ai
Gydwybod (3 chrair Chred a Briduw

75. Tair addysg arbennig a gafas Genedl y Cymry,
Cyntaf er yn oes oesoedd oedd y Gwyddanod cyn nog amser
Prydain ab Aedd Mawr. ail oedd Barddas fal ai dysgid gan
y Beirdd gwedi 'r caffaeliad o henynt—Trydydd y ffydd
ynghrist yn oreu o'r Tair.

Sef yn gyntaf y bu 'r Gwyddanod yn ben-doethion ac
athrawon Cenedl y Cymry, a gwedi dodi braint a Defod
iddynt yn Amser Prydain ab Aedd Mawr, ^{gelwid Beirdd}_{doded enw Beirdd}
arnynt, a dodi Barddas ar a wypynt, ac nid oes na chof na
gwybod am y Gwyddanod namyn Enw Tydain Tad Awen
yr hwn a wnaeth Gerdd Gymraeg gyntaf erioed, ac o'i gerdd
ef y cafwyd deall goreu ar y Barddas a Barddoniaeth, ac o

---

[1] Al. " learning."

[2] Al. " belief."   [3] Al. " the name Bards was bestowed upon them."

may require it of him, that is to say : to recite the points of the Cymric language ; the privileges and usages of the Bards of the Isle of Britain ; and the privileges and usages of the nation of the Cymry, and their sovereignty.

70. The three rudiments of the Bards of the Isle of Britain : word ; letter ; and symbol. Al. word ; symbol ; and letter.

71. Three men who are entitled to the endowment of country : a Bard ; a judge ; and a warrior.

72. The three primary descriptive mediums of the Bards of the Isle of Britain : song ; allegory ; and usage.

73. The three stocks of law : conscience ; truth ; and cogency. Al. and occasion.

The three materials of every rite and law : truth ; knowledge ;[1] and conscience.

74. The three relics of oath[2] and asseveration of the Bards of the Isle of Britain : the ten commandments ; the gospel of John ; and averment in the face of the sun and light. Others say : the ten commandments ; the gospel of John ; and a Bard declaring upon his word and conscience. According to others : a Bard ; a judge ; and a juror declaring upon his word and conscience.

75. The three especial instructions which the nation of the Cymry obtained : the first was that of the Gwyddoniaid before the time of Prydain, son of Aedd the Great, from the age of ages ; the second was Bardism, as taught by the Bards, after they were instituted ; the third, the faith in Christ, which was the best of the three. That is to say, first, the Gwyddoniaid were the principal philosophers and teachers of the nation of the Cymry, and when privilege and usage were conferred upon them in the time of Prydain, son of Aedd the Great, they were called Bards,[3] and what they knew was designated Bardism. There is no memorial or knowledge of the Gwyddoniaid, except the name of Tydain, the father of Awen, who first of all men composed a Cymric song ; and it was from his song that the best comprehension of Bardism and poetry was obtained,

K

hynny gwnaethpwyd Beirdd Braint a Defod o gyngor ac
addysg y Tri Chyntefig, sef, Plennydd, Alawn, a Gwron.

76. O Dripheth y cafwyd Barddoniaeth. O gof a gwybod er yn oes oesoedd—o gerdd Tydain ab Tudno, sef oedd
Hwnnw Tydain Tad Awen — ac o Awen o Dduw gan
Bwyll ac Ystyr a Deall. (*al* Tydain ab Tydnaw. Tud-
nawf qu? Noah?)

77. Tri pheth y Bydd Bardd, sef Pen a Phont, ai ddy-
falu ef yn bont am y dwg ef dros gors anwybodaeth—A Diogel lle bo Anniogel am nas bydd arf yn ei erbyn nac yn
erbyn ai cyfymdaith—a Braint i ddifraint, sef yw hynny ei
nawdd ef. sef y mae dywediad fal hynn — a fynno fod yn
ben bid bont, a fynno fod yn bont bid Bardd, o fod yn fardd
Bid Ben, o Ben bid bont.

78. Gwel rif 27 Tair gosteg Gyffredin y sydd, a pha
bynag ai rhybydd, ai haer, ai gwaedd, ai gwad, a rodder
bydded wrth bob un o'r tair dan rybydd undydd a blwyddyn—sef ydynt, Maes arglwydd—Cyrch golychwyd—a gorsedd Beirdd. (qu? hinc the Glam. expression of Gwadu
coed, maes, a mynydd, Cyhoeddi Coed maes a mynydd &c.

    neu fal hynn.

Tair Gosteg gyffredin y sydd. Cyrch golychwyd—Maes
Arglwydd—a gorsedd Beirdd—*Al.* Tri lle y mae cynnal
gosteg a rhybydd hyd ynghyfnod undydd a blwyddyn, &c.
ac ynddynt cynnal pob Gwaedd uwch adwedd, ac uwch adneu, ac uwch adfan.

---

[1] Al. " Tydain, son of Tydnaw." Tud-nawf, qu. Noah ?

[2] There is evidently an allusion to this Bardic dogma in one of the Mabinogion :—" Bendigeid Vran came to land, and the fleet with him by the bank of
the river. ' Lord,' said his chieftains, ' knowest thou the nature of this river,
that nothing can go across it, and there is no bridge over it ? ' ' What,' said
they, ' is thy counsel concerning a bridge ? ' ' There is none,' said he, ' except
that he who will be chief let him be a bridge. I will be so,' said he. And then
was that saying first uttered, and it is still used as a proverb. And when he had
lain down across the river, hurdles were placed upon him, and the host passed
over thereby."—Mabinogi, Branwen the Daughter of Llyr.

Gwilym Tew (1433—1470) describes our Saviour as

    Ein *pont* ein *pen*.—Our *bridge* and our *chief*.

and hence were instituted Bards of privilege and usage, by means of the counsel and instruction of the three primary ones, Plennydd, Alawn, and Gwron.

76. From three things was Bardism obtained: from memory and knowledge from the age of ages; from the song of Tydain, son of Tudno,[1] that is, Tydain, the father of Awen; and from Awen from God by means of reason, sense, and understanding.

77. A Bard will be three things, namely: a chief and a bridge, being resembled to a bridge, because he conveys over the morass of ignorance; security where there is insecurity, because there will be no weapon against him or against his fellow traveller; and a privilege for the unprivileged, that is, his protection. Accordingly it is said: he who would be chief, let him be a bridge; he who would be a bridge, let him be a Bard; from being a Bard, let him be a chief; from being a chief, let him be a bridge.[2]

78. There are three common announcements, and whether it be notice, assertion, cry, or denial that is issued, it ought to be according to one of the three, under the notice of a year and a day, namely: the field of a lord; the resort of worship; and the Gorsedd of Bards.[3]

Or thus:

There are three common announcements: the resort of worship; the field of a lord; and the Gorsedd of Bards. Otherwise: three places in which proclamation and notice are to be issued until the expiration of a year and a day, &c., and in them are to be uttered every cry of restoration, of re-assertion, and of re-arrangement.

And Lewys Daron, (1580—1600,) in his Elegy on Tudur Aled, applies the same expressions to him :—

> Pwy a fu *benn*, pa fab oedd,
> Pwy ond Tudur, pont ydoedd.

> Who was *chief?* What son was he?
> Who but Tudur? He was a bridge.

[3] Qu. Whether the Glamorgan expressions, " Gwadu coed, maes, a mynydd," " Cyhoeddi coed, maes, a mynydd," &c., are derived from these announcements?

79. Tair Gorsedd gadarn Ynys Prydain, Gorsedd gwlad ac arlwydd—Gorsedd Beirdd—a gorsedd Cynghyd Cynnal. E.A.W. Tair Prif orsedd Ynys Prydain &c.

80. Tair Priforsedd Beirdd Ynys Prydain, Gorsedd Moel Meriw, — Gorsedd Beisgawen, — a Gorsedd Bryn Gwyddon. *al.* Moel Efwr—Beisgawen—a Bryn Gwyddon.

81. gwel rif 39. a 41. Tair gwaith y rhoddwyd y farddoniaeth ar Raith gwlad a Chenedl. sef yn gyntaf pan ai trefnwyd ac ai Breiniwyd gyntaf yn amser Prydain ab Aedd Mawr—ail yn amser Bran ap Llyr—Trydydd yn amser Gruffudd ab Cynan, a braint nad elai neb wrth gerdd nag addysg o'r Byd onid ymmraint a nawdd Beirdd Ynys Prydain.

82. Tri Bannogion Gwladoliaeth—Bardd yn Addysg— Fferyllt yn amddiffyn—a Llafurwr yn ymborth—a braint Cywiriaid cynhwynawl Gwlad a Chenedl y Cymry a ddylit iddynt o ba wlad a Chenedl bynnag y bont.

83. Tri pheth nid oes a el yn eu herbyn—Hen Gerdd— Hen Gof — a Hen * gelfyddyd wrth Gerdd — (*al* a Hen * Ddefod.)

84. Tri dyn a gyfanneddant Lys (*al* Lys a llan) Bardd, gof, a Thelyniwr (Bardd, fferyllt, a Thelynor. *vel* Bardd— gwr wrth gerdd dant a fferyllt)

Tri dyn a wnant gyfannedd lle bont, Bardd, Gof, a *Thelynwr* (*al.* a *llafurwr*)

85. Tri phrif ofynion y sydd ar Fardd—cynnal cof a gwybod—cynnal heddwch a syberwyd—a chynnal addysg a deddfoldeb.

86. Tri thrwydded Bardd—ei bum erwi rhyddion—ei gylch clera—ai rodd am a wnêl herwydd ei gelfyddyd i'r un ai caffo.

---

[1] Al. "and an ancient usage." [2] Al. "a court and village."

[3] Al. "a labourer."

79. The three firm Gorsedds of the Isle of Britain : the Gorsedd of country and lord; the Gorsedd of Bards; and the Gorsedd of federate support. Others say : the three principal Gorsedds of the Isle of Britain, &c.

80. The three principal Gorsedds of the Isle of Britain : the Gorsedd of Meriw hill; the Gorsedd of Beiscawen; and the Gorsedd of Bryn Gwyddon. Al. the hill of Evwr; Beiscawen; and Bryn Gwyddon.

81. Three times was Bardism submitted to the verdict of country and nation, namely : first, when it was originally arranged and privileged in the time of Prydain, son of Aedd the Great; secondly, in the time of Bran, son of Llyr; thirdly, in the time of Gruffudd, son of Cynan, and it was so secured that no one should be initiated in any song or learning whatsoever, but under the privilege and protection of the Bards of the Isle of Britain.

82, The three characteristics of a community : a Bard teaching; an artist defending; and a labourer providing food; and they are entitled to the privilege of innate loyalists of the country and nation of the Cymry, of whatever country and nation they may be.

83. Three things which cannot be contravened : an ancient song; an ancient memorial; and an ancient art of poetry.[1]

84. Three men who socially constitute a court :[2] a Bard; a smith; and a harpist. Al. a Bard; a metallurgist; and a harpist. Or : a Bard; a man of instrumental song; and a metallurgist.

Three men who establish a social habitation wherever they may be : a Bard; a smith; and a harpist.[3]

85. Three principal things required of a Bard : to preserve memorial and knowledge; to preserve peace and courtesy; and to preserve instruction and morality.

86. The three maintenances of a Bard : his five free acres; his circuit of minstrelsy; and his fee for what he does, in virtue of his art, to another.

87. Tri thrwyddedog Llys—Bardd—Ynad—a Golych-wydwr.

88. (Gwel rif 66) Tri chynnal Gwladoldeb—Barddas—Yngneidiaeth—a Llafuriaeth.

89. Tair atgorfa gyffredin y sydd—Cyrch Beirdd yng-orsedd a golychwyd—Cyrch Dygynnill Gwlad ac Arlwydd wrth Raith a Chyfraith—a chyrch arodraeth (al cylch aron—vel cyfar—vel arawd—vel aryddiaeth) a braint i wryw a benyw eu cyrchu.

90. Tair atgorfa wahanred y sydd a braint i fenyw yn-ddynt, nid amgen Helwriaeth — milwriaeth — a chynghyd Cynnal.

91. Ar dripheth y dylai Fardd Drefnu a bod yn wr wrth Gadair Neithiorau au rhoi ar gof a Chadw,—y Campau breiniolion nid amgen na phedair-Camp-ar hugain Cenedl y Cymry. a chadw tangnef a deddfoldeb ynddynt, a barnu arnynt yn y bo iawn—a chadw cof a dosparth ar Fonedd y genedl ar Cyfoeth y bo ynddi ei gadair ai drwydded, fal nad elo anghof ac anach ac o hynny coll ar fraint gynhenid, a lle nas gwnelo hynn, colli ei dda wrth gerdd dros dair blyn-edd.

92. Gwel 54 Tri Dyn ni ddylit ac nis gellir Beirdd o honynt—Diog—Balch—a Chelwyddog.

93. Gwel rif 57—64 &c. Tair gwarant y sydd gallu Bardd o nebun a'i chwenycho—gair Bardd Llinolingerdd a ddywetto ar ei gydwybod—Gair Pennaeth sef Arglwydd neu Ynad—a gair Deuddeg o gywiriaid Gwlad. a barnu Offeiriad ymmraint Bardd Llinolingerdd, gan mai Derwydd ym mraint swydd a Dyled ydyw ef.

94. Y Tri phwnc cyntaf y dylai Fardd eu dysgu a'u hystyried, Credu pob peth—anghredu pob peth—a chredu ni waeth beth. E.a.w. — Tri phwnc cyntaf Barddas, vel Triphwnc Addysg cyntaf Bardd, &c.

87. The three licentiates of court : a Bard ; a judge ; and a worshipper.

88. The three supports of government : Bardism ; judicature ; and labour.

89. There are three common departures : the resort of Bards to Gorsedd and worship ; the resort to a convention of country and lord, which is regulated by jury and law; and the resort to aration ; both male and female being privileged to resort to them.

90. There are three peculiar departures, a female being privileged to join in them : hunting ; warfare ; and a convention of federation.

91. In respect of three things ought a Bard to regulate matters, and to be a man of Chair : nuptial festivities, which he ought to chronicle and register ; the royal games, that is, the twenty-four games of the nation of the Cymry, which he ought to see are conducted in peace and morality, and which he must arbitrate justly; and the genealogy of the nation and territory where his Chair and endowment may be, in respect of which he ought to keep a memorial and system, lest innate privilege should suffer oblivion, and blemish, and consequently loss ; if he attends not to these things, he shall lose the remuneration of his song for three years.

92. Three men who ought not, and cannot be made Bards : the idle ; the proud ; and the liar.

93. There are three guarantees which will enable any one who wishes to be made a Bard : the word of a Bard of poetic lineage, who shall affirm upon his conscience ; the word of a chief, that is, a lord, or a judge; and the word of twelve true and loyal men of country. A priest is adjudged to have the same privilege as a Bard of poetic lineage, since he is a Druid in virtue of office and duty.

94. The three first points, which a Bard ought to teach and consider : to believe every thing; to disbelieve every thing; and to believe it matters not what. Others say : the three first points of Bardism ; or, a Bard's three first points of instruction, &c.

95. (Gwel rif 74) Tri chrair cred a Briduw Beirdd Ynys Prydain—y dengair deddf—Efengyl Ieuan—ac wyneb haul a llygad goleuni. (*al.* ac edrych yn llygad haul ac wyneb goleuni) sef pan ydd eler wrth friduw rhoddi 'r ddwy law yn gymmhleth byssedd y naill yn y llall, a'u pwysaw parth y creiriau a ddywespwyd ar y ddwyfron.

96. (Gwel rif 63) Tri awdurdawd Cerdd dafod y sydd, Cyfiawnder iaith a chaniadaeth, gan nas gellir credu amgen herwydd Braint y Prydydd,—Cyfiawnder ystyr a datgan, can nas gellir credu amgen wrth bwyll ac ansawdd herwydd dyled a Braint y Prydydd.—a Braint Gorsedd sef yw hynny Barn a phlaid Tair Cadair wrth Gerdd a elont gan Ddefodau Beirdd Ynys Prydain—sef au galwant y Beirdd Braint Gorsedd gyfallwy.

97. (Gwel rif 4) Tair ffordd y cynhelir yn gyfiawn Barddoniaeth Beirdd Ynys Prydain, sef trwy Lafar Gorsedd—Can gyfallwy—a Defod wrth Gof gwlad a gorsedd. E.a.w. Llafar Gorsedd—Can Gorsedd—a Defod Gorsedd. —E.a.w. Cof Can—Cof Llafar. a Chof coelbren (sef Llythyr)

98. (Gwel rif. 7) Tri syrth Prifeirdd Ynys Prydain, Bairdd Braint neu Brydydd i Lywodraethu a chadw cof— Derwydd i athrawiaethu—ac Ofydd i wellhau dysg a Gwybodaeth.

99. Tair ymgais o ddyled y sydd ar Fardd, un yw cynnill a dysgu Gwybodau—ail yw Athrawiaethu—a Thrydydd yw Heddych gan gan yrru Cydfod a thangnef lle bo amryson ac ymdrin. a diweddu ar gywrysedd, can nid defod na gwedd i Fardd a wnelo _{yngwrth}^{yn erbyn} y pethau hynn.

100. Tair ymdrafod a fyddant ryddion i Fardd, ac i bob un arall o frodorion Gwlad a Chenedl, sef yw y rhai hynny

---

[1] Al. " and looking in the eye of the sun and the face of light."

95. The three relics of belief and asseveration of the Bards of the Isle of Britain : the ten commandments ; the gospel of John; and the face of the sun and eye of light.[1] And when one makes an asseveration, he is to fold his two hands, placing the fingers of the one between those of the other, and pressing them on the breast, towards the relics mentioned.

96. There are three authorities of vocal song : just language and versification, since none other can be believed according to the privilege of a poet; just import and recitation, since none other can be believed according to reason and nature in respect of the duty and privilege of a poet; and the privilege of Gorsedd, that is, the judgment and favour of three Chairs of song, which are held according to the privileges of the Bards of the Isle of Britain, being called by the Bards the privilege of an efficient Gorsedd.

97. In three ways is the Bardism of the Bards of the Isle of Britain properly maintained, namely : by means of the voice of Gorsedd; an efficient Gorsedd; and usage according to the memory of country and Gorsedd. Others say : the voice of Gorsedd ; the song of Gorsedd ; and the usage of Gorsedd. Others say : the memorial of song ; the memorial of voice ; and the memorial of Coelbren, that is, letter.

98. The three sorts of the primitive Bards of the Isle of Britain : a Bard of privilege, or poet, to rule, and to record ; a Druid, to teach ; and an Ovate, to improve learning and knowledge.

99. There are three endeavours, which are obligatory upon a Bard : one is, to accumulate and teach sciences; the second is, to instruct; and the third is, to pacify, by introducing concord and tranquillity where there is contention and quarrelling, and putting an end to strife ; for it is not according to usage, or becoming, that a Bard should do contrary to these things.

100. There are three pursuits which are lawful to a Bard, and to every other native of country and nation, that

L

Helwriaeth—ac Arddoriaeth—a maeronyddiaeth—can mai
wrth y rhai hynny y caffant bawb eu hymborth, ac nis dylit
na nag na negydd arnynt nag attal a'u chwenychai. (*vel* nac
attal o honynt i neb a'u chwenychai.) E.a.w. aryddiaeth,
maeronyddiaeth — a meddyginiaeth, can mai trafodaethau
gwellhâd wrth danc a chynneddf yw y rhai hynny a'r Tair
trafodion cyffredin a'u gelwir.

101. Tri pheth amraint i Fardd ymdrafod a hwynt—
can nad yw iawn y pethau hynny iddaw ef, sef *Fferylldod*
a'r _{honn gelfyddyd nid oes &c.}^{hynn nid oes a wnelo} ef namyn ei gwellhau oi bwyll ai addysg, ai wybodaeth ai athrawiaeth, can mai gwr wrth len yw
efe. A *Rhyfel*, can nas dylid arf noeth yn ei law ef yn
erbynnu, can mai gwr wrth heddwch a thangnef yw efe.
Trydydd yw *Cyfnewidiaeth* can mai gwr wrth gynneddf a
chyfiawnder yw efe, ac ef a ddylai fod wrth ei swydd o
addysgu gwlad a chenedl—ac achos y pethau hynn y bernir
nas dylid crefft i fardd amgen nai swydd ai gelfyddyd wrth
gerdd a Barddoniaeth, rhag Llwgr, a gwaethygiad, a choll
ar a ddylid o Fardd a Barddoniaeth a rhag nas gallo Bardd
o fod wrth grefft gynnal myfyrdawd ar y pethau a weddant
ar Fardd a Barddas, ac ar Lên a Gwybodau awenbwyll. ac
iawn iddaw y tair trafodiaeth gyffredin.

102. Tair rhyw wledd gyffredin a fyddant wrth drefn a
Llywedigaeth Beirdd Ynys Prydain, sef *Cyntaf* yw gwleddoedd y *pedair Alban*—*Ail* yw gwleddoedd Golychwyd ar
fannau Lleuad—*Trydydd* Gwleddoedd gwlad a chenedl gan
orfoledd a gwaredigaeth, a'u cynnal dan osteg a Rhybydd
Deugeinnydd. E.a.w.

Tair Gwleddoedd Gyferddawn a fyddant yn Nawdd
Beirdd Ynys Prydain, ac iddynt bawb ei rodd o'r tair
Dawnged, sef mêl, peillon, a Blith, nid amgen, Gwleddoedd
cyfarwys dan osteg deugeinydd, a gwleddoedd Alban — a

---

[1] "Al. "nor should they be restrained from such as may desire them."

is to say : hunting; tillage; and pastoral cares ; for it is by means of those things that all persons obtain food, and they ought not to be denied or prohibited, nor should such as may desire them be restrained.[1] Others say : tillage; pastoral cares; and medicine; for these are pursuits of improvement, consequent upon peace and morality, and are called the three common pursuits.

101. Three things which a Bard is not privileged to engage in, since they are not proper for him. Metallurgy, with which art he has nothing to do, except to improve it, according to his reason, learning, knowledge, and doctrine, for he is a man of literature. War, since there ought to be no naked weapon in his hand against others, for he is a man of peace and tranquillity. The third is commerce, for he is a man of primary law and justice, and he ought to attend to his office of instructing country and nation. And because of these things it is deemed that a Bard ought not to have any trade other than his office and art, in respect of song and Bardism, lest what ought to belong to Bard and Bardism should suffer loss and deterioration, and lest a Bard, by following a trade, may not be able to practise meditation in respect of the things which are suitable to Bard and Bardism, and to literature and genial sciences; nevertheless, the three common pursuits are proper for him.

102. The three common feasts, which are conducted and arranged by the Bards of the Isle of Britain, namely : the first are the feasts of the four albans ; the second are the feasts of worship at the quarters of the moon; the third are the feasts of country and nation, because of a triumph and deliverance ; which are to be held under the proclamation and notice of forty days.

Others say :

There are three contributory feasts under the protection of the Bards of the Isle of Britain, at which all have their portion of the three tributes, namely, honey, meal, and milk, that is to say : the feasts of co-aration under the proclamation of forty days ; the feasts of alban ; and the feasts

gwleddoedd golychwyd — a braint yw i Feirdd drefnu ynddynt, ac ynddynt cael rhoddion o'r tair Ced gyferddawn
sef yw y rhai hynny *yd*, a *blith* a *mel*. (*al* ydged (vel peillged—blithged—a melged.) sef au gelwir rhoddion cyfarwys
Beirdd, sef wrth aradr y byddant.

103. Tair gwledd arall y sydd, a syberwyd yw i Fardd
drefnu arnynt, sef yw y rhai hynny *Gwledd Pencenedl*—a
Gwledd Neithior—a *gwledd gwyl Bentan*, sef y bydd honno
man y bo derchafael pum maen Pentan yn orsaf cyfannedd,
ac ynnynt rhoddion y Cwmmwd a'r Genedl hyd y nawfed
ach—a dogn o'r rhoddion cyferddawn y gwleddoedd hynny
a fyddant i'r Beirdd, ac o âr ac o fuarth, ac o goedwal y
byddant, mal y bo hawsaf eu cael a'u rhoddi—ac i Fardd ei
syberwyd can nad oes namyn syberwyd i Fardd yn Tair
Gwleddoedd hynny.

104. Tair Gosteg y sydd—un yw gosteg dan Rybydd
un dydd a blwyddyn a than yr osteg honn y dylit pob
Gwaedd Gadarn fal y mae Gwaedd uwch adwedd — a
gwaedd uwch adneu — a gwaedd uwch adfan a'u cynnal
ymhob Gorsedd Gwlad ac Arlwydd—a phob Gorsedd Beirdd
—a phob Cyrch Golychwyd.—Ail yw gosteg deugeinydd ac
wrth honno y bydd pob Gwledd gyffredin gwlad a chenedl,
a phob gorsedd ormes sef Gorsedd ormes a elwir yr un a fo
angen ei chynnal achos Gormes Gorwlad ac Estron—neu
ddifrawd ac anraith yng ngwlad, ac achos gorfod i wlad ac
Arlwydd neu Feirdd neu eraill gan raid gwlad a chenedl
ymgynnill yngorsedd a chanu Corn Gwlad yn ymbarotoad
Rhyfel ac amddiffyn a gwared, a chynnal yr osteg honn ym
mhob cyrch Golychwyd a phob Llys cwmmwd, ac wrth
Gorn Cân ymhob Tref a fo bump Annedd ynddi.—Trydydd yw Gosteg Barod fal y mae Datgan Llysdanc yngorsedd Gwlad ac Arlwydd ac yngorsedd Beirdd ac yngorsedd

---

[1] Al. "corn contribution ; milk contribution ; and honey contribution."

of worship. It is privileged for Bards to preside over them, and to receive presents at them out of the three contributory gifts, which are corn, milk, and honey ;[1] and they are called the Bards' gifts of co-aration, because they refer to the plough.

103. There are three other feasts, which by courtesy a Bard regulates, namely: the feast of the head of kindred ; the feast of marriage ; and the feast of the fire back, which takes place where five fire back stones are raised as a station of social abode. In them the gifts of the comot and nation are presented, as far as the ninth generation ; and the Bards receive a portion of the contributory gifts of those feasts, being taken from tilth, fold, and wood covert, according as it may be easiest to obtain and to give them. They are given by courtesy to a Bard, for it is only the right of courtesy that a Bard is entitled to at these three feasts.

104. There are three proclamations. One is a proclamation under the notice of a year and a day, and it is under that proclamation that every substantial cry should be issued, such as the cry of restoration, the cry of re-assertion, and the cry of re-arrangement, which are to be published in every Gorsedd of country and lord, in every Gorsedd of Bards, and in every resort of worship. The second is the proclamation of forty days, according to which every common feast of country and nation, and every Gorsedd of oppression are held—a Gorsedd of oppression being the name given to that which requires to be held in consequence of oppression by a border country or stranger, or of depredation and pillage in a country, whereby there is a peremptory occasion for country and lord, or Bards, or others, in the cause of country and nation, to assemble in Gorsedd, and to blow the horn of country preparatory to war, defence, and deliverance. This proclamation is to be made in every resort of worship, and in every court of comot, and by sound of horn in every town, which contains five inhabited houses. The third is the ready proclamation, such as the recitation of juridical peace in the Gorsedd of country and

ddygynnill, ac ymhob Llys ynad a chyfraith, ac ymhob
Cyrch Golychwyd, a gwedi y Cyhoedder Llysdanc nid
rhydd i neb arf noeth yn erbynnu, a rhydd i bawb parth
Gwlad a chenedl, ac aillt ac Estron gyrch ger bron cyd ac
ydd aroso yn nawdd y Llysdanc heb arf heb osawd, ar neb
a fo amgen nid ^rhydd_braint iddo Lysdanc eithr wrth ddifrod ac
anraith ai bernir.   Braint i ddeuddeg o gywiriaid gwlad a
chenedl ddamgynnill, heb arf heb osawd o byddant wrth
Lysdanc ai gyhoeddi cyn y gwnelont yn ol eu rhaid a
gwedi cyhoeddi 'r Llysdanc myned herwydd eu rhaid yn
Llys—ac yn honno dabru Corn gwlad dan osteg deugeinydd, a myned wrth raith Gwlad a Chenedl, a Braint yw i'r
Raith honno dadebru Corn Gwlad a myned gan eu rhaid a'u
hachos dan osteg a Rhybydd undydd a blwyddyn y naill ai
yngorsedd Gwlad ac Arlwydd ai yngorsedd ddygynnill, ai
yngorsedd Beirdd, a Llys 12 Cywiriaid a fo fal dywespwyd
a elwir Llys Cyffro, a Chyffro Gwlad can nas gallant wrth
y rhaid ar achos amgen na Chyffro 'r Llys ar orsedd a fo
achos wrthi.

105.   Tri pheth rhydd i fardd eu cymmortha ynghylch
Clera sef ydynt y tri phrif osymddaith nid amgen Yd—
Blith — a Mel, ac nid iawn i Fardd cymmortha gosymddaith namyn y tair osymddaith gyferddawn—cas nis gellir
amgen iddynt a fo Gosymddaith yn nawdd Duw ai dangnef.
ac or tair Gosymddaith gyferddawn y bydd pob rhoddion
cyferddawn yngwleddoedd y pedair Alban, ac yngwledd

---

[1] Al. "privileged."

lord, in the Gorsedd of Bards, in the Gorsedd of convention, in every court of judge and law, and in every resort of worship. And when juridical peace is proclaimed, it is not lawful for any one to bear a naked weapon of offence, whilst it is lawful for all, in respect of country and nation, alien and stranger, to be present, as long as they shall remain under the protection of the juridical peace, without a weapon, without assault; whereas he who conducts himself otherwise is not allowed[1] to enjoy juridical peace, but is adjudged to be a man deprived of privilege and exposed to warfare. Twelve true and loyal men of country and nation have the privilege of meeting together, without a weapon, without assault, in right of juridical peace, which must be proclaimed, before they perform what is necessary; and when the juridical peace is proclaimed, they must go to court, in respect of what is necessary, and there awake the horn of country under the proclamation of forty days, and submit to the verdict of country and nation, which verdict is privileged to awake the horn of country. And they must proceed to deal with their wants and requirements under the proclamation and notice of a year and a day, either in the Gorsedd of country and lord, or in the Gorsedd of convention, or in the Gorsedd of Bards. The court of twelve true and loyal men, constituted as already mentioned, is called the court of agitation, and the agitation of country, since they can have nothing to do with the necessity and occasion otherwise than by means of the agitation of the court and Gorsedd of which there is need.

105. Three things which it is lawful for a Bard to exact in his circuit of minstrelsy, being the three principal provisions, namely: corn; milk; and honey; nor is it lawful for a Bard to exact provisions, except the three contributory provisions, for nothing else may be given which is a provision under the protection of God and His peace. And from the three contributory provisions are all contributory gifts in the feasts of the four albans, and in the feasts of

Golychwyd a phob Gwledd arall a fyddont yn nawdd Duw
ai dangnef.

106.   Tair Gwledd a farner yn nawdd Duw ai Dangnef,
sef gwleddoedd y pedair Alban—Gwleddoedd gwared gwlad
a chenedl a fydd dan osteg deugeinydd, a rhoddion ynddynt
o'r Tair Ced gyferddawn, gan bawb or genedl — a dogn o'r
rhoddion hynny i Feirdd ac i dlawd, ac i Estron a el yn
nawdd Duw a Beirdd Ynys Prydain.

107.   Tair gwledd arall syberwyd yw eu bod yn nawdd
Duw a Beirdd Ynys Prydain, nid amgen, gwledd Pencenedl
— a gwledd Cyfarwys — a gwledd gwylbentan, a rhoddion
cyferddawn or tri phrif osymddaith.   E.a.w. o ar—o fuarth
—ac o wyddwal, a dogn i Fardd, ac i dlawd, ac i Estron a
el yn Nawdd Duw ai dangnef, sef yw hynny myned yn
nawdd Beirdd Ynys Prydain wrth Gosteg deigeinydd.—
E.a.w. sef y bydd y tair arllad, un o ar arall o fuarth, ac
arall o wyddwal, (neu o fel neu ossai ffrwythau coed.

108.   Tri bannog freiniolion gwlad, Barddoniaeth—Yngneidiaeth — a Fferylltaeth, can nis gellir eu cynnal onid
wrth fraint, ac nid rhaid i bawb ei medru.   E.a.w. Ysgol-
heiccdod—Yngneidiaeth, a Chrefftoriaeth.   E.a.w. Ysgol-
heigiaeth—Crefft—a Chyfnewid.

109.   Tair Canghen Barddoniaeth, Ofyddiaeth, Prydyddiaeth, a Golychwydoriaeth.

110.   Tair Cangen fferylltaeth, Gofaniaeth, Saerniaeth,
a meddyginiaeth.

111.   Tair cangen ysgoheigiaeth, Barddoniaeth, Yngneidiaeth, a chynghelloriaeth.

112.   Tri breiniog annhiriog y sydd, Bardd, Gof, a Saer,

worship, and in every other feast, which may be under the protection of God and His peace.

106. There are three feasts which are deemed under the protection of God and His peace, namely : the feasts of the four albans ; the feasts of deliverance of country and nation, which take place under the proclamation of forty days, when gifts are presented from the three contributory aids by all men of the nation ; and a portion of those gifts is for Bards, the poor, and stranger, who are under the protection of God and the Bards of the Isle of Britain.

107. There are three other feasts which are by courtesy under the protection of God and the Bards of the Isle of Britain, namely : the feast of the head of kindred ; the feast of co-aration ; and the feast of the fire back ; at which gifts are contributed from the three principal provisions. Others say : from tilth ; fold ; and wood covert ; with a portion to the Bard, the poor, and the stranger, who may be under the protection of God and His peace, that is, under the protection of the Bards of the Isle of Britain pursuant to the proclamation of forty days. Others say : the three oblations : one from tilth ; another from fold ; and another from wood covert :—or, of honey, or the juice of the fruit of trees.

108. The three privileged specialities of country : Bardism ; judicature ; and metallurgy ; since they cannot be maintained except by privilege, and all are not required to know them. Others say : scholarship ; judicature ; and trade. Others say : scholarship ; trade ; and commerce.

109. The three branches of Bardism : Ovatism ; poetry ; and worship.

110. The three branches of artizanship : metallurgy ; carpentry ; and medicine.

111. The three branches of scholarship : Bardism ; judicature ; and chancellorship.

112. The three landless ones who are privileged : a Bard ; a smith ; and a carpenter ; for they have the privilege of free maintenance, though they may not be possessed

M

—sef y bydd braint Trwydded rydd iddynt, cyd na bont
wrth fraint o fonedd cynhenid, ac o hynny tiriawg.

113. Tri Breiniog tiriawg y sydd Cymro gan fonedd
cynhenid, sef hynny o'r nawfed ach yn Gymro, ac i bob un
ei bumerwi rhyddion.—A Bardd neu Yngnad a wnelo Gymmod cadarn rhwng gwlad a gorwlad, sef lle nid oes raith
arnynt, ac wynt yn anghymmod — * ac estrongad a ennillo
frwydr a gorfod ymhlaid Cenedl y Cymry, yn erbyn eu
gelynion, sef y dylit tir a braint Cymry cynhenid iddynt.
al. * estrongad ynnill ymhlaid Cenedl y Cymry.

114. Tair cyfran gyfrydd y dylit i bob Cymro cynhenid, tiriogaeth o bumerwi rhyddion — Budd a braint swydd o
wybodaeth—a rhyddyd corphorawl, ac nis dylid eu naccau i
neb a fo brodor o Gymro cynhenid. E.A.W. Tir rhydd,
gwybodaeth, a rhyddyd—E.a.w. Gwaith Duw Dad—Gwybodaeth—a rhyddyd, cans nis dylit naccau i neb ei gyfran
o'r tripheth hynn.

115. Tair cyfran anghyfrydd y sydd, sef nid rhydd i
neb ond au meddo ei ran ynddynt sef un yw petheu a font o
waith Duw megis nerth corph a deall. Gwraig, a phlant.
Ail yw a wnelo ddyn oi bwyll ai ddeall ai gelfyddyd ai
alluoedd corphorawl ei hunan, fel y mae ty, a dodrefn, a
gwisgoedd, a pheiriannau, a phob oi allu ai gymmhwyll, ai
ddefnydd ei hun, sef braint iddo y cyfan a wnelo ac a gaffo
ef oi gamp ai gelfyddyd, ai wybodaeth ei hun. Yn drydyd
nis dylai neb ran yn y fraint anghyfran a gaffo gan wr neu
y gan wlad a chenedl, neu ygan wyr wrth swydd a dosparth,
o ddyled ymraint ai dirper, fal y bydd braint Teyrn, neu
Yngnad, neu fardd, neu un swydd arall ba bynnag wrth
raid gwr, neu wlad a chenedl.

116. Trirhyw ddyledogion mawl a chof Cerdd a Barddoniaeth—pob glan a daionus o gamp a defawd—pob hardd a

---

[1] Al. "a foreign army that wins in behalf of the nation of the Cymry."

of the privilege of innate nobility, and consequently endowed with land.

113. There are three privileged proprietors of land: a Cymro of innate nobility, that is, he who is a Cymro in the ninth descent, and every one who is such is entitled to his five free acres; a Bard, or judge, who makes firm peace between country and border country, that is, where they are not subjected to juridical verdict, and are at variance; and a foreign army that may win a battle and victory in behalf of the nation of the Cymry,[1] over their enemies, for they are entitled to land and the privilege of innate Cymry.

114. Three free allotments which are due in common to every innate Cymro: five free acres of landed property; the benefit and privilege attached to the function of science; and corporal freedom. These should not be denied to any native who is a genuine Cymro. Others say: free land; knowledge; and liberty. Others say: the work of God the Father; knowledge; and liberty; for no one should be denied his share of these three things.

115. There are three shares which are not free for all, that is, none but the possessor is allowed to participate in them. One, the things, which are of God's creation, such as strength of body and intellect, a wife, and children. The second is, what man makes of his own reason, understanding, art, and bodily faculties, such as a house, furniture, dresses, and implements, and every thing that is produced by his own ability, devise, and material — he being privileged to have the whole of what he makes and obtains by means of his own skill, art, and science. Thirdly, no one is entitled to the incommunicable privilege which another receives from a person, or from country and nation, or from men of office and system, as duly deserving it, such as the privilege of a king, or a judge, or a Bard, or any other office whatsoever according to the requirement of man, or of country and nation.

116. The three proper subjects of praise, and of the memorial of song and Bardism: every quality and usage

serchog o bryd a gwedd — a phob ymbwyll a chelfyddyd er lles Byd a bywyd a ellir heb o hanaw nac afles nac afraid a fo cydbwys ai lesioldeb.

117. Tair anraith Byd — Arglwydd heb gyfiawnder— ^{Ynad}_{brawdwr} heb drugaredd—a Bardd heb ddysg.

118. Tri chadernyd gwladoldeb, Arglwydd Cyfiawn— Brawdwr Trugarawg—a Bardd dysgedig a deddfawl.

119. Tri Nawdd Gwlad a Chenedl, Cadair Beirdd— Llysoedd gwlad ac Ynad—ac arad yn ei gorchwyl.

120. Tri thryfydoldeb Cerdd dafawd a'r nas ceffir y rhain nis gellir ei bod herwydd addysg Beirdd Ynys Prydain—Addysg daioni—cof am foliannus ar ddyn a digwydd —a diddanwch diargywedd, ac er cadarnhau y rhai hynn y trefnwyd Dosparth Beirdd a Barddoniaeth.

121. Tair Deddf gadarn Beirdd Ynys Prydain a Chenedl y Cymry, Barn wrth Fraint a Defod gorsedd gan raith gorseddogion herwydd y trechaf o nifer; Barn wrth raith a defod gwlad a Chenedl dan osteg a Rhybydd, a myned o honno wrth daw a llafar gwlad a Chenedl, gan y trechaf o nifer; a Barn yr Rwyf wrth Bwyll ag ansawdd gan angen a gorfod, lle nis gellir un o'r ddwy eraill.

122. Gwel rif 8. Tri Bardd Graddol y sydd; Prifardd, Derwyddfardd, ac Ofyddfardd. E.a.w. Tri rhyw Prifeirdd y sydd; Prydydd sef Bardd Trwyddedawg, ag arnaw y mae Prydu, a Chynnal Cof a Phennoriaeth Gorsedd a chynnal, sef hynny Llywyddiaethu yngorsedd a gair ei air ef ar bawb ynghadair a gorsedd. Ofydd, ag arnaw y mae

---

[1] Ni nawdd fydd arad heb heieirn, heb had.

The plough is no sanctuary without the irons, or without seed.

Taliesin.

that are pure and good; every form and appearance that are beautiful and lovely; and every contrivance and art for the benefit of the public and life, which are not productive of disadvantage and uselessness of equal weight with its utility.

117. The three depredations of the world : a lord without justice; a judge without mercy; and a Bard without learning.

118. The three stabilities of the social state : a just lord; a merciful judge; and a learned and moral Bard.

119. The three sanctuaries of country and nation : the Chair of Bards; the courts of country and judge; and a plough at work.[1]

120. The three essences of vocal song, and where they are not found, it cannot be in accordance with the instruction of the Bards of the Isle of Britain : the doctrine of goodness; the memorial of what is commendable in man and circumstance; and harmless amusement; and it was with the view of confirming these that the system of Bards and Bardism was ordained.

121. The three firm laws of the Bards of the Isle of Britain and the nation of the Cymry : judgment according to the privilege and usage of Gorsedd, by means of the verdict of presidents, and which is formed by a majority of votes; judgment according to the verdict and usage of country and nation under proclamation and notice, submitted to the silence and voice of country and nation by a majority of votes; and impulsive judgment according to reason and nature brought about by necessity and obligation, where neither of the other two can be obtained.

122. There are three graduated Bards : the Primitive Bard; the Druid-bard; and the Ovate-bard. Others say : There are three kinds of Primitive Bards : a Poet, or licensed Bard, on whom it is incumbent to poetize, and to maintain the memorial and supremacy of Gorsedd, and to maintain, that is, to rule in Gorsedd, and his word is to be paramount in Chair and Gorsedd; an Ovate, on whom

ymawenu, a gwellhau Dysg a Gwybodau, — a Derwydd, ac
arnaw y mae cynnal athrawiaeth a chyrch golychwyd, — a
Lle na bo Derwydd dosparthus o radd Cadair, braint yw i'r
Prydydd gynnal addysg a Golychwyd, can mai arnaw ef o
gysefin ofynion a swyddau a Dyled Celfyddyd y mae Cynnal addysg Golychwyd.

123. Tair gorsedd Cerdd gadarn y sydd; Gorsedd o
brif arfer a Defawd Cenedl y Cymry er yn oes oesoedd cyn
Cof a gwybod, ai hamserau bannau haul a lleuad : Gorsedd
Gorddawd gan Gof, ai hamserau y Tair prif wyl arbennig,
nid amgen y Pasg ar Sulgwyn, ar Nadolig, a gorsedd ddamwain anhyspys o amserau, sef y bydd dydd priodas Brenin,
dydd gwisgaw corn,* a dydd corn heddwch.

TRIOEDD BEIRDD CYMMRU

a dynnwyd or hen Lyfrau gan Risiart Iorwerth, ac a ddangoswyd gantho, ynghadair Tir Iarll ac a farnwyd o flaen
honno yn awdurdodawl, ac fe gafwyd iddynt wedi hynny
Gadair ymhob un o'r tair Talaith.

TRIOEDD BEIRDD CYMRU.

Llymma Drioedd a ddangoswyd ger bron Cadair Tir iarll
gan Risiart Iorwerth mab Iorwerth Fynglwyd (o Llyfr
Thomas Hopcin o Langrallo) un o lyfrau Thos. ab Ifan o
Dre Brynn.

1. Tri Bardd Caw y sydd, Cyntaf Prifardd neu Bryd-

---

* A mistake apparently for " coron."

[1] I.e. the proclamation of peace by means of a horn.

[2] See Vol. i. p. 73, note.

[3] Thomas Hopkin was the son of Hopkin Thomas, who wrote the *Greal* and
other works, about the year 1350. John Hopkins, the versifier of the Psalms,
was descended from this family.

[4] Thomas ab Evan, or Bevan, was a good poet and critic, who flourished between 1660 and 1700.

it is incumbent to genialize and to improve learning and sciences; and a Druid, on whom it is incumbent to maintain instruction and a meeting of worship—and where there is no regular Druid having a Chair degree, the Poet is privileged to maintain instruction and worship, for it belongs to him in virtue of original requirement and offices, and obligation of art to maintain the instruction of worship.

123. There are three firm Gorsedds of song: a Gorsedd according to the primitive practice and usage of the nation of the Cymry from the age of ages, before memory and knowledge, its times being the points of the sun and moon; an institutional Gorsedd within memory, its times being the three principal and special festivals, namely, Easter, Whitsunday, and Christmas; and an incidental Gorsedd, its times being unknown, such as the marriage day of a king, the day of coronation, and the day of the horn of peace.[1]

THE TRIADS OF THE BARDS OF CYMRU,

Extracted from the Old Books by Richard Iorwerth, and exhibited by him in the Chair of Tir Iarll, and adjudged before it as authoritative; after that, they obtained a Chair in each of the three provinces.

THE TRIADS OF THE BARDS OF CYMRU.

The following are the Triads which were exhibited before the Chair of Tir Iarll by Richard Iorwerth, son of Iorwerth the Grey-haired.[2] From the Book of Thomas Hopkin[3] of Llangrallo—one of the Books of Thomas, son of Evan,[4] of Tre Bryn.

1. There are three Banded[5] Bards. The first is the Primitive Bard, or Poet, whose function and art are to

---

[5] Cathlau clau cerddau *caw.*
Hymns and incessant songs of the *band.*—Cynddelw.

ydd, ai swydd ai gelfyddyd yw Prydu, a chynnal cof cadwedig am bob moliannus ar wr a gweithred a chanu mawl i
bob moliannus a daionus a weddo parth a fo teilwng a haedd-
iannus, a dysgu ar ei gerdd pob daionus parth addysg a
defodau, a chynnal cof ac addysg y gelfyddyd wrth gerdd, a
phob Breiniau a defodau a ddoded ar Feirdd Ynys Prydain,
a'u haddysgu ar gerdd ddosparthus herwydd cyfiawn gelfyddyd Cerdd dafawd Beirdd yr Hen Gymry: a dyled yw
arnaw drefnu a dosparthu herwydd Breiniau a defodau yr
Hen Gymry, ym mhob Cadair ac Eisteddfod a gorsedd wrth
gerdd dafawd, ac arnaw y mae cadw a chynnal yr Iaith
Gymraeg yn ddiledryw a dilediaith ai dysgu yn gywir herwydd ei hansawdd ai dosparth gynhenid a dyledawg.

Ail yw Arwyddfardd, ai swydd ai gelfyddyd yw Cof ac
addysg a chyfarwyddyd, ac arwyddaw gweithredoedd daionus a moliannus, a rhoi ar gof Llyfr ac ysgrifen achoedd
a Bonedd Cenedl y Cymry, a'u Breiniau a'u defodau fal a'u
gwypper, rhag digwyddaw ar genedl y Cymry y lledryw a'r
lledach a ddiffrwythant Fonedd a Breiniau cenedl, ac o
hynny digwyddaw ammraint a chamfraint, a phob annosparth yn unwedd ag y bu digwydd y Cenhedloedd annysg-
edig na chawsant yn eu plith nac awen o Dduw na Beirdd
na Barddoniaeth herwydd yr awen honno. A dyled arnaw
yw dysgu darllain ac ysgrifennu yr iaith gymraeg ai llyfrau
ai cherddau yn gyfiawn gywirgamp, a gwybod Breiniau a
Defodau Beirdd Cenedl y Cymry, a'u hansawdd a'u han-
fodau, ac ef a ddylai wrthfaeddu pob ammonedd, a phob
ammraint, a phob camfraint, a phob anneddf ac annefawd,
rhag llygru Cenedl y Cymry a'u breiniau au defodau moliannus, a'u hiaith a'u cynhwynolder, a'u cynhenidrwydd
moliannus.

Trydydd yw Posfardd ai gelfyddyd yw Cerdd dafawd
herwydd dychymmygfawr addysg a chelfyddyd gynnilgamp

poetize, and to preserve the memorial of every thing that is commendable in man or deed — to celebrate in song every thing that is commendable and good, as would be fitting in respect of what is meritorious and deserving — to teach in song every thing that is good in respect of doctrine and usages, and to maintain the memorial and teaching of the art of song, and all the privileges and usages which have been conferred upon the Bards of the Isle of Britain, and to teach them in methodical song, according to the proper art of vocal song of the Bards of the Ancient Cymry ; and it is his duty to arrange and systematize matters, according to the privileges and usages of the Ancient Cymry, in every Chair and Eisteddvod, and Gorsedd of vocal song ; it is incumbent upon him also to preserve and maintain the Cymric language free from degeneracy and corruption, and to teach it correctly, according to its quality and original and proper arrangement. The second is the Herald-bard, whose office and art are memorial, instruction, and history—to symbolize good and laudable deeds, and to record in book and writing the genealogies and descent of the nation of the Cymry, their privileges and usages, so that they may be known, lest there should happen to the nation of the Cymry that degeneracy and ignobleness which impoverish the descent and privileges of a nation, and hence ensue non privilege and false privilege, and every lack of system, as has been the case with those unlearned nations, among which neither Awen from God, nor Bards, nor Bardism proceeding from that Awen, have been found. It is his duty to learn to read and to write the Cymric language, and to commit it to book and song properly and correctly, and to know the privileges and usages of the Bards of the nation of the Cymry, with their nature and essence. He ought also to impugn all ignobleness, all lack of privilege, all false privilege, and all illegality and disusage, lest the nation of the Cymry, their privileges and laudable usages, their language, innateness, and celebrated antiquity should suffer corruption. The third is the Post-bard, whose art is vocal song according to the inventive

N

y Beirdd diweddar, a dwyn ar addysg bob gwybodaeth a
doethineb a chelfyddydau a defodau daionus a moliannus, a
dosparthu gwybodau newyddion herwydd rhyw, a rhif, ac
amser, a lle, ac achos, ac urddas, a hynn y sydd rhwng y
Prifardd ar Posfardd, Prifardd a ddylai arwain gydag ef a
fu oi ol o'r hen oesoedd, a'r Posfardd a ddylai alw atto a
welo efe oi flaen; a threfnu ar y pethau hynn a wna yr
arwyddfardd herwydd y bo 'r lles a'r gofyn, a'r ansawdd,
a'r hanfod, ar amser, ar urddas ; ac o'r pethau hynn gyrru
addysg a gwybodau, a doethineb, a chelfyddyd, ac urddas,
ac anrhydedd ar genedl a gwlad y Cymmry, fal y gwedd i
ddaionnus a moliannus.

2.   Tair unbengerdd y sydd, Prydu, a chanu Telyn a
thant, a Chyfarwyddyd.

3.   Tri rhyw wr wrth Gerdd dafawd y sydd, Cyntaf,
Prydydd, ai swydd yw Prydu a chanu yn ddosparthus
herwydd y gelfyddyd wrth Gerdd, ac yn warantedig ei
awdurdawd, ac yn ddysgedig ei ymdawr, ac yn awenaidd
ei ddychymmyg, ac yn bwyllgar ei arfaeth, ac yn ddalben-
nig ei amcan, a chadw cof am fraint a defawd ac addysg o
hengerdd, a barn ar gerdd Dafawd, a chof moliannus am
bob gwr a gweithred a fernir yn foliannus, a hwya gallu
dwyn cof am achoedd a bonedd cenedl y Cymry, a'u hanfod
a'u hansawdd, a chanu 'n farddonïaidd ar Destyn fal y bo
hawddaf deall a dysgu a chofiaw y gerdd, er addysg a diddanwch ai dysgo ac ai hatgano, ac au clyw.—Ail yw Teuluwr, a hwnnw a fydd Cerddawr o Brydydd gwarantedig ei
awdurdawd, herwydd y dylit ar Brydydd wrth Fraint a
Defod yr hen Gymry, ai swydd yw canu yn Deulüaidd ar
destyn ac arfaeth, a chanu yn amlwg ei ddychymmyg ac yn
serchogaidd ei fyfyrdawd, ac arail a dysgu defodau daionus

---

[1] These three Bards are mentioned by Edmund Prys :—

Prifardd, arwyddfardd raddfawl,
A *phosfardd* nid anardd dawl.

Primitive Bard, Herald-bard of honourable degree,
And *Post-bard ;* the selection is not unhandsome.

instruction and skilful art of the later Bards, and to impart instruction in every science, wisdom, arts, and good and laudable usages, and to systematize new sciences according to kind, number, time, place, occasion, and dignity.[1] And this is the distinction between the Primitive Bard and the Post-bard: the Primitive Bard ought to bring with him what has been behind him from old ages, and the Post-bard ought to call to him what he sees before him; whilst the Herald-bard arranges these things according as the advantage, requirement, nature, essence, time, and dignity of them may demand; and to bestow instruction, sciences, wisdom, art, dignity, and honour out of them upon the nation and country of the Cymry, as befits what is good and praiseworthy.

2. There are three supremacies of song: to poetize; to play the harp and stringed instrument; and to teach history.

3. There are three kinds of men of vocal song. The first is the Poet, whose function is to poetize, and to sing methodically, according to the art of song—being of warranted authority, of learned pursuit, of genial imagination, of discreet intention, and of regular purpose, to keep the memorial of privilege, usage, and instruction derived from ancient song, to pronounce judgment upon vocal song, to keep laudable memorial of every man and deed that are adjudged to be commendable, to preserve a record of the genealogies and descent of the nation of the Cymry — their derivation and condition, and to sing poetically upon a subject in such a manner as would be easiest to understand, learn, and remember the song, for the instruction and amusement of those who may learn, recite, and hear it. The second is the Family Bard, or a minstrel who is a poet of warranted authority, as becomes a poet according to the privilege and usage of the Ancient Cymry; and his function is to sing domestically upon a subject and proposition, to sing with a clear imagination, and with affectionate meditation, to regulate and teach good, noble, and moral usages,

a bonheddigaidd a deddfolion, a chanu serch heb serthedd, a
mawl heb Druth, a Dychan heb waradwydd, ac addysg yn
ddiddan a diddanwch yn addysg. yn ol y bo hawsaf dysgu
a deall a chofiaw y gerdd ac arnaw ef ai gerdd y mae Dosparth a barn Cadair ac Eisteddfod y Cyfoeth y bo ei drigfa,
ac y mae na chano ac nas dysgo ar ei gerdd a fo anweddus
ei glywed ai ddysgu herwydd y sydd ar ddefodau daionus a
gweddus eu harfer. a brawd ffydd a chydymaith yw efe i
Brydydd o Fardd Cadeiriawg gwarantedig ac yn nawdd a
braint ei gadair, a rhydd yw myned Cerdd Deulüaidd gerbron Cadarn * a barnu arni herwydd o barth rhyw y ddosparth sydd arni y dylid, ac nid un ei Dosparth a honno ar
gerdd orchestol Prydydd Cadeiriawg a fo arnaw gynnal ei
gadair yn erbyn ei gystedlyddion, eithr hi a ddosparther
herwydd ei chymraeg, a daionusder ei haddysg, a gloywder
ei myfyrdawd, ai chymraeg, a hawsder ei dysgu ai deall ai
chofiaw ai dwyn ar erddigan ac arwest.—Trydydd yw Clerwr, ac iddo y mae clera ac ymsennu a goganu, a gwarth-
ruddaw, ac ymddyfalu, ac ymserthu, ac ymbil ac ymddyrïaw
gwers tragwers, er diddanu a llawenhau meddwl, ac nid oes
arnaw nac ar ei gerdd na dosparth na barn, na braint Cadair, na defawd ar ei swydd a'i gelfyddyd, namyn bod wrth
farn gwlad a chyfraith, ac na wnelo yn eu herbyn. Sef y
gelwir y Triwyr hynn wrth gerdd dafawd — Bardd Cadair,
Bardd Teulu, ac Oferfardd, ac arnynt y mae tair cainc cerdd
Dafawd, nid amgen na Barddoniaeth sef yw hynny Prydyddiaeth, a Theuluwriaeth, a Chlerwriaeth.

4. Tri achos Beirdd a Barddoniaeth y sydd, cynnal cof
cyfiawn yn gadwedig am a fu gynt ai gwr, ai gweithred, ai
gwybodau—addysgu defodau daionus, a gwybodau a wnant
gyfanneddiant, ai celfyddyd, ai doethineb, ai deddfoldeb—a

---

* "Cadair" is probably meant.

and to sing love without frivolity, praise without flattery, satire without reproach, instruction in an amusing way, and amusement in an instructive way, as may be easiest to learn, understand, and remember the song. Upon him and his song are conferred the system and judgment of the Chair and Eisteddvod of the territory, in which may be his abode; but, in conformity with good usages, and such as are meet to be practised, he must neither sing nor teach in song what is not fitting to be heard or taught. He is a brother in the faith and companion to a Poet, who is a Chaired Bard, authorized by, and under the protection and privilege of his Chair. It is lawful to refer a domestic song to a Chair, and it ought to be judged according to the kind of system which is peculiar to it, for its system is not the same as that which belongs to the extraordinary song of a Chaired Poet, who has to maintain his Chair against his fellow competitors, but is arranged according to its Cymraeg, the goodness of its instruction, the lucidity of its meditation and Cymraeg, and the facility of learning, understanding, and remembering it, and of clothing it in harmony and music. The third is the Minstrel, who is authorized to stroll, to censure, to satirize, to reproach, to mock, to abuse, to supplicate, and to recite lyrics in a dialogue, for the sake of amusing and rejoicing the mind. Neither he nor his song is endowed with a system, judgment, or privilege of Chair, nor is there any usage attached to his office or art, further than that they are subject to the judgment of country and law, and that he should do nothing against them. These three persons of vocal song are called Chair Bard, Family Bard, and Irregular Bard; and to them belong the three branches of vocal song, namely, Bardism, that is, Poetry, Domesticity, and Minstrelsy.

4. There are three occasions for Bards and Bardism: to maintain and preserve just memorial of what were formerly, whether man, or deed, or sciences; to teach good usages, and sciences which promote social inhabitation, whether they be art, or wisdom, or morality; and to amuse, rejoice,

diddanu a llawenhau, a chyfanneddu meddwl a deall a serch, a dyfyrru amser yn ddiannoeth, canys y pethau a gyfanneddant wlad a Thudwedd. ac y dygir Trefn a dosparth gwlad ar genedl a chiwed, yn y modd a gafwyd yn hawsaf, a diddanaf, a chadarnaf.

5. Tripheth, herwydd ai dosparther, y dylai Fardd o Brydydd Cadeiriawg eu gwybod, cyntaf yw y ddosparth ar gerdd dafawd ai chelfyddyd, ai pherthynasau,—ail yw Dosparth Breiniau a Defodau y gwyr wrth Gerdd Dafawd a thant, a threfnu a dosparthu herwyddwynt, canys ar briffardd o Brydydd y mae hynny. — Trydydd yw Dosparthu ar gyfarwyddyd a gwybodau Barddonïaidd sef Bannau doethineb yr hen Gymry, ac achoedd a Bonedd Cenedl y Cymry, au Brenhinoedd au Tywysogion au Dyledogion Cynhwynawl a'u gweithredoedd moliannus, ac ardderchogiaethau cenedl y Cymry. a rhoi 'r cyfan ar gof cerdd a Dosparth gyfiawn herwydd Defodau Beirdd yr Hen Gymry.

6. Tair dyledswydd arbennigion Bardd wrth Fraint a Defawd yr Hen Gymry. Cadw a chynnal Breiniau Cenedl y Cymry; Cadw a chynnal y Iaith Gymraeg yn ddilediaith, a cadw a chynnal Defodau a gwybodau daionus a moliannus a hynn i gyd ar Gerdd Dafawd ddosparthus yn nawdd a Braint Cadair ac Eisteddfod, sef er cadw a chynnal y petheu hynn y dychymmygwyd ac y trefnwyd Cerdd Dafawd a Beirdd a Barddoniaeth, ac a ddoded ar hynny Fraint a dyled yng nghadair ac Eisteddfod.

7. Tripheth a waherddir ar Fardd o Athraw Cadeiriog. Un yw Celfyddyd a dysgeidiaeth anneddfawl a drygionus: Gweithredoedd a Defodau anneddfolion ; ac ymgyfathrachu a gwŷr a gwerinoedd anneddfolion, canys diffrwythaw cyfanneddrwydd gwlad a chenedl a wnant y pethau hynn. ac am hynny ni wedd ar Brydydd anneddfoldeb, na'i ryw na'i rith,

and occupy the mind, intellect, and affection, and to while away the time not unwisely. For they are what make country and district socially inhabitable, and whereby the arrangement and system of country are conferred upon nation and tribe, in the way found to be most practicable, most diverting, and most permanent.

5. There are three things, which, according to their arrangements, a Bard, who is a Chaired Poet, ought to know. The first is the system of vocal song, its art, and appurtenances. The second is the system of the privileges and usages of men of vocal and instrumental song, and how to arrange and regulate them, for that is the duty of a poet who is a primitive Bard. The third is how to arrange Bardic history and sciences, or the principal features of the wisdom of the Ancient Cymry, and the genealogies and descent of the nation of the Cymry, their kings, princes, and innate nobility, with their laudable deeds, and the excellences of the nation of the Cymry; and to place the whole on the record of song, and in proper arrangement, according to the usages of the Bards of the Ancient Cymry.

6. The three special duties of a Bard according to the privilege and usage of the Ancient Cymry : to preserve and maintain the privileges of the nation of the Cymry ; to preserve and maintain the Cymric language free from corruption ; and to preserve and maintain good and laudable usages and sciences—and all this by means of a systematic vocal song, under the protection and privilege of Chair and Eisteddvod. That is, it was for the purpose of preserving and maintaining these things that vocal song, Bards, and Bardism were devised and appointed; and on the same were conferred privilege and obligation in Chair and Eisteddvod.

7. There are three things which are forbidden to a Bard, being a Chaired Teacher : an immoral and wicked art or learning ; immoral acts and usages ; and intercourse with immoral men and society ; for these things will spoil the social inhabitation of country and nation. On that account, immorality, its kind or form, are not becoming to

canys canllaw pob deddfoldeb a chyfanneddiaeth yw Bardd
herwydd ei swydd ai ddyled. ac er cadarnhau hynny y
doded iddaw nawdd gwlad a gorwlad, a Braint rhag arall
mal y gallai efe gadw a chynnal cyfanneddiaeth a deddfoldeb, a'u haddysgu yn gyfiawn.

8.   Tripheth anhepcor ar Fardd y sydd nid amgen,
Iawn ganu, Iawn ddysgu, ac Iawn farnu.

9.   Tripheth o gysefin ddyled herwydd nawdd a braint
arbennig y sydd i Fardd wrth Fraint a Defawd yr Hen
Gymry; Ei dir yn rhydd, sef hynny ei bumerwi rhyddion;
ai washail yn rhad lle bynnag ydd elo herwydd ei swydd ai
gelfyddyd wrth gerdd a hynny y gan Arglwydd y Cyfoeth
lle ydd elo; ai air yn air heb air neb yn air arnaw ef tra bai
iddaw ei radd ai gadair.

10.   Tair gradd dysgyblaeth y sydd ar gerdd dafawd a
Barddoniaeth nid amgen, Cyntaf yw Dysgybl Ysbas, ail yw
Dysgybl dysgyblaidd, Trydydd yw Dysgybl pencerddaidd.

Dysgybl ysbas a ddylai wybod dosparth y silltau, a'r
ymadroddion herwydd llyfrau dosparth y cyhydeddau, a
dosparthu ar Fesurau Cerdd Deuluaidd Canys dysgyblaeth
Cerdd dafawd yw honno, a chanu ar bump or mesureu hynny
yn awenyddawl yn marn Pencerdd a ddywetto ar ei air ai
gydwybod y gellir Prydydd o honaw, hefyd efe a ddylai
wybod y deddfau a'r defodau y sydd ar ei ddysgyblaeth.

Dysgybl dysgyblaidd a ddylai wybod heblaw a wyr Dysgybl ysbas, dosparth y mesurau a'r cymmeriadau, a chanu ar
y naw mesur cysefinion, a'u dangos o'i waith ei hun yn warantedig ar air neu y dan law ei athraw, ac ef a ddylai wybod
y pumtheg bai cyffredin a'u gochel, ac efe a ddylai wybod

a Poet, since a Bard is the ballustrade of morality and social
inhabitation, according to his office and duty; and it was
to confirm the same that he was invested with the protection
of country and border country, and distinctive privilege,
that he might preserve and maintain social inhabitation and
morality, and teach them accurately.

8. There are three things indispensable in a Bard,
namely: that he should sing properly; that he should
teach properly; and that he should judge properly.

9. There are three things in right of primary obligation,
by special protection and privilege, to which a Bard according to the privilege and usage of the Ancient Cymry is
entitled: that his land should be free, namely, his five free
acres; that his wassail should be gratuitous, wherever he
may go, in virtue of his office and art of song — the same
being supplied to him by the lord of the territory, which he
may visit; and that his word should be paramount, no
person's word being superior, as long as his degree and
Chair remain to him.

10. There are three disciplinary degrees attached to
vocal song and Bardism, namely: the first is a probationary Disciple; the second is a pupil Disciple; the third
is a master Disciple. A probationary Disciple ought to
know the system of syllables and sentences, according to
the Books of the system of metricities, and how to arrange
the metres of domestic song, for that belongs to the discipline of vocal song, and to sing in five of those metres
poetically according to the opinion of a master of song, who
shall say upon his word and conscience that he is competent
to be a poet; he ought also to know the laws and usages which relate to his discipleship. A pupil Disciple
ought to know, in addition to what a probationary Disciple
knows, the system of metres and resumptions, and to be
able to sing in the nine primary metres, and to exhibit the
same as his own composition, warranted by the word, or
under the hand of his Teacher; he ought to know, and to
avoid the fifteen common faults; he ought also to know the

hefyd y defodau a ddylit wrth gynnal Cadair ac Eisteddfod,
a medru dosparth achau bonedd a chyfarwyddyd.

Dysgybl Pencerddaidd a ddylai wybod y cyfan a ddylai 'r
dysgybl dysgyblaidd ei wybod, a chyda hynny canu 'n
ddysgyblaidd ar yr holl fesurau cadeiriawg a medru dosparth eu hansawdd a'u rhywiau, a gochel yr holl feiau a
medru cyfarwyddyd oddiwrth y Prifeirdd wrth Fraint a
defawd yr Hen Gymry, a dwyn achoedd Tywysogion a
bonheddigion cynhwynawl Cenedl y Cymry, a chyfarwyddyd am eu holl weithredoedd a'u defodau moliannus, a gwybod breiniau Cenedl y Cymry a'u hanfod au hansawdd, a
medru dwyn ar gof yr holl bethau hynn gerbron Cadair, a
medru rhoi ar lyfr yn ddosparthus y cyfan, a medru trefnu
a dosparthu Cadair ac Eisteddfod ym marn Bardd o Bencerdd Cadeiriawg, a medru Bannau doethineb yr Hen Gymry, a dosparth gyfiawn ar y Iaith Gymraeg ai holl silltau ai
geiriau, ai hymadroddion, ai hysgrifenny yn gyfiawn a dosparthus, ac efe a ddylai wybod ar ei gof ai lafar holl freiniau
a defodau Beirdd yr Hen Gymry, a'r ddosparth gyfiawn
arnynt a chof a gwybod am yr hen Brifeirdd a'u Cerddi, au
llyfrau, ar hollgyfarwyddyd y sydd oddiwrthynt, a phan
ddangos efe oi ganu ei hunan yr holl fesurau cadeiriawg
herwydd eu rhywiau o gysefin ansawdd yn gerddoriaeth
Bencerddaidd hawl iddo gadair, a gwedi y caffo efe dair,
athraw Cadeiriawg y bydd, ac iddaw 'r nawdd a'r Breiniau
a ddoded ar Feirdd wrth Fraint a Defawd yr Hen Gymry.
a chyn y bo iddaw Gadair bernir ef yn gydymaith i Bencerdd.

11.   Tair dognaeth y sydd ar roddion Beirdd herwydd
graddeu eu dysgyblaeth au hansawdd, nid amgen,

Rhodd dysgybl ysbas am ei gerdd ar bob un o'r tair gwyl
arbennig yw pedwar ar hugain, o bydd gwarantedig ar air ei

usages necessary in holding a Chair and Eisteddvod, and to be skilled in the genealogies of the nobility, and in history. A master Disciple ought to know the whole that the pupil Disciple ought to know, and therewith to sing like a disciple in all the chaired metres, to know the system of their quality and kinds, to avoid all the faults, to be skilled in history, as taught by the primitive Bards according to the privilege and usage of the Ancient Cymry, to trace the pedigrees of the innate princes and noblemen of the nation of the Cymry, to be acquainted with the history of all their laudable deeds and usages, to know the privileges of the nation of the Cymry, their substance and quality, to be able to record all these things before a Chair, to commit the whole methodically to book, to regulate and arrange a Chair and Eisteddvod, according to the judgment of a Bard, who is a chaired master of song, and to know the articles of the wisdom of the Ancient Cymry, and proper arrangement of the Cymric language, and all its syllables, words, and sentences, and to write them properly and systematically ; he ought to know in memory and viva voce all the privileges and usages of the Bards of the Ancient Cymry, and their proper arrangement, and the memorial and knowledge respecting the ancient primitive Bards, their songs, and Books, and all the history which is derived from them. And when, by means of his own singing, he shall exhibit all the chaired metres, according to their kinds founded upon primary quality, to be a masterly science of music, he is entitled to a Chair ; and when he shall have obtained three, he will become a Chaired Teacher, and be entitled to the protection and privileges conferred upon Bards according to the privilege and usage of the Ancient Cymry. And before he obtains a Chair, he is deemed as the companion of a chief of song.

11. There are three apportionments of the fees of Bards, in respect of the degrees of their discipleship and quality. The fee of a probationary Disciple for his song, on each of the three special festivals, is twenty-four pence, if he be

athraw neu o dan ei law ef, a rhydd yw syberwyd, cydna
bo rydd ceisio amgen nac a fo ddefodawl o rodd.

Rhodd dysgybl dysgyblaidd am ei gerdd, o bydd gwarantedig yw deugein, sef yw hynny triswllt a grôd, ac nid rhydd
iddo fwy na hynny o hawl a gofyn, cyd bo rhydd syberwyd.

Rhodd Dysgybl pencerddaidd yw pedwar ugeint, sef chwe-
swllt ac wythceiniawg, a bod wrth warant gair neu law ei
Athraw, ac nid hawl iddo dros hynny, namyn derbyn syberwyd.

y rhoddion hynn a geffir y gan Arglwydd y Cyfoeth am
a ganer o gerdd cof ac addysg, ac a ddosparther o gyfarwyddyd, neu a ddyccer o achau bonedd wrth achos cyfreith-
iawl megis y bydd hawl tir, a braint cenedl y Cymry, a
neithiawr a phob dysgybl yn warantedig y dan law neu ar
air ei Athraw, ac Athraw yn warantedig wrth farn a braint
a gradd Cadair. ac o cheir rhodd am gerdd neu am gyfarwyddyd ar un o'r gwyleu, ni cheffir ar un o'r lleill rodd am
yr un dangos. rhodd hefyd a ddylit i'r Bardd herwydd ei
radd gan a genir iddynt neu a ddangoser o gyfarwyddyd, ar
rhoddion hynn a fyddant ossymddaith Beirdd yn nysgybl-
aeth.

12.   Tri gossymddaith y sydd i Fardd herwydd braint
ei swydd ai gelfyddyd.   Pum erwi rhyddion, ceiniog o bob
aradr o fewn y cwmmwd a rodder iddo ygan arglwydd y
cyfoeth. ai roddion defodol herwydd ei swydd ai gelfyddyd.

13.   Am dripheth y dylit rhoddion i Fardd herwydd ei
radd, am y gerdd dafawd a gano wrth arch a damuned ai
caffo, ac am yr ach a'r cyfarwyddyd y rhotho efe ymhob
hawl tir, ac ymhob hawl bonedd a braint Cenedl a gwlad, ac
am y Cyfarwyddyd a rotho y dan ei law a geisier am a fu
gynt ac am a fynner ei ddysgu o'r Iaith Gymraeg parth ei

warranted by the word, or under the hand of his Teacher;
and courtesy is free to him, though it is not lawful for him
to seek more than the customary fee. The fee of a pupil
Disciple for his song, if warranted, is forty pence, that
is, three shillings and a groat; and he is not, of claim
and requirement, entitled to more, though he is entitled to
courtesy. The fee of a master Disciple is eighty pence,
that is, six shillings and eight pence, warranted, as he must
be, by the word or hand of his Teacher, and he has no claim
to any thing beyond that, except the reception of courtesy.
These fees are received from the lord of the territory, for the
song of memorial and instruction which is sung, and for the
history which is analyzed, or for the pedigrees of descent
which are traced, in pursuance of some lawful cause, such as
a claim for land, the privilege of the nation of the Cymry, and
nuptial festivity—each Disciple being authorized under the
hand, or by the word, of his Teacher, and his Teacher being
authorized by the judgment, privilege, and degree of Chair.
And if a fee be received for a song or narrative on one of
the festivals, a fee shall not be received on any of the others
for the same exhibition. A fee is due also to a Bard, according to his degree, from those to whom he may sing, or
exhibit a narrative; and these gifts shall constitute the tra-
velling provisions of Bards during their discipleship.

12. There are three provisions for a Bard, according to
the privilege of his office and art: five free acres; a penny
from every plough in the comot assigned to him by the lord
of the territory; and his customary fees in respect of his
office and art.

13. For three things ought fees to be paid to a Bard,
according to his degree: for the vocal song which he shall
sing at the bidding and desire of him who hears it; for the
pedigree and information which he shall supply in every
claim for land, and in every claim for the nobility and privilege of nation and country; and for any required information which he shall give under his hand, respecting what
occurred formerly, and respecting what is desired to be

darllain ai hysgrifennu a'r dosparth y sydd arni, ac ar fardd
y mae y pethau hynn o hawl a chyfiawnder a braint ei
swydd ai gelfyddyd wrth gerdd.

14.   Tair deddf y sydd ar Fardd o Athraw Cadeiriawg
abarth ei ddysgyblon. Cyntaf nas cymmero atto amgen
nac un o bob gradd ar unwaith, Ail yw nas gadawo efe iddynt gymmeryd attynt ddysgyblion na gwneuthur o honynt
ddysgyblion, can ni wedd i ddysgybl wneuthur dysgybl arall. a thrydydd nac ymarferont y gwyr wrth gerdd dafawd
a cherdd dant megis canu crwth neu delyn, neu gynnal ac
ymarfer a chrefft a chelfyddyd o'r byd pa un bynnag oddi-
eithr y gelfyddyd wrth gerdd dafawd, ai pherthynasau.

15.   Tripheth y dylai Athraw wiliaw rhagddynt ar ei
ddysgyblon rhag eu myned yn annosparthus ac yn ormes
gwlad a theulu lle ydd elont ac y byddont, ac yn anysgedig
parth eu celfyddyd ac yn anghyfannedd-gamp o fod felly.

Cyntaf yw na wnelont weithredoedd anneddfolion nac ymarfer a defodau anneddfolion, nac ymgyrch i leoedd anneddfolion sef nac ymarferont a lledrad a Brad a chynllwyn ac
ymladdau, a godineb a phutteindra a chynnenau, ac ymrys-
onau, a thwyll a gormes a chablu a gwaradwyddaw, a sennu,
a goganu, a gwatwar a dynwared, a meddwdawd, ac na lun-
iont gelwydd ar neb nac am un peth na'i ddywedyd ar ol
arall, ac na wnelont rigymmau drygfoes ac anweddus er
anfoddloni gwr a gwlad, ac er dwyn llwgr ar gampau daionus, a llygru defodau moliannus, ac nad elont i Dafarneu, ar
lle bo chwarëon anghyfreithlawn, a lle byddo cyrch meddw-
on ac anudonwyr a lladron a Bradwyr, a phutteiniaid a
phob rhyw grwydraid a rhodiaid a phob drwgweithredwyr a
rhai aflywodraethgar, megis y rhai a lygrant arian y brenin
ai gynhwysiadau, ac na wnelont eu hunain nac ymarfer a
chwareuon anneddfolion megis Cardiau a disiau, ac na chwa-
rëont y cyfryw chwareuon am nac arian nac am unrhyw

learned of the Cymric language, as to the reading, writing, and arranging of it. These things belong to a Bard in virtue of the claim, justice, and privilege of his office and art of song.

14. There are three laws incumbent upon a Bard, who is a Chaired Teacher, relative to his Disciples. The first is, that he take to himself only one of each degree at once. The second, that he suffer them not to take disciples, or to make disciples, for it is not fitting that a disciple should make another disciple. And the third, that the men of vocal song associate not with men of instrumental song, by playing the violin or harp, or that they follow and practise no trade or art whatsoever, except the art of vocal song and its appurtenances.

15. Three things which a Teacher ought to guard against in his Disciples, lest they should become irregular, oppressive to country and family whither they may go, and where they may be, illiterate as to their art, and consequently unsociable. The first is, that they should not commit any immoral deeds, or practise any immoral usages, or frequent any immoral places ; that is, that they should not habituate themselves to theft, treachery, waylaying, fighting, adultery, fornication, contentions, quarrels, deceit, oppression, blaspheming, reproaching, scoffing, lampooning, mocking, mimicking, and drunkenness, that they should tell no falsehood of any man or thing, or repeat it after another, that they should compose no immoral or indecent rhymes to displease man and country, to bring corruption into good qualities, and to corrupt commendable usages, that they should not go to taverns, and places where there are illegal plays, and which are the resort of drunkards, perjurers, thieves, traitors, harlots, all kinds of vagrants, tramps, all evildoers, and those who are disaffected to the government, such as those who alloy the king's money, and abuse his writs, that they should not commit or practise any immoral plays, such as cards and dice, that they should not play such plays for money, or any goods, profit, or gain

dda neu ged ac ynnill yn y byd, Ac nad elont i leoedd cudd
anghyfreithlawn, ac nad ymarferont a rhiniau anneddfolion a
Bradongar, ac nas gwnelont gyfeillach a nebryw ddrygddyn-
ion ai gwryw ai benyw y bont, ac na wnelont unrhyw ansyberwyd or byd tuagat na gwraig na morwyn lle y byddont ;
ac os gwnant hwy y dysgyblion y petheu hynn o anfodd eu
hathrawon, ac yn erbyn eu cyngor a'u Dosparth hwynt, colli
eu clera a'u rhoddion, au holl dda wrth gerdd a wnant hyd
ymhen y tair blynedd, a dwyn poen ffin a charchar au rhoi
wrth farn cyfraith a phawb yn swyddogion arnynt, a dwyn
y maint a fo yn eu cylch o'u da wrth gerdd, canys gwyr
wrth gerdd a ddylynt ymarfer a defodau daionus a chyf-
anedd a thangnefeddus, a chyfiawn, a dwyn ymadroddion
teg a hawddgar ac heddychlon, a bod yn garedig ac yn
ufudd ac yn gymmydogaethgar, a bod wrth raid ac achos
Brenin a Gwlad ac Arglwydd ac ynad iddeu cyfarwyddaw,
au cadarnhau, a'u harwedd ymhob peth a wnelont, ac a
wnelo eu swyddogion.

Ail yw ar yr Athraw parth ac at eu ddysgyblon dysgu
iddynt y gelfyddyd wrth Gerdd dafawd ai holl berthynasau,
a holl freiniau a defodau Beirdd wrth fraint a defawd yr
Hen Gymry, herwydd eu dosparth au hansawdd a'u hanfod,
a holl Freiniau Cenedl y Cymry, ar defodau a'r gwybodau
moliannus a ddylaint fod ar gof a gwybod gan Feirdd y
Cymry, ac a berthyn i Feirdd eu gwybod au dysgu yn ath-
rawiaethgar. ac efe a ddylai ddysgu iddynt yr Iaith Gymraeg herwydd cyfiawnder ei dosparth, ai hysgrifennu yn
gyfiawn, a dysgu 'r ddosparth a'r drefn y sydd ar gyfarwyddyd a dwyn achau bonedd ac a berthyn, ar hynny o
freiniau, ac ef a ddylai dysgu iddynt y drefn y dycer ar
gof a wypper ac a ddysger herwydd dosparth y sydd ar
hynny o gainc celfyddyd Bardd, sef y modd a ddyccer ar
gof ar gerdd ac ar lafar ac ar ddefawd ac ar lyfr. ac ef a
ddylai 'r Athraw farnu ar a wnelont y dysgyblon ai cerdd

whatsoever, that they should not frequent any secret, illegal places, that they should not make use of immoral and treasonable charms, that they should form no intimacy with any evil persons, whether male or female, and that they should show no discourtesy whatsoever to either wife or maid, wherever they may be. But if they, the Disciples, should do these things against the will of their Teachers, and contrary to their advice and system, they shall forfeit their minstrelsy and fees, and all the goods attached to their song, until the expiration of three years, and bear the penalty of a fine and imprisonment, being tried by the judgment of law, and all being officers over them, and divesting them of the amount of goods, which may be attached to their song in their respective circuits. For men of song ought to practise good, sociable, peaceable, and just usages, to use fair, amiable, and pacific speeches, to be kind, obedient, and neighbourly, and to be at the necessity and requirement of king, country, lord, and judge, to direct, support, and guide them in all things that they, and their officers, may do. The second duty of the Teacher towards his Disciples is to teach them the art of vocal song, and all that belongs to it, all the privileges and usages of the Bards according to the privilege and usage of the Ancient Cymry, as to their arrangement, quality, and substance, all the privileges of the nation of the Cymry, and the commendable usages and sciences, which ought to be remembered and known by the Bards of the Cymry, and which it appertains to Bards to know and to teach dogmatically; he ought also to teach them the Cymric tongue, as to the correctness of its arrangement, to write it correctly, to teach the system and order of history, and to trace the descent of nobility, and what belongs to such privileges; he ought also to teach them the order of recording what is known and learned in respect of the system which appertains to that branch of Bardic art, that is, the mode of recording in song, speech, usage, and book; and the Teacher ought to judge what the Disciples do, whether it be vocal song or history, to see that

P

dafawd ai cyfarwyddyd y bo, a gweled bod hynny 'n ddosparthus, ai warantu ar ei Air ac y dan ei law.

Trydydd yw arnaw trefnu 'n ddosparthus ar glera ei
ddysgyblon, ac efe a ddylai ymorelwi a hwynt fis o leiaf o
flaen pob gwyl a gwledd y bo defodawl i Feirdd westeïaeth
a chlera arni, fal y mae y tair gwyl arbennig, a gwledd
neithiawr gwr bonheddig o uchelwr cynhwynawl, a gwledd
gwyl mabsant, a gwledd Cadair ac Eisteddfod a fo pen pob
tair blynedd, ac ynddi y bydd rhoddion Arglwydd y Cyfoeth, a chyn y gwylau ar gwleddoedd hynn y dylai Athraw
farnu ar gerdd ei ddysgyblon, a gwarantu ar ei air a than ei
law a fo cyfiawn, ai cerdd dafawd ai cyfarwyddyd y bo, a
dangos i bob un i ba le ydd elo rhag myned gormodd i'r
unlle o honynt, ag nad elo fwy nag un i dy gwr o ddegpunt
yn y flwyddyn o Rent iddaw, a dau i dy uchelwr a fo iddaw
ugeinpunt yn y flwyddyn o fywyd, ac wrth hynny o drefn
at wr a fai uwch ei rent, oni wahodder yn amgen gan wr ty
o fonheddig dyledawg, ac ni wedd i Fardd fyned at anfon-
heddig rhag ei lygru, ac o hynny dwyn o honaw ach
yngham ac yn amgen nac y dylai ei bod.

Ni ddylai un or gwyr hynn wrth gerdd dafawd fyned o'r
ty y delei iddaw ar y cyntaf tra pharai yr wyl neu'r wledd
neu'r mabsant honno, heb gennad gwr y ty, wrth wahoddiad
arall, ac o gwna colli ei glera, ac od a o dy i dy rhaid yw ei
ddala fal crwydryn a rhodiad anghyfreithawl, heb warant
heb awdurdawd, a dwyn ei glera oddiarnaw, ai roi wrth raid
y tlodion, ac o brwysga efe yn y wledd, neu wneuthur o
honaw un ansyberwyd arall, colli ei rodd ai glera, a lle nas
gwilio yr Athraw ar a ddangoswyd yma, colli ei fraint ai
gadair hyd ymhen y tair blynedd, ac nid rhydd iddo ddysgyblon wedi hynny o anllywodraeth.

such be regular, and to guarantee it upon his word, and under his hand. His third duty is to arrange systematically the strolling minstrelsy of his Disciples, and he ought to confer with them a month at least before every holiday and festival, on which it is customary for Bards to hold their visitation and go on circuit, such as the three principal festivals, the nuptial feast of a gentleman, who is an innate freeholder, the feast of the patron saint, and the feast of Chair and Eisteddvod, which is held at the end of every three years, and in which gifts from the lord of the territory are presented. Before these holidays and festivals the Teacher ought to judge the song of his Disciples, to guarantee, upon his word and under his hand, whatever is right, whether it be vocal song or history, and to show every one where he is to go, lest too many of them should go to the same place, and that no more than one should go to the house of a person whose rental is ten pounds a year, and two to the house of a freeholder, whose property is twenty pounds a year, and in proportion to the house of a person whose rental is higher, unless a different number be invited by the householder, being a proprietary gentleman. It is not becoming that a Bard should visit an ignoble person, lest he be corrupted, and hence trace descent unjustly and differently to what it ought to be. None of these men of vocal song should depart from the house he came to at first, whilst the said holiday, or feast, or wake, lasted, at the invitation of another, without the permission of the master of the house; and if he should do so, he shall forfeit his right of minstrelsy. Should he go from house to house, he must be apprehended as a vagrant, and a lawless tramp, without warranty, without authority, be divested of his right of minstrelsy, and placed in the situation of the poor. If he get drunk at the feast, or commit any other act of discourtesy, he shall forfeit his fee and right of minstrelsy. And if the Teacher guard not in respect of the particulars here shown, he shall lose his privilege and Chair until the end of three years, nor will it be lawful for him to have Disciples after such irregularity.

16. (Gwel 39) Am dripheth y dilit dwyn oddiar Fardd ei radd ai Fraint wrth Gerdd, ac nis gellir hwynt iddaw eilwaith tra fo byw, cyntaf am ddadrin cyfrinach a gymmero arno ef, herwydd ei swydd ai fraint wrth gerdd. ail am Furn a chynllwyn a myned yn ryfelwr yny bo arf yn ei erbyn hyd nas gallo fyned yng ngwlad a gorwlad wrth raid ac achos gwlad ac Arglwydd, ac yng nghysswyn gwlad a gorwlad herwydd ei swydd ai fraint wrth Gerdd a Barddoniaeth, ai nawdd cywlad ym mraint Cysswyn Cywlad Brenhinoedd y Cymry. ar ddosparth y sydd ar hynny. Trydydd am ddywedyd Celwydd yn ystig yn ei Gerdd hyd nas gellir gair ei air ef, ac nis o honaw a fo raid ac achos y rwng gwlad o gorwlad, ac yn hawl ac atteb gwlad a chyfoeth, ac o gwna efe y tripheth hynn nis gellir yn ei einioes iddaw fraint a nawdd a da wrth gerdd a Barddoniaeth.

17. O drille y tynner gwaed ar Fardd pan ai diradder, sef oi dalcen, ac o'i fronn, ac o'i arffed ; sef hynny o gelloedd y bywyd a'r enaid a'u rhagfannau, a Brenin y Cyfoeth a'i tynn a blaen cledd ger bron eisteddfod Beirdd, a ger bronn Llys gwlad ac Arglwydd, a Llys Ynad a Chyfraith, a ger bron gwlad a gwerin mewn tair Llann ar y Sulieu yng nghyfnod y tair Gŵyl Arbennig, o fewn i'r Cyfoeth lle bytho, ac yn oes y gwr a ddiradder felly nis gellir iddo na braint na nawdd nac un da pa bynnag o'r byd wrth gerdd a Barddoniaeth.

18. Am dripheth y cyll bardd ei fraint ai nawdd ai radd a'i holl dda wrth gerdd hyd ym mhen saith mlynedd, sef am Ledrad, ac am odineb, ac am dringardawd hyd ymladd, can nis dylit y pethau hynn ar fardd.

19. Am dripheth y cyll gwr wrth Gerdd ei radd hyd

16. For three things ought a Bard to be deprived of his degree and privilege of song, and be rendered incapable of recovering them as long as he lives. The first, for divulging a secret which he holds, in respect of his office and privilege of song. The second, for murder and waylaying, and for enlisting as a soldier, thus exposing himself to weapons, so that he cannot visit country and border country at the call and necessity of country and lord, and in pursuance of a treaty between country and border country, according to his office and privilege of song and Bardism, and his protection of federate country in right of a federal treaty between the kings of the Cymry, and the system which appertains to it. The third, for pertinaciously telling a falsehood in his song, so that his word cannot become paramount, and cannot avail between country and border country, or in any investigation between country and territory. Should he do these three things, he cannot, whilst he lives, have privilege, protection, and property in right of song and Bardism.

17. From three places in a Bard is blood to be drawn, when he is degraded, namely : from his forehead ; from his breast ; and from his groin ; that is, from the receptacles of life and the soul, and their vicinities. It is drawn by the king of the territory with the point of the sword before an Eisteddvod of Bards, before the court of country and lord, before the court of judge and law, and before the country and people, in three churches on the Sundays which occur at the periods of the three principal festivals, within the territory where he may be, and, during life, the man so degraded cannot have privilege, or protection, or any property whatsoever in right of song and Bardism.

18. For three things will a Bard lose his privilege, protection, degree, and all the goods which he possesses in right of song, until the end of seven years, namely : for theft ; adultery ; and pugnacity ; for a Bard ought not to be guilty of these things.

19. For three things will a man of song lose his degree

ymhen y tair blynedd, am butteindra, am Feddwdod, ac am ymgynglynu a phoblach anneddfolion a drwg parth y gair a honnir am danynt.

20.   Am dripheth y syrth Bardd o Athraw Cadeiriawg i radd dysgyblaeth gyssefin ac ai gweddo herwydd ei annysg ai anneddfoldeb; cyntaf am fai ar ei gerdd nas gallo ac nas gwyppo ei ddifeiaw : Ail am annefawd parth ymddwyn a buchedd na wedd ar Fardd o Athraw ; Trydydd lle nas gallo gadw a chynnal ei gadair yn erbyn ei gystedlyddion.

21.   Tri rhyw gerddawr y sydd rydd iddynt glera yn eu cylchoedd cyfreithawl o fewn i'r cyfoeth y pont unwaith yn y flwyddyn. ac unwaith bob tair blynedd drwy holl Gymru benbaladr.   Cyntaf yw Bardd o Bencerdd Cadeiriawg, ai rodd am ei gerdd neu amgen ag a wnelo parth ei swydd ai gelfyddyd yw pedwar ugain, lle na bo ragammod, a lle bo nid rhydd iddo erchi dros chweugein o rodd neu o dda nai werth yn y byd dan colli ei glera ai dda wrth gerdd, ac a fo gantho ai roddi wrth raid Brenin y Cyfoeth lle gwnelo'r annefawd anraith.— Ail yw dysgybl dysgyblaidd ai rodd yw pedwar ugain os ysbas y bydd, os dysgyblaith yna deugein, ac os Pencerddaidd pedwar ugeint, ac nid rhydd i ammodi 'n ragfynedig am a fo mwy heb warantrwydd ei Athraw. ac o gwna efe hynny, colli ei glera.   Rhodd dysgygbl Pencerddaidd yw pedwar ugain, ac un ddeddf yw ef a'r dysgyblion eraill parth rhagammod, can nas dylaint y dysgyblon farnu ar a wnelont eithr eu hathraw a farn iddynt ac nis gellir ammod heb farnu ar a fo wrth yr ammod a wneler. sef y bydd athraw cadeiriawg wrth farn ei gadair ai nawdd ai fraint herwydd ei radd. a dysgybl o bob gradd a

until the end of three years : for adultery; for drunkenness ; and for associating with people of an immoral and bad character.

20. For three things will a Bard, who is a Chaired Teacher, fall to the rank of primary discipleship, and what befits his illiterateness and immorality : first, for a fault in his song, which he cannot, and knows not how to correct ; secondly, for immorality in respect of conduct and life unbecoming a Bard, who is a teacher ; thirdly, where he cannot keep and maintain his Chair against his fellow competitors.

21. There are three minstrels, who are permitted to stroll in their lawful circuits within the territory, in which they may be, once a year, and three times a year through the whole of Cymru universally. The first is a Bard, who is a chaired chief of song, the fee due for his song, or any other performance of his office and art, being eighty pence, where there has been no previous contract, and where it is not lawful for him to demand more than six score pence in the way of fees or chattels, or their value in any form, under the pain of forfeiting his right of minstrelsy, the goods attached to his song, and whatever he possesses ; and the same shall be given up in behalf of the king of the territory, where the immoral party shall have committed the wrong. The second is a pupil Disciple, whose fee is four score pence, if he be probationary; if disciplinary, then forty pence, and if chief of song, four score pence. It is not lawful to contract before hand for a greater remuneration without the warranty of his Teacher ; and if he does so, he shall forfeit his right of minstrelsy. The fee of a chief of song Disciple is four score pence ; and in respect of precontract the same law stands for him as for the other Disciples, for the Disciples ought not to judge their own works, but their Teacher will judge for them, and there can be no contract without judging what is bound by the contract made. For a Chaired Teacher is bound by the judgment of his Chair, protection, and privilege, according to his de-

fydd wrth farn ei Athraw. — Trydydd yw *Clerwr*, o wr
anafus megis a fo dall neu gloff. a rhydd i hwnnw glera a
chanu yn ei sefyll hyd onis erchir iddo amgen : Ac nis dylit
cennad Arglwydd y Cyfoeth i amgen o wyr no hynn glera
lle na bo iddynt raddau Cadeiriawg.

22.   Tair hawl y sydd ar Fardd ac nid rhydd iddo ei
rodd na'i radd lle nas gwnelo yn eu herwydd

Cyntaf yw cynnal cof ar gerdd ddosparthus am weithredoedd moliannus Tywysogion ac Arglwyddi, a Doethion, a
Dyledogion cynhwynawl, a phob Teilyngwas Cenedl y Cymry ; er clod iddynt hwy, ac er dangos ir oes y sydd ac a
ddel yr hynn a ddylynt herwydd Defawd, a gweithred, ac
ymddwyn, ac ymgais ymhob moliannus, er addysg ac an-
nogaeth, a chynhaliad y petheu hynn i genedl y Cymry, ac
er y sydd ddiddan o'u gwybod.

Ail yw Cynnal yr Iaith Gymraeg ai haddysgu herwydd
ei hanfod ai hansawdd ai dosparth i'r neb ai chwennycho, a
dysgu ei hysgrifennu yn gyfiawn a dysgu y sydd arni ym-
mherthynas ei Barddoniaeth a Cherdd Dafawd a'u perthynasau.

Trydydd yw cynnal cof achoedd, a neithioreu, fal nas
dygwyddo ledach ar Deulu dyledog a chynhwynawl o Genedl y Cymry, *a dwyn ach y Gwr* or nawfed ach lle nas gellir
ei ddwyn o ddyledawglin a wypper o hanfod cyn cof am
dani sef y bydd honno Tywysawglwydd neu Frehyr lwyth,
a hynn rhag myned ar ledach ac aillt, ac alltud a thaiawg
difraint y Fraint ar nawdd nas dylit i ddyn o'r byd namyn
i Gymro dyledawg, neu Gymraes Gynhwynawl. *A dwyn
ach y wraig* o Eppil a Bonedd fam a Thad, o Gymry cynhwynawl lle y bo felly er braint iddi o gymraes gynhwynawl
yr hynn nis gellir i Alldudes neu i ferch o fab Aillt, sef nad

gree; and a Disciple of every degree by the judgment of his Teacher. The third is the Minstrel, who may be a maimed person, such as blind or lame; it will be lawful for him to perform his minstrelsy and to sing standing, until he be requested to do otherwise. The permission of the lord of the territory ought not to be given to other than these to go on circuit, where they have no chaired degrees.

22. A Bard has three claims, and he is not entitled to his fee or degree, where he acts not according to them. The first is, to maintain in a methodical song the memorial of the commendable deeds of princes, lords, wise men, innate proprietors, and every worthy servant of the nation of the Cymry, for their own praise, and in order to shew the present and future generations what is incumbent upon them in respect of usage, act, conduct, and aim in all that is praiseworthy, for the instruction, promotion, and maintenance of these things to the nation of the Cymry, and for the amusement which arises from the knowledge of them. The second is, to uphold the Cymric language, and to teach it, as to its substance, quality, and arrangement, to such as may desire, to teach the proper writing of it, and to teach what in it refers to Bardism, vocal song, and their appurtenances. The third is, to maintain the memorial of genealogies, and nuptial feasts, lest any proprietary and innate family of the nation of the Cymry should happen to suffer degeneracy. The man's descent should be traced from the ninth generation, when it cannot be traced from a proprietary lineage, the derivation of which is known before memory, the same being a princely tribe or a baronial tribe. This is, lest the privilege and protection, which are due to no man whatsoever, except to a proprietary Cymro, or an innate Cymraes, should befal the degenerate, the alien, the foreigner, and the unprivileged villain. The woman's descent should be traced on the father's and mother's side, as to posterity and origin, from innate Cymry, such being a privilege to her, being an innate Cymraes, which cannot be to a foreign woman, or to the daughter of an alien; for the latter does

oes i honno fraint Cymraes ddyledawg cyd nas llygro merch
o aillt ac Alldudes ach a bonedd ei gwr ai phlant, sef yr
achoseu hynn y dylit ddwyn a chynnal ar gof a chadw
achoedd bonedd Cenedl y Cymry yn gyfiawn er gwybod
rhwng Ach a lledach, ac am Frodor ac Alldud. ac am Aillt
a Brehyr, ac am hynn herwydd ei swydd ai gelfyddyd wrth
gerdd iawn yw i Fardd ei rodd wrth fraint a defawd, a
cheiniog o bob aradr, a lle nas ceir arian dwyn gafael, ai
roddi wrth farn deuddengwyr Gwlad. ac am hynn o ddosparth, ymhob neithiawr iawn a dyled bod yn Fardd wrth
Fraint Cadair a Gorsedd, ac ar Arglwydd y Cyfoeth y mae
dosparthu hynny, rhag myned yn ammraint y pumerwi
rhyddion, ac er a fai iawn a dyledus yn hynn o betheu y
trefnwyd dosparth gyntaf ar ddwyn achau bonedd.

23. (24) Tripheth a ddylit ar y neb a ddywetto ei fod
yn arwyddfardd Un yw gwybod Achau Tywysogion a Brenhinoedd, a Boneddigion y Cymry. Ail yw Cyfarwyddyd y
Prifeirdd. Trydydd yw gwarant o gyfiawn awdurdawd a
dangos, oi radd ai gadair, a lle bo a ddywetto ei fod yn arwyddfardd heb arnaw y petheu hynny, rhaid yw ei ddal fal
crwydryn ai roi yngharchar onis gwaretto Arglwydd y Cyfoeth ef.

24. (23) Tripheth a ddylit ar a ddywetto ei fod yn
Brifardd. Un yw y Gelfyddyd wrth Gerdd ai pherthynasau ac y sydd arni herwydd Dosparth Beirdd yr hên
Gymry. Ail yw Cyfarwydd Beirdd Ynys Prydain, herwydd dosparth y sydd ar hynny. Trydydd yw Defodau
moliannus a Buchedd i argywedd, ac o fod hynny arnaw,
iawn iddaw ei Gadair.

25. Tripheth a ddylit ar a ddywetto ei fod yn Bosfardd.

not possess the privilege of a proprietary Cymraes, though an alien or a foreign woman does not corrupt the lineage and descent of her husband and children. For these reasons the genealogical descent of the nation of the Cymry ought to be traced, kept in memory, and preserved accurately, in order to distinguish between noble and mean descent, and in respect of native and foreigner, and of alien and baron. On this account, in right of his office, and the art of his song, a Bard is entitled to his fee by privilege and usage, and a penny from every plough; and where money cannot be obtained, he should make a seizure, and submit it to the judgment of twelve men of country. And because of this system, in every nuptial feast it is right and proper that the Bard should be under the privilege of a Chair and Gorsedd; and it appertains to the lord of the territory to make that arrangement, lest the five free acres should lack privilege. It was, in order that these particulars should be conducted rightly and duly, that the system of compiling the lineages of descent was first arranged.

23. There are three things required in him who says he is a Herald-bard. One is, that he should know the genealogies of the princes, kings, and nobles of the Cymry. The second is, the information of the primitive Bards. The third is, a properly authorized and exhibited warranty of his degree and Chair. He who says that he is a Herald-bard without possessing these requisites must be apprehended as a vagrant, and put in prison until the lord of the territory gives him deliverance.

24. There are three things required in him who says that he is a Primitive Bard. One is, the art of song and its relatives, and what belongs to it according to the system of the Bards of the Ancient Cymry. The second is, the information of the Bards of the Isle of Britain, according to the system into which it is reduced. The third are, commendable usages and irreproachable conduct. Whoever possesses these qualifications is entitled to his Chair.

25. There are three things required in him who says

Un yw y Gelfyddyd wrth Gerdd herwydd dychymygfawr gywreinrwydd y Beirdd diweddar, Ail yw medru darllain Cymraeg ai hysgrifennu yn berffaith.   Trydydd yw medru atteb a ofynner iddaw herwydd a ddywed y Doethion.

26.   Tripheth a ddylit ar a ddywetto ei fod yn Fardd o Athraw Cadeiriawg un yw a ddylit ar y Prifardd.   Ail yw a ddylit ar yr Arwyddfardd; Trydydd yw a ddylit ar y Posfardd, ac o bydd hynny arnaw iawn yw iddaw ei radd ai fraint o Athraw Cadeiriawg.

27.   Trille y dylit cynnal Cadair ac Eisteddfod Beirdd a gwyr wrth Gerdd dafawd a thant, sef y bydd y gwyr wrth Gerdd dant Cadair ac Eisteddfod Beirdd, un yw Cadlas egored yngoleuni haul, sef tra bydd haul ar yr awyr, ac yngolwg ac yng ngwybod gwlad a chenedl, herwydd Defawd a chyfraith ac oni bydd arfer tair blynedd wedi bod ar y lle rhaid rhaid yw ei roi ar wybod a chlyw gwlad ac Arglwydd wrth rybudd cyfreithawl dan osteg undydd a blwyddyn, a chynnal y rhybudd dan osteg fal hynny dros dair blynedd yna defodawl fydd y lle ac arnaw fraint Beirdd a Chadair, Ail yw Llysoedd Arglwydd y Cyfoeth ai Yngnaid, Canys llïoedd egored au bernir herwydd braint y sydd arnynt. Trydydd yw y llannoedd, sef yr Eglwysi, sef y bernir y rheini yn egored ac yngoleuni dydd, ac yngwybodaeth a chlyw gwlad a chenedl ac Arglwydd a Chyfraith, ac nis gellir na gwarant nac awdurdawd, na braint, na gair dros Gadair ac Eisteddfod na dim ac a wneler wrth Gerdd Daf- awd parth braint a gwarantrwydd, namyn a wneler yn y llïoedd egored wrth fraint a Defawd gwlad a chyfraith.

28.   Mewn Trille y rhoddir rhybydd dan osteg undydd a blwyddyn, Un yw ymmhob Llys Arglwydd ac ynad a

that he is a Post-bard. One is, the art of song, according to the inventive skill of the later Bards. The second is, to be able to read Cymraeg, and to write it accurately. The third is, to be able to answer questions put to him according to the sayings of wise men.

26. There are three things required in him who says that he is a Bard, in virtue of being a Chaired Teacher. One is, that which is required in a Primitive Bard. The second is, that which is required in a Herald-bard. The third is, that which is required in a Post-bard. If he is possessed of these qualifications, he is entitled to his degree and privilege as a Chaired Teacher.

27. In three places ought a Chair and Eisteddvod of Bards and men of vocal and instrumental song (a Chair in the case of men of instrumental song, and an Eisteddvod in the case of Bards) to be held. One is, an open yard, in the light of the sun, that is, whilst the sun is in the firmament, and in the sight and knowledge of country and nation, according to usage and law; and unless the place has had the usage of three years, it must be submitted to the knowledge and hearing of country and lord by means of a legal notice under the proclamation of a year and a day, the notice being given under such a proclamation for three years. The place will then be institutional, having the privilege of Bards and Chair. The second are, the courts of the lord of the territory and his judges, for they are deemed open places, in respect of the privilege which belongs to them. The third are, the sacred enclosures, or churches, for they are deemed open, and as being in the light of day, and in the knowledge and hearing of country and nation, and lord and law. There can be no warranty or authority, or privilege, or word, in respect of Chair and Eisteddvod, or anything that is done relative to vocal song as to privilege and security, but for what is done in the open places, according to the privilege and usage of country and law.

28. In three places is notice to be given under the proclamation of a year and a day. One is, in every court of

Chyfraith, Ail yw ymmhob Llann ac Eglwys yn y Cyfoeth,
Trydydd yw, ymmhob Ffair a marchnad yn y Cyfoeth. ac
yna breiniawl fydd a rother yn nawdd y rhybydd hynny
dan osteg undydd a blwyddyn ac nis dylit yn ei erbyn, onid
a ellir cyn pen y tair blynedd, herwydd Breiniau a Defodau
yr hen Gymry, a Breiniau a Defodau Beirdd Ynys Prydain,
canys yn nawdd y rhyw rybudd a hynny y dechreuasant yr
hen Gymry pob Breiniau a Defodau a phob Cyfraith a Chyfrwym, a phob Trefn a Dosparth wrth fraint ac yn nawdd
gwlad a Chenedl, ar y sydd ac a fu yn arfer a Dospartheu
Cenedl y Cymry, a byth nis dylid yn amgen gan na Gwlad
nac arglwydd na chan hawl na gwrthhawl nac yn ol ac ym
mraint y Drefn honn ar Ddospartheu Gwlad a Chenedl.

29.   Tair Gwarant ac awdurdawd Cadair wrth Gerdd ac
Eisteddfod Beirdd y sydd, o bydd ei chynnal yn yr un a
fynner a fo cyflwydd o'r Llｃoedd breiniawl egored, ac yn ei
hamser egored yngoleuni haul. Un yw Cynghor a Chynghyd Triwyr wrth Gerdd o Feirdd Cadeiriawg herwydd
Braint a Defawd yr Hen Gymry, neu a font herwydd
Braint a Defawd Beirdd Ynys Prydain, sef y bydd Gair
eu gair hwy lle byddont yn warant ar Gerdd dafawd a
Barddoniaeth ac a berthyn ar hynny parth Breiniau a Defodau. Ail yw nawdd a braint deuddeg o ddyledogion yn
gywiriaid Gwlad a Chyfoeth dan osteg a rhybydd Cyfreithawl, a hynn o nawdd lle na bo tri Bardd Cadeiriawg
ynghadair, sef malpai nas bai ond Dau, neu Un, neu wyr
wrth Gerdd wrth hawl na fuant Cyn no hynny yn gadeir-
iawg. Trydydd yw nawdd Arglwydd y Cyfoeth neu dri oi
Yngneid, eisoes dywedir y gellir nawdd o un Yngnad Cyfoeth lle bo wrth rybudd a gosteg gyfreithawl, a nawdd
Arglwydd y Cyfoeth a ellir o'r a geffir o dan ei law yn

---

[1] " Llan " seems to be synonymous with the Latin *fanum*, and the Greek
τιμένος. Its original meaning was simply an *inclosure*, but in later times the
term was applied exclusively, in its simple form, to an area enclosed for public
worship, or a church.

lord, and judge, and law. The second is, in every llan[1] and church in the territory. The third is, in every fair and market in the territory. Then what is rendered under the protection of the said notice after the proclamation of a year and a day is privileged, and ought to receive no opposition except what may be offered before the end of the three years, according to the privileges and usages of the Ancient Cymry, and the privileges and usages of the Bards of the Isle of Britain. For it was under the protection of such a notice that the Ancient Cymry began all privileges and usages, every law and contract, and every order and system according to the privilege, and under the protection of country and nation, relative to those who practise and have practised the arrangements of the nation of the Cymry. And nothing should ever be done either by country or by lord, by claim or by counter claim, other than according to, and in virtue of, this order of the systems of country and nation.

29. There are three guarantees and authorities of Chair of song and Eisteddvod of Bards, if it be held in one or other, as may be convenient, of the open and privileged places, and at its open time in the light of the sun. One is, the counsel and communion of three men of song who are Chaired Bards according to the privilege and usage of the Bards of the Isle of Britain, for the testimony of their word, wherever they may be, will be a warrant for vocal song, and Bardism, and whatever appertains to the same in respect of privileges and usages. The second is, the protection and privilege of twelve proprietors, being true men of country and territory, under lawful proclamation and notice, which protection is given where there are no three Chaired Bards in Chair, as if where there are only two or one, or only men of song by claim, who have not been chaired previously. The third is, the protection of the lord of the territory, or of three of his judges—nevertheless it is said that the protection of one territorial judge will avail, if given under lawful notice and proclamation; and the protection of the lord of the territory will suffice, if warranted under his hand,

warantedig, lle na bo Cyttrem efe, ac oni bydd un neu 'r
llall o'r tri hynn, nis gellir cynnal Cadair ac Eisteddfod
Ddefodawl a Chyfreithawl, herwydd braint a defawd yr
Hen Gymry.

30.   Tri amseroedd egored y sydd, ac arnynt rhydd yw
cynnal Cadair ac Eisteddfod, un ydynt tri phrifgyfnod haul,
sef y dyddiau au gwyleu au tradwyeu, y delo 'r haul i gyfnod cyhydedd y gwanwyn, ac i gyfnod hirddydd haf, ac i
gyfnod cyhydedd y mesyryd, ac i gyfnod byrddydd y gauaf;
ail ydynt y tair Gwyl Arbennigion sef y Pasg, a'r Sulgwyn,
a'r nadolig: Trydydd yw dyddiau Llys a Chyfraith yn y
mannau, ar amser o ddydd, a gynhelir y llysoedd hynny,
ac nid mewn amgen o fann. a lle bo achos a rhaid wrth amseroedd eraill, rhaid yw eu rhoddi wrth rhybydd dan osteg
undydd a blwyddyn herwydd Defawd a chyfraith.

31.   O dair ffordd y greddir Bardd, cyntaf yw o ddysgyblaeth y gan Athraw o Fardd Cadeiriawg yny wyppo 'r
gelfyddyd wrth Gerdd ac y sydd arni parth swydd a Dyled,
ac yny wyppo Freiniau a Defodau 'r Beirdd, a'r gwybodau
eraill a berthynant ar Fardd a Barddoniaeth, a gallu o honaw atteb drosto ei hun lle ydd elo ynghyrch haul ym mraint
a nawdd ei Athraw ; a hynny arnaw, gradd a chadair iddaw.

Ail yw ym mraint Gwybodau a medru ar gelfyddyd
Cerdd dafawd ai pherthynasau, a Breiniau a defodau Beirdd
a Barddoniaeth ac y sydd arnynt, a dangos o honaw ganu
yn ddosparthus a difai oi waith ei hunan, a medru o honaw
ddarllain Cymraeg yn berffaith ai ysgrifennu ai ddosparthu
yn gyfiawn can mai o hynny ac nid yn amgen y gellir ei
wybodau ef heb addysg dysgyblaeth, a gofyn arnaw yw
dangos y petheu hynn oll o flaen Cadair ac Eisteddfod, a
lle nis gellir gwrtheb, gradd a Chadair iddaw ym mraint ei

though he himself may not be present. And unless there be one or other of these three, an institutional and lawful Chair or Eisteddvod, according to the privilege and usage of the Ancient Cymry, cannot be held.

30. There are three open times, on which it is lawful to hold a Chair and Eisteddvod. One is, the three principal periods of the sun, that is, the days, their festivals, and their third days, on which the sun enters the point of the equinox of spring, the point of the long day of summer, the point of the equinox of autumn, and the point of the short day of winter. The second, the three principal festivals, namely, Easter, Whitsunday, and Christmas. The third, the days of court and law, in the places, and at the time of day, where and when those courts are held, and in no other place. But where there may be need and occasion for other times, notice of them must be given under the proclamation of a year and a day, according to usage and law.

31. In three ways is a Bard graduated. The first is, after discipleship, under a Teacher who is a Chaired Bard, until he shall have known the art of song, and what belongs to it in respect of office and duty, and until he shall have known the privileges and usages of the Bards, and the other sciences which appertain to Bard and Bardism, and become capable of answering for himself where he is examined under the privilege and protection of his Teacher. Being possessed of these qualifications, he is entitled to a degree and Chair. The second is, in virtue of sciences, and from being skilled in the art of vocal song, and its appurtenances, and the privileges and usages of Bards and Bardism, and what belongs to them, and from having exhibited methodical and faultless singing of his own composition, and being able to read Cymraeg accurately, and to write and arrange it properly, because it is from those things, and not otherwise, that his sciences can accrue without the teaching of discipleship. It is required of him to exhibit all these things before a Chair and Eisteddvod, and where there can be no objection, he is entitled to a degree and Chair in virtue of his sciences, and

R

wybodau, a hynn a elwir gradd a Chadair o Balledigaeth, neu, o ddywediad arall, gradd Beblig, gan mai wrth farn a phabl cadair ac Eisteddfod, ac nid dysgyblaeth ac Athraw ai gradder.

Trydydd yw, lle nas gellir Cadair ac Eisteddfod ddefodawl, ac o hynny analledigaeth ar farn wrth gerdd a Barddoniaeth eisieu Beirdd a Chadeirogion, myned ar farn Gwlad a Chenedl dan rybydd a gosteg undydd a blwyddyn, ac o anallu gwrtheb a myned o gyfiawnder yn ei erbyn, gradd i'r Bardd, a chynnal y rhydd honno dan osteg undydd a blwyddyn hyd ymmhen y tair blynedd, yna cadarnhau gradd iddaw a chadair, ac yn hynn o ffaig nis gellir ar eu wybodeu ai gelfyddyd ef amgen na barn gwlad a Chenedl ai doethion Ac nis gellir dosparth arnynt amgen na barn herwydd pwyll ac ansawdd a gorfod, can nas gellir amgen na hynn eisieu Beirdd a Ac nis gellir Dosparth o annosparth amgen nag ym mraint Pwyll ac Ansawdd a gorfod, au rhoddi wrth farn a rhaith gadarn gwlad a Chenedl dan rybydd a gosteg gyfreithawl hyd ymhen y tair blynedd. Ac yn hynn o fodd y graddwyd y Beirdd cyssefinion y gan genedl y Cymry, ac y trefnwyd Dosparth ar Feirdd a Barddoniaeth ac ar Freiniau a defodau a weddai iddynt cyn bod na Bardd nac Athraw na Chadair, na dosparth ar ddim or byd parth Cerdd dafawd a Beirdd a Barddoniaeth, a'r radd honn alwir gradd a chadair hir-rhaith gadarn gwlad a chenedl ym mraint a nawdd cyssefin gwlad a chenedl y Cymry. A Rhaith Gadarn gwlad a chenedl y gelwir hyn o drefn a dosparth wrth rybydd dan osteg undydd a blwyddyn, gan mai cadarnaf o bob rhaith a dosparth, ac o fodd amgen nis gellir yn gyfiawn ddechreuad ar drefn a dosparth o'r byd parth gwlad a chenedl, nac ar gyfraith a chyfrwym,

they are called the degree and Chair of faculty, or, as it is otherwise said, a faculty degree, since it is by the judgment and faculty of Chair and Eisteddvod, and not by means of discipleship and teacher, that he is graduated. The third is, where no customary Chair and Eisteddvod can be obtained, and hence there is an impossibility of receiving the judgment of song and Bardism, through the want of Bards and Chaired men, by submitting to the judgment of country and nation under the notice and proclamation of a year and a day; and where there can be no objection, or just opposition, then a degree ought to be conferred upon the Bard. The said notice ought to be issued under the proclamation of a year and a day until the end of three years, when a degree and Chair should be confirmed to him. And in this crisis, his sciences and art cannot receive other than the judgment of country and nation and its wise men, and they can have no system other than judgment according to reason, nature, and cogency, because other than this cannot be had from the want of Bards, nor can system arise from the lack of system other than in virtue of reason, nature, and cogency, the same being submitted to the firm judgment and verdict of country and nation, under legal notice and proclamation until the end of the three years. It was after this manner that the primary Bards were graduated by the nation of the Cymry, and the system of Bards and Bardism, and of the privileges and usages which befit them, before there was either a Bard, or Teacher, or Chair, or arrangement of any thing whatsoever relative to vocal song and Bards and Bardism. This degree is called the long-established and firm degree and chair of country and nation, under the primary privilege and protection of the country and nation of the Cymry. And this arrangement or system, after notice under the proclamation of a year and a day, is called the firm verdict of country and nation, for it is the firmest of all verdicts and systems. There cannot, in any other way, be a beginning properly of any arrangement and system in respect of country and nation, as to law and contract, and

nac ar Fraint a defawd, nac adnewyddu ar ddim o'r byd
gwedi y darffo unwaith am dano, am hynny Cadarn ar bob
Cadarn y bernir y Rhaith a'r ddosparth honn. a rhydd yw
i bob Dyledawg a Chynhwynawl, a chynhenid o genedl y
Cymry ei dodi, ni waeth ai Cyfiawn ai anghyfiawn y bo ei
hawl, Gwlad a Chenedl ai barn.

32.   Tri galw gorddyfned y sydd ar Feirdd Ynys Prydain, Un yw Beirdd wrth Fraint Cadair a Gorsedd, a hynny
a berthyn i bawb o Feirdd, a reddir yng nghadair ac Eisteddfod, herwydd y dospartheu y sydd ar hynny.   Ail yw
Beirdd wrth Fraint a Defawd Beirdd Ynys Prydain, ac a
berthyn ar a radder yn Fardd o ba ffordd bynnag y bo
hynny herwydd y dospartheu y sydd ar hynny o betheu.
Trydydd yw Beirdd wrth Fraint a Defawd yr Hen Gymru,
ac ni pherthyn hynn ar amgen na Phrifardd o Brydydd sef
yr oedd efe cyn bod y ddwy radd eraill ar Feirdd, sef arwyddfeirdd a Phosfeirdd a chynn bod na dosparth na threfn
na gradd nac enw iddynt, a chyn no dyfod y Cymry i Ynys
Prydain yr oedd iddynt Brifeirdd o Brydyddion ac iddynt
freiniau a defodeu a dosparth.   Ac yn Ynys Prydain y
trefnwyd y ddwy radd eraill ar Feirdd, a'r ddosparth ar
gofynion y sydd arnynt, a'r Breiniau a berthyn iddynt, Am
hynny Prydydd yn unig neu Brifardd arbennig y dylit ei
alw yn Fardd wrth fraint a defawd yr Hen Gymry, cyd bo
efe eisoes yn Fardd wrth fraint Cadair a Gorsedd, ac hefyd
wrth Fraint a Defawd Beirdd Ynys Prydain, a chyd y
gelwir Tydain Tad Awen, a Rhuawn Hen, a Madawg ab
Alchnoe, a Chadawg gwr gwerin, ac Erddyled leuferawg, ac
Arianrod ferch Mynwar, yn Feirdd a Barddesi wrth fraint
a Defawd yr hen Gymry, ni iawn eu galw wrth fraint a
defawd Beirdd Ynys * can nad oeddent hwy wedi cael eu

---

* "Prydain" seems to have been inadvertently omitted by the copyist.

privilege and usage; nor can any thing whatsoever be renewed, when it has once perished. Therefore, firm above all
that is firm is this verdict and system adjudged to be; and
it is lawful for every proprietor, native, and innate man of
the nation of the Cymry, to appeal to it; whether his claim
be just or unjust, the country and nation will judge it.

32. There are three customary vocations among the
Bards of the Isle of Britain. One consists of the Bards
according to the privilege of Chair and Gorsedd, which includes all Bards that are graduated in Chair and Eisteddд-
vod, in respect of the systems which are attached to them.
The second are the Bards according to the privilege and
usage of the Bards of the Isle of Britain, and includes such
as are graduated in any way whatsoever, in respect of the
system which is attached to those particulars. The third
are the Bards according to the privilege and usage of the
Ancient Cymry, which include none other than a Primitive
Bard, being a Poet, for he existed before the two other degrees of Bards, namely, the Herald-bards, and Post-bards,
and before they had a system, or order, or degree, or name;
and before the arrival of the Cymry in the Isle of Britain,
they had Primitive Bards, being Poets, who possessed privileges, usages, and a system. It was in the Isle of Britain
that the two other degrees of Bards were appointed, as well
as their system and requirements, and the privileges which
appertain to them. Therefore, a Poet only, or a special
primitive Bard, ought to be designated a Bard according to
the privilege and usage of the Ancient Cymry, though he
may be already a Bard according to the privilege of Chair
and Gorsedd; and also according to the privilege and usage
of the Bards of the Isle of Britain. And although Tydain,
the father of Awen, and Rhuawn the Aged, and Madog, son
of Alchnoe, and Cadog the Peasant, and Erddyled the Lu-
minous, and Arianrod, daughter of Mynwar, were Bards
and Bardesses, according to the privilege and usage of the
Ancient Cymry, it is not right to call them according to
the privilege and usage of the Bards of the Isle of Britain,

dechreuad y prydieu hynny. ac eisoes eraill a ddywedant y
dylit galw Beirdd wrth fraint a defawd Beirdd Ynys Prydain yn feirdd wrth fraint a defawd yr Hen Gymry achos
mai gan yr hen Gymry y trefnwyd hwynt yn Ynys Prydain gyntaf, cyd y gellir ynawr feirdd na bont felly ac er
hynny yn Feirdd wrth fraint a defawd yr hen Gymry, ac
or rhyw hynn y dylit barnu y Prydyddion doethion a chyw-
reint a chelfyddgar a geffir tra byddo Cadair ac Eisteddfod
yng nghwsg sef y pryd hynny ni ellir na nod na dyled arnynt nag iddynt, namyn Awen o Dduw a deall, a barn
gwlad a chenedl, yn ail y bu Beirdd cyssefin Cenedl y
Cymry o'r dechreuad, cyn bod amgen iddynt o fraint na
defod na dosparth.

33. Tri Chysefiniaid Beirdd Ynys Prydain Plennydd
Ac Alawn a Gwrawn. sef yn amser Prydain ab Aedd Mawr
y buant, ar Triwyr hynn a wnaethant gyntaf drefn a dosparth gyfreithawl ar Feirdd a Barddoniaeth ac a ddodasant
arnynt Freiniau a defodau Cadair a Gorsedd a nawdd gwlad
a chenedl a nawdd cyfrwym cywlad, a nawdd arglwydd a
chyfoeth, ac achos y gwnaed hynn oedd er cynnal cof a
chadw am a fu gynt yn deilyngaf a theilyngfawl ar wr a
gweithred, a deddf a defawd, a daionus a moliannus; ac er
dysgu doethineb a phob gwybodeu daionus ac er cefnogi 'r
da, a gwarrogi 'r drwg. A chan rhaith gwlad a chenedl a
than Osteg a rhybydd gyfreithawl, a Phrydain ab Aedd
Mawr yn Benrhaith ac yn Benteyrnedd pan y bu hynn, a
llyma fal y bu dechreuad y Rhyw a elwir Beirdd wrth
Fraint a defawd Beirdd Ynys Prydain.

34. Tair nawdd o fraint y sydd i Feirdd Ynys Prydain. Un yw nawdd Gwlad a Chenedl, sef hynny ei bumerwi rhyddion ymmraint ei gelfyddyd ai swydd wrth Gerdd,

because they did not originate in those times. Nevertheless, others say, that Bards according to the privilege and usage of the Bards of the Isle of Britain should be called Bards according to the privilege and usage of the Ancient Cymry, because it was by the Ancient Cymry that they were first instituted in the Isle of Britain, though there may be Bards now who are not so appointed, and yet are Bards according to the privilege and usage of the Ancient Cymry. Of this kind ought to be deemed the wise, ingenious, and skilful Poets, who are found whilst a Chair and Eisteddvod are dormant; for at that time they can exhibit no mark or obligation, except Awen from God, understanding, and the judgment of country and nation, similarly to what was the case with the primary Bards of the nation of the Cymry, before they had any other privilege, usage, or syste m.

33. The three primary Bards of the Isle of Britain: Plennydd; Alawn; and Gwron; who lived in the time of Prydain, son of Aedd the Great. It was these three persons that first legally arranged and systematized Bards and Bardism, and conferred on them the privileges and usages of Chair and Gorsedd, the protection of country and nation, the connecting protection of federate country, and the protection of lord and territory. And the reason why this was done was, in order to preserve the memorial and record of what was formerly most worthy and commendable in respect of man and deed, law and usage, and of what was good and praiseworthy, and in order to teach wisdom and all good sciences, and to encourage the good and subdue the evil. This was effected by the verdict of country and nation, and under legal proclamation and notice, Prydain, son of Aedd the Great, being supreme of jury and supreme of princes, at the time. Thus did originate the class, called Bards according to the privilege and usage of the Bards of the Isle of Britain.

34. There are three privileged protections to the Bards of the Isle of Britain. One is, the protection of country and nation, that is, his five free acres in right of his art and

a phob braint gosymmaith. Ail yw na bo arf yn ei erbyn,
nac arnaw ddwyn arf ynghyrch a gosawd rhyfel. Trydydd
yw bod Gair ei air ef ar bawb, ac Gair eiddo neb arnaw ef.

Ail nawdd yw nawdd Cyfrwym cywlad, sef bod rhydd
iddo fyned yng ngwlad a gorwlad heb yn ei erbyn nag arf
na gorfod, na gair na gwrtheb ai yn heddwch ai yn rhyfel y
bo y gwledydd yr elo. Sef hynny mal y gallo fyned yn bo
rhaid er gyrru heddwch a chyfiawnder y rhwng y gwledydd
a fythont yn dwyn rhyfel a chynllwyn y naill ar y llall.

Trydydd nawdd yw nawdd ei gadair, sef y neb ydd elo
yn ei nawdd hi nid oes namyn barn ger ei bronn ai di-
nawdd, ac od a Caeth yn ei nawdd hi rhydd fyddai, ac i
bawb y mae myned yn ei nawdd er cael addysg a deall ar
wybodau ac ar a wnelo felly ni ellir ei ofyn yn rhaid gwlad
ac Arglwydd yn amgen nac a wyppo ac a fo iawn iddo wrth
Gerdd a Barddoniaeth can mai ym mraint dysgybl Bardd a
cherdd dafawd y saif efe. cans iawn i fardd a fynno er gyrru
addysg a gwybodau a chyfiawnder a thangnef ar wlad a
chenedl, ac ar wlad a gorwlad, ac er galledigaeth y pethau
hynn y doded y sydd herwydd y dospartheu ar fardd a
Barddoniaeth.

35. Tri Beirdd Llen o Brifeirdd wrth fraint a defawd
Beirdd yr Hen Gymry a fuant gyntaf o'u hanfod a'u hansawdd, sef oeddynt Taliesin Ben Beirdd a Merddin ab Mor-
fryn, a Merddin Emrys, sef au gelwir y tri phrifeirdd Llen
am wneuthur o honynt Lyfrau a dospartheu ysgrifennedig
ar y gelfyddyd wrth Gerdd ac a berthyn iddi, ac ym mraint
eu llyfreu hwy, ac ymmraint Defod a chof Cadair ac Eisteddfod y mae cynnal Barddoniaeth Beirdd Ynys Prydain

office of song, and every privilege of viaticum. The second is, that there shall be no weapon against him, and that he shall not bear a weapon in the march and onset of war. The third is, that his word shall be a word superior to all, and that the word of nobody shall be superior to him. The second protection is the connecting privilege of a federate country, that is, that he shall be permitted to go into country and border country, opposed by neither weapon nor force, neither word nor contradiction, whether the countries which he visits shall be at peace or war. This is done, that he may be enabled to go, as necessity requires, to introduce peace and justice between the countries which bring war and ambuscade one against the other. The third protection is the protection of his Chair; that is, whoever defers to its protection cannot, except by judgment before it, become unprotected; and should a bond appeal to its protection, he shall go free; and all are allowed to be under its protection, in order to obtain instruction and understanding in sciences. Of him, who is thus circumstanced, nothing can be asked in the service of country and lord, other than what he knows, and what befits him in respect of song and Bardism, for it is in right of a Bardic disciple and vocal song that he stands. And a Bard may adopt what course he pleases to impart instruction, sciences, justice, and peace to country and nation, and to country and border country; and it was for facilitating these things, that what exists, in respect of the systems of Bard and Bardism, was appointed.

35. The three literary Bards, being primitive Bards according to the privilege and usage of the Bards of the Ancient Cymry, who first derived their essence and quality from them, namely: Taliesin, the Chief of Bards; Merddin, son of Morvryn; and Merddin Emrys. That is, they are called the three literary primitive Bards, because they made written books and arrangements of the art of song, and what appertains to it. And it is in virtue of their books, and in virtue of the usage, and memorial of Chair and Eisteddvod, that the Bardism of the Bards of the Isle of Britain is to be

S

ac a berthynant ar hynny. ac nid rhydd cadair na Gradd i'r neb na bo gantho gyfarwyddyd oddiwrth y tri phrifeirdd Llen a enwyd, a medr ar eu llyfreu a wnaethant hwy, yn gyntefigion eu bath.

36.   Tair Dyledswydd arbennig y sydd ar Deulüwr, yn y lle y bo, Dysgu darllain ac ysgrifennu 'r Iaith Gymraeg, Dysgu syberwyd teuluaidd a defodau daionus herwydd Cyfiawnder a chariad—a chadw cof am a berthyn i'r Teuluoedd y bo efe athraw iddynt.

37.   Tripheth y sydd ar Fardd neu brydydd a fo eirchiad, Cyntaf nad archo na da na dim arall o'r byd ar gerdd dafawd heb gennad y perchennog, ail nad archo dros gwerth chweugain o ddim yn y byd. Trydydd nas danfono Gerdd Archiad, nac unrhyw Gerdd arall o'r Byd gyda gwr wrth gerdd dant, dan boen colli ei dda wrth Gerdd hyd ymhenn y tair blynedd, a phob rhodd a gosymaith a ddylit iddaw o fraint a ant i Arglwydd y Cyfoeth.

38.   Tri chrair Bridiw Beirdd Ynys Prydain—y dengair deddf Efengyl Ieuan — a dywedyd o fardd ar ei air ai gydwybod.

39.   Tripheth y sydd ac am danynt y *Cyll Bardd ei gadair* hyd ym mhen y tair blynedd. Un yw gwall cof a chadw ar a ddylai—Ail yw dwyn arf yn rhyfel—Trydydd yw anghadw ei rin. ac eraill a wedant nis gellir Adwedd iddaw o'i gadair yn ei einioes o gwna efe y petheu hynn.

40.   Tri Unben Gwladogaeth, *Barddoniaeth*, ac ar hynny y mae addysg a phob athrawiaeth Llen a deddfoldeb a dwyfoldeb—*Yngneidiaeth*, ac ar hynny y mae dosparthu a gyrru barn a chyfiawnder, yn y bo achos, herwydd breiniau a defodau gwlad a chenedl, ac herwydd iawn a chyfraith, ar a elo yn eu herbyn. Tywysogaeth neu Arglwyddiaeth ac ar

maintained. Nor is a Chair or degree granted to any one who has no information derived from the said three literary primitive Bards, and skill in the books which they made, being the first of their kind.

36. There are three special duties incumbent upon a Family Bard, wherever he may be: to teach the reading and writing of the Cymric language; to teach domestic politeness, and good manners, in respect of justice and love; and to keep a record of what belongs to the families in which he is tutor.

37. There are three things required in a Bard or Poet, who is a supplicant. First, that he should ask neither goods nor any thing else whatsoever by means of vocal song, without the permission of the owner. Secondly, that he should not ask for any thing above the value of six score pence. Thirdly, that he should not send a supplicatory song, nor any other song whatsoever, with a man of instrumental song, under the pain of losing the goods attached to his song until the end of three years; and every fee and provision, to which he is privileged, shall go to the lord of the territory.

38. The three relics of adjuration of the Bards of the Isle of Britain: the ten commandments; the gospel of John; and the affirmation of a Bard upon his word and conscience.

39. There are three things for which a Bard will lose his Chair until the end of three years. One is, defect of memorial and record in respect of what ought to be remembered. The second is, bearing a weapon in war. The third is, divulging his secret. Others say: his Chair cannot be restored to him during life, if he does these things.

40. The three monarchs of government: Bardism, to which belong learning, and every doctrine of literature, morality, and godliness; judicature, which has to distribute and do judgment and justice where there is occasion, according to the privileges and usages of country and nation, and according to right and law, to those who may oppose them; and the office of a king or lord, on which depends the de-

hynny y mae amddiffyn gwlad a chenedl a dosparthu ar
hynny o beth herwydd braint a defawd gwlad a chenedl; ac
o bydd achos herwydd rhaith gwlad dan rybydd a gosteg
deugeinnydd. ac heb y tri hynn nis gellir Cyfannedd gadarn
ar wlad a Chenedl.

41. Trilliw gorwisg Bardd o Athraw cadeiriawg, a rhydd
iddo yr un a fynno, cyd y bo'r wisg honno pa un bynnag o'r
lliwiau y bo yn gwbl gyfunlliw, sef y cyfunlliw yn arwydd
gwirionedd sef cyfunlliw hwnnw ^{ar} bob amser ac ymhob damwain—Un yw Assur, neu las awyr, yn arwyddaw heddwch
a Thangnef yn ail i awyr hinon haf, yn nhes eglur ysblen-
nydd heb niwl heb gwmmwl. Ail yw Gwyrdd yn arwydd
dysg a doethineb gwybodau a darddant ac a dyfant yn hardd
fal gwyrddlysiau 'r meusydd yn hyfrydu perchen llygad au
gwêl. Trydydd yw gwynn yn arwydd Dwyfoldeb a phob
pur a diniwed, a phob iawn a chyfiawn, canys y rhain a
fyddant yn gyfliw haul a goleuni yn ddisgleirwyn ysblen-
nydd. a gwyn a ddylit ei wisgaw pan ydd eler ynghyrch
golychwyd. ar Assur pan ydd eler yng nghadair a gorsedd
—a'r gwyrdd, lle ' dd eler yn Athraw Teuluaidd, sef ymhob
un o'r lliwieu hynn y saif y cyfunlliw yn arwydd *gwir*. ac
nid rhydd i amgen na bardd Cadeiriawg eu gwisgaw, ac nid
iawn iddaw eu cymmysg, ac o gwna efe hynny ym mraint
ac urddas dysgybl ai cymmerir, cans o'r trilliwieu hynn yn
ogymmysg y bydd gwisg dysgybl ac ynddi nid iawn unlliw
arall o'r byd, a'r lliwieu barddonïaidd y gelwir y rhain.

42. Tri swyddeu cyssefinion Bardd—Cynnal heddwch a
Thangnef—cynnal a gwellhau defodau daionus—a chynnal
cof am ddaioni a gwybodau, a gweithredoedd moliannus.

43. Tair deddf gyssefin y sydd ar Fardd parth ac at a
wnelo ei hun—cadw ei air—cadw ei gyfrin—a chadw heddwch.

fence of country and nation, and the arrangement of the same, according to the privilege and usage of country and nation, and if there be occasion, according to the verdict of country under the notice and proclamation of forty days. Without these three there can be no firm social abode for country and nation.

41. The robe of a Bard, being a Chaired Teacher, is of three colours, and he may adopt whichever he pleases, provided the robe, of whichever of the colours it is, be entirely unicoloured, for unicolour is the symbol of truth, that being unicoloured at all times, and under all circumstances. One is azure, or sky-blue, signifying peace and tranquillity, which are similar to the sky of summer weather, during clear and resplendent heat, without mist, without a cloud. The second is green, the symbol of learning and the wisdom of sciences, which spring and grow beautifully like the green herbs of the fields, rejoicing the owner of the eyes that behold them. The third is white, the symbol of godliness and all purity and innocence, and all right and justice; for these are of the same colour as the sun and light, glitteringly and splendidly white. White ought to be worn in the resort of worship; azure in Chair and Gorsedd; and green, when one becomes a domestic tutor. And each of these colours should be unicoloured, as significative of truth. Nor is it lawful for other than a Chaired Bard to wear them, and it is not right for him to mix them, but should he do so, it must be under the privilege and dignity of a Disciple : because the robe of a Disciple consists of the three colours mixed, and should not admit of any other unicolour whatsoever:—and these are called the Bardic colours.

42. The three primary offices of a Bard: to maintain peace and tranquillity ; to maintain and improve good usages; and to maintain the memorial of goodness, sciences, and laudable deeds.

43. There are three primary laws incumbent upon a Bard in respect of what he does himself: to keep his word; to keep his secret; and to keep the peace.

44. Tair deddf ochel y sydd ar Fardd, gochel diogi a
thra llesgedd can mai gwr yw wrth ymgais ac ymbrawf—
gochel cynnen a chywryssedd can mae gwr yw efe wrth gariad a thangnef—a gochel ffolineb ac anneddfoldeb ac anadd-
wynder, can mai gwr yw efe, wrth bwyll a deall ac Awen o
Dduw.

45. Tair sail gwybodaeth y dylai Bardd eu hystyriaw
a'u trafod Pwyll—ansawdd—a gorfod.

46. Tair athrawiaeth a ofynnir gan Fardd, can wrth
bwyll a doethineb deddfawl — a llafar herwydd cof a defod
Gorsedd a Golychwyd. ac ymddwyn herwydd Defodau a
chynneddfau addwyn a daionus.

47. Tripheth ni ddylai Brydydd o Fardd Cadeiriawg
eu dwyn — arfau. anfoes, ac anfawl. cans swydd arnaw yw
gyrru heddwch a thangnef — a chadarnhau addwynder, a
moliannu pob daionus.

48. Tripheth molianus ar Fardd, serchogrwydd gwresog
—Ehawnder araf—a Phwyll ymgeisgar.

49. Tripheth nis gellir eu hepcor ar Fardd, Awen wrth
Gerdd—Gwybodau 'r gelfyddyd wrth Gerdd, a chynneddfau
addwynion a daionus.

50. Tri chyflwydd Bardd a Barddoniaeth, addwynhau a
gwerinaw cenedl—cyfanneddu gwlad—a gwellhau gwybodau.

51. Tri dyn nis byddant wrth gledd nac wrth gorn,
Bardd, Fferyllt, a Benyw.

52. Tair celfyddyd a fyddant yn nawdd ac wrth ddeddf
Beirdd cenedl y Cymry. Cerdd Dant — Llenyddiaeth sef
darllain Cymraeg ai ysgrifennu a meddyginiaeth.

53. Tri phoen gwlad, Arglwydd Anneddfawl—Cyfoeth-
awg disyfyd, a Bardd anwybodus.

54. Tripheth anferth ar Fardd, anwybodaeth — anhynawsder—ac anneddfoldeb.

55. Tripheth ni weddant ar gerdd dafawd Farddonïaidd

44. There are three laws of avoidance incumbent upon a Bard: to avoid idleness and extreme slothfulness, since he is a man of exertion and experience; to avoid strife and contention, since he is a man of love and peace; and to avoid folly, immorality, and uncourteousness, since he is a man of reason, understanding, and Awen from God.

45. There are three foundations of knowledge, which a Bard ought to consider and discuss: reason; nature; and impulse.

46. There are three instructions required of a Bard: a song according to reason and moral wisdom; oral tradition according to the memorial and usage of Gorsedd and worship; and demeanour, according to polite and good usages and habits.

47. Three things which a Poet, being a Chaired Bard, ought not to bear: arms; rudeness; and dispraise; for it is his function to promote peace and tranquillity, to encourage courtesy, and to praise every thing that is good.

48. Three things commendable in a Bard: warm affection; gentle boldness; and energetic reason.

49. Three things which cannot be dispensed with in a Bard: awen of song; the sciences of the art of song; and courteous and good qualities.

50. The three successful objects of a Bard and Bardism: to polish and civilize a nation; to render a country socially inhabitable; and to improve sciences.

51. Three persons who are exempt from sword and horn: a Bard; a metallurgist; and a female.

52. The three arts which are under the protection and law of the nation of the Cymry: instrumental song; literature, that is, reading and writing Cymraeg; and medicine.

53. The three penalties of a country: a wicked lord; a rich upstart; and an ignorant Bard.

54. Three things monstrous in a Bard: ignorance; incivility; and immorality.

55. Three things which ill become a Bardic vocal song:

—Cof am anfad ac anferth—Llygredigaeth deddf a syberwyd, a gwrthladd diddanwch.

56. Tripheth nid oes a el yn eu herbyn. Defawd Cadair. Llafar a chof Cadair, a Hengerdd wrth fraint Cadair.

57. Tri dyn nis gellir, ac nis dylit Beirdd o honynt,
Balch—diog—a Chelwyddog.

58. Tripheth anhepcor i Fardd, Awen o Dduw—addysg
Athraw—ac ymgais ei hunan.

59. Tripheth nis dylai Cerddawr o Fardd Cadeiriawg
eu dattrin, Cyfrinach Beirdd, gwir argyweddus—a gwarth-
usder ei gyfaill.

60. Tri choel Cerddawr Tafawd — Coel Cerdd — Coel
Gwyddor—a Choel ymbwyll.

61. Tri chyfrin cyspar cerd — Awen, dysg, a chyn-
heddfa daionus, ac hebddynt nis gellir cerd berffaith.

62. Tri ymglywed bardd, ymglywed ar gwir a chyfiawn,
ymglywed ai galon ai serchiadau—ac ymglywed ai awen ai
alledigaethau.

63. Tri pheth a ddylit eu deall a'u gwybod ar gerdd
dafawd ai pherthynasai ac ar bob peth arall o'r byd. sef
ydynt Bannogion,—adfannogion—ac ammanogion. a lle nas
gwypper y rhain nis gellir na dosparth na chelfyddyd gyfiawn ar ddim o'r byd, sef o'u gwybod au deall y cair ddeall
ar ansawdd y gelfyddyd ydd ymgeisier a hi, ac y gwnëir
trefn a dosparth arni, fal y bo hawdd a serchog ei dysgu ai
chofio ai hymarfer.

64. Tri pheth anhepcor ar bob celfyddyd a gwybydd-
iaeth. ei dysgu, ei chofio, ai hymarfer.

65. Tripheth ni gellir Cerdd dafawd hebddynt, gwybodaeth, awen, a chynhyrfiad.

66. Tri chynhyrfiad Cerdd, serch tuag at hardd a da-

the memorial of what is impious and monstrous ; the abuse of law and courtesy ; and resistance to amusement.

56. Three things which cannot be contravened : the usage of Chair ; the voice and memorial of Chair ; and an ancient song according to the privilege of Chair.

57. Three men who cannot, and ought not to be made Bards : the proud ; the indolent ; and the false.

58. Three things indispensable in a Bard : Awen from God ; the instruction of a teacher ; and individual exertion.

59. Three things which a songster, being a Chaired Bard, ought not to reveal : the secret of the Bards ; injurious truth ; and the disgrace of his friend.

60. The three credibilities of a vocal minstrel : the credibility of song ; the credibility of alphabet ; and the credibility of consideration.

61. The three co-equal secrets of song : awen ; learning ; and good principles ; and without them there can be no perfect song.

62. The three mutual feelings of a Bard : to feel mutually with truth and justice ; to feel mutually with his heart and affections ; and to feel mutually with his awen and its capabilities.

63. Three things which ought to be understood and known in a vocal song and its appurtenances, and in every other thing whatsoever, namely : points ; divisions ; and individualities. And when these are not known, there can be no arrangement or just art in respect of any thing ; whilst by knowing and understanding them, the nature of the art sought after is understood, and is reduced to order and method, in such a way as it would be an easy and loving matter to learn, remember, and practise the same.

64. Three things indispensable in every art and science : to learn ; to remember ; and to practise them.

65. Three things, without which there can be no vocal song : knowledge ; awen ; and impulse.

66. The three impulses of song : affection towards the beautiful and good ; the consciousness of duty ; and remu-

T

ionus, cydwybodolder dyled — a gobr o ged a chanmoliaeth
dynion da doethinebgar.

67.   Tri rhagoroldeb Celfyddyd, sef hawsder ei dysgu—
y diddanwch o'i dysgu, a lles a buddioldeb o'i dysgu.

68.   Tri pheth a wnant y gelfyddyd wrth gerdd y peth y
dylei fod Eglurdeb dysg a dosparth — godidowgrwydd y
gelfyddyd ai dosparth, ac anianoldeb y gelfyddyd ai pherthynasau.

69.   Tair braint bardd.   Coelio ei air ai wediad—Cys-
ymmaeth man ydd elo, ac nad elo oi anfodd wrth raid a
swydd gwlad.

70.   Tripheth y dylai Fardd eu chwiliaw a gwiliaw arnynt, Ei anwydau,—ei Farn gyssefin—a phob newyddoldeb.

71.   Tripheth y dylai Athraw o Fardd awengar eu
gwneuthur, mangraffu ar ymbwyll celfyddyd, manddos-
parthu ar a ddealler.—a manddangos ar a ddysgo.

72.   Tair cynneddf a ddylit ar Fardd, bod yn Athraw-
iaethgar—bod yn haelionus Barn ac ymbwyll—a bod yn
ddeddfawl ei Fuchedd.

73.   Tri pheth y dylai Fardd ddarymgais eu gwellhau—
ei athrylith awenawl—ei gelfyddyd wrth gerdd—ai gyn-
heddfau buchedd.

74.   Tripheth a wna Brydydd dysgedig, gwellhâu addysg
a gwybodau—cyfanneddu gwlad a chenedl—a gwneuthur ei
enw ei hun yn dragwyddawl.   (Al. a pheri cof tragwyddawl
am ei enw ei hun.   E.a.w. a thragwyddoli ei enw ei hun.)

75.   Mewn tripheth y gwelir ansawdd pob celfyddydau a
gwybodau. sef yn eu hegwyddorion—yn eu cyferbynieid—
ac yn eu peiriadau.

76. *   Tair budd celfyddyd a gwybodau, ynnill a fo daionus ympryd a bywyd—gwared rhag a fo drwg o ddigwydd,

---

* In MS. it is 77, and the following Triads are numbered accordingly down
to 84 inclusive.

neration from the contributions and commendation of good
and philosophical men.

67. The three excellences of art, namely : the facility of
learning it ; the amusement of learning it ; and the benefit
and advantage of learning it.

68. Three things that will make the art of song what it
should be : perspicuity of learning and arrangement ; the
excellency of the art and its arrangement; and the natural-
ness of the art and its appurtenances.

69. The three privileges of a Bard : that his word and
saying should be believed; provisions wherever he goes ;
and that he should not against his will be made to adminis-
ter to the necessity, or to fill the office of country.

70. Three things which a Bard ought to examine, and
watch over : his passions ; his innate judgment ; and every
novelty.

71. Three things which a Teacher, being a poetic Bard,
ought to do : to observe accurately the reason of art ; to
analyze accurately what is understood ; and to show accurately what is learned.

72. The three primary laws which ought to be incumbent upon a Bard : to be fond of teaching; to be liberal of
judgment and reason ; and to be moral as to conduct.

73. Three things which a Bard ought to endeavour to
improve : his poetic genius ; his art of song ; and the principles of his conduct.

74. Three things will make a learned Poet : to improve
learning and sciences ; to promote the sociable inhabitation
of country and nation ; and to make his own name immortal. Others say : and to cause his own name to be ever-
lastingly remembered. Others say : and to immortalize his
own name.

75. In three things is seen the nature of all arts and
sciences, namely : in their principles; in their counterparts;
and in their effects.

76. The three advantages of art and sciences : the gain
of what is good in respect of abstinence and living ; deliver-

o feddwl, ac o weithred, a harddwch dosparthus er diddanu meddwl a golwg.

77. Tair colofn dyledswydd Bardd, Iawn ddysgu—Iawn ganu—ac Iawn farnu.

78. Tair effaith awen gyfiawn, Haelioni—gwarineb—a llawenydd.

79. Tri chyfeillion awengyfiawn, deall, ystyriaeth, ac amynedd.

80. Tripheth a gynhyddant awen, ei hiawn arfer—eu mynych arfer—a llwyddiant o'i harfer.

81. Tripheth ni ddyly cerddawr eu credu, gogan clerwr lle y prytto Prydydd;—a chanu Angerdd o Brydydd canmoledig ag awdurdawd iddaw; — a'r pethau ni allant fod herwydd y doethion; megis a ddywed annoethion nas dylit rhoddi gwallt a dorrer lle ai caffo yr adar, a'r cyfryw betheu oferchwedl, nas cafwyd erioed o benn doeth a deallus, ac yn unrhyw a hynn yw credu na fuant farw nac Arthur nac Owain Glyndyfrdwy, ac nis gellir mai gwir hynny.

82. O dripheth y cyll brydydd ei awdurdawd, camddysgu lle y dylai iawn ddysg—dywedyd celwydd ar ei gerdd yn ystig,—a goganu lle nas dylit.

83. Tripheth ni ddyly cerddawr eu Celu, gwirionedd diargywedd; a Barn ar gerddwriaeth — a chlod dyledus dynion da.

84. * Tripheth a barant garu cerddawr dysgu 'n ewyllysgar—canu yn gariadgar—a dwyn gair da.

85. Tair harddgamp ar gerddawr, Cynnildeb, Cyfundeb, a chywirdeb.

86. Tripheth serchawg ar Gerddawr, bod yn ddiddangerth,—bod yn ddifalch,—ac ymarfer a chlodforedd.

---

* In MS. it is 86, and the following Triads are numbered accordingly to the end.

ance from what is bad in regard to contingency, mind, and deed; and regular beauty to cheer the mind and sight.

77. The three columns of a Bard's duty: to teach properly; to sing properly; and to judge properly.

78. The three effects of just awen: generosity; gentleness; and joy.

79. The three friends of just awen: understanding; reflection; and patience.

80. Three things that will augment awen: to exercise it properly; to exercise it frequently; and to exercise it successfully.

81. Three things which a songster ought not to believe: the satire of an itinerant minstrel, where a poet poetizes; an unpoetic song by a commended and authorized poet; and the things which, in the estimation of wise men, cannot be, as when the ignorant say that the hair which is cut ought not to be placed where the birds can get it, and such vain superstitions that never came from the head of a wise and intelligent person. Of the same character is it, to believe that neither Arthur nor Owain Glyndwr are dead, for such cannot be true.

82. For three things shall a poet lose his authority: for teaching wrongly where he ought to teach correctly; for pertinaciously uttering a falsehood in his song; and for satyrizing where he ought not.

83. Three things which a minstrel ought not to conceal: innocuous truth; judgment upon poetry; and the praise due to good men.

84. Three things that will make a minstrel to be beloved: to teach willingly; to sing lovingly; and to bear a good name.

85. The three beautiful qualities in a minstrel: economy; concord; and integrity.

86. Three things that are amiable in a minstrel: to be poetically amusing; to be void of pride; and to be given to praise.

87. Tripheth a lygrant awen Cerddawr — Trameddw-
dawd—tragodineb—a sarrugrwydd.

88. Tripheth a ^{amlhânt}_{wellhant} awen Cerddawr — Hengerdd —
Barddoniaeth — a Chadwedigaethau daionus a diddan.

89. Triphrif gyfreidiau Bardd—gwybodau dosparthus—
Deddfoldeb cariadus—a braint gorsedd.

90. Tair harddgamp ar Fardd, Ufudd-dawd—Dysgeidiaeth—a serchogrwydd.

91. Tair colofn celfyddyd—Pwyll Ansawdd, a gorfod,
ac o iawn ddeall ar y rhai hynn y mae cadernyd gwybodau.

92. Tri hawddgarwch a ddylit ar Fardd a Phrydydd,
cyfarwyddaw anghyfarwydd—tawelu amryson, a threfnu ar
chwareuon gwleddolder. E.a.w. A threfnu ar chwareugamp
a gwleddolder.

93. Tripheth a ddylai fod ar bob chwareuon. Iachau 'r
corph, diddanu 'r meddwl, a bod yn ddiniwed.

94. Tri thawedogaeth Bardd, ar wirionedd argyweddus,
ar farn afraid, ac ar bob anhysbys.

95. Tripheth parchus i Gerddawr, Tylwyth da—cyfeillion da—a buchedd dda.

96. Tri ammodoldeb y sydd ar brydydd, cynnal iaith y
Cymry—cynnal cof achau a neithioreu—a chynnal cof addysg am Freiniau a gwybodau Cenedl y Cymry.

97. Tri gwellynogion Cerdd a Barddoniaeth, addysg—
ymgais—a gobrwyon.

98. Tri gobrwyon Cerdd dafawd a phob gwybodau daionus—Ced ac ynnill—canmoliaeth ac anrhydedd—a boddlondeb meddwl a chydwybod o'r lles a'r daioni peiriedig a
wnelo.

99. Tri menwedigion Byd—Bardd—Fferyllt,—ac ardd-
wr, sef au gelwir felly am y bydd gwell pob byw o honynt

---

¹ Al. " augment."

² Others say : " and to regulate games and festivities."

87. Three things that will corrupt a minstrel's awen : excessive drunkenness ; excessive incontinence ; and surliness.

88. Three things that will improve[1] a minstrel's awen : an ancient song ; Bardism ; and good and amusing traditions.

89. The three principal necessaries of a Bard : systematic sciences ; amiable morality ; and the privilege of Gorsedd.

90. Three beautiful qualities in a Bard : obedience ; learning ; and affectionate disposition.

91. The three columns of art : reason ; nature ; and cogency ; and it is from understanding these things properly that ensues the permanence of sciences.

92. The three amiable traits which a Bard ought to possess : to direct the unskilful ; to put an end to contention ; and to regulate festal plays.[2]

93. All plays ought to tend to three things : to heal the body ; to amuse the mind ; and to be innocent.

94. The three silent reserves of a Bard : in respect of injurious truth ; in respect of unnecessary judgment ; and in respect of every thing uncertain.

95. Three things respectable for a minstrel : good family ; good friends ; and good conduct.

96. There are three conditions incumbent upon a poet : to maintain the language of the Cymry ; to keep a record of genealogies and nuptial festivities ; and to preserve an instructive memorial of the privileges and sciences of the nation of the Cymry.

97. The three ameliorations of song and Bardism : instruction ; exertion ; and rewards.

98. The three rewards of vocal song and all good sciences : tribute and gain ; praise and honour ; and contentment of mind and conscience arising from the benefit and good which they eventually cause.

99. The three benefactors of the world : a Bard ; a metallurgist ; and an agriculturist ; they are so called because

a'u gwybodau, ac ni bydd gwaeth dim or byw. A Phencyf-annedd gwlad a'u bernir.

100. Tri Phabledigion Beirdd Ynys Prydain, *Teuluwr* ac arnaw y mae Athrawiaeth Deuluaidd herwydd Cerdd dafawd a dosparth Gwybodau a defodau Teuluaidd, a dodi ar gerdd y Cof ar Cadw o honynt — Ail yw Atgeiniad ac arnaw y mae Datganu ynghadair a gorsedd ar gan ac ar Lafar, a dwyn gwaedd a gosteg yn rybydd gwlad a Chenedl ynghyfoeth y lle y bo Drefedig. Trydydd yw gwr wrth Gerdd dant, ac arnaw y mae Telynoriaeth a Chrythoriaeth, ac yn nawdd Beirdd Ynys Prydain y mae Cerdd Dant heb arni amgen yn y byd parth Breiniau a defodau, ac am hynny e'u gelwir y tri Phabledigion Beirdd a Barddoniaeth.

101. Tri chyfatgan Beirdd Cymry, Cerdd Dafawd, Dam-meg, a chynnefawd.

102. Tair swydd dyled Bardd wrth raid ac achos gwlad a chenedl y sydd—un yw Cynnal golychwyd. Ail yw Cen-hadoriaeth rhwng gwlad a gorwlad — Trydydd yw gyrru Tanc a Chymmod lle y byther ynghyfrysedd.

103. Tair Cynneddf dyled y sydd ar Fardd herwydd ei ddyled wrth raid ac achos gwlad a chenedl. Un yw chwilio am a fo gwir. Ail yw Cyfrinach a rother iddaw herwydd ei swydd ai fraint wrth Gerdd. Trydydd yw ymddwyn cyn-neddfol wrth danc a chyfiawnder.

104. Tair rhagorfraint Bardd — sef *un*, ei ossymmaeth yn rhad lle bynnag ydd elo ym mraint ei swyddogaeth wrth gerdd—ail yw nas dycco ef, ac nas dyccer lle bo efe, arf noeth yn erbynnu—Trydydd yw Gair ei air ef ar bawb.

105. Tri gossymmaith Bardd, Ei bumerwi rhyddion—ei aberthged—ai drythgwd.

every living being will benefit by them and their sciences, whilst no living thing will be the worse. And they are deemed the chief settlers of the country.

100. The three faculty Bards of the Isle of Britain. A family Bard, on whom depends domestic instruction, according to vocal song, and the system of domestic sciences and usages; and he is to commit to song the memorial and record of the same. The second is a reciter, whose function is to recite in Chair and Gorsedd, by means of song and speech: and to issue cry and proclamation, as notice to country and nation, in the territory where he resides. The third is a man of instrumental song, on whom depends the art of playing the harp and violin; and instrumental song is under the protection of the Bards of the Isle of Britain, without any other privileges and usages. Therefore they are called the three faculty ones of Bards and Bardism.

101. The three primary recitations of the Bards of the Cymry: vocal song; parable; and custom.

102. There are three functions incumbent upon a Bard, according to the necessity and requirement of country and nation. One is, to maintain religious worship. The second is, to conduct an embassy between country and border country. The third is, to introduce peace and concord where there is contention.

103. There are three primary laws incumbent upon a Bard in respect of his obligation as to the necessity and requirement of country and nation. One is, to search for what is true. The second is, the secret imposed upon him in respect of his office and privilege of song. The third is, to conduct himself morally according to peace and justice.

104. The three distinguished privileges of a Bard. One, gratuitous provision, wherever he goes, in right of his office of song. The second is, that he bear not, and there should not be borne in his presence, a naked weapon of offence. The third is, that his word should be paramount over all.

105. The three provisions of a Bard; his five free acres; his offerings; aud his contribution bag.

U

106. Tri noddedigaeth Beirdd Cenedl y Cymry—noddi dysg, sef celfyddyd gwybodaeth—noddi heddwch a Thangnef—a noddi gwirionedd a chyfiawnder. Canys erddynt y petheu hynn y mae Bardd, ac nid Bardd ni wnelo erddynt.

107. Tri gofal Beirdd Cymry, coledd gwybodau daionus —coledd gwybodau daionus *—coledd heddwch a Thangnef —a gloywi gwirionedd a chyfiawnder.

108. O dripheth y cafwyd Barddoniaeth — Awen o Dduw — deall dyn — a syrth anian.

109. Tripheth y dylei Bardd eu gwneuthur—gwrando ar bob peth yn ofalus — edrych ar bob peth yn llwyr — a thewi yn gadarn oni bo achos cadarn yn galw am ei lafar.

110. Tri pheth y dyly Bardd eu gwneuthur ar ei gerdd ac ar ei ymddwyn, mwyhau gwybodau — Llaryeiddaw moes a chynneddf — a diddanu meddwl.

111. Tair dyled ymgais y sydd ar Fardd—Cynnul dysg a gwybodau — athrawiaethu anwybodus — a heddychu lle y bo cywryssedd, ac ymdrin.

112. Tair ymdrafod ryddion a fyddant gyfiawn i Fardd ac i bawb au chwenychant, Helwriaeth — Arddoriaeth — a Maerdÿaeth, cans wrth y rhai hynny y cant bawb eu gossymmaeth, ac nis dylit naccâu arnynt.

113. Tri thrwyddedog Llys, Bardd—Ynad—a Golychwydwr.

114. Tri chynnal gwladoldeb — Barddoniaeth — Yneidiaeth — a Llafuriaeth.

115. Tri dyn a wnant gyfannedd lle bont, Bardd — Gof — a Thelynwr.

116. O dripheth y mae cadernyd Gwybodau Barddoniaeth. Cyntaf Awen o Dduw, yn ymmod ystyrbwyll a

* Sic in MS.

106. The three protections required of the Bards of the nation of the Cymry : to protect learning, or the art of knowledge ; to protect peace and tranquillity ; and to protect truth and justice. . For a Bard exists on account of these things, and he is no Bard who does not act in their behalf.

107. The three cares of the Bards of the Cymry : to cultivate good sciences; to cultivate peace and tranquillity ; and to illustrate truth and justice.

108. From three things was Bardism obtained : Awen from God ; the intellect of man ; and the tendency of nature.

109. Three things which a Bard ought to do : to listen carefully to every thing ; to look fully at every thing ; and to hold his peace soundly unless there be sound reason for his speech.

110. Three things which a Bard ought to practise in his song and in his conduct: to increase sciences; to soften manners and customs ; and to console the mind.

111. There are three energetic duties incumbent upon a Bard : to accumulate learning and sciences ; to instruct the ignorant ; and to make peace where there are contention and variance.

112. The three free pursuits which are lawful for a Bard and all who may desire them : hunting ; tillage ; and dairy-work ; for it is by means of these things that all persons obtain their maintenance, and they ought not to be prohibited.

113. The three licentiates of court : a Bard ; a judge ; and a worshipper.

114. The three supports of government : Bardism ; judicature ; and labour.

115. Three men who will constitute a social abode wherever they are : a Bard ; a smith ; and a harpist.

116. From three things ensues the firmness of the sciences of Bardism : the first is, Awen from God moving consideration and intelligence ; the second, memory and

deall—ail o gof a gwybod er yn oes oesoedd—Trydydd o
Gerdd Tydain ab Tudnaw, sef hwnnw Tydain Tad Awen.

117.   Tair addysg arbennig y cawsant genedl * y Cyntaf
oeddynt y Gwyddanod er yn oes oesoedd—ail ydoedd y
Beirdd wedi amser Prydain ab Aedd Mawr—Trydydd yw
y ffydd ynghrist, ac o'r Tair hynn y mae gwybodau Cenedl
y Cymry.

118.   Tri gweinyddiaid gwybodau Beirdd y Cymry. Can
—arwydd—a llythyr—a goreu y bernir Cân, am nas achos
amgen o gelfyddyd ar ei chadwedigaeth na chof a synwyr
anianawl, sef hynny celfyddyd o Dduw.

119.   Tri chof Beirdd Cymry—Hengerdd—gorddawd—
a llythyr.

120.   Am dri pheth y mae ar Feirdd Cymru gynnal cof
a gwybod, *Cyntaf* yr iaith Gymraeg—*ail* achoedd a Bonedd
y Cymry—Trydydd, Breiniau a Defodau Beirdd a Chenedl
y Cymry.

121.   Tri pheth nis gellir a el yn eu herbyn.   Hengerdd
y Prifeirdd—a chof cadair wrth Gerdd—a Rhaith gwlad a
chenedl, sef o'r tri hynn y cynnelir cof ac awdurdawd Breiniau, a defodau, a gwybodau Beirdd a Chenedl y Cymry.

122.   Tair Colofn hawl Beirdd Cymry, Cerdd y Prifeirdd
—Cof a defodau Cadair—a Rhaith Trichannyn.

123.   Tri lle y sydd iawn cynnal Cadair wrth Gerdd.
Tyleu Penegor—Eglwys—a Llys Cyfraith.

124.   Tri amseroedd Cadair ac Eisteddfod.—Pedryfan-
noedd haul, sef dau gyfnod Cyhydedd—un y gwanwyn, a'r
llall y mesyryd †—a dyddiau gwyl golychwyd—a dyddiau
Llys a chyfraith.

---

* " Y Cymry," ought evidently to be supplied.

† The other points, which are the summer and winter solstices, have not been
explained.

knowledge from the age of ages; the third the song of Tydain, son of Tudnaw, that is, Tydain, the father of Awen.

117. The three special learnings which the nation of the Cymry obtained. The first was, that of the Gwyddoniaid from the age of ages. The second was, that of the Bards, after the time of Prydain, the son of Aedd the Great. The third is, the faith in Christ. Out of these three arise the sciences of the nation of the Cymry.

118. The three ministers of the sciences of the Bards of the Cymry: song; symbol; and letter; of which song is adjudged to be the best, because there is no occasion for any other art for its preservation than memory and natural sense, that is, art from God.

119. The three memorials of the Bards of the Cymry: an ancient song; institute; and letter.

120. Of three things ought the Bards of the Cymry to maintain the memorial and record: the first of the Cymric language; the second, of the genealogies and descent of the Cymry; the third, of the privileges and usages of the Bards and nation of the Cymry.

121. Three things which cannot be contravened: an ancient song of the primitive Bards; the memorial of the Chair of song; and the verdict of country and nation. That is, from these three are maintained the memorial and authority of the privileges, usages, and sciences of the Bards and nation of the Cymry.

122. The three columns of claim of the Bards of the Cymry: the song of the primitive Bards; the memorial and usages of Chair; and the verdict of three hundred men.

123. There are three places in which it is proper to hold a Chair of song: an uncovered elevation; a church; and the court of law.

124. The three times of Chair and Eisteddvod: the four points of the sun, that is, the two periods of the equinox, one in the spring, and the other in the autumn; the holidays of worship; and the days of court and law.

125. Trille nawdd cyffredin y sydd, ac nis gellir yn-ddynt arf yn erbyn neb o'r Byd, Cadair Beirdd—Llysoedd gwlad ac ynad—a Chyfarchwel golychwyd.

126. Tri meib rhydd o gaeth — Bardd — ysgolhaig — a Fferyll.

127. Tair braint urddasawl Bardd, Trwydded lle ydd elo—afnoeth arf lle bytho—a gair ei air ef ar bawb.

128. Tair braint gynhwynawl Bardd, Llafar ei bwyll lle y bytho — aflafariaeth lle a phryd y mynno can mai gwr wrth rin a Chyfrinach ydyw — ac nad elo namyn oi fodd wrth raid gwlad a swyddogaeth. namyn a berthyno ar ei swydd ai gelfyddyd wrth gerdd a gwybodau Barddonïaidd.

129. Tri gochel Bardd, gochel dwyn arfau can nad arf yn ei erbyn nac yngwlad nac yngorwlad,—gochel anfoes ac anneddfoldeb, can mai gwr wrth bwyll deddfoldeb a chyfiawn ymddwyn yw efe—a gochel diogi, can mai gwr wrth ymgais ydyw efe.

130. Tri Brenogion gwlad a Chenedl, Bardd—ysgol-haig—a Fferyllt, sef y bydd eu tir yn rhydd iddynt, a'r fraint a ddylit o hynny, sef Brodoriaeth.

131. Tri rhyw Bardd y sydd, Cyntaf — Prifardd, ai addysg yw can a chof llafar—ail arwyddfardd ai addysg yw arwydd a chymmhwyll cyfluniadau—Trydydd Posfardd ai addysg yw darllain Cymraeg ai ysgrifennu ac yn hynny o fodd cynnal cof a gwybod.

132. Tri pheth y dylai Fardd eu gwneuthur, dysgu 'n graff a welo ac a glywo—cadw yn graff a ddysgo—a dangos yn graff a wyppo.

133. Tri Athraw dyn, Cyntaf yw addysg o ddichwain,

125. There are three places of common sanctuary, in which no weapon may be used against any person whatsoever: the Chair of Bards; the courts of country and judge; and the assembly of worship.

126. Three persons who are free from bond: a Bard; a scholar; and an artizan.

127. The three dignified privileges of a Bard: maintenance wherever he goes; that there should be no naked weapon where he is; and that his word should be paramount over all.

128. The three innate privileges of a Bard: that his meaning be vocal wherever he may be; that he should keep silence where and when he pleases, for he is a man of secrecy and mystery; and that he should not, unless willingly, enter upon the service and office of his country, except in what relates to his office and art of song and Bardic sciences.

129. The three avoidances of a Bard: to avoid bearing arms, for there ought to be no weapon against him either in country or border country; to avoid rudeness and immorality, for he is a man subject to the law of morality and correct conduct; and to avoid indolence, for he is a man of exertion.

130. The three privileged ones of country and nation: a Bard; a scholar; and a metallurgist; that is, their land shall be free to them, and they are entitled to the privilege which ought to arise therefrom, that is, social rights.

131. There are three kinds of Bards. The first is the Primitive Bard, whose instruction consists of song and oral tradition. The second is the Herald-bard, whose instruction consists of symbol, and the import of pictures. The third is the Post-bard, whose instruction consists in reading and writing Cymraeg, memorial and knowledge being thereby maintained.

132. Three things which a Bard ought to do: to learn minutely what he sees and hears; to keep closely what he learns; and to exhibit accurately what he knows.

133. The three teachers of man. The first is, instruc-

sef o weled a chlywed—ail yw deall anianawl yn ystyriaw
—Trydydd yw rhadferthwch Duw sef hynny Awen. ac or
tri hynn y mae Pwyll Barddoniaeth.

134.　Tri Bannogion Barddoniaeth Cof — Addysg — a
Thangnef.

135.　Tripheth y dylei Fardd eu cadarnhau, a'u rhoi 'n
benn ar bob pen, Gwirionedd, Tangnefedd, a Phwyll gwybodau.

136.　Tri rhyw a ddylynt Fawl a chof am danynt. pob
glan a daionus o gamp a defawd — pob hardd a serchog o
bryd ac ansawdd—a phob ymbwyll celfydd a fo mwy y lles
na'r afles o honaw.

137.　Trirhyw drïoedd a fu o'r dechreuad gan Feirdd
Cymry, sef Trioedd Braint a defawd — Trïoedd golychwyd
—a Thrïoedd cerdd.

138.　Tri chadernyd gwladoldeb—Brawdwr cyfiawn—
Arglwydd trugarawg—a Bardd doeth a dysgedig.

Ac felly y terfynant y saith ugain Trioedd Beirdd Cymry
a dynnwyd o'r hen Lyfrau awdurdodawl gan Risiart ab
Iorwerth Fynglwyd.

TRIOEDD BEIRDD YNYS PRYDAIN.

Llyma Trioedd Beirdd Ynys Prydain a'r $^{cof a'r}$ son y sydd
$^{ar}_{gan}$Lafar Gorsedd am danynt, a'u hanfod a'u hansawdd.

Pan ddaethant y Cymmry gyntaf i Ynys Prydain o *wlad
yr Haf* llu y buant cyn no hynny, ydd oedd y Brifwybod-
aeth a'r Doethineb gyntefig yng nghadw ac ar addysg gan y
Gwyddoniaid sef oeddent y rheini Prydyddion yn berchen
Awen o Dduw cyn caffael a bod addysg o Ddyn a chyn
trefnu a Dosparthu Cadair wrth Gerdd, a Breiniau a Defodau i Feirdd ac ar Farddoniaeth, a'r Prydyddion hynny,

---

[1] It is evident from this statement that there are two Triads missing, which
accounts, moreover, for the numerical irregularity which we have noticed.

[2] " The memorial " does not occur in all the MSS.　　[3] Al. " by."

tion derived from circumstance, that is, from seeing and hearing. The second is, natural understanding giving heed. The third is, the grace of God, that is, Awen. And from these three comes the import of Bardism.

134. The three prominent features of Bardism : memorial ; instruction ; and peace.

135. Three things which a Bard ought to confirm, and to make supreme over every thing that is supreme : truth ; peace ; and the import of sciences.

136. Three kinds of things ought to be praised and remembered : every thing that is pure and good as to quality and custom ; every thing that is beautiful and amiable in form and nature ; and every clever device from which arises a greater amount of advantage than of disadvantage.

137. There have been three kinds of Triads from the beginning by the Bards of the Cymry, namely : the Triads of privilege and usage ; the Triads of worship ; and the Triads of song.

138. The three fundamentalities of government : a just judge ; a merciful lord ; and a wise and learned Bard.

And thus end the seven score[1] Triads of the Bards of th Cymry, which were extracted from the ancient Books of authority by Richard, son of Iorwerth the Grey-haired.

THE TRIADS OF THE BARDS OF THE ISLE OF BRITAIN.

Here are the Triads of the Bards of the Isle of Britain, with the memorial[2] and account which exist in[3] the voice of Gorsedd respecting them, their origin and nature.

When the Cymry first came into the island of Britain from the Summer Country, where they were previously, the primitive knowledge and original wisdom were kept and taught by the Gwyddoniaid, who were Poets possessed of Awen from God before the invention and existence of instruction from man, and before the Chair of song, and privileges and usages for Bards and relative to Bardism were

sef y Gwyddoniaid, a gadwasant ar gof cân a cherdd Dafawd y Prifwybodau daionus a gafwyd gyntaf ar ddeall drwy
Awen o Dduw, ac ynol hirfod o amser y cafwyd o genedl y
Cymmry Bardd o Brydydd a elwid *Tydain Tad Awen*, a
doethaf o'r holl Brydyddion ydoedd efe, a mwyaf ei awen o
Dduw, ac efe a wnaeth drefn ar Gerdd Dafawd ac ar Farddoniaeth, ac a wnaeth drefn ar Freiniau a defodau a weddynt
ar Fardd a Barddoniaeth, a'r Beirdd hynny a elwid Beirdd
wrth Fraint a Defawd yr Hen Gymmry, ac wrth y drefn a
wnaeth Dydain y cynhaliwyd Cerdd Dafawd a Barddoniaeth
dros hir o amser hyd pan y gwnaeth Brydain ab Aedd
Mawr Gystlwn Cywlad ar Ynys Prydain a'i Chenhedloedd,
ac am i Dydain wneuthur hynn o drefn gyntaf ar gerdd
dafawd a Barddoniaeth, ac am y gwybodau a gafwyd ynddo
ef yn well nag ym mewn arall parth Cerdd dafawd ai pherthynasau, ac am mai trwyddaw efe, ac a wnaeth o drefn a
dosparth, y cafwyd gyntaf addysg a chelfyddyd wrth gerdd
dafawd a gwybodau Barddoniaeth yn ddosparthus, y gelwid
ef *Tydain Tad Awen*, a rhai a ddywedant mai cyn dyfodiad
y Cymmry i ynys Prydain y bu Tydain, ond nis gellir digon
o wybod am hynny.

A Thydain a gymmerwys atto wyr ieuainc doethion yn
berchen awen o Dduw iddeu hathrawiaethu au haddysgu yn
y gwybodau wrth Gerdd dafawd a doethineb, ac wrth hyn o
drefn a dosparth y bu'r Gwybodau hynn gan y Prydyddion
a'r gwyddoniaid hyd amser Prydain ab Aedd Mawr, a gwedi
iddaw efe drefnu Unbenaeth a'r holl Ynys Prydain ai Chenhedloedd ai Brenhinoedd ai Thywysogion ai harglwyddi efe
a beris ir Prydyddion ddangos eu gwybodau, a'r cof ar cadw
ac oedd am danynt, a gwedi cael hynny y chwiliwyd pwy
doethaf a gwybodusaf o'r Prydyddion, a goreu o honynt a
gafwyd yn hynny o bethau a berthynynt i Gerdd dafawd a
gwybodau doethineb oeddynt Plennydd ac Alawn a Gwron,

arranged and regulated. And those Poets, or Gwyddon-iaid, preserved, by means of the memorial of poetry and vocal song, the good primitive sciences, which were first understood by means of Awen from God. And after a long space of time, there was found from among the nation of the Cymry a Bard, being a Poet, called Tydain the father of Awen, who was the wisest of all the Poets, and he reduced vocal song and Bardism into order, and arranged the privileges and usages that were proper for Bard and Bardism. Those Bards were called Bards according to the privilege and usage of the Ancient Cymry. It was according to the arrangement made by Tydain, that vocal song and Bardism were maintained for a long time, until Prydain, the son of Aedd the Great, formed a confederacy in the island of Britain, and among its nations. And, because it was Tydain that first made this arrangement of vocal song and Bardism, and because the sciences which he possessed were superior to those possessed by any other person, in respect of vocal song and its relatives, and because it was through him, and the order and system which he made, that regular instruction and art in regard to vocal song and the sciences of Bardism, were first obtained, he was called Tydain, father of Awen. Some say, that it was before the arrival of the Cymry in the island of Britain, Tydain lived; but there is no sufficient information on that point.

Tydain took to him certain young and wise men, endued with Awen from God, to be taught and instructed in the sciences of vocal song and wisdom; and it was according to this arrangement and system that such sciences were held by the Poets and Gwyddoniaid until the time of Prydain, son of Aedd the Great. And when he had appointed a sovereignty over all the island of Britain and its nations, kings, princes, and lords, he ordered the Poets to exhibit their sciences, and the memorial and record in which they were preserved; and when that was done, search was made as to who were the wisest and most knowing of the Poets, when Plennydd, Alawn, and Gwron, were found to be the

a hwy a gyfarfuant yng Nghadair ac yno trefnu Gwaedd
uwch adwydd a wnaethant dan osteg a rhybydd undydd a
blwyddyn a myned wrth raith gadarn gwlad a chenedl, ac
yn y waedd honno rhoddi gwys a gwahawdd i bawb o'r
Prydyddion a'r Gwyddoniaid a fedrant ar Gerdd dafawd, a
gwybodau doethineb, a breiniau a defodau yr Hen gymry.
ddyfod ynghadair a gorsedd yn yr amlwg ac yng ngolwg
haul ac wyneb goleuni, a yno y daethant bawb a fedrant ar
Awen a gwybodau wrth Gerdd dafawd a'u perthynasau, ac
yno y trefnwyd Breiniau a defodau, a dosparth arnynt a
weddynt ar Feirdd a Barddoniaeth a doethineb a Chyfrinach Barddas, a threfnu a defodi hefyd y Tair syrth ar
Feirdd a Barddoniaeth a gwybodau Barddas a wnaethpwyd,
nid amgen, Prifardd neu Brydydd Trwyddedawg, wrth
Fraint a Defawd yr hen Gymry, a Derwydd ac ef yn wr o
Fardd wrth wybodau cysefinion y Gwyddoniaid, ac Ofydd
yn Fardd wrth wybodau o ddychymmyg a dichwain, a
rhoddi 'r cyfan a wnaethant ar gadw a chof Beirdd Ynys
Prydain, sef ydynt Can Gorsedd, Llafar Gorsedd, a Defawd
Gorsedd, rhag ei myned ar goll ac anghof, a gwedi myned
parth hynn o bethau wrth Raith gadarn Gwlad a Chenedl
nid amgen na Gwaedd Gwlad dan rybydd a gosteg undydd
a blwyddyn, hyd ynghyfallwy, a'r Triwyr hynn sef Plennydd, Alawn, a Gwron, a fuant yn dri chyntefigion Beirdd
Gorseddogion Ynys Prydain, sef cysefinogion oeddynt wrth
Freiniau a Defodau Beirdd Ynys Prydain pa rai a drefnwyd
ac a ddefodwyd ac a ddeddfwyd ac a ddosparthwyd yn yr
orsedd honno yn nawdd a braint gwlad a chenedl wrth
Raith Gadarn, ac yna cymmeryd attynt eraill o'r Prydyddion gwybodusaf a wnaeth y Tri chyntefigfeirdd ac enwoccaf
o'r rhai hynny y cafwyd, Madawc, a Chenwyn, ac Anllawdd, sef oeddynt y Tri cyntaf a raddwyd o addysg a

best as to those particulars which appertained to vocal song
and the sciences of wisdom. And they met in Chair, where
they issued the cry of restoration under the proclamation
and notice of a year and a day, and deferred to the substantial verdict of country and nation. In that cry they cited
and invited all the Poets and Gwyddoniaid who were skilled
in vocal song, the sciences of wisdom, and the privileges and
usages of the Ancient Cymry, to repair to Chair and Gorsedd about to be held openly, in the sight of the sun and eye
of light. And thither came all who were versed in awen
and the sciences of vocal song, and their appurtenances;
and there were arranged and systematized such privileges
and usages as were suitable to Bards and Bardism, and the
wisdom and secret of Bardism; and there were also arranged
and instituted the three classes of Bards and Bardism and
the sciences of Bardism, namely, the Primitive Bard or licensed Poet, according to the privilege and usage of the
Ancient Cymry, the Druid, being a Bard according to the
primary sciences of the Gwyddoniaid, and the Ovate, being
a Bard according to sciences derived from imagination and
circumstance. And they committed the whole to the record
and memorial of the Bards of the Isle of Britain, which are
the song of Gorsedd, the voice of Gorsedd, and the usage of
Gorsedd, lest they should become lost or forgotten. And
when, in respect of these things, they had appealed to the
firm verdict of country and nation, that is, the cry of country, under the notice and proclamation of a year and a day,
until the period of efficiency, these three men, Plennydd,
Alawn, and Gwron, were the three primary presiding Bards
of the Isle of Britain, that is to say, they were primary
according to the privileges and usages of the Bards of the
Isle of Britain, which were arranged, instituted, legalized,
and systematized in that Gorsedd, under the protection and
privilege of country and nation, by a firm verdict. Then
the primary Bards took to them others of the most knowing
poets, the most celebrated of whom were found to be Madog,
Cenwyn, and Anllawdd, being the three first that were, after

Throfedigaeth yn Feirdd gorseddog herwydd y Drefn a'r
Ddosparth a wnaethpwyd fal y dangoswyd, ac arnynt y
rhoddwyd cynnal a chadw y trichof, a Barnu a threfnu
ynghadair a gorsedd, a chymmeryd Trofedigion ac Awenyddion iddeu haddysgu yng ngwybodau Cerdd dafawd a'u
pherthynasau, a chadw rhag ei llygru y Trifwybodaeth a'r
Iaith Gymraeg, a chof am bob daionus a moliannus ar wr a
gweithred a damwain.

Ac yn yr amser hynny y defodwyd ac y breiniwyd y tri
Ofyddion cyntefig, sef oeddynt, Cadawc ab Myl mur Mawredd, a Thrysin ab Erbal, a Rhuawn gerdd arian—ac ar yr
Ofyddion y dodwyd ac a ddefodwyd cynnull Gwybodau
Barddoniaidd a daionus o ba ddichwain bynnag, ac o ba
awen a dychymmyg bynnag a'u rhoddi ar farn Cadair a
Gorsedd. ac wrth bwyll a barn a dosparth Celfyddyd. Ac
yn yr amser hynny hefyd y defodwyd ac y breiniwyd yn
Dderwyddon Meiwyn Fardd, a Rhiallon asgellawg ab Prydain ab Aedd Mawr, a Berwyn ab Arthrawd, ac arnynt y
rhoddwyd cynnal Golychwyd a'r Gwybodau a berthynynt i
hynny herwydd y Tri chof, a herwydd a gaid wrth Farn
Cadair a Gorsedd, a'r Tri thriwyr hynn y gyd a'r Tri
Chyntefigion a fuant y deuddeg cysefinogion Beirdd Gorseddawg wrth Fraint a defawd Beirdd Ynys Prydain sef o
gysefinder ydynt rhag nad oedd o'u rhyw a'u syrth rai o'u
blaen hwynt. A'r Deuddeg cysefinion au bernir am eu bod
o'r un Orsedd Gysefin, ac o honynt y cafwyd gyntaf Tair
syrth Beirdd Ynys Prydain, ac yn ol y dywedir yma y
dangosant yr Athrawon a'r Beirdd dysgedig Tair syrth o
hanfod ac Ansawdd Beirdd Ynys Prydain. Ac yn yr Orsedd gysefin a soniwyd am dani wrth fraint a defawd Beirdd
Ynys Prydain, y gwnaethpwyd dosparth gadarn a rif a

instruction and discipleship, graduated presiding Bards, according to the arrangement and system which were made, as already shewn. And they were enjoined to maintain and preserve the three memorials, to judge and rule in Chair and Gorsedd, to take disciples and aspirants to be instructed in the sciences of vocal song and its appurtenances, to keep from corruption the primary knowledge and Cymric language, and to record every thing good and laudable in man, deed, and event.

It was in those days that the three primary Ovates, Cadog, son of Myl, the Wall of Greatness, Trysin, son of Erbal, and Rhuawn of the Silver Song, were instituted and privileged. The Ovates were appointed and enjoined to collect Bardic and good sciences, from whatever incident, and from whatever awen and imagination, to submit them to the judgment of Chair and Gorsedd, and to regulate them according to the sense, judgment, and system of art. In those days, also, were instituted and privileged, as Druids, Meiwyn, the Bard; Rhiwallon the Winged, son of Prydain, son of Aedd the Great; and Berwyn, son of Arthrawd. And they were enjoined to maintain religious worship, and the sciences appertaining thereto, according to the three memorials, and according to the result of the judgment of Chair and Gorsedd. These three triads of men, together with the three primaries, were the twelve primary Bards of Gorsedd according to the privilege and usage of the Bards of the Isle of Britain. That is, they are primary because none of their kind and sort existed before them; and they are deemed the twelve primaries, because they belonged to the same primary Gorsedd. And it was from them that were obtained first the three degrees of the Bards of the Isle of Britain; and it is according to what is here said, that the teachers and learned Bards point out three degrees of the substance and nature of the Bards of the Isle of Britain. In the primary Gorsedd, which has been mentioned, according to the privilege and usage of the Bards of the Isle of Britain, figures and numbers were reduced to a fundamental

rhifedi nid amgen no fal hynn, Tair Rhif Gadarn y sydd,
yr un Cyntaf, a'r Tri Cyntaf a wnant liaws, a'r trithrioedd
cyntaf a wnant luosydd neu liaws gadarn sef yw hynny
naw, ac od eir ymhellach syrthio i ansawdd Undawd a wna
rif fal y mae deg, canys o un i ddeg, ac o ddeg i ddeg degau
sef hynny cant, ac yn unwedd a hynny ydd eir o un cant
hyd ddeg sef y bydd hynny mil, ac o un mil i ddeg sef
hynny myrdd, ac wrth hynn o ddosparth hyd a fynner, ac
wrth bwyll yr un Cadarn ydd eir fal y dangoswyd, ac wrth
bwyll y lliaws gadarn sef tri ydd eir hyd y tri thrioedd yn
Liosydd Cadarn can nis gellir undawd ar un o fannau rhifedi yn amgen nac a ddangoswyd o un i ddeg, ac am hynny
lluosawg a chadarn ar luosawg yw tri a thrioedd can nis
gellir a myned hyd y gellir amgen na lliawsogrwydd arnynt,
ac ym mraint hynn o ansawdd y cafwyd trioedd ar bob peth
herwydd dosparth anianawl ac wrth bwyll a deall, a gorfod,
can nid oes un nac undawd ar unpeth mewn byd a bod, namyn ar Dduw a gwirionedd ac un cyfnod rhyddyd, ac
ymhob undawd arall y bydd lliaws parth ansawdd a bannau,
ac o hynn o ddeall ar ansawdd rhif y dodwyd Llafar Gorsedd Beirdd Ynys Prydain ar fesur Tri a Thrioedd, ac ar
hynn o drefn y dosparthant Beirdd Ynys Prydain eu dysg,
a'u celfyddyd, a'u doethineb a'u holl wybodau wrth Gerdd a
Barddoniaeth gan mai ar y lleiaf lluosawg y mae hawsaf
dosparthu prifannau pob gwybodau a chelfyddyd a phob
trefn ar ddoethineb. ac ar hynn o drefn y mae hawsaf
dysgu a chofiaw a fo raid parth y bo achos ei ddysgu ai
wybod, ac ymhob cadair wrth gerdd a gorsedd y mae 'n
gofyn datganu Trioedd Beirdd Ynys Prydain er cynnal cof
a chadw ar holl wybodau Beirdd Ynys Prydain, ac nis